FoxPro 2.6 for Windows™

UNLEASHED

Edward Jones
Derek Sutton

D1210757

SAMS PUBLISHING

A Division of Macmillan Computer Publishing
201 West 103rd Street, Indianapolis, IN 46290

Copyright © 1994 by Sams Publishing

Trademarks

Contents

Part II   Advanced FoxPro

Part IV Programming in FoxPro

Acknowledgments

This book would not have been possible without the help of a number of dedicated individuals. We would like to thank Rosemarie Graham, James Grass, Phillip W. Paxton, Matthew Usher, and many others on the team at Sams Publishing. We would also like to thank Menachem Bazian, Barbara Dove, Linda Joyce Wright, and William R. Beem for their careful review of the manuscript. And thanks to all of our friends and families for putting up with our crankiness during one of the more intense book production periods in recent memory.

Dedication

From Derek Sutton—

To my Mom, thanks for putting up with me during this project, and believing in me when no one else would; finally, we can leave for North Carolina.

To Ana Banana, gracias para tu amistad y a por ayudarme ver mas alla, y estas "cosas" de mi personalidad, eres mas que una amiga, que te vaya bien en tus viajes por el mundo, recuerda, siempre voy a estar aqui si me necesitas.

About the Authors

Edward Jones is the author of more than 30 computer books, including many best-sellers in the area of databases. He specializes in providing clear and understandable books at the novice to advanced level. Jones also provides consulting, planning, software development, and training for federal government agencies, law firms, and corporate clients in the greater Washington, DC area. He has designed and provided personnel management software to an installed base of approximately 100 companies nationwide, and provides consulting services through Computer Support Group of Annandale, Virginia. As a writer, Jones has published articles in Lotus, Databased Advisor, and DBMS magazines.

Derek Sutton is a journalist and college-level student in the computer sciences, who also provides consulting services in the database management area.

Introduction

Welcome to FoxPro, one of Microsoft's database managers for Windows. FoxPro brings the advantages of XBase compatibility to the Windows arena, without sacrificing speed or performance in the bargain. And FoxPro's strengths as a development environment provide serious users with the necessary tools to offer custom Windows database applications. This book is designed to help you maximize on those strengths offered by FoxPro.

Organization

This book is divided into six parts. Part I is designed to help you quickly put FoxPro to work and provides a detailed look at the basic "interactive" usage of FoxPro. Part II details the more advanced features of FoxPro. Part III details the many ways in which you can go beyond the typical interactive use of FoxPro, by detailing topics such as data-sharing with other software, designing graphs, and creating complete applications. Part IV delves into programming, using the powerful FoxPro Basic language that is built into the program. Part V provides coverage of advanced programming techniques, such as the use of the FoxPro API and DDE functions, and multiuser techniques. Part VI provides a reference of FoxPro commands and functions.

Part I / FoxPro Basics

Chapter 1, "First Things First," provides an overall look at FoxPro and offers an explanation of the basics of FoxPro, hints on proper database planning, hardware requirements, and installation techniques.

Chapter 2, "Maximizing the FoxPro User Interface," covers the FoxPro user interface, with a slant towards the effective use of the FoxPro Catalog Manager (which is new to version 2.6 of FoxPro).

Chapter 3, "Creating and Working with Tables," covers creating tables, how to open and use tables, adding and changing fields, saving the structure, basic data entry, and changing the structure of a table.

Chapter 4, "Adding and Changing Data," details adding data, adding data to memo fields, adding data to general fields, using FoxPro's Edit mode, working with the Browse mode, using the Browse menu, splitting the Browse window, displaying multiple databases in Browse mode, finding records, deleting records, and recalling deleted records.

Chapter 5, "Arranging Data," details ways in which you can keep your data in order. Topics covered include indexing from the menus, indexing from the Command Window, working on multiple fields, ascending versus descending sorts, selective sorts with a FOR clause, and a discussion of when to index versus when to sort.

Chapter 6, "Performing Queries with RQBE," covers RQBE (Relational Query By Example) in FoxPro. Topics detailed include defining and running queries, choosing query fields, choosing an order, grouping the results, choosing an output destination, creating sample queries, saving queries, and reusing saved queries.

Chapter 7, "Queries with Commands," covers queries that can be built through the use of FoxPro commands. Topics in this chapter include how expressions are used as part of FoxPro commands; using LOCATE and CONTINUE; using FIND and SEEK; and the use of the SET FILTER TO command.

Chapter 8, "Creating and Using Simple Screens," covers the creation of screen forms through the use of the automated screen-design features, which are new to FoxPro 2.6. Topics include using FoxPro's AutoScreen feature, using the Screen Wizard to create a screen, using and navigating within an existing screen, changing existing screens with the ScreenWizard, and saving changes to a screen.

Chapter 9, "Creating and Using Simple Reports," starts coverage of the topics of reports, a vital part of your work with data. Topics covered include how you can create "instant" reports with the AutoReport button, creating different types of reports with the Report Wizards, how reports can be saved for later use, and how you can create simple reports with the use of FoxPro commands.

Part II / Advanced FoxPro

Chapter 10, "Working with FoxPro's Relational Powers," details effective planning for relational databases, how relational queries can be used to extract data from multiple tables, effectively utilizing the results of a multiple query, how to create multiple reports, and how the relational environment can be established.

Chapter 11, "Designing and Customizing Screens," covers the manual creation of screens within FoxPro. Topics covered include creating screen controls, working with controls, adding sections, working with list boxes, combination boxes, check boxes, editing regions for memo fields, and radio buttons, the addition of control buttons to perform command tasks, and how to add custom design effects to a screen.

Chapter 12, "Designing and Customizing Reports," covers the manual creation of reports within FoxPro. Topics covered in this chapter include creating and working with report fields and expressions, adding grouping to reports, sorting to produce reports with data in the desired order, and how to add custom design effects to a report.

Chapter 13, "Using Expressions and Functions," details the use of expressions to obtain desired data within a screen or a report, and shows how the FoxPro Expression Builder can be used to quickly design needed expressions.

Chapter 14, "Producing Mailings," details how you can produce mailing labels, how to generate form letters (both with and without graphic elements) from within FoxPro, and how to generate form letters using Word for Windows or other Windows word processors.

Part III / Extending FoxPro

Chapter 15, "Creating Applications with FoxPro," covers how simple applications can be created with no programming through the use of the FoxPro Applications Generator. Topics covered in this chapter include starting the FoxApp utility, choosing the base table, relating another table, creating or modifying a screen, building the application, and using the application.

Chapter 16, "Sharing Data with Other Programs," covers the topics that relate to sharing data with other programs, including importing data from other programs, exporting data, and how you can use OLE to share data with other Windows programs.

Chapter 17, "Working with Graphs," details how you can create graphs based on data retrieved through queries, and how different styles of graphs can be displayed, edited, and printed using MS Graph (which is provided with the Windows version of FoxPro).

Chapter 18, "Power Techniques for Power Users," covers an assortment of advanced techniques, including working with dates, working with memo fields, international issues, maximizing Rushmore (which is FoxPro's internal technique used to speed data retrieval), and optimizing FoxPro for speed.

Part IV / Programming in FoxPro

Chapter 19, "FoxPro Programming Basics," provides an introduction to FoxPro programming. Topics covered include creating programs, using the FoxPro Editor, and using common programming concepts such as constants, variables, and operators within your FoxPro programs.

Chapter 20, "Program Flow in a FoxPro Program," covers how multiple program modules are used to build a complex FoxPro application, and how program flow is controlled within a program.

Chapter 21, "Programming for Data Entry and Editing," details programming techniques that can be used for the management of data-entry and editing routines within a FoxPro application.

Chapter 22, "Programming for Reporting Needs," details programming techniques used to meet reporting needs within an application.

Chapter 23, "Pulling It All Together," details how the Menu Builder and Project Manager, along with the FoxPro power tools and the programming techniques covered in the previous four chapters can be used in the design and implementation of complete FoxPro applications.

Chapter 24, "Debugging Techniques," details techniques used to find errors within FoxPro programs.

Part V / Advanced Programming

Chapter 25, "The Event-Driven User Interface," details techniques you can use in developing FoxPro applications that behave like Windows applications.

Chapter 26, "Multiuser Programming and Techniques," explains programming tools and techniques for writing programs in a network environment.

Chapter 27, "Programming with DDE," covers the use of Dynamic Data Exchange (DDE), and how Windows DDE functions can be used within FoxPro programs to communicate with other Windows applications.

Chapter 28, "Working with the FoxPro API," details the use of the Application Program Interface, and how it can be used to extend the capabilities of FoxPro through the inclusion of C or assembler routines.

Chapter 29, "Cross-Platform and Migration Tips and Techniques," details the techniques you can use when working with FoxPro applications across platforms, and when migrating applications from other database managers into FoxPro.

Chapter 30, "Developing Online Help," shows how you can add online help to your applications, and how you can provide help screens that are context-sensitive, or attuned to the area of an application that a user is in.

Part VI / Reference

Chapter 31, "Command Reference," provides a listing complete with syntax and descriptions for all FoxPro commands.

Chapter 32, "Function Reference," provides a listing complete with syntax and descriptions for all FoxPro functions.

Appendix

Appendix A, "Third-Party Products," provides a reference of third-party add-ons that can be used with FoxPro.

Assumptions

This book was written with the assumption that you are already familiar with Microsoft Windows. If you are not yet familiar with Windows, you should consider taking the Windows Tutorial (in Windows, open the Help menu and choose Tutorial), or you can refer to your Windows documentation for specifics about Windows.

How to Use This Book

The best way to learn to put FoxPro to effective use is to work with the program. Toward that end, this book and the accompanying disk provide databases that you can use with the hands-on examples that are detailed throughout the book. The book is also designed to appeal to those who may have some exposure to FoxPro, but who wish to go well beyond the basics in specific areas. The book doesn't tie you to a planned learning track, so feel free to jump around and consider the subjects that are of the most interest to you.

1

PART

FoxPro Basics

First Things First

IN THIS CHAPTER

Welcome to FoxPro, Microsoft's high-end offering in the Windows database arena. If you are coming to FoxPro from another database manager such as dBASE or Paradox, you'll find that FoxPro offers many improvements over other database managers, including raw speed; the ability to run virtually all existing dBASE programs; and cross-platform compatibility, with similar versions for Windows, DOS, and the Macintosh. If you are upgrading from a previous version of FoxPro there are other advantages. For the first time, novice users can accomplish many common database tasks in FoxPro by using the Catalog Manager and some of the wizards that are available as guides. Both the Catalog Manager and the wizards are new to version 2.6 of FoxPro.

FoxPro follows the popular relational database model in which data is represented in a series of rows and columns, similar to the arrangement of a spreadsheet. Figure 1.1 shows names and addresses stored in a FoxPro table.

FIGURE 1.1.

Names and addresses stored in FoxPro.

Microsoft FoxPro

File Edit Database Record Program Run Browse Window Help

```
Command
set default to c:\fpw26\tutorial
USE customer.dbf EXCLUSIVE
browse
```

	Customer					
Cno	Company	Contact	Address	City	State	Zip
14021	1st Computers	Jeff W. Culbertson	5111 Parkway	Brookline	MA	02146
18232	1st Data Reductions	Dennis Johnson	360 Riverview Farm Street	New Orleans	LA	70113
12082	1st Software Systems Ltd.	Rance Sivren	23433 Chapel 121	Houston	TX	77035
12840	1st Survey	Robert Hepworth	733 Peeler 86th	Dallas	TX	75234
A8872	A Beck Pertamina	Jim Ansarti	4001 Rowed Rd	Arlington	MA	02174
A8818	A. Arts Computers	Darryl Roudebush	3305 Plantation Avenue	Melrose	MA	02176
A6459	A. Bloomington Biz	Phil Putnam	6300 East Drive	Tallahassee	FL	32301
A6188	AZ Inc	Tom Totah	2041 Wilshire Blvd	Taunton	MA	02780
A5181	Abbymark Velonex	Isador Sweet	2139 Bridge Sciller	Dallas	TX	75201
A3964	Acres Tree Solutions	Russell Kmickle	621 Ferndale Ste Park	Sparta	NJ	07871
A3882	Add Associates	Len Silverman	318 N Sante Fe Ave Office L	Novato	CA	94947
A1046	Add Inc	Bert Crawford	253 Mitchell St	Boulder	CO	80303
A7249	Adder Incorporated	Brenda Cartwright	1237 Bering Belleview	Warren	MI	48093
A3835	Adv. Software	Barbara H. Martin	600 114th Ave Se A1a	Arlington	MA	02174
A3061	Advantage Computer School	Duane Marshall	3784 Van Dyke Suite Street	San Jose	CA	95131

Customer   Record: 1/500   Exclusive   Ins

Each row of the table contains an individual record, and each column consists of one field of the table. In Figure 1.1, Last Name, First Name, Address, City, State, and ZIP code are all separate fields. In the relational model, all your data can be broken down into a series of such tables.

With a relational database, you'll typically have a number of different tables that contain related data. For example, in a database designed to track the donations made to a charitable organization, you might have one table with the names of the organization members and another containing donation amounts. You could establish relationships between the two tables, based on a common field contained in both tables. Figure 1.2 shows data from two related tables displayed simultaneously in FoxPro.

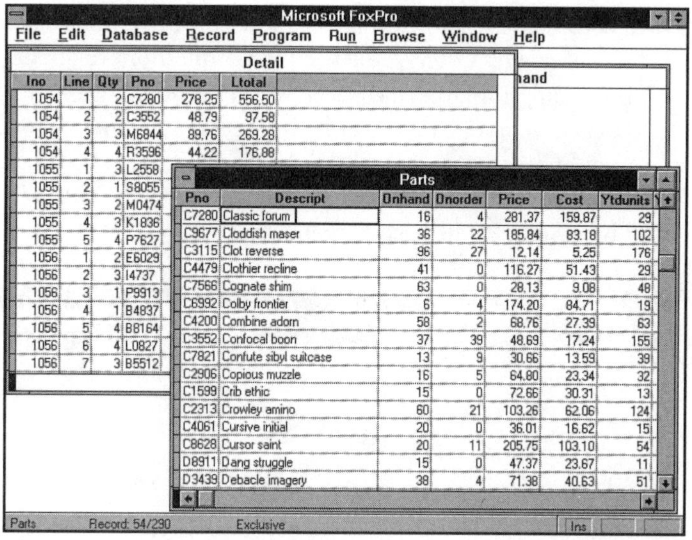

FIGURE 1.2.

A display of related tables.

FoxPro lets you create *screens* for data entry and record editing. Screens (called "forms" in some database managers) provide an easy way to view existing records, or to add new records to a table. While the tabular layout of data presented by a table may suffice for viewing large numbers of records, it usually is not the most convenient way to examine a single record. When you are working with individual records, screens are generally more convenient. Figure 1.3 shows a record from a table displayed within a screen.

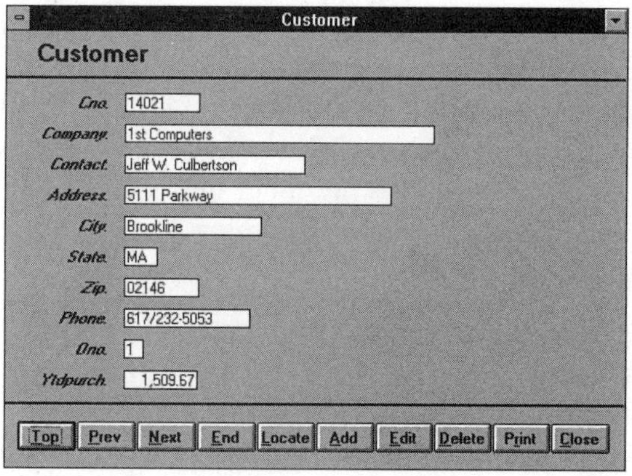

FIGURE 1.3.

Tables displayed within a screen.

While virtually all database managers (and even most spreadsheets) let you create forms for database data entry, FoxPro screens offer more. With screen wizards, you can create screens with buttons that the users can click to search for records or print data.

You have the full range of Windows graphical capabilities when it comes to designing screens in FoxPro; you can include various fonts, colors, and shading effects.

Once your data exists within tables in FoxPro, you phrase questions about your data in the form of *queries*. Often you'll need to ask questions to obtain specific information, such as "How many employees have been with the company for five years or more?" or "Which customers have not placed an order in the last 12 months?" In FoxPro, you can ask these questions by creating and using queries. (See Figure 1.4.) With queries, you can view data from multiple tables, select specific fields or records, sort records, and use the data provided by a query as the basis for reports.

FIGURE 1.4.

A sample query.

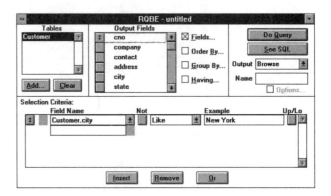

One way you can formulate queries in FoxPro is by filling in a graphical Query-By-Example window. Relational Query-By-Example, or RQBE, is a common technique used to retrieve data from relational databases. RQBE was designed by IBM in the 1970s, to provide users (who were not necessarily programmers) with an easy way to retrieve data. Starting with Borland's Paradox, RQBE has been implemented in a number of PC-based database products. But the graphical nature of FoxPro's RQBE makes queries easier to compose than with DOS-based products; instead of having to type a precise syntax for field names, you can simply click and drag fields onto a query grid. Complex expressions can be easily designed with the aid of the FoxPro's Expression Builder. Also, if you are accustomed to making queries by typing dBASE-style commands, you can continue to use this technique in FoxPro.

The ultimate objective of most databases is to provide reports of some sort, whether in printed form or displayed on-screen. FoxPro provides great flexibility in report design and generation through a visual report-designer interface. As with forms, reports can show data from a single table, or they can be relational; they can provide selected subsets of data, or they can provide overall summaries; and with the aid of the report wizards, reports can be easily created to meet a variety of needs. Figure 1.5 shows an example of a completed report in Print Preview.

FIGURE 1.5.

A report in Print Preview.

FoxPro lets you design your own reports from scratch, or modify the reports created by the report wizards. The report in Figure 1.5 is shown in its design view in Figure 1.6.

FIGURE 1.6.

A report in design view.

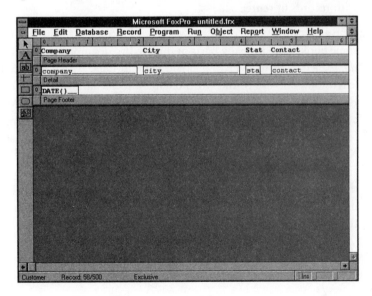

Databases, Defined

Before you create and work with data in FoxPro, it's helpful to clarify this book's terminology. Microsoft says that FoxPro is a *relational database management system.* A database management system (DBMS) is a system of tools that enables you to manage data stored in a database. *Relational* means that FoxPro lets you establish and work with relationships between multiple tables of related data.

According to a general definition, a *database* is a collection of tables which contains *records* (or rows) of data. (The stricter definition of a database involves some rules that PC database managers find difficult to follow completely, but this type of discussion is beyond the scope of this text.) The records in tables of a database are made up of *fields*, the individual categories of your data. In Figure 1.1, shown previously, each record of the table contains the data associated with a different individual, including last name, first name, address, and so on. Each category or column in the table is a field; hence, Lastname is a field, as are Firstname, Address, City, and so forth. With relational databases, it is customary to have more than one table to manage all of your data. For instance, a system for tracking video rentals to members of a video club might have a table with a listing of all the club members, another table with a listing of all the videos in stock, and a third table with records of rented videos.

One area of possible confusion with FoxPro relates to the use of the word database. In some books (and in many parts of the FoxPro documentation and help screens), the term *database* is used to refer to a single table of data, which is stored in a file with a .DBF extension. The use of the word database to mean a single table is actually the result of FoxPro's roots in the world of XBase. (XBase is a term used to describe all database management systems that use data files written in the dBASE file format.) The original dBASE II stored all tables in individual files (called database files) and assigned a .DBF extension. XBase products like FoxPro have been adhering to this standard since the days of dBASE II. Because of this, FoxPro tables are still routinely referred to as databases, even though this goes against the generally accepted definition. In this book, the word *table* will be used to refer to an individual table of FoxPro data. For your own purposes, keep in mind that FoxPro tables and FoxPro database files refer to the same thing.

FoxPro and the Big Picture

It is also important to understand where FoxPro fits into the computer arena from a historical perspective, because such insight will give you a better idea of FoxPro's capabilities. FoxPro was designed to provide a database migration path into the Windows graphical environment while maintaining maximum compatibility with existing database applications written in an XBase-compatible environment.

Different products in the database market approach relational database management differently. FoxPro has successfully carved its own broad market segment. Microsoft provides two very different products in the Windows database management market: FoxPro and Access appeal to the interactive user, the user who doesn't need compatibility with XBase program code. Access also appeals to the user who doesn't know database commands or programming, and has no desire to learn. While Access includes a powerful programming language, one can build applications of surprising complexity without knowing the language.

FoxPro, on the other hand, is aimed at the user who is on a higher level than the typical Access user. FoxPro excels in the hands of those who are willing to get their feet wet in the programming area. Because its roots are in dBASE, FoxPro is compatible with dBASE database files and, to a large degree, with XBase program code. In the past, the "no pain, no gain" scenario has applied to FoxPro. A common complaint was that the program was, by nature of its power, not very easy to use. But many of the improvements made to version 2.6 of FoxPro were designed to address that specific need. In particular, the wizards provided with FoxPro 2.6 make it possible for novice users to perform most common FoxPro tasks without an intricate knowledge of commands or complex menu sequences.

FoxPro vs. dBASE

Historically, the database market for IBM-compatible PCs was initially defined by the product known (in various incarnations) as dBASE. Originally marketed by a long-gone company named Ashton-Tate and now owned by Borland, dBASE set the standard for database management on the PC in the 1980s. There were other database managers for the PC before dBASE, but none had the market success of dBASE. dBASE II became entrenched as the first dominant database manager for personal computers. (There was no dBASE I, but that is a long story woven in the annals of micro trivia!) In spite of its popularity, dBASE II had severe limitations. It could open only two database files at once, was limited to a maximum of 32 fields, was horrendously slow at sorting, and required some convoluted programming to deal with date values. Its successor, dBASE III, addressed all of these weaknesses, but maintained the dBASE reputation of being a difficult product to master. dBASE III Plus was later introduced with further improvements. Other companies, in response to user demands for a "better" dBASE, produced a slew of dBASE-compatible products in the 1980s. These software packages were designed to provide compatibility with dBASE data files and programs, and also to offer more features. One of the best of these offerings was FoxBase, a software package produced by a small but savvy company out of Perrysburg, Ohio, known as Fox Software. As dBASE evolved from dBASE III to dBASE III Plus and dBASE IV, Fox Software upstaged its competition by introducing FoxBase Plus, followed by FoxBase for the Macintosh. The FoxBase products offered more speed and programming power than dBASE III and dBASE III Plus. However, the FoxBase programs remained difficult to use, and in the DOS arena, FoxBase still had the limitations of a DOS-based product using a character-based interface.

Enter Windows...

To counter general complaints about ease-of-use, Microsoft developed Windows in the late 1980s. Prior to Windows, competing DOS products set their own standards for even the most basic operations (such as printing a file). Using an industry standard, originally developed by IBM, called Common User Access (CUA) as a model, Microsoft developed Windows to provide a consistent user interface that different software products could run under. The graphical user interface (GUI) had been popularized earlier in the Apple Macintosh environment, and was based on pioneering work done at Xerox Corporation's Palo Alto Research Center. The hoped-for benefit was that once you knew how to use one program under Windows, you could use other Windows programs with less instruction. Initial versions of Windows were slow and sorely lacking in many areas, and the product made rather small inroads into the PC marketplace. In 1990, Microsoft released a major upgrade that cured many deficiencies, priced it reasonably, and the rest is history. Windows sales exceeded 10 million copies by the end of 1992, and Windows became the standard installed software on all IBM-compatible PCs sold at the retail level. Along with the success of Windows came a demand for Windows software, and database managers were initially slow to fill the gap. Long after word processors like Word for Windows and Ami Pro and spreadsheets like Excel appeared, database managers had not made major inroads to the Windows arena. A few "niche" products such as Software Publishing's Superbase 4 and Computer Associates' dbFAST appeared, but these products were not considered to be major successes in the Windows database field.

Around the time that Windows was gaining popularity, Fox Software introduced the first version of FoxPro for DOS. By this time, most persons in the computer field recognized the benefits of the graphical user interface. However, much of the available hardware was dragging behind the promise of the GUI environment, and the people at Fox Software wanted to bring the benefits of the GUI environment to a character-based interface. In doing so, speed of operation would not be sacrificed to GUI design. The result, FoxPro for DOS, was an unqualified success. Users liked being able to design Windows-like database applications on machines that had little or no chance of running Windows.

As hardware continued to improve and come up to the demands of Windows, Fox Software continued to improve FoxPro, and the development of a Windows version became part of the natural progression. At about the same time FoxPro for Windows was in development, Microsoft was in the process of acquiring Fox Software. The Microsoft/Fox merger brought a number of benefits: the Fox Software developers continued to develop FoxPro at Microsoft; and FoxPro and Access, Microsoft's other Windows database manager, were able to share technologies. Access 2, for example, makes use of FoxPro's patented Rushmore technology to gain speed, while version 2.6 of FoxPro provides wizards, which are ease-of-use features inherited from Access.

The Advantages of Windows

As a Windows product, FoxPro supports full data exchange with other Windows products. FoxPro has the ability to import and export data using many different formats, including ASCII text, Lotus 1-2-3, Paradox (import only), and dBASE. FoxPro provides support for Object Linking and Embedding (OLE) and Dynamic Data Exchange (DDE), which enables you to share live data between FoxPro and other Windows applications. Figure 1.7, for example, shows a graphic from Windows Paintbrush pasted into a field of a FoxPro table. With the OLE capabilities in FoxPro, the graphic can change, and the changes are automatically reflected in the FoxPro table.

FIGURE 1.7.

A Paintbrush graphic pasted into a FoxPro table through a form.

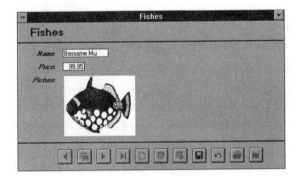

Proper Database Planning

Before getting into the development and use of FoxPro databases, a few words are needed about the overall design of your database. All too often, careful planning is neglected in the design of a database. This is particularly true with relational database management software, because many users have come over to the new generation of Windows products from the spreadsheet world. Lack of planning is a trait shared by both computer programmers and developers because so many find that developing applications or writing code is far more enjoyable than planning database designs on paper. Nevertheless, the structure of the tables and the relationships between them are at the heart of every database application. If the users of a database are to benefit, the design of the database must be properly planned from the start.

When you are planning the design, or structure, of a database, it often helps to tackle the problem from the output side. The database's output can be reports or responses to queries from users. How do users want their reports formatted? How will users formulate their queries? Once the desired output has been defined, you can begin to refine the necessary input data to produce the desired output.

While juggling output requirements and input specifications, keep in mind that most database management systems involve the use of multiple tables, and the varying relationships between those tables. A personnel tracking system, for example, might contain a salaries database and a benefits database, with a relationship drawn between common employee numbers contained in both files.

To effectively plan a database, list both the input and the output requirements on paper. Then refer to those requirements as you begin to define the necessary names of fields, types of fields, and sizes of fields. If possible, discuss the revised list of database fields with the future users of the system. They may not know the mechanics of programming, but likely will have a good idea of what will and won't work when it comes to the design of their database. Implementing a planning process as a part of database design will save *significant* additional effort and frustration later, as major changes to the database structure and dependent applications will be far less likely to occur.

For those unfamiliar with the esoterics of database design, time spent becoming familiar with the recommended design process is necessary. All the power of FoxPro, with its wizards and on-line help, won't salvage a poorly planned and implemented database. There are a minimum of three steps involved in the database planning process: *data definition*, *data refinement*, and *normalization*.

> *Data Definition:* During this step, you identify the data needs. With these needs identified, you can outline (on paper first, not while in the Table Design window of FoxPro) the desired fields that are needed for your tables. If you are building a system that is modeled after an existing paper-based system, you have a head start. Study the existing forms and reports that serve as input and output for the system, and plan the required fields that will best accommodate your data. As mentioned earlier, talking to users can save time and reduce wasted effort. One refinement that's not necessary at this stage is the separation of fields into multiple tables; this is performed during the second and third steps of the overall process.
>
> *Data Refinement:* During this phase of the design process, you begin to group parts of your data into logical categories. At this point, you can begin thinking about whether all the data should be contained in a single table, or whether it should be divided into a number of smaller tables. The smaller tables should follow your logical categories; for example, you might have categories such as CUSTOMERS, ORDERS, and PRODUCTS; CLIENTS and TIME SPENT; DOCTORS, PATIENTS, and OFFICE VISITS; VIDEO MEMBERS and VIDEO RENTALS; and so on. At this stage, you also refine your list of fields as needed, so that they more closely model the actual data to be stored within the tables. Upon examination, you may find that certain single fields need to be split

into more than one field (an "address" field, for example, may need to be restructured as a "street address" and an "apartment number" field).

Normalization: During this final step, you complete the necessary division of your fields into individual tables. The object here is to eliminate redundancies between the proposed tables and take advantage of the fact that FoxPro is a relational database. Textbooks on database design point out that normalization can often be taken through a series of steps, with each step reducing redundancies between tables. For instance, a first glance at a database for tracking customers and their orders might contain two tables: one for customer names and addresses, and another for customer orders. This might appear sufficient, but as records would be added to the Orders table, a redundancy would become apparent—many records would contain descriptions of the same items, ordered over and over by different customers. The solution to the redundancy would be to add a third table of inventory items, related to the Orders table by means of an item number. Depending on the complexity of the application, additional related tables might well be needed to eliminate all redundancies from the database design. Besides making for good database design, normalization can greatly reduce the work involved in data entry, as well as reduce the possibility of errors. Given the preceding example, the addition of an inventory table means that during data entry for each order, all that's needed is an order number. A complete description and cost of each item is not needed.

Keep in mind that even after all steps of the process are complete, no database design is set in stone. Changes may become necessary at a later time, and FoxPro will accommodate such changes. But proper planning from the outset can minimize such changes, and reduce effort later.

Hardware Requirements

Your computer must meet certain minimum hardware requirements to use Microsoft FoxPro for Windows. The following are the minimum requirements.

- An IBM-compatible computer capable of running Windows (minimum 386SX or better processor)

- A hard disk or network file server (disk space needed varies depending on how much of FoxPro you install and the amount of data and programs you store)

- 4 megabytes of memory or more (8MB or more, while not required, will do wonders for performance)

- An IBM-compatible VGA or other graphics card compatible with Microsoft Windows, version 3.0 or above

- A Microsoft mouse or other compatible pointing device
- Microsoft MS-DOS or IBM PC-DOS, version 3.1 or above
- Microsoft Windows, version 3.0 or above running in enhanced mode
- For operations on a network, network software that supports a network basic input/output system (NetBIOS)

Installation

FoxPro comes as several disks and assorted manuals. If you have not already made backup copies of the program disks, it is always a wise idea to do so before installing the program. (If you are unfamiliar with how to make backup copies of disks, refer to your Windows documentation for details.)

Installation

You can install FoxPro on your computer by performing the following steps:

1. Start Windows in the usual manner. (On most PCs, you can do this by typing WIN at the DOS prompt.)
2. Insert the Microsoft FoxPro Setup Disk in your disk drive.
3. Open the Windows File menu (press Alt+F), and choose Run.
4. In the Run dialog box which appears, enter **A:SETUP** (if the setup disk is in drive A:) or **B:SETUP** (if the setup disk is in drive B:), then click OK or press Enter.

The installation process will start, and you can follow the directions that appear on the screen to complete the installation. Some of the questions and prompts you will see include the following:

- FoxPro will ask you to enter your name, and the name of your company, in a dialog box. If FoxPro was already installed on another system using the same disks, you will see a warning box informing you of copyright regulations. Choose Continue from this dialog box to proceed with the installation (or choose Cancel Setup to cancel the process).
- FoxPro will ask in which directory you want to install the program. By default, FoxPro suggests C:\FPW26 as a directory name, although you can change this to any valid drive and path name.
- FoxPro gives you a choice between installing all of the program, specific parts of the program (custom installation), or a minimum installation of the program. If you choose custom installation, you are presented with check boxes that let you

choose which parts of the program you want to install. For example, you can choose to omit the tutorial to save on disk space. If you select the complete installation, FoxPro will require roughly 12MB of disk space to install the program. If you choose the minimum installation, FoxPro will require roughly 4MB of disk space.

■ FoxPro prompts for each additional disk as it is needed. When prompted, insert the specified disk in the drive, and click OK.

NOTE

If you are installing FoxPro on a network, you will see questions about the type of network in use. For additional details on installing FoxPro on a network, refer to "Setting Up FoxPro on a Network" in your *Microsoft FoxPro User's Guide*.

Once the installation process is complete, you are returned to the Windows desktop. A new program group containing FoxPro will have been added to your desktop. You can open the program group, and double-click the FoxPro icon within the group to start the program.

Chapter Summary

For computer users who need the power and flexibility traditionally offered by XBase along with the ease of use afforded by Windows, FoxPro 2.6 meets those needs in a first-class way. The Catalog Manager of FoxPro 2.6 makes it possible for novice users to perform complex database management tasks with FoxPro, while the power of the XBase programming language remains for those who prefer to have full access to that power. The remaining chapters in Part I of this book will discuss how you can quickly put FoxPro to work, using the Catalog Manager, the menu options, and the available FoxPro commands.

Maximizing the FoxPro User Interface

2

This chapter details the user interface behind FoxPro for Windows. Topics in this chapter include the use of the Catalog Manager, mouse and window techniques, and the effective use of menus, windows, and dialog boxes. Much of this chapter serves as a reference for those who are unfamiliar with the FoxPro interface. When you can't recall where a specific menu option is located, you can refer to this chapter to find it.

Version 2.6 of FoxPro is flexible among database managers in that it actually provides three methods of interacting with the program: a Catalog Manager, a menu system, and a Command Window. The different methods of working with FoxPro will appeal to different types of users. The Catalog Manager feature of FoxPro is new to version 2.6, and it makes it possible to work in FoxPro without a knowledge of menu options or commands. In general, the Catalog Manager, which is discussed in this chapter, will appeal both to novice users and to those who prefer to be insulated from the complexities of FoxPro. The menu system provides more flexibility than the Catalog Manager, while still shielding users from needing an intricate knowledge of FoxPro commands. Finally, the Command Window lets experienced users address the full power of FoxPro through interactive commands.

> **TIP**
>
> Those who are upgrading to FoxPro from older versions of XBase products will likely be most comfortable with the use of the Command Window. In the Command Window, you can type FoxPro commands (most of which are compatible with other XBase products).

Starting FoxPro

When FoxPro is first started (by double-clicking the FoxPro icon in the FoxPro for Windows program group), an introductory screen appears. (See Figure 2.1.)

The screen provides buttons that you can click to choose any of the following options. You may not see this screen if it has been turned off; once you check the "Don't display this introductory screen again" option, it no longer appears on startup.

- **Proceed to the Catalog Manager.** Clicking this option takes you to FoxPro's Catalog Manager, which you can use to accomplish most common types of database tasks.

- **Proceed to the Menu System and Command Window.** Clicking this option takes you to the FoxPro desktop, which contains the menus and the Command Window. You can choose to use either menu options or FoxPro commands to accomplish your work in FoxPro.

- **Explore a sample catalog.** This option lets you work with a sample catalog that includes files containing sample data. This option is normally used by those who are just learning to use the program.

- **Don't display this introductory screen again.** This option turns off the introductory screen. After choosing this option, FoxPro will start up the next time in whatever mode you left the program in when you exited. For example, if you chose to use the Catalog Manager, FoxPro will next start up in the Catalog Manager. If you chose to use the menus and Command Window, FoxPro will display these upon the next startup.

FIGURE 2.1.

The introductory startup screen.

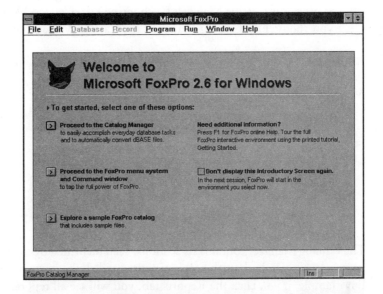

If you are at the FoxPro menus and Command Window and prefer to use the Catalog Manager, you can easily switch to the Catalog Manager by choosing File, Catalog Manager from the FoxPro menus. If you are in the Catalog Manager and want to switch to the menus and the Command Window, press Ctrl+F4 when the Catalog Manager is the active window, and click Switch to Command Window in the dialog box that appears. The material which follows discusses both the Catalog Manager and the use of FoxPro menu options in greater detail.

Using the Catalog Manager

The Catalog Manager is a user-friendly graphical interface that enables you to organize your database work in a file-folder type system. FoxPro catalogs can be thought of as containers to store database-related items you work with on a regular basis. Tables, queries, screens, reports, labels, and programs can all be stored in FoxPro catalogs. You can also use a feature of the Catalog Manager, called AutoMigrate, to easily bring in dBASE III and dBASE IV files.

If FoxPro doesn't automatically enter the Catalog Manager when you start the program, you can get to the Catalog Manager by choosing File, Catalog Manager from the menus. Once you choose File, Catalog Manager, the Catalog Manager appears (See Figure 2.2).

FIGURE 2.2.

The FoxPro Catalog Manager.

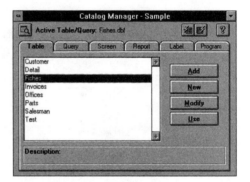

The Catalog Manager contains six sections, each identified by a corresponding tab. Once you click on any tab, that tab becomes active, and all the items related to that tab appear. For example, if you click the Reports tab, you will see all reports stored in that catalog. Buttons that appear in the Catalog Manager let you perform tasks which are appropriate to the item you've selected. For example, with tables as the selected item types, buttons are available to add a table to the catalog, to create a new table, to modify an existing table, or to put a table into use. The various options of the Catalog Manager that you can use to perform database tasks are covered in more detail throughout the book. For example, Chapter 3, "Creating and Working with Tables," tells you how to create new tables from the Catalog Manager, as well as from the menus or from within the Command Window. It helps to be familiar with the Catalog Manager on an overall basis if you plan to make extensive use of it.

Keep in mind that there are limitations to the Catalog Manager. The Catalog Manager can be thought of as the least-intimidating way to use FoxPro, but it's designed to accomplish only the more common database tasks. If what you need to do often leans towards the unusual, you may find that the Catalog Manager won't always let you accomplish what you desire. The FoxPro menus go a wide step beyond what is possible with the Catalog Manager, and the use of FoxPro commands through the Command Window provides the most power of all. For that reason, a significant portion of this book (Chapters 23 and 24) details the specific use of FoxPro commands and functions.

About the FoxPro Menu System

When you start FoxPro with the Command Window with the menus active (or if you switch from the Catalog Manager to the Command Window and menus), you see the FoxPro desktop. (See Figure 2.3.) The menu system appears as part of the desktop, at the top of the screen.

FIGURE 2.3.

The FoxPro desktop.

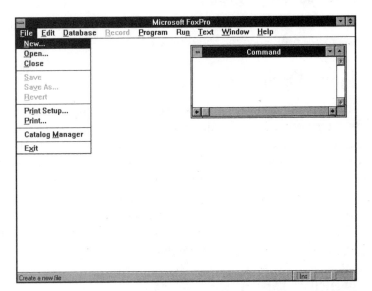

The FoxPro menu system has four parts: a menu bar, menu pads (which reside along the menu bar), pull-down menus (which open from the menu pads), and menu options. When you open a menu by clicking the desired menu pad with the mouse, or by pressing Alt+ the underlined letter in the menu pad, the pull-down menu drops from the menu pad, and you can choose a desired option. In Figure 2.3, the File menu is open and the available choices displayed.

Menu Bar

The menu bar appears at the top of the FoxPro window and the names of the individual pull-down menus are shown. Not only is this menu bar a standard way of working with FoxPro, but it also is representative of the interface design for most FoxPro applications. Using the Applications Generator or FoxPro programs of your own design, you can create custom applications that use menu options similar to those in the FoxPro menu bar.

Menu Pads

The menu pads are placed horizontally along the menu bar, and each pad is the name of a corresponding pull-down menu. If a menu pad is dimmed, the pad is disabled and doesn't apply to the current operation. In Figure 2.3, for example, the Record menu pad is dimmed because no table is open and the options under the Record menu would not apply. Depending on the operation being performed, specific menu pads may be added to the menu bar by FoxPro, or existing pads removed.

Pull-down Menus

Pull-down menus (called *popup menus* by some) are rectangular boxes that pull down from the menu pads when the pad is selected.

Menu Options

Each pull-down menu contains menu options relevant to the area in which you are working. If an option is dimmed, it is not available. For example, in Figure 2.3, shown previously, the Save, Save As, and Revert options are unavailable, because no file is currently open. The options that are followed by an ellipse (...) cause dialog boxes to appear when selected. Some menu options also contain Ctrl+key combinations, which can be used as shortcut keys for those menu selections. For example, the Window menu contains a Cycle option with a Ctrl+F1 designation, and a Command option with a Ctrl+F2 designation. Therefore, pressing Ctrl+F1 from anywhere in FoxPro would be the equivalent to opening the Window menu and choosing Cycle.

Making Menu Selections

You can make menu selections with either the keyboard or the mouse, and there are advantages to each method. Mouse usage tends to be intuitive and easy to understand, while the keyboard appeals to many persons who find mouse navigation difficult. To use the mouse to select a desired menu option, click the menu by name on the menu pad with the left mouse button, then click the desired option from the pull-down menu that opens. To use the keyboard to choose a desired menu option, press Alt+ the underlined letter of the desired menu pad to open the pull-down menu, then press the underlined letter that corresponds to the desired menu option. For example, to open a file, you could press Alt+F (to open the File menu), followed by the letter "O" (for the "Open" choice).

If you open a menu and then decide that you would rather do something else, you can cancel the menu selection. From the keyboard, press the Esc key. Or, with the mouse, you can click anywhere outside of the menu that is open.

About Dialog Boxes

As mentioned earlier, menu boxes that are followed by ellipses (...) display a *dialog box* asking for additional information when selected. Dialog boxes contain the specific settings that are related to the chosen command, along with the assumptions that FoxPro makes for that command. Figure 2.4 shows the dialog box that appears when you choose File, Print Setup. You can select OK (by clicking the OK button or pressing Enter) to accept the settings shown in the dialog box, or you can change any of them. Dialog boxes vary as to the available options within them, but they all contain some or all of the elements described in the following paragraphs.

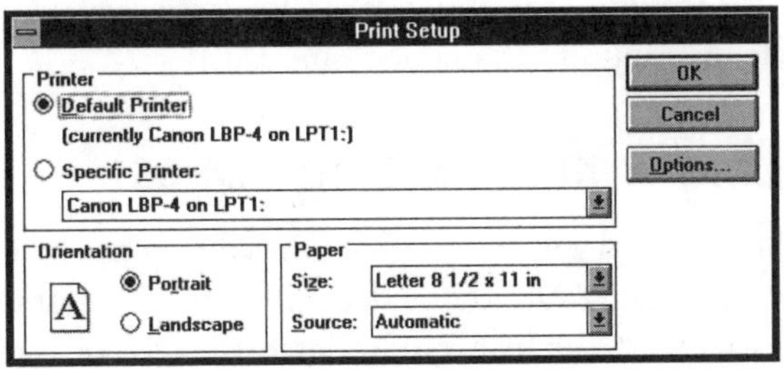

FIGURE 2.4.

The File, Print Setup dialog box.

Command Buttons

These are rectangular buttons with rounded corners. They implement commands or other actions, or display an additional dialog box. Most dialog boxes contain command buttons that say OK, Cancel, or Close, used to confirm or cancel an action. When the term in a command button is followed by an ellipse, choosing that button will cause another dialog box to appear. A command button labeled Options indicates that more options are available if you select the button.

Option Buttons

These are buttons with rounded corners that can be turned on or off. The button is filled in when the option is turned on, and is blank when the option is switched off.

Text Boxes

These are rectangles that accept text you enter in response to a prompt, such as a file name or a numeric value for a margin setting. Text boxes that accept numeric values may also have double arrows at the right edge of the box (also known as *spinners*). Mouse users can click on the arrows to increase or decrease the value entered. Text boxes are sometimes combined with list boxes (described below) to form *combination boxes*. In a combination box, you can either type your selection in the text box or choose a selection from the list box.

List Boxes

These contain lists of available choices, such as file names or font styles. Some list boxes display all possible choices, along with a scroll bar that lets you view the choices. Other list boxes are called *drop-down* boxes. These initially show just one choice. To see additional choices, you click on the down arrow at the side of the list box or Tab to the list box and press the down arrow key.

Check Boxes

These are circles that contain a smaller, shaded circle to indicate when the option beside them is turned on. If the option is off, the circle is blank. (In some versions of Windows, the circle may appear as a diamond instead.)

Working with the Dialog Boxes

With the keyboard you can move within a dialog box by using the Tab and the Shift+Tab keys, or by pressing Alt+ the underlined letter of an option name. The OK and Cancel buttons can be chosen by pressing Enter (for OK) or Esc (for Cancel). You can open list boxes from the keyboard by using the Tab key to move to the desired list box, then press the down arrow key to open the list. Once the list is open, you can navigate within it with the up and down arrow keys; when the desired option is highlighted within the list, press Enter to select it.

Mouse users have less of a hassle with the mouse: just click the desired option. To turn the option buttons or check boxes on or off, click the desired button or box. To open a list box, click the arrow anywhere within the box.

The Available FoxPro Menu Options

The following paragraphs provide a summary of the FoxPro menu options. Keep in mind that where ellipses appear with the named commands, choosing the command displays a dialog box with more options.

File Menu

The File menu (shown previously in Figure 2.3), lets you create new files, open existing files, and save changes to files. Various options within the File menu also provide access to system hardware such as disk drives and printers. The following options are available from the File menu:

>**New...:** This option displays the New dialog box (see Figure 2.5), from which you can select the desired file type in the dialog box to begin creating the desired

type of file. This may include a table (also known as a database), program, text file, index file, report, label, screen, menu, query, or project. (How you create the different types of files is discussed throughout the book.)

FIGURE 2.5.

The New dialog box.

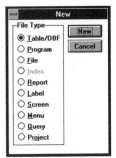

Open...: This option displays the Open dialog box (see Figure 2.6), which you can use to open an existing file. You can use the Drive and Directory list boxes that appear in the Open dialog box to browse among the different disk drives and directories. File types appear in the order of their extensions. You can click in the List Files of Type box to choose a different file type to open. When you do this, the extension changes correspondingly.

FIGURE 2.6.

The Open dialog box.

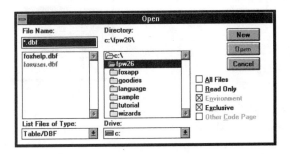

Close: This option closes the current window and removes it from the FoxPro desktop.

Save: This option saves the active file, and writes any changes to disk without closing the active file. If more than one file is open under FoxPro, choosing Save saves only the file that's in the active window.

Save As...: This option displays the Save As... dialog box, which you can use to copy the active file to disk under a new file name.

Revert: Use this option to abandon all modifications to the open file, and return to the last saved version of the file. Before this happens, FoxPro asks if you want to discard the changes you've made to the file. In effect, this is an alternate method of closing a file without saving the changes, then reopening the file.

Print Setup...: This option displays the Print Setup dialog box. (See Figure 2.7.) You can use the options in this dialog box to specify printer options such as the printer to be used, page size, margins, and page orientation.

FIGURE 2.7.

The Print Setup dialog box.

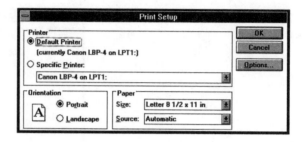

Print...: This option displays the Print dialog box. (See Figure 2.8.) You can use the options within this dialog box to print the contents of the active window, or to print the contents of a file that is not open (by clicking the File button and choosing the desired file in the dialog box that appears). You can also choose options such as whether line numbers appear with the printed file, and whether page ejects should be sent to the printer before or after printing starts.

FIGURE 2.8.

The Print dialog box.

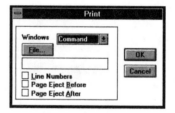

Catalog Manager...: This option starts the Catalog Manager, which you can use to access dBASE IV and FoxPro catalogs. (The Catalog Manager was described in further detail earlier in this chapter.)

Exit: This option closes FoxPro and exits to Windows.

Edit Menu

The various options of the Edit menu are used to provide text-editing functions. Most Edit menu options relate to the editing of text, but the Insert Object, Change Link, and Convert to Static options are specifically used with OLE (Object Linking and Embedding) objects. The Edit menu OLE options are available only for a general field of a table that is open. General fields can be used to store different types of Windows data, such as pictures or sound. (General Fields are discussed in more detail in Chapter 3.) The Edit menu contains the following options:

Undo: This option reverses your most recent editing action.

Redo: This option reverses your most recent Undo.

Cut: This option removes selected text and places it in the Clipboard.

Copy: This option duplicates the selected text and places an image of the selection in the Clipboard.

Paste: This option places cut or copied text (the contents of the Clipboard) at the cursor location.

Paste Special...: This option displays a Paste Special dialog box. You can use the options in this dialog box to move OLE objects to general fields.

Clear: This option removes the selected text without placing it on the Clipboard.

Insert Object...: This option displays the Insert Object dialog box, which can be used to insert an OLE object in a general field.

Object...: This option activates an OLE object.

Change Link...: This option displays the Edit Link dialog box, which can be used to update a link to an object.

Convert To Static: This option changes a linked or embedded OLE object to a static picture.

Select All: This option selects all objects or text in the active window (except for Browse windows, which do not allow selections of all data contained).

GoTo Line...: This option displays the GoTo Line dialog box, which can be used to move the cursor to a specified line number.

Find...: This option displays the Find dialog box, which can be used to search for text.

Find Again: This option repeats the text search started with the Find option.

Replace And Find Again: This option substitutes new text and continues the search.

Replace All: This option substitutes new text for all occurrences of the specified text.

Preferences...: This option displays the Preferences dialog box. You can use the options in this dialog box to set your save, justification, and editing preferences.

Database Menu

When you open the Database menu, you see the available options used for performing operations on tables, and for printing reports and labels. The following options are provided on this menu:

Setup...: This option displays the Setup dialog box, which you can use to make modifications to an existing table, or to perform maintenance on a table.

Browse: This option opens a Browse window into the active table. From the Browse window, you can easily edit the information in a table.

Append From...: This option displays the Append From dialog box, which is used to move data from another table to the currently active table.

Copy To...: This option displays the Copy To dialog box, which is used to move data from the currently active table to another table.

Sort...: This option displays the Sort dialog box, which you can use to create a new table of data that is in a different order than that of the active table.

Total...: This option displays the Total dialog box, which you can use to sum the values in specified fields of the active table.

Average...: This option displays the Average dialog box, which you can use to calculate the average of a specified expression.

Count...: This option displays the Count dialog box, which you can use to display the number of records that meet specified criteria.

Sum...: This option displays the Sum dialog box, which you can use to calculate the sum of a specified expression.

Calculate...: This option displays the Calculate dialog box, which you can use to calculate financial or statistical value based on a specific expression.

Report...: This option starts the Report Writer, which can be used to produce a report from the active table. Report... enables you to run a predefined report. To create a new report, use File, New.

Label...: This option starts the Label Writer, which can be used to produce a set of labels from the active table. Label... enables you to run a predefined label. To create a new label, use File, New.

Pack: This option removes records marked for deletion from the active table.

Reindex: This option rebuilds any open index files associated with the active table.

Record Menu

On the Record menu you will find commands used to perform operations on records in the table that is currently active. The following options are provided on this menu:

Append: This option opens an edit window in append mode.

Change: This option opens an edit window in change mode.

GoTo...: This option opens the GoTo dialog box, which you can use to move to a specific record.

Locate...: This option displays the Locate dialog box, which can be used to find a specific record based on the specifications that you enter into the dialog box.

Continue: This option continues a LOCATE command, searching for the next record that meets the specified conditions.

Seek...: This option displays the Seek dialog box, which can be used to search for a record in a table when a corresponding index is active.

Replace...: This option displays the Replace dialog box, which is used to change a record or a series of records.

Delete...: This option displays the Delete dialog box, which is used to delete a record or a series of records.

Recall...: This option displays the Recall dialog box, which is used to remove the delete tag from one or more records.

Program Menu

The Program menu contains options you'll find useful when running or writing programs in FoxPro. The options include the following:

Do...: This option displays the Do dialog box, which can be used to run a program.

Cancel: This option ends program execution and returns control to FoxPro.

Resume: This option continues operation of a program that was suspended.

Debug: This option opens the Debug window, which is used to show variables as a program runs.

Trace: This option opens the Trace window, which can be used to follow a program in a step-by-step sequence.

Compile...: This option displays the Compile dialog box, which is used to convert a program's source code to object code.

Generate...: This option displays the Generate dialog box. The options in this dialog box are used to generate source code based on an item (such as a screen) created with one of FoxPro's power tools.

Macros...: This option displays the Macro Edit dialog box, which is used to define macros.

Beautify... This option displays the Beautification Options dialog box, which is used to make cosmetic changes to a program.

FoxDoc: This option opens the FoxDoc dialog box. FoxDoc is a utility that is useful in documenting your FoxPro programs.

Run Menu

The Run menu provides fast access to FoxPro's power tools. The menu options are:

New Query: Use this option to open a blank RQBE Window, where you can begin creating a new query.

Query: Use this option to open a RQBE Window containing an existing query.

Screen: You can use this option to run an existing screen program by selecting the screen program name from the list and choosing Run, or you can create a new screen by choosing New to display the Screen Design Window.

Report: Use this option to run an existing report by selecting the report name in the dialog box that appears. In this dialog box, you can choose whether you want the report output to appear in a Page Preview window, or to be sent to a printer or a file. Or, you can create a new report by selecting New in the dialog box to open a Report Layout Window.

Label: Use this option to run an existing label form by selecting the label name in the dialog box that appears. In this dialog box, you can choose whether you want the label output to appear in a Page Preview window, or to be sent to a printer or a file. Or, you can create a new label form by selecting New in the dialog box to open a Label Form Layout Window.

Application: This option displays the Open dialog box. You can use this dialog box to run an existing application, or you can create a new application by choosing New from the dialog box to load the FoxPro Application Generator (FOXAPP).

Wizard: When you choose this option, an additional menu appears, with a choice of wizards. You can choose the desired wizard to run it.

Text Menu

The Text menu provides a number of text formatting options, as detailed below.

Font...: This option displays the Font dialog box, used to choose a desired font, font style, and size.

Enlarge Font: This option enlarges the font size for a text file (or for the data displayed in the active window) to the next available point size.

Reduce Font: This option reduces the font size for a text file (or for the data displayed in the active window) to the next available point size.

Single Space: This option changes the line spacing for a text file to single space.

1 1/2 Space: This option changes the line spacing for a text file to 1 1/2.

Double Space: This option changes the line spacing for a text file to double space.

Indent: This option moves selected lines to the next tab stop.

Undent: This option moves selected indented lines back to the prior tab stop.

Spelling...: This option runs FoxPro's spell checker.

Window Menu

You can use the various Window menu options to work with windows on the FoxPro desktop. The menu provides the following options:

Hide: This option hides a window (it makes the window invisible without closing the window).

Clear: This option clears the current window, removing any information from it.

Cycle: This option moves open windows to the top in sequential order.

Command: This option brings the Command window to the front.

View: This option displays the View Window. You can use the View window to establish relationships between tables, to change various settings within FoxPro, and to specify work areas.

Window: This portion of the menu contains a list of all windows that are currently open on the FoxPro desktop. You can choose any window by name to bring it to the front.

Help Menu

The Help menu contains information about FoxPro features, support, and special topics under the following options:

Contents: This option displays a table of contents containing the Help topics.

Search for Help On...: This option displays the Help Search dialog box, which you can use to find help on a specific topic.

How to Use Help: This option displays a dialog box that details different ways in which you can use FoxPro's help system.

dBASE Help...: This option displays help that's useful to users who have upgraded to FoxPro from dBASE.

About FoxPro...: This option displays information about FoxPro, including system configuration, and FoxPro support.

Calculator: This option displays the Calculator desk accessory.

Calendar/Diary: This option displays the Calendar/Diary desk accessory.

Filer: This option displays the Filer desk accessory.

Puzzle: This option displays the Puzzle desk accessory.

Chapter Summary

This chapter provided an overview of the user interface provided with FoxPro for Windows. Probably the most important point to realize is that with FoxPro, you are not locked into a single style of doing things. Depending on your comfort level and your familiarity with the program, you can use commands, menu options, or the Catalog Manager to work in FoxPro. A familiarity with all three methods will provide you with the most in terms of flexibility.

Creating and Working with Tables

Chapter 1, "First Things First," introduced tables for storing data within FoxPro. Tables can be considered to be *containers* for your data—all data that is stored in FoxPro is stored in tables. In a relational database manager like FoxPro, most applications require the use of a collection of tables, each of which is used to store data about a different subject. For users not accustomed to designing relational databases, proper table planning is the most challenging part of the job. If you are new to this area, you should carefully consider the topic "Proper Database Planning" in Chapter 1.

Creating a Database Automatically with the Table Wizards

The Table Wizards provide an easy way for FoxPro users to create tables for common business and personal applications. A major portion of this chapter details the specific kinds of tables you can create. (For reference, a section detailing each of the available table types possible with the wizards is included at the end of this chapter.) When you begin the table creation process using the Table Wizards, FoxPro displays a Table Wizard dialog box. Using the various options within the dialog box, you can select from common table types, including inventory, customers, or business contacts. For each sample table, you're presented with a list of proposed fields, any or all of which can be included in your table. When you complete your responses in the dialog box, FoxPro builds the table for you.

Paying Attention to Database Design

Out of necessity, database design arises as a consideration when using the wizards to design your tables. A natural question may be "why consider database design when the Table Wizards make table creation automatic?" It's the ease of table creation in such an automated manner that makes a warning about database design necessary. The Table Wizards are a significant step forward in making database design easier, but there are things the Table Wizards will do and things they won't. In a nutshell, the wizards help you lay out individual table designs, with appropriate fields and field types. However, the wizards will *not* establish any relationships between multiple tables. Nor will they identify where relationships might be needed, or even where the normalization process is necessary (in other words, when you should be using multiple tables). When you create your tables without the wizards, you're forced to think about table design and how your tables relate to the overall picture. When you use an automated process like a wizard, it's easy to forget about the rest of the picture. You should recognize that when creating databases of any complexity, even with the wizards, you'll need to do some of the design work on your own. Careful planning remains a part of the table creation process, even when you use the Table Wizards.

Creating a Table with the Wizards

To create a table with the Table Wizards, you can be at the Catalog Manager, or you can choose Run, Wizard, Table from the menus. From the Catalog Manager, perform the following steps:

1. Click the Table tab, then click New. When you do so, FoxPro displays the Create Table dialog box. (See Figure 3.1.)

FIGURE 3.1.

The Create Table dialog box.

2. Click the Table Wizard button. FoxPro displays the first of the Table Wizard dialog boxes. (See Figure 3.2.)

FIGURE 3.2.

The first Table Wizard dialog box.

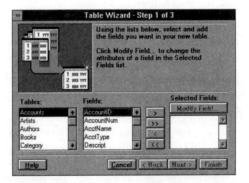

The first Table Wizard dialog box presents a list of possible table designs in the list box at the left side of the dialog box. For each table type, a list of possible fields appears in the Fields portion in the center of the dialog box. As you choose fields for inclusion in the table design, they will be placed at the right side of the dialog box in the Selected Fields list box.

3. Scroll in the Tables list box as needed, and click the desired table design. When you do so, the corresponding list of fields for that design appears in the Fields list box.

4. Using the angle bracket buttons, add the fields you want by clicking each field in the Fields list box to select it, then clicking the right-angle bracket button to add

the field to the Selected Fields list. Alternatively, you can double-click any field in the Fields list box to add it to the Selected Fields list box. You can also click the double right-angle bracket button, to add all the fields to the Selected Fields list box.

5. When satisfied with the proposed fields, click Next. You see the second Table Wizard dialog box, shown in Figure 3.3.

FIGURE 3.3.

The second Table Wizard dialog box.

At this point, the Table Wizard needs to know if you want to add an *index* to sort the records. You can choose one or more fields that will serve as the index to maintain the records in a specific order. (You'll learn more about indexing in Chapter 5, "Arranging Data.") If you don't want to arrange the records in any specific order, just click Next to bypass this dialog box.

6. Click each field you want to sort by selecting the field. Click Ascending or Descending as desired, then click the Add button in the center of the dialog box to move the field into the Sort Order list box. If you make a mistake, you can click the Remove button to remove any unwanted fields from the Sort Order list box. When done adding the desired fields, click Next.

TIP

If you want to arrange the records based on a sort order of more than one field, be sure to add the most important fields first. For example, if you want to arrange the records in a mailing list by state and then by city, add the State field first, then add the City field.

The next dialog box informs you that the process is completed. By using the buttons in this dialog box (see Figure 3.4), you can save the table, save the table and open it in a Browse window, save the table and create a default screen (called AutoScreen), which is useful for data entry and editing, or modify the structure of the table. Click the desired option, then click Finish to proceed. Whichever option you choose, you are prompted to enter a name for the table. Since FoxPro saves tables as individual files under the operating system, you are limited to the same restrictions when naming files as you are under your operating system. Assuming you're using DOS, this means table names of eight characters or less, with no spaces.

FIGURE 3.4.

The final Table Wizard dialog box.

Depending on which table design you choose in the Tables list box that appears in the first dialog box, the Table Wizards propose a different table structure that can be used as is, or modified as you prefer. Later in this chapter, you'll find listings of the structures for all the different tables that can be created with the Table Wizards.

Creating a Table Manually

Before creating a table manually, you'll need to know the field names and field types you plan to use in the table. (If you are already using paper forms to collect the data in your application, the forms can serve as a model for your field names and field types.) FoxPro 2.6 gives you three ways to create a table without the aid of the wizards. You can click in the Command Window and enter CREATE filename, where "filename" is the name of the table that you want to create. Or, from the Catalog Manager, you can click the Table tab, then click the New button, and click New Table in the next dialog box that appears. Finally, from the menus, you can choose File, New. In the dialog box that appears, you should click Table/DBF, then click New.

With any of these methods, the Table Structure dialog box appears. (See Figure 3.5.) The Table Structure box enables you to name the fields in your database. When you name a field, the name can contain up to 10 characters. Names that are too long or have illegal characters (such as spaces) are not accepted.

The data type that you choose for a field determines what kind of data you can enter into it and the amount of storage space available for the data. FoxPro tables can use any one of seven types of fields; these are shown in the menu that appears if you click in the Type column. (See Figure 3.6.)

FIGURE 3.5.

The Table Structure dialog box.

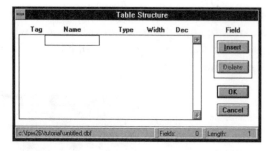

FIGURE 3.6.

The menu of available data types.

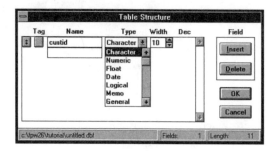

If you don't select one of the data types, FoxPro defaults to the Character data type. The available data types and their uses are detailed in the following list.

Character fields Use character fields to store any type of characters, such as customer names, product names, and addresses. Character fields can contain any combination of text and numbers, of up to 254 characters in length. Numbers that you don't intend to perform calculations on, such as part numbers, patient ID numbers, or phone numbers, should be stored in character fields. If you need to store more than 254 characters, use a memo field instead.

Numeric fields This type of field stores numbers, with or without decimals. Only numbers, a minus sign (the hyphen), or a decimal point are allowed in this field; commas cannot be entered. Although commas are not allowed, you can format reports that show commas. Up to 20 digits can be entered in the field and FoxPro maintains numeric accuracy to 16 digits.

TIP

Use Numeric fields only for numbers that you are going to perform calculations on. Use character fields for such items as phone numbers.

Float fields This is a variation of the numeric field. This type handles numbers with floating decimal points. As with numeric fields, you can enter the minus sign. Float fields are accurate up to 16 digits.

Date fields Use this field type to store date values. FoxPro automatically adds the slashes if six digits are entered in a date field. All leading zeros must be included for the day and month when adding data to a date field. Validation of existent dates is automatic; you cannot enter invalid dates (such as 02/31/93). Date fields can be useful in calculations, as FoxPro lets you perform date-based arithmetic. You could, for example, subtract one date field from another in a report, to come up with the number of days between both dates.

Logical fields These fields consist of single letters that represent the true or false value, such as T for true or Y for yes, F for false or N for no.

Memo fields A memo field allows large blocks of text to be stored in a database. In theory, an unlimited amount of data can be stored here, but the practical limits are the size of your hard drive. Memo fields are ideal for items like employee job descriptions, product descriptions, article abstracts, or other long paragraphs of text.

General fields This field is used to store pictures, sound, spreadsheets, word-processing documents, or any other type of OLE data that can be imported from other windows applications. (Chapter 17, "Working with Graphs," shows how this type of information can be shared.)

You can choose the type of field you want under the type column by either typing the first letter of the desired field type, or by clicking the arrow in the drop down list box. You can also use the arrow keys to scroll through the field types in the drop down list box, and press Enter to choose a type from the list.

After choosing a field type, you can click in the Width column, or press the Tab key to move to the Width column. (Note that the Date, Logical, Memo, and General field types have preset widths that are automatically entered by FoxPro.) For character fields, you can enter the desired width, then move on to defining the next field. For numeric and float fields, once you enter the width, you also need to enter the desired number of decimal places in the Dec column to the right of the Width column.

Once you have defined the specifications needed for the field, press Tab to move to the next successive field. You can also use the Insert and Delete buttons in the dialog box to insert new fields between existing fields in a table structure or to delete a field from a table structure. Continue to define the desired fields of the table, and when done, click OK. If you used the CREATE *filename* syntax in the Command Window to start the process, FoxPro will not ask for a table name; otherwise, you will be prompted for a name that the table will be saved under.

A Note About Index Tags

As you add fields to the table structure, you will see a Tag button appear to the left of each field name. The Tag button, which is initially blank, represents a way to add an *index tag* to a field of a table. Index tags are used to speed searches and keep table records in order by means of an index. Chapter 5 provides additional details on the topic of indexes. You can click the Tag button to add an index based on the selected field. Clicking the button once adds an up-pointing arrow to the button, indicating that an index will be added in ascending order. Clicking the button again changes the arrow to a down-pointing one, indicating that the added index will be in descending order. Clicking the button once more removes the arrow, indicating that there will be no index tag added to that field.

An Example of Table Creation

To get an idea of the methods used to create tables (and to make use of a table that will be used as an example throughout this book), you can create a Customer file that will be used for a mail-order bookstore. After going through the database planning process, the bookstore employees have proposed the following list of fields:

```
CustID
Lastname
Firstname
Address
City
State
ZIP Code
Phone
```

Purchases	(a numeric field that tracks the number of books bought)
Since	(a date field that shows how long the person has been on the list)
Desires	(a memo field that contains notes about the reader's preferences)

The field titled "CustID" is an example of a field that uses numbers, but should be defined as a character field because there are no calculations taking place with the data stored in this field. (The use of a numeric field for fields, which at first glance may seem to contain numbers, can pose a problem with the use of social security numbers, for example. FoxPro ignores everything after the hyphen, which results in an incorrect entry.)

From the menus, choose File, New. In the dialog box that appears, click Table/DBF, then click New to start the table creation process. (If you are at the Catalog Manager, click the Table tab, then click New, then click New Table in the next dialog box that appears, and enter the name BUYERS for the table.) When the Table Structure dialog box appears, type CustID for the first field name, then press Tab to move on to the Type column.

For the field type, choose Character. (Character is the default type so you can press Tab and move to the Width column.) Regarding widths, keep in mind that character widths can be up to 254 characters in length but numeric fields are limited to a width of 20. (Logical fields are fixed at one character, memo date fields are fixed at eight, while memo and general fields are fixed at 10 characters.) In our example database, the CustID field will be three digits in length, so enter 3 as the desired width, then press Tab to move to the name column for the next field.

You can finish building the database structure by entering the following information:

Enter Lastname as the name of the second field and press tab. Leave this field's type as a character field, press tab again, and enter a field width of 15 characters. Then press Tab again to move to the definition of the next field. For the third field, enter Firstname for the field name and press Tab, as it too is a character field. Press Tab again and enter 15 as the field width. Press Tab again to begin defining the fourth field.

For the fourth field enter Address as the field name, Character for the field type, and 25 for the width. The fifth field will be City, Character for field type, and 15 for field width. Next, enter State for the field name, Character for the field type, and 2 for the field width.

Next is the field for ZIP code. ZIP codes contain numbers, but 10 digit ZIP codes have hyphens. Therefore, you will use a character field since in a numeric field the rest of the number would be ignored. Enter ZIPcode for the field name, Character for the field type, and 10 for the field width. The next field, Phone numbers, will also use a character field. Enter Phone for the field name, Character for the field type, and 12 for the field width. The next field, Purchases, will be a numeric field. Enter Purchases for the name, Numeric for the field type, 3 for the width, and 0 for the decimal places.

For the last two fields, add a field called Since, and make it a Date field. Then, add a field called Desires, and make it a memo field.

As you are creating a table, some noteworthy statistics appear at the bottom of the dialog box. These statistics show the number of fields created thus far, and the total length (based on the combined width of all of the fields). These statistics change as you add fields to the database.

When you have defined the fields for the example table, click the OK button in the dialog box. Depending on how you started the process, you may or may not be prompted for a name to save the table under. If you are prompted for a name, enter BUYERS as a table name, and click OK. Finally, you will see a dialog box asking if you want to input records at this time. Choose "Yes" from the dialog box. At this time, the table opens in a window in what is know as FoxPro Change/Edit mode and is ready for the addition of data. (See Figure 3.7.)

FIGURE 3.7.

A data entry window.

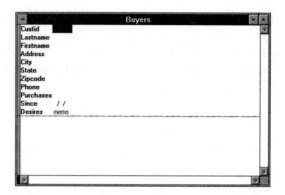

Adding Information to a File

With the structure definition completed, you can proceed to add data to the table. Notice that the layout of the simple form, shown in Figure 3.7, matches the structure of the table as defined earlier. If you had not set up this database and immediately proceeded into the data entry mode, you could add data (to an existing table) by first opening the table with the USE command in the command window (type USE *filename*, where *filename* is the name you saved the file under). You also can choose File, Open from the menus, and enter or select a file by name from the Open dialog box. From the Catalog Manager, you can click the Table tab to highlight the desired table, then click the table by name, then click Use. Any of these methods will open a table in the current work area.

Once the table is open, choose Record, Append from the menus, or enter APPEND in the Command Window to bring up a simple on-screen form for data entry. If you are at the Catalog Manager, click the AutoScreen button to have FoxPro create a screen that you can use for adding records. (Chapter 8, "Creating and Using Simple Screens," provides more details on the use of screens.)

Add the following record to the example table. Note that the memo field data is not included, because FoxPro uses a special technique for adding data to the memo field. This method is detailed later.

> Custid: 101
> Lastname: Roberts
> Firstname: Jamie
> Address: 118 Main Street
> City: Reston
> State: VA
> ZIP Code: 22091
> Phone: 703-555-2321

Purchases: 11
Since: 03/12/92

Correcting Mistakes

If you need to correct any mistakes made during the data entry process, click the desired column to place the insertion pointer there, or use the Tab key or Shift+Tab to move to the column where you want to make changes. To add new characters between existing ones, place the cursor in the desired location and insert the changes. Pressing the INS key takes you out of insert mode. When not in insert mode, any characters typed overwrite existing ones.

Once you complete the entry of the data described in the preceding sample record, the cursor will be located at the memo field.

Adding Data to a Memo Field

To add data to a memo field, either double-click in the field, or tab to the field and press Ctrl+PgDn or Ctrl+Home. With either method, another window appears. (See Figure 3.8.)

FIGURE 3.8.

The Window into memo field.

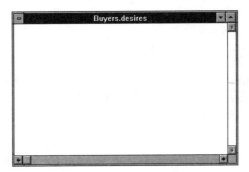

You can type the text of the memo into that window. Use either method to open the memo window for the example record, and type the following text into the memo window:

```
Science-fiction; fan of Asimov, Bradbury, and L. Niven.
```

As you are typing in a memo window, you can use the same editing keys (the cursor keys and the Backspace and Delete keys) as you would use to correct text in any Windows application. When done with your changes, close the memo window by pressing Ctrl+F4, or by double-clicking its Close box in the upper-left corner of the window. You can also use the Ctrl+W key combination. (This is a holdover from the days of dBASE III and FoxBase.) Note that pressing Esc abandons any changes made to the field.

TIP

If you work with memo fields regularly, you can use Windows cut-and-paste techniques to move large amounts of text from other applications into the contents of FoxPro memo fields. For example, to take a paragraph of text from a Word for Windows document into a memo field, you could open the document in Word for Windows, select the desired paragraph using normal selection techniques, and choose Edit/Copy from the menus. You would then switch back to FoxPro, open the memo window for the desired field of the desired record, and choose Edit/Paste to copy the contents into the memo field.

Use the PgDn or down-arrow key to move to the next record in the table. Add the remainder of the records shown here to the table (remember to use the Ctrl+PgDn key combination to get into the memo fields).

Custid: 102
Lastname: Sanderson
Firstname: Lucy
Address: 931 Thames Ct., Apt. 2C
City: Herndon
State: VA
ZIP code: 22070
Phone: 703-555-5681
Purchases: 25
Since: 06/17/89
Desires: American and world history, computer programming texts

Custid: 103
Lastname: Smith
Firstname: Larry
Address: 142 Haven Way
City: Kensington
State: MD
ZIP code: 31025
Phone: 301-555-2815
Purchases: 3
Since: 12/10/93
Desires: travel books and videos

Custid: 104
Lastname: Jones
Firstname: Nikki
Address: 8000 Watergate Circle
City: Washington
State: DC
ZIP code: 20005
Phone: 202-555-1586
Purchases: 12
Since: 11/22/89
Desires: travel, health and fitness

Custid: 105
Lastname: Hernandez
Firstname: Maria
Address: 19012 Pimmit Drive
City: Towson
State: MD
ZIP code: 30309
Phone: 301-555-6725
Purchases: 8
Since: 10/14/92
Desires: books on aviation and pilot safety

Custid: 106
Lastname: Jones
Firstname: Jarel
Address: 1412 Wyldewood Way
City: McLean
State: VA
ZIP code: 22035
Phone: 703-555-9091
Purchases: 12
Since: 10/22/92
Desires: graphic novels and collect-
able out-of-print comic books

Custid: 107
Lastname: Ziebermann
Firstname: Daniel
Address: 235 White Oak Way
City: Arlington
State: VA
ZIP code: 22032
Phone: 703-555-2114
Purchases: 7
Since: 08/15/92
Desires: science and technology,
computers

Custid: 108
Lastname: O'Neill
Firstname: John
Address: 12555 Lee Highway West
City: Merrifield
State: VA
ZIP code: 22045
Phone: 703-555-9256
Purchases: 14
Since: 10/02/91
Desires: photography

Custid: 109
Lastname: Bannerton
Firstname: Alicia
Address: 107 Embassy Row
City: Falls Church
State: VA
ZIP code: 22046
Phone: 703-555-1200
Purchases: 16
Since: 04/15/90
Desires: home improvement,
landscaping techniques

An Introduction to Browse

It is difficult to view a number of records on the screen at the same time, and most people prefer to view data that's stored in a database in a tabular form of some sort. For this reason, FoxPro offers a Browse mode that is used in a number of circumstances. The next chapter will cover the Browse mode in detail, but the following provides a short introduction to the topic.

If you are following the example, choose Browse from the database menu, or in the Command Window, type BROWSE. (Browse can also be chosen from the Browse menu, but unless you are appending or editing a file, the Browse menu will not appear as a menu choice.) After choosing Browse from the Database menu, the table appears in Browse mode. (See Figure 3.9.) FoxPro's Browse mode allows for the display of a large amount of information at the same time.

FIGURE 3.9.

FoxPro's Browse mode.

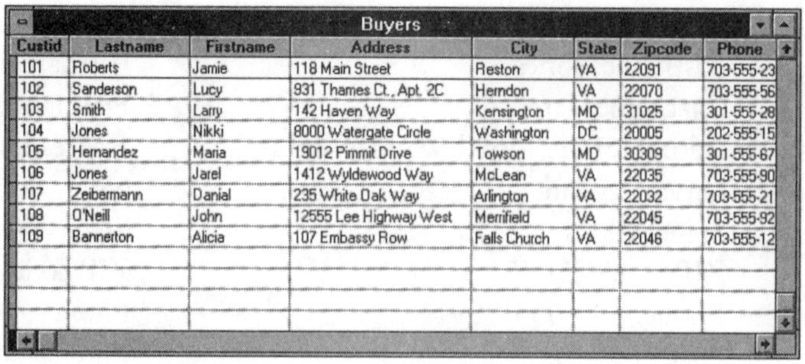

Custid	Lastname	Firstname	Address	City	State	Zipcode	Phone
101	Roberts	Jamie	118 Main Street	Reston	VA	22091	703-555-23
102	Sanderson	Lucy	931 Thames Ct., Apt. 2C	Herndon	VA	22070	703-555-55
103	Smith	Larry	142 Haven Way	Kensington	MD	31025	301-555-28
104	Jones	Nikki	8000 Watergate Circle	Washington	DC	20005	202-555-15
105	Hernandez	Maria	19012 Pimmit Drive	Towson	MD	30309	301-555-67
106	Jones	Jarel	1412 Wyldewood Way	McLean	VA	22035	703-555-90
107	Zeibermann	Danial	235 White Oak Way	Arlington	VA	22032	703-555-21
108	O'Neill	John	12555 Lee Highway West	Merrifield	VA	22045	703-555-92
109	Bannerton	Alicia	107 Embassy Row	Falls Church	VA	22046	703-555-12

Moving around in Browse mode differs somewhat from keyboard movement using the simple data-entry screen you used earlier. You can use the PgUp and PgDn keys to move up and down by a screen full of records at a time. (If the Browse window contains less than a screen full of records, these keys will have no visual effect, although the record pointer will move between the first and last records.) The up and down arrows move between records, and the Tab and Shift+Tab keys move between fields. The mouse can also be used to move to desired locations in the database. Also the scroll bars can be used to navigate within the window. There are a number of options available for the Browse mode, and they are covered in the next chapter in detail.

Obtaining a Quick Report

Only a few menu options are needed to create a report. (More detailed options that you can use to create a report are described in Chapter 9, "Creating and Using Simple Reports.") This example report shows how quickly a report can be created.

1. From the menus, choose File, New. In the New dialog box that appears, click Report, then New. In a moment, a blank report appears (reports are discussed at length in Chapter 9 and Chapter 12, "Designing and Customizing Reports").

2. Open the Report menu, and choose Quick Report. The Quick Report dialog box appears. (See Figure 3.10.) In this dialog box, you are given the option of a tabular layout (the button on the left) or a columnar layout (the button on the right).

FIGURE 3.10.

The Quick Report dialog box.

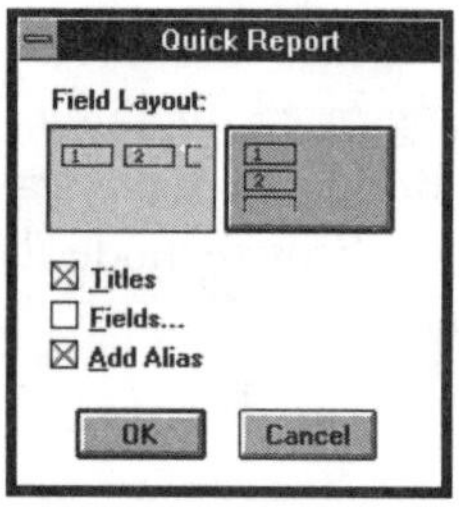

3. Click the form-oriented button (the one on the right). Making this choice causes the information to appear in a stacked fashion on the screen. (There is also a titles option that controls whether the field names appear as titles beside the contents of the field or not. The fields option is used to control which fields are included in the report. If you want all the options to appear in the report, you can leave these options set at their defaults. The add alias option is used with relational reports, which are covered in Chapter 12.)

4. Click OK.

5. If you want to see how the report will look on screen before you print it, choose Report, Page Preview from the menu. A page preview of the report appears. (See Figure 3.11.) You can place the mouse at any location in the window and click to get a close-up look at that portion of the page. You can also use the Next and Previous buttons in the dialog box, to move between pages of the report. When done with the preview, click OK to return to the report's design.

FIGURE 3.11.

Page Preview of a report.

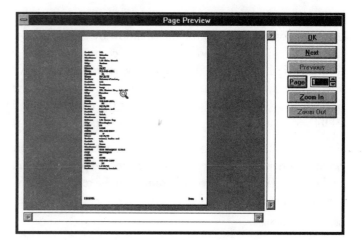

6. After clicking OK, open the File menu and choose Save. The Save As dialog box appears and you are prompted for a report name. Type BUYERS, then click Save. When asked if you want to save the environment information, answer Yes.

7. Choose File, Close to close the report. Then, choose Run, Report. In the Open dialog box, double-click BUYERS.FRX as the report name. When you do so, the Run Report dialog box appears. (See Figure 3.12.) Click To Print in this dialog box, then click Run to run the report.

FIGURE 3.12.

*The Run Report
dialog box.*

Useful Commands for Working with Data

As this book emphasizes, you can get more accomplished through the use of commands entered directly into the command window. And in most cases, commands are faster than wading your way through numerous menu options and dialog boxes. This section of the chapter provides some useful commands for working with data.

Using the EDIT Command

The EDIT command is used to modify existing records in a database. The command is used most often in the Command Window by experienced users as a quick way to make changes to a database. Upon entry of the command, EDIT, the user is presented with a form identical to the form that appears when you enter the APPEND command, or when you choose Record, Append from the menus. However, instead of displaying a blank set of fields, FoxPro displays the contents of the current field. Therefore, to effectively use EDIT, you must position the FoxPro record pointer at the record that is to be edited.

FoxPro marks its position within a table by means of an internal marker called the record pointer. When a table is first opened, the record pointer normally points to the first record in the table. The FoxPro record pointer can be repositioned with the GO command. The syntax for the command is:

```
GO <record number>
GO TOP
GO BOTTOM
```

where the record number desired is entered following the command. As an option, entering GO TOP will cause the record pointer to move to the beginning of the table, while GO BOTTOM will cause the record pointer to move to the end of the table. As an example, to move the record pointer to record number 5 in a table, the proper command would be:

```
GO 5
```

Once the record pointer is positioned at the desired record, entry of the EDIT command would then cause the record to be displayed within a fill-in form.

When editing a record, the cursor keys can be used to move within the record. If the cursor is at the first field in the table, pressing the up-arrow key will result in the prior record being displayed (unless there is no prior record, in which case pressing the up arrow has no effect). Similarly, if the cursor is at the last field of a record, pressing the down arrow key will result in the next record being displayed, unless there is no next record (in which case the key has no effect). The INSERT key can be used to switch back and forth between "insert" and "overwrite" mode. In insert mode, all characters typed when the cursor is among existing characters will cause those characters to move to the right, while overwrite mode results in new characters overwriting any existing characters on the screen. A complete description of editing keys available when using EDIT or APPEND is shown in Table 3.1.

Table 3.1. A description of EDIT or APPEND keys.

Key	Result
Left Arrow	Cursor left one character
Right Arrow	Cursor right one character
Up Arrow	Cursor up one field
Down Arrow	Cursor down one field
Home	Cursor to beginning of field
End	Cursor to end of field
PgUp	Scroll up record
PgDn	Scroll down record
Ins	Switch in and out of insert mode
Del	Delete character at cursor location
Ctrl+End or Ctrl+W	Save record
Escape	Exit without saving changes

Opening and Closing Tables with Commands

Once a FoxPro table exists, it must be opened before any file operations can be performed on that table. From the Command Window, the USE command is used to open an existing table. The syntax for this command is:

```
USE <filename>
```

where filename is the name of the table to be opened. (The .DBF extension is assumed by FoxPro; all tables are saved with a .DBF extension, unless you specify otherwise when you save the table). In response to the USE command, FoxPro will open the table, and the record pointer will be placed at the first record in the table. All commands entered following the USE command will perform their desired functions on the table that has been opened with the USE command. As an example, to open a table named CLIENTS, the command would be:

```
USE CLIENTS
```

Tables can be closed with a number of commands. The CLOSE DATABASES command will close the table in use. The CLOSE ALL command will close the table, and any other files that may be open as a result of other FoxPro commands. Alternatively, the USE command can be used to close a table. If no filename is specified following the USE command, the table in use will be closed without an additional table being opened.

Viewing and Displaying Data with Commands

Data can be viewed with the LIST and DISPLAY commands. The syntax for the LIST command is:

```
LIST <ALL/NEXT X/record no.><fieldnames><FOR condition><TO PRINT>
```

The LIST command can be used without specifying the names of desired fields to produce a list of all fields within the table, as shown in this example, with the following results:

```
USE MAILER
LIST
Record#  LAST_NAME       FIRST_NAME       ADDRESS_1
ADDRESS_2 CITY       STATE ZIP_CODE  CUSTNO COUNTRY
      1  Jones           Ed               2318 Lake Newport Rd
         Reston     VA    22090      23245
      3  Johnson         Larry            2915 Freetown Court
         Reston     VA    22090      23299
      4  Jones           Benjamin         3412 Fayetteville St #2B
         Durham     NC    27705      23248
      6  Canion          Ron              3 Nice House Lane
         Woodlands  TX    74087      18145
      7  Roberts         Clayborne        1415 Buena Vista Ave
         Hollywood  CA    90043      10509
```

To produce a list of the contents of the LAST_NAME, ADDRESS_1, CITY, STATE, and ZIP_CODE fields, the following commands could be used, with the resultant display:

```
USE MAILER
LIST LAST_NAME, ADDRESS_1, CITY, STATE, ZIP
Record#  last_name       address_1         city       state   zip_code
1        Jones           2370 Southgate Sq.  Reston     VA     22090
2        Smith           4343 East Orange Ave San Jose CA     95404
3        Johnson         2311 Freetown Court Reston     VA     22090
4        Jones           3412 Fayetteville St Durham    NC     27705
5        Miller          345 Plano Road      Plano      TX     75090
6        Canion          3 Nice House Lane   Woodlands  TX     74087
7        Roberts         1415 Buena Vista Ave Hollywood CA     90043
```

The DISPLAY command performs a similar function, but in its default mode, DISPLAY shows only chosen records that are selected through the use of a qualifying expression. For example, entering LIST with no qualifier lists all the records, while entering DISPLAY with no qualifier displays only the current record. The syntax for the DISPLAY command is:

```
DISPLAY <ALL/NEXT X/record number><fieldnames><FOR condition><TO
PRINT>
```

The default use of the command is simply DISPLAY, which causes the current record to be displayed, as shown:

```
go 4
display
Record#  LAST_NAME    FIRST_NAME   ADDRESS_1        ADDRESS_2
CITY      STATE ZIP_CODE   CUSTNO
     4   Jones        Benjamin     3412 Fayetteville  #2B
Durham   NC    27705      23248
```

By specifying a scope (ALL, NEXT X where X is a numeric value, or a record number), all records, a group of records in succession, or an individual record can be displayed:

```
display all last_name, first_name, address_1, city
Record#  last_name    first_name   address_1        city
     1   Jones        Benjamin     3412 Fayetteville St Durham
     2   Roberts      Clayborne    1415 Buena Vista Ave Hollywood
     3   Miller       Larry        345 Plano Road       Plano
     4   Jones        Ed           2318 Lake Newport Rd Reston
     5   Johnson      Larry        2915 Freetown Court  Reston
     6   Smith        William      4343 East Orange Ave San Jose
     7   Canion       Ron          3 Nice House Lane    Woodlands

go top
display next 3 last_name, first_name, address_1, city

Record#  last_name    address_1         city
     1   Jones        Benjamin     3412 Fayetteville St Durham
     2   Roberts      Clayborne    1415 Buena Vista Ave Hollywood
     3   Miller       Larry        345 Plano Road       Plano

display record 3

Record#  LAST_NAME    FIRST_NAME   ADDRESS_1        ADDRESS_2  CITY
     STATE ZIP_CODE   CUSTNO
     3   Miller       Larry        345 Plano Road     Suite 405  Plano
     TX    75090      101
```

The FOR option can be used to specify conditions for the records that will be shown with both DISPLAY and LIST, as shown in the following examples:

```
display all last_name for city = "Reston"
 Record#  last_name
     1   Jones
     3   Johnson
```

```
list last_name, address_1 for zip_code > "60000"
  Record#  last_name       address_1
        2  Smith           4343 East Orange Ave
        5  Miller          345 Plano Road
        6  Canion          3 Nice House Lane
        7  Roberts         1415 Buena Vista Ave
```

If the TO PRINT option is added to the end of the LIST or DISPLAY command, the results of the command will be printed on the printer and displayed on the screen.

There is one difference between a LIST and a DISPLAY ALL command; the DISPLAY ALL command will pause as each screen fills, and a key must be pressed to continue screen output. The LIST command will display all data without any screen pauses.

Table Types Created by the Table Wizards

This section of the chapter provides a look at each of the available tables produced by the FoxPro Table Wizards. For each one, you'll find here a list of suggested fields, and a figure showing the default form created by the Table Wizard if you check the "Save table and open a default screen" option in the last Table Wizard dialog box.

The fields used by each of the table designs are outlined on the remaining pages of this chapter. In each case, all the default fields and field names were accepted in the Table Wizard dialog box. Keep in mind that the Table Wizards do not force you to add all the proposed fields, or use the proposed field names; you can modify the designs suggested by the Table Wizards as you prefer, by making the desired changes in the dialog boxes presented by the wizards.

Table 3.2. The suggested fields for the Accounts table.

Field	Field Name	Type	Width	Dec	Index
1	ACCOUNTID	Character	15		
2	ACCOUNTNUM	Character	15		
3	ACCTNAME	Character	30		
4	ACCTTYPE	Character	20		
5	DESCRIPT	Memo	10		
6	STARTDATE	Date	8		
7	TAXABLE	Logical	1		
8	UNITS	Numeric	5		
9	TOTALDUE	Numeric	15		
10	NOTE	Memo	10		

Figure 3.13 shows the default form for the Accounts table created by the Table Wizards.

FIGURE 3.13.

The form created for Accounts table.

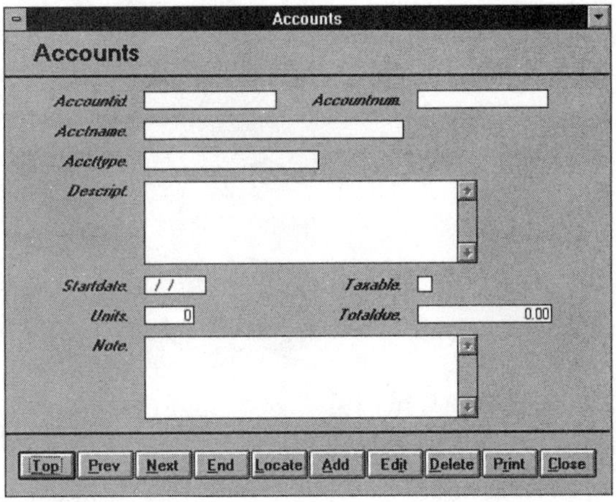

Table 3.3. The suggested fields for the Artists table.

Field	Field Name	Type	Width	Dec	Index
1	ARTISTID	Character	15		
2	FIRSTNAME	Character	15		
3	LASTNAME	Character	20		
4	NATIONALIT	Character	15		
5	BIRTHDATE	Date	8		
6	BIRTHPLACE	Character	30		
7	TRAINLOC	Character	30		
8	DATEDEATH	Date	8		
9	PHOTOGRAPH	General	10		
10	NOTE	Memo	10		

Figure 3.14 shows the default form for the Artists table created by the Table Wizards.

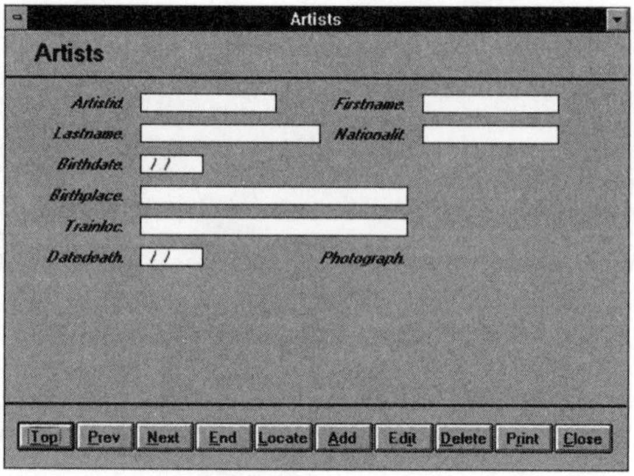

Artists

FIGURE 3.14.

*The form created for
Artists table.*

Table 3.4. The suggested fields for the Authors table.

Field	Field Name	Type	Width	Dec	Index
1	AUTHORID	Character	15		
2	FIRSTNAME	Character	15		
3	LASTNAME	Character	20		
4	NATIONALIT	Character	15		
5	BIRTHDATE	Date	8		
6	BIRTHPLACE	Character	30		
7	TRAINLOC	Character	30		
8	MAJORINFLU	Memo	10		
9	DATEDEATH	Date	8		
10	PHOTOGRAPH	General	10		
11	NOTE	Memo	10		

Figure 3.15 shows the default form for the Authors table created by the Table Wizards.

FIGURE 3.15.

*The form created for
Authors table.*

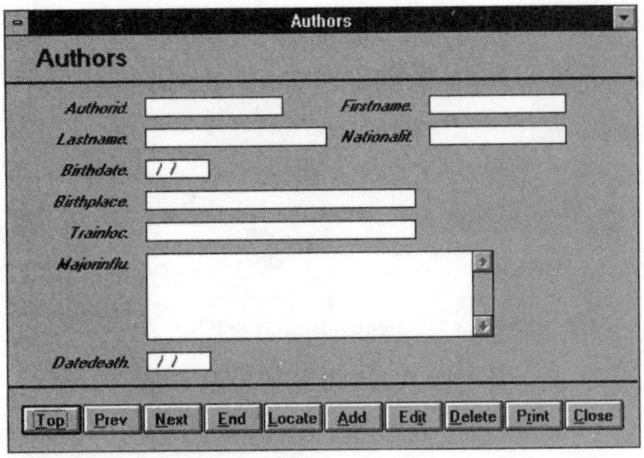

Table 3.5. The suggested fields for the Books table.

Field	Field Name	Type	Width	Dec	Index
1	BOOKCOLLID	Character	15		
2	AUTHORID	Character	15		
3	CATEGORYID	Character	15		
4	TITLE	Character	15		
5	COPYRDATE	Date	8		
6	ISBNNUMBER	Character	15		
7	PUBNAME	Character	30		
8	PURCHPRICE	Numeric	15	2	
9	EDITIONNUM	Numeric	5		
10	COVERTYPE	Character	15		
11	DATEPURCH	Date	8		
12	PAGES	Numeric	5		
13	SHELFNUM	Numeric	5		
14	NOTE	Memo	10		

Figure 3.16 shows the default form for the Books table created by the Table Wizards.

FIGURE 3.16.

The form created for Books table.

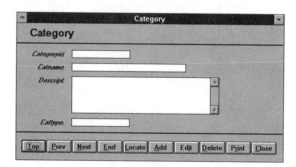

Table 3.6. The suggested fields for the Category table.

Field	Field Name	Type	Width	Dec	Index
1	CATEGORYID	Character	15		
2	CATNAME	Character	30		
3	DESCRIPT	Memo	10		
4	CATTYPE	Character	15		

Figure 3.17 shows the default form for the Category table created by the Table Wizards.

FIGURE 3.17.

The form created for Category table.

Table 3.7. The suggested fields for the Classes table.

Field	Field Name	Type	Width	Dec	Index
1	CLASSID	Character	15		
2	CLASSNAME	Character	30		
3	DEPTNAME	Character	20		
4	DEPTNUMBER	Character	15		

Field	Field Name	Type	Width	Dec	Index
5	SECNUMBER	Character	15		
6	INSTRUCTOR	Character	20		
7	TERM	Character	15		
8	UNITS	Numeric	5		
9	YEAR	Character	4		
10	NOTE	Memo	10		

Figure 3.18 shows the default form for the Classes table created by the Table Wizards.

FIGURE 3.18.

The form created for Classes table.

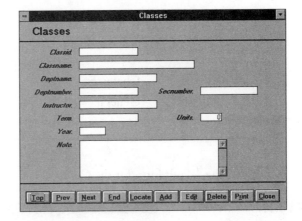

Table 3.8. The suggested fields for the Contacts table.

Field	Field Name	Type	Width	Dec	Index
1	CONTACTID	Character	15		
2	PREFIX	Character	15		
3	FIRSTNAME	Character	15		
4	LASTNAME	Character	20		
5	SUFFIX	Character	10		
6	ORGNAME	Character	30		
7	ADDRESS	Character	80		
8	CITY	Character	30		
9	STATE	Character	2		
10	POSTALCODE	Character	10		

continues

Table 3.8. continued

Field	Field Name	Type	Width	Dec	Index
11	REGION	Character	15		
12	COUNTRY	Character	15		
13	WORKPHONE	Character	20		
14	HOMEPHONE	Character	20		
15	FAX	Character	20		
16	MOBILPHONE	Character	20		
17	EMAILNAME	Character	20		
18	BIRTHDATE	Date	8		
19	CONTACTTYP	Character	15		
20	LASTMEET	Date	8		
21	ACTITEMS	Memo	10		
22	REFERREDBY	Character	20		
23	PHOTOGRAPH	General	10		
24	NOTE	Memo	10		

Figure 3.19 shows the default form for the Contacts table created by the Table Wizards.

FIGURE 3.19.

*The form created for
Contacts table.*

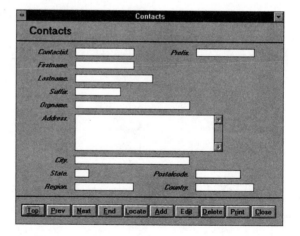

Table 3.9. The suggested fields for the Customer table.

Field	Field Name	Type	Width	Dec	Index
1	CUSTOMERID	Character	15		
2	FIRSTNAME	Character	15		
3	LASTNAME	Character	20		
4	ORGNAME	Character	30		
5	ADDRESS	Character	80		
6	CITY	Character	30		
7	STATE	Character	2		
8	REGION	Character	15		
9	POSTALCODE	Character	10		
10	COUNTRY	Character	15		
11	CONTNAME	Character	20		
12	PHONENUM	Character	15		
13	CONTTITLE	Character	15		
14	FAX	Character	20		
15	CATEGORYID	Character	15		
16	NOTE	Memo	10		

Figure 3.20 shows the default form for the Customer table created by the Table Wizards.

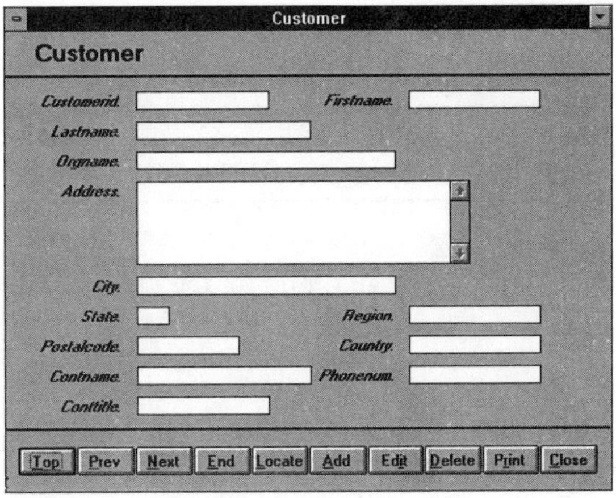

FIGURE 3.20.

The form created for Customer table.

Table 3.10. The suggested fields for the Delivery table.

Field	Field Name	Type	Width	Dec	Index
1	DELIVERYID	Character	15		
2	CUSTOMERID	Character	15		
3	ORDERID	Character	15		
4	EMPLOYEEID	Character	15		
5	SHIPPEDVIA	Character	20		
6	SHIPTRCODE	Character	15		
7	SHIPPHONE	Character	20		
8	SHIPDATE	Date	8		
9	SHIPFROM	Character	20		
10	DESTADDR	Character	50		
11	DESTCITY	Character	20		
12	DESTSTATE	Character	2		
13	DESTPOSTAL	Character	10		
14	DESTCTRY	Character	20		
15	ARRDATTIME	Character	20		
16	PKGCURLOCA	Character	30		
17	PKGDIMEN	Character	15		
18	PKGWEIGHT	Numeric	5		
19	PICKUPLOCA	Character	30		
20	PICKUPDATE	Character	30		
21	RECEIVEDBY	Character	20		
22	FREIGHTCHG	Numeric	15	2	
23	NOTE	Memo	10		

Figure 3.21 shows the default form for the Delivery table created by the Table Wizards.

FIGURE 3.21.

The form created for Delivery table.

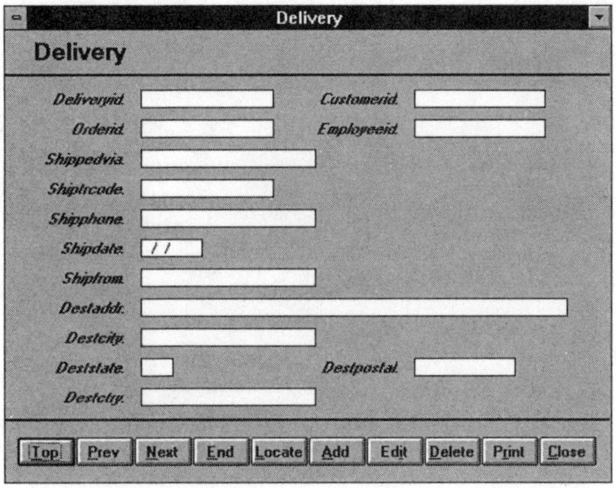

Table 3.11. The suggested fields for the Diet Log table.

Field	Field Name	Type	Width	Dec	Index
1	DIETLOGID	Character	15		
2	PERSONID	Character	15		
3	DIETTYPE	Character	20		
4	WHICHMEAL	Character	10		
5	DATERECORD	Date	8		
6	GRAMSCARBO	Numeric	7	2	
7	GRAMSPROT	Numeric	7	2	
8	GRAMSFAT	Numeric	7	2	
9	TOTALCALOR	Numeric	5		
10	MILLIGRAMS	Numeric	5		
11	VITAMINS	Character	30		
12	NOTE	Memo	10		

Figure 3.22 shows the default form for the Diet Log table created by the Table Wizards.

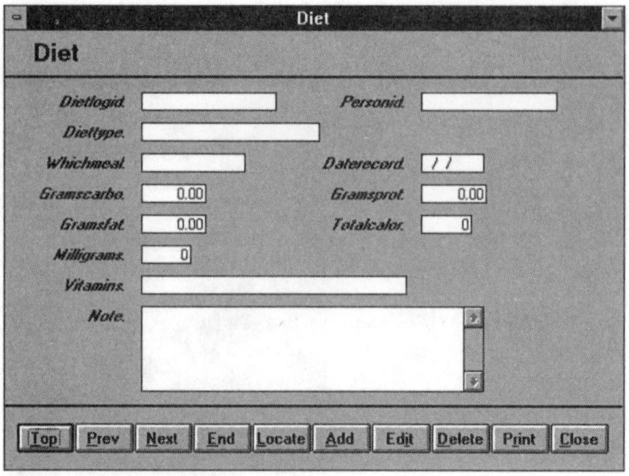

FIGURE 3.22.

The form created for Diet Log table.

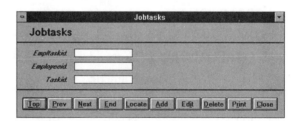

Table 3.12. The suggested fields for the Employee Tasks table.

Field	Field Name	Type	Width	Dec	Index
1	EMPLTASKID	Character	15		
2	EMPLOYEEID	Character	15		
3	TASKID	Character	15		

Figure 3.23 shows the default form for the Employee Tasks table created by the Table Wizards.

FIGURE 3.23.

The form created for Employee Tasks table.

Table 3.13. The suggested fields for the Employee table.

Field	Field Name	Type	Width	Dec	Index
1	EMPLOYEEID	Character	15		
2	SOCIALSEC	Character	15		
3	NTLEMPNUM	Character	30		

Field	Field Name	Type	Width	Dec	Index
4	FIRSTNAME	Character	15		
5	MIDNAME	Character	10		
6	LASTNAME	Character	20		
7	TITLE	Character	15		
8	EMAILNAME	Character	20		
9	EXTENSION	Character	4		
10	ADDRESS	Character	80		
11	CITY	Character	30		
12	STATE	Character	2		
13	REGION	Character	15		
14	POSTALCODE	Character	10		
15	COUNTRY	Character	15		
16	HOMEPHONE	Character	20		
17	WORKPHONE	Character	20		
18	DEPTNAME	Character	20		
19	CATEGORYID	Character	15		
20	BIRTHDATE	Date	8		
21	DATEHIRED	Date	8		
22	SUPERVISOR	Character	15		
23	SPOUSENAME	Character	20		
24	EMERNAME	Character	20		
25	EMERPHONE	Character	20		
26	PHOTOGRAPH	General	10		
27	NOTE	Memo	10		

Figure 3.24 shows the default form for the Employee table created by the Table Wizards.

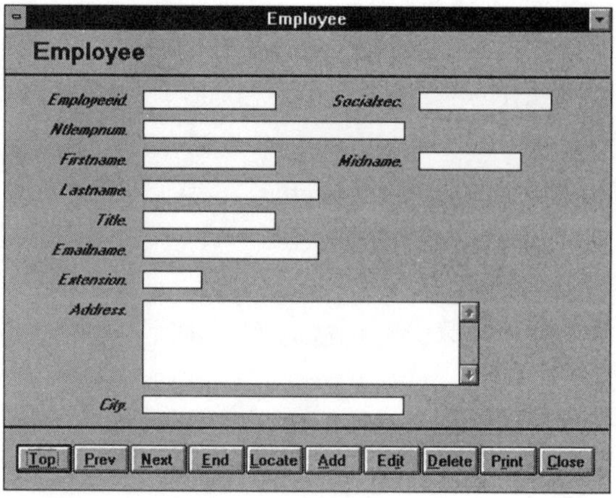

FIGURE 3.24.

The form created for Employee table.

Table 3.14. The suggested fields for the Events table.

Field	Field Name	Type	Width	Dec	Index
1	EVENTID	Character	15		
2	EVENTNAME	Character	30		
3	EVENTTYPE	Character	15		
4	STATUS	Character	10		
5	LOCATION	Character	30		
6	STARTDATE	Date	8		
7	ENDDATE	Date	8		
8	STARTTIME	Character	15		
9	ENDTIME	Character	15		
10	CONFIRMED	Logical	1		
11	AVAILSPACE	Numeric	5		
12	COSTPERSON	Numeric	15	2	
13	DESCRIPT	Memo	10		
14	NOTE	Memo	10		

Figure 3.25 shows the default form for the Events table created by the Table Wizards.

FIGURE 3.25.

The form created for Events table.

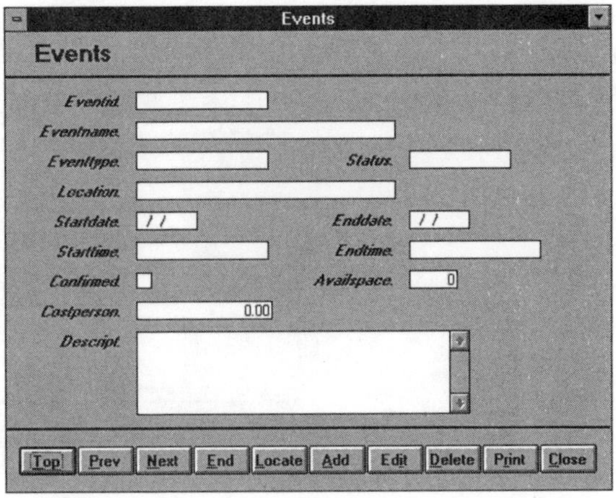

Table 3.15. The suggested fields for the Exercise Log table.

Field	Field Name	Type	Width	Dec	Index
1	EXERLOGID	Character	15		
2	PERSONID	Character	15		
3	ACTIVITY	Character	30		
4	WORKOUTDAT	Date	8		
5	EXERTYPE	Character	15		
6	AEROANAERO	Character	10		
7	TIMEEXER	Character	20		
8	DISTTRAVEL	Numeric	10		
9	RESTPULSE	Numeric	5		
10	MAXPULSE	Numeric	5		
11	CALSBURNED	Numeric	5		
12	HOURSSLEEP	Numeric	5		
13	NOTE	Memo	10		

Figure 3.26 shows the default form for the Exercise Log table created by the Table Wizards.

FIGURE 3.26.

The form created for
Exercise Log table.

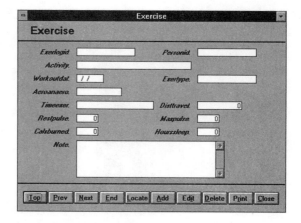

Table 3.16. The suggested fields for the Expenses table.

Field	Field Name	Type	Width	Dec	Index
1	EXPENSEID	Character	15		
2	EMPLOYEEID	Character	15		
3	CATEGORYID	Character	15		
4	EXPENSTYPE	Character	20		
5	PURPOSEEXP	Character	50		
6	AMTSPENT	Numeric	15	2	
7	DESCEXPENS	Memo	10		
8	DATEPURCH	Date	8		
9	DATESUBMIT	Date	8		
10	ADVAMOUNT	Numeric	15	2	
11	PYMTMETHOD	Character	15		

Figure 3.27 shows the default form for the Expenses table created by the Table Wizards.

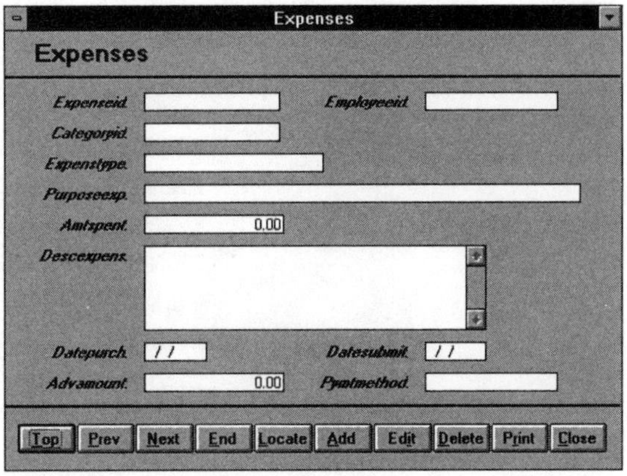

FIGURE 3.27.

The form created for Expenses table.

Table 3.17. The suggested fields for the Fixed Assets table.

Field	Field Name	Type	Width	Dec	Index
1	FIXEDASSET	Character	15		
2	CATEGORYID	Character	15		
3	ASSETNAME	Character	30		
4	MAKE	Character	20		
5	MODEL	Character	20		
6	MODELNUM	Character	20		
7	SERIALNUM	Character	30		
8	BEGINVALUE	Numeric	15	2	
9	DEPRMETHOD	Character	15		
10	DEPRRATE	Numeric	5		
11	CURRENTVAL	Numeric	15	2	
12	COMMENTS	Memo	10		
13	DESCRIPT	Memo	10		

Figure 3.28 shows the default form for the Fixed Assets table created by the Table Wizards.

FIGURE 3.28.

The form created for Fixed Assets table.

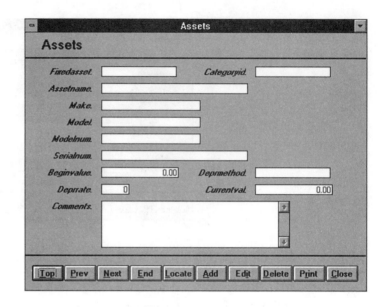

Table 3.18. The suggested fields for the Friends table.

Field	Field Name	Type	Width	Dec	Index
1	FRIENDID	Character	15		
2	FIRSTNAME	Character	15		
3	LASTNAME	Character	20		
4	NICKNAME	Character	15		
5	SPOUSENAME	Character	20		
6	CHILDNAMES	Character	30		
7	ADDRESS	Character	80		
8	CITY	Character	30		
9	STATE	Character	2		
10	REGION	Character	15		
11	POSTALCODE	Character	10		
12	COUNTRY	Character	15		
13	HOMEPHONE	Character	20		
14	WORKPHONE	Character	20		
15	MOBILPHONE	Character	20		
16	ALTPHONE	Character	20		
17	FAX	Character	20		

Field	Field Name	Type	Width	Dec	Index
18	EMAILADDR	Character	30		
19	CISID	Character	15		
20	BIRTHDATE	Date	8		
21	DATEUPDATE	Date	8		
22	LASTTALKED	Date	8		
23	HOBBIES	Character	50		
24	HEALTHPROB	Memo	10		
25	PHOTOGRAPH	General	10		
26	NOTE	Memo	10		

Figure 3.29 shows the default form for the Friends table created by the Table Wizards.

FIGURE 3.29.

The form created for Friends table.

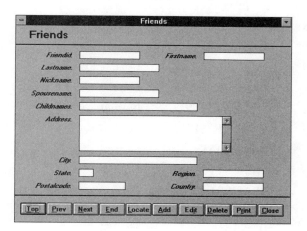

Table 3.19. The suggested fields for the Guests table.

Field	Field Name	Type	Width	Dec	Index
1	GUESTID	Character	15		
2	PREFIX	Character	15		
3	FIRSTNAME	Character	15		
4	LASTNAME	Character	20		
5	SPOUSENAME	Character	20		
6	CHILDNAMES	Character	30		

continues

Table 3.19. continued

Field	Field Name	Type	Width	Dec	Index
7	ADDRESS	Character	80		
8	CITY	Character	30		
9	STATE	Character	2		
10	REGION	Character	15		
11	POSTALCODE	Character	10		
12	COUNTRY	Character	15		
13	HOMEPHONE	Character	20		
14	WORKPHONE	Character	20		
15	MOBILPHONE	Character	20		
16	FAX	Character	20		
17	ALTPHONE	Character	20		
18	EMAILADDR	Character	30		
19	CISID	Character	15		
20	DATEUPDATE	Date	8		
21	LASTTALKED	Date	8		
22	NUMATTEND	Numeric	5		
23	CONFIRMED	Logical	1		
24	NEEDDAYCAR	Logical	1		
25	HEALTHPROB	Memo	10		
26	PLACESTAY	Character	20		
27	ROOMNUM	Numeric	5		
28	INDATTIME	Character	20		
29	OUTDATTIME	Character	20		
30	CHECKEDIN	Logical	1		
31	GIFTGIVEN	Character	20		
32	THANKSSENT	Logical	1		
33	NOTE	Memo	10		

Figure 3.30 shows the default form for the Guests table created by the Table Wizards.

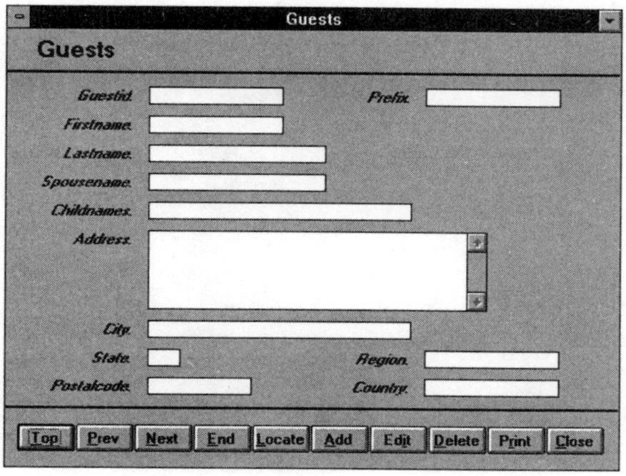

FIGURE 3.30.

The form created for Guests table.

Table 3.20. The suggested fields for the Household table.

Field	Field Name	Type	Width	Dec	Index
1	HOUSEINVID	Memo	10		
2	ITEMNAME	Character	20		
3	ITEMTYPE	Character	15		
4	DESCRIPT	Memo	10		
5	ROOM	Numeric	5		
6	MANUFACT	Character	30		
7	MODEL	Character	20		
8	MODELNUM	Character	20		
9	SERIALNUM	Character	30		
10	DATEPURCH	Date	8		
11	PLACEPURCH	Character	20		
12	PURCHPRICE	Numeric	15	2	
13	APPRVALUE	Numeric	15	2	
14	INSURED	Logical	1		
15	NOTE	Memo	10		
16	PHOTOGRAPH	General	10		

Figure 3.31 shows the default form for the Household table created by the Table Wizards.

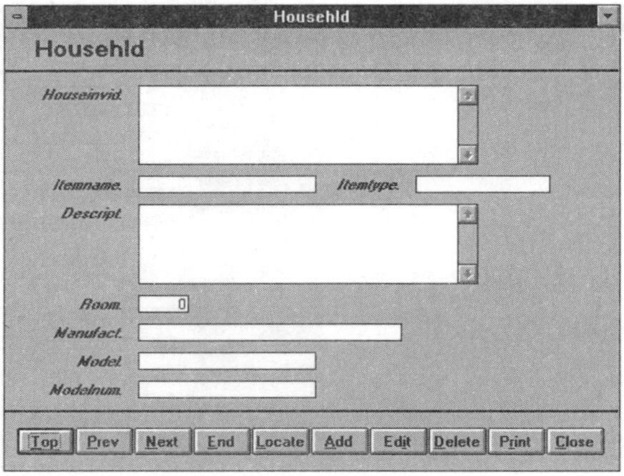

FIGURE 3.31.

*The form created for
Household table.*

Table 3.21. The suggested fields for the Investments table.

Field	Field Name	Type	Width	Dec	Index
1	INVESTMENT	Character	15		
2	ACCOUNTID	Character	15		
3	SECNAME	Character	20		
4	SECSYMBOL	Character	4		
5	SECTYPE	Character	20		
6	SHARESOWN	Numeric	5		
7	ACTION	Character	20		
8	TYPE	Character	15		
9	CLEAR	Logical	1		
10	NOTE	Memo	10		

Figure 3.32 shows the default form for the Investments table created by the Table Wizards.

FIGURE 3.32.

The form created for Investments table.

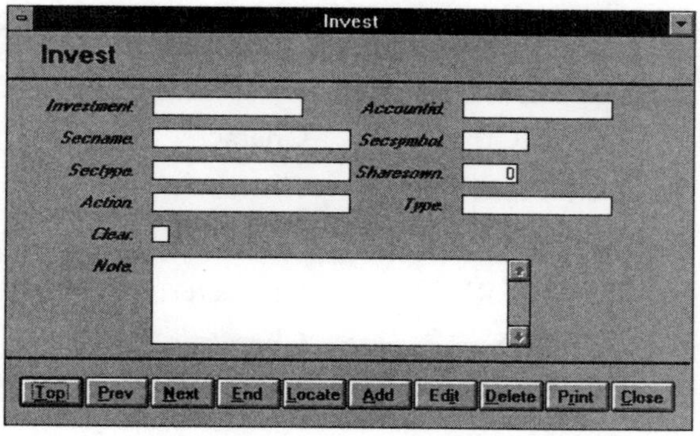

Table 3.22. The suggested fields for the Invoice Details table.

Field	Field Name	Type	Width	Dec	Index
1	INVDETID	Character	15		
2	INVOICEID	Character	15		
3	ORDERID	Character	15		
4	PRODUCTID	Character	15		
5	QUANTITY	Numeric	10		
6	PRICEUNIT	Numeric	7	2	
7	PYMTTERMS	Character	20		
8	DISCOUNT	Numeric	5		

Figure 3.33 shows the default form for the Invoice Details table created by the Table Wizards.

FIGURE 3.33.

The form created for Invoice Details table.

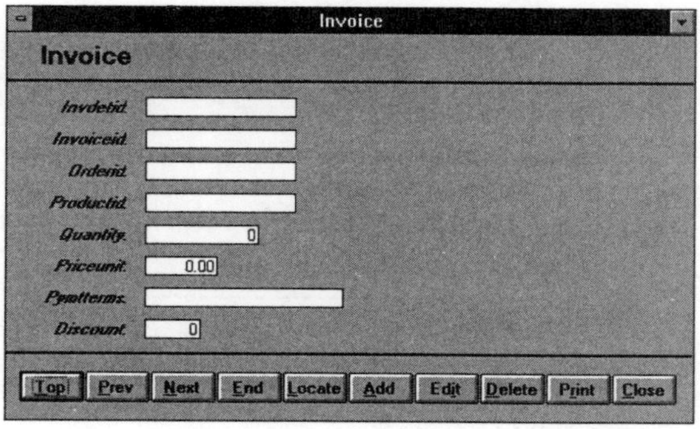

Table 3.23. The suggested fields for the Invoices table.

Field	Field Name	Type	Width	Dec	Index
1	INVOICEID	Character	15		
2	CUSTOMERID	Character	15		
3	EMPLOYEEID	Character	15		
4	DELIVERYID	Character	15		
5	STATUS	Character	10		
6	INVDATE	Date	8		
7	SALESPERS	Character	20		
8	SHIPDATE	Date	8		
9	SHIPPEDTO	Character	30		
10	SHIPPEDVIA	Character	20		
11	SHIPCOST	Numeric	15	2	
12	NOTE	Memo	10		

Figure 3.34 shows the default form for the Invoices table created by the Table Wizards.

FIGURE 3.34.

The form created for Invoices table.

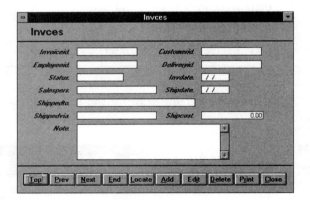

Table 3.24. The suggested fields for the Mailing List table.

Field	Field Name	Type	Width	Dec	Index
1	MAILLISTID	Character	15		
2	PREFIX	Character	15		
3	FIRSTNAME	Character	15		

Field	Field Name	Type	Width	Dec	Index
4	MIDNAME	Character	10		
5	LASTNAME	Character	20		
6	SUFFIX	Character	10		
7	NICKNAME	Character	15		
8	TITLE	Character	15		
9	ORGNAME	Character	30		
10	ADDRESS	Character	80		
11	CITY	Character	30		
12	STATE	Character	2		
13	REGION	Character	15		
14	POSTALCODE	Character	10		
15	COUNTRY	Character	15		
16	HOMEPHONE	Character	20		
17	WORKPHONE	Character	20		
18	MOBILPHONE	Character	20		
19	FAX	Character	20		
20	ALTPHONE	Character	20		
21	EMAILADDR	Character	30		
22	CISID	Character	15		
23	BIRTHDATE	Date	8		
24	NATIONALIT	Character	15		
25	EMERNAME	Character	20		
26	EMERPHONE	Character	20		
27	DATEUPDATE	Date	8		
28	MEMBERSHIP	Character	15		
29	DATEJOINED	Date	8		
30	PLEDGEAMT	Numeric	15	2	
31	PLGPDDATE	Date	8		
32	DUESAMOUNT	Numeric	15	2	
33	DUESPDDATE	Date	8		
34	HOBBIES	Character	50		

continues

Table 3.24. continued

Field	Field Name	Type	Width	Dec	Index
35	HEALTHPROB	Memo	10		
36	PHOTOGRAPH	General	10		
37	NOTE	Memo	10		

Figure 3.35 shows the default form for the Mailing List table created by the Table Wizards.

FIGURE 3.35.

The form created for Mailing List table.

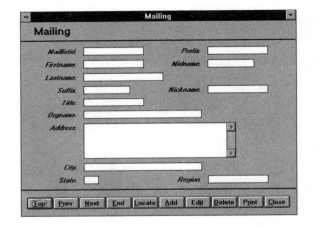

Table 3.25. The suggested fields for the Music table.

Field	Field Name	Type	Width	Dec	Index
1	MUSCOLLID	Character	15		
2	ARTISTID	Character	15		
3	CATEGORYID	Character	15		
4	GROUPNAME	Character	20		
5	TITLE	Character	15		
6	RECLABEL	Character	20		
7	YEARRELSD	Character	4		
8	FORMAT	Character	15		
9	NUMTRACKS	Numeric	5		
10	DATEPURCH	Date	8		
11	PURCHPRICE	Numeric	15	2	

Field	Field Name	Type	Width	Dec	Index
12	NOTE	Memo	10		
13	PHOTOGRAPH	General	10		
14	SAMSNDCLIP	General	10		

Figure 3.36 shows the default form for the Music table created by the Table Wizards.

FIGURE 3.36.

The form created for Music table.

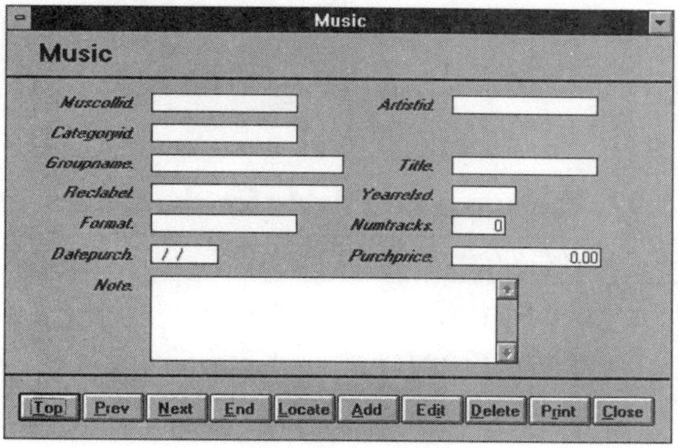

Table 3.26. The suggested fields for the Order Details table.

Field	Field Name	Type	Width	Dec	Index
1	ORDERDETID	Character	15		
2	ORDERID	Character	15		
3	PRODUCTID	Character	15		
4	DATESOLD	Date	8		
5	QUANTITY	Numeric	10		
6	UNITPRICE	Numeric	15	2	
7	DISCOUNT	Numeric	5		
8	SALEPRICE	Numeric	15	2	
9	SALESTAX	Numeric	15	2	
10	PYMTTERMS	Character	20		

Figure 3.37 shows the default form for the Order Details table created by the Table Wizards.

FIGURE 3.37.

The form created for Order Details table.

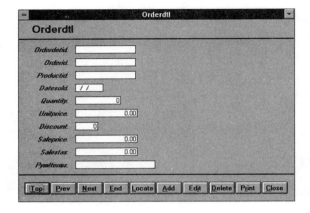

Table 3.27. The suggested fields for the Orders table.

Field	Field Name	Type	Width	Dec	Index
1	ORDERID	Character	15		
2	CUSTOMERID	Character	15		
3	EMPLOYEEID	Character	15		
4	ORDERDATE	Date	8		
5	REQUIREDBY	Date	8		
6	PROMISEDBY	Date	8		
7	SHIPNAME	Character	30		
8	SHIPADDR	Character	50		
9	SHIPCITY	Character	15		
10	SHIPSTATE	Character	2		
11	SHIPREGION	Character	15		
12	SHIPPOSTAL	Character	10		
13	SHIPCTRY	Character	15		
14	SHIPDATE	Date	8		
15	SHIPVIA	Character	15		
16	FREIGHTCHG	Numeric	15	2	

Figure 3.38 shows the default form for the Orders table created by the Table Wizards.

FIGURE 3.38.

*The form created for
Orders table.*

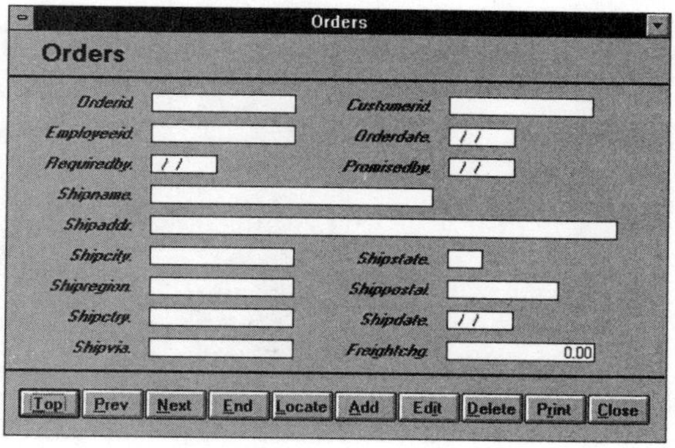

Table 3.28. The suggested fields for the Payments table.

Field	Field Name	Type	Width	Dec	Index
1	PAYMENTID	Character	15		
2	CUSTOMERID	Character	15		
3	ORDERID	Character	15		
4	RESERVID	Character	15		
5	CATEGORYID	Character	15		
6	PYMTAMOUNT	Numeric	15	2	
7	PYMTDATE	Date	8		
8	PYMTMETHOD	Character	15		
9	CHECKNUM	Numeric	5		
10	CARDTYPE	Character	15		
11	CARDNUMBER	Character	20		
12	CARDNAME	Character	20		
13	CARDEXPIRE	Date	8		
14	PYMTTERMS	Character	20		
15	NOTE	Memo	10		

Figure 3.39 shows the default form for the Payments table created by the Table Wizards.

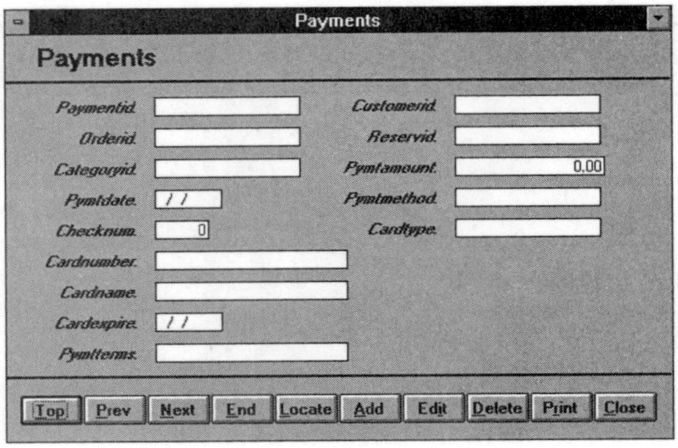

FIGURE 3.39.

The form created for Payments table.

Table 3.29. The suggested fields for the Photos table.

Field	Field Name	Type	Width	Dec	Index
1	PHOTOID	Character	15		
2	FILMID	Character	15		
3	CATEGORYID	Character	15		
4	DATETAKEN	Date	8		
5	TIMETAKEN	Character	20		
6	PLACETAKEN	Character	50		
7	SUBJNAME	Character	30		
8	SUBJADDR	Character	80		
9	SUBJPHONE	Character	20		
10	CAMERA	Character	20		
11	LENSUSED	Character	15		
12	APERTURE	Character	10		
13	SHUTTERSPD	Character	10		
14	FILTERUSED	Character	15		
15	FLASH	Logical	1		
16	PRINTSIZE	Character	15		
17	NOTE	Memo	10		

Figure 3.40 shows the default form for the Photos table created by the Table Wizards.

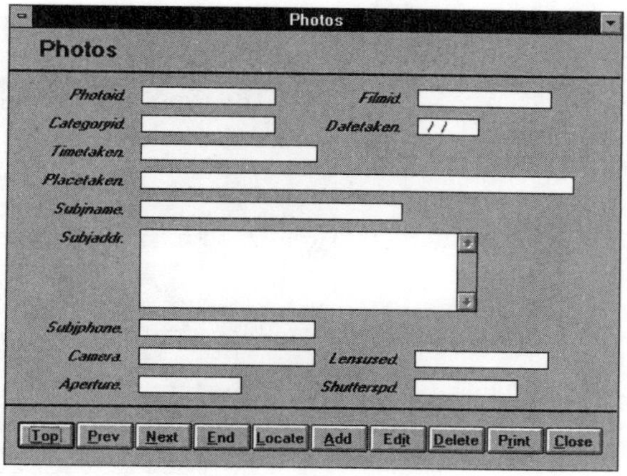

FIGURE 3.40.

The form created for Photos table.

Table 3.30. The suggested fields for the Plants table.

Field	Field Name	Type	Width	Dec	Index
1	PLANTID	Character	15		
2	COMMNAME	Character	30		
3	GENUS	Character	30		
4	SPECIES	Character	30		
5	FLOWERING	Logical	1		
6	LIGHTPREF	Character	10		
7	TEMPPREF	Character	15		
8	FERTFREQ	Character	20		
9	WATERFREQ	Character	10		
10	DATEPURCH	Date	8		
11	PLACEPURCH	Character	20		
12	DATEPLANT	Date	8		
13	DATEREPOTT	Date	8		
14	DATEPRUNED	Date	8		
15	DATEFERT	Date	8		
16	DATEWATER	Date	8		
17	PHOTOGRAPH	General	10		
18	NOTE	Memo	10		

Figure 3.41 shows the default form for the Plants table created by the Table Wizards.

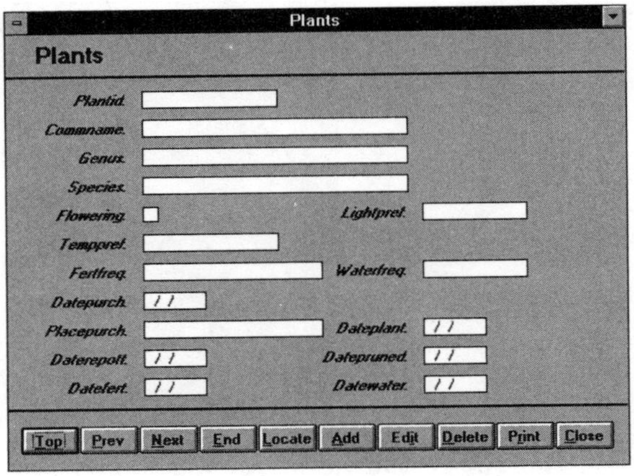

FIGURE 3.41.

The form created for Plants table.

Table 3.31. The suggested fields for the Products table.

Field	Field Name	Type	Width	Dec	Index
1	PRODUCTID	Character	15		
2	PRODNAME	Character	20		
3	CATEGORYID	Character	15		
4	SUPPLIERID	Character	15		
5	SERIALNUM	Character	30		
6	UNINSTOCK	Numeric	10		
7	UNONORDER	Numeric	10		
8	UNITPRICE	Numeric	15	2	
9	REORDERLVL	Numeric	10		
10	DISCONTD	Logical	1		

Figure 3.42 shows the default form for the Products table created by the Table Wizards.

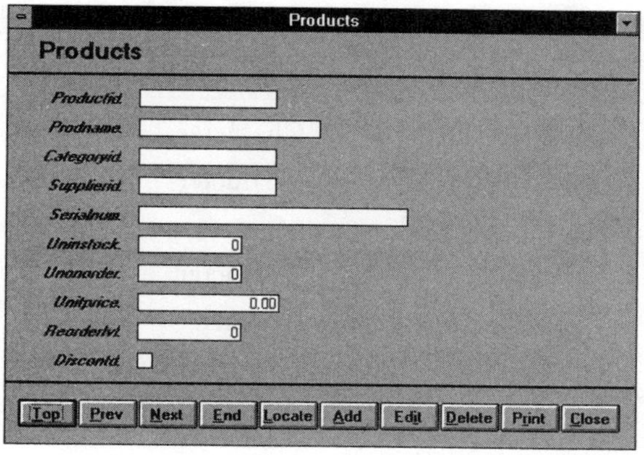

FIGURE 3.42.

The form created for Products table.

Table 3.32. The suggested fields for the Projects table.

Field	Field Name	Type	Width	Dec	Index
1	PROJECTID	Character	15		
2	PROJNAME	Character	20		
3	CUSTOMERID	Character	15		
4	CATEGORYID	Character	15		
5	PROJLEAD	Character	20		
6	PROJDESC	Memo	10		
7	PROJTMMEMB	Memo	10		
8	NOTE	Memo	10		

Figure 3.43 shows the default form for the Projects table created by the Table Wizards.

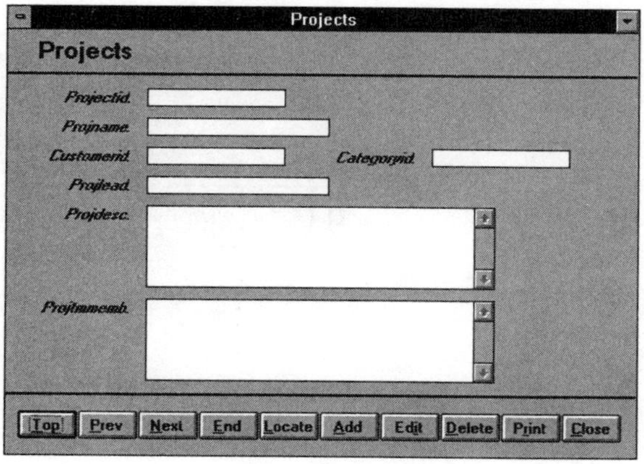

FIGURE 3.43.

The form created for Projects table.

Table 3.33. The suggested fields for the Recipes table.

Field	Field Name	Type	Width	Dec	Index
1	RECIPEID	Character	15		
2	RECIPENAME	Character	20		
3	RECIPEDESC	Memo	10		
4	SOURCE	Character	20		
5	WHICHMEAL	Character	10		
6	VEGETARIAN	Logical	1		
7	TIMETOPREP	Character	20		
8	NUMSERVING	Numeric	5		
9	CALSSERV	Numeric	5		
10	NUTRITINFO	Memo	10		
11	INGREDIENT	Memo	10		
12	INSTREXP	Memo	10		
13	QTYONHAND	Numeric	5		
14	NOTE	Memo	10		
15	PHOTOGRAPH	General	10		

Figure 3.44 shows the default form for the Recipes table created by the Table Wizards.

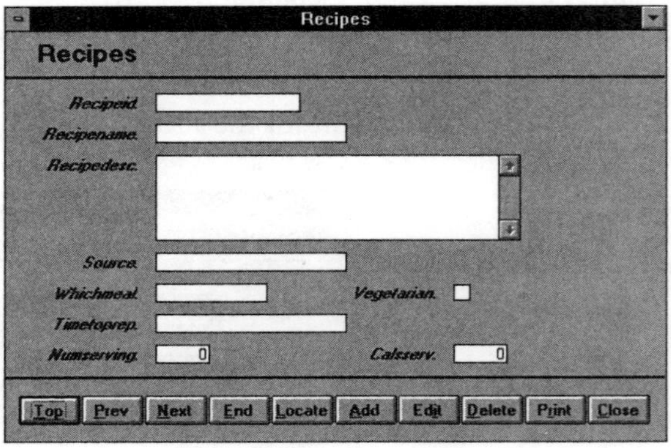

FIGURE 3.44.

The form created for Recipes table.

Table 3.34. The suggested fields for the Reservations table.

Field	Field Name	Type	Width	Dec	Index
1	RESERVID	Character	15		
2	CUSTOMERID	Character	15		
3	EVENTID	Character	15		
4	EMPLOYEEID	Character	15		
5	QTYRESERVE	Numeric	10		
6	RESERVDATE	Date	8		
7	DEPOSITDUE	Numeric	15	2	
8	TOTALDUE	Numeric	15	2	
9	AMOUNTPAID	Numeric	15	2	
10	CONFIRMED	Logical	1		
11	NOTE	Memo	10		

Figure 3.45 shows the default form for the Reservations table created by the Table Wizards.

FIGURE 3.45.

The form created for Reservations table.

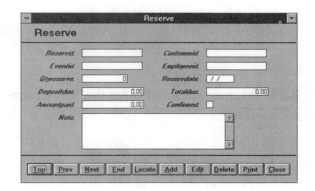

Table 3.35. The suggested fields for the Rolls of Film table.

Field	Field Name	Type	Width	Dec	Index
1	FILMID	Character	15		
2	FILMTYPE	Character	10		
3	FILMSPEED	Character	10		
4	COLORFILM	Logical	1		

continues

Table 3.35. continued

Field	Field Name	Type	Width	Dec	Index
5	FILMEXPDAT	Date	8		
6	DATEDEVEL	Date	8		
7	DEVELOPBY	Character	20		
8	NOTE	Memo	10		

Figure 3.46 shows the default form for the Rolls of Film table created by the Table Wizards.

FIGURE 3.46.

The form created for Rolls of Film table.

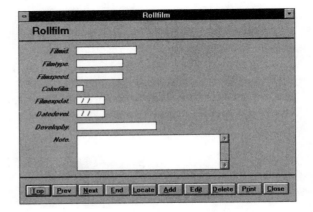

Table 3.36. The suggested fields for the Service table.

Field	Field Name	Type	Width	Dec	Index
1	SERVRECID	Character	15		
2	FIXEDASSET	Character	15		
3	SERVDATE	Date	8		
4	EMPLOYEEID	Character	15		
5	DESCPROB	Memo	10		
6	DESCSERV	Memo	10		
7	DATEPROM	Date	8		
8	DATEDELIV	Date	8		
9	RECEIVEDBY	Character	20		
10	LABORHOURS	Numeric	15	2	

Field	Field Name	Type	Width	Dec	Index
11	LABORHRACT	Numeric	5		
12	PARTSREPL	Memo	10		
13	ESTDCOST	Numeric	15	2	
14	ACTUALCOST	Numeric	15	2	
15	PVSERVDATE	Date	8		
16	MILESSINCE	Numeric	10		
17	HOURSSINCE	Numeric	10		
18	NEXTSERV	Date	8		
19	AUTHORIZED	Character	20		

FIGURE 3.47.

The form created for Service table.

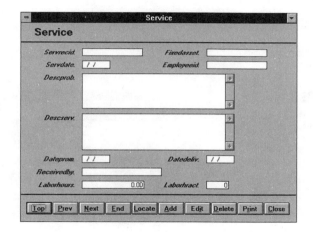

Figure 3.47 shows the default form for the Service table created by the Table Wizards.

Table 3.37. The suggested fields for the first Students table.

Field	Field Name	Type	Width	Dec	Index
1	STUDENTID	Character	15		
2	FIRSTNAME	Character	15		
3	MIDNAME	Character	10		
4	LASTNAME	Character	20		
5	PARENTNAME	Character	30		

continues

Table 3.37. continued

Field	Field Name	Type	Width	Dec	Index
6	ADDRESS	Character	80		
7	CITY	Character	30		
8	STATE	Character	2		
9	REGION	Character	15		
10	POSTALCODE	Character	10		
11	PHONENUM	Character	15		
12	EMAILNAME	Character	20		
13	MAJOR	Character	20		
14	NOTE	Memo	10		

Figure 3.48 shows the default form for the first Students table created by the Table Wizards.

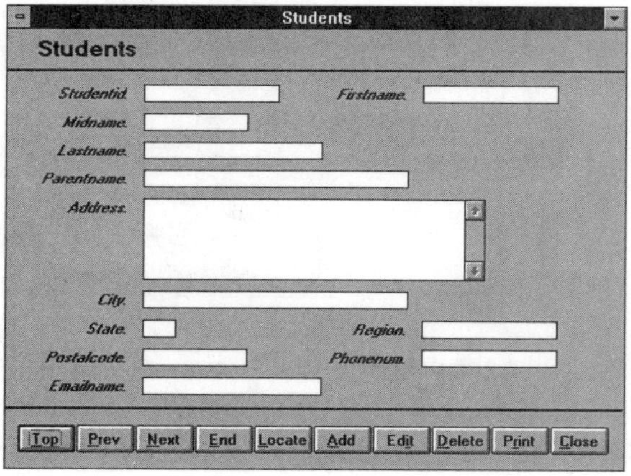

FIGURE 3.48.

The form created for first Students table.

Table 3.38. The suggested fields for the second Students table.

Field	Field Name	Type	Width	Dec	Index
1	STUCLASSID	Character	15		
2	CLASSID	Character	15		
3	STUDENTID	Character	15		
4	GRADE	Character	10		

Figure 3.49 shows the default form for the second Students table created by the Table Wizards.

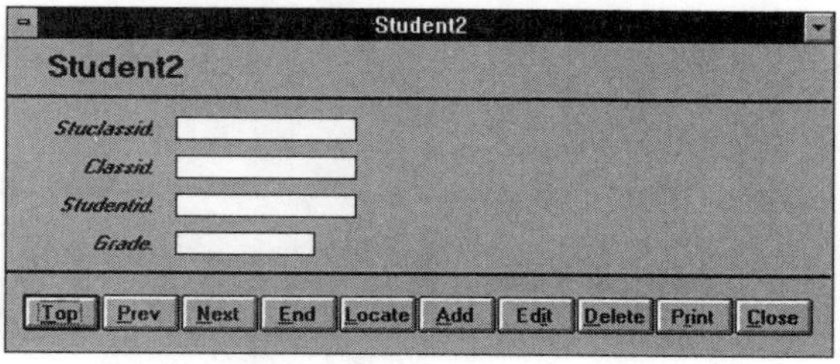

FIGURE 3.49.

The form created for second Students table.

Table 3.39. The suggested fields for the Suppliers table.

Field	Field Name	Type	Width	Dec	Index
1	SUPPLIERID	Character	15		
2	SUPPLNAME	Character	20		
3	CONTNAME	Character	20		
4	CONTTITLE	Character	15		
5	ADDRESS	Character	80		
6	CITY	Character	30		
7	POSTALCODE	Character	10		
8	REGION	Character	15		
9	COUNTRY	Character	15		
10	PHONENUM	Character	15		
11	FAX	Character	20		
12	PYMTTERMS	Character	20		
13	NOTE	Memo	10		

Figure 3.50 shows the default form for the Suppliers table created by the Table Wizards.

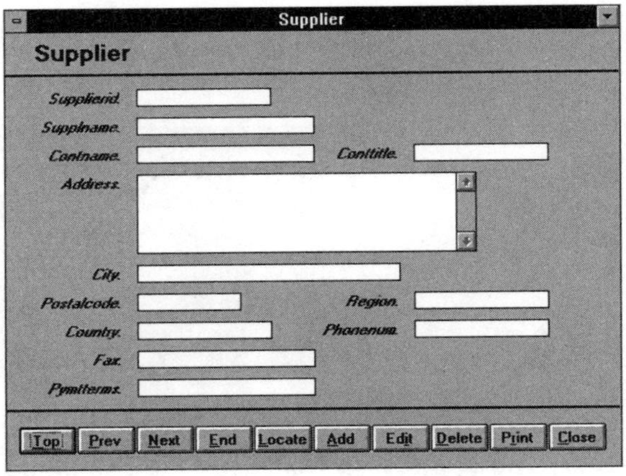

FIGURE 3.50.

The form created for Suppliers table.

Table 3.40. The suggested fields for the Tasks table.

Field	Field Name	Type	Width	Dec	Index
1	TASKID	Character	15		
2	TASKDESC	Memo	10		
3	STARTDATE	Date	8		
4	ENDDATE	Date	8		
5	NOTE	Memo	10		

Figure 3.51 shows the default form for the Tasks table created by the Table Wizards.

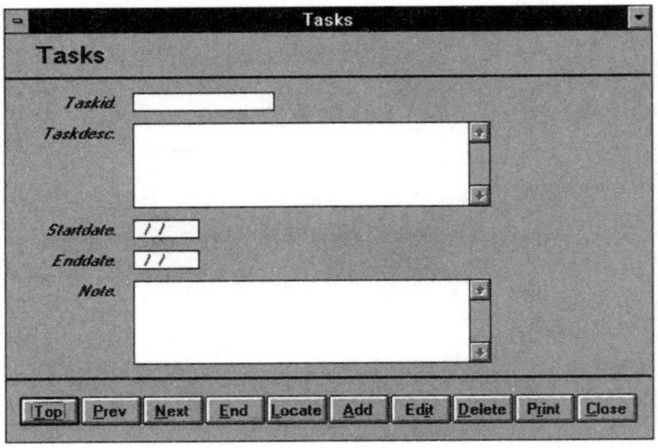

FIGURE 3.51.

The form created for Tasks table.

Table 3.41. The suggested fields for the Time Billed table.

Field	Field Name	Type	Width	Dec	Index
1	TIMEBILLED	Character	15		
2	CUSTOMERID	Character	15		
3	PROJECTID	Character	15		
4	EMPLOYEEID	Character	15		
5	BILLDATE	Date	8		
6	HOURLYRATE	Numeric	7	2	
7	NUMBILLHRS	Numeric	7	2	
8	NOTE	Memo	10		

Figure 3.52 shows the default form for the Time Billed table created by the Table Wizards.

FIGURE 3.52.

The form created for Time Billed table.

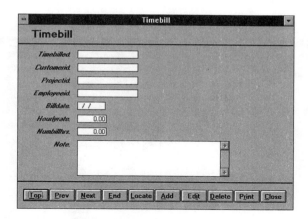

Table 3.42. The suggested fields for the Transactions table.

Field	Field Name	Type	Width	Dec	Index
1	TRANSACTID	Character	15		
2	ACCOUNTID	Character	15		
3	CATEGORYID	Character	15		
4	PAYMENTID	Character	15		
5	TRANSNUM	Numeric	5		

continues

Table 3.42. continued

Field	Field Name	Type	Width	Dec	Index
6	TRANSDATE	Date	8		
7	REFNUMBER	Character	20		
8	DEPOSITAMT	Float	20	2	
9	INTEARNED	Numeric	15	2	
10	PURSELDATE	Date	8		
11	PSPRICE	Numeric	15	2	
12	SERVCHARGE	Numeric	15	2	
13	TAXABLE	Logical	1		
14	NOTE	Memo	10		

Figure 3.53 shows the default form for the Transactions table created by the Table Wizards.

FIGURE 3.53.

The form created for Transactions table.

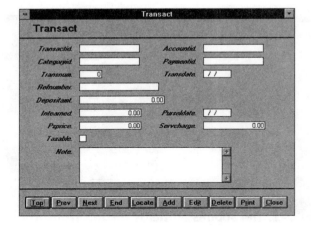

Table 3.43. The suggested fields for the Video table.

Field	Field Name	Type	Width	Dec	Index
1	VIDEOCOLID	Character	15		
2	CATEGORYID	Character	15		
3	MOVIETITLE	Character	30		
4	LDGACTRESS	Character	20		

Field	Field Name	Type	Width	Dec	Index
5	LEADACTOR	Character	20		
6	DIRECTOR	Character	20		
7	PRODUCER	Character	20		
8	YEARRELSD	Character	4		
9	RATING	Numeric	5		
10	SUBJECT	Character	50		
11	LENGTH	Numeric	15	2	
12	DATACQREC	Date	8		
13	PURCHREC	Character	10		
14	PURCHAT	Character	20		
15	PURCHPRICE	Numeric	15	2	
16	REVIEW	Memo	10		
17	DATEERASED	Date	8		
18	SAMVIDCLIP	General	10		
19	NOTE	Memo	10		

Figure 3.54 shows the default form for the Video table created by the Table Wizards.

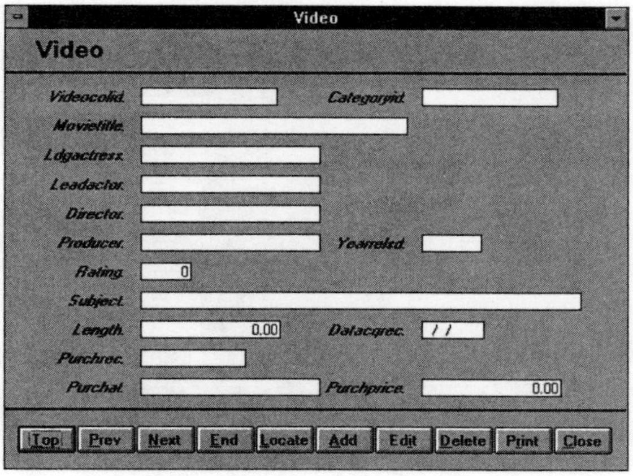

FIGURE 3.54.

The form created for Video table.

Table 3.44. The suggested fields for the Wine List table.

Field	Field Name	Type	Width	Dec	Index
1	WINELISTID	Character	15		
2	WINENAME	Character	20		
3	VINEYARD	Character	20		
4	VARIETY	Character	20		
5	VINTAGE	Character	50		
6	WINETYPE	Character	15		
7	COLOR	Character	15		
8	SWEETORDRY	Character	10		
9	CTRYORIGIN	Character	20		
10	REGION	Character	15		
11	SERVINSTR	Memo	10		
12	PCTALCOHOL	Numeric	7	2	
13	NOTE	Memo	10		

Figure 3.55 shows the default form for the Wine List table created by the Table Wizards.

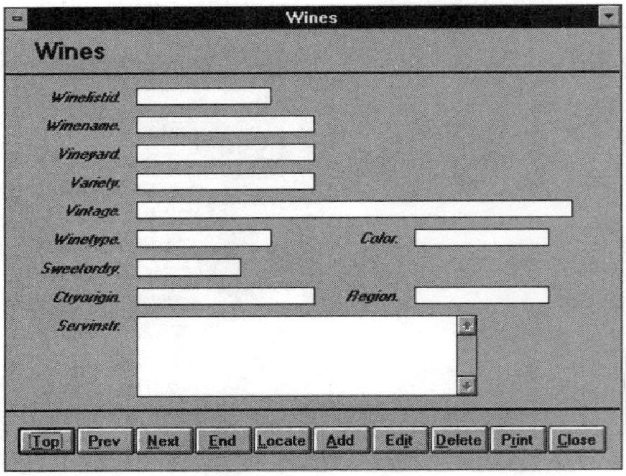

FIGURE 3.55.

The form created for Wine List table.

Chapter Summary

The very basis of your data in any relational database is your tables, and this chapter provided details on opening and using tables, adding, deleting, and changing fields, and using the Table Wizards (which are new to FoxPro 2.6) to aid in the creation of tables aimed at common business tasks. In Chapter 4, "Adding and Changing Data," you'll learn how to get data into your tables, and how to effectively manage that data.

Adding and Changing Data

The previous chapter briefly introduced the subject of adding and editing data. This chapter provides more detailed techniques that you can utilize to ease the task of getting data into your table.

In FoxPro you can use any of three approaches to add data. You can open a screen from within the Catalog Manager, you can choose Record, Append from the menus, or you can enter the APPEND command into the Command Window.

Adding and Changing Data from the Catalog Manager

The easiest way to add or change data from the Catalog Manager is to open a screen, which you can then use for the data entry. (Screens will be covered in more detail in Chapter 8, "Creating and Using Simple Screens.") If you have not already created and saved a screen, you can first click the Table tab in the Catalog Manager, click the table you want to add the data to, and click the Use button to place that table in use. Next, click the AutoScreen button at the upper-right side of the dialog box; it's the button resembling a tiny picture of a form with a lightning bolt above it. (See Figure 4.1.)

FIGURE 4.1.

The Catalog Manager and location of AutoScreen button.

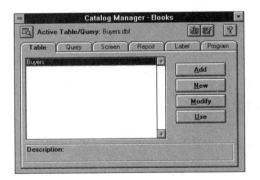

Once you click the button, FoxPro creates a default screen. (On computers with just 4MB of memory, this process may take a while.) When the screen is completed, it appears similar to the one shown in Figure 4.2. In this example, the BUYERS.DBF table (created as part of the exercise in the prior chapter) was used as the table for the screen.

You can click the Add button at the bottom of the screen, which moves FoxPro to a new blank record. You can then proceed to add the desired data, using the Tab key to move between fields of the screen. When done with the addition, click the Save button. You can then click the Add button if you want to add another record, or click the Close button if you are done with the additions.

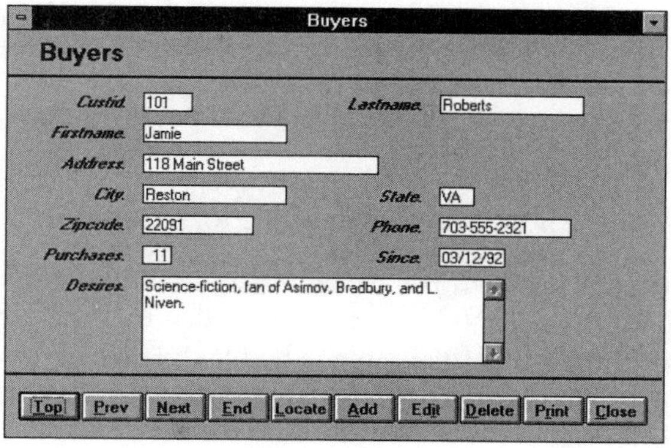

FIGURE 4.2.

A new screen based on BUYERS table.

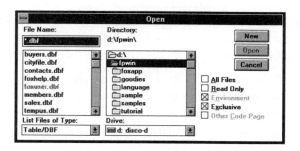

If you created a screen earlier using the Catalog Manager, you can use that screen at any time to add records. To open an existing screen, click the Screen tab in the Catalog Manager, then click the screen to select it and click Run (or just double-click the screen by name). The screen will load, and a record will appear. You can then click the Add button to add a new record.

Adding and Changing Data from the Menus and Command Window

If you are at the menus, before you can add or edit data you must first place a table in use. To open the table, choose File, Open. The Open dialog box appears. (See Figure 4.3.)

FIGURE 4.3.

The Open dialog box.

Since FoxPro assigns all tables an extension of .DBF by default, only files with this extension appear in the dialog box. (You can include extensions other than .DBF with tables. This is risky, since FoxPro assumes the .DBF extension and may not be able to readily find tables if you name them with extensions other than .DBF.) You can use the Drives and Directory list boxes to navigate among the available directories and disk drives on your system. Click the desired table to open in the File Name list box to select it, then click Open to open the table.

If you prefer the Command Window, you can open any table with the USE command, as mentioned in Chapter 3, "Creating and Working with Tables." In the Command Window, enter

```
USE filename
```

where *filename* is the name of the table that you want to open.

Once the table is open, you can add data by choosing Record, Append from the menus, or by entering APPEND in the Command Window. With either method, a blank record is added to the end of the table. The blank record appears in FoxPro's default Append window (see Figure 4.4), with the fields matching the fields in the order they occur within the table.

FIGURE 4.4.

The default Append window.

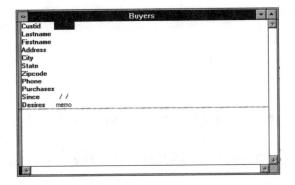

Once you've entered the Append command or chosen Record, Append from the menus, FoxPro places you in append mode. This means that as you leave the last field of a new record with the down arrow or the PgDn key, another new record is automatically added. You remain in append mode until you close the window, or use the Ctrl+End or Ctrl+W key combinations.

To modify your data in existing records, the Change command can be entered in the Command Window, or you can choose Record, Change from the menus. With either method, a record appears in FoxPro's default Change/Edit window. (See Figure 4.5.) Once in Change mode, you can make any desired changes to the records. By pressing the up or down arrow keys you will move up or down one field at a time. If you continue to press the down arrow key past the last field, the cursor will move to the next record. Pressing the up arrow key will eventually move you to the prior record unless you are at the beginning of a table. Mouse users can make changes to any field by clicking in the desired field and entering the desired changes.

Seasoned users of the XBase language may be accustomed to finding a desired record and entering the EDIT command to make the changes. The CHANGE command is functionally identical to the EDIT command, so you can enter either CHANGE or EDIT in the Command Window, and get the same results.

FIGURE 4.5.

The default Change/Edit window.

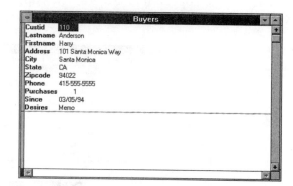

Entering Data in a General Field

In FoxPro General fields are used to store any type of OLE data from other windows applications. A brief description of how to enter data in a General field is provided here; more detailed information is found in Chapter 17, "Working with Graphs."

When a table is created and it contains a general field, entering information is a simple matter. The data to insert in the general field should first be placed into the Windows Clipboard using Windows cut-and-paste techniques. You can switch to the other Windows program, select the desired object in the other application, and choose Edit/Copy to copy the data to the Windows Clipboard.

Once the data is in the Windows Clipboard, switch back to FoxPro and open the general field by double-clicking on it. The general field opens into a window, ready for the entry of data. Choose Paste from the Edit menu (or press Ctrl+V) to paste the object to the general field.

About the Record Menu Options

With a table in use, you can use the various menu options on the Record menu to locate specific records for editing. (Each of these options also has an equivalent command that can be used in the Command Window.) If you open the Record menu, it appears with the options shown in Figure 4.6.

The Append option adds a blank record and places you within that record. The GoTo and Locate options can be useful in quickly finding a record to edit. Locate can search for data based on a specific field or expression (this technique will be detailed shortly). GoTo can take you to a specific record by number so you can edit that record. Choose GoTo from the record menu, and you will see the GoTo dialog box. (See Figure 4.7.) There you will find four choices, Top, Bottom, Record, and Skip. These features all facilitate movement within a table.

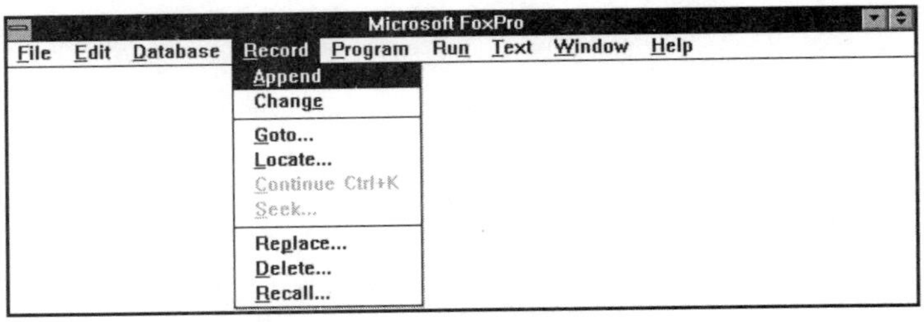

FIGURE 4.6.

The Record menu.

FIGURE 4.7.

The GoTo dialog box.

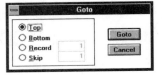

If you choose Top, the record pointer moves to the top of the table. The Bottom option moves the pointer to the bottom of the table. The Skip option moves the pointer by a certain number of records which you specify. The number 1 appears in the entry field, as the option assumes you want to skip by one record. You also can enter the number you want including negative numbers to go backwards. For example, you could enter -5 to go back by five records, or you could enter 5 to go forward five records. If you select the Record option, you can enter the record number desired and the pointer will move to that particular record number.

These options work well when you know the record number to be edited, but very often this is not the case. In many cases, a search of some type is needed. This can be done with Locate, Continue, and Seek options, which also are located on the Record menu. Seek does a search based on the use of an index, so the search must be based on the field used to build the index. (Locate and Continue, by comparison, do not need an index to function.)

Finding Records to Edit with Locate

Choose the Locate from the Record menu to find records when no index is in use or to search based on multiple fields. Figure 4.8 shows the dialog box which appears when you choose Record, Locate from the menus. There are three choices: Scope, For, and While.

FIGURE 4.8.

The Locate dialog box.

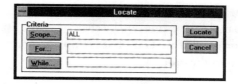

The Scope option lets you limit the scope of your search. Clicking on the Scope option reveals another dialog box with four options: All, Next, Record, and Rest. The All choice is the default, and leaving it selected causes the Locate option to consider all records as part of the search. The Next option Tells FoxPro to look at a certain span of records starting with the location of the pointer, based on the number you enter. You could also choose Record and enter a record number. (The usefulness of this option is a bit questionable, because if you knew the record number you wouldn't need to search to begin with.) The Rest option applies the Locate option to the records from the pointer to the end of the table—in effect telling FoxPro to start from wherever it is at in the table and search the rest of the table.

On the Locate menu, the While and For options are generally the most useful. The While option works best with an index, but the For option can be used on any field whether there is an index or Not. Figure 4.9 shows the FoxPro Expression Builder dialog box, which appears after choosing For in the Locate Dialog Box.

FIGURE 4.9.

The Expression Builder dialog box.

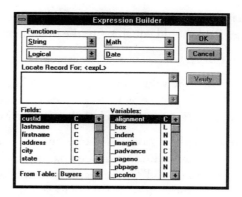

In the Locate Record for <expL> portion of the dialog box, you enter an *expression* that tells FoxPro what to locate. An expression is the combination of the Field names, operations, and constants which all equate to a certain value. For example:

```
Lastname = "Hernandez"
```

is an expression, as is

```
Purchases > 5.
```

You can enter your expression by typing it into the Locate Record for <expL> text box. You can also build the expression by clicking in the list boxes within the dialog box, or use a combination of both methods. For example, a typical expression to search for data would be something in the order of

```
Locate for fieldname = search term
```

where *fieldname* would be the name of the field you wanted to search, and *search term* would be the data you were seeking. In the Expression Builder, you could build such an expression by first double-clicking the field name in the Fields Box. The field name you choose then appears in the Locate Record For <expL> text box. (You could also type the field name in the text box if desired.) Next, you would need to enter an operator (such as an equal sign). These can be found in the Logical drop down menu box. (Normally the quicker method is to just type the operator.) Finally you would enter the desired search value. Enter Text expressions with quotation marks around them. Numbers must be entered exactly as they are stored in the numeric field and dates can be entered surrounded with curly braces ({}), or they can be entered using the CTOD conversion function. For example, CTOD("3/20/94") causes the expression to be evaluated as a date value.

As part of your expressions, include the AND and OR operators. These tell FoxPro whether to look for a match to all the conditions or only one of them. For example the expression

```
Lastname = "Hernandez" And Purchases = 5
```

indicates that the value in the Lastname field should equal Hernandez and the value in the Purchases field should equal 3. On the other hand, an expression like

```
Lastname = "Hernandez" or Lastname = "Anderson"
```

would indicate that the value in the Lastname field could be either of these values. Note that most versiions of XBase required periods surrounding the AND and OR keywords. In FoxPro, these periods can be included or omitted with the same results.

You can verify that the expression you've entered is a valid one, by clicking the Verify button in the Expression Builder dialog box. If the expression is valid, the screen briefly displays "Expression is valid" in the Status Bar at the bottom of the FoxPro window. You can click OK to complete the entry in the Expression Builder, and again reveal the Locate dialog box. Finally, click on Locate to activate the search.

The use of Locate finds the record (assuming it exists), but it does nothing to force its display. If you want to view or edit the record, you'll need to choose Record, Change from the menus (or enter the equivalent CHANGE command in the Command Window).

Using Browse Mode

FoxPro's Browse mode displays a number of records at the same time, in a spreadsheet-like (tabular) format. To enter the Browse mode, type BROWSE in the Command window or choose Database, Browse from the Database menu. (If you choose Database, Browse and the records appear but in a Change/Edit fashion, open the Browse menu and choose Browse to change to the Browse mode of display.) Figure 4.10 shows the records of a table in Browse mode. You can experiment with the options covered in this section by opening a table that has a large number of records. You can use your own table, or copy the MEMBERS.DBF table from the disk that accompanies this book to your working directory, and then open that table by choosing File, Open and selecting MEMBERS.DBF in the Open dialog box.

FIGURE 4.10.

Records of a table in Browse mode.

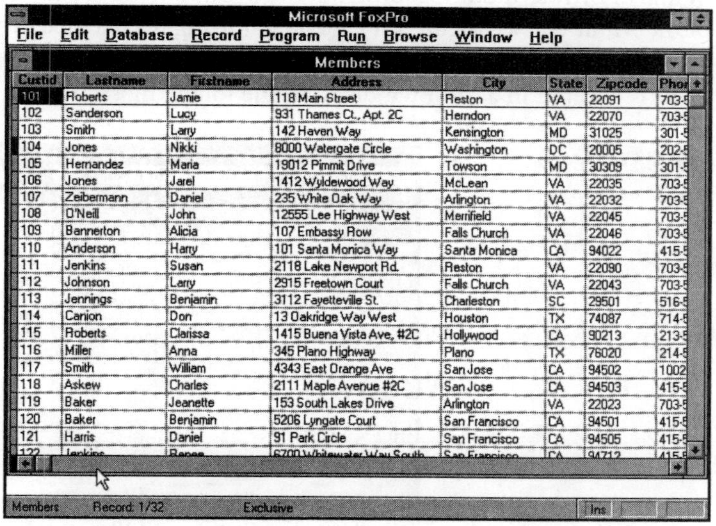

The records that are not visible in the window can be seen by pressing PgDn or PgUp. If the table has too many fields to be seen within the width of the window, the rest of the fields will appear to the right of the window's edge and can be reached by using the arrow keys or the Tab key. The scroll bars can also be used—clicking and dragging on the boxes causes the screen to move in the direction the box is dragged. The position of the boxes are relative to your position in the file. For example, if you are two-thirds of the way down the box, you are two-thirds down in the file. The scroll bar at the bottom the screen works in a horizontal manner and the scroll bar at the right works in a vertical fashion.

Records can be edited while in Browse mode. The changes can be entered as if you were in Change/Edit mode. Memo fields also can be edited in Browse mode in the same way as in edit mode; double-click the memo field to open a window to enter the changes.

Double-clicking the control menu icon closes the memo window (or you can press Ctrl+F4). You can also close a memo window by opening the control menu with Alt+Hyphen and choosing Close.

Records can also be added by choosing Append from the Browse menu. This enables you to add new records to a table. (Note that you can also use Ctrl+N to add a single blank record, although doing so does not put you into append mode.) With either of these techniques, a new blank record appears at the end of the table, and FoxPro automatically switches to Append mode. While you remain within a Browse style of display, pressing the down arrow or PgDn keys adds a new record.

Browse Menu Options

While in Browse mode a new menu, the Browse menu is added to the menu bar at the top of the window. (See Figure 4.11.) The following is a detailed description of these options. (Note that most of these options also have shortcuts keys.) The use of these various options is covered in additional detail in the following sections.

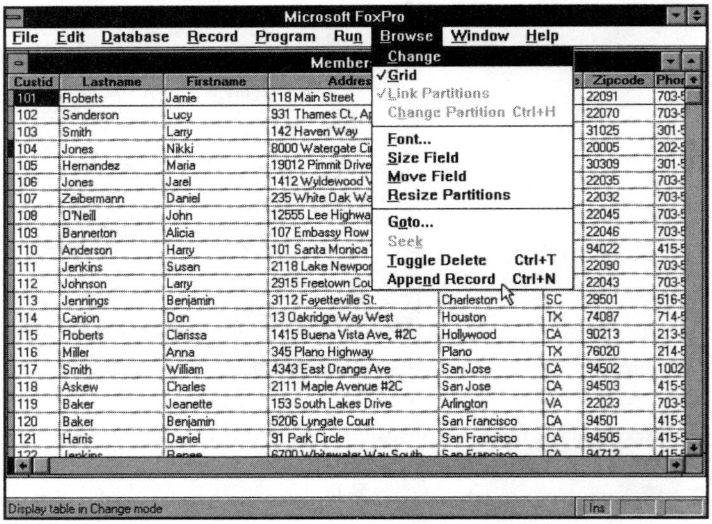

FIGURE 4.11.

The Browse menu.

Change: This option shows the file in the browse window in full-screen edit form. This is functionally equivalent to using the CHANGE or EDIT command in the Command Window.

Grid: This option causes the vertical and horizontal lines to appear between the columns and rows. Choosing this option turns the grid lines on or off.

Link Partitions: If a window is divided in two parts, this option links or unlinks the two parts of the window. The option is a toggle; choosing the option alternately turns it on or off. (When turned on, a check mark appears beside the option name in the menu.) If Link Partitions is turned off, the cursor moves independently within the two partitions. If Link Partitions is turned on, the cursor moves through the two partitions in synchronization.

Change Partition: If a window is divided into two partitions this option alternately switches between the partitions.

Font: This option enables you to choose a font, font size, and font style for use in the Browse window.

Size Field: Selecting this option resizes a field. Tab to the desired field, choose this option and use the arrow keys to resize the field. Any key (except arrow keys) completes the resizing. (Sizing also can be done with the mouse, as discussed shortly.)

Move Field: Select this option to move a field. Move to the field you wish to move, select Move Field, use the arrow keys to relocate the field, and then press any key except the arrow keys to place the field in the desired area. (Moving can also be done with the mouse, as discussed shortly.)

Resize Partitions: This option enables you to change the size of existing partitions, or lets you restore a split window to its full size. From the menus, choose this option and then use the left arrow and right arrow keys to open, close, or change the size of existing partitions. Pressing any key except the arrow keys completes the option.

GoTo: This option is equivalent to choosing GoTo from the Change menu. It is used to go to a specific record.

Seek: This option is used to find an indexed record. (Indexing is covered in detail in Chapter 5, "Arranging Data.")

Toggle Delete: This marks a record for deletion at a later time. (This option can also be activated by pressing Ctrl+T.)

Append Record: Choosing this option adds a blank record at the end of the table for the addition of new data.

Changing Fonts

Changing the font or font size can make records easier to read. To change fonts, choose Browse, Font from the menus. The Font dialog box will appear. (See Figure 4.12.)

Click on the font you want and click the desired point size. You also have choices in the font style box of Regular, Italic, Bold, and Bold Italic. When you've selected your options, click OK to apply the font changes to the table. The font chosen can make a significant change to the appearance of the information in the table. For example, Figure 4.13 shows a table using Arial 8-point, while Figure 4.14 shows a table using Times New Roman 12-point.

FIGURE 4.12.

The Font dialog box.

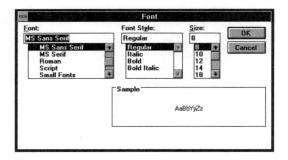

FIGURE 4.13.

A Browse window using Arial font, 8-point size.

Custid	Lastname	Firstname	Address	City	State	Zipcode	Phon
101	Roberts	Jamie	118 Main Street	Reston	VA	22091	703-
102	Sanderson	Lucy	931 Thames Ct., Apt. 2C	Herndon	VA	22070	703-
103	Smith	Larry	142 Haven Way	Kensington	MD	31025	301-
104	Jones	Nikki	8000 Watergate Circle	Washington	DC	20005	202-
105	Hernandez	Maria	19012 Pimmit Drive	Towson	MD	30309	301-
106	Jones	Jarel	1412 Wyldewood Way	McLean	VA	22035	703-
107	Zeibermann	Daniel	235 White Oak Way	Arlington	VA	22032	703-
108	O'Neill	John	12555 Lee Highway West	Merrifield	VA	22045	703-
109	Bannerton	Alicia	107 Embassy Row	Falls Church	VA	22046	703-
110	Anderson	Harry	101 Santa Monica Way	Santa Monica	CA	94022	415-
111	Jenkins	Susan	2118 Lake Newport Rd.	Reston	VA	22090	703-
112	Johnson	Larry	2915 Freetown Court	Falls Church	VA	22043	703-
113	Jennings	Benjamin	3112 Fayetteville St.	Charleston	SC	29501	516-
114	Canion	Don	13 Oakridge Way West	Houston	TX	74087	714-
115	Roberts	Clarissa	1415 Buena Vista Ave, #2C	Hollywood	CA	90213	213-
116	Miller	Anna	345 Plano Highway	Plano	TX	76020	214-
117	Smith	William	4343 East Orange Ave	San Jose	CA	94502	1002
118	Askew	Charles	2111 Maple Avenue #2C	San Jose	CA	94503	415-
119	Baker	Jeanette	153 South Lakes Drive	Arlington	VA	22023	703-
120	Baker	Benjamin	5206 Lyngate Court	San Francisco	CA	94501	415-

Members   Record: 18/32   Exclusive   Ins

FIGURE 4.14.

A Browse window using Times New Roman font, 12-point size.

Custid	Lastname	Firstname	Address	City	State
101	Roberts	Jamie	118 Main Street	Reston	VA
102	Sanderson	Lucy	931 Thames Ct., Apt. 2C	Herndon	VA
103	Smith	Larry	142 Haven Way	Kensington	MD
104	Jones	Nikki	8000 Watergate Circle	Washington	DC
105	Hernandez	Maria	19012 Pimmit Drive	Towson	MD
106	Jones	Jarel	1412 Wyldewood Way	McLean	VA
107	Zeibermann	Daniel	235 White Oak Way	Arlington	VA
108	O'Neill	John	12555 Lee Highway West	Merrifield	VA
109	Bannerton	Alicia	107 Embassy Row	Falls Church	VA
110	Anderson	Harry	101 Santa Monica Way	Santa Monica	CA
111	Jenkins	Susan	2118 Lake Newport Rd.	Reston	VA
112	Johnson	Larry	2915 Freetown Court	Falls Church	VA
113	Jennings	Benjamin	3112 Fayetteville St.	Charleston	SC
114	Canion	Don	13 Oakridge Way West	Houston	TX
115	Roberts	Clarissa	1415 Buena Vista Ave. #2C	Hollywood	CA

Members   Record: 15/32   Exclusive   Ins

Manipulation of the Window

Several options exist for the manipulation of the window in Foxpro. The maximize button allows for the displaying of the maximum number of records at a time. The Browse window can be split by using the mouse or the Resize Partitions option. Placing the mouse over the split bar changes the pointer to resemble an arrow with two heads. Dragging the split bar in the bottom scroll bar splits the Browse window. (See Figure 4.15.)

FIGURE 4.15.

A Browse window after splitting.

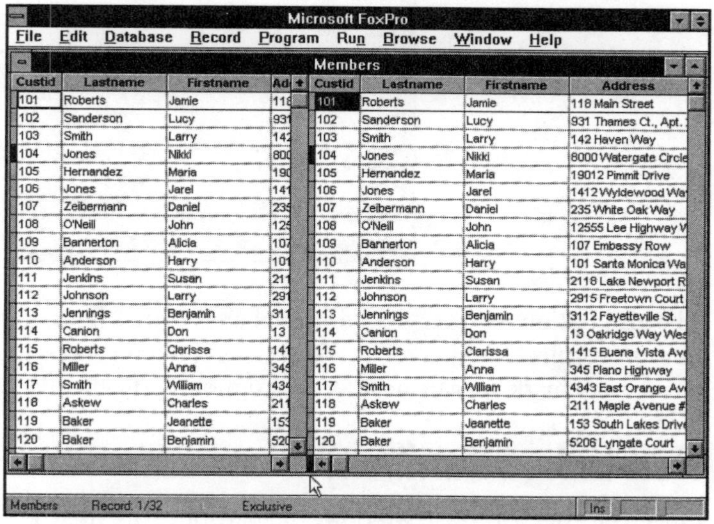

You can also use the menu options to split a window, by choosing Resize Partitions from the Browse menu, then pressing the right arrow key until the window splits.

Simultaneous Use of Edit and Browse Mode

If you make one partition of a Browse window active (by clicking anywhere on it), the Change option of the Browse menu can then be used to show records within that partition in Edit mode while in the Browse window. This trick gives you a view of the records in a tabular form and a full record view simultaneously. (See Figure 4.16.) The Ctrl+H key combination lets you switch between partitions (you can also open the Browse menu and choose Change Partitions to accomplish the same result). Moving up and down in the left portions causes the record and the corresponding field to appear at the right. While the active partition contains an Edit-style of display, the first option on the Browse menu changes to Browse. You can select this option to change the active partition from Edit mode back to Browse mode.

FIGURE 4.16.

A simultaneous view of Edit and Browse modes in same window.

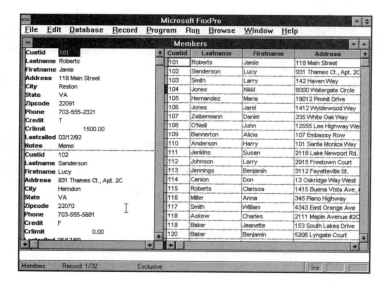

The grid option removes the horizontal and vertical lines between the records. The option is a toggle; choosing it turns grid lines either on and off. If the grid lines are turned on, a check mark appears next to Grid option in the menu.

Non-Linked Partitions

Once you split a Browse window, the partitions are linked. This means that when you move in one, the other normally "follows." You can tell whether the partitions are linked by looking at the Link Partitions option on the Browse menu. If there is a check mark beside the option, it has been activated.

Changing Field Sizes and Positions

The field width and the order of the fields in a Browse window can be rearranged at will. Clicking on the field's right border in the heading area of the field and then dragging the border changes the field width. Changing the location is done much the same way—by clicking and dragging on the heading itself. To change the field's width, place the mouse pointer on the right edge of the field heading area of the first name field. When you are in the correct area, the pointer will change to a double arrow. Click and drag the edge, and the field will narrow by a corresponding amount. (You can also use the Browse, Size Field option of the menus to resize the field. Place the cursor in the field you want to size, choose Browse, Size Field, then use the left or right arrow key to widen the field as desired, and press Enter.)

To change the location of a field, place the mouse pointer anywhere in the field heading area that is not on the border, then click and drag the field to the desired location elsewhere in the header. (You can also use the Browse, Move Field option of the menus to move the field to a different location. Place the cursor in the field you want to move, choose Browse, Move Field, use the left or right arrow key to move the field to the desired location, and press Enter.)

Using Browse with Commands

From the command window, with any table in use you can enter BROWSE to open a Browse window into that table, but this only scratches the surface of what you can do with the Browse mode from a command standpoint. Using commands, you actually have more flexibility with Browse than you can attain with menu options. You can enter commands that open a Browse window containing certain fields of a table, and you can restrict editing.

You can enter the BROWSE command along with a list of specified fields, in which case only those fields will be available for editing. For example, the command

```
BROWSE FIELDS LASTNAME, FIRSTNAME, ADDRESS, CITY, STATE
```

would display only those fields named in the command line for each record. You can also specify the FREEZE option to restrict editing to a specific field, preventing changes to any other field. For instance, the command

```
BROWSE FIELDS LASTNAME, FIRSTNAME, PURCHASES FREEZE PURCHASES
```

would display only those fields listed. Of those fields, only the PURCHASES field would be available for editing.

The BROWSE command offers a specific option for locking one or more columns in the left partition of a window, while allowing other columns to pan across the screen in a right partition. You can enter BROWSE LOCK *numeric expression,* where *numeric expression* contains a number indicating the number of fields that should be locked at the left side of the screen. As an example, the command,

```
BROWSE LOCK 2
```

creates a display that keeps the first two fields in the database always visible in the left partition, while the other fields can be viewed in the right partition. (Note that entering BROWSE LOCK 0 turns off the ability to create multiple partitions.)

Use the NOFOLLOW option with indexed tables (see the next chapter for an explanation of indexing). After you have edited a field in an indexed table, BROWSE normally repositions the display to maintain position according to the index. If you want to prevent this from happening, add the NOFOLLOW option to the BROWSE command.

Add the NOAPPEND option to the BROWSE command to prevent users from adding records while in the BROWSE mode. In a similar fashion, the NOEDIT option prevents editing, while the NODELETE option prevents deletions with Ctrl+T. The NOMENU option denies access to the Browse menu while in Browse mode. All four of these options are powerful tools for restricting access to Browse when you use the command within a FoxPro program. Programming is discussed beginning with Chapter 19, "FoxPro Programming Basics."

The WINDOW option is a useful one (particularly within FoxPro programs) when you want to limit the Browse display to a predefined portion of a screen. (You must first use the DEFINE WINDOW command to define the name and screen parameters of the window.) For example:

```
DEFINE WINDOW MyScreen FROM 2,10 TO 12,60
BROWSE WINDOW MyScreen
```

The first statement defines the window "MyScreen" as having coordinates from row 2, column 10 to row 12, column 60. (When translated to the Windows environment, such coordinates are measured in characters using FoxPro's system font.) The second statement causes the Browse display to appear within the predefined window. The WINDOW option can be combined with other options of the BROWSE command, to provide precise control of a Browse window while in a FoxPro program. As an example, the statement

```
BROWSE NOAPPEND NOEDIT NODELETE NOMENU WINDOW MyScreen
```

would present the Browse display within the defined window, while preventing any modifications to the data and denying access to the Browse option that normally appears on the menu bar.

Deleting and Recalling Records

As with all XBase-compatible database systems, deleting records is a two-step process in FoxPro. First, you use the Record, Delete menu option or the DELETE command in the Command Window to mark the desired record for deletion. You can repeat this step for as many records as you want to delete. When you want to make the deletions permanent, you use the Database, Pack menu option or its equivalent PACK command. While this two-step approach may seem cumbersome to those who have worked with database managers outside of the realm of XBase, it has the inherent advantage of making it difficult to lose records by accidental deletions.

When the Delete command is entered or Record, Delete is chosen form the menus, the record is marked for deletion by FoxPro, but not actually deleted. This built-in protection provides you with the opportunity to change your mind and recall the record.

To prepare a record for Deletion, first move to the desired record. Enter DELETE in the Command Window, or choose Record, Delete from the menus. If you use the menus, you will see the Delete dialog box. (See Figure 4.17.) If at that time you only care to mark the current record for deletion, ignore all of the options and just click delete.

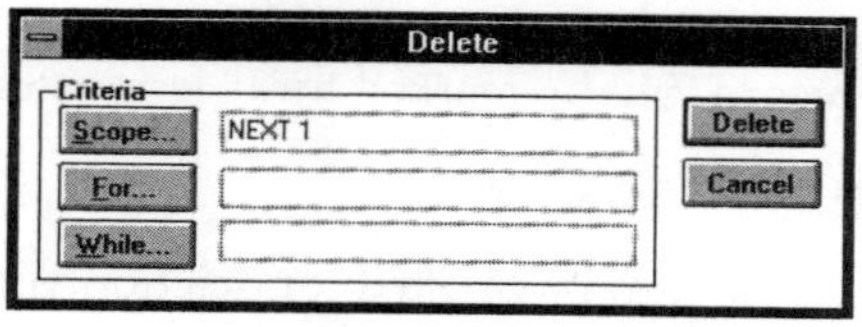

FIGURE 4.17.

The Delete dialog box.

A locate command or menu option, followed by a delete command or menu option, can be used to find a particular record and mark it for deletion. Remember, the format for locate is

The scope option allows for the choosing of a group of records for deletion. Choosing All records marks all records for deletion. Next*n*, (*n* representing a number such as in Next 5), is useful in the deletion of a contiguous group of records. The Rest option functions based on the location of the record pointer, and marks all records form the current one to the end of the file. The While option isn't recommended if you are making simple deletions. The While option works best with an indexed field; for example, if a table was indexed on the basis of City names, you could delete all records "while City = Omaha" to mark all the records with "Omaha" in the City field for deletion. (Indexed fields are discussed in Chapter 5.)

TIP

FoxPro provides another way to delete records while in the Browse window. You can delete records by clicking on the rectangular shaded area at the immediate left of the records leftmost field. When you do this, the gray area turns black and the record is marked for deletion.

A locate command or menu option, followed by a delete command or menu option, can be used to find a particular record and mark it for deletion. Remember, the format for locate is

```
Locate for fieldname = search term
```

When searching character fields the search term must be surrounded by quotation marks. Capitalization inside the quotes must also match. If you are searching a numeric field only the number need be entered.

If you prefer to do your deletions from the Command Window, the syntax for the DELETE command is

```
DELETE [scope] [WHILE condition] [FOR condition]
```

The command can be used with a scope (ALL, NEXT *n*, REST), or with a specific record number. If no scope is specified, the current record (wherever FoxPro's record pointer is located) will be marked for deletion. As an example, if the record pointer is currently at record 7, then the command

```
DELETE
```

would cause record 7 to be marked for deletion. The command

```
DELETE RECORD4
```

would cause record 4 to be marked for deletion. You can see that deleted records are not physically removed from a table by deleting one or more records and then opening a Browse window for the table. The records marked for deletion still appear in the window, but the shaded area at the left edge of the Browse window (beside the affected record) is black, as shown in Figure 4.18.

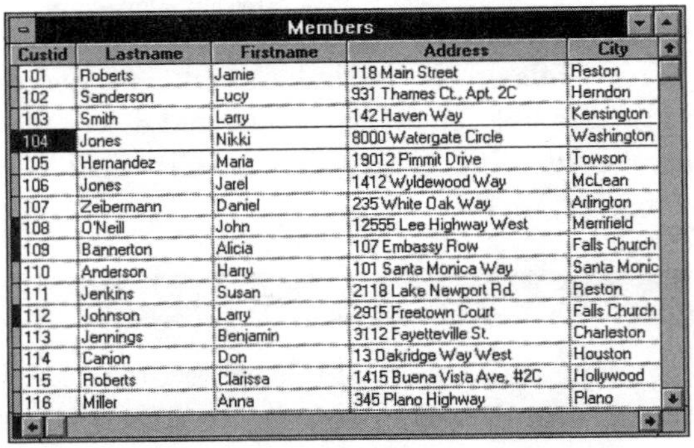

FIGURE 4.18.

Records marked for deletion in Browse window.

Custid	Lastname	Firstname	Address	City
101	Roberts	Jamie	118 Main Street	Reston
102	Sanderson	Lucy	931 Thames Ct., Apt. 2C	Herndon
103	Smith	Larry	142 Haven Way	Kensington
104	Jones	Nikki	8000 Watergate Circle	Washington
105	Hernandez	Maria	19012 Pimmit Drive	Towson
106	Jones	Jarel	1412 Wyldewood Way	McLean
107	Zeibermann	Daniel	235 White Oak Way	Arlington
108	O'Neill	John	12555 Lee Highway West	Merrifield
109	Bannerton	Alicia	107 Embassy Row	Falls Church
110	Anderson	Harry	101 Santa Monica Way	Santa Monic
111	Jenkins	Susan	2118 Lake Newport Rd.	Reston
112	Johnson	Larry	2915 Freetown Court	Falls Church
113	Jennings	Benjamin	3112 Fayetteville St.	Charleston
114	Canion	Don	13 Oakridge Way West	Houston
115	Roberts	Clarissa	1415 Buena Vista Ave, #2C	Hollywood
116	Miller	Anna	345 Plano Highway	Plano

If you prefer not to see the records you have marked for deletion, you can hide them from normal view by entering SET DELETED ON in the Command Window.

In FoxPro more than one record can be deleted at once if the records are in sequential order. Consider the following commands:

```
GOTO 5
DELETE NEXT 4
```

This enables you to delete four records at the same time, beginning with record 5 in the table.

As mentioned, deleted records are normally still visible within a table, and they can be "unmarked" from the deleted status by choosing Record, Recall from the menus, or by entering the equivalent RECALL command. A Recall menu option or command has the opposite effect as the Delete menu option or command—it removes the deletion marker from the affected record. From the menus, you use the option in a manner similar to the

Delete menu option—choose Record, Recall from the menus. When you do so, you will see the Recall dialog box, containing the same Scope, For, and While options that are provided in the Delete dialog box. If you just wish to recall the current record, ignore all of the options and click delete. You also can use the scope, for, or while options as detailed earlier to choose a group of records to be recalled.

From the Command Window, the RECALL command uses a syntax that is identical to that of the DELETE command, namely:

```
RECALL [scope] [WHILE condition] [FOR condition]
```

Examples of the use of the RECALL command include:

```
RECALL NEXT 7
RECALL ALL
RECALL NEXT 200 FOR STATUS = "paid"
RECALL ALL FOR LASTNAME = "Carter" .AND. SALARY <= 7.50
```

Packing a Table

The Pack option of the Database menu and its equivalent PACK command are used to remove all records marked for deletion from a table. The PACK command also renumbers all the remaining records, so that disk space consumed by the table is minimized. If an index is open at the time the Pack option or command is used, the index is updated. While you can perform a pack immediately after deleting a record, it is time consuming, particularly with large tables. Many FoxPro programmers prefer to perform a pack infrequently in their applications because it is so time consuming. You can leave records marked for deletion in the table and make those records appear to have been deleted by using the SET DELETED ON command. A pack operation can then be done on a weekly or monthly basis to recover disk space.

To perform a pack, choose Database, Pack, or enter PACK in the Command Window. FoxPro displays a confirmation dialog, asking if you want to pack the database. Click Yes in the dialog box, and all records marked for deletion are removed and the remaining records renumbered.

You can empty a table by entering DELETE ALL followed by PACK in the Command Window. A faster alternative to empty an entire table is to use the ZAP command. ZAP will delete all records from the active table. Unlike DELETE ALL, the ZAP command provides no way to restore erased records. You could not issue a RECALL ALL command after you had issued a ZAP command. Because ZAP is such a destructive command, it asks for confirmation first by displaying a dialog box. You must confirm the operation before that table will be emptied of its contents.

Chapter Summary

This chapter examined the use of the Catalog Manager, menu options, and commands used to add and edit data in your tables, with a particular emphasis on the flexibility of the Browse mode. As you work with FoxPro, you'll be able to use these techniques along with others to use FoxPro fully in an interactive mode, as well as to better design and implement any database applications.

Arranging Data

This chapter provides the tips and techniques you'll need to keep your data in order, by means of *indexing* and/or *sorting*. In FoxPro, as in any XBase system, data is kept in a desired order using one of two methods: indexing or sorting. While indexing is by far the more common of the two, there are times when sorting makes sense. With indexing, a separate file is used to provide a reference to how the records in the original table should be arranged. With sorting, the data is physically copied in the desired order to a new table. The first part of this chapter will look at the more commonly-used (and more complex) technique, indexing, in detail. The second portion of the chapter covers sorting, and provides examples of when sorting can be a viable alternative to indexing.

Indexing, Defined

When you add an index to a FoxPro table, you establish an order in which your records will be arranged, without modifying the original table. FoxPro creates a separate index, which contains record numbers and a minimum of one field (or expression based on fields) from the corresponding table. The fields contained within the index are used to indicate the desired record number in the corresponding table. In effect, the index is a *virtual index* of the table. Although the records within the associated table may not be sorted in any fashion physically, the table will appear to be sorted in the manner of the index. An excellent analogy for understanding how FoxPro indexes work is to compare the FoxPro index to the index in the back of a book. Just as a book index is a separate section that provides reference to where data is physically located elsewhere in the book, a FoxPro index provides a reference for FoxPro as to where a record is physically located. FoxPro then uses this reference to display or print your data in the desired order. In FoxPro, you can create indexes with all three user interfaces: the Catalog Manger, the menus, and the Command Window.

The Benefits of Indexing

Partly because FoxPro offers so many variations on indexing, PC users new to FoxPro sometimes wonder when indexing is necessary, if ever. Seasoned XBase professionals know that indexing is a fundamental part of database operations. In most Browse windows and with most reports, you'll want to see your data in order, and indexing helps you accomplish this need. Indexing serves two purposes readily apparent to the FoxPro user: it keeps your data in a certain order, and it speeds up searches when the searches are on fields or expressions contained in the index. The presence of indexes can also speed up FoxPro's query-by-example process, as certain queries require indexes. FoxPro builds these needed indexes behind the scenes, but if the needed indexes already exist, FoxPro will save time by using the existing indexes during the query process.

Along with the benefits comes a disadvantage: indexing can adversely affect overall performance. As you make changes to records in a table, FoxPro updates any index that is open to reflect the changes to the table. With a large number of indexes open, this can have a degrading effect on performance. Each time you add a new record, for example, all the open indexes must be updated to reflect the addition. You'll want to strike a balance between flexibility and performance by opening indexes that are truly needed, while avoiding adding unnecessary indexes.

Types of Indexes

In the early days of XBase, only one type of index was possible: separate index files were created, with the index data stored outside of the database (*.DBF) file. Everything was done from the command level (there were no menus or helpful interfaces like the Catalog Manager in those days), and each time you wanted to use an index file, it had to be opened along with the database file which contained the table. This led to a confusing directory structure with applications of any complexity—a single table could easily have a half-dozen different index files to help keep things in order different ways. If your application used five or six different tables, the tables and corresponding index files alone could add 50 or more files to a single subdirectory. When dBASE IV was introduced, it offered a technique that solved the problem of multiple index files cluttering a directory. With dBASE IV, *index tags* could be added to the database file containing the table itself. Different index tags could be added to a single database file, called a *compound index file*. FoxPro adopted this strategy to maintain compatibility with dBASE IV. This means that in FoxPro you have two ways of indexing information: the use of a compound index file containing one or more index tags, or the creation of single index files (in line with the indexing technique from the early days of XBase). Compound index files in FoxPro have a .CDX extension, while single index files are assigned an .IDX extension. Which type of index you create depends on how you create the index. From the Command Window, you can use different commands (discussed in this chapter) to create index tags, or to create separate index files. From the menus, certain options in the Index dialog box let you specify whether an index that you create is added to a compound index file, or stored separately. The only area where you do not have a choice is when you create indexes through the Catalog Manager. An index added through the Catalog Manager will be stored in a compound index file. (You can however, place single index files that were created outside the Catalog Manager in use from within the Catalog Manager.)

In general, it is advantageous to stick with the use of compound index files. One reason to use the older style of separate index files is when you need to maintain compatibility with early versions of FoxPro (versions 1.x), or with other XBase products (dBASE III Plus).

A Note About the Structural Compound Index File

One special compound index file is the *structural compound index file*, a fancy name for a compound index file that has the same name as the database file containing the table, but with a .CDX extension. The only special aspect of this index is that FoxPro automatically looks for it whenever a table is first opened. If FoxPro finds a file with a .CDX extension that has the same name as the table's filename, FoxPro opens that compound index file automatically, and puts it in use. This means that as you make changes to the records in that table, the index tags in the compound index file are updated automatically.

Indexing from the Catalog Manager

When you're using the Catalog Manager, you can add or change indexes with the Data, Add Modify Indexes option. (This menu option is only available in the Catalog Manager, so don't look for it elsewhere in FoxPro.) Indexes added through the Catalog Manager are automatically placed in the structural compound index file for the table that's in use. You can create an index with the following steps:

1. Place the desired table in use, if it isn't already. (In the Catalog Manager, click the Table tab, then click the desired table to select it, then click Use.)

2. From the menus, choose Data, Add/Modify Indexes. The Add/Modify Indexes dialog box opens. (See Figure 5.1.)

FIGURE 5.1.

The Add/Modify Indexes dialog box.

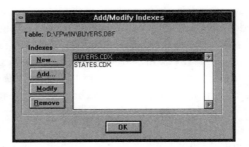

3. Click the desired index file in the list box to select it.

4. Click Modify (this button lets you modify the index that's currently in use. Unless you've changed it, the Catalog Manager uses the structural compound index file). The Change Index dialog box appears. (See Figure 5.2.) In the Available Fields portion of the dialog box, you see all the fields of the table.

FIGURE 5.2.

*The Change Index
dialog box.*

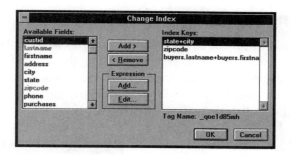

5. Select the desired field from the list to base the index on, and click the Add button to add it to the Index Keys portion of the dialog box. When you want to base the index on an expression (like a combination of fields), you can click the Add button under Expression (in the center of the dialog box), and manually type the expression in the Expression text box that appears in the Create Expression dialog box. When done, click OK. You can also click the Expression button in the Create Expression dialog box, and use the Expression Builder, which appears to construct an expression. (An example that follows shows how you can do this.)

6. When done choosing the fields or building the expressions that will create the desired tags (called *index keys* in the Create Index dialog box), click OK, to build the indexes.

About the Choices in the Add/Modify Index Dialog Box

When you choose Data, Add/Modify Indexes from the menus, the Add/Modify Indexes dialog box (see Figure 5.1), which contains four buttons: New, Add, Modify, and Remove, appears. The list box within this dialog box shows the available indexes. The buttons serve the following purposes:

New...: Use this button to display the Create Index dialog box, which you can use to create a new index on the active table in the current catalog.

Add...: Use this button to display the Open dialog box, which you can use to add an index to the current catalog. You can add either a compound (.CDX) index file or an single index (.IDX) file using this button.

Modify: Use this button to display the Change Index dialog box, which you can use to modify the current index.

Remove: Use this button to remove an index from the current catalog. (Doing so does not erase the index file; it just removes it from view in the catalog.)

Putting the Index in Use

While you can create as many indexes as you wish (within the limits of your hard disk), only one index can be *active*, or controlling the order of the records, at one time. From the Catalog Manager, you decide which index should be the active index with the Data, Order Table menu option. From the menus, choose Data, Order Table, to display the Order Table dialog box. (See Figure 5.3.)

FIGURE 5.3.

The Order Table dialog box.

In the Available Tags/Indexes list box, click the desired index you want to use to control the order of the records. Then click Ascending or Descending as desired. Finally, click the Set Order button, to put your chosen order in effect. From this point on, the records will appear in the order specified. Note that the dialog box also contains a No Order button. You can click this button to cancel the effects of an index that you chose previously. After clicking this button, the records appear in *natural order*, or the order in which they were originally entered into the table.

Indexing on Multiple Fields from the Catalog Manager

A common need is to index on more than one field. For example, you might want to see the records for a mailing list arranged in order of states, and where states are the same, in order of city names. You can do so by building an expression that combines more than one field, with the aid of the Expression Builder. To create an index on multiple fields, use these steps:

1. Place the desired table in use, if it isn't already. (In the Catalog Manager, click the Table tab, click the desired table to select it, then click Use.)

2. From the menus, choose Data, Add/Modify Indexes to open the Add/Modify Indexes dialog box (shown previously in Figure 5.1).

3. Click the desired index file in the list box to select it.

4. Click Modify to open the Change Index dialog box.

5. In the Expression portion of the dialog box, click Add to add a new expression. (The expression that you build will contain the combination of fields that you want the index to be based on.)

6. In the Create Expression dialog box that next appears, click the Expression button. When you do so, FoxPro's Expression Builder appears. (See Figure 5.4.)

FIGURE 5.4.

The Expression Builder.

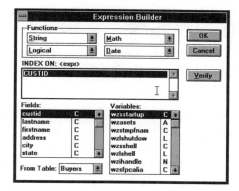

7. In the Fields list box, double-click the first field name that you want to use.

8. In the Functions portion of the Expression Builder, click the arrow beside String, and choose the plus symbol from the drop-down list box.

9. Double-click the next field you want to use as the basis for the index.

10. Repeat steps 8 and 9 for any more fields you want to base the index on.

11. Click OK. The expression that will be used to build your index appears in the Create Expression dialog box. (See Figure 5.5.)

FIGURE 5.5.

A completed Expression in the Create Expression dialog box.

12. In the Create Expression dialog box, click OK to close it. Then click OK again in the Change Index dialog box to close it, and click OK in the Add Indexes dialog box to close it. At this point, your index based on more than one field has been added to the index file.

An Example: Creating and Using Indexes with the Catalog Manager

If you created the BUYERS.DBF table in Chapter 3, "Creating and Working with Tables," (or if you've copied the table from the disk provided with this book into your working directory), you can perform the steps shown here to demonstrate how you can work with indexes from within the Catalog Manager. The steps outlined will build two indexes—one based on ZIP Codes, and one based on a combination of last and first names. Perform the following steps to build these indexes and see the results:

1. If you are not already at the Catalog Manager, choose File, Catalog Manager.

2. Click the Table tab, then click Buyers to select it, then click Use.

3. Choose Data, Add/Modify Indexes to open the Add/Modify Indexes dialog box.

4. If BUYERS.CDX is not already selected in the list box, click it to select it. Then, click Modify. (Doing this lets you modify the existing structural compound index file, BUYERS.CDX. In your own applications, you could also choose to create another compound index file, by using the New button.)

5. When the Change Index dialog box appears, click Zipcode, then click Add, to add this field as a tag to the compound index file.

6. Click OK to close the dialog box. Then click OK in the Add/Modify Indexes dialog box to close it.

The index has been added, but you will need to put it in use to see the effects. Perform these steps to do so:

1. From the menus, choose Data, Order Table to open the Order Table dialog box.

2. In the list box, click BUYERS:ZIPCODE to select it. With the default of Ascending selected in the dialog box, click Set Order , then click OK, to place the index in active use.

3. To see the results of the index, click the Browse button at the upper-left corner of the Catalog Manager. A Browse window into the table opens, and if you scroll over until the Zipcode field comes into view, you will see that the records are arranged in ascending order of ZIP codes. (See Figure 5.6.)

FIGURE 5.6.

Data arranged in order of Zipcodes.

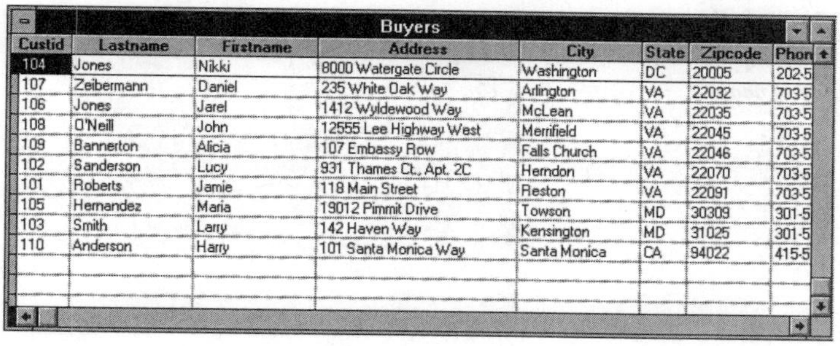

Custid	Lastname	Firstname	Address	City	State	Zipcode	Phon
104	Jones	Nikki	8000 Watergate Circle	Washington	DC	20005	202-5
107	Zeibermann	Daniel	235 White Oak Way	Arlington	VA	22032	703-5
106	Jones	Jarel	1412 Wyldewood Way	McLean	VA	22035	703-5
108	O'Neill	John	12555 Lee Highway West	Merrifield	VA	22045	703-5
109	Bannerton	Alicia	107 Embassy Row	Falls Church	VA	22046	703-5
102	Sanderson	Lucy	931 Thames Ct., Apt. 2C	Herndon	VA	22070	703-5
101	Roberts	Jamie	118 Main Street	Reston	VA	22091	703-5
105	Hernandez	Maria	19012 Pimmit Drive	Towson	MD	30309	301-5
103	Smith	Larry	142 Haven Way	Kensington	MD	31025	301-5
110	Anderson	Harry	101 Santa Monica Way	Santa Monica	CA	94022	415-5

To try the example of adding another index that is based on more than one field, perform the following steps.

1. Press Ctrl+F4 to put away the Browse window.

2. Choose Data, Add/Modify Indexes to open the Add/Modify Indexes dialog box.

3. If BUYERS.CDX is not already selected in the list box, click it to select it. Then, click Modify to open the Change Index dialog box.

4. In the Expression portion of the dialog box, click Add. When you do so, a Create Expression dialog box appears.

5. Click in the Tag text box, and enter **Names** as a tag name.

6. In the Create Expression dialog box, click the Expression button to reveal the Expression Builder.

7. In the Fields list box of the Expression Builder, double-click the Lastname field.

8. In the Functions portion of the dialog box, click the arrow beside String to open the String drop-down list box, and click the plus symbol.

9. In the Fields list box of the Expression Builder, double-click the Firstname field.

10. Click OK to close the Expression Builder.

11. Click OK to close the Create Expression dialog box. Click OK to close the Change Indexes dialog box, and click OK again to close the Add/Modify Indexes dialog box.

12. To put the new index into use, choose Data, Order Table to open the Order Table dialog box.

13. In the list box, click BUYERS:NAMES to select it. With the default of Ascending selected in the dialog box, click Set Order, then click OK, to place the index in active use.

14. To see the results of the index, click the Browse button at the upper-left corner of the Catalog Manager. A Browse window into the table opens, and if you scroll over until the Zipcode field comes into view, you will see that the records are arranged in ascending order of last names, and where the last names are the same, in order of first names. (See Figure 5.7.)

FIGURE 5.7.

Data arranged in order of names.

Custid	Lastname	Firstname	Address	City	State	Zipcode
110	Anderson	Harry	101 Santa Monica Way	Santa Monica	CA	94022
109	Bannerton	Alicia	107 Embassy Row	Falls Church	VA	22046
105	Hernandez	Maria	19012 Pimmit Drive	Towson	MD	30309
106	Jones	Jarel	1412 Wyldewood Way	McLean	VA	22035
104	Jones	Nikki	8000 Watergate Circle	Washington	DC	20005
108	O'Neill	John	12555 Lee Highway West	Merrifield	VA	22045
101	Roberts	Jamie	118 Main Street	Reston	VA	22091
102	Sanderson	Lucy	931 Thames Ct., Apt. 2C	Herndon	VA	22070
103	Smith	Larry	142 Haven Way	Kensington	MD	31025
107	Zeibermann	Daniel	235 White Oak Way	Arlington	VA	22032

Indexing from the Menus

If you are not using the Catalog Manager but prefer to stick with menu options (as opposed to the use of commands), you can create indexes by choosing File, New from the menus, clicking Index in the New dialog box that appears, and clicking OK. When you do so, the Index dialog box appears. (See Figure 5.8.)

FIGURE 5.8.

The Index dialog box.

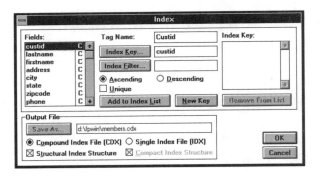

With the options provided in this dialog box, you can create compound (.CDX) or single (.IDX) index files. Your index can be based on a field, which you choose by double-clicking the desired field in the Fields list box, or by typing the field name into the text box beside the Index Key button. You also can base the index on an expression (such as a combination of two or more fields) by clicking the Index Key button to bring up the FoxPro Expression Builder. After you've designed an expression using the Expression Builder, click OK to close the Expression Builder dialog box and return to the Index dialog box.

The Index Filter button, when clicked, causes the Expression Builder to appear, which you can use to enter a For Clause that will limit the index to a specific group of records. (This technique is further detailed under the heading "Selective Indexing" later in this chapter.) The Ascending and Descending buttons let you choose ascending or descending order for the index. (Note that these buttons are disabled if you choose .IDX-style indexes.)

Near the center of the dialog box are three buttons labeled Add to Index List, New Key, and Remove From List. The Add to Index List button places the tag in the existing Index Key list, at the right side of the dialog box. The New Key button clears the existing tag name from the Index Key list box and Tag Name text boxes, so you can create a new index key. The Remove From List button removes the selected index tag from the Index Key list.

The Unique Check box allows the selection of a unique index, where duplicate entries of the indexed field or expression are ignored by FoxPro.

The lower portion of the dialog box, titled Output File, contains the specifications that define the type of index file you will create. You can choose Compound Index File (.CDX) or Single Index File (.IDX). If you choose Compound Index File, you can turn on or off the Structural Index option. When checked, the index tags named in the Index dialog box are added to the structural compound index file (the one that always has the same name as the table). If you choose Single Index File, you can specify a filename for the .IDX file, by entering the name in the Save As text box, or by clicking the Save As button, and entering or selecting a filename in the Save As dialog box that appears. When creating single index files, you must also decide whether to leave the Compact Index Structure check box turned on. With this option on, single index files created by FoxPro save space, but are not compatible with version 1.x of FoxPro, or with FoxBase+ or FoxBase Mac. When you are done with all the options in the Index dialog box, click OK to create the specified indexes.

Placing Indexes in Use from the Menus

With many indexes in existence at any one time, you must choose which index you want to be active. From the menus, you can do this with the Database, Setup option. Choose Database, Setup, and you will see the Setup dialog box. (See Figure 5.9.)

FIGURE 5.9.

The Setup dialog box.

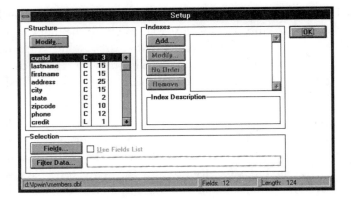

In the Indexes portion of the dialog box, you will see the names of all indexes (you can scroll within the list box if there are too many indexes to be viewed at one time). Click the desired index you want to use to select it, then click the Set Order button to make that index the active index. Finally, click OK to close the dialog box.

An Example: Creating and Using Indexes from the Menus

If you created the BUYERS.DBF table in Chapter 3 (or if you've copied the table from the disk provided with this book into your working directory), you can perform the steps shown here to demonstrate how you can work with indexes using the Index dialog box. Perform the following steps to build an index and see the results:

1. Open the BUYERS.DBF table, if it is not already open (choose File, Open, and double-click BUYERS.DBF in the list box.)

2. Choose File, New. In the New dialog box that appears, click Index, then click New.

3. In the Index dialog box, turn off the Structural Index Structure check box. (For this example, you'll create a new compound index file and put it in use.)

4. Click the Save As button. In the Save As dialog box that appears, enter **BUYER2.CDX** as a filename for the next compound index file, then click OK.

5. Double-click the Zipcode field. When you do so, it will be added to the Index Key list in the dialog box. (See Figure 5.10.)

FIGURE 5.10.

The Index dialog box with Zipcode added as new index key.

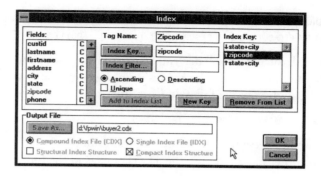

6. Click in the Tag Name text box, and enter **Towns** as a tag name.

7. Click the Index Key button in the dialog box, to bring up the Expression Builder. (You will use the Expression Builder to add another index tag that's based on a combination of two fields, State and City.)

8. In the Fields list box, double-click the State field.

9. In the Functions portion of the Expression Builder, click the arrow beside String to open the String drop-down list box, and click the plus symbol.

10. In the Fields list box, double-click the City field.

11. Click OK to close the Expression Builder dialog box.

12. In the Index dialog box, click the Add to Index List button, to add the second index tag to the Index Key list. At this point, two index tags (one based on ZIP codes and the other based on a combination of states and cities) will exist within the compound index file that will be created.

13. Click the OK button to create the index.

14. Choose Database, Setup from the menus, to open the Setup dialog box.

15. In the Indexes list box, click Buyer2:Zipcode to select it.

16. Click Set Order, then click OK.

17. Choose Database, Browse from the menus, to open a Browse window into the table. If you scroll over in the table, you will see that the records are arranged in order of ZIP codes.

Indexing with Commands

From the command level, the creation of indexes is done with the INDEX command, a command that's familiar to any user of a previous XBase product. In FoxPro, the syntax for the index command is

```
INDEX ON expression TO idx file ¦ TAG tag name [OF cdx file] [FOR logical expression]
[COMPACT] [ASCENDING ¦ DESCENDING] [UNIQUE] [ADDITIVE]
```

and the basic syntax will determine whether the command you enter adds an index tag to a compound index file, or creates a single index file. If you enter a command with the TAG clause, as in the following example:

```
INDEX ON LASTNAME+FIRSTNAME TAG NAMES
```

then an index tag (called "names" in this example) is added to a compound index file. If, on the other hand, you use the TO clause, as in the following example:

```
INDEX ON LASTNAME+FIRSTNAME TO NAMES
```

then a single index file (with a filename of NAMES.IDX in this case) is created by FoxPro.

If you use the TAG clause but you do not specify a .CDX filename, the index tag that's created is automatically added to the structural compound index file. (If no structural compound index file exists, FoxPro creates one.) As an example, the following commands

```
USE BUYERS
INDEX ON ZIPCODE TAG ZIPS
```

would create an index tag called "zips", and that index tag would be added to BUYERS.CDX, which is the structural compound index file for the BUYERS table. On the other hand, the following commands

```
USE BUYERS
INDEX ON ZIPCODE TAG ZIPS OF MAILING
```

would create an index tag called "zips", and that index tag would be added to a compound index file called MAILING.CDX. (If MAILING.CDX did not exist, FoxPro would create it.)

From the command level, you can put indexes into use at the same time that you open tables, by including the index names as a part of the USE command. The complete syntax for the USE command is:

```
USE filename [INDEX index file list ¦ [ORDER [index tag ¦ idx index file ¦ [TAG] tag
name [OF cdx file] [ASCENDING ¦ DESCENDING]]]]
```

Hence, you could name index tags (or single index files) that should be opened and maintained as part of the USE command. For example, the following command

```
USE BUYERS ORDER TAG ZIPCODE
```

would open the table named BUYERS.DBF, and set the index tag to the tag named zipcode in the structural compound index file. (Because no OF *cdx filename* clause was specified, FoxPro assumes that the tag can be found in the structural compound index file.)

An index file, whether it is a compound index or a single index file, can be opened independently of the USE command with the SET INDEX TO command. As an example, to specify an index file named USERS as the active index file, you could enter the command

```
SET INDEX TO USERS
```

and once the index is opened, it is updated automatically as records are added or edited.

When using multiple tags in a compound index file, you can change the tag, which is in active use with the SET ORDER command. As an example, if you create three index tags based on lastname, city, and state with commands like these:

```
USE MAILER
INDEX ON LASTNAME TAG NAMES
INDEX ON CITY TAG CITIES
INDEX ON STATE TAG STATES
```

then STATES would be the active index tag, because it was the tag most recently created. You could change the active index to the City field with the command

```
SET ORDER TO CITIES
```

and the other tags would remain open (and would therefore be updated as changes were made to the table), but the records would appear in the order of the contents of the City field.

TIP

Using the DESCENDING clause along with the SET ORDER TO command will cause the data to be arranged in descending order, regardless of how the tag was ordered when it was created.

Indexing on Different Field Types

One limitation of indexing (which can be annoying at times) is that when you index on multiple fields, the fields must all be of the same data type. If you try to mix data types as part of the same INDEX command, FoxPro complains with an error message. For example, if you enter a command like

```
INDEX ON STATE + CRLIMIT TAG PEOPLE
```

you see a dialog box warning you of a type mismatch in the expression, and FoxPro does not create the index. Because State is a character field and Crlimit is a numeric field, a type mismatch occurs and the index can't be created. All is not lost, however. When you need to index in this manner, you can use FoxPro *functions* to convert the field types so that they are compatible. Use the STR() function to convert the contents of a numeric field to characters, and use the DTOS() function to convert a date field to a string of characters. The overall syntax for the INDEX command, used in this manner, becomes

```
INDEX ON character field + STR(numeric field) + DTOS(date field) TAG index tag name
```

or with individual index files,

```
INDEX ON character field + STR(numeric field) + DTOS(date field) TO .CDX index file name
```

As an example, you can accomplish the task described above (indexing the Buyers table on a combination of the State and Credit limit fields) with a command like this

```
INDEX ON STATE + STR(CRLIMIT) TAG PEOPLE
```

and the results shown here

```
LIST
<...show results...>
```

indicate that the index tag places the data in order of States, and where the States are the same, by credit limits.

Selective Indexing

One lesser-known technique that can prove useful in certain situations is that of *selective indexing*, where you purposely create an index that contains only those records meeting a certain criteria. From the menus, this can be done by clicking the Index Filter button in the Index dialog box that appears when you choose File, New, then Index. From the command level, you can do this by including a FOR clause along with the INDEX command.

For example, if you open the BUYERS.DBF table, then choose File, New, click index in the New dialog box that appears, and then click New, you will notice that the Index dialog box that appears (shown previously in Figure 5.7) contains an Index Filter button, near the center of the dialog box. If you click this button, the Expression Builder appears, this time containing a text box labeled For clause <ExpL>. (See Figure 5.11.)

FIGURE 5.11.

The Expression Builder containing For Clause text box.

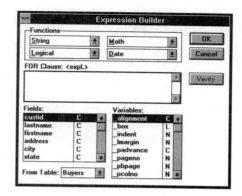

In the text box, you can manually type an expression that limits the records to be included in the index. Or, you can build the expression using the list boxes in the Expression Builder. As an example, building an expression such as

```
STATE = "MD"
```

would limit the index to only those records containing the abbreviation for Maryland in the State field.

From the command level, you would accomplish selective indexing with the INDEX command along with this type of syntax:

```
INDEX ON expression TAG tagname [OF .cdx filename] FOR condition
```

or, if you wanted to create a single index file, you would use the syntax,

```
INDEX ON expression TO .idx filename FOR condition
```

and the *condition* would be any expression that FoxPro can determine to be logically true or false. Using the same example of only those records from Maryland, you could use a command like

```
INDEX ON LASTNAME+FIRSTNAME TAG NAMES FOR STATE = "MD"
```

and the resulting index would cause the records to be arranged in order of the Lastname and Firstname fields, but only the records for the Maryland residents would be included in the index. Hence, whenever the index is made active, the table appears to contain only those records with "MD" in the State field.

Seasoned XBase users who have always done things from a command level might be tempted to accomplish this sort of selective data retrieval by setting an ordinary index, followed by the use of a SET FILTER command, but there is a speed advantage to this kind of selective indexing. Using an INDEX ON...FOR variation of the INDEX command as described here is generally faster than using an INDEX command followed by a SET FILTER command. This is particularly true when retrieving data from large tables.

Using REINDEX

If you open and modify a table without remembering to activate an accompanying index file, the index won't reflect the actual contents of the table. (This potential problem is one good reason to keep all your index tags in the structural compound index file; since it is automatically opened along with the table, you don't have to remember to activate it.) To solve this problem if and when it occurs, activate the desired index, then use the REINDEX command. (Enter REINDEX in the Command Window.) The REINDEX command tells FoxPro to update all currently open indexes.

Sorting

While indexing is the technique commonly used to keep things in order in FoxPro, it is not the only method. A lesser-used technique is *sorting*. With sorting, the records in the table are copied in a specified order to a new table. For example, if you sort a table based on a customer ID field in ascending order, the records are copied to the new table in ascending order of the customer ID numbers. When FoxPro sorts a table, the results are always copied to a new file. It's not possible to sort a table into itself. (This drawback highlights one of the primary disadvantages of sorting; significant disk space can be consumed, as you always create another table as a result of the sorting process.)

Sorting is somewhat of a holdover from the days of dBASE II, which did not support indexing. As sorting has fallen out of favor over the years, the Catalog Manager doesn't provide a way to do it. For novice users, this really isn't a drawback, as you should only consider sorting if it offers clear advantages over indexing.

Sorting from the Menus

You can sort a file from the menus by performing the following steps:

1. Choose Database, Sort. The Sort Order dialog box opens. (See Figure 5.12.)

FIGURE 5.12.

The Sort Order dialog box.

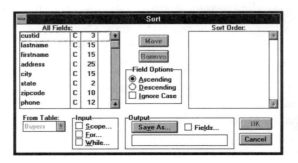

2. In the All Fields list box, double-click the field or fields that you want to base the sort on. As you double-click each field, that field is added to the Sort Order list box, at the right side of the dialog box. The fields you add first get the highest priority in the sorting order.

3. For each field that you add, click Ascending or Descending in the Field Options portion of the dialog box, as desired. If you want FoxPro to ignore the case of letters during the sort, click the Ignore Case check box.

4. In the Output portion of the dialog box, click in the text box below Save As, and enter a name for the new table. (You can also click the Save As button to open a Save As dialog box, which you can use to change drives and/or directories.)

5. When done with the options in the Sort dialog box, click OK to perform the sort.

Once you have completed the sort, you can open the new table just as you would open any table under FoxPro, and use the data as desired.

Sorting from the Command Level

You can perform sorts at the command level by entering a SORT command. The basic form of this command has the following syntax:

```
SORT ON fieldname1[/A/C/D], fieldname2[/A/C/D],...fieldnameX[/A/C/D] [ASCENDING/
DESCENDING] TO new filename
```

As indicated by the syntax, you can sort on one or more fields. The ASCENDING/DESCENDING option is used to indicate whether the sorted file will be arranged in ascending or descending order. (The default value of FoxPro is ascending.) The /A and /D options provide the ability to sort in ascending or descending order on a single field. Character fields, when sorted in alphabetical order, display one trait of XBase that can be annoying—uppercase letters have a higher value than their lowercase counterparts. As a result, records containing character fields are sorted to list fields in order of A through Z, then a through z. You can solve this problem by including the /C option, which tells FoxPro to ignore the case of the letters during the sort.

If more than one field is named within the SORT command, the table is sorted in priority order according to the named fields. If date fields are chosen as a sort field, the sorted table is in chronological order. (You cannot sort on memo or general fields.) As an example, to sort the BUYERS.DBF table alphabetically by city and store the sorted output in a table called CITYFILE.DBF, you could use the following commands:

```
USE BUYERS
SORT ON CITY TO CITYFILE
```

Before the sort the records might look like this:

```
Record#  CUSTID  LASTNAME       FIRSTNAME       CITY            STATE
      1  101     Roberts        Jamie           Reston          VA
      2  102     Sanderson      Lucy            Herndon         VA
      3  103     Smith          Larry           Kensington      MD
      4  104     Jones          Nikki           Washington      DC
      5  105     Hernandez      Maria           Towson          MD
      6  106     Jones          Jarel           McLean          VA
      7  107     Zeibermann     Daniel          Arlington       VA
      8  108     O'Neill        John            Merrifield      VA
      9  109     Bannerton      Alicia          Falls Church    VA
     10  110     Anderson       Harry           Santa Monica    CA
```

After the sort the records would look like this:

```
Record#  CUSTID  LASTNAME       FIRSTNAME       CITY            STATE
      1  107     Zeibermann     Daniel          Arlington       VA
      2  109     Bannerton      Alicia          Falls Church    VA
      3  102     Sanderson      Lucy            Herndon         VA
      4  103     Smith          Larry           Kensington      MD
      5  106     Jones          Jarel           McLean          VA
      6  108     O'Neill        John            Merrifield      VA
      7  101     Roberts        Jamie           Reston          VA
      8  110     Anderson       Harry           Santa Monica    CA
      9  105     Hernandez      Maria           Towson          MD
     10  104     Jones          Nikki           Washington      DC
```

To sort on a combination of the Lastname and Firstname fields, with the Firstname fields arranged in descending order, and the Lastname field having priority over the Firstname field, you could use the following commands:

```
USE BUYERS
SORT ON LASTNAME, FIRSTNAME /D TO CITYFILE
```

and following the sort, the records would appear like this:

```
Record#  CUSTID  LASTNAME       FIRSTNAME       CITY            STATE
      1  110     Anderson       Harry           Santa Monica    CA
      2  109     Bannerton      Alicia          Falls Church    VA
      3  105     Hernandez      Maria           Towson          MD
      4  104     Jones          Nikki           Washington      DC
      5  106     Jones          Jarel           McLean          VA
      6  108     O'Neill        John            Merrifield      VA
      7  101     Roberts        Jamie           Reston          VA
      8  102     Sanderson      Lucy            Herndon         VA
      9  103     Smith          Larry           Kensington      MD
     10  107     Zeibermann     Daniel          Arlington       VA
```

Sorting Selected Records and Fields

By default, when you perform a sort operation, all the records in the source table are rearranged and written to the new destination table. Also, all fields from the source table appear in the destination table. FoxPro provides the flexibility of changing this default behavior of a sort. You can execute a sort which copies only selected records that meet a certain condition to the destination table. You can also execute a sort which copies specific fields from the source table to the destination table.

To produce a sorted file containing selected records, use the FOR clause along with the SORT command. The syntax for the SORT command, used in this manner, is

```
SORT ON fieldname1, fieldname2,... fieldnameX TO newfile FOR condition
```

and the expression you include as *condition* defines which records appear in the new table. As an example, using the Buyers table as the original table, you could produce a table containing only records of buyers residing in Virginia with a command like

```
SORT TO JUSTVA ON LASTNAME, FIRSTNAME FOR STATE = "VA"
```

and if you use the subsequent commands shown below to open the new table and list some of the fields, you see the results:

```
USE JUSTVA
LIST LASTNAME, FIRSTNAME, CITY, STATE
```

Record#	LASTNAME	FIRSTNAME	CITY	STATE
1	Bannerton	Alicia	Falls Church	VA
2	Jones	Jarel	McLean	VA
3	O'Neill	John	Merrifield	VA
4	Roberts	Jamie	Reston	VA
5	Sanderson	Lucy	Herndon	VA
6	Zeibermann	Daniel	Arlington	VA

If you want to include specific fields in the new table, add the FIELDS *fieldlist* clause to the SORT command. Include the keyword FIELDS, followed by a list of the specific fields that you want to see in the new table. For example, you could create a sorted table based on the Buyers table but containing only the Lastname, Firstname, Address, City, State, and Zipcode fields by using a SORT statement like the following,

```
SORT ON ZIPCODE TO MAILER FIELDS LASTNAME, FIRSTNAME, ADDRESS, CITY, STATE, ZIPCODE
```

and like all optional clauses used in a SORT command, you can combine these clauses if desired, to create a sorted table that contains selected records and selected fields from the original table.

If you prefer working from the menus, you can use the check boxes in the Sort dialog box labeled For Clause and Fields, to accomplish the same results. Click the For Clause check box to bring up the Expression Builder, where you can build an expression which defines which records are selected as a part of the sort. Click the Fields box to display a Fields dialog box, which you can then use to limit the available fields that will be included in the results of the sort.

This type of selective sorting can be quite useful when you want a fast way to create data files that can be used with other software. For example, with a personnel file, you might need to copy just the names and salaries from a table to a file that the accounting department will import into a spreadsheet. The selective use of the SORT command is ideal for this task, since most spreadsheets can easily import a file in dBASE file format.

Why Not Sort?

While sorting does the job as far as rearranging the order of a table, it is usually not the best method for doing so. There are three main disadvantages to sorting a table. First, unless a selective sort is done with a FOR or WHILE clause, a new table as large as the original table is created as a consequence of the sort. This not only wastes disk space, it can make sorting large tables impossible on a system with limited disk space. Second, sorting is a slow process compared to the faster alternative of indexing. Finally, if you add records to the sorted table, it must be sorted all over again to keep the records in order. For all of these reasons, indexing is recommended over sorting.

One area where sorting can be useful is on local area networks, when a specific subset of data is needed in a specific order, to produce a report. You may prefer to perform a sort to create a separate table. The new table can then be used for the reporting needs and deleted when the report is completed. This keeps the main table available for the use of others on the network.

Chapter Summary

This chapter detailed indexing and sorting, the methods that you use to keep tables in order. While indexing is by far the most common technique, both methods have their places in different situations. Note too that records can also be placed in a specific order as part of a query that retrieves the specific data you need. The topic of queries and how you can design them are detailed in Chapter 6, "Performing Queries with RQBE."

Performing Queries
with RQBE

In FoxPro, a significant part of your work involves queries. With queries, you ask questions about the data stored in tables, and FoxPro provides an answer in the form of a subset of records that meet the conditions specified by the query. The most common reason for designing queries is to select desired fields and records. This is a particular need with relational databases, as queries in FoxPro offer one easy method of obtaining needed data from multiple tables. (Another method of querying for specific data is to use FoxPro commands; this approach is detailed in Chapter 7, "Queries with Commands.")

In FoxPro, you perform queries through the use of the Relational Query By Example (RQBE) facility. When you create FoxPro queries through the RQBE facility, FoxPro translates the specifications of the query into SQL SELECT commands. SQL, or Structured Query Language, is a data retrieval and manipulation language originally developed by IBM scientists in the 1970s. A major part of the SQL language is the SELECT command, which can be used to obtain a subset of data meeting a specific condition.

As part of the overall query process, FoxPro also utilizes a patented query optimization process called *Rushmore* to perform the query and retrieve the results faster. When you create your queries using the RQBE facility, FoxPro utilizes Rushmore automatically to obtain the fastest results.

Figure 6.1 shows an example of a query's design. Figure 6.2 shows the data produced as a result of the query. You can select specific fields for inclusion in the query, and by means of criteria, include certain records in the result. For example, in a table of book club members, you might want to see just the name, address, and member-since date for all members living in a certain city. You could structure a query to obtain this specific data.

FIGURE 6.1.

A query's design.

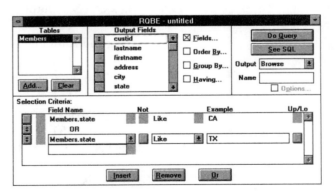

FoxPro queries also provide a vital tool to the developer of serious applications. In other database managers (like dBASE), selected data was routinely provided with a series of commands, often stored within programs. XBase developers are universally familiar with DO..ENDDO loops, where multiple lines of program code perform repetitive operations that process certain records. Since FoxPro is an XBase compatible language, you can use the same approach if comfortable with it, but this is not required. In FoxPro, a single query using query-by-example can replace dozens of lines of programming code in XBase. And the SQL statements that make up the heart of any query in query-by-example can be used within any FoxPro program to obtain specific data.

FIGURE 6.2.

The resulting data from query's design.

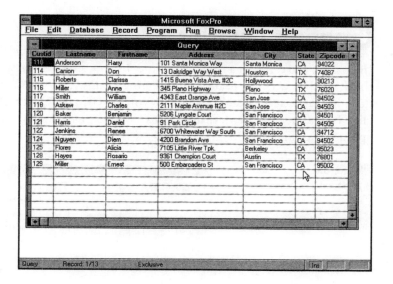

You can do all of the following tasks with the aid of queries:

- Selecting desired fields. By clicking the Fields check box of a query window and adding or removing fields in another dialog box which appears, you specify which fields should be included in the data. In tables with large numbers of fields, you can get just the fields you need for a particular task, and ignore the rest. As an example, in a personnel table, you could look at just the employee names and salary information, without having to deal with addresses, phone numbers, and a host of other unwanted personal data.

- Selecting desired records. By entering conditions in a Criteria row of the query window, you can limit the records made available by the query. As an example, you might be interested in seeing only your customers located in Miami. By entering City = "Miami" in the Selection Criteria area of the query window, you would be telling the query to retrieve only those records where Miami appears in the City field.

- Sort records. You can specify a sorting order within queries, to control whether records appear in ascending or descending order based on the contents of one or more fields. When you sort on multiple fields, you can establish a sorting priority by moving the fields around in the Query Grid. For example, in a query that retrieves selected records from a national mailing list, you might sort by State, and where the States are equal, by City.

■ Perform grouping. You can specify that queries are divided into groups of data, based on the contents of a field or fields.

Creating Queries

In FoxPro, you can start a new query either by choosing File, New and selecting Query in the dialog box which appears, or by entering CREATE QUERY in the Command Window. If you are at the Catalog Manager, you can click the Query tab, then click New, and click New Query in the next dialog box. With either method, a blank RQBE Window appears. (See Figure 6.3.)

FIGURE 6.3.

A blank RQBE window.

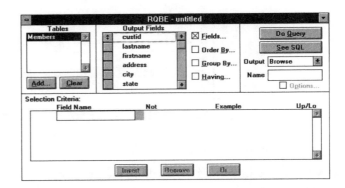

The general steps you follow once the RQBE window has been opened are:

■ Add the table or tables you want to use in the query. In non-relational queries, a single table serves as the source of the records. By default, FoxPro adds any table that is open in the current work area to the RQBE Window.

■ Select any desired join conditions, if you are creating a relational query. Queries can be relational, where two or more tables provide the record source for the query. (See Figure 6.4.) In the figure, the presence of two tables (Customer and Offices) and the matching fields in the selection criteria, "Offices.ono Like Customer.ono" indicate the presence of a relationship.

■ Add the fields that you want to include in the query. You can click the Fields check box, to display the RQBE Select Fields dialog box. Using this dialog box, you can choose the fields you want to appear in your query's results.

Chapter 6

FIGURE 6.4.

A relational query.

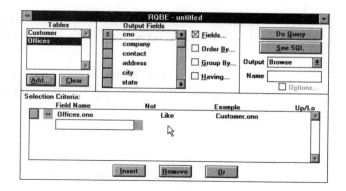

Add any needed criteria to identify which records should appear in the query results. With query-by-example, you enter criteria into the Selection Criteria portion of the RQBE Window. The criteria are then used by FoxPro to select the desired records. For example, entering "State LIKE VA" in a row of the Selection Criteria area would retrieve all records where the letters "VA," an abbreviation for Virginia, appear in the State field of the table. (See Figure 6.5.)

FIGURE 6.5.

Criteria to retrieve records with VA in State field.

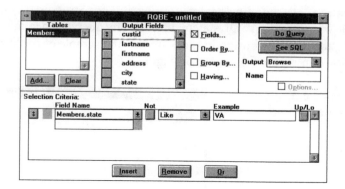

Add any sorting selections desired to arrange the data. FoxPro lets you sort within a query, in ascending or descending order, by clicking the Order By check box of the RQBE Window. Doing so causes the RQBE Order By dialog box to appear, and you can then select one or more fields as the basis for the sort, as well as the direction (ascending or descending). You can sort on a single field or on a combination of fields.

Select the desired destination for the query results. By default, FoxPro sends the results of the query to a Browse window. You can change this default, and instead direct the query results to a report or a stored label format, or to a new table. You can also send the results of a query to a temporary location called a *cursor*, which can be useful for specialized operations when working directly with the SQL language.

■ Run the query. Once the query is completed, you can run it by clicking the Do Query button in the RQBE Window. When the query runs, the results appear in a browse window. Visually, the RQBE window appears identical to the browse window for a table, but its contents are based on the query specifications and not on a table.

Outside of these basic steps, there's much more that can be done with queries in FoxPro. You can perform math operations as part of the queries and provide averages or sum totals of numeric fields. The criteria can range from simple to quite complex. You can structure your criteria to provide a range of data based on AND and OR conditions—and you can save queries for later use.

SQL Behind the Scenes

When you fill in the desired options in the RQBE Window and run a query, FoxPro generates a corresponding statement using SQL, or Structured Query Language. You can see the corresponding SQL statement while any query is open in the active window by clicking the See SQL button in the window. An example of the SQL statement for the query shown in Figure 6.5 appears in Figure 6.6.

FIGURE 6.6.

The Figure 6.5 SQL statement.

```
untitled.qpr [Read Only]
SELECT *;
  FROM Members;
  WHERE Members.state = "VA"
```

If you are familiar with the SQL language, you may prefer to enter the SQL statements generated by queries into the Command Window to obtain the same results. You can also use the SQL statements within your FoxPro programs.

An Example: Creating a Simple Query

This chapter makes extensive use of examples because the best way to learn the complete use of FoxPro queries is to work with them. To provide realistic examples without typing in dozens of records, the chapter uses the example data in the Members table provided on the disk that accompanies this book. Copy the file (MEMBERS.DBF) from the disk into your FoxPro working directory. Then, choose File, Open, and select MEMBERS.DBF in the Open dialog box to open the table.

To create a query that retrieves selected fields (the company name, contact name, and address) from those records where the company is based in California, follow the steps show here:

1. From the menus, choose File, New.

2. In the New dialog box, click Query, then click New. Doing so causes a blank RQBE Window to appear. (See Figure 6.3, shown previously.) Note that because the Members table is open, it appears by name in the Tables list box at the upper left corner of the RQBE Window.

   By default, FoxPro adds all fields of the table to the query. For this simple example this is fine. (The chapter details how you can change this assumption.)

3. Click under Field Name in the Selection Criteria portion of the dialog box, and choose Members.State from the list box which opens. When you do so, the "Like" operator automatically appears in the center of the Selection Criteria portion of the dialog box.

4. Click in the Example box, and type CA (the two letter abbreviation for California). At this point, your query should resemble the example in Figure 6.7.

FIGURE 6.7.

A completed example of a query.

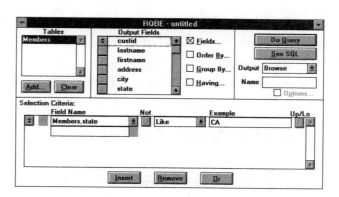

5. Click the Do Query button in the window. The query runs and provides the results, which should resemble those shown in Figure 6.8. (In the figure, the window has been maximized so the State column is visible.)

FIGURE 6.8.
The results of the sample query.

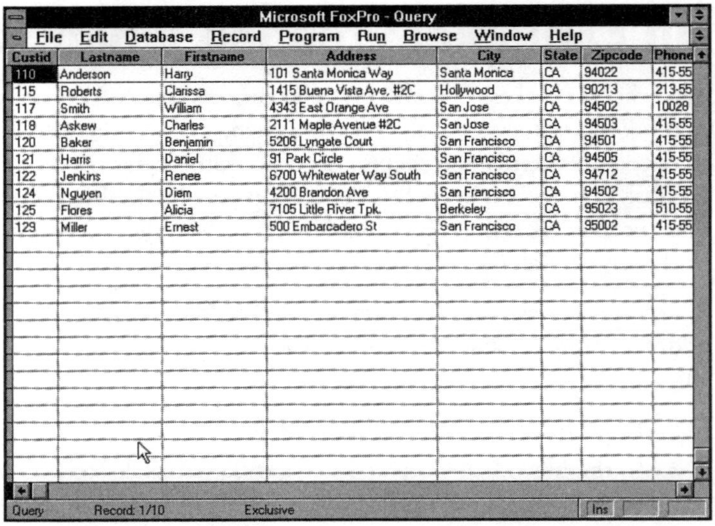
Microsoft FoxPro - Query
File Edit Database Record Program Run Browse Window Help
Custid Lastname Firstname Address City State Zipcode Phone
110 Anderson Harry 101 Santa Monica Way Santa Monica CA 94022 415-55
115 Roberts Clarissa 1415 Buena Vista Ave, #2C Hollywood CA 90213 213-55
117 Smith William 4343 East Orange Ave San Jose CA 94502 10028
118 Askew Charles 2111 Maple Avenue #2C San Jose CA 94503 415-55
120 Baker Benjamin 5206 Lyngate Court San Francisco CA 94501 415-55
121 Harris Daniel 91 Park Circle San Francisco CA 94505 415-55
122 Jenkins Renee 6700 Whitewater Way South San Francisco CA 94712 415-55
124 Nguyen Diem 4200 Brandon Ave San Francisco CA 94502 415-55
125 Flores Alicia 7105 Little River Tpk. Berkeley CA 95023 510-55
129 Miller Ernest 500 Embarcadero St San Francisco CA 95002 415-55
Query
Record: 1/10
Exclusive
Ins

More About the RQBE Window

As mentioned earlier, the first step in performing a query is to open a blank RQBE Window. For reference, the parts of the RQBE Window are shown again. (See Figure 6.7, shown previously.)

Before bringing up the RQBE Window, you must open a table in the current work area. (You can open additional tables later if you are creating a relational query, but you must have at least one table open before you can bring up the RQBE Window.)

When a new RQBE Window initially appears, the name *untitled* appears beside the abbreviation RQBE in the window's title bar. (If you later save the query, the name it is saved under replaces the "untitled" designation.)

You can consider the RQBE Window to have two halves: an upper half, which you use to set the *query specifications*, and a lower half, which you use to define *selection criteria* that determine the records to be selected by the query.

Changing the Query Specifications

The Tables list box, in the upper left corner of the RQBE Window, displays the tables that are available for use by the query. The table that was open in the current work area when you opened the RQBE Window appears by name in the Tables list box. You can

To **Russell**

Date 4/9/96   Time 1:10   A.M. **P.M.**

WHILE YOU WERE OUT

M _Jackie Aherns_

of _MIS_

Phone _546 - 5596_

Area Code	Number	Extension

TELEPHONED	☒	PLEASE CALL	☒
CALLED TO SEE YOU		WILL CALL AGAIN	
WANTS TO SEE YOU		URGENT	
RETURNED YOUR CALL		

Message _Inquired about work._

_65D-1111_

Fran

Operator

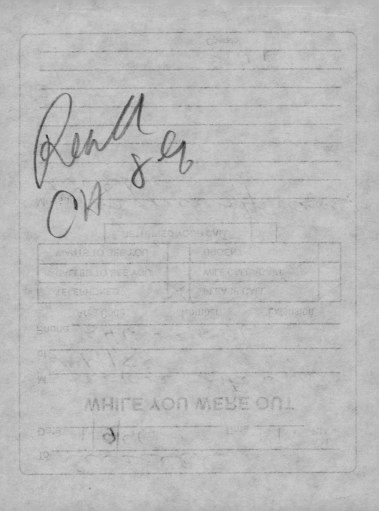

add additional tables to the list box by clicking the Add button below the list and selecting the additional tables desired. This technique is used when building relational queries, a topic covered in Chapter 10, "Working with FoxPro's Relational Powers."

To the right of the Tables list box appears the Output Fields list box. This list box displays all fields which appear in the results of your query. By default, FoxPro assumes you want to see all the fields in your selected table in the results of the query. If this is the case, leave the Fields box checked. You can also choose selected fields for inclusion in the query by clicking the Fields check box. When you do so, the RQBE Select Fields dialog box appears. (See Figure 6.9.)

FIGURE 6.9.

The RQBE Select Fields dialog box.

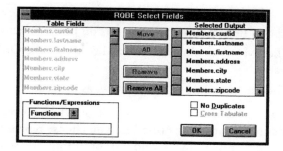

To remove a field from the list, click the unwanted field, then click the Remove button. Repeat this step for any fields you don't want in the query. With tables that have a large number of fields, you may find it faster to click the Remove All button, to remove all the fields from the query. Then, click each desired field followed by the Add button (or double-click the desired field) to add it to the Selected Output portion of the dialog box.

Eliminating Duplicates from the Query Results

When you click the Fields check box to bring up the RQBE Select Fields dialog box, you may also notice the No Duplicates check box within this dialog box. (See Figure 6.9.) Turning on this option tells FoxPro to remove all duplicate rows from the query's results. (Duplicate rows are those records in which all the fields match.)

Determining the Order of the Query Results

Below the Fields check box appears an Order By check box, which you use to specify a sort order for the results of the query. When you click this box, an RQBE Order By dialog box appears. (See Figure 6.10.)

FIGURE 6.10.

The RQBE Order By dialog box.

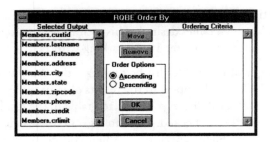

To select the fields that determine the order of the data in the query results, perform these steps:

1. Click a field that you want to sort on in the Selected Output list box to select it.
2. Click Move, to move the selected field into the Ordering Criteria portion of the dialog box.
3. Choose Ascending or Descending, as desired.

If you want to base the sort on more than one field, you can select multiple fields, in order of the desired priority. The first field you choose represents the first level of sorting, the second field represents the second level of sorting, and so on. Once you are done with the options in the dialog box, click OK.

Adding Grouping to the Query Results

FoxPro also provides the option of grouping the results of your query, based on a specific field. (For example, you might want to see the results of a query of customers divided into groups of states.) You can establish grouping by clicking the Group By check box. When you do this, the RQBE Group By dialog box appears. (See Figure 6.11.) You can select the field or fields which control how the results of the query will be grouped. To select a field for grouping, click the field then click the Move button, or just double-click the field. When done selecting desired fields, click OK to close the dialog box.

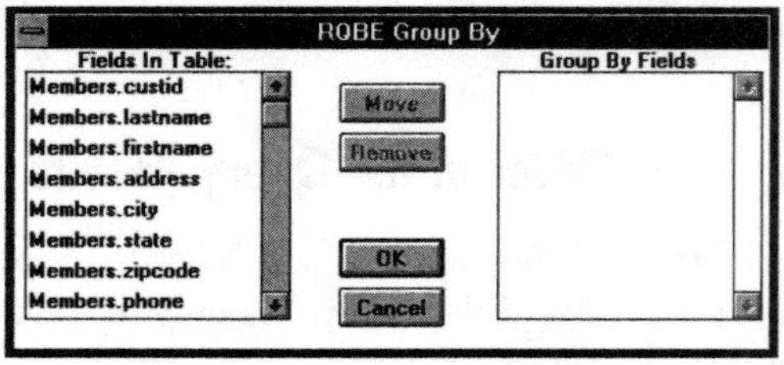

FIGURE 6.11.

The RQBE Group By dialog box.

The upper right portion of the RQBE Window contains buttons that let you run the query (Do Query) or see the equivalent SQL Statement (See SQL). Also in this area is the Output popup, which lets you specify where the results of the query are sent. You can choose Browse, Report/Label, Table/DBF, Cursor, or Graph. Browse (which is the default) directs the output of the query to a Browse window. The Report/Label option sends the output to a stored report or label file of your choice, so that a report or mailing labels based on the query can be generated. The Table/DBF option is used to store the results of the query to a new table, and the Cursor option sends the query results to a temporary database. The database appears in the View window, and can be used for any on-the-spot browsing or reporting needs. (Once you close the temporary database, it is lost. If you want a permanent copy of the results, direct the output to a new table, rather than to a cursor.) Choosing Graph causes the output of the query to be directed to a graph designed with Microsoft Graph.

Directing a Query's Output to a Report

By default, FoxPro sends the output of a query you design into a Browse window. While you often want to see the results of a query in this fashion, many times you may want a printed copy of the data. You have a wide range of options to choose from if you select Report/Label in the Output list box of the RQBE Window, and then check the Options check box. When you do this, the RQBE Display Options dialog box appears. (See Figure 6.12.)

FIGURE 6.12.

The RQBE Display Options dialog box.

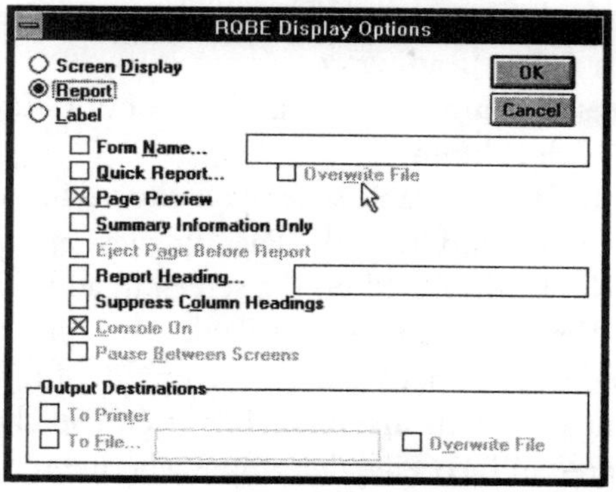

The RQBE Display Options dialog box enables you to format the report and/or label options and establish your desired output destinations. The dialog box contains three radio buttons labeled Screen Display, Report, and Label. Screen Display, which is the default, causes the query's output to be directed to the screen. You can turn on the Report button to have the query's output sent to a stored report form, or you can turn on the Label button to have the query's output sent to a stored label form to generate mailing labels.

The remainder of the options in the dialog box are used to control the various aspects of your chosen output: screen, report, or labels. Some of the options are available with specific choices of output, and not with others. For instance, the Page Preview option is available if you check Report or Label at the top of the dialog box, but not if you check Screen Output. Options which don't apply to a particular style of output are dimmed. The remaining options serve the purposes detailed as follows:

Form Name: Available when you choose Report or Label, this option causes an Open File dialog box to appear. You can then select an existing report or label form file from the list box, or enter an existing name in the text box.

Quick Report: Available when you choose Report, this option displays the RQBE Quick Report dialog box, which you can use to create a quick report. (Quick reports are discussed in detail in Chapter 9, "Creating and Using Simple Reports.")

Overwrite File: Available when you choose Quick Report, this option causes an existing report with the same filename to be overwritten by the new quick report.

Page Preview: Available when Report or Label is selected, this option directs the output to a Page Preview window instead of to the printer.

Summary Information Only: When checked, this option displays summary information instead of the entire report.

Eject Page Before Report: This option sends a page eject before report printing begins.

Report Heading: Available when you choose Report, the text box can be used to enter a heading for the report in the text box. You can also click in the Report Heading check box to display the Expression Builder, which can then be used to create a report heading.

Suppress Column Headings: This option turns off the display of headings at the top of each column.

Console On: Available when you choose Screen Display or when you choose Report Form and leave the Page Preview option unchecked, this option causes output to be displayed on the screen in addition to being sent to the printer.

Pause Between Screens: Available when you choose Screen Display, this option causes output to pause after a screen full of information.

Output Destinations: Available when you choose Screen Display, these options, to Printer and To File, determine whether screen output should also be sent to the printer, or stored in a disk file. Check the desired option, and if you turn on the To File option, add a filename where the output should be stored. As an option, you can click the To File check box to display the Save As dialog box, where you can enter a file name or select an existing file. If the Overwrite File option is checked, FoxPro overwrites the output file if it exists.

Saving and Running Queries

Queries can be saved for reuse at a later time, an important benefit if you perform the same query repeatedly. To save a query, choose File, Save from the menus while the query is open in the active window. If the query is being saved for the first time, FoxPro displays the Save As dialog box, and you can enter a desired filename and click OK to save the query. (If the query has been saved previously, you won't see the Save As dialog box; FoxPro just saves the latest changes to the query.) You can also just close a query by double-clicking the window's Close box, or by pressing Ctrl+F4. If the query has not been saved, FoxPro asks if you want to save the changes to the untitled query. Answer Yes, and the Save As dialog box appears, where you can enter a name for the query.

To run an existing query, choose Run, Query from the menus, select the desired query by name in the Open dialog box which appears, then click Open. The query opens and runs, with the output directed to whatever device was specified in the saved query. You can also run a query from the command level, by entering the command,

```
DO queryname.QPR
```

where *queryname* is the name you saved the query under.

Modifying Existing Queries

To modify a previously saved query, choose File, Open from the menus. In the Open dialog box which appears, choose Query under the List Files of Type list box, to display only the queries in the current directory. Click the desired query in the list box to select it, and click Open. The chosen query opens in the RQBE Window, and you can make the desired changes to the query.

You can also open a query for modifications from the command level, by entering the command,

```
MODIFY QUERY queryname
```

where *queryname* is the name you saved the query under earlier.

Specifying Criteria

To provide the specific data you want in the query, specify the criteria in one or more rows in the Selection Criteria portion of the dialog box. Effective criteria design is a major part of working with queries. For that reason, most of the second half of this chapter deals with entering criteria. The criteria constitute an *expression* which tells FoxPro how to limit the data retrieved. As an example, for a City field, you might use **City like New York** as a criterion, to retrieve all records with New York in the City field. For a Salary field, you might use a criterion of **Ytdsales between 2000 and 5000** to retrieve all records with year-to-date sales amounts between the two values shown. If you were using an On Hand field of an Inventory table, you might use **Onhand Less Than 5** to show all records with an inventory of less than five items.

FoxPro divides the expression into three parts: the *field name*, the *comparison operator*, and the *example*. FoxPro makes entry of the expression easier, by providing pull-down boxes for the field name and comparison operator selections, leaving you with the task of entering the proper examples to achieve your desired results. To enter your selection criteria, first click under Field Name to open the Field Name list box. (See Figure 6.13.)

FIGURE 6.13.

The RQBE Window with Field Name list box open.

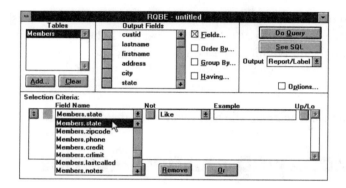

Note that while field names are what you want in nearly all cases, FoxPro doesn't limit you to only field names. You can also use the Field Name list box to build an expression of your own devising, by choosing <expression...> at the bottom of the list box, and using FoxPro's Expression Builder which appears.

Once you choose a field, the default comparison operator, Like, appears in the center of the Selection Criteria area. If you click the arrow beside the Like entry, the list box of comparison operators opens, showing your available choices: Like, Exactly Like, More Than, Less Than, Between, and In. The comparison operators can be used to perform the following types of comparisons between data:

> **Like:** This option (which is the default) specifies that the field must match the example text before the record is included in the query's output. As an example, "MEMBERS.STATE Like N" would match records from North Carolina, North Dakota, and Nebraska.
> **Exactly Like:** Specifies that the field must exactly match the example text, character for character, before the record is included in the query's output.

More Than: Specifies that the field must be greater than the value in the example text before the record is included in the query's output.

Less Than: Specifies that the field must be less than the value in the example text before the record is included in the query's output.

Between: Specifies that the field must be greater than or equal to the lower value and less than or equal to the higher value provided in the example before the record is included in the query's output. As an example, "MEMBERS.DATECALLED Between 06/01/93,06/30/93" would match records for the month of June, 1993).

In: Specifies that the field must match one of several comma-delineated examples in the example text before the record is included in the query's output.

The Up/Lo check box, at the right edge of the Selection Criteria area, can be checked to tell FoxPro to ignore capitalization of character data when the query runs.

The real power of select queries lies in effectively formulating the different criteria that obtain the needed data. FoxPro doesn't limit you to the simple kind of criteria entered in the sample query shown earlier in the chapter. You can use the operators described previously to build complex expressions. These operators, and how they can be used in criteria, are detailed in the examples throughout the rest of this chapter.

Using Text-Based Criteria

Literal text is a common entry in the Selection Criteria area of the RQBE Window. With Literal text, you use text entries to find a given name, such as that of a particular department, city, or country. As an example, you might want to specifically see the records of all members living in the city of San Francisco. Perform the following steps to do so:

1. Choose File, New. Click Query in the dialog box which appears, then click New.

2. Under Selection Criteria, click in the Field Name list box, and choose Members.City.

3. Leave Like selected as the desired comparison operator.

4. Click in the Example text box, and type **San Francisco** in the box.

5. Click the Do Query button in the dialog box. The result, shown in Figure 6.14, shows all records that contain the desired text in the city field. When done examining the data, press Ctrl+F4 to close the Browse window. Press Ctrl+F4 again to close the query dialog box, and answer "No" to the "Save Changes" prompt.

FIGURE 6.14.

The results of a simple query using text.

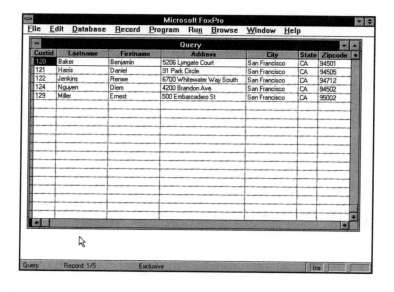

Using Numeric Criteria

You can make use of the More than, Less than, and Between operators, as well as the Like operator, to obtain the desired matching data. These are commonly used with numeric values, although they can be used with text as well. You can try an example of numeric data to find all members with credit limits greater than $700, for example, by performing the following steps:

1. Choose File, New. Click Query in the dialog box which appears, then click New.
2. Under Selection Criteria, click in the Field Name list box, and choose Members.Crlimit.
3. Choose More Than as the desired comparison operator.
4. Click in the Example text box, and type **700** in the box.
5. Click the Do Query button in the dialog box. The result, shown in Figure 6.15, shows all records that contain members with a credit limit greater than $700. When done examining the data, press Ctrl+F4 to close the Browse window. Press Ctrl+F4 again to close the query dialog box, and answer "No" to the "Save Changes" prompt.

When working with numeric values, keep in mind that the Like and Exactly Like operators have the same mathematic effect as an equal symbol. Therefore, if you were constructing a query and you wanted to find all members with a credit limit of precisely $800, you could structure the selection criteria as **Members.crlimit Like 800** or **Members.crlimit Exactly Like 800** to obtain the desired data.

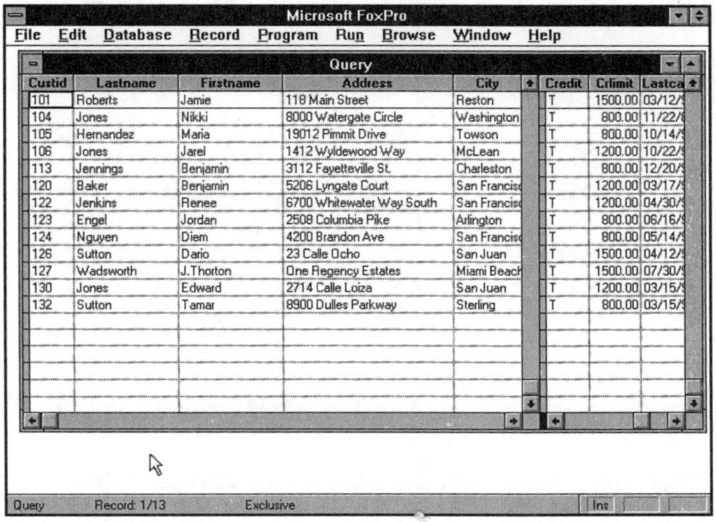

FIGURE 6.15.

The results of query using a numeric value.

Using Date-Based Criteria

Besides working with text values, you can select records based on a date value, or on a range of dates. The More than, Less than, and Between operators can be used to perform date-based logic. You could, for example, select all records with a hire date later than June 1, 1992 by entering **more than 6/1/92** as the criteria. As an example of date logic, you might want to find all members who were contacted in 1993. Perform the following steps to do so:

1. Choose File, New, and click Query in the dialog box which appears, then click New.
2. Under Selection Criteria, click in the Field Name list box, and choose Members.Lastcalled.
3. Choose Between as the desired comparison operator.
4. Click in the Example text box, and type **1/1/93,12/31/93** in the box.
5. Click the Do Query button in the dialog box. The result, shown in Figure 6.16, shows all records that contain a date within 1993 in the Lastcalled field. When done examining the data, press Ctrl+F4 to close the Browse window. Press Ctrl+F4 again to close the query dialog box, and answer "No" to the "Save Changes" prompt.

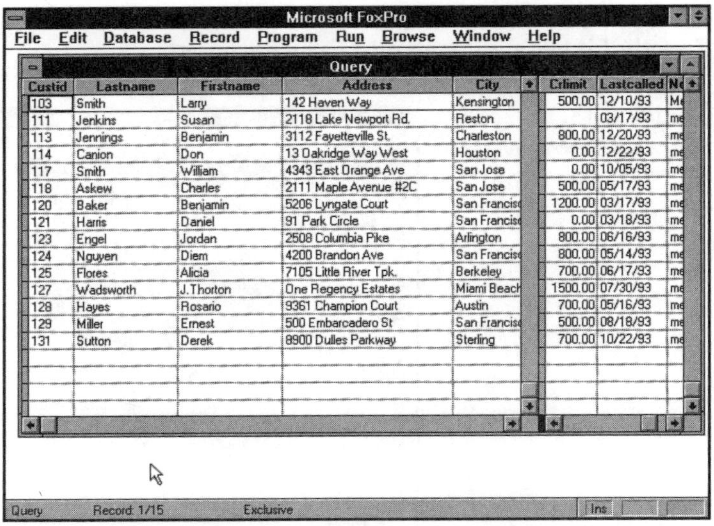

FIGURE 6.16.

The results of range-based query using a date.

Searching for Dates Based on the Current Date

You can include the Date() function to structure queries that retrieve data based on the current date, according to the PC's clock. As an example, after selecting a date field and choosing Between as a comparison operator, in the Example text box you could enter an expression like the following

```
1/1/93, date()
```

and this would translate to any dates between January 1, 1993 and the current date according to the PC's clock. An expression like

```
date()-30, date()
```

would translate to all dates within the last 30 days.

Searching for Logical Values

When constructing queries to retrieve values based on a logical (true/false) field, note that you must use .T. to indicate true, and .F. to indicate false (the letters must be surrounded with periods). As an example, since the Credit field in the Members table is a logical field, a query with a selection criterion of **Members.credit Like .T.** would retrieve all the records with a value of "true" in the Credit field.

Including Wildcard Characters

When entering expressions, you may find the use of *wildcard* characters to be helpful. You can use valid wildcards to find groups of records where the entries match a specific pattern. Note that the wildcard character in FoxPro's query-by-example is *not* the usual asterisk and/or question mark combination that's common to DOS commands; instead, FoxPro uses the percent symbol (%) to indicate any sequence of zero or more characters. As an example, you might use the selection criterion

```
Members.lastname Like J%n
```

to find names like Johnson, Jarlan, and James-Harrison. If you wanted to locate part of a string within a string of text, you would use a pattern with the search text surrounded by percent symbols. For example, **%der%** would find any records with the letters "der" located within the search text.

You can try an example of a wildcard in a query, to find certain records in the Members table with a Lastname that begin with the letter "J" and end with "s" by performing these steps:

1. Choose File, New, and click Query in the dialog box which appears, then click New.

2. Under Selection Criteria, click in the Field Name list box, and choose Members.Lastname.

3. Choose Like as the desired comparison operator.

4. Click in the Example text box, and type **J%s** in the box.

5. Click the Do Query button in the dialog box. The result (see Figure 6.17) shows all records that contain lastnames beginning with "J" and ending with "s." When done examining the data, press Ctrl+F4 to close the Browse window. Press Ctrl+F4 again to close the query dialog box, and answer "No" to the "Save Changes" prompt.

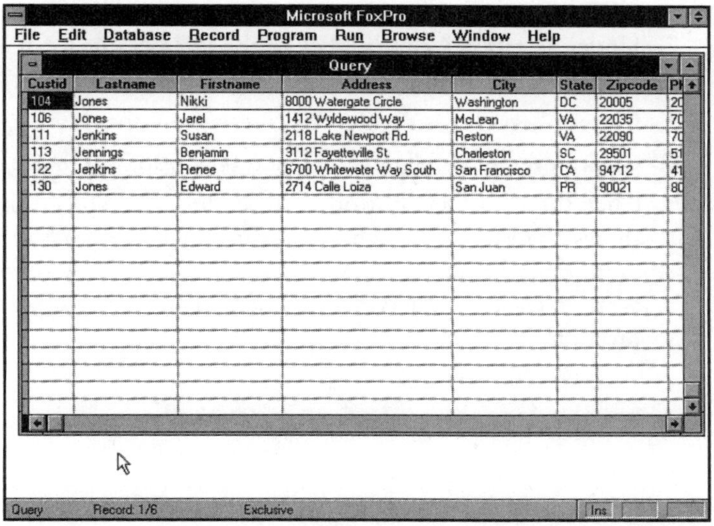

FIGURE 6.17.

The results of query using like operator and wildcard.

Using a Range of Values

One of the most common uses of queries is to select records that fall inside a certain range of values. As an example, you might want to see all sales that occurred between January 1 and June 31 of a particular year, or all products that sell for between $20 and $50. With ranges, you use the **between** comparison operator to structure your expressions. Examples of valid criteria for selecting ranges of data appear in Table 6.1.

Table 6.1. Valid criteria for selecting ranges of data.

Selection Criteria	Meaning
Crlimit Between 500, 1000	All values between 500 and 1000, inclusive from a field called CRLIMIT
Lastcalled Between 1/1/94, 6/30/94	All dates from January 1 through June 30 of 1994 in a field called LASTCALLED
Age Less Than 21	All values under 21 in a field called AGE
Quantity More Than 200	All values greater than 200 in a field called QUANTITY
More Than "M"	All text values starting with "M" through the end of the alphabet

For example, to see all members with credit limits between $500 and $700, perform the following steps:

1. Choose File, New, and click Query in the dialog box which appears, then click New.
2. Under Selection Criteria, click in the Field Name list box, and choose Members.Crlimit.
3. Choose Between as the desired comparison operator.
4. Click in the Example text box, and type **500,700** in the box.
5. Click the Do Query button in the dialog box. The result, shown in Figure 6.18, shows all records that contain credit limits between $500 and $700. When done examining the data, press Ctrl+F4 to close the Browse window. Press Ctrl+F4 again to close the query dialog box, and answer "No" to the "Save Changes" prompt.

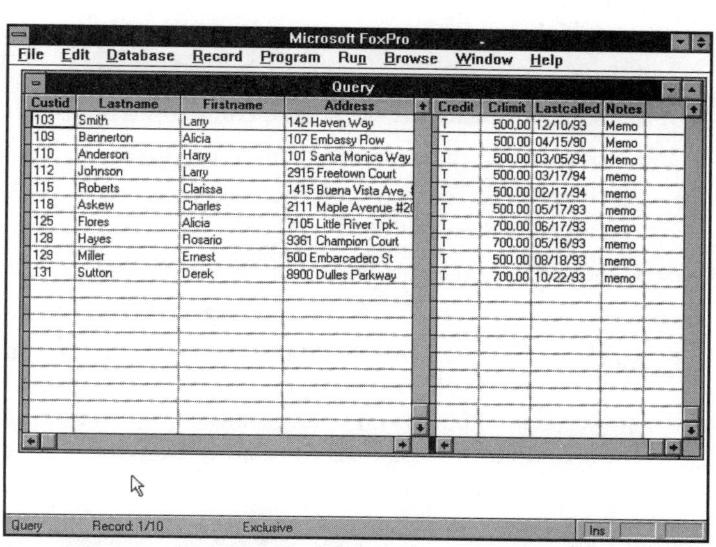

FIGURE 6.18.

The results of range-based query using numeric amounts.

Using the In Operator

Until now, the practice queries have demonstrated the use of the Like and Between comparison operators. Another operator that FoxPro provides is the In operator, which can be used to find records that contain a group of individual values. As an example, to find those members whose lastnames are Jenkins, Baker, and Sutton, you could specify a selection criterion such as

```
Members.Lastname In Jenkins,Baker,Sutton
```

to accomplish this task.

Using AND-Based Criteria

Anytime you need to retrieve selected data based on more than one condition, and each of the conditions must be true, you have a query that is using AND-based logic. For example, you might want to see all members who have credit limits over $700, *and* were contacted in 1993. Because one named criterion *and* another named criterion must be true for the record to be selected, this type of criterion is known as AND-based logic. You create such expressions by filling in as many rows in the Selection Criteria portion of the dialog box as are needed to accomplish the selection. To see how this works, you can duplicate the example described previously (all members who have credit limits over $700, and were contacted in 1993) by performing these steps:

1. Choose File, New, and click Query in the dialog box which appears, then click New.

2. Under Selection Criteria, click in the Field Name list box, and choose Members.Crlimit.

3. Choose More Than as the desired comparison operator.

4. Click in the Example text box, and type **700** in the box.

5. Click in the second row of the Selection Criteria area under Field Name, and choose Members.Lastcalled.

6. Choose Between as the desired comparison operator.

7. Click in the Example text box, and type **1/1/93,12/31/93** in the box.

8. Click the Do Query button in the dialog box. The result, shown in Figure 6.19, shows all records for members last contacted in 1993, whose credit limits are greater than $700. When done examining the data, press Ctrl+F4 to close the Browse window. Press Ctrl+F4 again to close the query dialog box, and answer "No" to the "Save Changes" prompt.

FIGURE 6.19.

The results of query using AND logic.

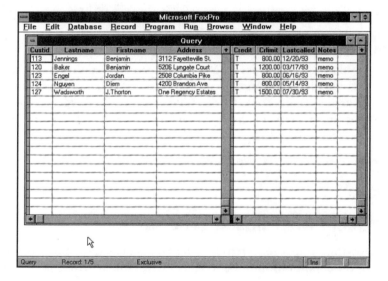

Using OR-Based Criteria

When you need to retrieve selected data based on any of a number of conditions, and only one of the conditions must be true, then you have a query that is using OR-based logic. As an example, you might want to see all members who reside in California *or* Texas *or* Maryland. Because any one of the three named criterion can be true for the record to be selected, this type of criterion is known as OR-based logic. One way to create OR-based logic in a query is to fill in the different criteria, one underneath the other. You click the Or button after each row of selection criteria, and you can continue to fill in as many rows with criteria as are necessary. To see how this works, you can duplicate the example described previously (all customers who are based in California or Texas or Maryland) by performing these steps:

1. Choose File, New, and click Query in the dialog box which appears, then click New.
2. Under Selection Criteria, click in the Field Name list box, and choose Members.State.
3. Leave Like selected as the desired comparison operator.
4. Click in the Example text box, and type **CA** in the box.
5. Click the Or button in the dialog box.
6. Click in the next row of the Selection Criteria area under Field Name, and again choose Members.State.
7. Leave Like selected as the desired comparison operator.
8. Click in the Example text box, and type **TX** in the box.
9. Click the Or button in the dialog box.
10. Click in the third row of the Selection Criteria area under Field Name, and again choose Members.State.
11. Leave Like selected as the desired comparison operator.
12. Click in the Example text box, and type **MD** in the box.
13. Click the Do Query button in the dialog box. The result, shown in Figure 6.20, shows all records for members living in any one of the three states named. When done examining the data, press Ctrl+F4 to close the Browse window. Press Ctrl+F4 again to close the query dialog box, and answer "No" to the "Save Changes" prompt.

FIGURE 6.20.

The results of query using OR logic.

Custid	Lastname	Firstname	Address	City	State	Zipcode	PI
103	Smith	Larry	142 Haven Way	Kensington	MD	31025	30
105	Hernandez	Maria	19012 Pimmit Drive	Towson	MD	30309	30
110	Anderson	Harry	101 Santa Monica Way	Santa Monica	CA	94022	41
114	Canion	Don	13 Oakridge Way West	Houston	TX	74087	71
115	Roberts	Clarissa	1415 Buena Vista Ave. #2C	Hollywood	CA	90213	21
116	Miller	Anna	345 Plano Highway	Plano	TX	76020	21
117	Smith	William	4343 East Orange Ave	San Jose	CA	94502	10
118	Askew	Charles	2111 Maple Avenue #2C	San Jose	CA	94503	41
120	Baker	Benjamin	5206 Lyngate Court	San Francisco	CA	94501	41
121	Harris	Daniel	91 Park Circle	San Francisco	CA	94505	41
122	Jenkins	Renee	6700 Whitewater Way South	San Francisco	CA	94712	41
124	Nguyen	Diem	4200 Brandon Ave	San Francisco	CA	94502	41
125	Flores	Alicia	7105 Little River Tpk.	Berkeley	CA	95023	51
128	Hayes	Rosario	9361 Champion Court	Austin	TX	76801	71
129	Miller	Ernest	500 Embarcadero St	San Francisco	CA	95002	41

Complex Queries

You can combine AND and OR conditions as necessary to obtain any subset of data you need. Suppose, for example, you needed to see all customers residing in either California or in Texas, who were last contacted in 1993. This combination of AND and OR logic can be duplicated with the following steps:

1. Choose File, New, and click Query in the dialog box which appears, then click New.

2. Under Selection Criteria, click in the Field Name list box, and choose Members.State.

3. Leave Like selected as the desired comparison operator.

4. Click in the Example text box, and type **CA** in the box.

5. Click in the second row of the Selection Criteria area under Field Name, and choose Members.Lastcalled.

6. Choose Between as the desired comparison operator.

7. Click in the Example text box, and type **1/1/93,12/31/93** in the box.

8. Click the Or button in the dialog box.

9. In the next row under Selection Criteria, click in the Field Name list box, and again choose Members.State.

10. Leave Like selected as the desired comparison operator.

11. Click in the Example text box, and this time type **TX** in the box.

12. Click in the next row of the Selection Criteria area under Field Name, and again choose Members.Lastcalled.

13. Choose Between as the desired comparison operator.

14. Click in the Example text box, and type **1/1/93,12/31/93** in the box.

15. Click the Do Query button in the dialog box. The result, shown in Figure 6.21, shows all records for members living in any one of the two states named, who were last contacted in 1993. When done examining the data, press Ctrl+F4 to close the Browse window. Press Ctrl+F4 again to close the query dialog box, and answer "No" to the "Save Changes" prompt.

Searching for Records That Don't Match a Value

You can use the NOT check box in the RQBE Window to select records that do not meet a specified condition. For example, you could enter an expression like **Members.State Like CA** in the Selection Criteria portion of a query, then check the Not button, to retrieve records with any entry in the State field but the abbreviation "CA."

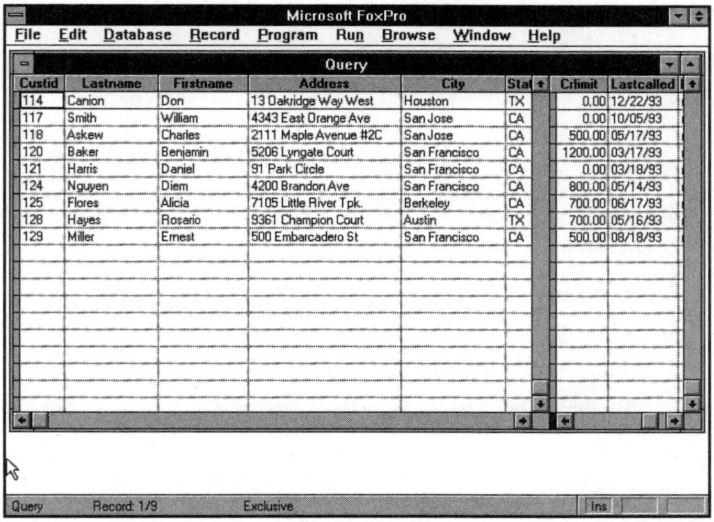
Microsoft FoxPro
File Edit Database Record Program Run Browse Window Help
Query
Custid Lastname Firstname Address City Stat Crlimit Lastcalled
114 Canion Don 13 Oakridge Way West Houston TX 0.00 12/22/93
117 Smith William 4343 East Orange Ave San Jose CA 0.00 10/05/93
118 Askew Charles 2111 Maple Avenue #2C San Jose CA 500.00 05/17/93
120 Baker Benjamin 5206 Lyngate Court San Francisco CA 1200.00 03/17/93
121 Harris Daniel 91 Park Circle San Francisco CA 0.00 03/18/93
124 Nguyen Diem 4200 Brandon Ave San Francisco CA 800.00 05/14/93
125 Flores Alicia 7105 Little River Tpk. Berkeley CA 700.00 06/17/93
128 Hayes Rosario 9361 Champion Court Austin TX 700.00 05/16/93
129 Miller Ernest 500 Embarcadero St San Francisco CA 500.00 08/18/93
Query Record: 1/9 Exclusive Ins

FIGURE 6.21.
The results of query using a combination of AND and OR logic.

Using Calculations in Queries

FoxPro lets you add calculated fields to a query, in addition to those fields which are part of a table's design. Calculated fields are used to display the results of calculations. These calculations are usually based on numeric fields in the tables. Calculated fields don't exist in any permanent location in the underlying tables. They exist only in the query where they are created.

You create a calculated field within a query by entering the expression which performs the calculation as an extra Output Field. You enter the desired expression that provides the calculation by clicking the Fields check box in the RQBE Window, and adding the expression in the Functions/Expressions portion of the RQBE Select Fields dialog box which appears.

As an example, if a query contained fields for Saleprice and Quantity, you could create a calculated field containing the total cost by entering an expression like this one as an extra Output Field:

```
Saleprice*Quantity
```

And when the query runs, FoxPro would multiply each of the values in the Saleprice field by the corresponding values in the Quantity field to produce the new value, which would be displayed in a calculated field within the query's results.

As an example, you can use the following steps to add a calculated field to a query that shows the value in the Crlimit field of the Members table, multiplied by 2. Perform these steps:

1. Choose File, New, and click Query in the dialog box which appears, then click New.

2. Under Selection Criteria, click in the Field Name list box, and choose Members.State.

3. Leave Like selected as the desired comparison operator.

4. Click in the Example text box, and type **CA** in the box.

5. Click the Fields check box. When you do so, the RQBE Select Fields dialog box appears. (See Figure 6.22.)

FIGURE 6.22.

The RQBE Select Fields dialog box.

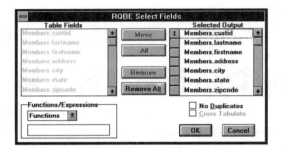

6. In the Functions/Expression portion of the dialog box (at the lower left corner), click inside the text box, and type the following expression:

Members.crlimit * 2

7. Click OK. You see a dialog box containing the message

```
Include Members.crlimit * 2 ?
```

8. Click OK in this dialog box to add the expression that results in the calculated field into the Selected Output portion of the RQBE Window.

9. Click the Do Query button in the dialog box. The result, shown in Figure 6.23, shows the calculated field added as the last field in the Browse window. When done examining the data, press Ctrl+F4 to close the Browse window. Press Ctrl+F4 again to close the query dialog box, and answer "No" to the "Save Changes" prompt.

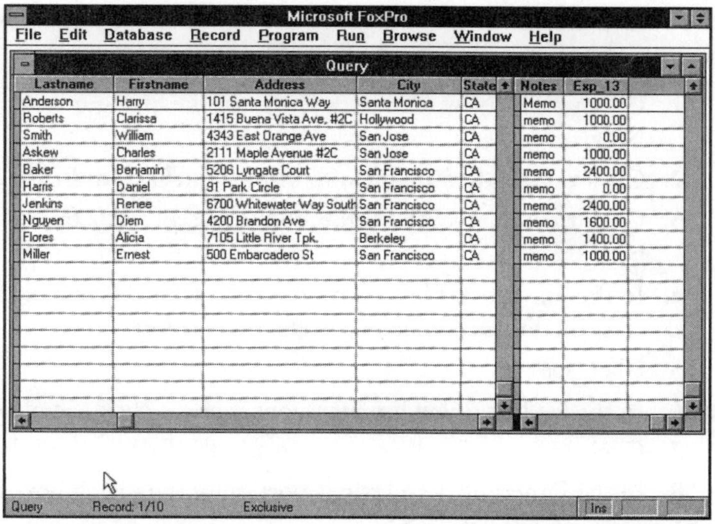
Microsoft FoxPro
File Edit Database Record Program Run Browse Window Help
Query
Lastname Firstname Address City State Notes Exp_13
Anderson Harry 101 Santa Monica Way Santa Monica CA Memo 1000.00
Roberts Clarissa 1415 Buena Vista Ave. #2C Hollywood CA memo 1000.00
Smith William 4343 East Orange Ave San Jose CA memo 0.00
Askew Charles 2111 Maple Avenue #2C San Jose CA memo 1000.00
Baker Benjamin 5206 Lyngate Court San Francisco CA memo 2400.00
Harris Daniel 91 Park Circle San Francisco CA memo 0.00
Jenkins Renee 6700 Whitewater Way South San Francisco CA memo 2400.00
Nguyen Diem 4200 Brandon Ave San Francisco CA memo 1600.00
Flores Alicia 7105 Little River Tpk. Berkeley CA memo 1400.00
Miller Ernest 500 Embarcadero St San Francisco CA memo 1000.00
Query Record: 1/10 Exclusive Ins

FIGURE 6.23.
The results of query using calculated field.

Creating Summary Queries

FoxPro offers the capability of building *summary queries*, which can summarize data in your tables. As an example, you might have a table of employee salaries, and you might want to know the average, minimum, and maximum salaries for a specific group of employees. These kinds of calculations can be performed by using column functions, such as `SUM()`, `AVG()`, `MIN()`, and `MAX()`, and by including these functions as expressions within the RQBE Window. Table 6.2 shows the available functions, and their meanings.

Table 6.2. Available column functions.

Table Function	*Meaning*
COUNT()	Counts the occurrences of values in a column
SUM()	Sums (totals) the values in a column
AVG()	Calculates the average of the values in a column
MIN()	Determines the minimum value in a column
MAX()	Determines the maximum value in a column

You can perform the following example to see how the column functions can be used to construct summary queries. Perform these steps:

1. Choose File, New, and click Query in the dialog box which appears, then click New.

2. Click the Fields check box, to display the Output Fields dialog box.

3. Click the Remove All button, to remove all fields from the Selected Fields list box.

4. In the Functions/Expressions portion of the dialog box (in the lower left corner), click the Functions arrow to open the list box.

5. Click SUM( ).

6. In the list box of fields which now appears, click Members.Crlimit to select it.

7. Click Move in the dialog box, to add the field to the Selected Output list box.

8. In the Functions/Expressions portion of the dialog box, again click the Functions arrow to open the list box.

9. Click AVG( ).

10. In the list box of fields which appears, click Members.Crlimit to select it.

11. Click Move in the dialog box, to add the field to the Selected Output list box.

12. In the Functions/Expressions portion of the dialog box, again click the Functions arrow to open the list box.

13. Click MAX( ).

14. In the list box of fields which appears, click Members.Crlimit to select it.

15. Click Move in the dialog box, to add the field to the Selected Output list box.

16. Click OK, to close the Output Fields dialog box.

17. Click Do Query, to run the query. The results, shown in Figure 6.24, show the sum, average, and maximum credit limits for the Members table. If you wanted to obtain these figures for a specific subset of records, you could do so by including appropriate selection criteria within the query. When done examining the data, press Ctrl+F4 to close the Browse window. Press Ctrl+F4 again to close the query dialog box, and answer "No" to the "Save Changes" prompt.

FIGURE 6.24.

The results of summary query.

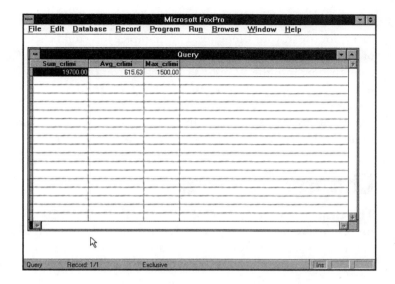

Using A Query's SQL Elsewhere

One important point to remember when working with queries is that underneath the flash and glitz of the RQBE Window lies an SQL statement that tells FoxPro how to retrieve the desired data. A knowledge of the SQL statements used by FoxPro can be quite useful, because you can enter the statements directly as commands (which can be a time saver if you are familiar with the syntax of SQL). More importantly, you can use the SQL statements within FoxPro programs that you write. (Programming in FoxPro is covered beginning with Chapter 19, "FoxPro Programming Basics.") With the RQBE Window for any query open on the screen, click the See SQL button, and a window containing the resulting query statement opens. Figure 6.25 shows an example of the query statement used to generate the query shown earlier, in Figure 6.24.

FIGURE 6.25.

A query's SQL statement.

You can use standard Windows cut-and-paste techniques to copy the text of the SQL statement, for use in your programs. For example, you could click and drag to select the text of the entire SQL statement in the window, and choose Edit/Copy from the menus to copy the text into the Windows Clipboard. You could then switch to editing a program in the FoxPro Editor (or in another Windows editor), and choose Edit/Paste from the menus to paste the SQL statement into the editor as a part of your program. Also keep in mind that any SQL statement can be typed directly into the Command Window, and the results will be identical to opening and running the query.

Chapter Summary

This chapter provided a detailed examination of what is arguably the most powerful feature of FoxPro, its query-by-example capability. The ultimate goal of most database management systems is to obtain the specific data that you need, and query-by-example is a fast, powerful, and easy way to accomplish this goal in FoxPro. Chapter 10 provides additional details on how you can use query-by-example in a relational fashion, to link tables and obtain needed relational data.

Queries with Commands

The ability to find information quickly in a database is invaluable when making decisions. For example, you may want to find all the customers with a certain balance on their account in order to send notices to them. In FoxPro, one of the ways that you can accomplish this is through the use of a query, performed with FoxPro commands. A query finds information in a database that fits the criteria set out in the expression used with one of the commands such as Locate, Seek, Find or Set Filter.

The Makeup of an Expression

A logical expression (an expression that evaluates as either true or false) must be included in a query that you compose using FoxPro commands. In Chapter 5, "Arranging Data," logical expressions were used to build indexes and perform sorts.

Expressions can contain one or more *functions* and *operators*. The logical functions are usually used in programming, but can also be found in everyday FoxPro use. One example of this is the EOF() function, which stands for end of file. When the pointer is located on the last record, and Skip is entered then EOF() becomes true. EOF() also becomes true if a query is executed and FoxPro does not find what you were looking for. The EOF() function is discussed in more detail in the programming section of this book.

Operators indicate the performance of the operator. For example, in the command

```
State = "TX" .OR. State = "CA"
```

the = operator signifies equivalency. The are four types of operators: relational, logical, arithmetical, and string operators.

Relational Operators

Relational operators are used to compare numbers, strings, or dates. For example, expressions such as Purchases = 12, Firstname = "Aaron," or Since = {11/12/93}. There are many different relational operators that can be used in FoxPro; the following is a list of the different relational operators in FoxPro and their meanings.

=	Equal to
<> or #	Not Equal to
<	Left operand is less than right operand
<=	Left operand is less than or equal to
>	Left operand is larger than the right operand
>=	Left operand is larger than or equal to right operand
$	Comparison of substring
==	Identical character string comparison

The double-equal symbol forces an identical comparison, which at times is what you need for a specific purpose. As an example, using the command

```
Lastname = "Will"
```

would return all the lastnames with those characters

Record#	Lastname
1	Will
7	Williamson
9	Willston

On the other hand, if you use the == operator, FoxPro only matches those exact characters and the result is exactly what you entered (in this case, "Will").

Logical Operators

Logical operators are used to create complex expressions involving true or false conditions. Sometimes it's necessary to find records that have two or more conditions. In those cases, the following logical operators can be used:

( )	Used to group expressions
.NOT. or !	The following expression must be untrue in order for the entire expression to be evaluated true
.AND.	Must meet the conditions before and after
.OR.	May meet either one of the conditions

Arithmetical Operators

Arithmetical operators are use for the construction of numerical expressions such as these:

Weight = 3 * 75
Weekly = (30 * 160) /4
Total = ((50+90)/3) * 5

The following is a list of the arithmetical operators with their meanings.

( )	Used for grouping
** or ^	Exponential
*	Multiplication
/	Division
%	Modulus (remainder)
+	Addition
-	Subtraction

Functions

FoxPro's built-in functions perform many common operations. Converting data and performing math operations are two common uses. In Chapter 5, functions were used to convert numbers in a numeric field to character strings. Functions can also be used to return system information. As an example of a function, you can enter the following in the command window:

```
? Time ()
```

This causes the current system time to appear.

String Operators

Both of the two string operators in FoxPro are used for string concatenations. the plus operator joins two strings. For example, using the plus symbol, as in the example here,

```
"Alberta " + "Sutton"
```

appears as

```
Alberta Sutton
```

The (-) sign is used to concatenate the strings. Replacing the plus sign with a minus sign in the previous example causes it to appear as AlbertaSutton.

Performing Queries with FoxPro Commands and Menu Options

Querying a database is usually done in order to find one record or to isolate a subgroup. To retrieve one record, the Locate and Seek commands from the record menu can be used. If you created the example Buyers table earlier (or copied it from the accompanying disk), enter USE BUYERS in the command window to activate the Buyers file. You will practice the Seek and Locate commands in the next two sections of this chapter using this table.

Locate from the Menus

After choosing Locate from the Record menu, the dialog box appears. (See Figure 7.1.) In the dialog box there are three options, Scope, For, and While. Scope reveals a dialog box with the options All, Next Record, and Rest. This options enables you to specify the limit on the search. All, which is the default, specifies that the search should include all of the records. The Next command with a number, is used to specify a group of records. For example, entering 5 limits the search to the next five records. Choosing Record and entering a record number moves the record pointer directly to the specified record. Rest is the last choice in this dialog box. This option is used to include all records from the pointer to the end of the file in the search.

FIGURE 7.1.

The Locate dialog box.

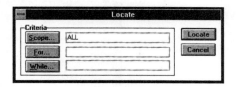

When you choose For or While from the previous dialog box, the expression builder appears. On the lower left side, the Field Names box is found. From this box field names can be selected to build the search expression. Once the field is selected, it appears in the Locate Record While/For Box (depending on which you selected, For or While.) The field names can also be typed in the Locate Record While window.

Clicking on the logical box allows for the selection of an operator from the menu. It may be faster to type the symbols into the clause. Note that both logical functions and operators are listed on the menu; these are grouped by data type.

In the For/While clause box, search value and text expression, should be surrounded by quotes. Numbers are entered as in a numeric field, and dates using curly braces.

If you are working with dates, you can surround them with curly braces ({}), or the CTOD() function can be used. Memo fields may also be included in the search condition.

To see if the syntax is correct in your expression, click the Verify button. If the expression is correct, then "Expression Valid" is briefly displayed at the bottom of the window. Clicking OK finishes your entry, and the Locate Box is again displayed. The search is begun by clicking the Locate button. The record is then found, but FoxPro does nothing to show it to you. If you want to see the record, you can enter DISPLAY in the Command Window or use the Edit or Change command.

As an example, with the Buyers table in use, choose Locate from the Record menu. Then click the For option for the dialog box. Enter the following in the Locate For <expL> text box of the Expression Builder:

```
Lastname = "Hernandez"
```

This can also be done by selecting lastname for the fields list and typing or choosing the equal sign from the logical menu, and entering the lastname in quotation marks.

Mouse users can also do this task with the mouse. Instead of typing, you can click the string Box and Select Text from the pull down menu that appears, then type the name.

Click OK and the Locate box reappears. Finally, click the Locate button, and the search is implemented. Now enter EDIT in the Command Window, and you see the desired record. (See Figure 7.2.)

FIGURE 7.2.

A located record.

The Continue Option

This command finds the next occurrence of a search term. Continue is located on the Record menu. This option helps in cases where the first record located is not the one desired. If no other record is found to meet the specifications, the "End of Locate Scope" message is displayed.

The Locate Command

From the command level, you can use the Locate command to perform a search. This command finds the first occurrence of a Record. The syntax is

```
Locate (scope) For condition
```

And *condition* evaluates to a logical expression, such as firstname = "Maria". The scope is optional, and can be used to limit the search in the database. Any one of four scopes can be used: Next*n*, All, Rest, and Record*n*. Next*n*, and Rest begin the search at the current record number. All sets the scope to the entire table, and Record*n* sets the search to a specific record number.

If all or rest has been chosen for the scope and the first record found is not the one desired, the Continue command can be used to find the next record to fit the criteria.

You can try an example of the Locate command at the Command Window, by entering the following:

```
LOCATE FOR CITY = "Falls Church"
DISPLAY
```

This is the result

```
Record#   Custid      Address          City          State
9         109         107 Embassy Row  Falls Church  VA
```

And you can enter CONTINUE to find the next occurrence of the same city name. When no additional records that meet the specified scope can be found, "End of Locate Scope" is displayed in the Status Bar, showing that there are no other records fitting the search criteria.

The Seek Option

The Seek option works faster that the Locate option due to its utilization of FoxPro indexes. The selection of Seek from the Record menu brings up the FoxPro Expression Builder. But in this case, the text box is labelled "Value to Seek." The Expression Builder is used much the same here as it was with the Locate command; you enter the desired seek expression in the Seek Value window. Only the expression is needed, because FoxPro knows which field or fields to base the search on, based on the active index file.

As an example of the use of the Seek option from the menus, you can first build an index for the Buyers table, by entering the following command in the Command Window:

```
INDEX ON LASTNAME TAG NAMES
```

Then choose Record, Seek from the menus. Next, enter Hernandez in the value to Seek box (don't forget quotation marks.) Click OK to implement the command, and the first occurrence is found in the index. If there are duplicates, the use of the Browse option helps to see all the records meeting the criteria.

The Seek Command

This command is equivalent to the Seek option. As with many commands, it can be faster than wading through menus and dialog boxes, in that you only have to enter the search value. The format is as follows:

```
Seek expression
```

The expression can consist of a number, a character string surrounded by quotation marks, a variable (variables are covered later in the programming section of this book), or a combination of constants, variables, and operators. The Seek command moves the record pointer to the specified record. For example, assuming that an index based on ZIP codes was active, you could use a command like

```
SEEK "90210"
```

to search for the first entry of that value in the ZIPCODE field.

The Find Command

This command is only available at the Command Window; you cannot perform a Find through the menus. This command also does an index search; therefore, an index must first be active. The format for the command is

```
FIND character string
```

where character string is a group of characters that do not need to be surrounded by quotation marks. You can try an example of the FIND command by entering the following statements in the Command Window:

```
INDEX ON LASTNAME TAG NAMES
FIND O'Neill
```

Enter DISPLAY in the Command Window, and the following is the result:

```
Record#        Lastname      Custid
8              O'Neill       108
```

Using the Set Filter Command to Select Subsets of Data

For some applications (such as pulling select addresses for a mailing list,) you need to select a group of records. There are a number of ways you can do this. The query-by-example techniques presented in Chapter 6, "Performing Queries with RQBE," outlined one way to select subgroups of records. Another way this can be done is by using the SET FILTER command. When a filter is set, only specified records—those meeting the conditions—are affected by the commands. The format is as follows:

```
SET FILTER TO condition
```

where *condition* is a logical expression, such as LASTNAME = "Edhard", to define a search. Once the command is entered, any subsequent commands which normally affect the entire database only affect those records that meet the conditions set by the filter. As an example, a command like

```
SET FILTER TO CITY = "Falls Church" .AND.  STATE = "VA"
```

limits the commands to the records that meet the criteria set out in the filter—those that live in Falls Church, VA. The Set Filter command is the equivalent of the filter command found on the Database/Setup menu. Record groups can also be isolated by using the Set Filter command followed by a LIST or BROWSE command.

Complex searches can also be done with SET FILTER, for example:

```
Set Filter to (HIREDAY >= {01/01/94} .AND. HIREDAY <= {12/31/94} .AND. State = "TX"
```

This filter would limit records available to those with a value in the HIREDAY field within 1994, and with a value of "TX" in the STATE field.

To find out if a filter is in effect, type DISPLAY STATUS or LIST STATUS in the Command Window. The result includes any filter that's currently in effect. You can also enter ? SET("FILTER") in the Command Window to display any filter that's in effect. To cancel the effects of filter, enter SET FILTER TO without any expression.

Chapter Summary

This chapter provided a look at the various commands and menu options that you can use to find the data you need in FoxPro. At times, the number of ways to find your data may seem confusing—there is not any correct way necessarily to do things in FoxPro. The flexibility of the different methods provides you with the most effective ways to do things under different circumstances.

Creating and Using Simple Screens

8

Screens provide another way to view data in FoxPro. While the Browse window displays your data in the familiar row-and-column screen art, screens let you view a record at a time, using any layout you prefer. Screens in FoxPro can be quickly created with the AutoScreen button on the Toolbar, or by means of the Screen Wizards. Screens can also be designed manually, through a Screen Design window which lets you drag objects (such as fields and text) to any desired location. Figure 8.1 shows a screen for editing that table's data. In this example, the screen was created in a single step, using the Catalog Manager's AutoScreen button.

FIGURE 8.1.

A screen for editing data.

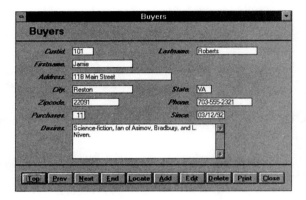

Screens can be based on queries, providing a painless way to view and edit information. For example, you might design a query to show all sales records for a given month. A screen could then be designed to view or edit the data for only those records. By basing the screen on the query (rather than on the entire table), the correct records are automatically made available to the screen whenever the screen is opened.

FoxPro screens go beyond providing data and text labels. With screens, you can display graphics, such as drawings, photos, or corporate logos. You can include calculated fields to provide totals or other summations of specific numeric information. Another important benefit of screens is that they provide the precise type of data needed. With a database, you could have several different screen designs with the same set of fields, to provide different "views" of relevant data.

Why Use Screens Over the Browse Window?

Screens offer a number of advantages over the Browse window, when it comes to data entry and editing. With the Browse window, you don't have a great deal of control over how your data is displayed. While it is true that you can move columns around, change row heights and column widths, and modify font sizes, these are pretty much the limits of what you can do with the appearance of a the Browse window. With screens, you can move the fields to any location you wish, not just to an area of a specific column. Screens can display data in row-oriented or column-oriented fashions, or a combination of both. While the Browse windows must follow a row-and-column format, screens essentially use a free-screen design. Screens also let you utilize color and shading within the controls, something that is not possible with the Browse windows. You can add lines, boxes, or drawings in the screen of bitmaps to enhance the screen's appearance.

Some types of data are better suited for display in screens than in Browse windows. Memo fields are hard to view in the Browse window, and general fields that contain pictures or other OLE data cannot be viewed in a Browse window. Finally, screens can contain options like list boxes or combination boxes to choose from among various options that you specify. List boxes and combination boxes are not possible in the Browse windows.

On What Should I Base My Screens?

Since FoxPro lets you base screens on tables or queries, some advance planning may be a wise idea to help make the most effective use of screens. If you intend to use the screen to examine any or all of the records in a single table, base the screen on the table. If you need to examine data from multiple tables—or if you need to examine a selected subset of data— base the screen on a query. When creating screens from the Catalog Manager using the New button, FoxPro displays a New Screen dialog box at the start of the process. (See Figure 8.2.) You use this dialog box to indicate which table or query the screen should be based upon. Note that when you base a screen on a query, FoxPro must run the query as it opens the screen. For this reason, screens that are based on large tables and/or complex queries may be slow to open.

FIGURE 8.2.
A New Screen dialog box.

Creating Simple Screens

This chapter details how you can create simple to moderately complex screens exclusively with the use of the AutoScreen button and with the aid of the ScreenWizards. (The AutoScreen button is available only through the Catalog Manager.) Note that Chapter

12, "Designing and Customizing Reports," details how you can add more features to screens you design or enhance manually.

Creating a Screen with the AutoScreen Button

The simplest way to create a screen is to make use of the AutoScreen button on the Toolbar. (If you are using a version of FoxPro prior to version 2.6, you won't have the use of this feature.) The AutoScreen button builds a default single-column screen for whatever table is in use at the time you click the button. Choose File, Catalog Manager to switch to the Catalog Manager (if you are not already there). Click the Table tab, then click Buyers to select it, then click Use to open the table. Next, click the AutoScreen button. When you do so, FoxPro builds a default screen for the table. An example of such a screen was shown previously in Figure 8.1.

Creating a Screen with the Screen Wizards

FoxPro provides an automated way to create a wide variety of common screens, with the aid of the ScreenWizards. Like other FoxPro wizards, the ScreenWizards step you through the process of screen creation, by asking a series of questions about the desired screen. The overall steps, which are described in more detail in the following paragraphs, are these:

1. With the Catalog Manager active, click the Screen button, then click New. When you do so, the Create Screen dialog box appears.

2. In the Select A Table/Query list box, choose the desired table or query that you want to base the screen upon.

3. Click the ScreenWizards button.

4. Follow the directions in the Wizard dialog boxes. In the last dialog box that appears, click the "Save and Run Screen" option then click Finish to begin entering or viewing data, or click the "Modify screen with design tool" option then click Finish to see the structure of the screen.

When you click the Screen tab in the Catalog Manager and then click New, the New Screen dialog box appears. (See Figure 8.2, shown previously.) Click the down arrow in the Select a Table/Query list box to display all the available tables and queries in the current directory. Once this is done, clicking the ScreenWizard button displays the first dialog box for the ScreenWizard.

Choosing the Desired Fields

The first dialog box presented by the ScreenWizard lets you choose the desired fields that are included in the screen. (See Figure 8.3.)

FIGURE 8.3.

A dialog box for choosing fields.

When you click a field in the Available Fields list box to select it, and then click the Add button, the field gets added to the Selected Fields list box. Alternately, you can double-click any field to add it to the Selected Fields list box. (As an option, you can also click the Add All button, to add all the fields to the list.) If you make a mistake and add an unwanted field, the Remove button can be used to remove a field you've already added from the Field Order on Screen list box, and the Remove All button removes all the fields. After adding the desired fields, click Next to proceed to the next dialog box.

> **TIP**
>
> You can add the fields in any order you like. The wizard doesn't force you to add fields in the order that they appear in the Available Fields list box. For example, if the Available Fields list box contains a Last Name field and directly beneath it, a First Name field, you could choose to add the First Name field to the Field Order on Screen list box, followed by the Last Name field. In the resulting screen, cursor movement would be into the First Name field, then into the Last Name field.

Choosing a Field to Sort the Records

If your screen is based on a table, the next dialog box presented by the Screen Wizard asks which fields you want to use to sort the records that appear in the screen. (See Figure 8.4.) (If you are basing the screen on a query, the wizard skips this step.) For example, if you are working with a mailing list, you might prefer the records to be sorted so that they appear in State order, and where states are the same, by City. In the Available Fields list box, click each field that you want to use to sort the records, then click the Add button. The ScreenWizard lets you pick up to three fields as the basis for a sort order. The first field you pick gets the highest priority in the sort, followed by the second field, then by the third field. After selecting the desired field or fields, click Ascending or Descending as desired, then click Next to proceed. Keep in mind that you can ignore this dialog box entirely and click Next without choosing any fields, in which case the records do not appear in any defined order when viewed through the screen.

FIGURE 8.4.

The dialog box for choosing sort order.

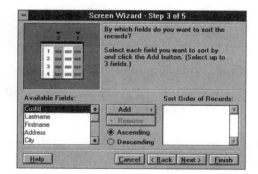

Choosing a Look for the Screen

The next dialog box presented by the ScreenWizards asks which look you want for the screen: standard, chiseled, shadowed, boxed, or embossed. The standard screen (see Figure 8.5), provides a simple combination of black text labels on a grey background, with fields in white text boxes. If you plan on manually changing a screen's design, this style of design can be easier to modify than the others. (The other screens use fancy tricks with shadowed highlighting that can make modifications difficult.)

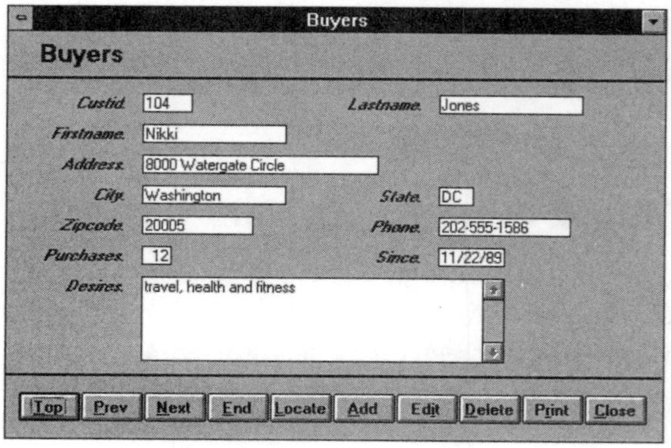

FIGURE 8.5.

The standard look for a screen.

The chiseled screen (see Figure 8.6), takes on an appearance similar to that of the standard screen, but all fields and the screen's title are underlined with a chiseled effect.

FIGURE 8.6.

The chiseled look for a screen.

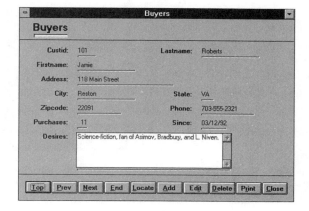

The shadowed look (see Figure 8.7), uses the same text, color, and background design as the standard look, but the fields are given a three-dimensional "drop shadow" effect. Note that this screen can be difficult to make manual design changes to, because in Design view, it is often difficult to place the fields and the corresponding shadows in the same relative positions after moving them.

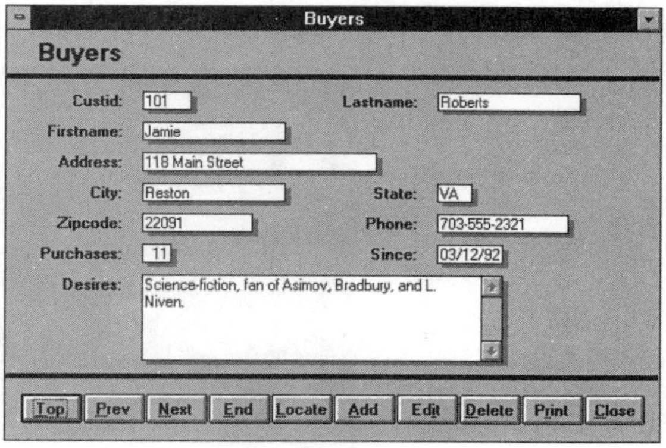

FIGURE 8.7.

The shadowed look for a screen.

The boxed look (see Figure 8.8), provides a screen with field labels in blue, and field data in black upon a white background, and the overall screen background in gray. Each combination of field label and field is enclosed in a white box, with the labels placed at the upper left. As with the shadowed look, the boxed look can present difficulties if you want to make manual changes, because it can be hard to keep the labels and fields in respective positions as you move them.

FIGURE 8.8.

The boxed look for a screen.

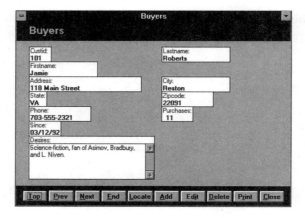

Finally, the embossed look provides black text for field labels and white text boxes for the fields, but the fields are given a sunken effect. (See Figure 8.9.) The screen's title is given an attractive drop-shadow look.

You can also click the Text or Picture button as desired, to choose whether you want the screen's navigation buttons to display text or pictures. The text of the buttons use terms such as "Next," "First," "Last," and "Prev," while the pictures use VCR-style buttons to represent these functions for moving around within a table. When done choosing an appearance for the screen and selecting the options for the buttons, you can click Next to proceed.

FIGURE 8.9.

The embossed look for a screen.

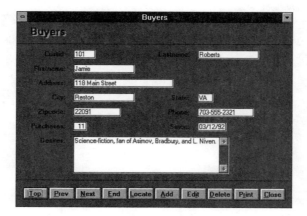

Completing the Design Process

The last ScreenWizards dialog box (see Figure 8.10), provides a box for entering a title for the screen, along with Open and Modify buttons. The default title is the same as the underlying table or query, but you can change this as desired. (This title is not used as a filename that the screen is saved under, instead it appears as a title in the upper left corner of the screen when the screen opens.) After entering a title, click the "Save and run screen" option, then click Finish to use the new screen with your data. You can also click "Modify screen with design tool," then click Finish, to open FoxPro's screen designer and make further modifications.

FIGURE 8.10.

The final dialog box for ScreenWizard.

You can also click "Save screen for later use" if you want to save the screen as-is, but don't plan to use it at the present time. Whichever choice you make, when you click Finish, FoxPro presents the Save As dialog box. (See Figure 8.11.) You must enter a filename that the screen is saved under. By default, screens are saved with an extension of .SCX.

FIGURE 8.11.

The Save As dialog box.

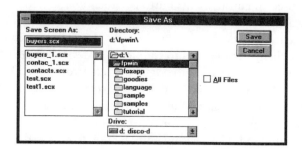

Even when you prefer to design your own screens, the Screen Wizards can often save time and effort by providing a screen that is close to what you want. Use the wizards to create a screen, then switch to Design view and make your desired changes. You'll find more on design techniques for screens in Chapter 11, "Designing and Customizing Screens."

Opening a Screen

Screens can be opened from the Catalog Manager by clicking on the screen name in the Catalog manager window. (If the Screen tab is not visible, it is necessary to first click the Screen tab in the Catalog Manager, so that all the stored screens appear.) You can then open the desired screen by clicking on its name. Doing so causes the screen to appear, with the first available record shown. (If an index is active, the first record that you see in the screen is the first record according to the index.) At the bottom of the screen appears a list of buttons for navigation among the records.

Navigating Within a Screen and Editing

Navigation within a screen is done by using the four navigation buttons at the bottom of the screen. The first button, Top, displays the first record on the screen with all its fields (shown previously in Figure 8.1). The next button is the Prev button, which displays the previous record on the screen. If you are at the beginning of the file and click this button, the message "Top of File" is displayed. The Next button displays the next record in the file, unless you are at the end of the file. The End button is the last of the navigation buttons and displays the last record in the file.

There are also six other buttons available. The Locate button opens a miniature Browse window and enables you to find a record and display it on the screen. The Add button can be used in editing. This button enables you to add a new record to the database by adding a blank record at the end of the file, and opening that record for data entry within the screen. The Edit button lets you edit the current record. Click the Edit button, and you can change the entries to the fields as desired. The TAB key can be used to move around the fields as well as the right and left arrow keys. Delete is another of the available buttons—it marks records for deletion. Records marked for deletion can't be viewed from any aspect of the Catalog Manager. When it comes to deleting records, keep in mind that a record cannot be recalled from the Catalog Manager. In order to do that you need to go to the Command Window and enter RECALL followed by the record number. The Print button is also located here, and enables you to print the current record or the entire record set. When you click Print, a Print dialog box appears. (See Figure 8.12.)

FIGURE 8.12.

A Print dialog box.

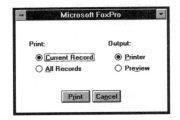

In this dialog box, you can click Current Record to print the current record, or click All Records to print all records in the table. The Output buttons let you choose the printer or a Page Preview window as a destination. Make your desired choices in the dialog box, then click Print to proceed. The last button in the screen, the Close button, closes the screen and returns you to the Catalog Manager.

An Example: Creating A Screen for the Buyers Table

You can perform the following steps to demonstrate how you can create a data entry screen for the Buyers table created in Chapter 3, "Creating and Working with Tables." Perform the following steps:

1. If the Buyers database is not open, click the Table tab in the Catalog Manager, click Buyers to select it, and click the Use button.

2. Click the Screen Tab in the Catalog Manager.

3. Click New. The Create Screen dialog box appears. Click the Screen Wizard to begin building a screen.

4. Next a dialog box appears that asks what fields you want in the screen. For this example, click Add All. Then, remove three of the fields. Click Purchases, then click the Remove button. Click Since, and click the Remove button. Finally, click Desires, and click the Remove button. Finally, click Next at the bottom of the screen.

5. The next dialog box asks which fields you want to sort (if the screen were based on a query, this step would be skipped.) Add the LASTNAME field, then add the FIRSTNAME field. (Doing so causes the records in the completed screen to appear in the order of last names, and where last names are the same, in order of first names.) There is also a choice for Ascending and Descending in the dialog box; leave it as Ascending, and click Next.

6. The next dialog box which appears enables you to select the style and button type for your screen. The choices are displayed in the upper left corner of the dialog box, as you choose them from the Select Style box. Scroll through the different types and see what they look like by moving the blue highlight to the name of the different style. Choose Chiseled, and click next.

7. The Final dialog box lets you enter a title for your screen. For this example, call it Buyers. Then click Finish.

8. Next, the Save As dialog box appears so that a file name can be given to your screen. Save the screen as Buyers2 and click save. The screen is now created.

When the screen is opened (by clicking on Buyers2 and clicking Run in the Catalog Manager) the screen bears the title Buyers, as it was named in the wizard dialog box.

If for some reason you desire to change your screen, click the Screen tab, click the desired screen in the window to select it, then click the modify button, and the Wizard steps you through the process. As an example of how you do this, click Modify now in the Catalog Manager. (Make sure Buyers is highlighted.) After choosing Modify, you are returned to the Screen Wizard dialog box entitled "Step 2 of 5," which enables you to select the fields to be included in the screen. Add the Purchases field to the Selected Fields Box. Click Finish, and you are taken to the last screen. Click Finish again, and the Save As dialog box appears. Save it as under the same name, and you are finished with the modification. This same method can be used to make more involved changes to an existing screen.

Chapter Summary

This chapter detailed the creation of screen forms with the automated features added to FoxPro version 2.6. For the first time in FoxPro's history, these features make it possible for you to work with custom screens with no knowledge of programming. You can, however, use manual screen design and programming techniques to go beyond what is possible with the Catalog Manager. Such techniques are covered in Chapter 11.

Creating and Using Simple Reports

9

Reports are the end result of much of your work in FoxPro—or in any database, for that matter. They provide a way to organize, format, display, or print desired information. FoxPro reports provide significant flexibility, especially if you are accustomed to the DOS-based database managers that were commonly used prior to the popularity of Windows. FoxPro reports let you combine elements such as data, text in a variety of formats, graphs, and graphic elements (lines, rectangles, and so on) to provide the precise report you need. You can quickly create reports with the AutoReport button available through the Catalog Manager, or you can use the Report Wizards (also available through the Catalog Manager) to guide you through the report design process, while maintaining some control over the report's type and appearance. You can also design your reports manually, using FoxPro's Report Writer to place the needed objects in a blank report. Figure 9.1 shows a report for a table of customers. In this example, the report was created in a single step with the AutoReport button on the Toolbar.

FIGURE 9.1.

An example of a report.

Buyers
03/30/94

Custid	Lastname	Firstname	Address
101	Roberts	Jamie	118 Main Street
102	Sanderson	Lucy	931 Thames Ct,. Apt. 2C
103	Smith	Larry	142 Haven Way
104	Jones	Nikki	8000 Watergate Circle
105	Hernandez	Maria	19012 Pimmit Drive
106	Jones	Jarel	1412 Wyldewood Way
107	Zeibermann	Daniel	235 White Oak Way
108	O'Neill	John	12555 Lee Highway West
109	Bannerton	Alicia	107 Embassy Row
110	Anderson	Harry	101 Santa Monica Way

While reports can be based on a table, another viable option is to base reports on queries. When a report is based on a table, the report includes every record in the table, and rarely is this what is needed. Most often, what's needed is a report that contains specific data: all sales during the first quarter, or all vacation destinations in the Caribbean, or all surgery records for a specific patient. When a report is based on a query, the SQL statement behind the query runs whenever the report is opened, and the desired subset of data automatically appears in the report. Reports can include graphics, stored in general fields of a table or pasted into blank areas as design elements.

While reports share many design elements with forms, there are some differences. Reports use a *band-oriented* approach, where the design of the report can be divided into different bands containing separate elements like headers, footers, and group titles. Reports also provide specialized options that let you group the data produced by the report.

Design Issues Behind Reports

Proper planning can save wasted time and avoid reports that don't provide users with needed information. In the area of report design, the job at hand is to take the raw data that's provided by a table or a query, and somehow transform that data into a printed report that provides needed information in a way that makes sense to the user. An effective methodology for producing a report might consist of steps like these:

1. Define the report's layout on paper
2. Design and implement the underlying table or query
3. Design the report in FoxPro
4. Preview or print the report

■ Define the Report's Layout on Paper. Before beginning work with the Report Wizards or with the manual design surfaces of FoxPro's Report Writer, you should have a concrete idea of what the report will look like—either on paper or mentally. A hand-drawn sketch passed around the ranks of those who use the system will do much to refine a report before anything is attempted on-screen. If you are using an existing manual system, or you are re-implementing an older computer-based application in FoxPro, you likely have the advantage of existing forms to use as a basis for comparison to your new designs. One point of warning: just because a report already exists in an older computer-based system does not mean it is the right model to use for designing an equivalent report in FoxPro. The existing report may have shortfalls in design, or you may be able to design a better report by taking advantage of FoxPro capabilities that the older system lacked. Again, getting the users of the report involved in the design process helps provide a report that accomplishes the needed task.

■ Design and Implement the Underlying Query. Unless you want a completely non-relational report that contains every iota of data in a table, you need a query to serve as the basis for the report. If the report is to be a relational one, you'll need to design a relational query (as outlined in Chapter 10, "Working with FoxPro's Relational Powers") to provide the desired fields from the different tables. Queries can provide the selected records, the desired fields, and the needed sort order for the data before it is processed in the report. For example, consider a database used by a video rental store, with tables for customers, videos in stock, and rental records. You might need a report that shows all customer tape rentals for a specific month. The query would need to retrieve the customer names from the Customers table, the video titles from the Videos table, and the rental dates from the Rentals table. The query would also need to select records for a specific month and produce the results before the report based on the query could provide the needed data.

■ Design the Report in FoxPro. Once the query exists, you can design the report using either the Report Wizards or the manual method of report design.

■ Preview or Print the Report. You can print or preview the report when done with design. From the Catalog Manager, click the report to select it, then click the Print button. From the menus, you can choose Run, Report, select the desired report in the Open dialog box, and click Run. From the Command Window, you can use the REPORT FORM command. All these methods are covered in this chapter.

Creating Simple Reports

This chapter details how you can create simple-to-moderately complex reports. The primary methods detailed are the use of the AutoReport button, and the use of the Report Wizards. Chapter 12, "Designing and Customizing Reports," contains additional information on how you can apply the more complex features of custom report design.

Creating a Report with the AutoReport Button

The Catalog Manager's AutoReport button can be used to quickly create a default single-column report. The AutoReport button builds a simple columnar report for any table or query that is selected or active when you click the button. To produce such a report, first switch to the Catalog Manager. Click the desired table or query to select it, then click the AutoReport button. (It's the button that resembles a notebook cover with the lightning bolt across it.) When you do so, FoxPro builds a default report for the table or query, and displays a Catalog Manager Print dialog box. (See Figure 9.2.) You can choose Printer and click OK to print the report, or click Page Preview, then click OK to see the report in Page Preview. An example of such a report was shown previously in Figure 9.1.

FIGURE 9.2.

The Catalog Manager Print dialog box.

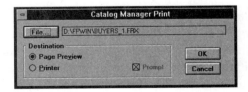

The type of report you get with this technique is a simple columnar report. The field names appear at the top of each page as column headings. A disadvantage of using the AutoReport button is that the resulting report only contains as many fields as will fit across a single page—any additional fields in the table or query are omitted from the report. You can get around this by designing a selective query that provides just the fields you need (assuming they will fit), or by customizing the report's design using techniques outlined in Chapter 12.

Creating a Report with the Report Wizards

The built-in Report Wizards provide an automated way to create a number of commonly used reports, by stepping you through the process of report design and asking a number of questions about the desired report. The overall steps, covered in detail in the paragraphs that follow, are these:

1. From the Catalog Manager, click the Report tab, then click New to display the New Report dialog box.

2. In the dialog box under Select A Table or Query, from the list choose the desired query or table to base the report on.

3. Click the Report Wizard button, then choose one of the following Wizards from the list: Group/Total, Multi-column, or Report Wizard. (The types are further detailed shortly.)

4. Follow the directions which appear in the dialog boxes. In the last dialog box, you can choose to display the report in Print Preview or in Design view.

When you click the Report tab in the Catalog Manager and then click New, the Create Report dialog box appears. (See Figure 9.3.)

FIGURE 9.3.

The Create Report dialog box.

Click the down arrow in the Select a Table/Query list box to display a list of all available tables and queries in the database. Then, click the desired query or table from which the report should draw its data. Finally, click the Report Wizard button. In a moment, the first dialog box for the Report Wizard appears. (See Figure 9.4.)

FIGURE 9.4.

The first Report Wizards dialog box.

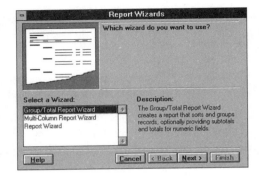

The first dialog box presented by the Report Wizards offers a choice of three report types that the wizard can produce: Group/Totals, Multi-column, or Report Wizard.

With groups/totals reports, the data is organized with the selected fields placed in columns and each record occupying a row. The records are optionally sorted and grouped according to a value that's based on a field. Numeric totals can be included for numeric fields. If totals are included in the design, FoxPro adds a grand total at the end of the report. Figure 9.5 shows an example of a groups/totals report.

FIGURE 9.5.

A groups/totals report.

Lastname	Firstname	City	State	Phone
Roberts	Jamie	Reston	VA	703-555-2321
Sanderson	Lucy	Herndon		703-555-5681
Smith	Larry	Kensington	MD	301-555-2815
Jones	Nikki	Washington	DC	202-555-1586
Hernandez	Maria	Towson	MD	301-555-6725
Jones	Jarel	McLean	VA	703-555-9091
Zelbermann	Daniel	Arlington		703-555-2114
O'Neill	John	Merrifield		703-555-9256
Bannerton	Alicia	Falls Church		703-555-1200
Anderson	Harry	Santa Monica	CA	415-555-5555

Multi-column reports divide the data into columns. Using this option, you can create a report that has up to three columns of data. Figure 9.6 shows an example of a multi-column report.

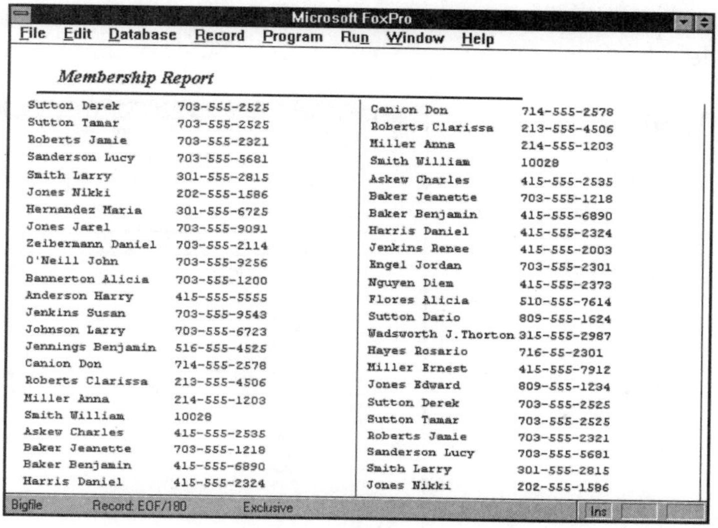

FIGURE 9.6.

A multi-column report.

The Report Wizards choice creates a report whose appearance varies, depending on the style and layout you select in the wizard dialog boxes.

Choosing a Look for the Report

The next dialog box presented by the Report Wizards asks which look you want for the report: executive, presentation, or ledger. The executive report (see Figure 9.7) adds thin double lines in the header and uses a default 14-point font for the header, and a default 10-point font for the remaining text.

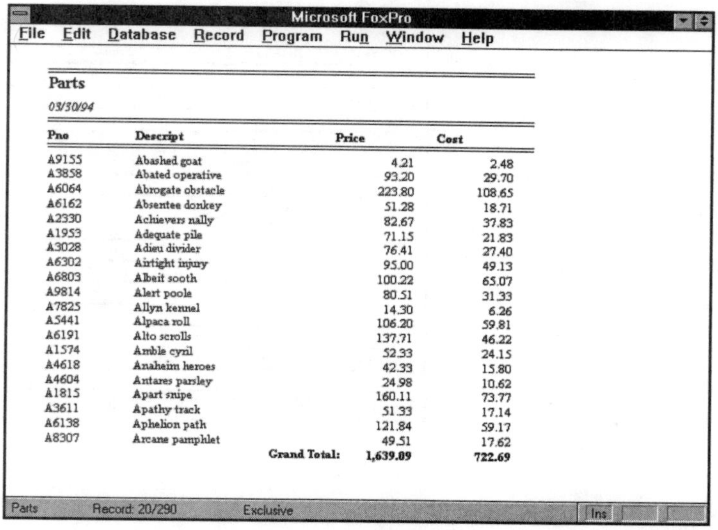

FIGURE 9.7.

The executive look for a report.

The presentation report (see Figure 9.8) adds thick single lines in the header and uses a default 14-point font for the header, and a 10-point font for the remaining text.

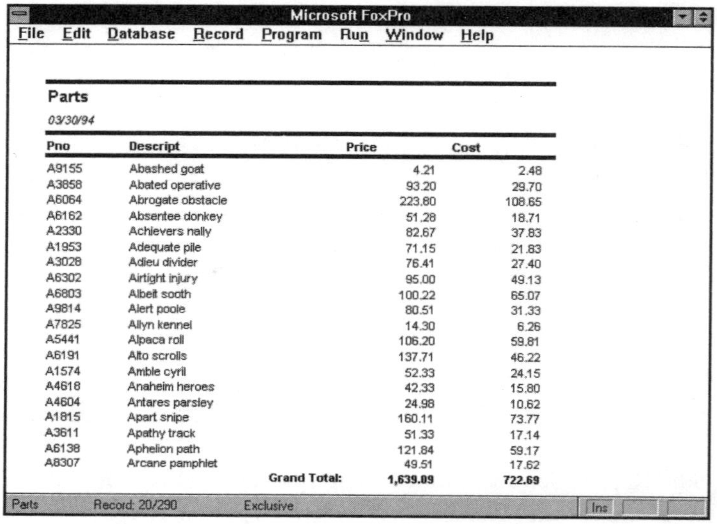

FIGURE 9.8.

The presentation look for a report.

The ledger look (see Figure 9.9) uses lines and fonts similar to those used by the executive style, but the data is enclosed in a spreadsheet-like grid formed by horizontal and vertical lines.

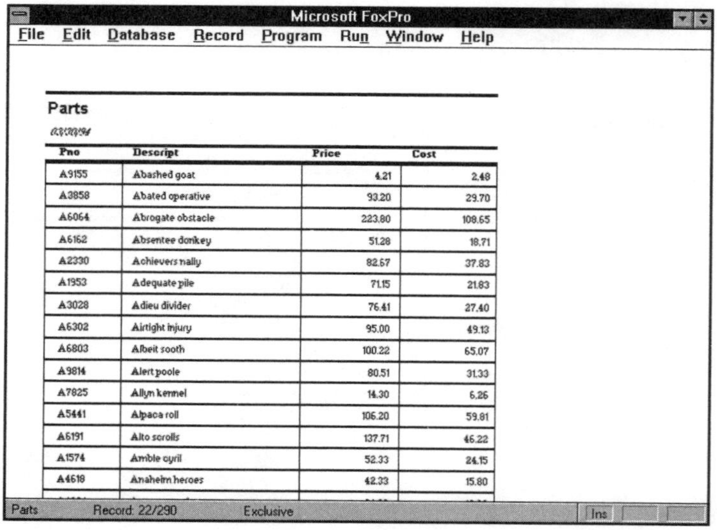

FIGURE 9.9.

The ledger look for a report.

> **TIP**
>
> Of the three styles of reports provided, the ledger look accommodates more data in a single page of printable space than the other styles.

As you click each option button in the dialog box, a representative sample of the report's appearance is displayed at the left side of the box. When done choosing an appearance for the report, click Next to proceed.

Choosing Fields for the Report

The next dialog box presented by the Report Wizard lets you choose the desired fields that are included in the report. (See Figure 9.10.)

FIGURE 9.10.

The dialog box for choosing fields.

When you click a field in the Available Fields list box to select it and then click the Add button, the field gets added to the Selected Fields list box. Alternately, you can double-click any field to add it to the Selected Fields list box. (As an option, you can also click the Add All button to add all the fields to the list.) If you make a mistake and add an un-wanted field, the Remove button can be used to remove a field you've already added from the Field Order on Screen list box. The Remove All button removes all the fields. After adding the desired fields, click Next to proceed to the next dialog box.

> **TIP**
>
> You can add the fields in any order you like. The wizard doesn't force you to add fields in the order that they appear in the Available Fields list box. For example, if the Available Fields list box contains a Last Name field and directly beneath it, a First Name field, you could choose to add the First Name field to the Selected Fields list box, followed by the Last Name field. In the resulting report, the First Name field would be to the left of the Last Name field.

Choosing Positioning for the Fields

If you chose Report Wizards as the desired report type, the next dialog box (see Figure 9.11) lets you decide how the fields should be positioned in the report. (You do not see this dialog box if you chose Groups/Totals as the desired report type.) Your choices in this dialog box are Horizontal and Vertical. Choose Horizontal to place the field titles horizontally across the top of the report. Or choose Vertical to place the field titles along the report's left margin. When done with the options in this dialog box, click Next.

FIGURE 9.11.

The dialog box for field positioning.

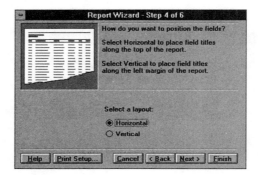

TIP

You can also click the Print Setup button in this dialog box to bring up the Print Setup dialog box, which lets you change paper sizes and select portrait or landscape orientation for the report.

If the fields you chose won't fit on the report using the positioning choice you made, FoxPro displays a dialog box warning when you click Next. (See Figure 9.12.) You can click the Adjust Fields button in the dialog box if you want to go back and remove certain fields, or you can click the Adjust Layout button in the dialog box to change the layout. You can also click the Ignore button, in which case FoxPro creates a report with as many fields as will fit.

FIGURE 9.12.

A dialog box warning that all fields won't fit.

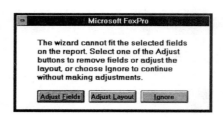

Completing the Design Process

The last Report Wizards dialog box (see Figure 9.13) provides a box for entering a title for the report, along with the options titled "Save Report for later use," "Save and print report," and "Modify report with design tool." After entering a desired title (which appears at the top of the first page of the report), click the "Save and print report" option, then click Finish to use the new report with your data. Or, click "Modify report with design tool" then click Finish to open FoxPro's Report Writer and make further modifications.

FIGURE 9.13.

The final dialog box for Report Wizard.

You can also click "Save report for later use" if you want to save the report as-is, but don't plan to use it at the present time. Whichever choice you make, when you click Finish, FoxPro presents the Save As dialog box. (See Figure 9.14.) You must enter a filename that the screen will be saved under. By default, reports are saved with an extension of .FRX.

FIGURE 9.14.

The Save As dialog box.

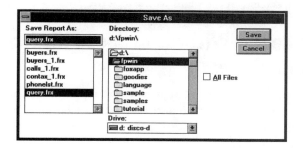

Even when you prefer to design your own screens, the Screen Wizards can often save time and effort by providing a screen that is close to what you want. Use the wizards to create a screen, then switch to Design view and make desired changes. You'll find more on design techniques for reports in Chapter 12.

How to Print the Report

In a nutshell, you can print a completed report with any of the following methods:

- From the Catalog Manager. Click the report to select it, then click the Print button. The Catalog Manager Print dialog box appears. (See Figure 9.2, shown previously.)

  Click Printer in this dialog box to print the report, or click Page Preview to display the report in preview mode. Then click OK to produce the report.

- From the menus, you can choose Run, Report, then select the desired report in the Open dialog box that appears, and click Run. In the Run Report dialog box that next appears, click Preview to display the report in preview mode, or click Print to sent the report's output to the printer. Finally, click Run to produce the report.

- From the Command Window, you can use the REPORT FORM command, with the following basic syntax:

```
REPORT FORM report filename [TO PRINT]
```

  and if the TO PRINT option is used, the report is printed; otherwise, it appears on screen, in the main window of the FoxPro desktop.

Use Report Wizards to Speed the Manual Report Design Process

Even when you prefer to design your own reports, the Report Wizards can often save time and effort by providing a report that is close to what you want. Use the wizards to create a report, then open the report in FoxPro's Report Writer and make any desired changes to the existing report.

Changing the Print Setup Options

FoxPro stores a number of print setup and page orientation settings with the report. You can change these once, and they remain in effect for that particular report until changed again. To set the page orientation and other print setup options for a report, perform these steps:

1. Open the existing report by choosing File/Open from the menus. In the Open dialog box that appears, change the List Files of Type option to Report, then click the desired report and click OK to open it.

2. Choose File/Print Setup from the menus. This causes the Print Setup dialog box to open. (See Figure 9.15.)

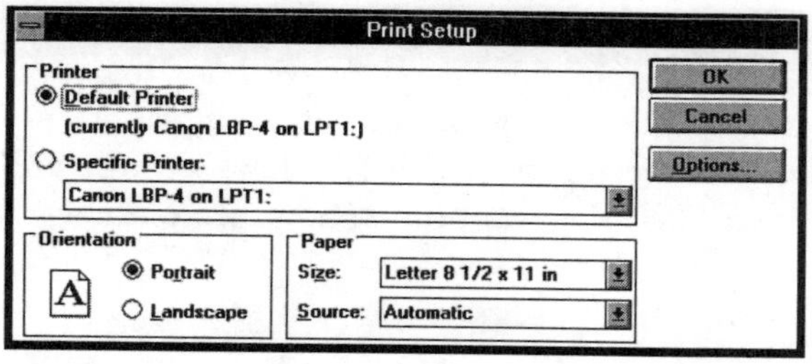

FIGURE 9.15.

The Print Setup dialog box.

3. In the Printer portion of the dialog box, choose the desired printer. (The drop-down list boxes contain all printers that have been installed for use with Windows on your system.)

4. In the Orientation portion of the dialog box, choose the desired orientation (portrait or landscape).

5. In the Paper portion of the dialog box, choose the desired paper size, then click OK.

By clicking the Options button in the dialog box, you can reveal additional options that apply to your specific printer. The dialog box that you see when you click the Options button varies, depending on your printer. Figure 9.16 shows an example of the dialog box that appears for the Canon LBP-4 laser printer.

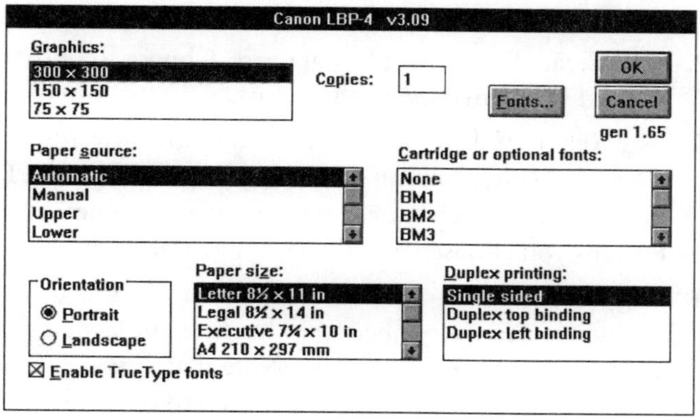

FIGURE 9.16.

The printer options dialog box for a Canon printer.

Because there are hundreds of printers on the market, it is impossible to explain all of the possible settings. Each printer's dialog box contains options applicable to that particular printer. In addition, most laser printers contain list boxes for choosing from various installed fonts and/or font cartridges. Your printer's documentation may be helpful in determining what fonts and other options can be used with your particular printer.

> **NOTE**
>
> When you click the Options button to display the printer's dialog box, the options you see are the default Windows settings for that printer. Changing these options is likely to affect printing in other Windows applications.

An Example: Creating a Report with the Report Wizards

As an example of a report design, you can use the following steps to create a report using both the AutoReport button and the Report Wizards. First, to create a default report with no additional steps involved, use the AutoReport button (located next to the AutoScreen button in the Catalog Manager). Clicking this button causes FoxPro to build a default report with no questions asked. This report can be previewed after its creation from the dialog box that appears. This is FoxPro's quick and easy way to create a report.

There are, of course, times when a more detailed report is needed. In those cases, the Report Wizards can be used. From the Catalog Manager, perform the following steps:

1. Click the Report tab from the Catalog Manager, then choose New for a new report.

2. The Create Report window appears. Choose Report Wizard to use the Report Wizard in the making of the report.

3. The Report Wizard asks which of the three wizards you want to use: Group Total Reports, Multi-Column Report, or Report Wizard. (The order of the successive dialog boxes, and what appears in each dialog box, is different depending on the options you choose.) For the example, follow the Report Wizard choice.

4. After you click Report Wizard, the next window to appear is the window that enables you to choose between the different layouts for the report. Choose Presentation for this example. (Note that as you choose the different layouts, a representation of each layout is displayed in the dialog box. This enables you to see the styles for the different types of layouts before implementing them.)

5. After choosing a report layout, you are asked which fields you want to include in your report. For the example, include only the Firstname, Lastname, Custid, and Phone fields, by clicking each field and then clicking the Add button. (This dialog box is also seen here if you choose Group Total reports as a report type. However, with the Multi-Column reports, this information is asked for as a fourth step. The third step asks for the number of columns to be included in the report.)

6. The next dialog box asks about the orientation of the report: Horizontal or Vertical. For this example, choose Vertical. (If you are creating a Group Total report, you are asked which field should be used as the basis for the grouping.)

7. The next dialog box asks which field should serve as the basis for the sort. This dialog box enables you to sort the report's output by specified fields. For the example, sort according to Custid by clicking the Custid field and clicking the right arrow button. Leave the default of ascending order selected, and click Next.

8. The next dialog box is the last you'll see as a part of the report's design process. By default, the report has the title Buyers (which is the same name as the underlying table). This can be changed if simply by backspacing and typing the new name. (Note that this name is not the filename that the report is saved under; rather, it simply serves as a title that appears on the first page of the report.) Enter Buyers Report as the title for the report. Also in this dialog box, you have the option of saving the report for later use, saving and printing the report, or modifying the report with the Report Writer tool. For this example, click the Save and Print the Report option.

9. When prompted for a filename to save the report under, save the report as BUYERSEG.

Regarding the overall process of creating a report with the Report Wizard, note that the Group/Total reports differs from the example report shown previously at step 5 as well. With Group/Total reports, this step sets different grouping options. Fields can be grouped according to the entire contents of each field, by first character, or the first two or three characters.

For example, If you grouped Sutton, Sanders, and Swanson, each of the names would appear in their own group. On the other hand, if you grouped by first letter, these names would appear in the same group. Numeric fields, by default, constitute each number a separate group. But if you choose to group by 20s, then 1-19 would appear as one group.

Producing Simple Reports from the Command Window

Another common way to produce reports in FoxPro is by entering commands. You can use the LIST and DISPLAY commands to generate simple listings of data. You also can use the REPORT FORM command to produce a report based on a report that was saved previously.

The LIST Command

The LIST command is one way of producing a simple report. The LIST... TO PRINTER command produces a simple columnar listing, with the output sent to the active window and to the default installed printer. The format of this command is as follows:

```
LIST [field1,field2..fieldn] TO PRINT
```

As an example, enter this command in the Command Window:

```
LIST CUSTID, LASTNAME, CITY, STATE TO PRINT
```

This command prints all the customer ID numbers, last names, cities, and states. If a laser printer is used, it may be necessary to enter the eject command to cause the paper to feed out of the printer.

You can also be more specific and add a FOR condition to the list to produce a more exact report. As an example, consider the following command:

```
LIST LASTNAME, FIRSTNAME, CUSTID FOR LASTNAME = "Jones" TO PRINT
```

This prints the last and first names, and customer ID numbers of the two buyers named Jones. As another example, a report can also be produced with only the customers with more than eight purchases with the following command:

```
LIST CUSTID, LASTNAME, PURCHASES FOR PURCHASES > 8
```

These are the results:

Record#	Custid	Lastname	Purchases
1	101	Roberts	11
2	102	Sanderson	25
4	104	Jones	12
6	106	Jones	12
8	108	O'Neill	14
9	109	Bannerton	16

At times it may be necessary to print a report using a condition based on a date field. This can be done using curly braces surrounding the date. For example, this command:

```
LIST CUSTID, LASTNAME, SINCE FOR SINCE<= {08/15/92} TO PRINT
```

lists the following records:

Record#	Custid	Lastname	Since
1	101	Roberts	03/12/92
2	102	Sanderson	06/17/89
4	104	Jones	11/22/89
7	107	Zeibermann	08/15/92
8	108	O'Neill	10/02/91
9	109	Bannerton	04/15/90

In this example, all of the dates in the SINCE field are prior or equal to 08/15/92.

Other conditions can be added to make the report even more in specific:

```
LIST CUSTID, LASTNAME, SINCE FOR SINCE <= {08/15/92} . And. STATE = "VA" TO PRINT
```

This command prints all the records with a date in the SINCE field before 08/15/92, who are residents of Virginia.

The REPORT FORM Command

The Report Form command can be used to produce stored reports. The syntax for the command is as follows:

```
REPORT FORM FILENAME [scope] [FOR expression] [WHILE expression] [TO PRINT/TO filename]
[PLAIN] [SUMMARY] [ NOEJECT] [HEADING "character expression"] [ENVIRONMENT]
```

The FOR and WHILE options let you specify conditions that control which reports are printed. Adding the TO PRINT option routes the output to the printer. The TO FILE option directs the report to a text file (the TO PRINT and the TO FILE clauses cannot be used at the same time).

The PLAIN option prints a report with no standard heading. The SUMMARY option is used to print reports with summary fields only. The NOEJECT option suppresses the formfeed codes that are normally sent to the printer. Custom headings can be added with the HEADING option, followed by a character expression. (The character expressions must be placed in quotation marks.)

The Environment option tells FoxPro to reestablish any environment that was saved when the report was saved. (The environment information records whether any filter is in effect, which fields are available through any use of the SET FIELDS command, and any relationships with other files. When a file is saved, the environment is saved also to a view file under the same name as the report (assuming you answer "Yes" to the "Save Environment?" question that appears when you save the report). This option saves you the trouble of opening a database and corresponding index files before printing the report.

Problems with Reports

As with any area of complex computer software, problems can arise in the printing of reports. Two of the most common problems, and their possible solutions, are described here:

Why Do I Get Extra Blank Pages Between Each Page?

This common printing problem occurs when the report's design surface is so large that it extends beyond the size of the printed page. The default settings for a report (visible in the dialog box when you choose File/Print Setup) are portrait orientation and 1-inch margins an all four sides. Subtract the margins from a standard 8 $1/2$-inch by 11-inch sheet of paper, and you are left with a *printable area* of 6 $1/2$ inches across, and 9 inches from top to bottom. (Users of international paper sizes must make the same type of calculations, subtracting the number of centimeters used by the margins from the paper size to come up with a printable area.) If the length or width of your report exceeds this printable area, FoxPro prints whatever portion of the report it could not fit on the original page onto an additional page. This is true even when the excess area contains no objects. FoxPro prints as many pages as are needed to display the full length and width of the report. When the excess area contains no objects, what you get is a blank page on every other page of the report. To remedy this situation, open the report in design mode and pull in the right and bottom edges of the design surface as much as possible. If the design surface is as small as possible and you still have the problem when printing the report, choose Report/Page Layout from the menus, and make sure that the margins are correct for your paper size. With most laser printers, you can reduce the margins from the 1-inch default to one-half inch on all sides, and still contain the data in the printer's limits of printable area.

> **TIP**
>
> You can save paper by performing a print preview to check for this problem before printing a newly designed report for the first time. Preview the report, and click the Next Record button in the navigation area at the bottom of the print preview window. If every other page is blank, you can go back into design mode and reduce the size of the report as necessary to solve this problem.

Why Is My Printer Printing Garbage, or Nothing at All?

If what you get bears absolutely no resemblance to what you see, chances are the problem lies outside of FoxPro. If the printer name that appears near the top of the Print dialog box doesn't match the printer that's connected to your computer, choose File/Print Setup from the menus, click the Specific Printer button, and make sure the correct printer is selected in the list box. Choose OK, and try the File/Print command again. If the correct printer is selected and you still can't print or the printing is garbage, the problem is likely to be in Windows itself, or in how it is installed on your system. FoxPro uses the Windows software (specifically, the Windows Print Manager) to manage all printing. If you can't print from another Windows application (like Notepad), you won't be able to print from FoxPro. If you can't print from any application in Windows, check the obvious: make sure the printer is properly connected, turned on, and on-line. Also, verify that you can print from the operating system itself (if you are running Windows atop a version of MS-DOS).

Chapter Summary

This chapter provided an introduction to reports, with an emphasis on the tools (such as the AutoReport button and the Report Wizards) you can use to quickly create a variety of reports. Chapter 12 gives much more detail, as well as additional coverage of more advanced reporting topics.

2

PART

Advanced FoxPro

Working with FoxPro's Relational Powers

This chapter details different ways in which you can take advantage of FoxPro's relational capabilities. FoxPro provides three different methods you can use to establish relationships. You can relate tables by building relational queries through the RQBE Window (introduced in Chapter 6, "Performing Queries with RQBE"). You can use FoxPro's View Window to establish relationships. You also can use the SET RELATION command—a method familiar to many XBase veterans. This chapter covers all three methods.

While you can use any methods you prefer, FoxPro is likely to provide better overall performance if you use the RQBE facility to design relational queries. The reason is that the SQL SELECT statements generated by the queries are automatically optimized with FoxPro's Rushmore technology. With the other methods, Rushmore only benefits performance if you open the necessary index files that optimize performance. With queries created in the RQBE facility, this is done automatically.

Relationships, Explained

The establishment of relationships is a fundamental part of *normalization*. Normalization (for those not schooled in the art of database design) is the process by which unnecessary redundancies in database design are eliminated. When working with relational databases, the normalization process helps you identify which data should be stored in which tables. To get the best results from the designs of your relational queries and the designs of your tables, it helps to have a firm idea, on paper or mentally, of how the tables should be laid out, and how relationships should be drawn whether done with queries or commands. Different types of relationships are possible in FoxPro, and you may want to take advantage of that fact in establishing the links in different ways between the fields of your tables.

In a relational database manager like FoxPro, you can have three different relationship types. They are *one-to-one*, *one-to-many*, and *many-to-many*. When one field of a single record within a table relates to one (and only one) record of another table, you have a one-to-one relationship. This kind of relationship is common in human resource or personnel management systems, because you often have a great deal of data split among different tables that concerns individual employees. One record in a table may contain an employee's ID number and all of the salary data for that employee. A corresponding record in another table may contain the employee's ID number and all health benefit information for that employee. The relationship between the two records in the two tables is a one-to-one relationship. Figure 10.1 illustrates the one-to-one type of relationship.

By far the most common type of relationship is the one-to-many relationship. With this type of relationship, one record in the first table relates to one or more records in the second table. A classic example of this type of relationship is customers and their orders in any order-entry system. A single customer may have many different orders in the system. (See Figure 10.2.) One record in the customers table has many matching records in the orders table. The records are linked on the basis of the Customer ID field, which is the common field between the two tables.

FIGURE 10.1.

A one-to-one relationship.

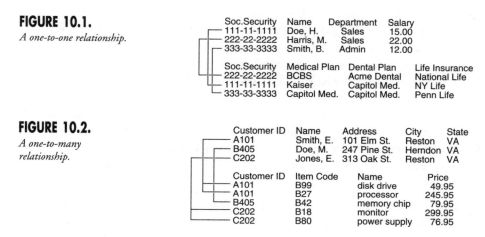

FIGURE 10.2.

A one-to-many relationship.

The third type of relationship is not as common as the first or second, but nevertheless arises from time to time. It is the many-to-many relationship. (See Figure 10.3.) With a many-to-many relationship, a field in several records in one table relates to a field in several records in another table. A typical example is the case of items in an inventory table and a table of suppliers for those items. The inventory table contains many items which come from one or more suppliers, and each supplier may provide more than one item. Many-to-many relationships are established through the use of "linking" tables.

FIGURE 10.3.

A many-to-many relationship.

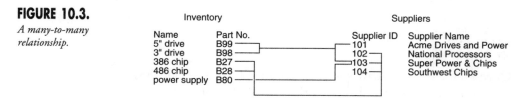

Following the example of many inventory items having many suppliers, an inventory table may contain the data about each item in the inventory, coded with a unique Stock Number for each item. Another table contains the name, address, and phone number of each supplier. In that table, a unique Supplier ID number is assigned to each supplier. To link the tables and create the many-to-many relationship, there must be another table containing just two fields: Stock Number and Supplier ID. The third table serves as the intermediate, or "linking" table between the other two tables, which contain the "many" data. When relating tables, it is always advantageous to have fields containing unique data so that relationships can be easily established.

About FoxPro and Work Areas

Whether you generate relational data by means of a query, through the View Window, or with SET RELATION commands, FoxPro manages things behind the scenes by opening tables in multiple work area. If you are using the SET RELATION command to establish relationships between tables, an understanding of the concept of work areas is a must. Even if you stick with the RQBE Window or the View Window to relate tables, it helps to understand what FoxPro is doing with work areas so that you know where to find the data you need. FoxPro can have up to 225 tables open at once, and each open table is held in a separate work area. By default, the work areas are numbered from 1 through 225. Work areas can also be given "alias" names which are more descriptive than the numbers. If no alias is assigned, each area assumes an alias that is the same as the name of the table, after the table is opened in that work area.

When a table is initially opened, FoxPro opens the file in work area 1 unless told otherwise. If you use RQBE to compose your relational queries, you need not worry about which work areas are chosen because FoxPro does this automatically. If you use the View Window (described later in this chapter), you can select work areas by number by clicking on the desired number in a list box shown in the View Window. From the Command Window, you'll choose work with the SELECT command, the syntax of which is

```
SELECT work area number[ALIASalias name]
```

Once the SELECT command is used to choose a work area, the desired table is opened. As an example, to open two table files ("Buyers" and "Donation") in work areas 1 and 2, these commands would be appropriate:

```
SELECT 1
USE BUYERS
SELECT 2
USE DONATION
```

Once a number of files have been opened, any file can be made the active file by selecting that work area, by its number or by the alias name. For example,

```
SELECT 2
```

makes the "Donation" table active, while the command

```
SELECT BUYERS
```

makes the "Buyers" table the active one. The active table is the table which is directly affected by FoxPro commands, such as APPEND, LIST, LOCATE, and so on. The portion of this chapter titled "Using the SET RELATION Command" further explores how you can use work areas and other commands at the command level to establish relationships between tables.

Creating Relational Queries with RQBE

Chapter 7, "Queries with Commands," discussed the use of the RQBE Window to create queries that can provide selected data for use in Browse windows, or in reports and labels. You can create queries of a relational nature, by using the Tables portion of the RQBE Window to add as many tables as are needed to the query. Each time you add a table, an RQBE Join Condition dialog box lets you define the relationship between the tables. To create a relational query using the RQBE Window, you open the first table you want to use, and start a new query (by choosing File, New and selecting Query then New in the dialog box, or by entering CREATE QUERY in the Command Window). With either of these steps, a new query appears in the RQBE Window. (See Figure 10.4.)

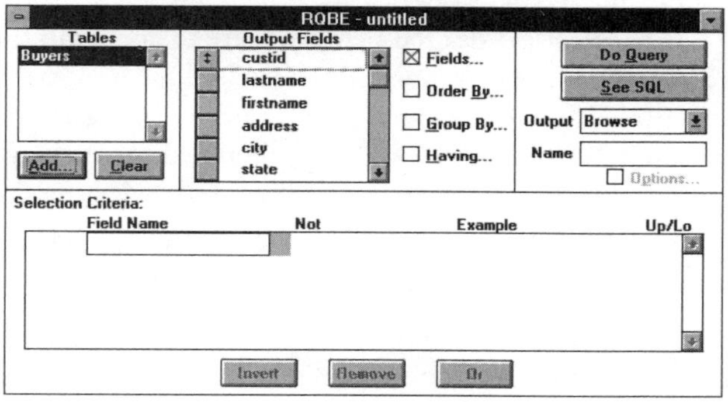

FIGURE 10.4.

The RQBE Query Window.

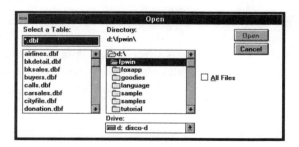

You then perform the following steps:

1. Click the Add button under the Tables list. The Open dialog box appears. (See Figure 10.5.)

FIGURE 10.5.

The Open dialog box.

2. Click the table you wish to add to the query, then click Open. The RQBE Join Condition dialog box appears. (See Figure 10.6.)

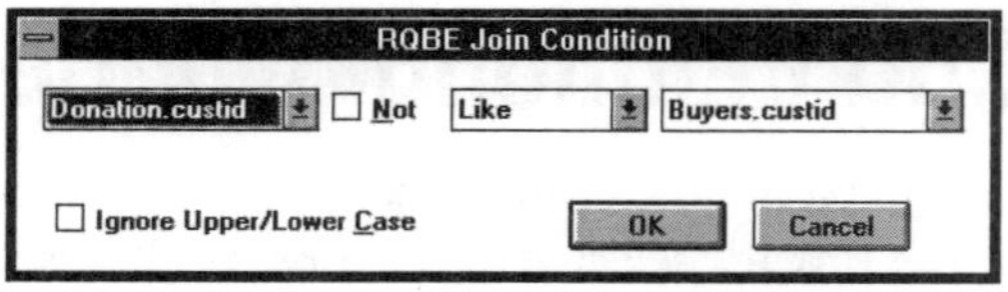

FIGURE 10.6.

The RQBE Join Condition dialog box.

3. In the Fields list boxes, choose the common field in both tables that is used to establish a link between the tables. (If two fields of the same name and same type exist in both tables, FoxPro automatically selects these fields in the list box, but you can change these defaults as desired.) The default of "Like" in the center of the dialog box should remain unchanged when relating tables with RQBE.

4. Repeat steps 2 and 3 for any additional tables that you want to add to the query.

5. Click the Fields check box to display the Select Fields dialog box. Use this dialog box to select the desired fields that are to appear in the query. (By default, all fields from the first table in the Tables list box appear in the Output Fields portion of the dialog box.) You can click the Fields check box and then click Remove All to remove all fields, then add the desired fields from both tables to the Selected Output list box. When done selecting the desired fields, click OK.

6. Fill in any other desired options for the query and choose a destination for the query's output in the Output list box. Click OK to run the query.

While the process sounds simple (and it is), it is important to note that correct results are dependent on effective database design. Your tables must have fields with matching data that can be used to establish the relationship, and the relationship must make sense for the query to yield the proper results. (This is just one more reason why the design of relational databases is not something to be taken lightly.)

An Example: Creating a Query Based on Two Tables

Assuming the BUYERS.DBF and DONATION.DBF tables have been copied from the accompanying disk to the working directory of your hard drive, you can perform the following steps to create a query that retrieves the names of persons in the Buyers table, and of donations associated with those persons stored in the Donations table:

1. Choose File, Open. Click BUYERS.DBF in the Open dialog box, then click Open to open the table.

2. Choose File, New. In the New dialog box, click Query, then click New to open a new query in the RQBE Window.

3. Under the Tables list box in the RQBE Window, click the Add button to add a second table to the list of tables used by the query. The Open dialog box again appears.

4. Click DONATION.DBF to select it, then click Open. At this point, the RQBE Join Condition dialog box appears (shown previously in Figure 10.6). Note that by default, FoxPro has assumed that the field called CUSTID in the Donations table should be linked to the field called CUSTID in the Buyers table. Since the fields have the same name and are of the same type, this is a logical assumption on FoxPro's part. In cases where FoxPro makes a wrong assumption, you can manually choose the desired field to establish the relational link by clicking the arrows in the list boxes, and selecting the matching fields.

5. Click OK to accept FoxPro's suggestion for the matching fields and close the dialog box. When you do so, the condition used to establish the relationship

```
Donation.custid Like Buyers.custid
```

appears in the Selection Criteria portion of the RQBE Window. (See Figure 10.7).

FIGURE 10.7.

The RQBE Window containing criteria used to relate tables.

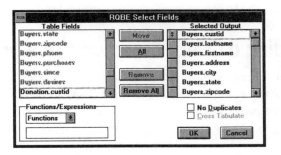

6. Click the Fields check box. The RQBE Select Fields dialog box appears. (See Figure 10.8).

FIGURE 10.8.

The RQBE Select Fields dialog box.

7. Click the Remove All button to remove all fields from the Selected Output list.

8. In the Table Fields list, double-click the following fields, one by one, to add them to the Selected Output list: Buyers.lastname, Buyers.firstname, Donation.date, and Donation.amount. Click OK.
9. With the Output set to Browse. click Do Query. The result (see Figure 10.9) shows the related data from the Buyers and Donations tables.

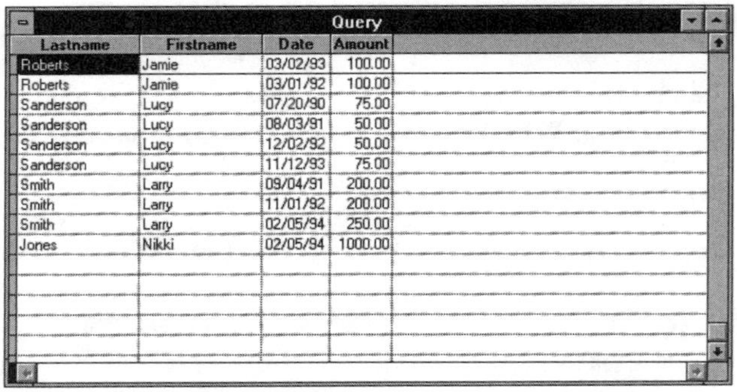

Lastname	Firstname	Date	Amount
Roberts	Jamie	03/02/93	100.00
Roberts	Jamie	03/01/92	100.00
Sanderson	Lucy	07/20/90	75.00
Sanderson	Lucy	08/03/91	50.00
Sanderson	Lucy	12/02/92	50.00
Sanderson	Lucy	11/12/93	75.00
Smith	Larry	09/04/91	200.00
Smith	Larry	11/01/92	200.00
Smith	Larry	02/05/94	250.00
Jones	Nikki	02/05/94	1000.00

FIGURE 10.9.
The results of the first relational query.

The key to retrieving the data from both tables simultaneously was the relational link, based on the CUSTID field. Note that the field used for the link need not appear in the query's output (it does not in this case). It is only important that FoxPro knows which field to use. You can see that FoxPro has used the CUSTID field if you examine the SQL statement generated by the query. If you close the query's Browse window and click the See SQL button in the RQBE Window, the SQL statement shown resembles the following:

```
SELECT Buyers.lastname, Buyers.firstname, Donation.date, Donation.amount;
 FROM Buyers, Donation;
 WHERE Donation.custid = Buyers.custid
```

and the WHERE clause at the end of the statement links the data, based on the matching CUSTID fields.

Building a Query Based on Three Tables

You can add more tables where necessary, to provide the data you need within a relational query. As an example, you can copy the BKSALES.DBF and BKDETAIL.DBF files from the accompanying disk into your working directory. The tables contain the following data, which you link by means of a query to show which books were ordered by which individuals:

(BKSALES.DBF)

CUSTID	DATE	INVID
101	03/02/94	901
101	03/07/94	905
101	04/02/94	908
104	03/04/94	902
104	04/01/94	907
107	03/05/94	903
105	03/06/94	904
103	03/08/94	906

(BKDETAIL.DBF)

INVID	TITLE	QUANTITY	PRICE
901	OS/2 Unleashed	1	34.95
901	FoxPro Unleashed	1	34.95
902	Access Unleashed	2	34.95
903	Teach Yourself Access	1	24.95
904	OS/2 Unleashed	1	34.95
904	FoxPro Unleashed	1	34.95
904	Corel Draw Unleashed	2	39.95
905	Teach Yourself C Programming	1	24.95
906	Teach Yourself FoxPro	1	24.95
906	FoxPro Unleashed	2	34.95
906	Access Unleashed	1	34.95
907	Teach Yourself C Programming	2	24.95
907	OS/2 Unleashed	1	34.95
908	Teach Yourself Access	1	24.95
908	Corel Draw Unleashed	1	39.95

In this case, what is needed is a relationship between the three tables. (See Figure 10.10).

FIGURE 10.10.

The relationship between three tables.

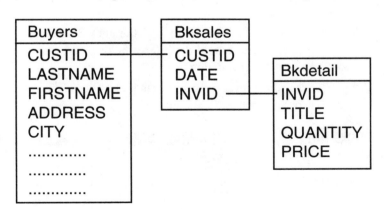

You can illustrate the kind of query needed to produce the data by closing the previous query (there is no need to save it), and performing the following steps:

1. If the Buyers table is not already open, choose File, Open, and click BUYERS.DBF in the Open dialog box, then click Open to open the table.

2. Choose File, New. In the New dialog box, click Query, then click New to open a new query in the RQBE Window.

3. Under the Tables list box in the RQBE Window, click the Add button to add a second table to the list of tables used by the query. The Open dialog box appears.

4. Click BKSALES.DBF to select it, then click Open.

5. The RQBE Join Condition dialog box that appears (shown previously in Figure 10.3) shows the common fields in both tables, by displaying the list box choices of "Bksales.custid Like Buyers.custid." Click OK to accept this setting.

6. Under the Tables list box in the RQBE Window, again click the Add button to open the Open dialog box so you can add a third table to the list of tables used by the query.

7. Click BKDETAIL.DBF to select it, then click Open.

8. The RQBE Join Condition dialog box which appears shows the common fields in these tables, by displaying the list box choices of "Bkdetail.invid Like Bksales.invid." Click OK to accept this setting.

9. In the Output Fields portion of the dialog box, click the Fields check box to display the RQBE Select Fields dialog box (shown previously in Figure 10.8).

10. Click Remove All to remove all fields from the query.

11. Double-click Buyers.Lastname and Buyers.Firstname to add these fields to the query.

12. Scroll down in the list box, and double-click Bksales.Date, to add this field to the query.

13. Scroll down in the list box, and double-click Bkdetail.Title, Bkdetail.Quantity, and Bkdetail.Price to add these three fields to the query. Click OK to close the RQBE Select Fields dialog box.

14. With the Output set to Browse, click Do Query. The results of the query appear in a Browse window. (See Figure 10.11.)

FIGURE 10.11.

The results of a query based on three tables in the Browse window.

Lastname	Firstname	Date	Title	Quantity	Price
Roberts	Jamie	03/02/94	OS/2 Unleashed	1	34.95
Roberts	Jamie	03/02/94	FoxPro Unleashed	1	34.95
Jones	Nikki	03/04/94	Access Unleashed	2	34.95
Zeibermann	Daniel	03/05/94	Teach Yourself Access	1	24.95
Hernandez	Maria	03/06/94	OS/2 Unleashed	1	34.95
Hernandez	Maria	03/06/94	FoxPro Unleashed	1	34.95
Hernandez	Maria	03/06/94	Corel Draw Unleashed	2	39.95
Roberts	Jamie	03/07/94	Teach Yourself C Programming	1	24.95
Smith	Larry	03/08/94	Teach Yourself FoxPro	1	24.95
Smith	Larry	03/08/94	FoxPro Unleashed	2	34.95
Smith	Larry	03/08/94	Access Unleashed	1	34.95
Jones	Nikki	04/01/94	Teach Yourself C Programming	2	24.95
Jones	Nikki	04/01/94	OS/2 Unleashed	1	34.95
Roberts	Jamie	04/02/94	Teach Yourself Access	1	24.95
Roberts	Jamie	04/02/94	Corel Draw Unleashed	1	39.95

You can see how a report based on the query can be quickly created, if you perform the following additional steps:

1. Close the Browse window, and change the choice under Output to Report/Label, then click the Options check box.

2. In the RQBE Display Options dialog box that appears, click Report. Then click the Quick Report button, and click OK in the Quick Report dialog box which appears to select the default options for the report.

3. Click OK in the RQBE Display Options dialog box to put away the dialog box.

4. Click Do Query. This time, a quick report containing the data appears in Page Preview mode.

5. When done previewing the report, choose File, Save from the menus. In the Save As dialog box that appears, call the new query BOOKS. Press Save, then press Ctrl+F4 to close the query window.

Using the View Window

Tables can also be related by means of FoxPro's View Window. For those who are familiar with menu-driven methods of working with tables in dBASE III Plus or dBASE IV, the View Window may be the most comfortable way of relating tables. However, it can be more awkward than the use of the RQBE Window, particularly with complex relationships. The tables must be indexed on the fields that are the basis of the relationship. In this respect, using the View Window differs significantly from the RQBE Window, which establishes any needed indexes automatically. If you are comfortable with the use of the RQBE Window to relate tables as discussed previously, you may choose to ignore this method of relating tables.

Close all open tables (you can enter CLEAR ALL in the Command Window to do this), then choose Window, View to open the View Window. (See Figure 10.12.) Notice there is a Toolbox on the left, and 225 work areas available in a list box.

FIGURE 10.12.

The View Window.

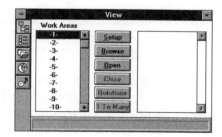

As an example, you can see how establishing relationships can be done in the View Window by performing the following steps:

1. Choose Open from the buttons in the center of the View Window.

2. Open the Buyers table in work area 1 by selecting it in the dialog box that appears and clicking Open.

3. Click work area 2 to select it.

4. Again, click Open. Select and open the Donation table.

   Now both tables are shown in their work areas. (See Figure 10.13.) At present, the Donation file is highlighted. This means it is the active table. Click Buyers to make it the active table. (This is done, because the table you are setting the relationship *out of* must be the active table.) At this point, you can establish the relationship between the two tables.

FIGURE 10.13.

The View Window with two tables open in separate work areas.

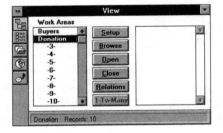

5. Click the Relations button in the center of the window. The table you selected as the parent table (Buyers) appears in the right portion of the dialog box, with a line pointing down and to the right.

6. Click Donation to select it as the child table. Next you see the Set Index Order box. This appears because no index was chosen. Choose Donation: CUSTID and click OK. The Expression Builder appears. Since the CUSTID field matches a field in the Buyers table, this field appears automatically in the Set Relation text box.

7. Since this is the desired field for the relationship, choose OK from the Expression Builder. The Donation table appears below the Buyers table in the right window of the View Window. (See Figure 10.14.)

With the Buyers table highlighted in the View Window, click the Browse button, then press Ctrl+F1 to return to the View menu. Select Donation from the Work Areas List Box and click Browse. Using the sizing techniques of Windows, move and size the windows as needed so the two of them can be viewed at once. Then switch to the parent table, Buyers, if you are not already there. As you move the cursor in the Buyers table you see the effects of the relationship. The Donation table changes as you select a record in the Buyers table, showing all the donations made by a certain person in the Buyers table. (See Figure 10.15.)

FIGURE 10.14.

The View Window with the relationship established.

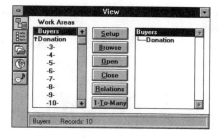

FIGURE 10.15.

The effects of the relationship shown in the Browse windows.

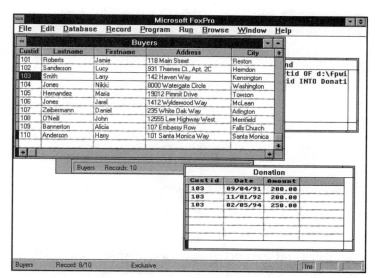

You can further demonstrate the effects of the relationship by switching to the Command Window and entering the following commands:

```
LIST BUYERS .LASTNAME, DONATION.DATE, DONATION.AMOUNT
```

The following is the result:

```
Record#   Buyers.LASTNAME  Donation.DATE    Donation.AMOUNT
      1   Roberts          03/02/93                  100.00
      2   Sanderson        07/20/90                   75.00
      3   Smith            09/04/91                  200.00
      4   Jones            02/05/94                 1000.00
```

```
5   Hernandez          /  /                0.00
6   Jones              /  /                0.00
7   Zeibermann         /  /                0.00
8   O'Neill            /  /                0.00
9   Bannerton          /  /                0.00
```

These same techniques can be used to generate reports. Don't forget that the relation must be established before the report can be generated. A section of Chapter 11, "Designing and Customizing Screens," covers the use of commands after a relation has been established.

Using the SET RELATION Command

Relationships are established at the command level with the use of the SET RELATION command. SET RELATION draws a relationship between a key field that is common to two or more tables, as illustrated here:

```
Customer.DBF
============
   CNAME
   CADDR1
   CADDR2            Orders.DBF
   CCITY             ============
   CSTATE               ITEMCODE
   CZIP                 DESCRIPT
   CPHONE               COLOR
   ACCTNUMB<========>ACCTNUMB
                        STYLE
```

The syntax for the SET RELATION command is

```
SET RELATION TO expression INTO alias
```

If, for example, the CUSTOMER table with the structure shown previously is open in work area 1 and the ORDERS table is open in work area 2, the SET RELATION command can be used to link the common field, ACCTNUMB. This means that whenever the record pointer is moved to a record in the ORDERS file, the record pointer in the CUSTOMER file is moved to the record containing the same account number. The file in the second work area must be indexed on the field or expression used to link the files, before the SET RELATION command can be used. The following example shows the effects of the SET RELATION command:

```
SELECT 1
USE CUSTOMER
INDEX ON ACCTNUMB TAG CUSTACC
SELECT 2
USE ORDERS
INDEX ON ACCTNUMB TAG ORDACC
SET RELATION TO ACCTNUMB INTO CUSTOMER
```

```
GO 3
DISPLAY
Record#   CUSTACCT DESCRIPT                      STOCKNO  PRICE
       3      1001 BrillaSol Super VGA Monitor      2523 179.90

SELECT CUSTOMER
DISPLAY CUSTNAME, CUSTACCT

Record#   CUSTNAME          CUSTACCT
       1  Smith, Jason          1001

 SELECT SALES
 GO 5
 DISPLAY

Record#   CUSTACCT DESCRIPT                      STOCKNO  PRICE
       5      1003 MS DOS Version 6.0             5117 249.95

 SELECT CUSTOMER
 DISPLAY CUSTNAME, CUSTACCT

Record#   CUSTNAME          CUSTACCT
       3  Richards, Jayne       1003
```

And reports could be designed which would produce the desired data from the linked tables once the SET RELATION command had been put into effect.

TIP

When you use SET RELATION to establish a relationship, it directly establishes a one-to-one relationship. This means that for each record accessed in the parent table, the record pointer in the child table moves to the first matching record. If you are working with a one-to-many relationship and accessing records by means of commands or with program code, you also need to use the SET SKIP command to indicate the presence of a one-to-many relationship. For details, see "Using SET SKIP" under the following subheading.

When multiple tables are in use by a program, fields from different tables can be specified within a command by giving the alias name for the work area, then an alias marker (which is a period (.)), then the name of the field. For example, the expression

```
CUSTOMER.CUSTCITY
```

would refer the CUSTCITY field in the customer table, even if it is in a different work area than the selected area. Consider the following program, and the results:

```
SELECT 1
USE CUSTOMER
INDEX ON CUSTACCT TAG CUSTACC
SELECT 2
USE SALES
```

```
INDEX ON CUSTACCT TAG SALESACC
SET RELATION TO CUSTACCT INTO CUSTOMER
LIST DESCRIPT, STOCKNO, PRICE, CUSTOMER.CUSTNAME, CUSTOMER.CUSTCITY

Hayes Smartcom software          4540 190.50 Leopold, Alvin    Queens
Prog. Ref. Guide to FoxPro       3009  39.95 Leopold, Alvin    Queens
BrillaSol Super VGA Monitor      2523 179.90 Smith,   Jason    Reston
MS DOS Version 6.0               5117 249.95 Sweeney, Eileen   Salem
MS DOS Version 6.0               5117 249.95 Richards, Jim     Raleigh
Ultimate Pack Rat software       2085  49.90 Richards, Jim     Raleigh
```

In the example, the LIST command is listing data simultaneously from two tables. Because the CUSTNAME and CUSTCITY fields are not contained within the active table, they must be identified with an alias name—in this case, CUSTOMER. Once a relation has been established with the SET RELATION command, alias names can then be used to indicate any field within the related tables. Alias names can also be used within expressions you place within the designs of your reports and mailing labels.

For example, in the case of our SALES and CUSTOMER tables, a columnar report containing customer name, account number, description, stock number, and price may be desired. The customer name and account number fields are contained within the CUSTOMER table, while the account number, description, stock number, and price fields are contained within the SALES table.

The four fields in the active table, CUSTACCT, DESCRIPT, STOCKNO, and PRICE, could be selected from the fields list when designing the report. Since the fifth field, CUSTNAME, is not in the active table but is in the related table open in the other work area, it can be referenced in a report, by using the fieldname along with the alias and pointer (.) symbol in the expression used in a report.

In the example report, the following expression was used as the field in the "customer name" column of the report:

```
CUSTOMER.CUSTNAME
```

Once the report has been created, use the SET RELATION and SELECT commands within the program to open the desired tables and draw the relation between the tables; then, use the REPORT FORM command to run the report. A sample program, using the following commands, provides this report:

```
SELECT 1
USE CUSTOMER
SET ORDER TO ACCOUNTS
SELECT 2
USE SALES
SET RELATION TO CUSTACCT INTO CUSTOMER
REPORT FORM RELATE TO PRINT
```

```
07/10/93
                              Relational Report
                              Uses Data From
                              Sales and Customer
                                  Tables.

Account Customer Name    Item Description            Stock    Cost
Number                                               Number

  1002 Leopold, Alvin    Hayes Smartcom software      4540  190.50
  1002 Leopold, Alvin    Prog. Ref. Guide to FoxPro   3009   39.95
  1001 Smith, Jason      BrillaSol Super VGA Monitor  2523  179.90
  1004 Sweeney, Eileen   MS DOS Version 6.0           5117  249.95
  1003 Richards, Jim     MS DOS Version 6.0           5117  249.95
  1003 Richards, Jim     Ultimate Pack Rat software   2085   49.90

*** Total ***

                                                            960.15
```

In the example described here, the listing and the report produce the desired results, because the previous relationship is a one-to-one relationship: for each sale in the sales table, there is one corresponding customer name in the customer table. One-to-many relationships, on the other hand, require the use of the SET SKIP command.

Using SET SKIP

Along with the SET RELATION command, the SET SKIP command is a vital tool when working with one-to-many relationships, and you need to access all the records in the child or "many" table that match the key value in the parent or "one" table. Think of the SET SKIP command as the way you identify one-to-many relationships when working from the command level or within program code in FoxPro. The problem with SET RELATION when used alone is that it creates a one-to-one relationship—for each record in the parent table, the record pointer in the child table moves to the first occurrence of a record with a matching key. With one-to-many relationships, the child table often contains multiple records that correspond to a single record in the parent table. By using the SET SKIP command after the SET RELATION command, you establish that the relationship is a one-to-many relationship. Then, as you move through the parent table, the record pointer stays on the same parent record until the record pointer in the child table moves through all the associated records. (The example of the Browse command in the following section visually demonstrates this effect.) The syntax for the SET SKIP command is

```
SET SKIP TO [alias1[alias2...aliasx]]
```

where each *alias* is the table or alias name for the related table. (The SET SKIP command is issued from the work area where the parent table is open.) In cases where one parent table is related to more than one child table, you can specify multiple alias names, separated by commas, to specify relationships with each child table. Assuming you have the Buyers and Donation tables on your system, and the Donation table has an index tag based on the CUSTID field, you can duplicate the problem with SET RELATION alone with commands like the following:

```
USE DONATION IN 2 ORDER CUSTID
USE BUYERS IN 1
SELECT BUYERS
SET RELATION TO CUSTID INTO DONATION
LIST LASTNAME, FIRSTNAME, DONATION.DATE, DONATION.AMOUNT
```

When you enter the commands, the resultant listing resembles the following:

	LASTNAME	FIRSTNAME	Donation.DATE	Donation.AMOUNT
1	Roberts	Jamie	03/02/93	100.00
2	Sanderson	Lucy	07/20/90	75.00
3	Smith	Larry	09/04/91	200.00
4	Jones	Nikki	02/05/94	1000.00
5	Hernandez	Maria	/ /	0.00
6	Jones	Jarel	/ /	0.00
7	Zeibermann	Daniel	/ /	0.00
8	O'Neill	John	/ /	0.00
9	Bannerton	Alicia	/ /	0.00
10	*Anderson	Harry	/ /	0.00

The problem is, all the donations for each person in the Buyers table don't appear, because only the first record in the child table is accessed with the SET RELATION command alone. But if you enter the following commands, to add the effects of SET SKIP and to repeat the listing:

```
SET SKIP TO DONATION
LIST LASTNAME, FIRSTNAME, DONATION.DATE, DONATION.AMOUNT
```

The results of the listing this time:

	LASTNAME	FIRSTNAME	Donation.DATE	Donation.AMOUNT
1	Roberts	Jamie	03/02/93	100.00
1	Roberts	Jamie	03/01/92	100.00
2	Sanderson	Lucy	07/20/90	75.00
2	Sanderson	Lucy	08/03/91	50.00
2	Sanderson	Lucy	12/02/92	50.00
2	Sanderson	Lucy	11/12/93	75.00
3	Smith	Larry	09/04/91	200.00
3	Smith	Larry	11/01/92	200.00
3	Smith	Larry	02/05/94	250.00
4	Jones	Nikki	02/05/94	1000.00
5	Hernandez	Maria	/ /	0.00
6	Jones	Jarel	/ /	0.00
7	Zeibermann	Daniel	/ /	0.00
8	O'Neill	John	/ /	0.00
9	Bannerton	Alicia	/ /	0.00
10	*Anderson	Harry	/ /	0.00

show the effects of the SET SKIP command, with all associated child table records (in this case, donations made) shown with each record from the parent table.

Keep in mind that this same technique, the use of SET SKIP after SET RELATION, also is needed before printing stored reports based on a one-to-many relationship. If SET SKIP is not used, the reports displays only the first record from the child table for each record in the parent table. This is one more reason for basing reports where possible on relational queries, as discussed previously in this chapter. When you base a report on the SQL statement that's generated by the RQBE Window, you don't have to concern yourself with setting relations or using commands like SET SKIP; FoxPro pulls the needed data from the needed tables automatically. In defense of SET RELATION and SET SKIP, there are times when advanced FoxPro users need these commands to get around the limitations of RQBE. A prime example is the situation where you have one parent table related to two (or more) child tables simultaneously, and want to pull data from the parent table and from both child tables into a report. This type of task cannot be handled properly through the RQBE Window, no matter how you try to structure the query's design. To do this, you have no choice but to use SET RELATION and SET SKIP commands, whether from the command level or within a FoxPro program.

Showing a One-to-Many Relationship in a Browse Window

One useful application of the SET RELATION and SET SKIP commands is to permit browsing within a one-to-many relationship. As mentioned previously, when SET SKIP is in effect, the record pointer in the parent table stays at a given record until the record pointer in the child table moves through all associated records. Once you have used SET RELATION and SET SKIP to establish the one-to-many relationship, you can use the FIELDS clause of the BROWSE command, along with alias names and field names to name the fields in the related table. Again using the Buyers and Donation tables as an example, the commands used to establish the relationship and open a Browse window could resemble the following:

```
USE DONATIONS IN 2 ORDER CUSTID
USE BUYERS IN 1
SELECT BUYERS
SET RELATION TO CUSTID INTO DONATION
SET SKIP TO DONATION
BROWSE FIELDS CUSTID, LASTNAME, FIRSTNAME, DONATION.DATE, DONATION.AMOUNT
```

The Browse command under these circumstances is shown in Figure 10.16. As shown, fields from the child table (Donation) are blank in cases where the parent table (Buyers) has no associated records in the child table. In cases where the parent table has multiple associated records in the child table, the parent data appears once, and the multiple child records appear.

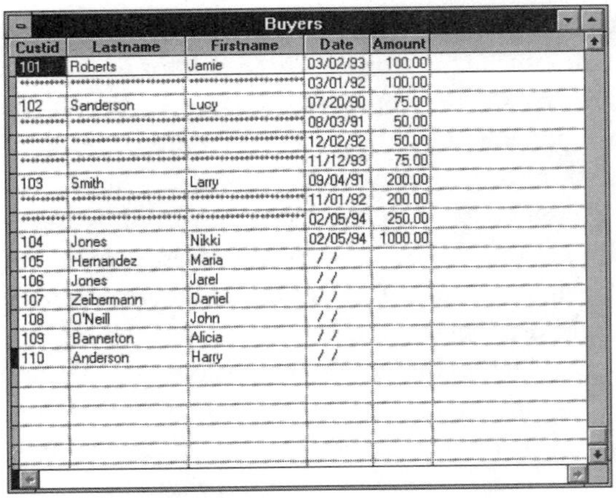

FIGURE 10.16.

The results of Browse with Fields clause after SET SKIP command.

Custid	Lastname	Firstname	Date	Amount
101	Roberts	Jamie	03/02/93	100.00
			03/01/92	100.00
102	Sanderson	Lucy	07/20/90	75.00
			08/03/91	50.00
			12/02/92	50.00
			11/12/93	75.00
103	Smith	Larry	09/04/91	200.00
			11/01/92	200.00
			02/05/94	250.00
104	Jones	Nikki	02/05/94	1000.00
105	Hernandez	Maria	/ /	
106	Jones	Jarel	/ /	
107	Zeibermann	Daniel	/ /	
108	O'Neill	John	/ /	
109	Bannerton	Alicia	/ /	
110	Anderson	Harry	/ /	

Notes About the Use of SET RELATION

The SET RELATION command is not limited to two tables. You can link a number of tables, as long as a common key field exists between any two linked tables. As an example, a customer table might be linked to a sales table by the customer account number; the sales table might be linked to a detailed inventory table by item stock number; and the inventory table might be linked to a table of pricing histories for each item, and also by stock number. Also, SET RELATION works best when you have matching contents in all of the records in the linked tables. If the linked table does not contain an entry matching the index key of the active table, the record pointer of the linked table is positioned at the end of the table, and any attempted retrieval of data returns a blank record.

If you are programming an application and the possibility of not finding a corresponding record exists, you may want to test for an end-of-file condition with an IF EOF() statement in an appropriate location of the program. (For more on programming, see Chapter 19, "FoxPro Programming Basics.") Existing relations may be cleared by using the SET RELATION TO command without specifying any table. You can also use the CLEAR ALL command to clear a relation (and close all open tables). Keep in mind the SET RELATION command takes priority over the SET DELETED ON and SET FILTER commands. Data contained in the related table is accessible, even if the records have been hidden by means of a filter, or marked for deletion. You won't have this problem in the active table (the one you are setting the relation from). In that work area, the SET FILTER and SET DELETED commands operate in a normal manner.

Using CREATE VIEW

FoxPro also provides the ability to create view files, which can save you some time in establishing an environment of related tables that you use regularly. View files are created with the CREATE VIEW *filename* FROM ENVIRONMENT command. A view file can be thought of as a record of all open tables, indexes, and relationships between tables. View files are given an extension of .VUE. When you enter CREATE VIEW FROM ENVIRONMENT in the Command Window or use the command within a program, FoxPro creates a view file based on any tables and indexes currently open and any relations currently specified.

Once a view file has been created, it can be used to establish the working environment at a later time with the SET VIEW TO *filename* command. By creating a view file and repeatedly using the SET VIEW command, you can avoid having to repeatedly select work areas and relations, since all of this information is stored in the view file. Consider the commands used and the listings which resulted in the following example:

```
SELECT 1
USE BUYERS ORDER CUSTID
SELECT 2
USE DONATION ORDER CUSTOMS
SELECT 1
SET RELATION TO CUSTID INTO DONATION
SET SKIP TO DONATION
CREATE VIEW DONATE FROM ENVIRONMENT
DISPLAY STATUS

Processor is 80386
Currently Selected Table:
Select area: 1, Table in Use:   D:\FPWIN\BUYERS.DBF  Alias: BUYERS
          Code page:    0
  Structural CDX file:   D:\FPWIN\BUYERS.CDX
        Index tag:   NAMES     Collate: Machine     Key: LASTNAME
Master Index tag:   CUSTID    Collate: Machine     Key: CUSTID
          Memo file:        D:\FPWIN\BUYERS.FPT
      Lock(s): Exclusive USE
        Related into:    Donation
            Relation:      CUSTID
          1-To-Many:    Donation

Select area: 2, Table in Use:   D:\FPWIN\DONATION.DBF  Alias: DONATION
          Code page:    0
  Structural CDX file:   D:\FPWIN\DONATION.CDX
        Index tag:  CUSTID     Collate: Machine     Key: CUSTID
Master Index tag:  CUSTOMS    Collate: Machine     Key: CUSTID
      Lock(s): Exclusive USE

Press any key to continue...
```

The work areas, open tables, and relation listed by the DISPLAY STATUS command are all contained within the view file, MYSALES.VUE. A CLEAR ALL command results in the closing of the tables and the clearing of the relation, as shown in the example:

```
CLEAR ALL
DISPLAY STATUS


Processor is 80386
File search path: D:\FPWIN
Default directory: D:\FPWIN
....
....
Press any key to continue...
```

Now that the view file exists, it can be used to open the files, work areas, and relations with a single SET VUE command, as shown here:

```
SET VIEW TO MYSALES
DISPLAY STATUS

Processor is 80386
Currently Selected Table:
Select area: 1, Table in Use:   D:\FPWIN\BUYERS.DBF  Alias: BUYERS
            Code page:   0
  Structural CDX file:   D:\FPWIN\BUYERS.CDX
        Index tag:   NAMES     Collate: Machine      Key: LASTNAME
Master Index tag:   CUSTID     Collate: Machine      Key: CUSTID
             Memo file:          D:\FPWIN\BUYERS.FPT
        Lock(s): Exclusive USE
          Related into:    Donation
               Relation:   CUSTID
            1-To-Many:     Donation

Select area: 2, Table in Use:   D:\FPWIN\DONATION.DBF  Alias: DONATION
            Code page:   0
  Structural CDX file:   D:\FPWIN\DONATION.CDX
        Index tag:   CUSTID        Collate: Machine      Key: CUSTID
Master Index tag:   CUSTOMS        Collate: Machine      Key: CUSTID
        Lock(s): Exclusive USE

Press any key to continue...
```

The last listing shows that the SET VIEW TO command has restored the environment, with the tables and indexes open, and the relationship established.

Creating Multitable Reports

Your relational data can be used to generate reports in a similar manner as when you work with data from individual tables. With reports, the most important point to remember is to make the environment that supports the relationships active before you run the report. You can do this either by opening a relational query and basing the report on the query, or by entering any necessary SET RELATION and SET SKIP commands before running the report.

When you create a new report, you can add desired fields from any of the tables involved in a relationship. For example, if you open the Books query (created earlier in this chapter as an example), then choose File, New followed by Report, a blank window into the Report Writer appears. If you then click the Field tool and click in the body of the report to add a field, the Report Expression dialog box appears. Click the Expression button in the dialog box to display FoxPro's Expression Builder. (See Figure 10.17.) If you click the From Table list box to open it, you see the names of the tables Buyers, Bksales, and Bkdetail in the list box. When you click the desired table, the fields for that table appear in the Fields list box. Double-click the desired field to add it to the report. (For more on the topic of custom report design, see Chapter 12, "Designing and Customizing Reports.")

FIGURE 10.17.

The Expression Builder.

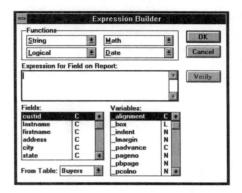

As a useful shortcut to relational report design, you can establish the environment by opening the query or using SET RELATION, opening a new report, and choosing Report, Quick Report from the menus. In the Quick Report dialog box which next appears, click the Fields check box to display the Field Picker. (See Figure 10.18.)

FIGURE 10.18.

The Field Picker.

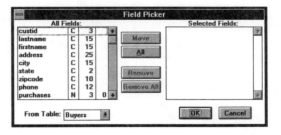

Note that in the Field Picker dialog box, the From Table list box contains the names of all tables established by your query, or by the use of the SET RELATION command. When you choose the desired table, its corresponding fields appear in the All Fields list box. You can double-click the desired fields to add them to the report.

Chapter Summary

This chapter has detailed one of the more important aspects of FoxPro: the use of the relational capabilities, and the different methods offered by FoxPro to establish relationships between tables. As this chapter has shown, most serious database applications benefit from the process of normalization—and the multiple tables which result can be linked together to provide the relational data you need in meaningful ways. The chapter placed a significant emphasis on detailing the different ways you can establish relationships in FoxPro. A familiarity with these methods offers you the most in terms of flexibility in getting the desired results from your relationships.

Designing and Customizing Screens

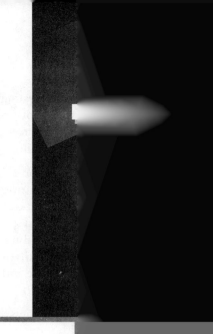

Chapter 8, "Creating and Using Simple Screens," introduced the topic of screens in FoxPro. That chapter covered how to create screens using the wizards, and introduced the basics behind using screens. This chapter examines the mechanics of screen design on a deeper level, with detailed coverage of how you can manually design and use complex screens.

Screens, as introduced in Chapter 8, let you examine records in a table by means of a custom layout. With custom screens that you create using FoxPro's Screen Builder power tool, you have a great deal of design flexibility. Not only can you place fields wherever desired, you can also add special types of controls, such as list and check boxes, radio buttons, and spinners. You also can add "code snippets" to screens. Code snippets are sequences of instructions, written in FoxPro's programming language, that further control the screen's behavior. These and other topics are covered in this chapter.

Before continuing, a word of advice is appropriate. To make effective use of screens that you custom design (that is, without the aid of the Screen Wizards), you need some familiarity with programming in FoxPro. (In this book, programming is covered beginning in Chapter 19, "FoxPro Programming Basics.") While you can create custom screens using FoxPro's Screen Builder without any programming, what you can do with those screens in a completely interactive context (outside of programming) is extremely limited. If you have no desire to get involved with FoxPro programming, consider only the following subheading of this chapter and stick with the exclusive use of the Screen Wizards for all your work with screens.

The Screen Wizards, Revisited

Chapter 8 provided considerable detail on the Screen Wizards, an integral feature of FoxPro 2.6 that makes it easy to create custom screens for adding and editing records. While it's not necessary to repeat the basics of using the Screen Wizards here, it is worth re-emphasizing that you can use the Screen Wizards to create custom screens with just the fields you want, while often saving a great deal of development time. Open any table you want to use as the basis of the screen with File, Open (or by entering the USE command in the Command Window). Then, choose Run, Wizard from the menus. From the submenu which appears, choose Screen. When you do this, the first of the Screen Wizard dialog boxes appears. You can choose the desired options in the dialog boxes to create the kind of screen you want, as detailed in Chapter 8. Figure 11.1 shows an example of a screen created through the use of the Screen Wizards.

Once the screen exists, you can run the screen at any time by choosing Run, Screen from the menus and choosing the desired screen in the dialog box. From the Command Window (or within a program) you can run the screen by entering DO *filename.SPR*, where *filename* is the name that the screen was saved under.

An important advantage to the approach of using the Screen Wizards is that the resultant screen already has a *control panel* (the row of buttons at the bottom of the screen) which can be used to navigate among the records. The Screen Wizard automatically creates the FoxPro program code necessary to include the control panel as part of the screen. As you see later, screens that you design with the Screen Builder don't have any controls added by default. You must create any desired controls, and add "code snippets" to tell FoxPro what actions should be taken when buttons in the control panel are pressed.

FIGURE 11.1.

A screen created using the Screen Wizards.

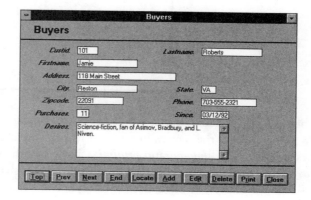

Types of Screens

FoxPro lets you create five different screen types with the Screen Builder. They are *desktop, user window, system window, dialog,* and *alert.* The desktop type of screen takes over the entire FoxPro desktop, while the other four screen types appear in windows that are contained within the FoxPro desktop. Figure 11.2 shows an example of a screen designed as a desktop.

FIGURE 11.2.

A screen using the desktop style of design.

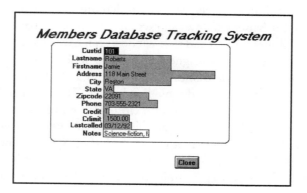

In contrast, Figure 11.3 shows an example of a screen placed in a user style of window.

FIGURE 11.3.

A screen using the user window style of design.

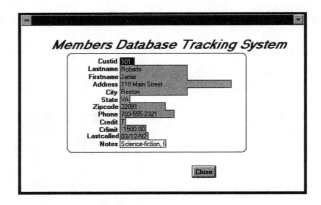

Each of the four "window" varieties of screens can be assigned *attributes,* which control what a user can do to the screen, in terms of its placement and size. Technically, the attributes are *close, float, shadow,* and *minimize.* Note that the shadow attribute is included only to keep screens compatible with FoxPro for DOS; shadow settings are ignored by FoxPro for Windows. The attributes are as explained here:

> **Close:** A window having the Close attribute can be closed, by double-clicking its Close button, or by choosing a Close option from a menu or pressing Ctrl+F4 when the window is active.
> **Float:** A window having the Float attribute can be moved within the FoxPro desktop.
> **Shadow:** A window having the Shadow attribute will, when opened under FoxPro for DOS, have a shadow behind it.
> **Minimize:** A window having the Minimize attribute can be minimized.

Which attributes a screen can have is determined by what type of window the screen resides in. Both user windows and system windows can have close, float, shadow, and minimize attributes. Dialog and alert windows can have float and shadow attributes. Any screen that is in a window is assigned a particular style of border: single, double, panel, or system. The single style frames the window in a single-line border, while the double-style frames the window in a double-line border. The Panel style frames the window with a wide border that lacks controls for closing, minimizing, or maximizing. The system style adds a wide border with controls. Note that the system, dialog, and alert window types all use specific border types that you can't change. System windows always use a system border, and alert and dialog windows always use a double border. Of all the window types which screens can occupy, only the user type lets you change the style of border.

Creating a Screen

To start FoxPro's Screen Builder, choose File, New. In the next dialog box, click Screen, then click New. At the command level, you also can enter CREATE SCREEN *filename*, where *filename* is the name that you want to save the screen under. (If you omit the name, FoxPro asks you for a name when you close the screen.) With either method, the Screen Builder appears within a window. When working with most screens, it helps to maximize the window so that you have room to work with a screen's design. Figure 11.4 shows an example of a new screen which appears when you use either of the methods detailed previously. Also note that the Screen menu is open in this figure. This menu is unique to the Screen Builder, and it contains various options which apply to your work with screens. The use of these options is covered when appropriate throughout this chapter.

FIGURE 11.4.

The Screen Builder with Screen menu open.

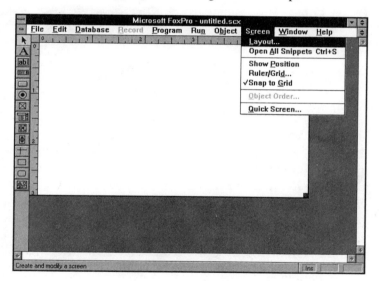

Choosing the Screen Type

To select the type of screen desired, choose Screen, Screen Layout from the menus. The Screen Layout dialog box appears. (See Figure 11.5.) (The options in this dialog box are covered in detail shortly.)

Click Window Style, and the Window Style dialog box appears. (See Figure 11.6.) As explained previously, in this dialog box, you use the Type list box to choose the desired window style: desktop, user, system, dialog, or alert. The Window Style dialog box also contains choices for the window's attributes and border. Keep in mind that depending on the type of window style chosen, the attribute and border settings may or may not be available. For example, if you choose alert, the options are dimmed, since alert windows have predefined double borders, and cannot be minimized or moved.

FIGURE 11.5.

The Screen Layout dialog box.

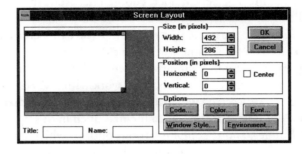

FIGURE 11.6.

The Window Style dialog box.

If you are designing a user window which you want the user to be able to minimize, use the Icon button in this dialog box to assign an icon of your choice to the minimized window. (The icon must be stored in a Windows .ICO file. You can create icons and store them to .ICO files with an Icon Editor, available from many bulletin boards and online services.) Clicking the Icon button displays a File dialog box, which you can use to choose the desired icon file. When you are done with the options in the Window Style dialog box, click OK to close the dialog box and reveal the Screen Layout dialog box underneath.

The options in the Screen Layout dialog box are divided into five sections: Size, Position, Options, Title, and Name. The screen's size, as measured in pixels, can be set using the Width and Height spinners in the Size portion of the dialog box. (Alternately, you can set the size of the screen by clicking and dragging the sizing rectangle in the lower-right corner of the drawing area.) The Horizontal and Vertical spinners in the Position portion of the dialog box let you change the position of a screen's drawing area, relative to the upper-left corner of the screen. (You can click the Center check box to center the drawing area within the screen.) The Title and Name text boxes are used to assign a title to a screen (it appears in the window's Title Bar), and to assign an optional name which can be used to refer to the screen from within FoxPro programs.

The Options portion of the dialog box contains buttons for Code, Colors, Font, Window Style (covered earlier), and Environment. The Code button displays a Screen Code dialog box, which you can use to specify program code which runs when you enter, exit, activate, deactivate, or refresh the screen. The Colors button displays a Screen Colors dialog box, which you use to specify a background color for the screen. The Font button displays a Font dialog box, which you use to change the default font used by the screen. The Environment button displays a dialog box which lets you save, restore, or clear the environment information.

Once you choose the desired options in the Screen Layout dialog box and click OK, you are left with the blank drawing area of the Screen Builder, ready to design your screen.

About the Screen Builder Tools

As you work with a screen's design, the left edge of the window contains a Toolbox. (See Figure 11.7.) You'll use the tools in the Toolbox to place various objects, such as fields, text, pictures, list boxes, check boxes, radio buttons, and so on, on the screen.

FIGURE 11.7.
The Toolbox.

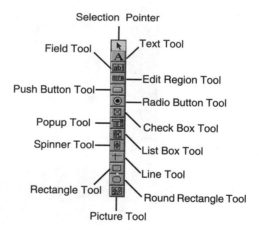

Selection Pointer

Field Tool — Text Tool

Push Button Tool — Edit Region Tool

Radio Button Tool

Popup Tool — Check Box Tool

Spinner Tool — List Box Tool

Line Tool

Rectangle Tool — Round Rectangle Tool

Picture Tool

Using the Quick Screen Option

In most cases, the easiest way to approach the process of custom screen design (other than using the Screen Wizards) is to use the Screen menu's Quick Screen option to create a default screen based on selected fields from a table. (Note that this menu option is available only before you make any additions to a blank screen.) After creating a default screen, you can make modifications to the screen as desired. To create a quick screen, choose Screen, Quick Screen from the menus. (If no table is open, you see an Open dialog box, where you can choose the table to base the quick screen on.) The Quick Screen dialog box appears. (See Figure 11.8.)

Choose the desired layout for the screen (columnar or form-oriented), and check any other desired options (these are explained more fully in the following paragraphs). Click OK. A default design for the screen appears in the Screen Builder window. (See Figure 11.9.)

FIGURE 11.8.

The Quick Screen dialog box.

FIGURE 11.9.

A default screen.

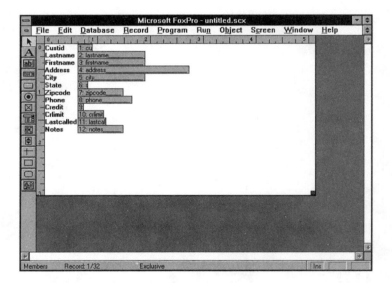

About the Quick Screen Dialog Box Options

The Quick Screen dialog box contains the buttons which let you choose the layout type (column-oriented or form-oriented), and check boxes for Titles, Fields, and Add Alias. Clicking the Column Layout button (the one on the left side of the dialog box) chooses a column-oriented layout, with the fields arranged in columns across the top of the page. Clicking the Row Layout button (the one on the right side of the dialog box) selects a row-oriented layout, with the fields arranged along the left margin of the screen.

The Titles check box, when checked, causes FoxPro to include a title along with each field placed in the screen. If you don't want the field names included in the screen, turn off the Titles check box.

The Fields check box can be used to select specific fields from the active table that should be included in the screen. By default, FoxPro includes all fields in a quick screen. If you click the Fields check box, the Field Picker appears, and you can click each desired field, followed by the Move button in the dialog box, to choose the fields you want in the screen. When done, click OK.

The Add Alias check box determines whether alias names are automatically added to the expressions on which fields that appear in the screen are based. Turning on this option is recommended if you plan to use the screens in a relational environment, where you have multiple tables open in different work areas, and if you plan to design a screen that takes its data from more than one table.

> **TIP**
>
> If you plan to use the same screen with different tables that have the same table structure, turn off the Alias option.

The Memory Variables check box, when checked, creates memory variables for all the fields. (Creating memory variables permits editing of table fields through program code you design, so that changes to the table can be validated, or discarded under control of your program.)

Adding Objects to the Screen

If you prefer to add objects to the screen manually (as opposed to using the Quick Screen option), you can use the techniques shown here as part of the screen design process. Note that the addition of buttons, check boxes, and lists requires some familiarity with FoxPro programming to be of any use. (This chapter shows how you can add those objects to a screen, but you need FoxPro program code to act on the choices made by users as they select the various objects you've placed in the screen.)

The precise method behind adding objects using the Toolbox varies depending on the type of object, but the overall process consists of these steps:

1. In the Toolbox, click the type of object you want to create.
2. Click in the screen where you want to place the upper-left corner of the object. In most cases, when you release the mouse, a dialog box appropriate to the object appears.
3. Fill in the desired options in any dialog box, then click OK to place the object.

Moving, Deleting, and Modifying Objects

FoxPro's Screen Builder classifies everything that you place in a screen as some type of *object.* You can manipulate the objects that you place on the screen in various ways. You can move them around, delete them, and place objects atop other objects. To move an object, first select the object by clicking it. (When an object is selected, it will be surrounded by small black rectangles called *handles.*) With the object selected, click anywhere within the object and drag to move it.

To resize an object, click any of its sizing handles, and drag them until the object assumes the desired size. (With lines, the sizing handles are the squares at the ends of the lines. With rectangular objects, they are the squares at the center of each side of the object.)

To delete an object, click the object to select it, then press the Delete key (or choose Edit, Cut from the menus).

You can also make use of various choices available from the Object menu, as you work with a screen's objects. Choosing Object, Align to Grid causes objects that you drag around to be aligned with the grid. Object, Bring to Front places an object atop another object, and Object, Send to Back moves an object behind another object. These options are useful when you purposely place one design element in a screen over another. For example, you might add a line to a screen and then place a smaller rectangle atop part of that line. Selecting the rectangle and choosing Object, Send to Back would place the rectangle behind the line, while choosing Object, Bring to Front would place the rectangle atop the line. Object, Center centers an object within the screen. If you select a number of objects (by holding the Shift key while clicking each desired object), you can choose Object, Group, to group the objects together so that they behave as if they are a single object. Selecting the combined object and choosing Object, Ungroup undoes this effect. The remaining options of the Object menu can be used to apply certain characteristics to various objects—such as lines and rectangles. These options are discussed at various places throughout this chapter.

Adding Fields

To add fields to the screen, click the Field tool in the Toolbox, then click at the location in the screen where you want to place the field's upper-left corner. A Field dialog box appears. (See Figure 11.10.)

In the Field portion of the dialog box, you can select the desired field type: Input Field (Get), or Output Field (Say). Input Fields, which are selected by default since they are most often used, enable users to enter and edit data in the field. Output Fields display the data in the field, but do not allow editing.

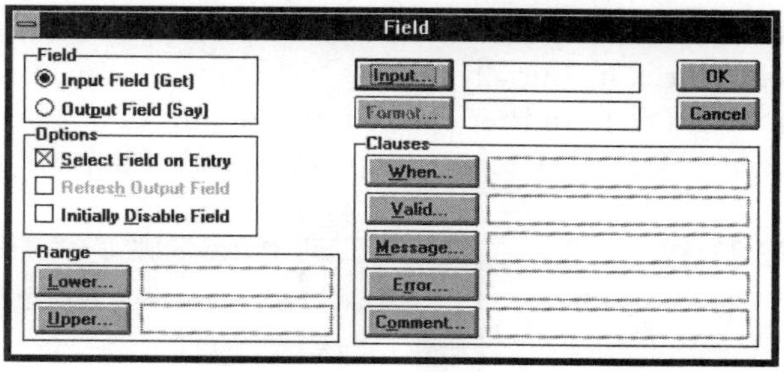

FIGURE 11.10.

A Field dialog box.

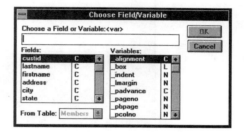

After choosing the field type, type the field's name along with any desired alias directly into the text box beside the Input button. You also can click the Input button to display a Choose Field/Variable dialog box. (See Figure 11.11.)

FIGURE 11.11.

The Choose Field/Variable dialog box.

In the Fields list of the dialog box, double-click the desired field. Click OK to close the dialog box. (Note that the Tables list box within this dialog box can be used to select another table, if you have established an environment where multiple tables are available for use. See Chapter 10, "Working with FoxPro's Relational Powers," for specifics on working with multiple tables.) When you close the Choose Field/Variable dialog box, the fieldname you selected appears in the text box to the right of the Input button within the Field dialog box. You can click OK again to place the field within the screen. Figure 11.12 shows an example of the result of placing a field.

The remaining options in the Field dialog box let you define a range of acceptable values for the field (using the Lower and Upper buttons), or add optional clauses which further control editing in the field. The Format button displays a Format dialog box, which is used to control how the data appears in the field. The When button lets you define a WHEN clause that must be true before editing is allowed. The Valid button lets you define a VALID clause that tests the validity of an entry. The Message button is used to add a message which appears in the Status Bar when the focus moves into the field. The Error button lets you enter a custom error message which appears if an entry doesn't meet the rules specified by a VALID clause. The Comment button lets you add a comment about the field you are placing in the screen. In the Options area of the dialog box, checking

Select Field on Entry causes the entire field to be selected when the focus is moved into the field. Checking Initially Disable Field causes the field to be initially disabled when the screen runs. (You can later enable it under control of a program, by including a SHOW *fieldname* ENABLE statement as part of a code snippet.)

FIGURE 11.12.

A Field added to a screen's design.

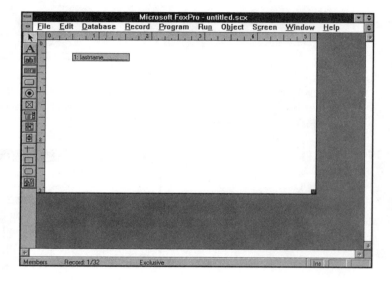

Adding Text to a Screen

Besides adding fields, you typically need to include text in forms. Figure 11.13 shows an example of text added to a form. Such text may be descriptive or explanatory, such as is used in field titles or captions. Text is added to forms with the use of the Text tool. (The Text tool is one of the few tools which, when used, does not cause a dialog box to appear.) To add text, click the Text tool in the Toolbox to select it, then click in the screen where you want to add the text and begin typing. The container that holds the text is flexible, and grows as needed to accommodate the text you add. You can press Enter at any point to begin a new line if you want to place text on multiple lines. Note that FoxPro does limit you to a maximum of 255 characters in any single text object. Click anywhere outside of the text when done (or click the Selection tool in the Toolbox) to complete the entry of the text.

You can change the text's appearance from the default font used by clicking the text to select it and choosing Object, Font to display the Font dialog box. (See Figure 11.14.) In the dialog box, choose a desired font, font size, and font style for the text. As you make the selections, samples of the text's appearance are shown within the dialog box. When done making selections, click OK to apply the selections to the text.

FIGURE 11.13.

Text added to a form.

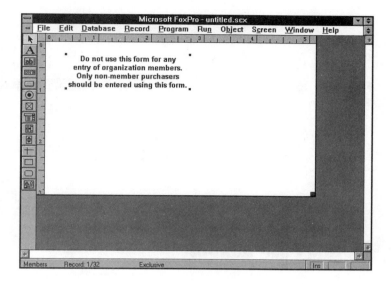

FIGURE 11.14.

The Font dialog box.

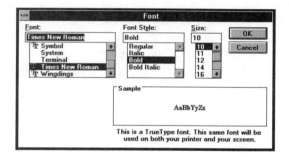

Placing Edit Regions

Edit regions are definable regions of the screen used for editing a field or a memory variable. Generally, they are used to display and edit the contents of memo fields. To place an edit region in the screen, click the Edit Region tool, then click in the Screen Design window at the desired location. The Edit Region dialog box opens. (See Figure 11.15.)

You can type the field's name along with any desired alias directly into the text box beside the Input button. Or you can click the Input button to display a Choose Field/Variable dialog box. (See Figure 11.11, shown previously.) Once the field has been named in the Input text box, the remaining options in the Edit Region dialog box are used to define a range of acceptable values for the field (using the Lower and Upper buttons), or add optional clauses (with the remaining buttons) which further control editing in the field. These options work as described earlier under "Adding Fields." Three options unique to this dialog box are "Scroll Bar on Edit Region" (which includes a scroll bar in the edit region),

"Allow Tabs in Edit Region" (which lets the user set and use tabs in the edit region) and "Character Length" (which lets you specify a maximum number of characters which can be entered in the region. If zero is specified, there is no limit).

FIGURE 11.15.

The Edit Region dialog box.

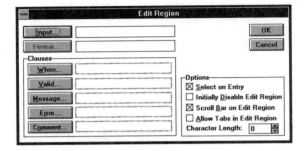

Placing Push Buttons

Push buttons are multiple choice selection buttons that resemble the rectangular grey buttons used in many of FoxPro's dialog boxes. You can use one or more push buttons in a screen whenever you want to provide a user with one or more choices. Depending on which button the user clicks, a numeric value is stored to the variable or table field you indicated when you designed the screen. (The number represents which button was pressed. You can act on that number within program code of a FoxPro program to determine what should happen next.)

To place push buttons for the screen, click the Push Button tool, then click in the Screen Design window, at the desired location. When you do so, the Push Button dialog box opens. (See Figure 11.16.)

FIGURE 11.16.

The Push Button dialog box.

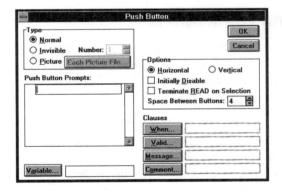

In the Type portion of the dialog box, you can choose Normal (which are visible buttons with text prompts), Invisible (which are transparent, and are normally placed over pictures or graphics), or Picture (which creates a button having a background based on a stored picture file). In the Push Button Prompts portion of the dialog box, enter the desired prompts for the buttons. For each button desired, type a prompt. Move to the next line and repeat this step if you want additional buttons. Under Options, check Horizontal or Vertical to indicate whether the buttons should be placed horizontally or vertically. Checking Initially Disable causes the buttons to be initially disabled when the screen runs. (You can later enable the buttons under control of a program, by including a SHOW GETS ENABLE statement as part of a code snippet.) The Terminate READ Upon Selection check box, when checked, causes the editing operation to be terminated when the user chooses any of the push buttons. The Space Between Buttons spinner can be used to set a spacing (measured in pixels) between each of the buttons.

You click in the Variable text box and type the name of the field or memory variable that the user's choice should be stored to. (You can also click the Variable button to display a Choose Field/Variable dialog box, which you can use to select an existing field or memory variable.) The field or variable should be of the character or numeric type, because the buttons you design will, when used, return a number indicating which button was pressed. (For example, if you add a group of four buttons and the user presses the third button, a value of 3 is stored in the field or variable in the Variable text box.)

The When button lets you define a WHEN clause that must be true before the push buttons can be selected. The Valid button lets you define a VALID clause that runs when any of the buttons are pressed. The Message button is used to add a MESSAGE clause that appears in the Status Bar when the focus moves to the buttons. The Error button lets you enter a custom error message that appears if the conditions specified by a VALID clause are not met when the buttons have the focus. The Comment button lets you add a comment about the buttons.

Placing Radio Buttons

Radio buttons, like push buttons, are multiple choice selection buttons. In appearance, they resemble the circular buttons used in many FoxPro dialog boxes. As with push buttons, you use radio buttons in a screen whenever you want to provide a user with one or more possible choices. Depending on which button the user clicks, a number value is stored to the variable or table field you indicated when you designed the screen. (The number represents which button was pressed; you can then act on that number within program code of a FoxPro program to determine what should happen next.)

To place radio buttons for the screen, click the Radio Button tool, then click in the Screen Design window, at the desired location. The Radio Button dialog box opens. (See Figure 11.17.)

In the Radio Button Prompts portion of the dialog box, enter the desired prompts for the buttons. For each button desired, type a prompt, and tab to the next line and repeat this step if you want additional buttons. The Picture buttons check box can be checked to include pictures instead of written prompts for the radio buttons.

FIGURE 11.17.

The Radio Button dialog box.

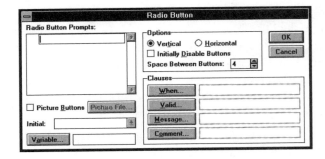

Under Options, check Horizontal or Vertical to indicate whether the buttons should be placed horizontally or vertically. Checking Initially Disable Buttons causes the buttons to be initially disabled when the screen runs. (You can later enable the buttons under control of a program, by including a SHOW GETS ENABLE statement as part of a code snippet.) The Space Between Buttons spinner can be used to set a spacing (measured in pixels) between each of the buttons. The Initial list box lets you select which of the buttons (in a list of more than one button) should be selected by default.

Click in the Variable text box and type the name of the field or memory variable that the user's choice should be stored to. (You can also click the Variable button to display a Choose Field/Variable dialog box, which you can use to select an existing field or memory variable.) The field or variable should be of the character or numeric type, as the group of buttons you design will, when used, return a number indicating which button was pressed. (For example, if you add a group of four buttons and the user presses the third button, a value of 3 is stored in the field or variable in the Variable text box.)

The When button lets you define a WHEN clause that must be true before the radio buttons can be selected. The Valid button lets you define a VALID clause that runs when any of the buttons are pressed. The Message button is used to add a MESSAGE clause which appears in the Status Bar when the focus moves to the buttons. The Error button lets you enter a custom error message which appears if the conditions specified by a VALID clause are not met when the buttons have the focus. The Comment button lets you add a comment about the buttons.

Placing Check Boxes

Check boxes are rectangular boxes which can be checked by the user, indicating a yes or no value. Check boxes can be used with numeric or logical fields or memory variables. When the user clicks the check box, a logical true gets stored to any logical field or memory variable, or a value of 1 gets stored to any numeric field or variable. If the box is not checked, a logical value of false gets stored to any logical field or memory variable, or a value of 0 gets stored to any numeric field or variable.

To place a check box for the screen, click the Check Box tool, then click in the Screen Design window at the desired location. The Check Box dialog box opens. (See Figure 11.18.)

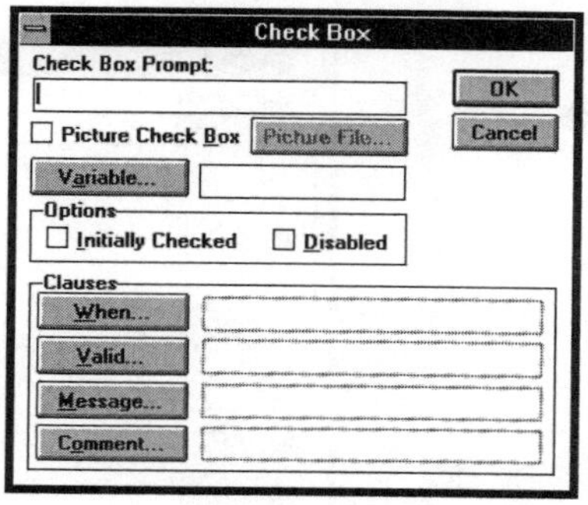

FIGURE 11.18.

The Check Box dialog box.

In the Check Box Prompt text box, enter the prompt that should appear beside the check box. The Picture Check Box option can be checked to include a picture instead of a written prompt for the check box. The Initially Checked option, when checked, causes the check box to be checked by default in the screen. The Disabled option, when checked, causes the check box to be initially disabled when the screen runs. (You can later enable the check box under control of a program, by including a SHOW GETS ENABLE statement as part of a code snippet.)

Click in the Variable text box and type the name of the field or memory variable that the user's choice should be stored to. (You can also click the Variable button to display a Choose Field/Variable dialog box, which you can use to select an existing field or memory variable.) The field or variable should be of the numeric or logical type, as the check box stores a numeric value of 0 (for no check) or 1 (for a check) to a numeric field or variable, and a value of false (for no check) or true (for a check) to a logical field.

The When button lets you define a WHEN clause that must be true before the check box can be clicked. The Valid button lets you define a VALID clause that runs when the focus moves to the check box. The Message button is used to add a MESSAGE clause that appears in the Status Bar when the focus moves to the check box. The Error button lets you enter a custom error message that appears if the conditions specified by a VALID clause are not met when the check box has the focus. The Comment button lets you add a comment about the check box.

Placing Popups

Popups are popup menu lists, which resemble the popup lists used throughout FoxPro. As with buttons, when you add a popup to a screen, you define all the items that appear in the popup by means of a dialog box.

To place a popup for the screen, click the Popup tool, then click in the Screen Design window, at the desired location. The Popup dialog box opens. (See Figure 11.19.)

FIGURE 11.19.

The Popup dialog box.

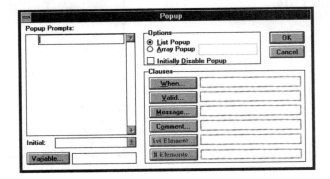

In the Popup Prompts portion of the dialog box, you enter the desired prompts for the available options in the list. (Note that this is not necessary if you use the Array Popup option in the dialog box, as explained shortly.) For each option desired, type a prompt, and move to the next line and repeat this step if you want additional options in the list. The Initial list box can be used to choose which prompt should be the prompt that initially appears within the popup.

You click in the Variable text box and type the name of the field or memory variable that the user's choice should be stored to. (You can also click the Variable button to display a Choose Field/Variable dialog box, which you can use to select an existing field or memory variable.) The field or variable should be of the character or numeric type. The popup you design will, when used, return a number indicating which option within the list was chosen. (For example, if you add a list of five items and the user selects the fourth item in the list, a value of 4 gets stored in the field or variable that you name in the Variable text box.)

In the Options portion of the dialog box, the List Popup option is used to tell FoxPro to define the popup based on the choices that you enter in the Popup Prompts area of the dialog box. The Array Popup option is used to tell FoxPro to base the popup choices on the contents of an existing array, stored in memory. The Initially Disable Popup option, when checked, causes the popup to be initially disabled when the screen runs. (You can later enable the popup under control of a program, by including a SHOW GETS ENABLE statement as part of a code snippet.)

The When button lets you define a WHEN clause that must be true before the popup can be selected. The Valid button lets you define a VALID clause that runs when the focus moves to the popup. The Message button is used to add a MESSAGE clause that appears in the Status Bar when the focus moves to the popup. The Error button lets you enter a custom error message that appears if the conditions specified by a VALID clause are not met when the popup has the focus. The Comment button lets you add a comment about the popup.

The 1st Element and # Elements buttons and corresponding text boxes are available when a popup is defined based on an array. Clicking the buttons displays the Code Snippet dialog box, which lets you specify the first element and the number of elements in the array.

Placing Lists

Lists are very similar to popups, but they show a scrollable list. The contents of the list can be based on an existing popup, values stored in an array in memory, files in a directory, records in a table, or available fields in a table's structure. To add a list to the screen, click the List tool, then drag to size in the Screen Design window at the desired location. The List dialog box opens. (See Figure 11.20.)

FIGURE 11.20.

The List dialog box.

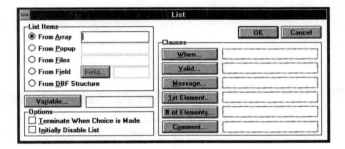

In the List Items portion of the dialog box, check the appropriate item to indicate where the choices in the list should come from (array, popup, files, field, or database (table) structure). If you choose Array, Popup, or Files, you must enter the corresponding name of the array, popup, or drive wildcards in the accompanying text box. If you choose Field, you can enter the field name, or click the Field button to display the Expression Builder, which you can use to select a field. If you choose From DBF Structure, the list comes from the table structure for the active table.

As with popups, click in the Variable text box and type the name of the field or memory variable that the user's choice should be stored to. (You can also click the Variable button to display a Choose Field/Variable dialog box, which you can use to select an existing field or memory variable.) The field or variable should be of the character or numeric type.

The list you design will, when used, return a number indicating which option within the list was chosen.

The Terminate When Choice is Made check box causes the operation to be terminated when the user chooses any of the items in the list. The Initially Disable List option causes the list to be initially disabled when the screen runs. (You can later enable the list under control of a program, by including a SHOW GETS ENABLE statement as part of a code snippet.)

The When button lets you define a WHEN clause that must be true before the list can be selected. The Valid button lets you define a VALID clause that runs when the focus moves to the list. The Message button is used to add a MESSAGE clause that appears in the Status Bar when the focus moves to the list. The Error button lets you enter a custom error message that appears if the conditions specified by a VALID clause are not met when the list has the focus. The Comment button lets you add a comment about the list.

The 1st Element and # Elements buttons and corresponding text boxes are available when a list is defined based on an array. Clicking the buttons displays the Code Snippet dialog box, which lets you specify the first element and the number of elements in the array.

Placing Spinners

You can include spinner controls in your screens. To add a spinner to the screen, click the Spinner tool, then drag to size in the Screen Design window. The Spinner dialog box opens. (See Figure 11.21.)

FIGURE 11.21.

The Spinner dialog box.

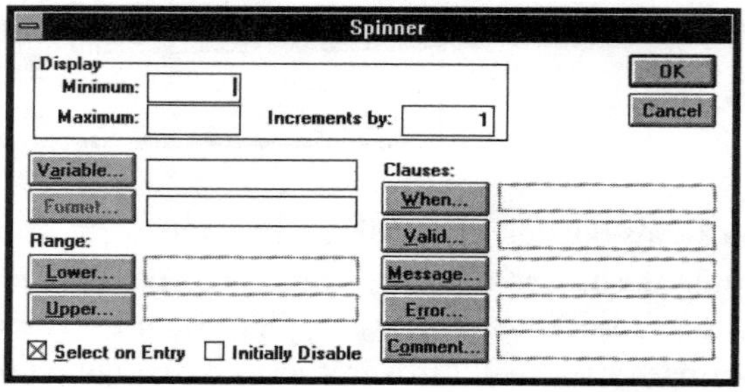

The options in the Spinner dialog box serve the following purposes:

Minimum and Maximum text boxes: In these boxes, you can enter the lowest and highest numeric values that are displayed in the spinner in the Minimum and Maximum text boxes.

Increments by text box: In this box, you can enter the incremental step by which values are displayed in the spinner in the Increments by text box. As an example, if you enter a Minimum value of 5 and an Increment by value of 5, clicking the up and down arrows in the resulting spinner displays multiples of five.

Variable button and text box: You click in the Variable text box and type the name of the field or memory variable that the user's choice should be stored to. (You can also click the Variable button to display a Choose Field/Variable dialog box, which you can use to select an existing field or memory variable.) The field or variable must be of the numeric type. The spinner will, when used, return a numeric value equal to what is displayed in the spinner.

Range push button: The minimum, maximum, and incremental values in the Display portion of the dialog box only affect the values shown in the spinner text box when the user clicks the up and down arrows. The user can still enter any numeric value in the spinner text box with the keyboard. To ensure that the data entered in the spinner is within the boundaries you want, set a range. (Note that you are not required to set both the upper and lower boundaries. If one boundary is omitted, that end of the range is ignored.)

Lower push button: When you click this button, the Code Snippet dialog box appears, which you can use to enter a procedure or expression to set the lowest allowable value that can be entered in the input field. (You can also enter the value by typing it into the text box next to the push button.) If the user inputs a value lower than the value you assign, a message with the allowed values appears in the status bar.

Upper push button: When you click this button the Code Snippet dialog box appears. Use this dialog box to enter a procedure or expression to set the highest allowable value that can be entered in the input field. (You can also enter the value by typing it into the text box next to the push button.) If the user inputs a value higher than the value you assign, a message with the allowed values appears in the status bar.

Drawing Lines

To draw a line in your screen, click the Line tool, position the cursor where you want one end of the line to be, and drag until the line is the desired length. You can change the characteristics of a line (its width, and whether it is solid or not) by clicking the line to select it, and choosing Object, Pen from the menus. From the submenu which appears, choose the desired option (hairline, 1 point through 6 point, dotted, dashed, dash-dot, and dash-dash-dot) for the type of line that you prefer. You can also select a line, and choose Object, Pen Color, to change the color used to draw the line.

Drawing Rectangles

To draw a rectangle on your screen, click the Rectangle tool, click in the screen where you want a corner of the rectangle to appear, and drag until the rectangle reaches the desired size. Once a rectangle exists, you can change many aspects of the rectangle's appearance. Click an existing rectangle to select it, then choose Object, Fill to select a fill pattern for the rectangle. You can use Object, Pen, to change the line style used by the rectangle; Object, Mode, to indicate whether the rectangle should be opaque or transparent; Object, Fill Color, to choose a fill color for the rectangle; and Object, Pen Color, to choose a color for the lines that form the rectangle.

Drawing Rounded Rectangles

To draw a rectangle with rounded corners, click the Rounded-rectangle tool, click in the screen where you want a corner of the rounded rectangle to appear, and drag until the rounded rectangle reaches the desired size. You can also specify how rounded the rectangle should be, by double-clicking the rounded-rectangle to display the Round Rectangle dialog box. (See Figure 11.22.) In this dialog box, you can choose the shape of the rounded rectangle, from oval to slightly rounded.

FIGURE 11.22.

The Rounded Rectangle dialog box.

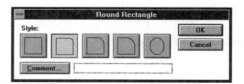

You can also apply the same changes to a rounded rectangle's appearance that you apply to a normal rectangle. After selecting the rounded rectangle, use the Object menu options to change the appearance of the rectangle.

Defining Pictures

To include a .BMP file or a picture that is stored in a general field of a table in the screen, click the picture tool, then click and drag to the desired size in the Screen Design window. The Screen Picture dialog box opens. (See Figure 11.23.)

Use this dialog box to tell FoxPro where to find the picture, and how to handle pictures that are not the same size as the frame they are in. When done selecting the desired options, click OK, and the picture appears within the screen's design. The options within the dialog box let you exercise control over where the picture comes from and how it is handled within the screen.

FIGURE 11.23.

The Screen Picture dialog box.

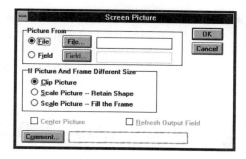

The Picture From area of the dialog box has File and Field radio buttons, and corresponding rectangular buttons and text boxes (where you can type in the name of a file or of a field). You use the options in this area to tell FoxPro where to find the picture that is placed in the screen. To include a single bit map picture in your screen, click the File radio button. Then, click the rectangular File... button to open a Picture dialog box that you can use to select the desired .BMP file. You can also type the name (including the path) of the .BMP file in the text box to the right of the File button. To base the picture on the contents of a general field of a table, click the Field radio button. Then, click the rectangular Field button to open a Choose Field/Variable dialog box, which you can use to select the desired field. Alternately, you can type the name of the field in the text box to the right of the Field button.

The If Picture and Frame Different Size area of the dialog box has three options, titled Clip Picture, Scale Picture-Retain Shape, and Scale Picture-Fill the Frame. When the picture is larger than the frame you added to the screen, the Clip Picture option tells FoxPro to clip the picture at the right and the bottom as required to fit within the frame. The Scale Picture-Retain Shape option tells FoxPro to show the entire picture, filling as much of the frame as possible while keeping the relative proportions of the bit-map picture. (This method of scaling helps avoid vertical or horizontal distortion.) The Scale Picture-Fill the Frame option shows the entire picture, filling the frame completely. Depending on the dimensions of the frame, this may cause horizontal or vertical distortion as FoxPro scales the picture to fit the frame.

The Center Picture check box is designed to be used along with pictures stored in general fields of a table. (Pictures in .BMP files that are placed in screens as design elements are not affected by this option.) Since bitmaps stored in general fields of a table can come in a variety of shapes and sizes, this option lets you tell FoxPro whether to center the pictures shown in the screen. When the bitmap stored in a general field is smaller than the frame, it appears in the upper-left corner of the frame unless you check Center Picture. Checking Center Picture ensures that pictures (stored in general fields) which are smaller than the frame are centered in the frame within the screen.

The Refresh Output Field check box is used when pictures come from the general field of a table. Turning on this option lets you update the picture in the frame with the picture in the general field for the current record. Finally, the Comment push button opens a Comment dialog box, where you can add comments about the picture. (Comments are purely for your reference, and do not appear in the screen.)

Saving Screens and Generating Code

Once you have finished the process of designing your screen, you can save it and generate the code that FoxPro uses to display it. To save the screen, choose File, Save from the menus. If you did not name the screen as part of the creation process, FoxPro displays a Save As dialog box, where you can enter a filename. By default, screens are saved with an .SCX extension. (The files that FoxPro saves are actually tables given this special extension, and FoxPro uses the tables to store the data about the screen's design.)

The screen which you save contains the design information behind the screen, but it cannot be used by FoxPro to actually display any data. To create a usable screen, you must generate screen code based on the screen's design. To do this, while the screen is still open, choose Program, Generate from the menus. The Generate dialog box appears. (See Figure 11.24.)

FIGURE 11.24.

The Generate dialog box.

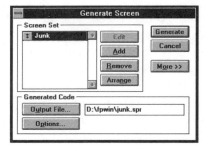

In the Screen Set portion of the dialog box, the screen you have designed appears by name. You can add other screens to this list by clicking the Add button, and choosing other screens in the dialog box. The Edit button can be used to edit the name of a screen, and the Remove button can be used to remove screens from the list.

In the Generated Code portion of the dialog box, the Output File text box contains the name that the generated code is saved under. By default, this is the same name that you saved the screen under, but with an .SPR extension. Use the Options button to display an additional dialog box which lets you add optional information (such as your name and company name as comments to the screen code).

The More button in the dialog box, when clicked, causes the dialog box to expand to reveal additional options. (See Figure 11.25.) (If you lack experience with FoxPro programming, these options may make little or no sense. Leave them set to their defaults if their purpose is unclear.) The options let you control whether the code generated by the screen should open tables on startup and close tables on exit; whether windows should be defined and released; whether a screen should be modal; and how the screen handles certain READ commands. When done with the options in the Generate Screen dialog box, click Generate. FoxPro generates the necessary screen code.

FIGURE 11.25.

The expanded Generate dialog box.

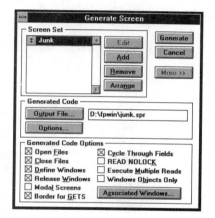

Using the Screen

With the screen code generated, put the screen to use by choosing Run, Screen and selecting the screen by name in the dialog box. Alternately, you can enter DO *filename.SPR*, where *filename* is the name you saved the screen under.

An Example: Creating a Custom Screen

You can use the steps outlined in the following procedure to see how the techniques described throughout this chapter can be used to design a custom screen.

1. In the Command Window, enter USE BUYERS to put the Buyers table into use.

2. In the Command Window, enter CREATE SCREEN to open the Screen Builder.

3. Choose Screen, Quick Screen from the menus, to open the Quick Screen dialog box.

4. Click the column layout button (the one on the right), then click OK to create a default screen.

5. Hold the Shift key, and while holding Shift click each of the fields and labels in the screen, to select all of the fields and labels simultaneously.

6. From the menus, choose Object, Group. Doing this groups the objects together, so they behave as a single object.

7. With the grouped object still selected, choose Object, Center from the menus to center the fields and labels within the screen horizontally.

8. Click within any of the fields, and drag the entire object down so it is centered vertically in the screen. At this point, your screen should resemble the example shown in Figure 11.26.

FIGURE 11.26.

A custom screen with fields and labels placed in center.

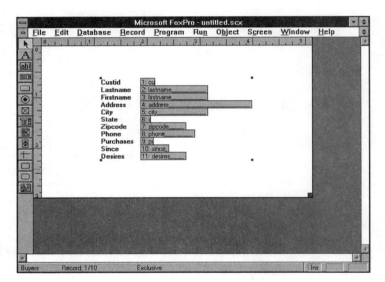

9. With the grouped object still selected, click Object, Ungroup.

10. Click anywhere outside of the fields and labels to deselect them, then click the last field, Desires, to select it (be sure you've selected the field, and not the text box).

11. Press the Delete key to delete the field. (Since this is a memo field, you replace the default field with an Edit Region that provides more room to edit the memo field's contents.)

12. In the Toolbox, click the Edit Region tool (the fourth tool down from the top).

13. Click just underneath the bottom left edge of the existing Since field. An Edit Region dialog box appears.

14. Click the Input button, to display the Choose Field/Variable dialog box. Scroll down in the Fields list box and double-click Desires. Click OK to close the

Field/Variable dialog box. Click OK again to close the Edit Region dialog box and place the field in the screen.

15. Click and drag the sizing handle at the center of the right edge of the field to reduce the field in size by roughly one-half inch. (You may have to widen the drawing area slightly or move the field slightly, to see the handles.) Then, click and drag the sizing handle at the center of the bottom edge of the field, to increase the depth by roughly 1 inch. Your screen should resemble the one shown in Figure 11.27.

FIGURE 11.27.

The screen after adding Edit Region.

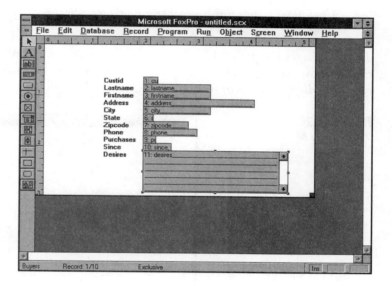

At this point, the necessary changes to the fields and text labels are complete. However, the form could use a little embellishing. You can perform the following steps to jazz up its appearance:

1. Click the sizing square at the lower-right corner of the screen's drawing area, and drag downwards to increase the depth of the screen's drawing area by roughly 1 inch. (This provides ample room for a control panel which is added in the exercise that follows this one.)

2. Click the Rounded Rectangle tool (the second tool from the bottom). Click above and to the left of the title of the first field (Custid), and drag down and to the right of the lower-right edge of the last field (Desires).

3. With the rounded rectangle still selected, choose Object, Pen Color. From the submenu, select another color which appeals to you.

4. Click the Text tool. Then click above the rectangle, near the center of the screen, and type **Buyers Screen**.

5. Click outside the text, then click the text to select it, and choose Object, Font. Choose a larger font and a font size (for this example, the choice was Times New Roman and 14-point). Click OK to apply the changes.

6. Choose File, Save from the menus, to save the design changes to the screen. When prompted for a name, call the screen **Buyer1**, and answer "Yes" to the prompt which asks if you want to save the environment information.

7. From the menus, choose Program, Generate. When the Generate Screen dialog box appears, click the Generate button to generate the screen code for the screen.

8. When FoxPro has finished generating the screen code, choose File, Close, to close the screen.

To try the screen, enter DO BUYER1.SPR in the Command Window. (You also could choose Run, Screen, and select Buyer1.spr in the dialog box which appears.) The screen runs, and displays a record from the Buyers table. (See Figure 11.28.)

FIGURE 11.28.

The completed Buyer1 Screen.

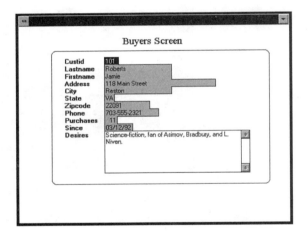

Adding a Control Panel to the Screen

If you try working with this screen, you quickly see the limitations of a screen which has no programming code added to allow user control. The screen shows the current record, and only the current record. With the screen visible, the PG UP and PG DN keys have no effect. Double-clicking the window's Close button also has no effect; to get out of the screen, you'll need to use the Esc key. You can move through the fields of the current record, but you cannot get to any other records in the table. Therefore, to use such a screen on an interactive basis would require you to move to the desired record from the Command Window or from the menus, then run the screen. You would need to do this for every record you wanted to edit, clearly a procedure that would be more trouble than it's worth. You can get around these limitations by adding a control panel to the screen. A control panel is nothing more than a group of push buttons that perform specific tasks. The buttons store a value to a memory variable, and that variable is acted on by a code snippet (a portion of FoxPro program code) that is stored with the screen. Perform the following steps to add the control panel to the existing form:

1. If necessary, press Esc to close the existing screen and get back to the Command Window.

2. Enter MODIFY SCREEN BUYER1 in the Command Window, to open the screen in design mode.

3. In the Toolbox, click the Push Button tool (the fifth one down from the top).

4. Click roughly one-quarter inch below the bottom of the rectangle around the fields, and about one-half inch from the left edge of the screen. The Push Button dialog box appears with the insertion pointer flashing in the Push Button Prompts portion of the dialog box.

5. Type **Top**, then press Tab. Type **Prior**, then press Tab; type **Next**, then press Tab; type **Bottom**, then press Tab; type **Append**, then press Tab; type **Delete**, then press Tab; and finally, type **Close** (but *don't* press Enter).

6. Click in the text box next to the Variable button, and type **chooser**. (This name is assigned to the memory variable that gets created when a button is pressed.)

7. Click the Valid button. A Code Snippet dialog box opens. (See Figure 11.29.) In this dialog box, enter the FoxPro program code necessary to respond to the value of the memory variable.

FIGURE 11.29.

A Code Snippet dialog box.

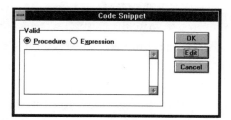

8. Leave the Procedure option (the default) checked, and enter the lines shown here in the Code Snippet dialog box:

```
DO CASE
CASE chooser = 1
      GO TOP
CASE chooser = 2
      IF EOF()
            GO TOP
      ELSE
            SKIP -1
```

```
        ENDIF
CASE chooser = 3
        IF EOF()
                GO BOTTOM
        ELSE
                SKIP 1
        ENDIF
CASE chooser = 4
        GO BOTTOM
CASE chooser = 5
        APPEND BLANK
CASE chooser = 6
        DELETE
CASE chooser = 7
        CLEAR READ
ENDCASE
SHOW GETS
RETURN
```

When done, check your work for errors, then click OK to close the Code Snippet dialog box. Then, click OK again in the Push Button dialog box to close it and add the push buttons to the screen.

9. Click outside the push buttons, then click any of the buttons to select them. With the buttons selected, choose Object, Center from the menus, to center the buttons horizontally in the screen.

10. Choose File, Save from the menus, to save the design changes to the screen.

11. From the menus, choose Program, Generate. When the Generate Screen dialog box appears, click the Generate button. Answer "Yes" to the prompt that asks if you want to overwrite the existing screen code.

12. When FoxPro has finished generating the screen code, choose File, Close, to close the screen.

To try the screen, enter DO BUYER1.SPR in the Command Window. (Alternately, you could also choose Run, Screen, and select Buyer1.spr in the dialog box which appears.) The screen runs, and this time it includes the control panel. (See Figure 11.30.)

Try using the buttons in the control panel to navigate within the table and to add or delete records. One aspect that's missing is a way to pack the table after a series of deletions are made. You could add another button (and the corresponding logic within the code snippet) to handle this task, or it could be handled elsewhere within an application. When you are done working with the screen, click the Close button to close it and return to the Command Window.

FIGURE 11.30.

The Buyer1 Screen with Control Panel added.

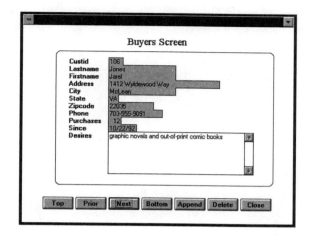

Chapter Summary

This chapter provided a detailed look at the Screen Builder, and the tools that it provides which you can use to design screens. Screens created with the Screen Builder are an important overall part of good applications design in FoxPro. Chapter 22, "Programming for Reporting Needs," and Chapter 24, "Debugging Techniques," provide additional details on how you can use FoxPro screens as an overall part of an application's design.

Designing and Customizing Reports

12

Chapter 9, "Creating and Using Simple Reports," introduced the topic of reports. That chapter showed how the Report Wizards could be used to create reports. This chapter builds on the science of report design on a deeper level, with a view towards the manual creation and use of reports.

To create reports manually with FoxPro, you use the Report Writer, one of FoxPro's menu power tools. The Report Writer is a visually-oriented interface used in the manual design of both reports and mailing labels. You create the desired report by placing different objects, such as fields, text, graphics, and expressions, into the report where desired. A Quick Report menu option can help you with some design tasks by providing a default layout for the report. When done with the report's design, you save the report. The file that is saved to disk can later be used to produce the desired report, on screen or through the default printer.

Types of Reports

Reports in FoxPro (or in any band-oriented report writer like FoxPro's) can be columnar or form-oriented reports. With columnar reports, the data for each field appears in a single column, with the title of each column at the top of the page. Figure 12.1 shows a column-oriented report. An advantage of this type of report is that it easily supports *grouping*, where groups of records meeting a certain condition are arranged together within the report. The report shown contains data that is grouped by States. Most reports which contain numeric data, along with totals, are column-oriented reports.

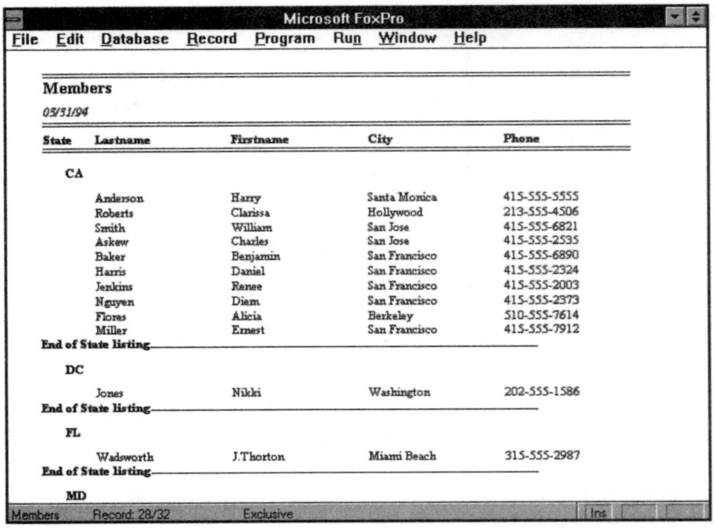

FIGURE 12.1.

A column-oriented report.

| Microsoft FoxPro |
| File Edit Database Record Program Run Window Help |

Members

03/31/94

State	Lastname	Firstname	City	Phone
CA				
	Anderson	Harry	Santa Monica	415-555-5555
	Roberts	Clarissa	Hollywood	213-555-4506
	Smith	William	San Jose	415-555-6821
	Askew	Charles	San Jose	415-555-2535
	Baker	Benjamin	San Francisco	415-555-6890
	Harris	Daniel	San Francisco	415-555-2324
	Jenkins	Renee	San Francisco	415-555-2003
	Nguyen	Diem	San Francisco	415-555-2373
	Flores	Alicia	Berkeley	510-555-7614
	Miller	Ernest	San Francisco	415-555-7912
End of State listing				
DC				
	Jones	Nikki	Washington	202-555-1586
End of State listing				
FL				
	Wadsworth	J.Thorton	Miami Beach	315-555-2987
End of State listing				
MD				

Members   Record: 28/32   Exclusive   Ins

A disadvantage of this type of report is that it is hard to fit a large number of fields on a single page, unless the fields happen to be extremely narrow. One way around this drawback is to print the report "sideways," or in landscape mode. However, the type of report desired may or may not lend itself to this kind of treatment.

With form-oriented reports, the resulting report displays or prints the data for each record in a separate section or page of the report. Fields are routinely placed in succession along the left side of the report. Figure 12.2 shows a form-oriented report. An advantage of this type of report is that you can place a large number of fields on each page; the corresponding disadvantage is that you cannot usually fit a large number of records on each page. Additionally, grouping is not as effective a technique with form-oriented reports as with column-oriented reports.

FIGURE 12.2.

A form-oriented report.

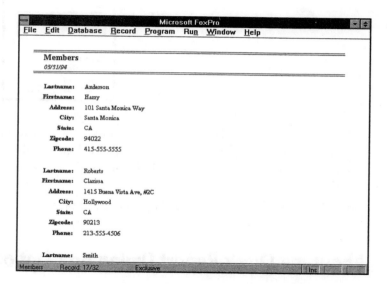

Creating Reports the Easy Way: With Quick Report

When you want to save time and let FoxPro make most design decisions, you can open a new report within the Report Writer, and use the Quick Report option of the Report menu to create a report with a default layout. Using this option, FoxPro provides the flexibility of producing column-oriented reports (where the data appears in columns) or form-oriented reports (where the data is arranged with one field beneath another). These are the steps you must perform to produce a quick report:

1. Open the table that the report is based on (choose File, Open and select the table by name in the dialog box, or enter USE *filename*, where *filename* is the name of the table).

2. From the menus, choose File, New, then click Report, then click New. In the Command Window, you can also enter CREATE REPORT.

3. When the Report Writer appears within a window, open the Report menu with the mouse or with Alt+O.

4. Choose Quick Report from the menu. When you do so, the Quick Report dialog box appears. (See Figure 12.3.)

FIGURE 12.3.

The Quick Report dialog box.

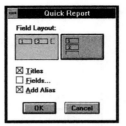

5. Choose the desired layout for the report (columnar or form-oriented), and check any other desired options (these are explained more fully in the following paragraphs). Click OK. A default design for the report appears in the Report Writer window.

6. Make any additional desired changes to the report, and choose File, Save to save the report.

About the Quick Report Dialog Box Options

The Quick Report dialog box (see Figure 12.3, shown previously) contains the buttons which let you choose the layout type (column-oriented or form-oriented), and check boxes for Titles, Fields, and Add Alias. Clicking the Column Layout button (the one on the left side of the dialog box) chooses a column-oriented layout, with the fields arranged in columns across the top of the page. Clicking the Row Layout button (the one on the right side of the dialog box) selects a row-oriented layout, with the fields arranged along the left margin of the report.

The Titles check box, when checked, causes FoxPro to include a title beside every field (in form-oriented reports) or above every field (in column-oriented reports). If you don't want the field names included in the report, turn off the Titles check box.

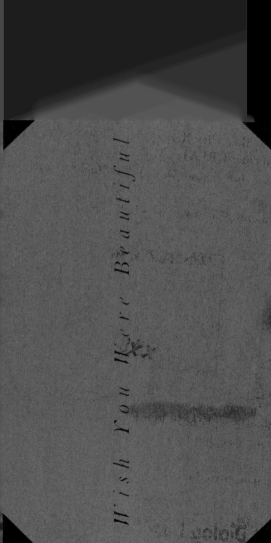

Roy Walsh

Opening Reception:
Saturday March 30 , 7 - 9 p.m.
March 30 - April 27, 1996.

26 Grand Street
New York City 10013
Tel/Fax 212 226 6361

Gallery Hours:
Wed through Sat, 12 - 6 p.m.

Russel Nelson
P.O. Box 251
Teaneck NJ 0266

The Fields check box can be used to select specific fields from the active table which should be included in the report. By default, FoxPro includes all fields in a quick report. If you turn on the Fields check box, the Field Picker appears, and you can click each desired field, followed by the Move button in the dialog box, to choose the fields you want in the report. When done, click OK.

The Add Alias check box determines whether alias names are automatically added to the expressions on which fields that appear in the report are based. Turning on this option is recommended if you plan to use the reports in a relational environment, where you have multiple tables open in different work areas, and you plan to design a report that takes its data from more than one table.

TIP

If you plan to use the same report with different tables that have the same table structure, turn off the Alias option. When you save the report, answer "No" to the prompt which asks if you want to save the environmental information.

Producing a Quick Report That's Based on a Query

One useful technique for quickly getting the precise data you need is to design a quick report that is based on a query. You can do this as part of the query design process, by changing the query's destination to Report/Label, clicking the Options check box, and choosing Quick Report in the next dialog box which appears. (For details on designing queries, refer to Chapter 6, "Performing Queries with RQBE.") These are the steps you need to follow to produce a quick report as a part of the query design process:

1. Open the RQBE Window using the techniques outlined in Chapter 6 and design the query that retrieves the desired records.
2. Click the arrow beside the Output list box, and change the query's output to Report/Label.
3. Click the Options check box. The RQBE Display Options dialog box appears. (See Figure 12.4.)

FIGURE 12.4.

The RQBE Display Options dialog box.

RQBE Display Options

○ Screen **D**isplay
● **Report**
○ **L**abel

☐ Form **N**ame...
☐ **Q**uick Report...   ☐ O**v**erwrite File
☒ **P**age Preview
☐ **S**ummary Information Only
☐ Eject P**a**ge Before Report
☐ Report **H**eading...
☐ Suppress Co**l**umn Headings
☒ **C**onsole On
☐ Pause **B**etween Screens

Output Destinations
☐ To Printer
☐ To **F**ile...   ☐ O**v**erwrite File

OK   Cancel

4. In the dialog box, click Report, then click the Quick Report option. The RQBE Quick Report dialog box appears. (See Figure 12.5.)

FIGURE 12.5.

The RQBE Quick Report dialog box.

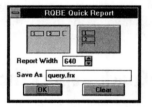

RQBE Quick Report

Report Width 640
Save As query.frx

OK   Clear

5. Click the Columnar Layout button (on the left side of the dialog box) or the Form Layout button (on the right side of the dialog box), to indicate the layout the quick report should use. Enter a name for the report in the Save As text box or leave the default name that FoxPro provides to accept it. Click OK to save the report.

6. In the RQBE Display Options dialog box, leave the Page Preview option turned on if you want to see the report in page preview mode. You also can turn off the Page Preview option and turn on the Output Destinations/To Printer option if you want the report printed. Click OK.

Upon completing these steps, the query can be saved (by choosing File, Save), and the query references the quick report by name when it is run. Running the query selects the specific data based on the query specifications and produce the report.

Working with a Report's Layout

When, for any reason, you prefer to design your report without the aid of the Quick Report option, you use the Report Writer as a working surface and add the desired fields, text, graphics, and other objects where you want them in the report. You can open a new report using any of the following three techniques:

- From the menus, choose File, New. Click Report in the dialog box which appears and click the New button.

- From the Catalog Manager, click the Report tab, click New, choose a table or query to base the report upon, and click the New Report button in the dialog box.

- From the Command Window, enter CREATE REPORT.

Any of these methods opens a window with a blank report within FoxPro's Report Writer tool.

To open an existing report, use any of these techniques:

- From the menus, choose File, Open. Change Type in the dialog box to Report, click the desired report by name, and click Open.

- From the Catalog Manager, click the Report tab, click the desired report by name to select it, and click the Modify button in the dialog box.

- From the Command Window, enter MODIFY REPORT *filename*, where *filename* is the name that the existing report was saved under.

With any of these methods, the existing report appears within a window in the Report Writer.

When you open a report in the Report Writer using any of these methods, you see a view similar to that shown in Figure 12.6. In report design, FoxPro uses the popular band-oriented approach. An understanding of what each band (or "section" of the report) is for is vital to the effective design of your reports. Where you place an object (such as text, an expression, or a field's contents) in a report determines exactly where the data prints, and how often.

If you did not assign a filename to a new report when you created it, FoxPro titles the report "Untitled" in the title bar, and adds an extension of .FRX. By default, FoxPro saves reports with this extension. When you later save the report, FoxPro asks for a filename, and it replaces the name "Untitled" with the name you assign.

> ## TIP
>
> If you want to create and work on two new reports at the same time, FoxPro gives you a problem. When you open one new report, FoxPro calls it "untitled.frx." If you then try to open a second new report and you don't assign it a name, FoxPro doesn't create another new report. Instead, FoxPro switches to the window that contains the existing report called "untitled.frx." The solution is to open the first new report, immediately save it under a filename, then open the second new report. You can then work on both reports while in design mode.

FIGURE 12.6.

An existing report in the Report Writer window.

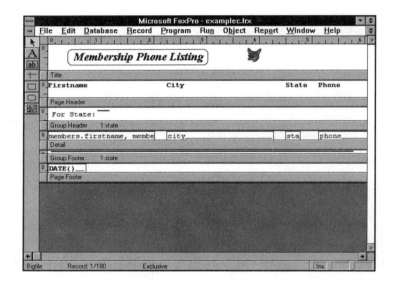

Reports normally contain a detail band, which contains the data that prints in the main portion of the report. Objects are placed within the report to determine what data is provided. The difference between designing reports and designing screens is that the objects placed in reports cannot by nature be interactive. Where screen objects could be used for interactive tasks like editing, report objects serve a one-way purpose—producing the data in on-screen or printed form. In addition to the detail band, reports often have title bands and summary bands, and page header and page footer bands. When designing a report, you see horizontal and vertical rulers, and you may also see a grid (unless these have been turned off with the Ruler/Grid option of the Report menu).

Titles and Summaries

The title band of a report contains any data which appears once, at the start of the report. The summary band also contains data that appears once in the report, at the end of the report. Title bands are commonly used for titles and the current date. The reports created by the Report Wizards place the title of the report in the title band. Summary bands are often used for summary information, such as grand totals for numeric fields that are desired only at the end of the report. If you want an object to appear once at the start of a report, add that object to the title band. If you want an object to appear once at the end of the report, add that object to the report's summary band.

Page Header and Page Footer Bands

Page header bands and page footer bands are also common in report designs. If you consider the actual printed pages that you expect to see from any hardcopy of a report, there will normally be information that you want to see once on each page. That page-repetitive data is what goes in the page header and footer bands of a report. Any data inserted into the page header band appears once at the top of each page, and any data inserted into the page footer band appears once at the bottom of each page. With the columnar reports designed by the Report Wizards, names of the fields appear in the page header bands, so that each page contains the field names at the start of the columns. If you want an object (such as text or a field) to appear once at the start of every page, add that object to the page header. If you want an object to appear once at the end of every page, place that object in the page footer.

Group Headers and Group Footer Bands

Reports can also contain optional group header bands and group footer bands. Group header bands and group footer bands let you arrange a report by groups. For example, you might want to see a mailing list printed by groups of residents of each country, and inside the country groupings, in groups by ZIP or postal codes. You would add group bands to the report to accomplish this task. (The adding of group bands to a report is covered later in this chapter.) Figure 12.7 shows an example of a report containing group sections in page preview mode. Figure 12.8 shows the same report in design mode. In the report's design, the State header and footer are the group sections that group the data alphabetically, by name of State.

FIGURE 12.7.

A report with group bands in page preview.

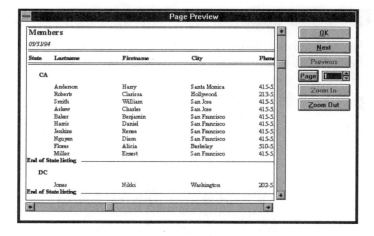

FIGURE 12.8.

A report with group bands in design mode.

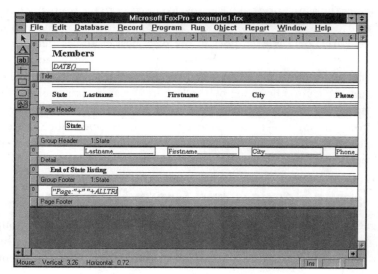

Column Headers and Column Footers

Reports in FoxPro can also contain multiple columns. (Multiple columns are added by choosing Report, Page Layout from the menus, and entering the desired number of columns in the dialog box.) When you have more than one column in a report, the data that you place in the Column Header appears at the top of each column, and data that you place in the Column Footer appears at the bottom of each column.

About the Report Menu Options

When you are designing a report, an additional menu titled Report appears on FoxPro's menu bar. The choices available within the Report menu are shown in Figure 12.9 and detailed in the following paragraphs.

FIGURE 12.9.

The Report Menu options.

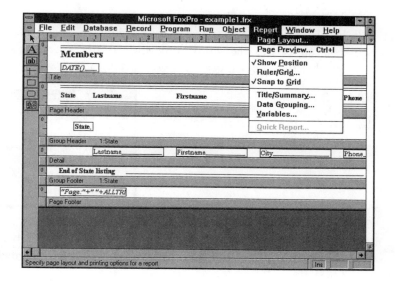

- Page Layout: This option causes the Page Layout dialog box to appear. (See Figure 12.10.) You can use the options within this dialog box to specify dimensions for the report, the number of columns and the order that multiple columns print in, and whether the print area encompasses the printable page, or the entire page. You can also access printer setup, environmental settings, and overall font settings, by clicking the Print Setup, Environment, or Font buttons in the dialog box. (These options are covered in detail shortly.)

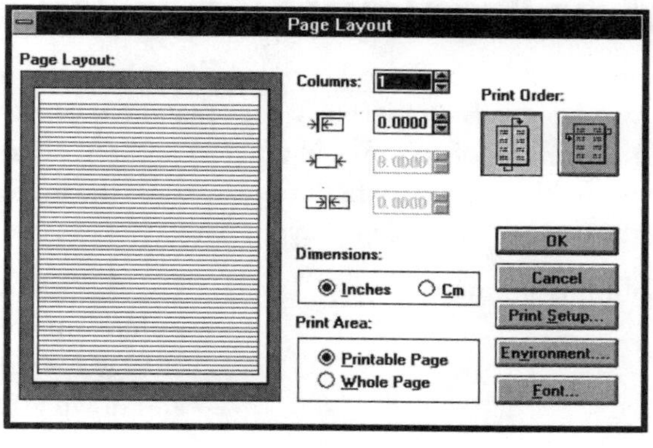

FIGURE 12.10.

The Page Layout dialog box.

■ Page Preview: This option displays the report in page preview mode. The option is useful for seeing how a report appears before it is printed.

■ Show Position: You can use this option to turn on and off the display of the position for the mouse pointer, or for a selected object. When this option is on, the position of the mouse pointer (or of an object that is selected) appears in the Status Bar.

■ Ruler/Grid: This option brings up a Ruler/Grid dialog box. (See Figure 12.11.) You can use this dialog box to specify what measurements are used by the rulers, whether ruler lines appear, and grid spacing.

FIGURE 12.11.

*The Ruler/Grid
dialog box.*

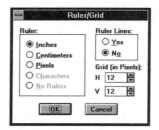

■ Snap To Grid: This option causes objects that you place in a report to snap to alignment with the grid (the objects are automatically aligned to the closest grid lines).

■ Title/Summary: You can use this option to add title bands or summary bands to a report.

■ Data Grouping: Use this option to add group bands to a report.

■ Variables: You can use this option to create memory variables, which can then be used within a report.

■ Quick Report: Use this option to create a default design for a report.

About the Page Layout Dialog Box

The options within the Page Layout dialog box (see Figure 12.10, shown previously), enables you to specify numerous values that affect the overall page layout. These values include the number of columns in a report and the distance between them; the left margin; the printable area; the default fonts used by the report; and the environmental setup. Each of the options in the Page Layout dialog box is detailed in the following paragraphs.

Columns spinner: Use this spinner to increase or decrease the number of columns in your report. You can change the value by clicking the spinner's up and down arrows, or by typing the desired value into the text box.

Left margin spinner:	Use this spinner to set the width of the left margin. You can change the value by clicking the spinner's up and down arrows, or by typing the desired value into the text box.
Column width spinner:	Use this spinner to set the width of the columns. You can change the value by clicking the spinner's up and down arrows, or by typing the desired value into the text box.
Space between columns spinner:	Use this spinner to set the width of the space between columns. You can change the value by clicking the spinner's up and down arrows, or by typing the desired value into the text box.
Dimensions area:	Use the buttons in this portion of the dialog box to indicate whether the measurements entered using the spinners are in inches, or in centimeters (cm).
Print Area area:	Use the options in this area to determine how printer margins are handled by the report. If you select the Printable Page button, the area of the page which is printed is determined according to the specifications of the default printer setup, and is shown within the box in the Page Layout area of the dialog box. If you select the Whole Page button, your report fills the entire page.
Print Order buttons:	Use these buttons to determine whether columns are filled from top to bottom beginning at the left side of the page, or whether rows are filled from left to right starting at the top of the page.
Print Setup button:	Use this button to open the Windows Print Setup dialog box, where you can change the default printer setup for the printer installed under Windows.
Environment button:	Use this button to open an Environment dialog box, which you can use to save the current environment, or to restore an environment that was previously saved.

Font... push button: Use this button to open the Font dialog box, which you can use to choose a default font, font size, and font style for objects added to the report.

About the Object Menu Options

When an object within a report is selected, the options of the Object menu are available. (See Figure 12.12.) These options are used for the following tasks:

Align to Grid: This option moves selected objects to align flush with the grid setting. If you have a group of fields, you can ensure that they line up perfectly by selecting the fields, then choosing Align To Grid.

Bring to Front: This option brings selected objects to the front, which means they show up above overlapping objects.

Send to Back: This option sends selected objects to the back, which means overlapping objects show up above them.

Center: This option moves an object horizontally to the center of its band. (The Center option has no effect on the vertical placement of the object.) Note that if you change the size of the report, you must select the object and choose Center again to re-center the object.

Group: This option joins selected objects. Once joined, you can move, cut, and paste them as if they were a single object.

Ungroup: This option separates previously grouped objects, so you can manipulate them individually.

Font: This option opens the Font dialog box, which you use to select a desired font, font style, and size for the characters in the selected object.

Text Alignment: This option displays another menu which lets you adjust the alignment and spacing of text within fields or text objects in the report. (Text objects must be on multiple lines before these options have any effect on them.) The menu contains these options:

Option	Description
Left	Left-justifies selected text.
Center	Centers selected text.
Right	Right-justifies selected text.

Single Space	Displays selected text single-spaced, with no blank lines appearing between lines of text.
1 1/2 Space	Displays selected text with 1 1/2 blank lines appearing between lines of text.
Double	Displays selected text double-spaced with one blank line appearing between lines of text.

Fill: This option displays another menu which lets you fill selected objects with one of seven hatched and cross-hatched patterns. (The default pattern is None.)

Pen: This option displays an additional menu which lets you set the point size and design pattern for lines and borders of rectangles and rounded rectangles in the report. The menu contains these options:

Option	Description
Hairline	One pixel width outline for the selected object.
1 Point	One point width outline for the selected object.
2 Point	Two point width outline for the selected object.
4 Point	Four point width outline for the selected object.
6 Point	Six point width outline for the selected object.
None	No outline for the selected object.
Dotted	Dotted line outline for the selected object.
Dashed	Dashed line outline for the selected object.
Dash-dot	Alternating dashes and dots for the outline.
Dash-dot-dot	Alternating dashes and two dots for the outline of the selected object.

Mode: This option displays an additional menu which lets you to determine whether the selected object is opaque or transparent. Mode only affects text objects, rectangles and rounded rectangles that have been assigned fill patterns.

Fill Color:	This option displays an additional menu which lets you choose one of 16 different fill colors for the selected object. If a fill pattern has been chosen for the object, the lines in the hatching or crosshatching pattern change to the selected color. If no fill pattern has been chosen, the fill color fills the selected object as a solid rather than as a pattern.
Pen Color:	This option displays an additional menu which lets you select one of 16 different pen colors for the selected object.

Using the Toolbox

At the left edge of the Report Writer window is a toolbox containing seven tools. (See Figure 12.12.) These tools are needed in the design of reports. You can use the tools to place the different objects (fields, text, graphics, and so on) in the report's design. To place an object in a report, first click the desired tool. Then click and drag in the Report Writer window to create the desired object. Note that when adding fields, you can click and drag to size the field, or you can just click where you want the field's upper-left corner to appear.

FIGURE 12.12.

The tools of the Toolbox.

> **TIP**
>
> You can add multiple objects of the same type to a report by first double-clicking the desired tool for that type of object. When you do this, the tool turns a dark grey, indicating it is the "locked" position. You can proceed to add the same type of object a number of times, without clicking the tool repeatedly.

Working with Objects

There are three different types of objects that you work with as you design reports: *text objects*, *field objects*, and *graphic objects*. Text objects contain text that you type directly into the report's design. Field objects are used to display data stored in fields, or data that's supplied by expressions or by user-defined functions. Graphic objects are pictures, lines, or rectangles. (Pictures in FoxPro reports must be stored either in general fields of a table, or as Windows Paintbrush files.)

As you add various objects to the report's design, you need to manipulate them in different ways. You can select them, resize and move them, and delete them when necessary. These are the steps needed to accomplish these tasks:

- To select an object, make sure the Selection tool (the upwards-pointing arrow) is selected in the Toolbox. Then, point to and click the desired object. When an object is selected, small rectangles surround it.

TIP

You can select multiple objects by holding the Shift key while clicking each object. You can also select all the objects within a band by double-clicking the band marker (directly beneath the band itself).

- To move an object, click and drag the desired object to the new location. Unlike the report writers in some database managers, FoxPro lets you drag objects between bands. For example, you could drag selected text from the Page Header band to the Page Footer band.
- To duplicate an object, first click the object to select it, and choose Edit, Copy from the menus. Then, choose Edit, Paste from the menus. When you do so, a copy of the object appears near its original location. You can then move the copy of the object to the desired location.
- To delete an object, select the object by clicking it, then press the Del key, or choose Edit, Cut from the menus.

Adding and Resizing Fields

The most common need when designing a report is the addition of fields to the report. To add fields, use the Field tool of the Toolbox. First click the Field tool in the Toolbox, then click in the report where you want the upper-left corner of the field to appear. When you do so, the Report Expression dialog box appears. Click Expression in this dialog box to reveal FoxPro's Expression Builder. In the Expression Builder, double-click the desired fieldname, then click OK to add the field to the Expression text box of the Report Expression dialog box.

To resize an existing field, click the field to select it (so that you can see its handles, the small rectangles that surround the field). Then click directly on any of the handles, and drag the handle in the desired direction, to resize the field as needed.

> **TIP**
>
> You can *concatenate* (combine on a textual basis) text fields with a space separating them, by double-clicking the name of the first field desired, typing a comma, and double-clicking the name of the next field desired. The comma tells FoxPro to separate the data with a space, and to remove trailing spaces. For example, assuming field names of FIRSTNAME and LASTNAME in a table, you could double-click the FIRSTNAME field in the Expression Builder, type a comma, and double-click the LASTNAME field, then click OK twice to insert the expression in the report. When printed, the expression would display the contents of the firstname field, followed by a space, followed by the contents of the lastname field.

Adding Text

To add text, typically used for titles or captions in a report, you use the Text tool. Click the Text tool, then click in the report where you want to begin the text to place a flashing insertion pointer at the desired location. Type the text. As you do so, it appears in the report.

When you are done typing the text, you can click anywhere outside of the text to complete the process. You can change the font and appearance of the text by clicking the text to select it. (When selected, the text is surrounded by four small rectangles.) With the text selected, choose Object, Font from the menus to open the Font dialog box. (See Figure 12.13.)

FIGURE 12.13.

The Font dialog box.

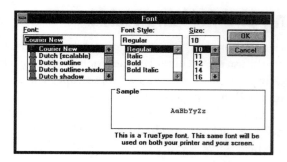

You can use the options in the Font dialog box to choose a desired font, font size, and style used for the font. When done selecting the desired options, click OK, and they take effect.

Drawing Lines and Rectangles

The Toolbox provides both a line tool and rectangle tools for drawing lines and rectangles. (You can draw two types of rectangles: ones with squared corners, and ones with rounded corners.) You can add visual emphasis to your reports by adding these design elements in appropriate locations.

To draw a line in a report, click the Line tool, place the cursor where you want an end of the line to be, and drag until the line is the desired length. To draw a rectangle in a report, click the Rectangle tool, place the cursor where you want a corner of the rectangle to be, and drag until the rectangle is the desired size. To draw a rectangle with rounded corners in a report, click the Rounded-Rectangle tool, place the cursor where you want a corner of the rounded rectangle to be, and drag until the rounded rectangle is the desired size. Note that you can specify how rounded the rectangle is by double-clicking on the rounded-rectangle object to open the Round Rectangle dialog box. In this dialog box, you can choose the shape of the rounded rectangle, from completely oval to slightly rounded.

Adding Title and Summary Bands

A new report which you create manually contains a Detail band, a Page Header band, and a Page Footer band by default. Title bands and Summary bands can be added by choosing Report, Title/Summary from the menus. When you do so, the Title/Summary dialog box appears. (See Figure 12.14.)

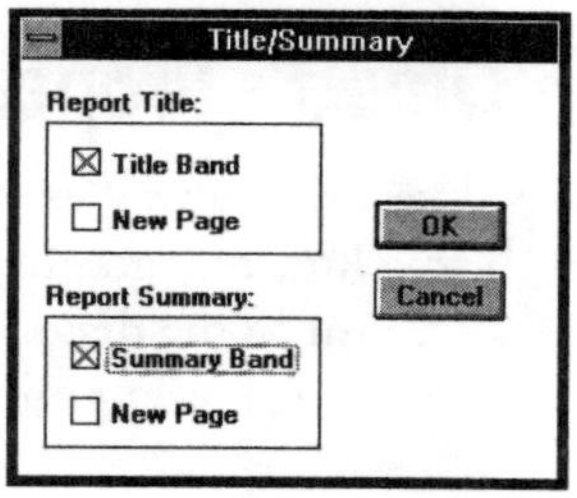

FIGURE 12.14.

The Title/Summary dialog box.

Under Report Title, click the Title Band option to add a Title band. Under Report Summary, click the Summary Band option to add a Summary band. With either option on, you can click the corresponding New Page option if you want the chosen band to always print its contents on a separate page. When done with the options, click OK. Once you've added a Title Band or a Summary Band to a report, add the desired objects to that band using the techniques outlined in this chapter.

Changing the Height of Bands

By default, FoxPro sets the size of any bands in a report to a minimum amount that's needed to enclose any fields. You can change the height of the bands using two methods. You can move the cursor to the left edge of the band's title line (where the cursor changes to the shape of a double-headed arrow), and click and drag the band upwards or downwards as desired. You can also double-click the rectangle at the left edge of the band's title line to open a dialog box for the band's height. (See Figure 12.15.) Double-click this dialog box, enter the desired value for the height, and click OK. You can turn on the Constant Height check box (which appears in this dialog box) if you do not want the band to adjust its height to accommodate lengthy data (like memo fields) that have been allowed to expand during printing.

FIGURE 12.15.

The dialog box for
adjusting band height.

TIP

If you don't want the Page Header or Page Footer bands that FoxPro adds to a new report by default, you can eliminate them by changing their heights to zero using either of the techniques discussed previously.

Modifying an Object's Properties

In FoxPro's Report Writer, an easy way exists to change the properties of a given object (such as a field, a text box, a line, or a graphic). Double-click the object, and a dialog box opens. The options that appear in the dialog box let you change the various properties of the selected object. Which dialog box appears depends on what type of object you double-click.

Modifying a Field's Properties

Double-click a field in a report, and the Report Expression dialog box appears. (See Figure 12.16.) As mentioned previously under "Adding and Resizing Fields," you use this dialog box to enter a fieldname or an expression that appears within the field. Clicking the Expression button displays the Expression Builder, which you can use to build a desired expression. Clicking the Format button causes the Format dialog box to appear, which you can use to specify different formatting options. (For more on these options, see "About the Format Dialog Box Options," which follows in this chapter.)

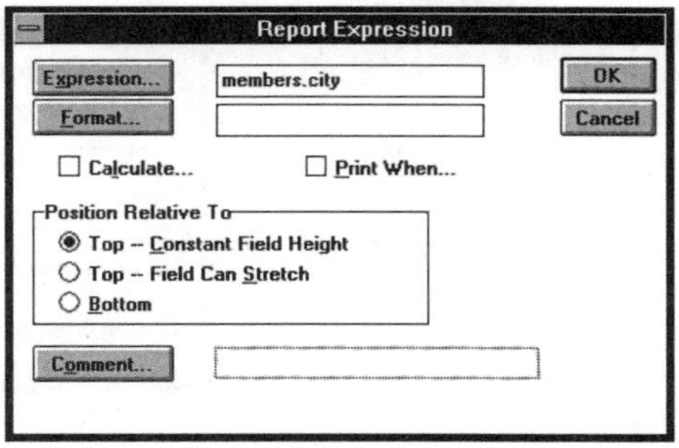

FIGURE 12.16.

The Report Expression dialog box.

The Calculate box, when checked, causes the Calculate Field dialog box to appear. (See Figure 12.17.) You can use this dialog box to establish a calculation for the expression. For example, if the expression is a field containing a numeric value, you could click Sum to obtain the sum of the values. The Reset list box in the Calculate Field dialog box lets you define whether the calculation occurs at the end of the report, at the end of each page, or at the end of each column (in reports having more than one column).

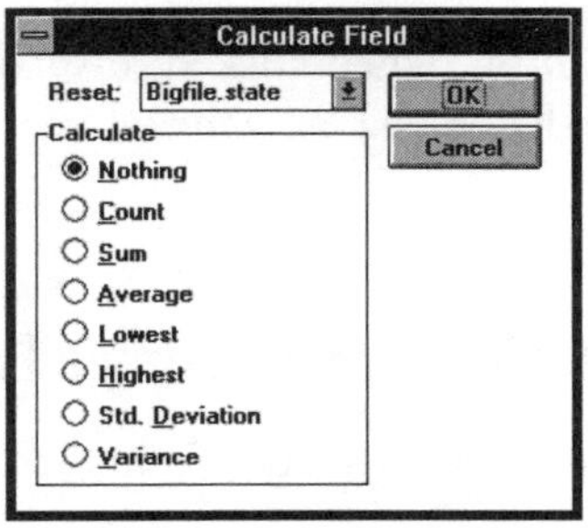

FIGURE 12.17.

The Calculate Field dialog box.

The Print When box, when checked, causes the Print When dialog box to appear. (See Figure 12.18.) You can use this dialog box to determine when the object is printed. By default, an object is printed whenever the contents of the band that contains it is printed, but you can use the options in this dialog box to change that default. For example, you can choose not to print values that repeat, and with reports that contain grouping, you can choose to print when the basis for the group changes. The Print Only When Expression is True check box lets you define another expression which then determines whether the field prints.

FIGURE 12.18.

*The Print When
dialog box.*

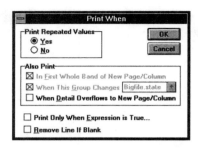

The Position Relative To portion of the Report Expression dialog box contains three options: Top–Constant Field Height, Top–Field Can Stretch, and Bottom. If you select Top–Constant Field Height, FoxPro maintains the position of the field relative to the top of the band and does not allow stretching of the field to accommodate lengthy data. If you select the Top–Field Can Stretch option, FoxPro maintains the position of the field relative to the top of the band and allows stretching of the field to accommodate lengthy data. If you select the Bottom button, FoxPro maintains the position of the field relative to the bottom of the band.

The Comment button, when clicked, displays a Comment dialog box. You can enter comments in this dialog box for your reference (they do not appear anywhere in the report).

Modifying Text, Line, and Rectangle Properties

Double-click a text object in a report, and the Text dialog box appears. (See Figure 12.19.)

FIGURE 12.19.

The Text dialog box.

Checking the Print When box causes the Print When dialog box to appear. (See Figure 12.18, shown previously.) Use the options in this dialog box to determine when the text prints, as described in the preceding paragraphs. The Position Relative To portion of the dialog box contains two options: Top, and Bottom. Use Top to position the text at the top of the report band, and Bottom to position the text at the bottom of the report band. The Comment button, when clicked, displays a Comment dialog box. You can enter comments in this dialog box for your reference (they do not appear anywhere in the report).

If you double-click a line in a report, the dialog box that appears is identical to the one shown in Figure 12.18, but with one difference: with a vertical line or rectangle, an additional check box titled "Stretch with Band" appears in the dialog box. If you turn on this option, the line or rectangle stretches along with the band.

If you double-click a rounded rectangle, a similar dialog box appears, but it also contains five different style buttons to apply five different styles of rounded rectangles. (See Figure 12.20.) In addition to specifying any of the options just described, you can click the desired style of rounded rectangle.

FIGURE 12.20.

The Round Rectangle dialog box.

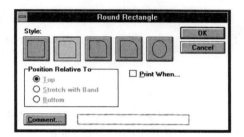

Modifying a Picture's Properties

If you double-click a picture in a report, a Report Picture dialog box appears. You can use the options in this dialog box to control where pictures in reports come from, when they should print, and how the size and scaling of the picture should be handled. For more specifics on the dialog box and the use of these options, refer to "Adding Graphics to a Report," which follows in this chapter.

About the Format Dialog Box Options

When you double-click a field to bring up the Report Expression dialog box and then click the Format button, the Format dialog box appears. (See Figure 12.21.) You can use the options in this dialog box to control the formatting applied to the selected field.

FIGURE 12.21.

The Format dialog box.

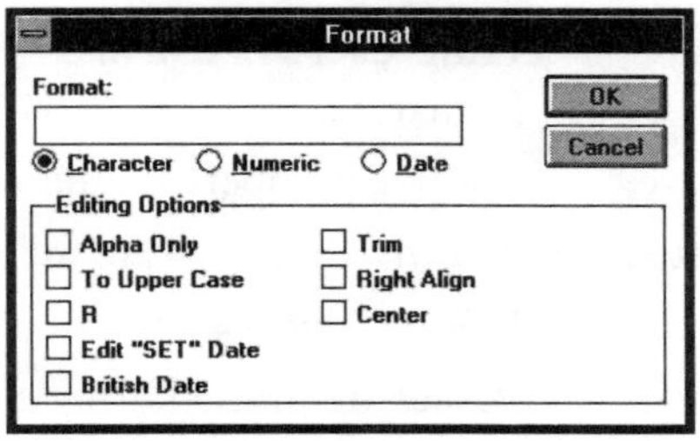

The Editing Options you see in this dialog box vary, depending on whether you select the Character, Numeric, or Date button. Table 12.1 shows the results of the options which you select in the Format dialog box when the Character button is selected.

Table 12.1. Results of Format dialog box options with Character selected.

Option	Result
Alpha Only	Allows only alphabetic characters
To Upper Case	Converts characters to uppercase
R	Displays characters, but does not store them
Edit SET Date	Prints data as a date using the SET DATE format that is in effect
British Date	Prints data as a date using the British (or European) date format
Trim	Strips leading and trailing blanks
Right Align	Prints data flush right
Center	Prints data centered

Table 12.2 shows the results of the options which you select in the Format dialog box when the Numeric button is selected.

Table 12.2. Results of Format dialog box options with Numeric selected.

Option	Result
Left Justify	Numeric data is aligned flush left
Blank if Zero	Field is blank if it contains a zero value
(Negative)	Negative numbers are enclosed in parenthesis
Edit SET Date	Prints data as a date using the SET DATE format that is in effect
British Date	Prints data as a date using the British (or European) date format
CR if Positive	Positive numbers are followed with the letters CR
DB if Negative	Negative numbers are followed with the letters DB
Leading Zero	Leading zeroes are printed
Currency	Values are printed using currency format
Scientific	Values are printed using scientific notation

Table 12.3 shows the results of the options which you select in the Format dialog box when the Character button is selected.

Table 12.3. Results of Format dialog box options with Date selected.

Option	Result
Edit SET Date	Prints data as a date using the SET DATE format that is in effect
British Date	Prints data as a date using the British (or European) date format

If you are familiar with the formatting codes used in the XBase language to format data, you can type those codes directly into the Format: text box that is in the dialog box. However, most users find it much easier to select the desired options by clicking the appropriate check boxes.

Adding Grouping to a Report

With most column-oriented reports (and many of a form-oriented nature), you'll want the data to appear subdivided into groups. For instance, if you were printing a report of employee phone numbers for a multinational corporation, you might need the report grouped by country, then by office or plant location within each country, then by department within each office or plant. Each of these categories would comprise a separate group. FoxPro's Report Writer overcomes the limitations of earlier XBase products by supporting up to 20 levels of grouping within a single report.

> **NOTE**
>
> A report that is grouped needs to have the underlying data arranged in an order that supports the group. Usually, this means creating an index (although you could technically accomplish the same result by sorting a table and basing the report on the sorted table). The point to remember is that you must put your data in order, whether by means of an index, a sort, or through an RQBE Query that orders the data, before it prints properly in a report that contains groups.

To add a group band, choose Report, Data Grouping from the menus. The Group dialog box appears. (See Figure 12.22.)

FIGURE 12.22.

The Data Grouping dialog box.

In the Group list box, you see the names of any existing groups you've added to the report. The Add, Change, and Delete buttons can be used to add a group, to change the specifications for an existing group, or to delete an existing group.

To add the group, click the Add button. The Group Info dialog box appears. (See Figure 12.23.) In this dialog box, you create and modify the expressions which controls the grouping in the report.

FIGURE 12.23.

The Group Info dialog box.

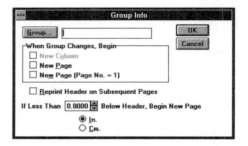

Click in the Group text box and type the desired expression, or click the Group button to bring up FoxPro's Expression Builder, where you can build the desired expression. When groups are used, the report begins a new group (or "breakpoint") each time the basis of the group expression changes. *Remember that when you use groups, you must index or sort the table on the field or expression used as the basis for the group.* For example, if a report is grouped on the basis of a Zipcode field within a table, the report contains a breakpoint, with any included subtotals of numeric fields or expressions, each time the contents of the Zipcode field changes. While many reports require the entry of a single fieldname as the expression, you use any valid FoxPro expression. For example, if you wanted the group to be based on a single field such as Zipcode, you would enter the field's name (in this example, **Zipcode**) as the expression in the Group text box. On the other hand, if a table was indexed on a combination of fields called Office and Department, and you wanted to base the grouping on that combination of fields, you could enter the expression **Office + Department** in the text box.

The "When Group Changes, Begin" portion of the dialog box contains three options: New Column, New Page, and New Page (Page No. = 1). The New Column box, when checked, causes a new column to start each time the group expression changes. (This option is only enabled if your report has more than one column. You can add columns to a report by choosing Report, Page Layout, and specifying the number of columns desired in the dialog box.) The New Page box, when checked, causes a page break to occur each time the group expression changes. The New Page (Page No. = 1) box, when checked, sets the page number to 1 each time the group expression changes.

The Reprint Header on Subsequent Pages box, when checked, tells FoxPro to reprint the header on each page spanned by the group.

The If Less Than spinner control lets you avoid having a group header print near the bottom of the page, while most of the detail lines associated with the header are printed on the next page. Use the spinner to choose a minimum distance from the bottom of the page that a group header is printed. (The Inches and Cm buttons let you specify whether the distances indicated by the spinner are measured in inches or centimeters.)

When done with the options in this dialog box, click OK. The dialog box closes to reveal the Data Grouping dialog box still beneath. You can click OK again to put away that dialog box. The new bands that you add appears in the report. However, by default, they occupy no space. You need to increase the width of the new bands to the amount you desire, using the techniques covered previously under "Changing a Band's Width."

Adding Graphics to a Report

One benefit of using FoxPro in the Windows environment is that you can add graphics to reports. These graphics can be from pictures that are stored in a general field of a FoxPro table or they can be design elements created in a drawing or paint program elsewhere in Windows. (Pictures which are used as design elements must be saved in Windows Paintbrush (.BMP) file format.) For example, Figure 12.24 shows a report with a picture has been copied into the Title band of the report as a design element. This picture appears at the top of the first page for every report printed.

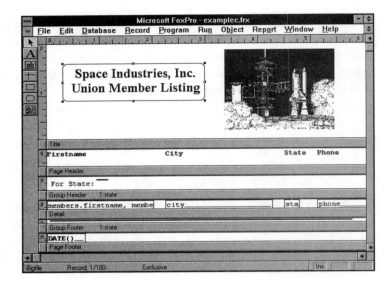

To add a picture to a report, perform the following steps:

1. Design the desired report, using the steps outlined in this chapter.

2. In the Toolbox, click the Picture tool.

3. Click at the desired starting location for the graphic, and drag to the desired ending location until the frame reaches the desired size for the picture. When you release the mouse, the Report Picture dialog box appears. (See Figure 12.25.)

4. Use the options in this dialog box (discussed in the following paragraphs) to tell FoxPro where to find the picture, and how to handle pictures that are not the same size as the frame they are in.

5. When done selecting the desired options, click OK. The picture then appears within the report's design. (See Figure 12.24.)

The Report Picture dialog box (see Figure 12.25) has the options described here which let you exercise control over where the picture comes from, and how it is handled within the report:

FIGURE 12.25.

*The Report Picture
dialog box.*

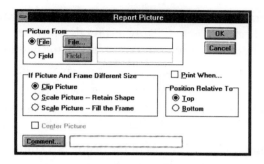

The Picture From area of the dialog box has File and Field radio buttons, and corresponding rectangular buttons and text boxes (where you can type in the name of a file or of a field). You use the options in this area to tell FoxPro where to find the picture that's placed in the report. To include a single bit map picture in your report, click the File radio button. Then, click the rectangular File... button to open a Picture dialog box which you can use to select the desired .BMP file. You can also type the name (including the path) of the .BMP file in the text box to the right of the File button. To base the picture on the contents of a general field of a table, click the Field radio button. Then, click the rectangular Field button to open a Choose Field/Variable dialog box, which you can use to select the desired field. Alternately, you can type the name of the field in the text box to the right of the Field button. Note that when general fields of a table contain a document other than a picture or a chart (such as Word for Windows documents, or Excel spreadsheets), an icon representing the object appears in the field that's printed in the report.

The If Picture and Frame Different Size area of the dialog box has three options, titled Clip Picture, Scale Picture-Retain Shape, and Scale Picture-Fill the Frame. When the picture is larger than the frame you added to the report, the Clip Picture option tells FoxPro to clip the picture at the right and the bottom as required to fit within the frame. The Scale Picture-Retain Shape option tells FoxPro to show the entire picture, filling as much of the frame as possible while keeping the relative proportions of the bit map picture. (This method of scaling helps avoid vertical or horizontal distortion.) The Scale Picture-Fill the Frame option shows the entire picture, filling the frame completely. Depending on the dimensions of the frame, this may cause horizontal or vertical distortion as FoxPro scales the picture to fit the frame.

The Center Picture check box is designed to be used along with pictures that are stored in general fields of a table. (Pictures in .BMP files that are placed in reports as design elements are not affected by this option.) Since bitmaps stored in general fields of a table can come in a variety of shapes and sizes, this option enables you to tell FoxPro whether to center the pictures shown in the report. When the bit map stored in a general field is smaller than the frame, it appears in the upper-left corner of the frame unless you check Center Picture. Checking Center Picture insures that pictures (stored in general fields) which are smaller than the frame are centered in the frame within the report.

The Print When... check box opens a Print When dialog box. You can use the options in this dialog box to tell FoxPro how often the picture should print (in relation to the band it is in), and under what conditions the picture should be printed. If you don't use any options in this dialog box, by default FoxPro always prints the picture.

The Position Relative To area of the dialog box contains two options: Top and Bottom. The Top button causes the picture to remain in the position you place it in the report, and maintain that position in relation to the top of the band. The Bottom button causes the picture to remain in the position you place it in the report, and maintain that position in relation to the bottom of the band.

The Comment push button opens a Comment dialog box, where you can add comments about the picture. (Comments are purely for your reference, and do not appear in the printed report.)

Previewing the Report

Once the report's design is complete, you can view it with actual data, by choosing Report, Page Preview from the menus. A preview of the report appears in a Page Preview window. (See Figure 12.26.)

> **TIP**
>
> You can use the preview feature at any time during the report's design to get an idea of how the report is shaping up during the design process.

FIGURE 12.26.

The Page Preview window containing a report.

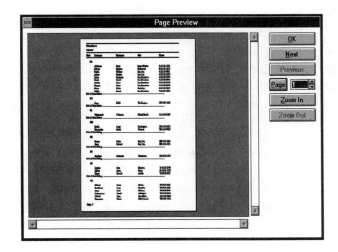

The preview mode of a report enables you to see what the report looks like before it is printed, complete with all fonts and design elements that are included in the report's design. The preview mode initially shows the entire page, in a reduced view, and the mouse pointer takes on the shape of a magnifying glass. By moving to any area of the report and alternately clicking, you can switch back and forth between a full-page view and a "zoomed" or enlarged view of the area. The right side of the window contains various buttons which you can use for navigation between pages of the report. Click the Next and Previous buttons to move to the next and previous pages of a report. You can also click the up and down arrows in the spinner to display a desired page number, then click the Page button to move to that page number. You can also click in the text box beside the spinner, type a page number, and click Page to move to that page number. The Zoom In and Zoom Out buttons are the equivalent of clicking in the report with the mouse—use Zoom In to switch to an enlarged view, and use Zoom Out to switch to a reduced view that shows a report's full page. When done previewing a report, click OK to return to the report's design.

Saving, Printing, and Displaying Reports

Chapter 9 provides details on saving and printing reports, both from the menus and from the Command Window. The overall techniques are touched on here purely as a reference. For details on these procedures, refer to Chapter 9.

To save the completed report, choose File, Save from the menus. If you did not assign the report a name when you started the report creation process, FoxPro displays the Save As dialog box. Enter a name for the file (assuming you are running DOS, filenames must be eight characters or less, with no spaces), then click Save. FoxPro saves the reports with a default extension of .FRX.

When a report is saved, FoxPro asks if you want to save the environment information. This refers to the surrounding "state of affairs" that exists when you save the report. This includes what tables are open, what indexes are active, any relationship that's established with the View dialog box or the SET RELATIONSHIP command, and any restrictions on available fields established with the SET FIELDS command. When you answer "Yes" to the "Save Environment?" prompt, FoxPro saves this information along with the report. This information can be useful to save along with the report, because you can then easily restore the environment when you run the report. You can do so by checking the Restore Environment check box in the Report dialog box which appears when you run a report by choosing Database, Report. You can also include the ENVIRONMENT clause along with a REPORT FORM command that you enter in the Command Window or call from within a FoxPro program.

To print a report using the menus, choose Run, Report, then select the desired report in the Open dialog box, and click Run. In the Run Report dialog box which next appears, click Preview to display the report in preview mode, or click Print to send the report's output to the printer. Click Run to produce the report. From the Command Window, you can print a report with the REPORT FORM command, with the following basic syntax:

```
REPORT FORM report filename [TO PRINT]
```

and if the TO PRINT option is used, the report is printed; otherwise, it appears on screen, in the main window of the FoxPro desktop.

You can also print reports by choosing Database, Report from the menus, and filling in the various options which appear in the Report dialog box. (See Figure 12.27.)

FIGURE 12.27.

The Report dialog box.

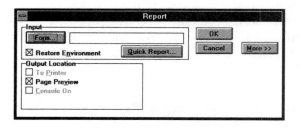

The Input portion of the dialog box contains a Form button, and a Form text box. You can enter the name of the stored report form in the text box or can click the button to display an Open dialog box, which you can then use to select a stored report form. The Restore Environment box, when checked, tells FoxPro to restore any environment that was saved at the time the report was saved. The Quick Report button displays the Quick Report dialog box, which you can use to create a new quick report. In the Output Location portion of the dialog box, you can choose Page Preview, or Printer. If you choose

Printer, you can also turn on the Console On option, which causes the report's output to appear in the active window as well as being sent to the default printer.

Clicking the More button in the Report dialog box causes the box to expand to reveal additional options. (See Figure 12.28.) The Scope, For, and While buttons can be used to specify conditions which determine the records that are included in the report. (For a discussion of using scope, for, and while, see Chapter 7, "Queries with Commands.") The First Page Heading Only causes the Page Header band to appear only on the initial page and omits it from subsequent pages. The No Initial Form Feed suppresses any initial form feed that would otherwise be sent to the printer before printing starts. The Summary Information Only option, when checked, causes the report to be printed without the data that's in the Detail band. The Heading option can be used to add another heading (one that is not a part of the report's design) to the report.

FIGURE 12.28.

The Expanded Report dialog box.

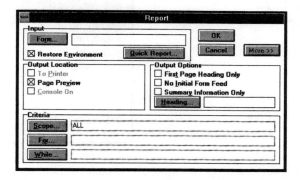

When done with the options in the Report dialog box, click OK in the dialog box to display or print the report.

An Exercise: Creating a Custom Report

You can follow the steps shown here to practice using the techniques described in this chapter. This exercise creates a custom report that uses multiple columns to display a phone directory. The report is grouped on the basis of the State field in the underlying table. The report uses the MEMBERS.DBF table that's stored on the accompanying disk. If you have not already copied MEMBERS.DBF from the disk into your working directory, you need to do so before you can follow this exercise. Perform the steps shown to create the report:

1. In the Command Window, enter USE MEMBERS to open the table.
2. In the Command Window, enter INDEX ON STATE TAG STATES to build and put into effect an index that supports the grouping which is added to the report.

3. Choose File, New, click Report, and click New to open a new report.

4. Click the Text tool. Then click in the Page Header band, about one inch to the right of the left edge and one-half inch down from the top, and type **Company Phone Listing**.

5. Click anywhere outside of the text, then click the text to select it. Choose Object, Font to open the Font dialog box, and choose a larger font of your choice, with a bold style.

6. Double-click the Field tool, to select it and lock in the selection.

7. In the Detail band, click roughly 1/2 inch to the right of the left edge and 1/2 inch down from the top of the band. The Report Expression dialog box appears. (See Figure 12.29.)

FIGURE 12.29.

The Report Expression dialog box.

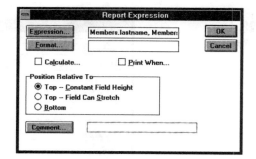

8. Click the Expression button to bring up the Expression Builder. In the Expression Builder, double-click the Lastname field, then type a comma, then double-click the Firstname field. Click OK to put away the Expression Builder. Click OK again to close the Report Expression dialog box.

9. In the Detail band, click roughly 1/4 inch to the right of the field that you just placed, to again display the Report Expression dialog box.

10. Click the Expression button to bring up the Expression Builder. In the Expression Builder, double-click the Phone field. Click OK to put away the Expression Builder, and click OK again to close the Report Expression dialog box.

11. Open the Report menu, and if the Snap to Grid option is on, turn it off by choosing this option. (You can tell when the option is on by the presence of a check mark that appears beside its name in the menu.)

12. Click the Rounded Rectangle tool in the Toolbox. Then click at a point just above and to the left of the title, and drag down and to the right until the rectangle fully encloses the text. If necessary, select the rectangle and move it so that the text appears evenly centered within the rectangle.

13. Click the Field tool in the Toolbox, then click in the Page Footer band, at a point roughly three inches to the right of the left edge and 1/2 inch down from the top of the band.

14. In the Report Expression dialog box, click the Expression button to bring up the Expression Builder.

15. In the Expression Builder, click the arrow to the right of the Date functions list box to open the list box. In the list box, double-click DATE().

16. Click OK to close the Expression Builder, and click OK again to close the Report Expression dialog box beneath it.

17. Choose Report, Page Layout from the menus to open the Page Layout dialog box.

18. Change the number of columns from one to two. Increase the distance between columns (the lowest spinner in the dialog box) to 0.5 inches, then click OK in the dialog box to close it.

19. Click the Line tool in the Toolbox. Then click at a point just to the right of the right edge of the Phone field, at the top of the Detail band, and drag straight down to the bottom of the Detail band. Doing so places a line to the right of each phone number, which helps divide the phone numbers in the left column from those in the right column. When you are done with this step, your report should resemble the one shown in Figure 12.30.

FIGURE 12.30.

The completed report in design mode.

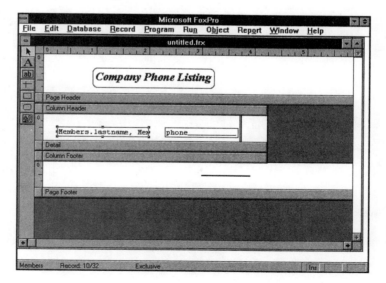

20. Choose File, Save from the menus. When prompted for a name, enter PHONELST as the desired name. Answer Yes to the prompt that asks if you want to save the environment information, and choose File, Close to close the report.

To produce the report, choose Run, Report, then select PHONELST.FRX in the Open dialog box which appears, and click Run. In the Run Report dialog box which next appears, click Preview if you want to display the report in preview mode, or click Print if you want to sent the report's output to the printer. Finally, click Run to produce the report.

Chapter Summary

This chapter provided an extensive reference to the techniques you use in designing and producing reports. In FoxPro, the secret to meeting your reporting needs is a complete familiarity with the Report Writer, as its capabilities make it possible to produce virtually any type of report imaginable. If you plan to call stored reports that you create from within FoxPro programs, be sure to consider the material in Chapter 22, "Programming for Reporting Needs," which shows how you can produce reports while under the control of a program.

Using Expressions and Functions

Expressions and functions come into regular use throughout FoxPro. As previously noted, you use them in queries—both when constructing queries through commands and when using the query-by-example facility. Expressions and functions are also particularly useful in forms and reports, where you can use them to calculate the values that appear in calculated fields. You can use expressions for any of the following tasks:

- Constructing queries within the RQBE Window
- Building queries with commands entered in the Command Window
- Adding a calculation to a form or a report
- Adding a system variable, such as the current date or time, to a form or report
- Provide totals or averages for an entire report, or for a group of records within a report

This chapter provides a more thorough look at how expressions are constructed and details how you can use different types of expressions and functions to obtain results like those described in the preceding list.

Expressions, Defined

An *expression* is a calculation, made up of any combination of functions, operators, constants, and fieldnames, which FoxPro evaluates to equal some kind of value. Typically, you use an expression because you need a value of some sort that cannot be directly obtained from a field of a table. For example, if a table of video sales contained a Quantity field and a Price field, you might use an expression in a report like this one

```
Quantity * Price
```

to return a value that is the result of the Quantity field multiplied by the Price field.

Parts of an Expression

An expression can include any needed combination of operators, fieldnames, functions, constants, and literal values. Figure 13.1 shows an expression, and the parts of that expression.

FIGURE 13.1.
The parts of an expression.

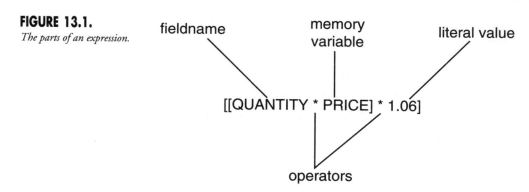

Operators

Most expressions use specific *operators,* which perform various operations on data to produce values. FoxPro provides *math operators* (for performing addition, subtraction, multiplication, and division), *assignment and comparison operators* (like equals, greater-than, and less-than) to assign and compare values, *logical operators* to deal with true and false values, and *concatenation operators* to combine character strings. Table 13.1 shows operators you'll commonly make use of in expressions.

Table 13.1. Operators used in expressions.

Math Operators	
*	Multiplication
+	Addition
-	Subtraction
/	Division
^	Exponentiation (raises one number to the power of another)

Assignment and Comparison Operators	
<	Less than
<=	Less than or equal to
>	Greater than
>=	Greater than or equal to
=	Equal to
<> or # or !	Not equal to
$	Contained within (used only with text strings)
==	Exactly equals (used only with text strings)

continues

Table 13.1. continued

Logical Operators	
.AND.	Both comparisons are true
.OR.	Either comparison is true
.NOT.	Entire comparison is true, of expression named by .NOT. is false

Concatenation	
+	String concatenation (combines two text strings)
, (comma)	String concatenation with trailing blanks trimmed and a space added between the two strings

Math Operators

You use math operators in FoxPro to produce numeric results. The usual operators of addition (+), subtraction (-), multiplication (*) and division (/) are present. In addition, FoxPro provides *unary minus* (where the minus sign changes a value into its negative equivalent), and exponentiation (raising a number to the power of another number).

Assignment and Comparison Operators

While the equal symbol may be common to math formulas, it isn't considered a math operation in FoxPro. In FoxPro, the equal sign is both an assignment operator and a comparison operator, used alone to assign values or used in combination with other operators to compare values. You use the equal sign alone to assign a value to an object or variable; for example, the statement `Salary = 12` assigns a value of 12 to the variable named Salary. The less-than and greater-than symbols can be used alone, or with the equal symbol as comparison operators. Used in this manner, the operators return a true or false value depending on the result of the expression. For example, a simple comparison of `5 < 9` would result in a logical true, while the result of `5 < NUMBER` would depend upon the value of the variable called NUMBER.

Logical Operators

You use the logical operators, .AND., .OR., and .NOT., to compare values and produce a logical true or false.

Concatenation

Use the concatenation operator (+) to combine text strings. For example, if a table has fields named Lastname and Firstname, you could produce a text string with the full name separated by a space with this expression:

```
trim(Firstname) + " " + LastName
```

You can also use the comma symbol as a concatenation operator to perform a similar function. When used between two expressions that evaluate as text, the comma concatenates (combines) the text strings, and inserts a space between them. Therefore, the expression

```
trim(Firstname),Lastname
```

would produce the same result as the expression shown earlier.

Operator Precedence

Note that there's a specific order, or precedence, in which math operations are performed. FoxPro performs exponentiation first, then negation (making a number a negative number), then multiplication and division, then addition and subtraction, then concatenation, then logical operations. In cases where operators maintain equal precedence (such as multiplication and division), the order of precedence is from left to right. You can use parentheses in your expressions to force a different order of precedence. When parentheses are used, FoxPro calculates from the innermost pair of parenthesis, and works outward.

Functions

Functions can be thought of as special-purpose programs, built into FoxPro, that perform tasks that would otherwise require large amounts of program code. Functions accept data, perform an internal calculation of some sort, and return data. You can use functions to convert data from one type to another, to perform specialized math operations, to test for various conditions, and to manipulate data in various ways. FoxPro contains dozens of functions for specialized purposes, such as finding the average of a group of values, looking up a field value within a specified set of records, converting characters of a string to uppercase, or returning a value representing the day of the week. You can see a complete list of all available functions by choosing Help/Contents from the menus, and clicking Commands and Functions under the Language Reference subheading.

Literals

Literals are actual values, such as text, numbers, or dates. Some examples of literals might be 36, 3/10/94, and Jayne Smith. Text literals must be enclosed in quotation marks, and dates must be enclosed in curly braces, as in {03/10/94}.

Entering Expressions in Screens and Reports

Expressions can be added to screens and reports with the Field tool, which is also used to add table fields to screen designs and to report designs. With screens, you open the screen in design mode, then you add an expression as a field using the following steps:

1. Click the Field tool in the Toolbox, then click and drag to place the field.
2. In the Field dialog box that opens, click Output Field (Say).
3. Click the Output button, to open the Expression Builder.
4. Type the expression, or use the Expression Builder to build it.

With reports, you open the report in design mode, then you add an expression as a field using the following steps:

1. Click the Field tool in the Toolbox, then click where you want the upper-left corner of the field to appear.
2. In the Report Expression dialog box that appears, click the Expression button to open the Expression Builder.
3. Type the expression or use the Expression Builder to build it.

In FoxPro, the Expression Builder can be a big help in adding expressions. Besides providing a way to construct expressions while minimizing possible syntax errors, the Expression Builder also contains a number of standard expressions for values such as the current date and time and the current page number of a report. (See Figure 13.2.)

FIGURE 13.2.

The Expression Builder.

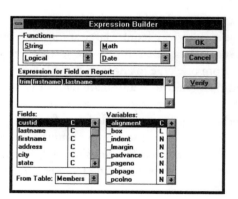

With the Expression Builder, you construct the desired expression by double-clicking the desired choices in the Functions list boxes, or the desired choices in the Fields and Variables list boxes to insert them where needed. As you double-click the desired items, they appear in the window in the center of the Expression Builder. As you build the expression, you can also type characters directly into the window at any time. When you are done constructing the expression, click OK to close the Expression Builder. The Verify button can be used to verify that a particular expression is valid to FoxPro. If the expression is valid, a message to that effect appears in the Status Bar when you click the button.

Using Concatenation

You can use the concatenation operator (+) to combine text strings within a field. This technique is commonly used in reports, to combine fields such as a last name, first name, and middle initial into a single field containing the full name, or to combine city, state, and postal code fields into a single field. For example, consider a table with fields named Lastname, Firstname, and Midinit. With such a table as the underlying table for a report, you could use an expression like the following within a text box control:

```
trim(Firstname) + " " + Midinit + ". " + Lastname
```

which might yield a text string like "Steve A. Hairston." In this example, if there were no entry in the Middle Initial field, you would get an unwanted space and a period. But this can be cured with the use of the IIF function, a topic that is covered later in this chapter.

When working with text, keep in mind that you can use the FoxPro string functions, including Left() and Right(), to print a portion of text. For example, if the underlying table or query contains a field called Midname and you want to display only the first character of whatever entry is in that field, you could use an expression like **Left(Midname,1)** to display the first character of that field's contents.

Working with Dates, Times, and Page Numbers

A common use for expressions within forms and reports is to show the current date or time, and in reports, the current page number or the total number of pages in the report. If you want to display the current date, time, or both, add a field using the Field tool, and enter any of the following expressions into the Expression Builder:

DATE()	(to display the current date)
TIME()	(to display the current time)
DTOC(DATE())+" "+TIME()	(to display the current date and time)
_PAGENO	(to display the current page number in a report)

Including Percentages in a Report

At times a report may include a numeric column of data such as a sale price for each item sold, and you may want to display another column beside the numeric column that shows each sales value as a percentage of the total sales. You can do this by first creating a memory variable that calculates the total for the field. You could use a command like

```
SUM SALES TO TOTSALES
```

to accomplish this. Then, you would add a calculated field to the report's Detail band. The field would contain the expression

```
(SALES/TOTSALES)*100
```

and the column that appears as a result of the field contains the calculated value. A disadvantage to this technique, from an interactive nature, is that you must remember to use the SUM command to create the memory variable before running the report. You can solve this problem by storing the commands to create the memory variable and then print the report in a program file, and you can then run the program each time you want to produce the report.

Including Running Totals in Reports

You can also use memory variables as part of expressions to display running totals in a report. Figure 13.3 shows a page preview of a report containing a field with donation amounts, and a running total of that field.

FIGURE 13.3.

Page preview of a report containing a running total.

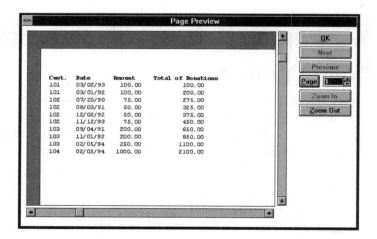

To add a variable to a report that can be used to display a running total, open the report in design mode, and choose Report, Variables from the menus. A Report Variables dialog box appears. Click Add, to display the Variable Definition dialog box. (See Figure 13.4.)

FIGURE 13.4.

A Variable Definition dialog box.

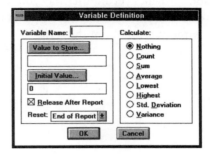

Enter a name for the variable in the Variable Name box, then click the Value to Store button. In the next dialog box, select the field to be used as the basis for the running total, and click OK. In the Calculate portion of the Variable Definition dialog box, click Sum, then OK. Finally, click OK to close the Variable Definition dialog box. You can then use the Field tool and the Report Expression dialog box (as detailed in Chapter 12, "Designing and Customizing Reports") to add the expression that calculates the running total to the report.

Using the IIF Function

The immediate IF function, or IIF(), can also be useful as part of an expression in forms and reports when you need to display one set of data if a condition is true, and another set of data if the condition is false. For instance, a field called Credit might contain a value of 1 indicating yes, and 0 indicating no. In a form or a report, you could indicate the value contained in the field with words rather than the numeric amounts with an expression like this one:

```
=IIF(CREDIT=1, "Yes", "No")
```

As another example, you might have a personnel report where you want to indicate how many weeks of vacation an employee receives; the company provides two weeks vacation once an employee has one or more years with the company. Assuming the table or query contains a field named Dayhired, you could display the amount of vacation in a form or report with an expression like the following:

```
IIF(DATE() - (DATE(DAYHIRED)) < 365, "none","two weeks")
```

You could place the entire expression within a field on a form or a report, and the form or report would display the appropriate amount of vacation for each employee.

Chapter Summary

This chapter detailed the use of expressions within FoxPro: queries, forms, and reports. Using expressions provides yet another way you can extend the power of FoxPro. Keep in mind that FoxPro's Expression Builder can be a significant aid in constructing expressions that run without errors from the start.

Producing Mailings

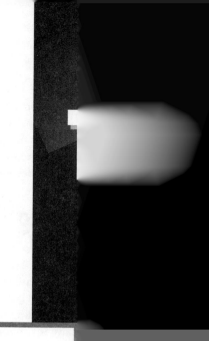

This chapter provides techniques you can use when dealing with mailings, which are a major business task handled by database software. Topics in this chapter include how you can produce mailing labels with the Label Wizard or by designing them manually, how you can generate form letters from within FoxPro, and how you can generate form letters by exporting files for use with Word for Windows and other word processors.

Creating Mailing Labels with the Label Wizard

Mailing labels are among the most common report types produced from database managers, and FoxPro is no slouch in this area. If you work through the Catalog Manager, FoxPro makes the mailing label creation process easy, through the addition of a wizard designed specifically for mailing labels. (You may want to first design a query that selects the desired records for the mailing labels before starting the wizard. With the query designed and saved, you can base the labels you create on that query.) From the Catalog Manager, use the following steps to create mailing labels:

1. Start the Catalog Manager if it is not already open (choose File, Catalog Manager).

2. Click the Label tab, then click New. The Create Label dialog box appears. (See Figure 14.1.)

FIGURE 14.1.

The Create Label dialog box.

3. In the Select a Table or Query list box, choose the query or table on which to base the labels, then click the Label Wizard button. The first of the Label Wizard dialog boxes appears. (See Figure 14.2.) This dialog box asks for a desired label size. Label sizes can be shown in both dimensions, English (using inches) or Metric (using centimeters). The labels use the common Avery office label numbers, available in most office supply stores, as a reference to label size. Use the English or Metric buttons in the dialog box to choose inches or centimeters, and click the desired label size to select it. When done choosing the desired options, click Next.

FIGURE 14.2.

The dialog box for desired label size.

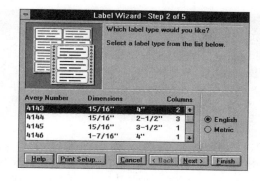

The next dialog box (see Figure 14.3) provides you with a list of fields from the underlying table or query. You can add any of these fields to the Selected Fields box by double-clicking, or by clicking the field followed by the right-arrow button. Also provided in the dialog box are punctuation buttons, which you use to add punctuation such as spaces, commas, and line breaks (or returns), and a Text box where you can type in text that appears in the label.

FIGURE 14.3.

The Label Wizard Mailing Label dialog box.

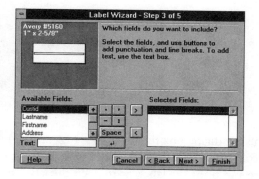

4. Add the desired fields to the label by clicking the field name in the list of fields to select it, and clicking the right-arrow button. (You can also just double-click the field.) To add a space or to add other punctuation, click the Space or the desired punctuation button. To move to a new line on the label, click the Return/Enter button. To add text in the label, type the desired text in the Text box, then click the right-arrow button to add the text to the label. As you add fields, punctuation, and text, the items you add appear in the Selected Fields box at the right side of the dialog box.

> **TIP**
>
> As you build the label, a representation of where the data will appear within the label appears in the upper-left corner of the dialog box, along with the chosen label's dimensions. This can be helpful for making sure that you don't add data that is too large for a particular label size.

5. When the label's design is complete, click Next. The next dialog box (see Figure 14.4) asks you to choose a sort order. Click the field or fields you want to determine the sort order followed by the Add button, and click Ascending or Descending, as desired. Click Next when done choosing a sort order. (Note that you can also click Next without specifying any sort order, in which case the labels are printed based on the order they occur in the underlying table or query.)

FIGURE 14.4.

The Label Wizard dialog box for choosing sort order.

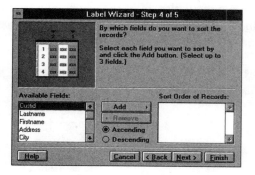

6. The last dialog box to appear (see Figure 14.5) informs you that the label design is completed. This box provides three buttons to save the label for later use, to save and print the label, or to open the label using FoxPro's Label Designer, so that you can make further modifications to the label's design.

FIGURE 14.5.

The last Label Wizard dialog box.

You can also click the Preview button in the dialog box, to see the labels in Page Preview mode before you save them. If you click the Preview button, the labels appear in a Page Preview window. (See Figure 14.6.) In the last Label Wizard dialog box, click the desired button, then click Finish to save the mailing labels or make changes to the design.

FIGURE 14.6.
A completed label design in Page Preview.

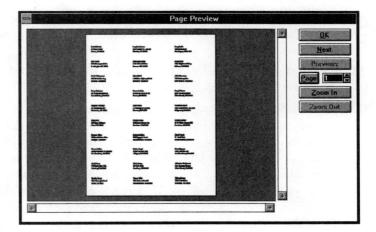

You can get to the Label Wizard from the menus, as well as from the Catalog Manager. From the menus, choose Run, Wizard, and from the next menu which appears, choose Label. The first Label Wizard dialog box appears and you can proceed to choose the desired options in the wizard dialog boxes to design the label.

Sample Project: Creating Mailing Labels

You can see how quickly you can use the Label Wizard to create mailing labels by designing labels for the members in the Buyers table. To try this, perform the following steps:

1. Start the Catalog Manager if it is not already open (choose File, Catalog Manager), and open the Books catalog.

2. Click the Label tab, then click New.

3. In the Select a Table or Query list box, choose Buyers.DBF. Then, click the Label Wizard button. In a moment, the first Label Wizard dialog box for the mailing labels appears (shown previously in Figure 14.2). The dialog box asks which label size you want to use. Click English, and scroll down in the list box and click Avery 5160, then click Next.

4. The next dialog box (shown previously in Figure 14.3) is used to lay out the design of the label. Double-click the First Name field, then click the Space button, then double-click the Last Name field.

5. Click the Return/Enter button to begin another line in the label.

6. Double-click the Address button, then click the Return/Enter button.

7. Scroll down in the list box, and double-click the City field.

8. Click the Comma button, then click the Space button, then double-click the State field.

9. Click the Space button, then double-click the Zipcode field. Finally, click the Next button.

10. The next dialog box (shown previously in Figure 14.4) asks which field you want to sort by. Double-click Zipcode, then click Next.

11. The last dialog box appears and asks whether you want to save the report for later use, save and print the report, or make further changes to the design. If you want to see the labels but not print them, click the Preview button. When you've finished examining the labels, click OK in the Page Preview window, click the "Save label for later use" option in the Label Wizard dialog box, then click Finish. If you want to print the labels, click the "Save and print label" option in the dialog box, then click Finish. When prompted for a name for the report, enter BUYLABEL and click Save. If you choose to preview the labels, they should resemble the example shown previously in Figure 14.5.

Printing Existing Mailing Labels

Once a mailing label exists, you can print the labels using any of the following methods:

■ From the Catalog Manager, click the Label tab, then click the desired label to select it, then click the Print button. The Catalog Manager Print dialog box appears. (See Figure 14.7.)

FIGURE 14.7.

The Catalog Manager Print dialog box.

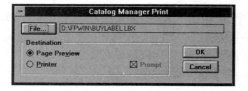

Click Printer in this dialog box to print the label, or click Page Preview to display the label in preview mode. Then, click OK to produce the labels.

■ From the menus, you can open the underlying table that the label is based upon (choose File, Open and click the desired table by name). Choose Run, Label, then select the desired label in the Open dialog box, and click Run. In the Run Label dialog box which next appears, click Preview to display the label in preview mode, or click To Print to send the label's output to the printer. Click Run to produce the label.

■ From the Command Window, use the LABEL FORM command, with the following basic syntax:

```
LABEL FORM label filename [SCOPE] [FOR condition] [WHILE condition] [TO PRINT]
```

and if the TO PRINT option is used, the label is printed; otherwise, it appears on screen, in the main window of the FoxPro desktop.

All of the clauses within the brackets, as with all commands, are optional. The SCOPE, FOR, and WHILE clauses are added to limit the records included in the mailing labels. (For a complete discussion of SCOPE, FOR, and WHILE, refer to Chapter 7, "Queries with Commands.") The TO PRINT option sends the labels to the printer.

You likely will want the labels to be printed in a certain order. To do this, you must index or sort the file before the labels are printed, so they are printed in the sorted or indexed order.

Use Label Wizards To Speed the Manual Label Design Process

Even when you prefer to design your own labels, the Label Wizards can often save time and effort by providing a label that is close to what you want. Use the wizards to create a label, then open the label in FoxPro's Label Designer tool and make any desired changes to the existing label.

Problems with Label Wizard Mailing Labels?

The Mailing Label Wizard creates report specifications for standard mailing labels. However, to do so, it makes some assumptions about your printer which may or may not be true. In particular, it assumes that it can print within a certain distance of each edge of the paper. Every Windows print driver can have a different "printable region," which is the rectangle on the printed page that FoxPro can print into. This rectangle may be smaller than the rectangle that the printer can actually print, due to the way that the print driver was designed. Therefore, you may not be able to print labels as close to the edge of the paper as you would prefer.

In general, the Label Wizard assumes that it can print within 1/4 inch of the edge of the paper. Early Hewlett-Packard LaserJets are notorious for creating problems with specifications like these, as they were designed to print only to within a half-inch of the paper's left and right edges. If you find that some of the text in your labels is getting cut off or is not getting printed at all, try going into design mode for the label and moving text items until all of the text prints. You may have to make the items smaller, choose a smaller font, and move them closer together to get everything to fit without having the label cut off at the edges of the page. If your printer has such a large top margin that you can't move your text items down far enough (or if doing so results in a visually crowded label), the next thing to try is to change the Print Setup margins so that the first label on each page is not used. To do this, choose Print Setup and add the height of your labels to the top margin provided by the Label Wizard. If you are having trouble with the last line of the last label getting cut off, you can use the same technique on the bottom margin to cause the last label on the page to be skipped.

Creating Mailing Labels Manually

Mailing labels can also be created manually from the Command window or from the menus. From the menus, choose File, New. In the New dialog box, click Label, then click New. From the Command Window, enter CREATE LABEL *filename,* where *filename* is the name that the label will be saved under. With either of these methods, the New Label dialog box appears. (See Figure 14.8.) This dialog box offers the different sizes for the labels, with heights, widths, and Avery office label numbers shown for each size.

FIGURE 14.8.

The New Label dialog box.

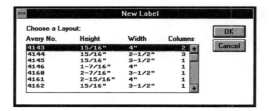

After choosing the label size, choose OK. A new report opens, with Column and Detail bands automatically added and sized to match the label size you chose. Figure 14.9 shows the report layout that appears as a result of choosing Avery 5160 as a label size.

FIGURE 14.9.

The report format for Avery 5160 Labels.

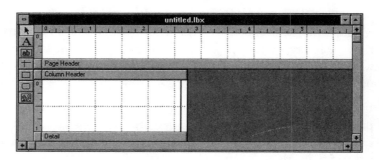

Fields can be added to the design area by clicking the Field Tool in the Toolbox. Then, click at the upper-left corner of the desired location to place the new field. After releasing the mouse, the Report Expression Box appears. In this box, click the Expression button and the Expression Builder appears. Using the Expression Builder, you can enter the desired field names, or build an expression containing field names or other data.

Since a label is just a specialized type of report with its dimensions and column layout suited for the label's size, the process of designing (adding fields, text, graphics and lines, and so on) is no different for labels than for reports. For specifics on designing reports, see Chapter 12, "Designing and Customizing Reports."

Saving Label Designs

When you have finished designing the label, save the design. To do this, choose File, Save from the menus and if prompted for a name, enter the desired filename. (If you named the label as part of a CREATE LABEL command when you started the process, FoxPro does not ask for a label name.)

Modifying Labels

To modify an existing label, use the command MODIFY LABEL *filename.* From the menus, you can also choose File, Open, then change Type to Label in the next dialog box, then choose the desired label name in the list box. Either method causes the Report Design window to appear, containing the label's layout. Double-click the desired field to display the Expression Builder, which allows you to make the desired changes to the fields in the label. You can use the techniques detailed in Chapter 12 to move fields, or add lines or graphics. When you have made the desired changes, choose File, Save from the menus to save your changes.

Designing Form Letters

In many cases when creating form letters it is necessary to export a file for use with a word processor. FoxPro has an advantage here, because it enables you to create form letters without leaving FoxPro. You can do this by designing reports that serve as form letters. First, increase the size of the Detail band in the Report Writer window. Then enter the text of the letter and the necessary fields within the band. You can add fields as needed within the letter. A Summary band should be added at the bottom, and the New Page option should be turned on for the Summary band, so each record prints on a different page.

To have a better understanding of how this works, you can create an example form letter with the following steps:

1. Open the Buyers table to begin the example.
2. Create a new report by entering CREATE REPORT LETTER1 in the Command Window. (You need to maximize the window to see the entire work area.)

3. At the left edge of the Page Header band is the sizing rectangle. Click the rectangle and drag it upwards to the top of the window. Also, at the left edge of the Detail band is another sizing rectangle; click and drag it to the bottom of the window to increase the size of the Detail band, to accommodate the text of a form letter.

4. Click on the text tool to begin entering text. About an inch and a half from the top of the window and a half-inch from the left margin enter the date, then click outside the date to deselect it.

5. Click the Field Tool, and just below the date click and drag and form a box roughly 1/4 inch high and 1 inch long. When you release the mouse, the Report Expression dialog box appears.

6. Click the Expression button and open the Expression Builder. Enter the following in the Expression for Field on Report text box:

```
TRIM(FIRSTNAME) , LASTNAME
```

The previous expression causes the contents of the Firstname field to appear trimmed of blank spaces and the contents of the Lastname field to appear with a leading space.

7. Click OK twice, in order to close the two dialog boxes. Align the new field with the text. (You may want to turn off the Report, Snap to Grid menu option to make aligning the field easier.)

8. Click the Field Tool again, and click and drag a rectangle 1/4-inch high and 2 1/2 inches long. Again when the mouse is released, the Report Expression box appears.

9. Click the Expression button to open the Expression Builder, and double-click the Address field in the Fields list box to place it in the Expression for Field text box.

10. Click OK twice to close the two dialog boxes, then align the new field with the name field.

To add the City, State, and Zipcode fields to the report, you need to create another field using the Field Tool from the Toolbar. Make the field roughly 1/4-inch high, and 2 inches long. In the Expression for Field on Report text box enter

```
TRIM(CITY) + ",  " + STATE + " " + ZIPCODE
```

This command causes the information to appear in the standard city-state-zipcode format.

Now, the remainder of the job is to enter is the text portion of the form letter. Click the Text tool, then click below the field you just placed, and enter the following:

```
Valued Member:
We thank you for your recent order and prompt payment. At
```

```
this time we would like to encourage you to renew your
membership. As the year comes to a close, just for your
renewal you will receive free, the book of your choice.
```

Click outside the text, then click the text tool again to select it. Click just below the paragraph you just typed to start another paragraph, and type the rest of the text shown here:

```
A friend may also be encouraged to join and receive the
selection of the month absolutely free. And for encouraging
a friend to join, you will receive the next two monthly
selections free. So act today to take advantage of this offer.
```

In this example, the two paragraphs are entered separately, because FoxPro imposes a limit of 255 characters in any single text object. When completed, the report resembles the example shown in Figure 14.10.

FIGURE 14.10.

A completed report which generates form letters.

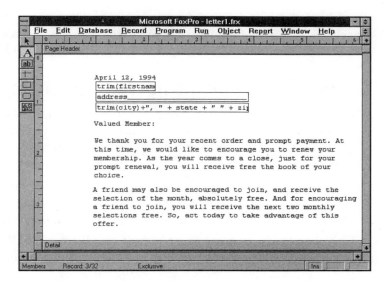

Finally, choose Report, Data Grouping from the menus, and in the dialog box that appears, add the custid field and turn on the New Page option to print each record on an aspirant page. At this point you can save the report, and print the form letters whenever desired by running the report. This technique for generating form letters works well if the letters are short, and if being able to easily edit the form letters is not of prime importance. With long letters, or with letters which must be repeatedly edited, you are likely better off creating merge files that can be used with your favorite word processor, as described in the sections which follow.

Exporting Data for Use in Word Processing

One of the common tasks that requires an exchange of data is the creation of form letters or other documents in word processing, based on data stored in FoxPro. This part of the chapter examines how users of word processing can use FoxPro data to create print merge documents (also known as "form letters"). You can export data from a FoxPro table or query in a variety of formats.

Creating a Print Merge in Word for Windows

The following description of the steps required to set up a merge for word processing will be general. However, since users of FoxPro often have a preference for other Microsoft products, the exercise which follows it will be designed for Word for Windows.

Creating a Mail Merge in Word Processing

1. Check the word processor's manual. Almost all word-processing programs will merge data from other programs, but the preferred format varies not only with the product you have, but with the *version* of the word processor you intend to use.

2. Use the Database, Copy menu option in FoxPro to export data for word processing. In the dialog box which appears when you choose this option, change the data type to the one required by your word-processing program.

3. If your word-processing program (like WordPerfect for DOS) has a conversion program to change data to merge input, run the conversion program.

4. In your word-processing program, follow the instructions for setting up the rest of the merge job.

An Example of a Print Merge Operation

Microsoft Word for Windows (versions 2.0 and 6.0) will link directly to a FoxPro file and pull all the variable information directly from the file. If your FoxPro file is a large one and you want to select only some records or some fields, you can use the database copy menu option to copy only the data you need.

To demonstrate how you can use FoxPro data along with the Print Merge facility in Word for Windows, the following exercise helps you combine a FoxPro file (created by exporting the data in the Buyers table) with a main document (created within Word for Windows) to generate form letters. Open the Members table if it is not already open, and perform these steps:

1. Choose Database/Copy To. The Copy To dialog box appears. (See Figure 14.11.)

FIGURE 14.11.

The Copy To dialog box.

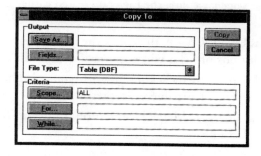

2. Click the Fields button to display the Field Picker dialog box.
3. Double-click the following fields: Lastname, Firstname, Address, City, State, and Zipcode. Click OK.
4. Click the arrow in the File Type list box, and leave the choice at dbf.
5. Click in the Save As text box, and enter the name WORDDATA.DOC as a filename. Click OK.
6. Click the Copy button in the dialog box to create the new file.

With the data exported, you can now proceed to the following steps, where you will attach the FoxPro file and create the main document containing the form letter itself. Use standard Windows techniques to switch to Word for Windows and perform the following steps.

1. Choose File, Print Merge (v2.0) or Tools, Mailmerge (v6.0) from the menus. You will see the Print Merge Setup dialog box (see Figure 14.12) or the version 6.0 Mail Merge screen.

FIGURE 14.12.

The Print Merge Setup dialog box.

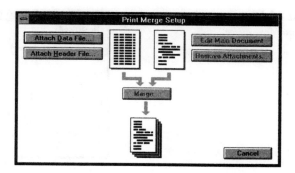

2. Click the Attach Data File button. A dialog box appears showing all document files in the current directory.

3. Type `worddata.dbf`, the file you created earlier in FoxPro, to select it, then click OK.

4. Press ENTER twice, then click the Insert Merge Field button in the Toolbar. In the list box of fields which appears, double-click Firstname.

5. Add a space, then click the Insert Merge Field button again. In the list box, double-click Lastname, then press ENTER.

6. Click the Insert Merge Field button. In the list box, double-click Address, then press ENTER.

7. Click the Insert Merge Field button. In the list box, double-click City, then add a comma and a space.

8. Click the Insert Merge Field button. In the list box, double-click State, then add a space.

9. Click the Insert Merge Field button. In the list box, double-click Zipcode, then press ENTER.

10. Press ENTER twice. Type the following text, using the Insert Merge Field button on the Toolbar to add the named fields in the locations indicated.

    ```
    You may have won $12 billion dollars! Surely you can only dream of what
    you and the <<Lastname>> family would do with $12 billion dollars! That
    trip to Spain... A new car... an entire car dealership... the space
    shuttle Atlantis... your very own savings and loan... all this and more
    can belong to the <<Lastname>> family of <<City>>, <<State>>.
    ```

11. With the letter completed, choose File/Print Merge from the menus. In the Print Merge Setup dialog box, click Merge. This causes the Print Merge dialog box to appear. (See Figure 14.13.)

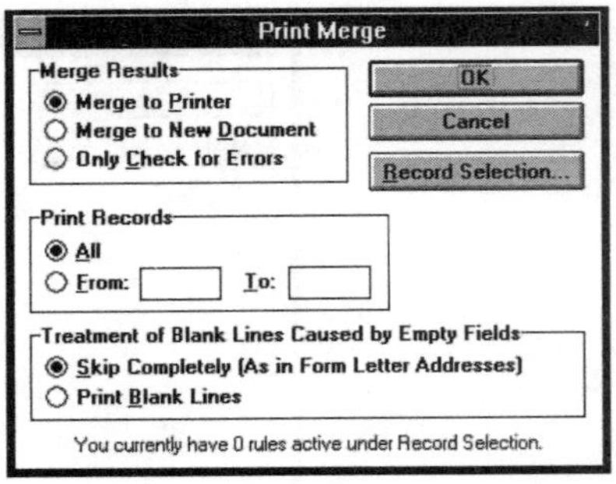

FIGURE 14.13.

The Print Merge dialog box.

12. Click the Merge to Printer option to select it to print the form letters. You can also click the Merge to New Document option to select it if you want to see the form letters in a separate document. (You could then save this document and print it later, using the usual techniques under Word for Windows.) Figure 14.4 shows an example of the Word for Windows document containing the form letters generated by this procedure.

FIGURE 14.14.

Form letters created using Word for Windows.

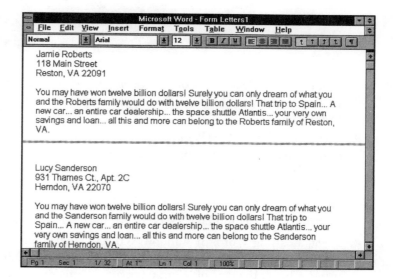

Using the Mail Merge Wizard

If you are using Word for Windows, Word for DOS, or another word processor, you can create exported files which can be used with your word processor to perform a mail merge, using the Mail Merge Wizard provided by FoxPro. The Mail Merge Wizard takes a FoxPro table, and uses it to create a data file that can be used by your particular word processor. You can then follow the steps that are appropriate for your word processor to merge this data file with a main document such as a form letter, labels, or a series of envelopes. You can use these steps to generate a data file with the Mail Merge Wizard:

1. Open the desired table that will supply the data for the mail merge (choose File, Open from the menus, or enter USE *filename* in the Command Window). Note that this step is not necessary if you start the Mail Merge Wizard from the Catalog Manager where you have already opened a table.

2. Choose Run, Wizard from the menus, and select Mail Merge from the submenu which appears. Or from the Catalog Manager, choose Tools, Mail Merge. With either method, the first of the Mail Merge Wizard dialog boxes appears. (See Figure 14.15.)

FIGURE 14.15.

The first Mail Merge Wizard dialog box.

From the list, select your word-processing program. If you select Word for MS-DOS, WordPerfect, or Other, the wizard skips to step 5 so you can complete the mail merge.

3. If you choose Word for Windows version 2.0 or 6.0, the next screen lets you create a new main document or select a main document which was created earlier. (If you need to create a main document, click the Create new document option, then click Next to continue. If you created a main document previously, click the Use existing document option and enter a filename, or click the File button to open the document, then click Next. At this point, the wizard will skip to step 5.

4. If you are using Word for Windows 6.0, and you choose to create a new main document, you are next asked to specify the type of main document you will be using. Choose the type of Word 6.0 main document you want to create: form letter, label, envelope, or catalog. (See your Word documentation for more details about these options.)

5. Click Finish. If you are using Word for Windows 2.0 or 6.0, choosing the Finish button starts Microsoft Word, and you can continue with the mail merge process. (Note: If your computer does not have enough memory to run FoxPro and Word at the same time, you will not be able to use the Wizards.) If you are using another word processor, choosing the Finish button displays FoxPro's Save As dialog box. You can enter a name and click Save to save the source document as a data file. Next, switch to your word processor and use the document you created as a data source for the mail merge.

Regardless of which method you use to generate the form letters, keep in mind that the data file exported from FoxPro is a snapshot of the data that exists at the time you exported the data. If you are generating form letters on a regular basis, you need to export the source of the data each time you want to generate form letters, to be sure that you have the most accurate data as the basis for your form letters.

Chapter Summary

This chapter has detailed how features of FoxPro can be used to implement mail-merge type operations quickly. One point to keep in mind is that if you use other Windows word processors, you may be able to use the techniques outlined in this chapter that apply to your particular processor. Experimentation with these techniques, in conjunction with your preferred word processor, can produce effective results.

3

PART

Extending FoxPro

Creating Applications
with FoxPro

15

This chapter details the use of FoxPro's Applications Generator, a utility used to create complete applications. An application is any collection of FoxPro objects you've created—tables, queries, screens, and reports—that are linked together through a series of menus to handle a specific task. You can use the Applications Generator provided with FoxPro to build simple applications that make use of one or two tables, and to perform basic editing, searching, and reporting functions. The Applications Generator does have its limits, but for prototyping or for providing users an easy way to deal with simple database management tasks, it is a useful tool. This chapter details the workings of the Applications Generator by describing the creation of an application using the BUYERS.DBF and DONATION.DBF tables created earlier (and also stored on the accompanying disk). You may want to copy those files to your working directory if you have not already done so.

Starting the Application Generator

To start the Application Generator, choose Run, Application from the menus. The Open menu will appear. Choose FOXAPP from the list box, then click New. Doing so starts the Application Generator. (See Figure 15.1.)

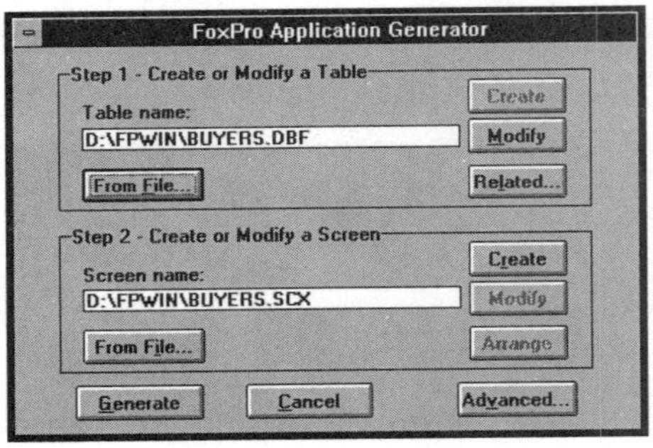

FIGURE 15.1.

*The Application
Generator.*

The Application Generator dialog box is divided into portions labeled Step 1 and Step 2. In the Step 1 portion of the dialog box, click the From File button. The Open dialog box appears. You now need to open the first table to use in the application. You can do this by choosing the desired directory in the list box to list the available tables in FoxPro. For this example, click BUYERS as the first table, then click Open. You are then returned to the Application Generator. Notice that the screen matching the Buyers table has been chosen by FoxPro automatically. If you choose not to use this screen, you may change it to a screen you have created by clicking the From File button in the Step 2 portion of the dialog box, and then selecting the desired screen. To work properly, the screen you choose must have fields which match those in the table you use. (You also have the option of creating another screen, using the methods discussed in Chapter 8, "Creating and Using Simple Screens," and Chapter 10, "Working with FoxPro's Relational Powers.")

At this point, if you do not wish to relate another table with the first one, click the Generate button, give the application a name, and create it by clicking OK. In many cases, though, it is necessary to use more than one table when generating an application. In these cases, click the Related button in the Step 1 portion of the dialog box to choose another table (which should be related with the first). The Related Tables dialog box appears. (See Figure 15.2.)

FIGURE 15.2.

The Related Tables dialog box.

If the table you want is not listed in the Related Tables box, click the Add button to retrieve it. Doing this causes the Open dialog box to appear. From this dialog box, you can choose the table you want to add to the Related Tables box. (In the example, since the Donation table is not already there, bring it to the Related Tables box by clicking the Add button and choosing the Donation table as the file from the Open dialog box.)

The Options for Donation.DBF dialog box next appears. (See Figure 15.3.) FoxPro has found the two matching fields in the two tables, and will use them as the related fields in the application. Click OK in this dialog box; after doing so, you are returned to the Related Tables box. In this box, you can choose Donation and click OK to save the database relations and window positions.

Next, click the Generate button in the Applications Generator. When you do so, the Save As dialog box appears with the name Buyers.app as the default name of the application. Click Save to save the application and begin its construction.

When the application is complete, a message appears informing you of that. Press any key, and the application appears. (See Figure 15.3.)

There are several menu options in the application, and a control panel at the bottom of the screen. Notice the Buyers file appears with the Donations file just below it (if one is on top of the other, you can click on the tile section of the window and drag it to a different section of the screen to make them both visible). As you move through the Buyers table, notice in the Donation table that each member who made donations has his corresponding donation amounts appear. For those who didn't make a contribution, blank records appear. The customer ID number is given in the Donation file along with the date and the amount of the donation. This lets you see the relationship between the two tables.

FIGURE 15.3.

The completed application.

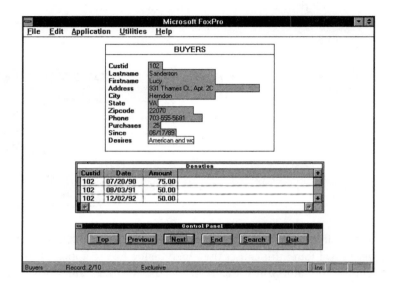

The options on the Control Panel perform the following tasks:

Top	This button moves you to the top of the Buyers file. In cases where the table is indexed, it moves you to the first record in the index.
Previous	This button moves you to the previous record in the database file. If you are at the first record, a message appears telling you so.
Next	This button moves you to the following record in the database file. If you are at the end, a message appears telling you so.
End	This button moves you to the end of the database file, or the last record in the index if the file is indexed.
Search	This button opens the Search For window (see Figure 15.4) and enables you to search for information in a record and a field. For example, choose search from the Control Panel and enter Sanderson in the Find box. You now need to tell FoxPro where to look for the information. (Custid is the default field that FoxPro looks at, but that is not the field Sanderson is located in.) Therefore, you need to choose Lastname from the In Field box by clicking on the arrow. Doing so opens the list box and lists all the available fields for the search. Choose Lastname, and click OK.

FoxPro searches for the first occurrence of the information in the find box and in the selected field.

Quit   This button exits the application and returns you to the Command Window or the Catalog Manager.

FIGURE 15.4.

The Search for window.

There are also several menu options available with the application running. The following is an explanation of each of the options available from the menus.

The File menu has one option available, Quit, which is used to exit the application. (The Quit button on the Control Panel performs the same function.)

The Applications menu (see Figure 15.5) has the most available options of the applications screen menus.

FIGURE 15.5.

The Applications menu.

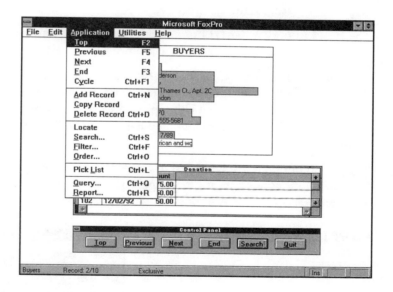

The first available option is the Top (F2) option. This is the same as the Top option from the Control Panel—it moves you to the top of the database file. Notice that the key is also listed beside each of the choices in the Applications menu.

The Previous option (F5) is used to return to the previous record in the database file.

The Next option (F4) moves you to the next record in the database file unless you are at the end of the file—in which case a message is displayed telling you so.

The End option (F3) moves you to the end of the file. If you are already there a message is displayed indicating such.

The Cycle option, (Ctrl+F1) is used to move between the two files and the Control Panel in a cycling fashion.

The Add Record (Ctrl+N) option adds a blank record to the end of the table, and moves you to that record where you can proceed to add the new data.

The Delete Record (Ctrl+D) enables you to delete the current record.

The Locate option lets you locate a record by selecting it from a browse screen.

The Search option, (Ctrl+S) is use to search for information in a field. Choosing this option opens the Search For box. At this box you are prompted to enter what is to be searched for. There is also an In Field box; here you can specify which field you want to look in for the information. FoxPro finds the first occurrence of the search term that you enter.

The Filter option (Ctrl+F) is used to set a filter on the database file. Choosing this option opens the expression builder window and enables you to set a filter on the database such as `Lastname = "Criollo" .or. "Arteaga"`.

The Pick List option (Ctrl+L) produces a list of all the records for the field of the table you are working with if there is one available.

The Query option (Ctrl+Q) is used to build a query on the database in use. After giving the query a name at the Save As box, the Relational Query by Example Window appears, where you can design a query. (This topic is discussed in detail in Chapter 6, "Performing Queries with RQBE.") After building the query in the RQBE Window, click Do Query to implement the query.

The Report option (Ctrl+R) is used to create a report. After choosing the Report option, the Print Options box appears. (See Figure 15.6.) You can create a report, modify an existing one, set up a printer, or print an existing report.

FIGURE 15.6.

The Print Options dialog box.

Choosing the Create Report option lets you create a quick report. (Chapter 9, "Creating and Using Simple Reports," and Chapter 12, "Designing and Customizing Reports," give a detailed explanation of reports.) When you choose this option, you are first prompted to save the report. The Report Writer window then opens, and you can change the design of the report as desired. (You are also given the option of modifying an existing report.)

The Printer Setup option displays the Windows printer setup dialog box, which enables you to change the default Windows printer.

The Print Report option prints the report that you select from the Open dialog box which next appears.

The next three options are all printer driver options. These options enable you to change the printer driver to the printer driver used by the report, the current printer driver, or no printer driver at all.

The Utilities menu provides three options: Refresh Screen, Construct Index, and Pack. The Refresh Screen option refreshes the display, a useful option to have when running on a network. On networks, records may have been changed by other users since they were displayed, particularly if you are looking at a number of records in a Browse window. Choosing Refresh Screen tells FoxPro to update the screen display with any changes that may have been made to the data. The Construct Index option, when chosen, rebuilds all index tags associated with the table's structural compound index file. The Pack option permanently removes all records marked for deletion from the table, the equivalent of performing a PACK command.

Finally, the application provides a Help menu, which has choices to let you define FoxPro macros, or bring up any of the FoxPro desktop tools (the calculator, calendar/diary, or puzzle).

Chapter Summary

The Applications Generator can provide you with complete applications which novice users can often use to work with data stored in FoxPro tables. As a development tool, you should recognize both its promise and its limitations. In general, the Applications Generator is suitable for only the simplest of applications. If your application uses no more than two tables, and the relationship between them is a one-to-many relationship (one record in the master table relates to one or more records in the related table), the Applications Generator may fit the bill. One aspect of development in which the Applications Generator can be very useful is when users are not sure of what they want, and you must experiment with different database designs. You can quickly develop applications to see if the tables, screens, queries, and reports involved are what's really needed. You can then use other more advanced FoxPro techniques (such as programming and project development) to build on what was learned with the use of the Applications Generator.

Sharing Data with Other Programs

With no PC being an island in today's world, existing data can come into FoxPro from a wide variety of sources, and FoxPro can export data in many formats for use in other programs. The capability of sharing data is particularly important in a world where mission-critical data can be found anywhere from older dBASE or Paradox for DOS files to SQL Servers stored on local area networks.

> **NOTE**
>
> One common use of exported data is to create form letters in word processors based on the exported data. With many word processors, you can export the data as fixed text, delimited text, or as dBASE files. You can then use the data in your word processor to produce the form letters (see your word processor's documentation for details). Using exported data to create form letters in Microsoft Word for Windows is not detailed in this chapter, because that task is detailed in Chapter 14, "Producing Mailings." If you need to create form letters in Word for Windows based on FoxPro data, see Chapter 14.

Many users come to a full-fledged database manager like FoxPro carrying established data-management needs that have outgrown a spreadsheet or a word processor. For example, a user might have dozens or even hundreds of expense records stored in a Lotus 1-2-3 spreadsheet. Or the office mailing list may have hundreds of names, stored in WordPerfect. Re-entry of this kind of data is not only incredibly time-consuming, it is also nearly always unnecessary. You can use the capabilities that FoxPro offers to move the existing data into a FoxPro table. When other departments within your organization need to get at your data, you can use those same capabilities to produce data in a file format that virtually any modern software package can work with.

> **TIP**
>
> If you regularly import or export data, you can combine the techniques learned in this chapter with those detailed in Chapter 19, "FoxPro Programming Basics," to create programs that import or export data. For more details on programming in FoxPro, see Chapter 19.

Using Data from dBASE

Many FoxPro users come to FoxPro from dBASE IV, dBASE III Plus, or dBASE III. Since dBASE and FoxPro are based on the same language (XBase), converting from one to the other is a simple matter. FoxPro 2.6 incorporates a specific technology designed to provide maximum compatibility with your existing dBASE files with a minimum of effort. When working from the Catalog Manager, FoxPro 2.6 utilizes a new technology known as *AutoMigrate*. AutoMigrate technology is activated when needed by the Catalog Manager. It works transparently to automatically convert your dBASE files for immediate use in FoxPro by modifying dBASE tables and creating new FoxPro screens, reports, labels, and queries based on the format of the existing dBASE files. This conversion requires no steps on your part, and it does not prevent you from using the files again in dBASE.

With the exception of tables which contain memo fields, all original dBASE files remain intact when they are converted for use in FoxPro. If your table has an index, AutoMigrate rebuilds it. In FoxPro for Windows, AutoMigrate also automatically transports files from MS-DOS to Windows.

AutoMigrate has the following effects on the dBASE files:

Tables (Databases):	AutoMigrate automatically converts dBASE tables when you use them.
Queries:	AutoMigrate converts dBASE queries to FoxPro RQBE query format when you modify them.
Screens (called forms in dBASE):	AutoMigrate converts dBASE forms to FoxPro screens when you modify or run them. Information about the fields, text objects, and design elements is copied from the design file in dBASE to a FoxPro .SCX file. Due to differences between DOS and Windows, the appearance of your converted screens may need minor modification.
Reports and Labels:	AutoMigrate converts dBASE reports and labels when you modify them or print them.
Programs:	Any dBASE programs run without conversion. (These are automatically recompiled in FoxPro.) While FoxPro is highly compatible with dBASE program code, there are a few commands unique to dBASE IV that FoxPro does not support. In cases where your dBASE IV programs use commands that are not supported by FoxPro, you will have to modify the programs to run properly. Also note that compiled dBASE IV programs (.FMO, .FRO, .LBO, and .DBO files) cannot run in FoxPro unless the source code (.PRG) or design file (.SCR, .FRG, .LBL) is available.

Of the hundreds of commands and functions present in the XBase language, only a few used by dBASE IV are not compatible with FoxPro 2.6. They are as follows:

```
BEGIN TRANSACTION
CONVERT
END TRANSACTION
PROTECT
ROLLBACK
USER( )
```

If your dBASE program uses any of the preceding commands, you need to remove them from the program before running the program in FoxPro. As these commands were not available in dBASE III or dBASE III Plus, any dBASE III/III Plus program can be run in FoxPro with no modifications.

Enhancing Compatibility with dBASE IV Programs

You can maximize compatibility with existing dBASE IV programs by issuing the command

```
SET COMPATIBLE DB4
```

in the Command Window. Doing so changes the way FoxPro executes certain commands and functions to more closely match the way dBASE IV behaves. In many cases, this is all that's needed to get a program written in dBASE IV up and running in FoxPro. As you work with the dBASE application, you may want to make changes to the program code to take advantage of FoxPro's features (such as its use of windows and pull-down menus).

Can I Maintain Files Shared Between dBASE and FoxPro?

In many network environments, users are faced with a situation where different users may need to work with the same data files, but they are doing so with different software packages. You may be using FoxPro, but other users may be using dBASE to work on the same data; hence, the question presented by this section's subheading arises. In a nutshell, the answer is "yes, but it's not a wise idea." The network file-locking mechanisms used by FoxPro and dBASE are incompatible with each other, and this can lead to conflicts on a network. Also, since the indexing schemes used by FoxPro and dBASE also differ, maintaining indexes for shared tables properly can become a logistical nightmare.

Importing Data from Other Software

FoxPro stores its files in the .DBF file format made popular by dBASE. However, other applications often store their information in files formatted differently. For example,

Microsoft Excel worksheet files store their information in .XLS extension, where as Lotus 1-2-3 version 3 files are stored in the .WK3 file extension.

Sometimes it you may desire to bring in information from one of the other applications to use in FoxPro. For example, you may want to import information from Lotus 1-2-3 version 3 to use in a FoxPro table, or you may want to export information to Lotus 1-2-3 to do advanced calculations.

FoxPro is at no loss in providing a way to work with information from other applications. In FoxPro there are several commands available for this. For *importing,* the bringing in of information from other applications, two commands are provided. There are also two commands available for *exporting,* the conversion of FoxPro information for use in other applications. Object Linking and Embedding (OLE) is also supported by FoxPro. This enables you to embed or link other Windows data to a general field in a FoxPro table.

Since most other applications save their files in different formats than FoxPro, they need to be converted in order to be used in FoxPro. FoxPro has the conversion routines built in to make the conversions. This feature makes the sharing of information with FoxPro easy.

TIP

Before spending time exporting data to another file format, check to see if the other software package can directly read FoxPro or dBASE IV data files. Due to the popularity of the dBASE data format, many software packages can work directly with data stored in the native format that FoxPro uses.

File Formats

FoxPro can transfer information stored in a number of file formats. They include Delimited, .SDF, .DIF, SYLK, .FW2, .RPD, and .WKS file formats. The following is a description of the different file formats FoxPro can use.

Delimited Format

Files that use the Delimited option contain data with fields separated by a specific character or characters (usually a comma). Each record occupies an individual line, and the line always ends with a carriage return and line feed. Within the record, each field is separated from the next field with a comma. Each character field is normally enclosed in quotation marks, and trailing blanks are stripped. The default separator of quotation marks can changed by adding a WITH <delimiter> option to the TYPE specification. For example, consider the Buyers table used in various parts of this text. The command

```
USE BUYERS
COPY TO FILEA.TXT FIELDS LASTNAME, FIRSTNAME, ADDRESS, CITY, STATE, ZIPCODE TYPE DELIMITED
```

copies the FoxPro data to a new file with data stored in the following format:

```
"Roberts","Jamie","118 Main Street","Reston","VA","22091"
"Sanderson","Lucy","931 Thames Ct., Apt. 2C","Herndon","VA","22070"
"Smith","Larry","142 Haven Way","Kensington","MD","31025"
"Jones","Nikki","8000 Watergate Circle","Washington","DC","20005"
"Hernandez","Maria","19012 Pimmit Drive","Towson","MD","30309"
"Jones","Jarel","1412 Wyldewood Way","McLean","VA","22035"
"Zeibermann","Danial","235 White Oak Way","Arlington","VA","22032"
"O'Neill","John","12555 Lee Highway West","Merrifield","VA","22045"
"Bannerton","Alicia","107 Embassy Row","Falls Church","VA","22046"
"Johnson","Ivan","","","",""
"Bannerton","Alicia","107 Embassy Row","Falls Church","VA","22046"
"Hernandez","Maria","19012 Pimmit Drive","Towson","MD","30309"
"Hernandez","Maria","19012 Pimmit Drive","Towson","MD","30309"
"Bannerton","Alicia","107 Embassy Row","Falls Church","VA","22046"
"Bannerton","Alicia","107 Embassy Row","Falls Church","VA","22046"
```

Date values in a database that is exported to a delimited format are represented by an eight-digit number. The first four digits indicate the year, the fifth and sixth digits indicate the month, and seventh and eighth digits indicate the day. Memo fields are not copied out to a delimited file. If there are any memo fields in the database, they will be dropped during the copying process and will not exist in the newly created file. A number of other software packages, including most PC-based database managers, can import files in delimited format.

.SDF Files

.SDF files store data in columnar fields, with an equal number of spaces between the start of each successive field. Each record represented by a line in an .SDF file is of equal length, and each line always ends with a carriage return and line feed. Spaces are used to pad the field contents, when necessary, so that the length of each record is identical. .SDF files are useful for transferring data to spreadsheets that don't accept the .DIF, .WKS, or SYLK file formats. The following commands create the .SDF file that follows:

```
USE DONATIONS
COPY TO FILEC .SDF FIELDS CUSTID, DATE, AMOUNT
        7 records copied
TYPE FILEC.TXT
10119930302 100.00
10119920301 100.00
10219900720  75.00
10219910803  50.00
10219921202  50.00
10219931112  75.00
10319910904 200.00
10319921101 200.00
10319940205 250.00
104199402051000.00
```

As with delimited files, .SDF files do not contain the contents of a memo field. Date fields are represented by an eight-digit number, with the first four digits being the year, the next two the month, and the last two being the day.

.DIF, SYLK, .FW2, .MOD, .RPD, and .WKS FILES

.DIF, SYLK, .FW2, .MOD, .RPD, and .WKS files are files containing data within a proprietary format that can be read by many other programs. The .DIF file internally resembles delimited files. .DIF was developed as an aid in transferring data from first-generation PC spreadsheet software packages. SYLK is used by Microsoft for a number of Microsoft application packages, including Multiplan, Chart, and File. Older Ashton-Tate products use the .RPD and .FW2 file formats. .RPD is Rapidfile file-manager format, and .FW2 files are used by Framework II. .MOD files are used by some versions of Microsoft's Multiplan. The .WKS format is used by Lotus 1-2-3 and by Symphony. Due to the popularity of Lotus 1-2-3, a number of other software packages can also work with files in .WKS format.

.DIF, SYLK, .RPD and .WKS files will not contain the contents of a memo field. Date fields are represented by an eight-digit number, with the first four digits being the year, the next two the month, and the last two being the day.

FOXPLUS Format

Files are created in dBASE III/III Plus and FoxBase Plus file formats by the FOXPLUS format. These format options help in importing and exporting files that contain memo fields.

FoxPro stores memo fields in a more efficient manner than most other dBASE-language products, but is not compatible with them. For this reason, an error message is received when you try to open a FoxPro database file with a memo field in products that accept dBASE files (Lotus 1-2-3, Excel, dBASE III Plus, dBASE IV, FoxBase, and FoxBase Plus).

You get around problems with other packages that can't deal with native FoxPro files with the use of the FOXPLUS option. This creates a file in the FoxBase/dBASE III Plus format. This allows the file to be read by any product that has the capacity to read dBASE files. Since FoxPro and dBASE III Plus use different methods of data storage, you need to use the FoxPLUS format when transferring data to dBASE III Plus. (If your file contains no memo fields, you do not need to use this format. dBASE III Plus works with the FoxPro data in its native format.)

NOTE

FoxPro also appends files from Rapidfile and Framework file formats. However, due to the age of these products, they are not discussed in detail in this chapter.

Importing Data

FoxPro has two commands available for importing data. The first, the Import command, creates a new table to place the imported information. The other command, the Append From command, adds information to an existing FoxPro table as opposed to creating a new file for the imported data. The Append From command also supports ASCII delimited and .SDF file formats, whereas the Import command does not.

Using Append From

FoxPro also provides a method to import files of the nine named file formats: DELIMITED, .SDF, .DIF, .MOD (Mutiplan 4.01), SYLK (Multiplan file format), .WKS (Lotus 1-2-3 format), DBASE II, .RPD (Rapid File file format), and .FW2 (Framework II file format). The Append From command can use the same Type option as are specified with the Copy To command. .WK1 is also available with the Append From command. This type supports Lotus 1-2-3, Release 2. The syntax for the command is:

```
Append From <filename> [WHILE <condition>] [FOR <condition>]
➥[Type DELIMITED, .SDF, DIF, MOD, SYLK, WKS, DBASE II, RPD, FW2]
```

If you are using the Delimited or .SDF Type options, and no extension is specified as a part of the filename, FoxPro assumes that the filename has an extension of .TXT. You therefore may need to specify the filename when using the .SDF or Delimited option of Append From. As an example of Append From, the command

```
APPEND FROM LOTUSFL1 TYPE WK1
```

would read in a file created by Lotus 1-2-3, Release 2, and append the contents of the file to the database currently in use. Note that when using Append From to read foreign files, the data structure must match that of the database that is to receive the data. With some applications, you may find it necessary to create a temporary database to hold the data imported from the foreign file. You can later transfer data from the temporary database into other databases on a selective basis.

Using Import

FoxPro offers specific commands, Append Memo and Copy Memo, which can be used to import and export the contents of memo fields. The Append Memo command writes the contents of a memo field out to a text file, while the Copy Memo command reads a text file into a memo field. The syntax for the Append Memo command is

```
APPEND MEMO memo field name FROM filename [OVERWRITE]
```

where *memo field name* contains the name of the memo field, and *filename* is the name of the file containing the text to be added to the memo field. An extension of .TXT is assumed for the text file; if the extension is different, it must be included with the filename. Text from the file is normally added to the memo field after any existing data in the memo field. If the Overwrite option is used, the text read in for the file will overwrite any existing text in the memo field.

The syntax for the Copy Memo command, used to copy the contents of the memo field to a file, is

```
COPY MEMO <memo field name>  TO  <filename> [ADDITIVE]
```

where *memo field name* is the name of the memo field, and *filename* is the name of the text file to be written. An extension of .TXT is assigned to the text file. If a different extension is desired, it must be included with the filename. If a file by the name specified already exists, it is normally overwritten by the Copy Memo command. The Additive option may be specified, in which case the memo field text is added to the end of any existing file.

Since the Append Memo and the Copy Memo commands work with the current record in the active database, it is up to your program to position the record pointer at the desired record. If you are exporting the memo field contents from a group of records, you can use the Copy Memo command within a Do While or a Scan...Endscan loop. Include the Additive option so that the exported file gets each successive memo field's contents added to the end of the file. An example of a program which copies the contents of a memo field to a text file follows:

```
CLEAR
SET ALTERNATE TO WPFILE.TXT
SET ALTERNATE ON
? "Memo fields from litigation file. Date 03/04/94
? "================================================="
?
CLOSE ALTERNATE
USE LITIGATE
DO WHILE .NOT. EOF()
     COPY MEMO COMMENTS TO WPFILE.TXT ADDITIVE
     SKIP
ENDDO
```

The Set Alternate commands are used to initially create the file as well as add a header. When the Additive option is used with Copy Memo, the named file must exist prior to the use of the Copy Memo command, or FoxPro displays an error message. The results of the preceding program appear in the form of ASCII text, as shown below:

```
Memo fields from litigation file. 03/04/94
======================================================
This may be the smoking gun we need. Phillips said that Jones promised him that he would
pay Phillips $300,000 to keep his mouth shut about the impending takeover. Conversation
took place in a bar on Wisconsin Avenue.
At this point the entire transaction began to unravel. First time that Phillips said
that he was considering retaining counsel and filling suit to block the takeover. This
is beginning to sound like a plot from a soap opera. Smith said if Phillips didn't stay
away from his spouse, he (Smith) would resort to draconian measures.
To further complicate matters, Jones claims to have hard evidence the president's
daughter has been laundering profits from her illegal exotic bird business through the
company.
```

The text file produced may then be imported into most word processors, using the Read ASCII File commands. (See your word processor manual for details.)

Exporting Data

The Copy To command can also be used to copy the contents of a database into foreign files, which you intend to export from FoxPro for use with other software. When you use Copy command. The TYPE option tells FoxPro which file format to use in writing the foreign file. The TYPE options include

```
DELIMITED
.SDF
DIF
MOD (Mutiplan 4.01)
SYLK (Multiplan file format)
WKS (Lotus 1-2-3 format)
DBASE II
RPD (Rapid File file format)
FW2 (Framework II file format)
FoxPlus (FoxBase+ or,dBASE II and III Plus with memo fields)
```

As an example of the use of the TYPE option, the following command creates a spreadsheet file that can be used by Lotus 1-2-3:

```
COPY TO OUTFILE FIELDS L_NAME, F_NAME_M_I, AGE, SALARY, TAXRATE TYPE WKS
```

There are two commands available in FoxPro for exporting data: the Export and Copy To commands. The Export command enables you to export information is FoxPro to other applications. The Copy To command enables you to copy part of a database to a file. For the most part, the two commands function equally, but the Copy To command must be use to export data in the ASCII format. This is useful since many applications support ASCII and .SDF formats.

The Export Command

This command can be used, for example, to export a table in FoxPro to another application. Export builds a database and accompanying screen form to be used with PFS:File, dBASEII, RapidFile, or Framework II. If used to export to PFS, the resulting PFS:File database uses all character fields. If a dBASE IV format file is open when the Export To command is used, the PFS:File screen form is based on the design of the dBASE IV format file. RapidFile and Framework II databases share field type characteristics with the dBASE IV database, except for memo fields, which are not be exported. The syntax for this command is:

```
Export To <filename> TYPE PFS/DBASEII/FW2/RPD
```

Copy To

This command copies part or all of a database to a specified file. A field list can be used to specify a list of fields that are included in the file being created. The Scope, For and While <condition> options can be used to specify condition that must apply before records are copied. The various Type options export non-dBASE IV files. The syntax for this command is:

```
COPY TO <filename> [<scope>] [FIELDS <field list>] [WHILE <condition>]
[FOR <condition>] [TYPE .SDF/DELIMITED/WKS/SYLK/DIF/RPE/FWZ/DBASEII/FOXPLUS]
```

Exercises in Transferring Data

The next section of this chapter deals with the transferring of files to different applications. Different packages are used in the examples. You may not have some of the packages in the examples. Because of this, you may not be able to follow all of the examples in this section. If you do not have the software in the example, try transferring data with some of your software.

Transferring Data To Lotus 1-2-3

FoxPro can read and write in most Lotus formats. Only the earliest versions of Lotus are not able to write and read FoxPro files which have been written out using the FOXPLUS file format.

Use the Copy To command to transfer files from FoxPro to Lotus with a Lotus file Type option. If memo fields are included in the database, use the FoxPLUS file type. To bring files in from Lotus 1-2-3 to FoxPro, open the existing FoxPro database and use the correct Type option of the Append command.

If you have Lotus 1-2-3 or Quattro Pro, which is 1-2-3 compatible, try the following example of transferring data. Enter these commands at the Command Window:

```
USE BUYERS
COPY TO 123DATA
```

Switch to the Windows Task List window and open Lotus. Use the File/Open command (or with older versions of 1-2-3, File/Load) to load the spreadsheet. The Set Column-Width command in Lotus can be used to fully display the information in the fields.

TIP

When data is transferred out of a spreadsheet to FoxPro, a worksheet file should be saved with only the data range for the worksheet. This does not include titles, explanatory text, or macro references.

Transferring Data to a Word Processor

In virtually all cases, word processors can deal with data stored in the ASCII format. For example, you might wish to create a document using your word processor that would contain a listing of the persons in the Buyers table. You could accomplish this with the following steps:

1. In the Command Window, enter USE BUYERS to open the table.
2. From the menus, choose Database, Copy To. The Copy To dialog box appears. (See Figure 16.1.)

FIGURE 16.1.

The Copy To dialog box.

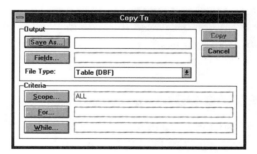

3. In the Copy To box under File Type, click the .SDF file type, then click Save As.
4. In the Save As dialog box, enter the name CALLS for the new file, and click OK. After naming the file, the Copy To box reappears with the assigned name in the Save As text box.

5. Click the Fields button, and the Field Picker window appears as shown in Figure 16.2. This dialog box lets you choose the fields you want to export to the file for use with your word processor.

FIGURE 16.2.

The Field Picker window.

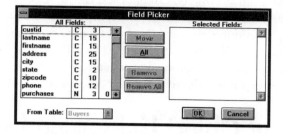

6. Double-click LASTNAME, CITY, STATE, and PHONE, then click OK.
7. Click the Copy button in the Copy To window to copy the file.
8. Press Ctrl+Esc to open the task list and open your word processor, then open the file in the directory you saved it in. If you are using Word for Windows, you see the Convert File box. Click OK for text only and the file appears in a format similar to that shown here:

Roberts	Reston	VA 703-555-2321
Sanderson	Herndon	VA 703-555-5681
Smith	Kensington	MD 301-555-2815
Jones	Washington	DC 202-555-1586
Hernandez	Towson	MD 301-555-6725
Jones	McLean	VA 703-555-9091
Zeibermann	Arlington	VA 703-555-2114
O'Neill	Merrifield	VA 703-555-9256
Bannerton	Falls Church	VA 703-555-1200
Bannerton	Falls Church	VA 703-555-1200
Hernandez	Towson	MD 301-555-6725
Hernandez	Towson	MD 301-555-6725
Bannerton	Falls Church	VA 703-555-1200
Bannerton	Falls Church	VA 703-555-1200

The information can then be edited the way you desire.

Using OLE Data and General Fields

This portion of the chapter details the concepts of OLE (Object Linking and Embedding), and shows how you can put these capabilities—inherent in FoxPro and recent versions of Windows—to work in your applications. Chapter 3, "Creating and Working with Tables," introduced the concept of the General field type, which can be used to store OLE data from other Windows applications. Such data could include pictures, spreadsheet cells, portions or all of word-processing documents, or even sound or video. OLE lets you merge much of the capabilities of other Windows software into FoxPro.

About Object Linking and Embedding

If you've worked with Windows to any great extent, you've probably already used OLE to some degree. Copying pictures from recent versions of Windows Paintbrush or other Windows graphics programs into a word-processing document makes use of OLE capabilities. OLE objects can be created using any Windows application that supports OLE. An OLE object can be a complete file (such as a Word for Windows document) or a portion of a file (such as a single paragraph from that same document). You can add OLE objects to an FoxPro table either by linking them or by embedding them.

Simply defined, Object Linking and Embedding is a Windows protocol, or set of communication rules, which permit objects stored in one Windows application to be linked or embedded in the documents of another Windows application. The one common requirement is that the Windows package that you are trying to use (in conjunction with FoxPro) supports OLE. Different Windows packages support OLE in different ways. Some Windows packages (including MS Graph and Windows Paintbrush) are only OLE *servers*, meaning they can supply data to other Windows packages, but they cannot accept OLE data. Some Windows packages are OLE *clients*, meaning they can accept OLE data but cannot supply OLE data to other software. FoxPro falls in this second category, as it can be an OLE client, but not an OLE server. Some packages can act as both clients and servers of data using OLE.

NOTE

Users of Windows version 3.0 should note that only linking is supported in Windows 3.0. If you want to use both the linking and embedding capabilities of Windows, you must upgrade to Windows 3.1 or higher, or have a Windows application installed which adds its own OLE 1.0 files, like Excel (version 4.0 or higher).

Before working with OLE, it is important to understand the difference between *linking* and *embedding*, as both have their advantages and disadvantages. The very names, linking and embedding, are key to the differences between the two. When you link to an OLE object, the object is stored elsewhere, and FoxPro maintains a link to the object. As an example, if a series of pictures in CorelDRAW! are linked to a general field for different records in a table, the drawings exist only in the CorelDRAW! subdirectory in which they were originally stored. Linking is the preferred method to use when you want the data shown in FoxPro to be updated whenever the data in the original Windows application changes. With linking, when data in the pictures changes, the data shown in the corresponding FoxPro table changes as well.

By comparison, when you embed an object into an FoxPro table, the object becomes a part of the FoxPro table. (It still exists in the original source directory, but the object in FoxPro is a virtual copy of the original source object.) Once the object is embedded, there is no longer any connection between it and the original object. This means that any changes made to the original object are not reflected in the embedded object. Using the same analogy of a series of CorelDRAW! images, if you embed the pictures into the FoxPro table, you can change them by double-clicking the images (which launches CorelDRAW!, where you can make the desired changes). However, the images are stored as a part of the FoxPro table, and the original application is used only to make changes to the object. The original CorelDRAW! image files would remain unchanged, regardless of changes made to the images while in FoxPro.

An advantage to embedding is that it keeps your application portable: you can copy the table to a disk that may be on another computer. As long as that computer has the same Windows applications used to create the objects, you can still work with the data. (With linked objects, moving tables between PCs could create major problems, as the drive and directory structures would probably not be identical between machines.) A serious disadvantage to embedding is the additional disk space consumed. Since the embedded objects are copies of the original data, significant additional disk space is used, particularly if the objects are of a type that consume a lot of space to begin with (like spreadsheets, sound, or video).

Editing OLE Objects in FoxPro

Once you have inserted an OLE object in an FoxPro table, you can edit that object by double-clicking it. This technique applies whether the object is linked or embedded. When you double-click the object, the original application used to create the object opens. You can make the desired changes to the object, and then choose File/Exit from the application's menus to return to FoxPro. Figure 16.3 shows an example of an object, in this case a Paintbrush picture, embedded in a general field of a FoxPro table.

FIGURE 16.3.

A Paintbrush picture stored in a general field.

Figure 16.4 shows the results when the picture in Figure 16.3 is double-clicked. Windows Paintbrush opens, containing the embedded image. Note that the image is titled "Paintbrush Picture in FoxPro," which reflects the name of the associated OLE container for the embedded object (in this case, a FoxPro table). Also, when Paintbrush opens, its File menu gets an additional choice titled "Exit and Return to FoxPro." This menu option lets the user exit from Paintbrush, at which point any changes made to the image while in Paintbrush appear in the embedded image in FoxPro.

FIGURE 16.4.

Windows Paintbrush containing an embedded image.

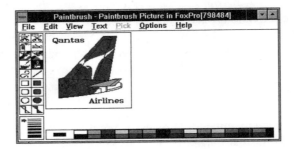

Inserting an OLE Object in a Field

Once you've created the tables and any screens you will use with the OLE data, you can proceed to embed or link OLE data to a field using the following steps.

To Embed an OLE Object in a Field

1. Open the table and begin editing data using your preferred method (such as the BROWSE or CHANGE commands, or their menu equivalents).

2. Move to the desired record where the OLE data should be embedded.

3. Double-click the general field where the OLE object should be added to open a window into the field.

4. From the menus, choose Edit, Insert Object. The Insert Object dialog box appears. (See Figure 16.5.)

FIGURE 16.5.

The Insert Object dialog box.

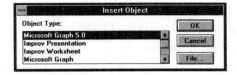

5. Under Object Type, click the desired type of object you want to embed, then click OK. When you do so, FoxPro launches the source application for the chosen object.

6. Use the source application to create the desired object.

7. In the source application, choose File, Exit and Return To FoxPro from the menus. (If the source application has no such command, choose File, Update. If neither command exists, check the documentation for the source application for the proper sequence of steps to update the embedded object and exit.) If you are asked whether you want to update the document before exiting, click Yes.

TIP

If the desired object you want to embed does not appear in the Object Type list box as a part of step 5, this is a hint that the Windows application you have in mind may not support OLE, or its name may not be present in the Windows registration file (REG.DAT). In such cases, you can often achieve satisfactory results by using Windows cut-and-paste techniques. Try switching to the application, select the desired data, and choose Edit, Copy. Switch back to FoxPro, click in the general field, and choose Edit, Paste.

To Link an Object to a Field

In addition to using embedding, you can also link data in another application (such as a Windows Paintbrush picture or cells of an Excel spreadsheet) to a field in an FoxPro table or form. To link the data, perform these steps:

1. In the source application (the application which will provide the data), open the file which contains the information you want to link to FoxPro.

2. Use the selection techniques appropriate to that program to select the desired information.

3. From the menus, choose Edit, Copy.

4. Switch to FoxPro (you can press Ctrl+Esc and choose FoxPro from the Task List), then open a form in Form view (or open the datasheet for a form, table, or query).

5. Move to the record where you want to link the data from the other application.

6. Double-click the desired field where you want to place the link to the data to open a window into the field.

7. From the menus, choose Edit, Paste Special. This causes a Paste Special dialog box to appear. (See Figure 16.6.)

FIGURE 16.6.

A Paste Special dialog box.

8. Choose the desired data type in the Data Type list box, then click the Paste Link option in the dialog box. Click OK. When you do this, FoxPro creates the link and displays the object in the general field when you double-click it to open a window into the field. If you are linking a spreadsheet or word processing document, an icon representing the document appears in the field.

Embedding an Existing OLE Object into a Field

When you have already created data in another Windows program that supports OLE, you can copy and paste all or a portion of the data as an OLE Object into a field of a form, table, or query. Perform the following steps to do this:

1. Open the other application, then open the document or file containing the data you want to place in FoxPro.

2. Use the selection techniques applicable to the other program to select the desired data.

3. From the application's menus, choose Edit, Copy to paste the data into the Windows Clipboard.

4. Switch to FoxPro (you can press Ctrl+Esc and choose FoxPro from the Task List), then move to the record where you want to link the data from the other application.

5. Double-click in the general field where you want to place the link to the data to open a window into the field.

6. From the menus, choose Edit, Paste. When you do so, FoxPro displays the data in the field.

Playing Sound and Video

If you store sound or video in a general field of a table, you can play the sound or the video using the following steps:

1. Open the table containing the data.

2. Find the desired record and click in the field that contains the sound or video you want to play.

3. Open the Edit command, and choose the appropriate Object command from the Edit menu.

4. From the submenu that appears, choose Play. (If the submenu has no Play option, choose Run.) When you do so, FoxPro plays the sound or video.

An example, if you paste sound objects using the Edit/Copy menu option of the Windows Media Player into general fields of a FoxPro table, FoxPro's Edit menu will contain a Sound Object menu option whenever you click in a field that contains sound data. You could click Sound Object, then click Play from the submenu to play the sound. You could also click Edit from the submenu to open the Media Player and edit the sound. (The use of Media Player requires the installation of sound drivers and compatible sound hardware. Refer to your Windows documentation for further details on Windows Media Player.)

Displaying the Contents of General Fields

As you work with your FoxPro data, you'll likely want to view and edit the contents of your general fields. One easy way to do this is to open a Browse window into the table, move to the general field and double-click it. You can then move and size both the Browse window and the window into the general field so you can see both windows simultaneously. Make the Browse window the active window by clicking it or choosing it by name from the Window menu. You can then move around among the records within the Browse window. As you do so, the corresponding data for the general field appears in the other window. (See Figure 16.7.)

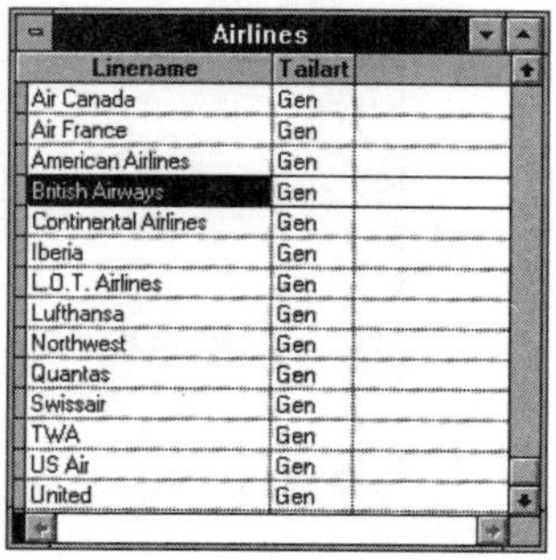

FIGURE 16.7.

A display of Browse window and general field data.

A Note About General Fields in Reports

You can use the techniques detailed in Chapter 12, "Designing and Customizing Reports," to add the contents of general fields to your reports. As that chapter noted, general fields can easily be added to a report's design by clicking the Picture tool when in the Report Writer and clicking and dragging in the report to add a picture frame that contains the general field. When you release the mouse button, the Report Picture dialog box appears. (See Figure 16.8.)

FIGURE 16.8.

The Report Picture dialog box.

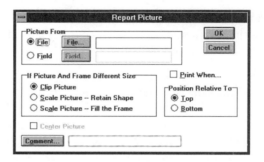

Click the Field radio button, then click the rectangular Field button to display a Choose Field dialog box. In this dialog box, double-click the name of the general field you want to place in the report, then click OK. Finally, click OK to put away the Report Picture dialog box. When you do so, a shaded rectangle representing the contents of the general field appears in the report's design. (See Figure 16.9.)

FIGURE 16.9.

An example of a report's design with a general field.

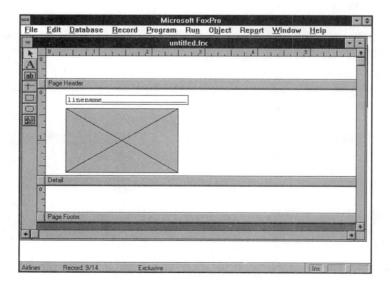

When you print the report, it displays the data stored in the general field as a graphic if a graphic is stored there, or as an icon representing the source application of a spreadsheet, word-processing document, sound or video clip, or other type of OLE data stored there. Figure 16.10 shows a completed version of the report described here.

FIGURE 16.10.

The completed report containing a general field.

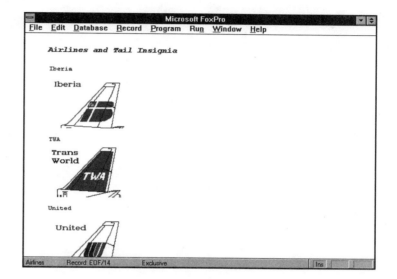

You can use the techniques detailed in Chapter 12 to enhance the report. Also, note that Chapter 12 details how you can add pictures that are stored in Windows Paintbrush format as design elements in your reports.

Chapter Summary

This chapter detailed the techniques you'll find useful when exchanging FoxPro data with other software, and when importing data from other software formats into FoxPro. Windows users have an advantage in that other Windows programs support additional features (such as the use of OLE) which make sharing data with FoxPro a less complex matter.

Working with Graphs

One feature of FoxPro that isn't offered by many database management packages is the capability to create business graphs. The graphs can be based on numeric data generated by a FoxPro query you design using the RQBE Window. When you direct the output of a query to a graph, a Graph Wizard runs automatically and asks the necessary questions to produce the graph. Once produced, the graph can be printed or stored in a general field of a FoxPro table. The graphs produced in FoxPro are generated with MS Graph, a Windows mini-application provided with many Microsoft applications (including FoxPro, Access, Word for Windows, and Excel for Windows).

A Typical Graph

Figure 17.1 shows a typical graph produced within FoxPro. (Graphs are also called *charts*; in fact, Microsoft uses the terms interchangeably.) Graphs are made up of *markers*, which represent the data produced by the query. The appearance of the markers changes, depending on the type of graph you tell the GraphWizard to create. In a bar graph or a column graph, the markers appear as horizontal or vertical bars. In a line graph, the markers appear as lines containing small symbols used for identification. In a pie chart, the markers are displayed as wedges of a pie. With the exception of pie charts, all graphs contain two axes: a horizontal axis known as the *category axis* and a vertical axis known as the *value axis*. Graphs can also contain titles and legends, which identify the markers. All these items can be defined and changed by means of the MS Graph application once the graph has been inserted into the general field of a table.

FIGURE 17.1.

A typical graph.

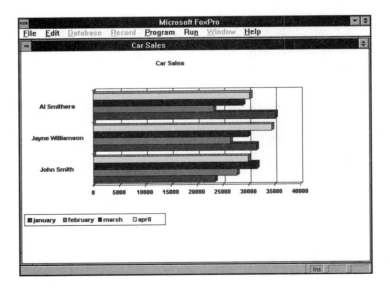

Preparing the Source of the Data

Before creating a graph, you need to prepare the source of the data on which the graph will be based. To do this, you need to design a query that retrieves the appropriate data. When the GraphWizard runs, it will generate a graph based on an existing query. If the query is not structured properly, the GraphWizard will be unable to produce a graph with the proper results. It's all too easy to overlook this fact and jump right into the creation of the graph, but the results may be unexpected. By its very nature, any table is likely to contain far more data than you want to graph at any time. Most likely you will want to base the data on some kind of summary, and that usually calls for refining the query to provide a summary of the data. If the graph is based on a single table's data, you can use that table as the underlying data source within the query. If the data comes from more than one table, then you'll need to design and save a relational query that will provide the data source. You'll want your query to contain the following:

- One or two fields that categorize the data. If the graph is to contain one horizontal axis, you'll use one field as a data category. If the graph is to contain two horizontal axes, you'll need two fields for this purpose. As an example, if you were tracking performance for a team of sales reps, you might use a field containing the names of the sales reps as a category. If you wanted to track some same sales reps by date, you might include two fields as categories in the graph: the name of the sales rep and the date the products were sold.

- One or more numeric fields that are summarized or averaged in the graph. Each field you add results in an additional *data series*, or a set of markers used to plot a specific group of data on the graph.

Creating a Graph

The following steps outline the overall process of creating a graph. After these steps comes an exercise that you can follow to demonstrate this process.

1. Using the RQBE Window, design the query that provides the data to be graphed. (For details on designing queries, see Chapter 6, "Performing Queries with RQBE.")

2. In the Output list box of the RQBE Window, change the query's output to Graph.

3. Save the query if desired, and click the Do Query button in the dialog box. This causes the first GraphWizard dialog box to appear, which asks what type of graph is desired. (See Figure 17.2.)

FIGURE 17.2.

*The first GraphWizard
dialog box.*

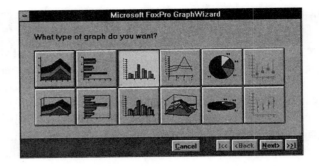

4. Click the desired graph type, then click Next.

5. In most cases, the next dialog box asks which fields you want to serve as the graph
   axis, and which fields should be used in the legend. (See Figure 17.3.) (With
   some types of pie charts, you do not see this dialog box.) Clicking the Swap
   button in the center of the dialog box swaps the fields used for the axis with the
   fields used for the legend. You can also select a field and use the > and < buttons
   to move just that field from the legend to the axis, or vice versa. Make the desired
   selections in this dialog box and click Next.

FIGURE 17.3.

*The dialog box asking
for choice of fields for
axis and legend.*

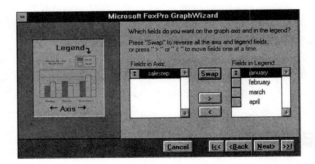

6. Another dialog box appears, asking for a title for the graph. Enter the desired title
   and click Next.

After clicking the Next button, MS Graph takes the data supplied by FoxPro and produces a graph according to the specifications given. A small image of the graph appears in
the last Graph Wizard dialog box. (See Figure 17.4.) From here, you can click Zoom to
zoom in on the graph, click Print to print the graph, or click Save As to save the graph to
a table (database file). If you zoom in on the graph, you can further customize it by double-
clicking it, and by using the techniques under "Using MS Graph to Customize the Graph"
later in this chapter.

FIGURE 17.4.

The last GraphWizard dialog box.

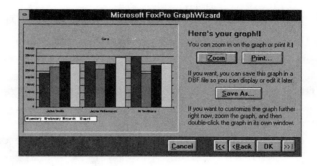

Note that if you click Save As, FoxPro displays the Save As dialog box, asking for a name for the table where the graph will be stored. When you enter a name, FoxPro creates a new table and adds a single record to it. The graph gets stored in the general field of that record.

An Example: Creating a Graph

You can demonstrate how the GraphWizard is used to create a graph by opening the CARSALES.DBF table. The CARSALES.DBF table is stored on the accompanying disk, and contains the data shown here.

```
(CARSALES.DBF)
SALESREP           JANUARY       FEBRUARY      MARCH        APRIL
John Smith         23490.30      27800.50      31560.00     29900.00
Jayne Williamson   31500.00      26450.50      29900.00     34500.00
Al Smithers        35200.00      23250.00      28890.50     30250.50
```

After you open the table, perform these steps to create a column graph representing the car sales for each sales rep:

1. From the menus, choose File, New. In the New dialog box that appears, click Query, then click New to open a new RQBE Window.

2. In this case, all the records are needed. The table is simple, so it contains only the data needed for the graph. Click in the Output list box of the RQBE Window, and change the query's output from Browse to Graph.

3. Click the Do Query button. The first GraphWizard dialog box appears. (See Figure 17.2, shown previously.)

4. Click the Bar Graph button (top row, third button from the left). Click Next.

5. The next dialog box that appears (see Figure 17.3, shown previously) asks which fields should serve as the axis, and which should serve as the legend. In this case, the default choices (which will place the sales rep names along the axis) are fine, so click Next.

6. The next dialog box asks for a title for the graph. Type **Car Sales**, and click Next.

The final dialog box shows a representation of the completed graph. Click the Zoom button, and you see an enlarged version of the graph in its own window. (See Figure 17.5).

FIGURE 17.5.

A completed graph based on car sales.

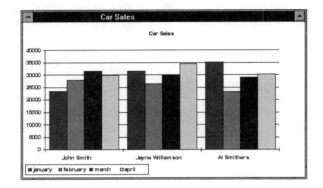

When done examining the graph, press Ctrl+F4 (or double-click the window's Close box) to close the graph window. If you desire a printed copy, click the Print button to print the graph.

About the Graph Types

MS Graph provides six different types of graphs: area, bar, column, line, pie, hi-low, and scatter. Each of the six types also provides numerous different style options so you can choose from a wide variety of possible graph designs. The available types of graphs and their possible uses are described here:

- Area graphs indicate the importance of data over a period of time. Visually, such graphs are cumulative in nature, as they highlight the magnitude of change rather than the rate of change.

- Bar graphs show individual figures at a specific time, offering a visual emphasis of different values oriented horizontally.

- Column graphs are similar in design to bar graphs, but are oriented vertically. Any passage of time is generally more apparent with a column graph.

- Line graphs are ideal for indicating trends in data that occur over a period of time. Line graphs are similar in design to area graphs, but line graphs highlight the rate of the change rather than the magnitude of the change.

- Pie charts identify the relationship between the pieces of a picture, or between a single part and the entire picture. Since each portion of the pie represents a part of the total series, a pie chart can represent only one data series at a time.

- Hi-low graphs are variations on line graphs. They show relationships among prices over a period of time, and are commonly used to indicate fluctuations in stock and commodity prices.

- Scatter graphs show relationships between various points of data, or plot two groups of numbers as one set of X and Y coordinates. Scatter graphs are routinely used to plot scientific data.

Experimentation in MS Graph is an excellent way to discover the available graphs and their various formats. As you create graphs with the aid of the wizard, you can select different options in the dialog box to see how different graph types are displayed.

Customizing a Graph

Because graphs are actually OLE objects produced by MS Graph, customization is a mixed bag at best. While you initially set the design aspects of the graph through the FoxPro GraphWizard, most aspects of the graph can be changed only by using MS Graph.

Using MS Graph to Customize the Graph

When you want to change a specific aspect of the graph itself, you must do it in MS Graph. You can open the graph inside of MS Graph by performing the following steps:

1. Open the table that contains the graph you want to modify. Find the record with the general field where the graph is stored, and double-click in the general field to open a window into the field. (If the graph is visible in the last GraphWizard dialog box, you can also double-click the graph to open it in a window, then double-click it again. Then skip to step 3.)

2. Double-click the graph.

When you do this, MS Graph starts and a window into MS Graph opens, containing the graph and a datasheet with the data being graphed. (See Figure 17.6.)

Since MS Graph is its own application independent of FoxPro, the menus are different than any you've worked with in FoxPro. A full discussion of all options presented by MS Graph is beyond the scope of this book, but you can refer to the MS Graph documentation packaged along with your FoxPro documentation. The following paragraphs do provide details on how you can perform the more common customizations of a graph.

- To change the graph type, open the Format menu and choose Chart. A Format Chart dialog box appears. (See Figure 17.7.) You can select area, bar, column, line, pie, or scatter from among the possible graph types, as well as choose two-dimensional (2-D) or three-dimensional (3-D) graph types. Depending on the type of graph chosen, various other options can be selected. For example, you can change the overlap and gap width of bars and columns, the angle of the first slice in a pie chart, and the depths used by 3-D charts. For some chart types, you can choose different styles by clicking a style shown in the Data View portion of the dialog box. When done choosing the desired options, click OK.

FIGURE 17.6.

MS Graph window containing a sample graph.

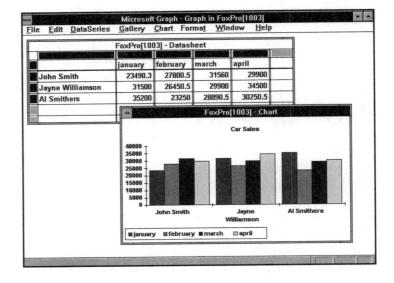

FIGURE 17.7.

The Chart Type dialog box.

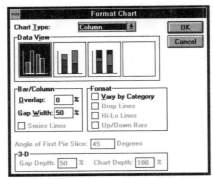

- To change the font used by axis labels or by a title or a legend in the graph, first select the axis labels or title containing the text, then choose Format, Font from the MS Graph menus. In the dialog box, select a desired font, font style, size, and color.

- To add a legend to an existing graph, choose Chart, Add Legend from the MS Graph menus. To delete an existing legend, choose Chart, Delete Legend. (The menu choice is a toggle, so if a legend is present, the menu choice is Delete

Legend. If a legend is not present, the menu choice is Add Legend.) To change the location of the legend, click the legend to select it and choose Format, Legend. In the dialog box that opens, select the desired location (bottom, corner, top, right, or left).

■ You can change the colors and patterns used for any data series by double-clicking the data series and choosing a desired color or pattern in the Area Patterns dialog box.

■ To change the settings or line styles used by an axis, double-click the axis to open the Axis Patterns dialog box and choose the desired settings.

Once you are done with the changes to the graph, choose File, Exit and Return to FoxPro from the MS Graph menus. The changes you made to the graph appear in FoxPro.

Adding a Graph Using External Data

You can use FoxPro to add a graph that contains data which is not stored in FoxPro, using the Datasheet window that is a part of MS Graph. When you want to do this, instead of using the GraphWizard to base the graph on existing FoxPro data, double-click in a general field of a table's record (where the graph will be stored), and choose Edit, Insert Object from the menus. When the Insert Object dialog box appears, choose MS Graph as the desired type of object. MS Graph starts automatically, and you can create the graph using the following steps. You can perform these steps to add a graph that is not based on any data in FoxPro:

1. Open any table that has a general field, and add a new record to that table.

2. Double-click in the general field of the record to open a window into the field.

3. From the menus, choose Edit, Insert Object. In the dialog box, click Microsoft Graph to select it, then click OK. In a moment, an MS Graph window opens which contains sample data for a graph in the Datasheet window, and a resulting column graph based on that sample data. (See Figure 17.8.)

4. Type your data directly into the Datasheet window (see the following section, "Entering Data in the Datasheet Window," for details.)

5. Use the Format/Chart Type options to select the desired type of graph. Add any other objects (such as legends or titles) with the options of the Insert menu.

6. When the graph is complete, choose File, Exit and Return to FoxPro. The graph is inserted into the general field of the FoxPro table. If you later want to make changes to the graph, double-click the field to open the graph in a window. Double-click the graph again and an MS Graph window containing the graph opens.

FIGURE 17.8.

*MS Graph window
containing sample data.*

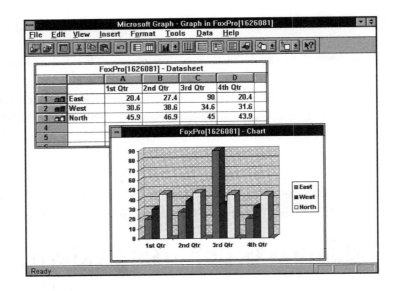

Entering Data in the Datasheet Window

To enter data in the Datasheet window, simply click in the desired cell and type the data directly into the cell. Enter a name for each *data series*, a label for each *category*, and a number for every value that is to be plotted in the graph. When you enter the data into the Datasheet window, MS Graph automatically creates a column chart. You can use the Format/Chart Type menu option to change this to whatever type of chart you want. When you include text in the cells—labels to the left of the values, headings above the values, or both—MS Graph uses the text to add labels and a legend to the graph. In Figure 17.8, shown previously, the labels (East, West, and North) in the first column of the Datasheet are used in the legend that appears in the graph. The headings (1st, 2nd, 3rd, and 4th Quarter) that appear above the values are used as labels in the graph.

You can move around in the datasheet with the cursor keys, or by clicking in any cell with the mouse. If a column is too narrow to accommodate your data, you can widen it. Just click on a cell in the desired column (or move to the cell with the cursor keys), choose Format/Column Width from the menus, enter the desired width in the dialog box that appears, and click OK (or press Enter).

Formatting Data in the Datasheet Window

You can format the numbers you have entered in the datasheet. The format that you apply to the numbers is used by MS Graph to determine the type of tick marks that appear on the chart axes. For example, if you use a format that includes dollar signs for the numbers entered in the datasheet, MS Graph places dollar signs before the numbers that appear along the vertical axis.

If you do not choose a specific number format, MS Graph displays the numbers using a default format called the General format. The General format displays numbers with as much precision as possible. If a number is too wide to fit in a cell, General format causes the number to be displayed using scientific notation. To change the format of the numbers in the datasheet, select the cell or cells you want to format. Choose Format/Number from the menus. In the Number dialog box that appears, select the desired number format, then click OK.

About Pie Charts

Because pie charts show the relationship between parts and a whole, you can plot only a single data series in a pie chart. If you enter more than one row or column of data in the Datasheet and choose Pie as the desired type of graph, MS Graph uses the data in the first row or column to build the graph. All additional data is ignored. (The commands available on the Data menu determine whether the chart is based on a row or a column.)

When working with pie charts, use the Data/Series in Rows or the Data/Series in Columns commands to tell MS Graph whether the graph should be drawn based on a data series stored in rows or a data series stored in columns. Open the Data menu and choose Series in Rows if your data series is stored in the row; choose Series in Columns if your data series is stored in the column.

Exiting from MS Graph

To exit from MS Graph, choose Exit and Return to FoxPro from the File menu. The graph will be updated with its latest version, and the MS Graph window will close. The graph will be stored in the general field of the record, and you can print the graph by including the contents of the general field in your reports.

Chapter Summary

This chapter has detailed how you can effectively use graphs from within FoxPro; no longer is it necessary (as it often is with older database managers) to export data to another program to create business graphs. If you often deal with numeric values, the use of graphs provides another way to highlight your information and emphasize trends. Additionally, if you use other Microsoft applications, you can use the techniques pertaining to MS Graph with many other Microsoft applications.

Power Techniques for Power Users

18

This chapter covers an assortment of topics which can be used to further extend FoxPro to get the most out of the software in combination with your specific applications. Note that some of the topics covered in this chapter assume a familiarity with FoxPro programming. If you are unfamiliar with the topic of programming in FoxPro, you will find coverage of that area beginning with Chapter 19, "FoxPro Programming Basics."

Handling Dates and Times

Like all variations on the XBase language, FoxPro has a date field type to handle the storage of dates. But just having the field type available doesn't solve all the potential problems involved in working with dates. Calculations must be performed, weekends must often be backed out of work time calculations, and holidays must be dealt with. To make matters worse, dates are not dealt with in an equal manner worldwide: 09-05-30 means September 5, 1930 to Americans; May 9, 1930 to most people in Europe; and May 30, 1909 to the Japanese. FoxPro offers a wide variety of commands and functions to deal with dates, but you have to know how to use them to achieve the desired results.

As far as FoxPro is concerned, dates are just a special kind of numeric value, and that is the key to using dates in calculations. FoxPro stores dates internally in the format YYYYMMDD. For example, 19940322 equates to March 22, 1994. This means that you can (to a degree) perform math operations on date values. You can add a number of days to a date, producing another date; or you can subtract a date from another date, providing the number of days between two dates. When working with date values in calculations, remember to enclose the dates in curly braces, so FoxPro knows that the value is a date. For example, the expression,

```
12/5/93 - 30
```

when evaluated by FoxPro, returns 29.97, because FoxPro takes 12 and divides it by 5, takes the result and divides it by 93, then subtracts 30 from the result. Obviously, this would not be what you want in an expression. On the other hand, the expression

```
{12/5/93} - 30
```

when evaluated by FoxPro, returns a date value of 11/5/93, or 30 days earlier than 12/5/93. You can add a number to a day to come up with a day in the future. For example, {1/30/94} + 30 yields 3/1/94, which is 30 days after 1/30/94. Expressions based on date calculations can often be useful in the design of your forms and reports. As an example, assuming the presence of a date field called DAYHIRED in a table, a report could contain a calculated field indicating the number of months on the job with an expression like the following in a field of the report:

```
Int((Date()-DAYHIRED)/12)
```

Dates can be displayed in a number of formats, depending on the SET DATE command or its equivalent Date setting within the View window. You can create a chronological index based on the contents of a date field by indexing on that field as you would index on any other field. For example, the command

```
INDEX ON HIREDATE TAG DATES
```

creates an index tag based on the contents of the date field, HIREDATE. To index in descending order, use the DESCENDING option of the INDEX command. (If you are indexing through the menus, you can also click the Descending button in the Index dialog box). If you must create indexes that are compatible with FoxPro 1.x or FoxBase (which could not create descending indexes), you can use a command like

```
INDEX ON CTOD("01/01/2199") - HIREDATE TO DATES
```

to build an index based on an expression that subtracts the date from some meaningless date in the future. Such an index has the characteristics of an index created in descending order, and the TO clause as past of the INDEX statement builds an index file that is compatible with FoxBase.

The display of dates in FoxPro can take on several formats, depending on the setting of the SET DATE command. The default value is American, which displays dates in a mm/dd/yy format (or, in a mm/dd/yyyy format if SET CENTURY is ON). Another useful choice for formats is ANSI (American National Standards Institute), which displays dates as yy.mm.dd (or yyyy.mm.dd if SET CENTURY is ON). If you transfer the contents of tables containing date fields to older software packages, or to mainframes, the other system will probably best deal with dates that are copied out in the ANSI format. The remaining options of the SET DATE command include British and French (both display as dd/mm/yy), Italian (displays as dd-mm-yy), German (displays as dd.mm.yy), Japanese (displays as yy/mm/dd), USA (mm-dd-yy), MDY (mm/dd/yy), DMY (dd/mm/yy), and YMD (yy/mm/dd). You can set the date format using the View Window, or with the SET DATE command. From the menus, choose Window, View to open the View Window, and click the globe button to display the International Settings. (See Figure 18.1.)

FIGURE 18.1.

The International settings in View Window.

Click in the Date list box, and choose the desired date setting from the list. (If you want to include all four characters of the year, turn on the Show Century check box.) From the Command Window, you can put a desired setting for the date display in effect with the SET DATE command. Enter SET DATE *type*, where *type* is one of the 11 acceptable formats- American, ANSI, British, French, German, Italian, Japanese, USA, MDY, DMY, or YMD.

If you need to break a date into character strings, you can do so with one of the date conversion functions. For example, you might want to spell out the date at the top of a report. You could enter an expression into a field of the report and place that field in the report's header. The expression could contain the following:

```
CDOW(DATE()) + ", " + CMONTH(DATE()) + " " + LTRIM(STR(DAY(DATE()))) + ", " +
LTRIM(STR(YEAR(DATE())))
```

and the expression would cause a date written like "Thursday, April 7, 1993" to appear in the report.

FoxPro offers a number of functions that convert dates to characters, character values to dates, and helps you to handle date data in other ways. Table 18.1 summarizes FoxPro's commonly-used date-related functions.

Table 18.1. Common date functions.

Function	Description
Between (d1,d2,d3)	Returns true if date d1 falls between dates d2 and d3.
CDOW(date value)	Returns the name of the day of the week that corresponds to the date value.
CMONTH(date value)	Returns the name of the month that corresponds to the date value.
CTOD(char. string)	Converts a character string to a date value. (The character string must be in a date format that matches the current settings of SET DATE and SET CENTURY.
DATE()	Returns the system date.
DAY(date value)	Returns a number corresponding to the day of the date value.
DMY(date value)	Returns the date in DD Month YY format, or in DD Month YYYY format if SET CENTURY is on.

Function	Description
DOW(date value)	Returns a number corresponding to the day of the week for the date value.
DTOC(date value,[1])	Converts the date value to a character string. If the optional 1 parameter is included, the character string takes the YYYYMMDD format (same as the DTOS() function).
DTOS(date value)	Converts the date value to a character string with the YYYYMMDD format.
EMPTY(date value)	Returns a logical true if the date value is empty.
GOMONTH(date value,*n*)	Returns a date which is *n* months before or after the date value.
MDY(date value)	Returns the date in Month DD, YY format, or in Month DD, YYYY format if SET CENTURY is on.
MONTH(date value)	Returns a number representing the month of the date value.
SECONDS()	Returns the number of seconds since midnight.
TIME()	Returns the system time as a character string in 24-hour format HH:MM:SS.
YEAR(date value)	Returns a four-digit number representing the year of the date value.

One area that may cause potential problems in a date-intensive application is how you handle dates that stretch into the 21st century. This is a problem that is going to haunt programmers and developers worldwide as systems (which were never designed to deal with anything but a 20th-century date) are maintained, for better or for worse, into and beyond the year 2000. For this reason, FoxPro provides the SET CENTURY command (and the equivalent Show Century check box in the View Window), which switches on the full four-digit display of dates. You must turn on the SET CENTURY setting if you want to enter, display, or edit dates outside of the 20th century.

Working with Memo Fields

Since their introduction in the earlier days of XBase, memo fields and commands for dealing with the contents of memo fields have become an important part of the XBase language.

The obvious reason for the use of memo fields is to accommodate the storage of lengthy text, particularly where that length may vary wildly between records. If you are working with a large amount of textual data, you can store that data in memo fields, and still maintain the ability to perform effective searches based on the contents of those fields.

Editing the Contents of Memo Fields

By default, a memo field in a Change/Edit or Browse window appears as a small field containing the word "memo" in lowercase letters if no data has been stored in the field, and initially capitalized ("Memo") if data has been stored in the field. Double-clicking the memo field opens a window into the field. However, there are better ways to display and edit a memo field. In screens, you can add an Edit Region that can be used to edit the field. (If you use the Screen Wizards to design a screen, any memo fields are placed into Edit Regions automatically.) Techniques for adding Edit Regions are covered in detail in Chapter 11, "Designing and Customizing Screens." In a nutshell, you perform these steps to add an Edit Region for editing memo fields to a screen's design:

1. Open the screen in design mode, and in the Toolbox, click the Edit Region tool (fourth tool down from the top).

2. Click in the screen where you want the Edit Region to appear, and drag until the rectangle reaches the desired size.

3. In the Edit Region dialog box, enter the name of the memo field in the Input text box, or click the Input button to display a Choose Field/Variable dialog box where you can select the desired field by name.

4. Click OK to place the field in the screen.

Figure 18.2 shows a completed screen containing an Edit Region added for the entry and editing of memo field data. By default, Edit Regions that you add contain scroll bars, which are useful for viewing memo field data that spans many paragraphs or pages.

FIGURE 18.2.

A screen with an Edit Region for adding and editing memo field data.

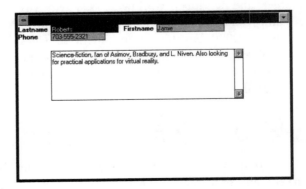

You can also use commands within a program to define, then open a window into a memo field. You can use FoxPro's SET WINDOW OF MEMO TO *windowname* command, to permit editing of a memo field within a window that you previously defined with the DEFINE WINDOW command. For instance, the following statements within a program

```
DEFINE WINDOW ForNotes SYSTEM FROM 10,5 TO 18,60
MODIFY MEMO Notes WINDOW ForNotes
```

would cause the contents of a memo field (called "Notes" in this example) to appear in the defined window. (See Figure 18.3.)

FIGURE 18.3.

The contents of a memo field displayed in a window.

Displaying Memo Field Data

You can display memo field data with the LIST or DISPLAY commands. Include the name of the memo field in a FIELDS clause as part of the LIST or DISPLAY command. If you do not do so, you get a column with just the word "memo" or "Memo" instead of the actual contents of the field. For example, the following command has the results shown:

```
USE PEOPLE
LIST OFF
```

LASTNAME	FIRSTNAME	PHONE	NOTES
Roberts	Jamie	703-555-2321	Memo
Sanderson	Lucy	703-555-5681	Memo
Smith	Larry	301-555-2815	Memo
Jones	Nikki	202-555-1586	Memo
Hernandez	Maria	301-555-6725	Memo
Jones	Jarel	703-555-9091	Memo
Zeibermann	Daniel	703-555-2114	Memo
O'Neill	John	703-555-9256	Memo
Bannerton	Alicia	703-555-1200	Memo

On the other hand, when a FIELDS clause includes the memo field by name, the results are distinctly different, as shown here:

```
USE PEOPLE
LIST LASTNAME, FIRSTNAME, NOTES
```

LASTNAME	FIRSTNAME	NOTES
Roberts	Jamie	Science-fiction, fan of Asimov, Bradbury, and L. Niven. Also looking for practical applications for virtual reality.
Sanderson	Lucy	American and world history, computer programming texts.

Smith	Larry	travel books and videos, with a particular interest in the Caribbean.
Jones	Nikki	travel, health and fitness
Hernandez	Maria	books on aviation and pilot safety.
Jones	Jarel	graphic novels and out-of-print comic books; preferential to X-Men classics.
Zeibermann	Daniel	science and technology, computers
O'Neill	John	photography
Bannerton	Alicia	home improvement, landscaping techniques, and any books that will help in the restoration of classic 1958 Porsche.

Note that when you list memo field data this way, FoxPro defaults to a width of 50 for the memo field data. This may or may not be ideal for your purposes; you can change this default width, by entering SET MEMOWIDTH TO *numeric expression*, where *numeric expression* is the desired width. For example, consider the same data as shown above, after the SET MEMOWIDTH statement is used to change the default width. In the listing that follows, the maximum memo width of 25 characters forces the memo field data to occupy more lines in the listing.

```
SETMEMOWIDTH TO 30
LIST LASTNAME, FIRSTNAME, CITY, PHONE, NOTES
```

LASTNAME	FIRSTNAME	NOTES
Roberts	Jamie	Science-fiction, fan of Asimov, Bradbury, and L. Niven. Also looking for practical applications for virtual reality.
Sanderson	Lucy	American and world history, computer programming texts.
Smith	Larry	travel books and videos, with a particular interest in the Caribbean.
Jones	Nikki	travel, health and fitness
Hernandez	Maria	books on aviation and pilot safety.
Jones	Jarel	graphic novels and out-of-print comic books; preferential to X-Men classics.
Zeibermann	Daniel	science and technology, computers

```
O'Neill          John          photography
Bannerton        Alicia        home improvement,
                               landscaping techniques,
                               and any books that will
                               help in the restoration
                               of classic 1958 Porsche.
```

Of course, you can also include memo fields in the stored reports that you create using FoxPro's Report Writer. An advantage of using stored reports is that FoxPro handles all formatting automatically. When placing memo fields within a report, you may want to turn on the Field Can Stretch option in the Report Expression dialog box to allow the stretching of the field to accommodate lengthy data.

A Note About Memo Field Incompatibilities

Keep in mind that earlier XBase products (including dBASE III Plus and FoxBase+) cannot read the contents of memo fields created with FoxPro. Use the FOXPLUS type option of the COPY TO command, as detailed in Chapter 16, "Sharing Data with Other Programs," to create tables with memo fields that are compatible with earlier XBase products.

Optimizing Performance

Performance is obviously a sort of "Holy Grail" among database users, if magazine ads that pit one product's speed against another are any indication. Since its inception, FoxPro has had a reputation for speed above all else. One could argue that some Windows database managers are easier to use than FoxPro. But if raw speed is what you're after, FoxPro is the product for you. With the capability to retrieve subsets of data from tables of more than 500,000 record in a matter of seconds, FoxPro is no slouch. However, for those who must press towards the ultimate goal of accomplishing everything in zero time, you can speed up an already fast product.

Normally you will want your indexes files and tags open so they can remain updated. But you must remember that this comes at a performance price. You can strike an effective balance between speed of data retrieval and speed of data entry and editing by building indexes that are used only as needed. For example, if a report that uses an unusual index key is printed only once a month, don't add a tag for that key to the structural compound index file. Instead, build the index as an individual (.IDX) index file before printing the report, and erase the index file when done with the report.

Another performance tip is that you should occasionally rebuild your compound index (.CDX) files. This can reduce the .CDX file size and improve performance. When recreating tags in a compound index file, you should first remove the tags using the DELETE TAG ALL command.

When SET DOHISTORY is left on, this noticeably reduces program execution. Be sure it is not left on from any debugging activities. For the same reason, be sure that unneeded SET TALK ON commands are not left within your programs.

The use of macro substitution (the & character in programs) should be kept to a minimum. The occurrences of the macro character can often be replaced with something else, such as an indirect reference or the use of the EVALUATE() function.

Another performance tip is to PACK your tables from time to time. Doing so reduces the size of the tables and improves performance. Use the PACK MEMO command to reduce size of associated memo files, particularly with tables where you often make changes to memo fields.

To improve the general performance of Browse commands, periodically SORT tables to the order that's most frequently used by your indexes.

To optimize performance during updates to records, use the following tips:

If you create applications with pre-set index tags, use as few tags as possible to accomplish the needed tasks within the application.

Create tags to support specific relationships, commonly-performed Seeks, Browse commands with Keys clauses, and all Rushmore-optimizable FOR clauses.

Where possible, use the "masterbase-childbase" or "batch-update" system of data entry, particularly with large tables. With this design approach, new records are not added to the main table, but are added to a temporary table with the same structure as the main table. After the data entry is completed, the new records can be added from the child table to the master table with the use of the APPEND FROM command. The module you use for the batch entry of records works at top speed, and lets the master table contain the tags that are needed to support your queries without slowing performance during the data entry process.

Keep Windows in Mind...

When looking to get the most in performance from FoxPro for Windows, remember that the overall Windows environment is also going to have an effect on how well FoxPro works. Like all Windows applications, FoxPro for Windows is dependent on a sufficient allocation of Windows' system resources to accomplish operations with reasonable speed. The more Windows applications you have running, the less that FoxPro can find in terms of system resources, so it makes sense to shut down any unneeded applications. On machines with only 4MB of RAM, it is a wise idea to run FoxPro without any other Windows applications open. Also, on 4MB machines, avoid the use of wallpaper (in Windows, open the Main window, double-click Control Panel, double-click Desktop, and change Wallpaper to None).

Optimizing for Rushmore

A significant reason behind FoxPro's claim to fame in the area of performance is *Rushmore*. Rushmore is a patent-pending technology that FoxPro uses to speed searches and data retrievals, and all versions of FoxPro since FoxPro 2.0 make use of it. Precisely how Rushmore works may be a closely-guarded Microsoft secret, but what Rushmore does with FoxPro commands is open knowledge. If you understand what Rushmore does, you can structure your data operations so that Rushmore can accomplish the most. Rushmore does the following:

1. Rushmore analyzes any commands that contain FOR *expression* clauses, and uses any available indexes to speed response time. (How much of a speed improvement is gained depends on how closely the expression included in the FOR clause matches the index key.) Rushmore can use any available indexes, whether they are tags of compound index files, or standard or compact index files in FoxPro's .IDX format.

2. Rushmore analyzes any SQL SELECT statements, and looks for available indexes to help speed processing of these statements. If no indexes exist that will help in the processing of an SQL SELECT statement, Rushmore builds temporary indexes as needed to effectively perform the query.

3. Rushmore analyzes SET FILTER statements, to see if the expression used as part of the statement can be optimized by Rushmore technology. If the expression is optimizable, Rushmore uses existing indexes to speed the execution of the SET FILTER statement.

In cases where Rushmore cannot *optimize* or speed the execution of a command, the operation occurs at speeds equivalent to those in versions of FoxPro prior to version 2.0. Also, note that in low memory situations, FoxPro may not be able to use Rushmore.

> **TIP**
>
> To take advantage of Rushmore when retrieving data from more than one table, you *must* use the SQL SELECT command (either by means of a query constructed through the RQBE Window, or by typing it directly into the Command Window). Rushmore is the basic technology used to optimize all SQL Queries.

One point to remember is that "available indexes" refers to indexes that are open, not just indexes that have been created at some point in time and may exist on the disk. If an index is not opened along with a table, Rushmore cannot make use of it. (This does not apply to SQL queries, where Rushmore automatically handles all indexing needs.) This is another argument in favor of storing all your indexes as tags in the structural compound index file, since these are opened automatically along with the table. Another point to remember is that for best performance, you should not set the order of the table. You can use a SET ORDER TO statement without naming an index (see the subheading "The SET ORDER Trick" later in this section).

In deciding how to structure your commands to get the most out of Rushmore, you need to determine whether or not an expression is *optimizable*. If an expression is optimizable, Rushmore can speed the execution of certain commands using that expression. Rushmore can optimize any of the following commands when a FOR clause is included, and when the expression itself is optimizable (as discussed in the following paragraphs):

AVERAGE	INDEX
BROWSE	LABEL
CALCULATE	LIST
CHANGE	LOCATE
COPY TO	RECALL
COPY TO ARRAY	REPLACE
COUNT	REPORT
DELETE	SCAN
DISPLAY	SORT
EDIT	SUM
EXPORT	TOTAL

For Rushmore to do any good, the FOR clause included with the above commands must be optimizable. FOR clauses are optimizable when indexes are available to support the use of the FOR clause. For example, you might have active index tags for a table based on the following expressions:

```
LASTNAME + FIRSTNAME
CUSTID
ZIPCODE
HIREDATE
```

and in such a case, the following expressions would be optimizable:

```
LASTNAME = "Miller"
LASTNAME = "Miller" .AND. FIRSTNAME = "Susan"
CUSTID = 1022
ZIPCODE >= "90210"
HIREDATE > {01/31/93}
```

Since the expression used by a FOR clause can be made up of more than one condition, the FOR clauses may be fully optimizable, partially optimizable, or not optimizable at all. Consider the command

```
LOCATE FOR LASTNAME = "Johnson"
```

In the past, serious XBase users would avoid such a command like the plague, because LOCATE was so slow when compared to the use of FIND or SEEK. But with Rushmore, if an index based on the LASTNAME field was created with a statement similar to

```
INDEX ON LASTNAME TAG NAMES
```

and assuming the index was active, the LOCATE command would find the desired data very quickly due to Rushmore's optimization. In this example, the LOCATE command is *fully optimizable*. By comparison, if the LOCATE command used a statement like

```
LOCATE FOR LASTNAME = "Johnson" .AND. FIRSTNAME = "Andrew"
```

and the index was constructed only on the basis of the LASTNAME field, the statement would be *partially optimizable* by Rushmore. To be fully optimizable in this case, you would need an active index with a key based on a combination of the LASTNAME and FIRSTNAME fields.

When trying to determine to what degree FOR clauses are optimizable, keep the following guidelines in mind:

- When all expressions in a FOR clause are optimizable, the clause is fully optimizable.

- The clause FOR *expression A* .AND. *expression B* is partially optimizable when *expression A* is optimizable, and *expression B* is not.

- The clause FOR *expression A* .OR. *expression B* is partially optimizable only when both *expression A* and *expression B* are at least partially optimizable.

- When no expressions in the FOR clause are optimizable, the clause is said to be *non-optimizable*.

When you build indexes, keep in mind some restrictions on Rushmore. Rushmore cannot work with indexes that created with the UNIQUE keyword, or with the INDEX FOR variation of the INDEX command. Rushmore also cannot work with indexes that contain database alias names within the index expression, or with indexes that use NOT operators as part of the index key. Finally, Rushmore cannot optimize any commands that contain WHILE clauses.

TIP

You can improve Rushmore's performance by setting DELETED to OFF, particularly with queries that return a large number of records.

Turning Rushmore Off

If for any reason you want to disable Rushmore, you can do so in one of two ways. You can add the keyword NOOPTIMIZE to any command that uses a FOR clause, and Rushmore will be disabled for that command. You can also enter SET OPTIMIZE OFF, and Rushmore will be disabled for all commands until you enter SET OPTIMIZE ON. One case where you should disable Rushmore is when you use a command (which could be optimized) that will modify the very index key used as part of the command's FOR clause. In such cases, Rushmore's internal record set could become out of sync, resulting in improper retrieval of data. You should disable Rushmore by adding the NOOPTIMIZE clause to the statement to prevent this from happening.

The SET ORDER Trick

In many cases, Rushmore works best when tables are in their *natural order* (that is, when no index is controlling the order of the records). You can put an open table in its natural order after indexes have been activated by using a

```
SET ORDER TO
```

statement, without naming any index after the word "TO."

A Note About Rushmore and Indexes

Since Rushmore does its work with FOR clauses and SET FILTER statements when supporting indexes are active, there may be a temptation to add an index tag that corresponds to most or all fields of a table. In most cases, this is not a good idea. Doing so can work wonders for the speed of searches and reporting. But the adding and editing of individual records can slow to a crawl, because each time a record is added or edited, all of the index tags for that record must be updated. You'll have to strike a balance between a sufficient number of indexes open to support effective data retrieval with the aid of Rushmore, while not slowing the data entry and editing process to an unacceptable level.

International Issues

FoxPro allows for a number of setting changes in the International section. The currency symbols used and the method of time display are among these. This section will deal with how to change the settings in the International settings by using the View window.

The date is the first thing that can be changed in the international section. Choose Window, View and click the globe icon at the left of the View box. This opens the international settings values. (See Figure 18.1, shown previously.) The current values are set at the American formats. Click the arrow beside Date: American, and you will see a list of countries, from which you can select the desired date format. You can also show the century by clicking on the show century option. The date delimiter enables you to change the delimiter that separates the months, dates, and years.

The currency symbol can also be changed, since not all countries use the same currency symbol. The symbol can also be moved from the left to the right of the numbers. Decimal places can also be changed from zero decimal places to up to 18 places.

Some prefer the 24 hour clock as opposed to the 12 hour clock. This can be changed simply by clicking the clock icon on the view window and changing from the 12 hour clock to the 24 hour clock.

Commands can also be used to change the international settings. These commands are listed here:

> For the date there is the Set Date *country* command.
> To add the century, enter Set Century On.
> To change the delimiter, enter Set Mark To "delimiter."
> To move the currency symbol, use Set Currency Right or Left.
> To change the decimal setting, enter Set Decimals To *number of decimal places desired.*
> To change the hours, enter Set Hours to 12 or 24.

Setting an International Sort Order

FoxPro provides the SET COLLATE TO command, which lets you specify a sorting or "collating" order that is adapted to a specific language. SET COLLATE can be used to properly sort and index your tables that contain accented characters, for any of the languages supported by FoxPro. For example, if you enter SET COLLATE TO SPANISH, a sort or index operation would consider "ch" and "ll" to be separate letters of the alphabet.

You specify the collation sequence with the command SET COLLATE TO *character expression,* where *character expression* is any of the following choices: DUTCH, GENERAL, ICELAND, MACHINE, NORDAN, SPANISH, and SWEFIN. These options are used for the languages shown in Table 18.2.

Table 18.2. Languages for Set Collate command.

DUTCH	Dutch
GENERAL	English, French, German, Modern Spanish, Portuguese, and other Western European languages

continues

Table 18.2. continued

ICELAND	Icelandic
MACHINE	Machine (the default collation sequence for earlier versions of FoxPro)
NORDAN	Norwegian, Danish
SPANISH	Traditional Spanish
SWEFIN	Swedish, Finnish

Note that once you use SET COLLATE, the new collating order takes effect for indexes that are created from then on. SET COLLATE does not affect the order of records according to previously-created indexes. This is advantageous because you can maintain different index orders for different languages by creating the indexes while SET COLLATE is set to different settings. The default for SET COLLATE is GENERAL, which matches the default collation order used by version 2.6 of FoxPro.

TIP

If you regularly use the same collation order, you can specify that order when you start FoxPro by including a line like this one in your FoxPro configuration file:

```
COLLATE = character expression
```

This is identical to issuing this command, SET COLLATE TO *character expression* from the Command Window.

When using a different collation order, keep in mind that FoxPro's Rushmore technology can only take advantage of indexes whose collation sequence match the current collation sequence. If you are building indexes to support several languages, make sure the current collation sequence matches the collation sequences for the active indexes and index tags.

Repairing Damaged Database Files

A somber saying says that there are only two kinds of computer users in this world: those who have lost data, and those who will. FoxPro is a complex database management system, and as with any complex system, there is always a possibility that data will be damaged or lost. As a developer, you can minimize the chances of data loss with good housekeeping techniques (opening files only when necessary and closing files as soon as possible, and including good backup routines in your programs). However, it helps to understand a little more than the average FoxPro user about how FoxPro stores data in a database file. Such knowledge may come in handy if one of your application files gets unexplainably damaged, and contrary to dire warnings, the users haven't performed a backup in two months.

A FoxPro database file consists of a file header, the file data (in the form of individual records), and an end-of-file marker (ASCII decimal-26 or hex-1A). The contents of the memo fields are another matter entirely; these are stored in a separate file with a .DBT extension. The memo field in the database (.DBF) file contains a pointer that is used to find the text in the associated .DBT file. The file header contains the date of the last file update, the number of records present in the file, a rather cryptic description of the database structure, and other information needed by FoxPro.

The contents of the fields are packed into records that are not delimited or separated with any special characters. Each record begins with one byte that contains a space (ASCII decimal 32, or 20 HEX) if the record is not deleted, and an asterisk (ASCII decimal 42, or 2A HEX) if it is deleted. FoxPro keeps a count of the number of records in a database by means of various hex codes stored in the file header. If the header is damaged or destroyed, you have run up against the more serious type of damage that can occur. FoxPro will think there are less records in the file than are actually present, or worse yet, will refuse to open the file and instead display the heart-stopping error message

```
Not a Table/DBF
```

when your program attempts to use the file. If the header has been damaged, any attempt to repair the damage requires a program that lets you edit the data contained in the header. If you are familiar with the DOS DEBUG utility, you can use it to change the contents of the header. (See your DOS manual for more instructions about DEBUG.) If the file is relatively small, you can use a good program editor (such as PC-Write, a "shareware" product available on bulletin boards) to edit the header in a word processing mode. In either case, make backup copies of the damaged file before attempting to perform any repairs. Once you have made a backup copy, you can attempt to manually calculate the proper HEX values, and rebuild the header to the point where FoxPro will recognize it as a valid database header. If FoxPro manages to open a file with a damaged header, the record count within the file should be immediately suspect. Because the record count is the last part of a header that is updated just before the file is closed, any system crash that occurs while a file is open will probably leave the header with an incorrect record count. You should use the COPY command to immediately create a new file, copying the records out to that file, with commands like:

```
USE Damaged
COPY TO GoodFile
```

When the COPY command has completed copying valid records out to the new file, it will update the recount count in the header of the new file with an accurate figure. The old file can then be deleted, and the new file substituted in its place.

Good Header, Bad Data

More common among trashed table files is a file that contains a valid header, but damaged data in the file. Your program performs an EDIT function, and the display for some of the records are garbled. When a LIST is performed, you get something that looks like this:

```
LNAME         FNAME        ADDRESS              CITY        STATE ZIP
Hobbs         Kerie        1607 Valencia Way    Reston      VA    22090
Hoffman       Carol        1569 Trails Edge Ln  Reston      VA    22091
Hoffman       Carol^!      1569 Trails Edge L n ResHogan          Debra
         982 Gr anby Court Ste rling    VA22070    Hummer       Annette
        1528 Sca ndia Circle Lee sburg  VA22075    Hunt         John W.
        1604 Sto we Road   Her ndon     VA22070    Hutcheson    Charles
```

For reasons unknown, random extra data has been introduced to your data file, resulting in a corruption of the database. The contents of the fields appear to straddle the field limits, and it appears that a re-keying of the data is the only way to proceed. Before resorting to such a drastic solution, try restoring the file first. Copy the file to another temporary file, and use that file for the attempt at database repair.

First, use the temporary file, and go to the first damaged record. Delete that record, and the record prior to it (in many cases, the record prior to the first record that appears damaged is the one that's causing the problem). Then, pack the database. These simple steps may (or may not) repair the damage.

If the problem still exists, you must resort to a program other than FoxPro that lets you directly edit the database file containing the table. Use DEBUG or a program editor to find the damaged record, and insert or remove HEX 20 (blank spaces) as needed until the data aligns properly within the fields when in FoxPro. You can probably manage to do this by deleting characters that don't appear to belong, and/or inserting spaces in the faulty record on a trial-and-error basis. Go in and out of BROWSE mode in FoxPro to check on the progress, until the data appears to fill the fields properly.

Random End-Of-File Marker

Another type of damage that occasionally occurs is when an extra end-of-file marker (HEX value 1A) gets placed somewhere in the database file. This is a commonly caused by abnormal exit; perhaps the system was rebooted before FoxPro had a chance to properly close the file.

Extra end-of-file markers cause FoxPro to behave in an interesting and baffling manner. The telltale signs are as follows: you enter LIST STRUCTURE, and FoxPro tells you that there are 198 records in the database. You do a LIST, and FoxPro shows you everything up to record number 82, then dumps you back at the command level. The BROWSE command gives you bizarre results, sometimes displaying some of the records, and sometimes displaying all of the records in a normal fashion. Your report and label-generating programs pretend that nothing exists above record 82. If you enter GO 84 to move to record number 84, and then enter a LIST NEXT 200, FoxPro then shows you the remaining records in the database.

What has happened is this: somehow an extra end-of-file character occupies a space at or near the end of record number 82. This problem can be corrected without leaving FoxPro (although if you are fluent with DEBUG or with your program editor, by all means use that route). Use the COPY command to copy the records prior to the end-of-file character to a temporary file, something like:

```
USE CLIENTS
COPY TO TEMP1
```

Then go to the record following the false end of file marker, and copy the remaining records to another table, such as with:

```
GO 84
COPY NEXT 9999 TO TEMP2
```

Then, use the first temporary file, and copy the records from the second file into the first with:

```
USE TEMP1
APPEND FROM TEMP2
```

Finally, delete your damaged file, and rename your temporary file to the name of the damaged file. At the most, you might lose one record with this approach.

Index Files

When a database has been damaged, all associated index files become immediately suspect. Any index files should be re-created from scratch before the application is used again. Don't use the REINDEX command, because it is possible that the structure of the index file has also been damaged.

Chapter Summary

The best time to think about recovering from the effects of damaged files is before such damage occurs. Assume the worst will happen, and take steps to provide recovery from system crashes. If your users don't remember backups, a forceful reminder using the RUN command to run DOS BACKUP regularly is a wise addition to any application. If money is no object when it comes to data security, recommend good surge protection, high-speed tape backup, and an uninterruptible power supply. Don't wait until someone calls frantically pleading for help to decide how you'll go about the business of crash recovery.

PART

4

Programming in FoxPro

FoxPro Programming Basics

This chapter provides an introduction to the real power behind FoxPro—programming. You'll learn how programs are created and executed under the FoxPro programming language, and how expressions, functions, and memory variables can be effectively used within your FoxPro programs.

Programming with FoxPro is made possible with command files, which are files made up of FoxPro commands. Any list of instructions or commands that directs the operation of a computer is a program, and FoxPro programs are simply lists of commands written in the FoxPro programming language. The FoxPro programming language makes use of the same commands that can be entered manually in the Command Window. Any series of commands that can be entered in the Command Window can also be stored in a text file. (The text file can be created by the editor that is built into FoxPro, or by any editor that can create normal text files composed of ASCII characters.) Files containing FoxPro commands are known as command files, or as programs. The two terms are often used interchangeably.

FoxPro programs can range from a simple list of a few commands to dozens of interrelated files containing hundreds of commands. When multiple files of commands are used to perform various tasks, the collection of files is often referred to as an application. For example, a number of command files may be designed to process the various transactions necessary within an accounting system. Those command files are referred to as an accounting application running under FoxPro. Much of the work done behind the scenes in FoxPro is done by FoxPro programs. The Catalog Manager, for instance, is a sophisticated FoxPro program.

The double method of dealing with commands is what makes programming in FoxPro possible. When it comes to commands, FoxPro can be used in one of two ways: in an interactive mode, which means entering commands one at a time in the Command Window; or in a program mode, by specifying the name of a command file. The program mode of FoxPro is invoked with the DO command. The syntax for this command is:

```
DO <filename>
```

where "filename" is a text file containing the individual FoxPro commands to be executed. The underlying operation of FoxPro is the same, whether in the interactive mode, or in the program mode. The only difference is that in the interactive mode, FoxPro reads commands from the keyboard, while in the program mode, FoxPro reads commands from a disk file. Each command contained within a command file occupies an individual line. Some programming languages allow more than one command on a single line, but FoxPro is not one of them.

A line within a FoxPro program normally begins with a command verb, which is a reserved FoxPro word such as DO or INDEX. The command verb is followed by a statement, which can be made up of a number of values or conditions that control the effect of the operation performed by the command. Lines of a program can start at the left margin, or they can be indented for easier reading. Lines cannot be longer than a maximum of 256 characters, including spaces.

A Simple Program

As an example of a simple programming task, it might be necessary to enter a series of commands that would open the Buyers table, index the file in alphabetical order by lastname, and display the contents of the last_name, address_1, city, state, and zip_code fields. In the Command Window, the commands to perform these tasks could be entered, with the following results:

```
USE BUYERS
INDEX ON LASTNAME TAG NAMES
```

and the results would resemble those shown here:

Record#	CUSTID	LASTNAME	FIRSTNAME	CITY	STATE
10	110	Anderson	Harry	Santa Monica	CA
9	109	Bannerton	Alicia	Falls Church	VA
5	105	Hernandez	Maria	Towson	MD
4	104	Jones	Nikki	Washington	DC
6	106	Jones	Jarel	McLean	VA
8	108	O'Neill	John	Merrifield	VA
1	101	Roberts	Jamie	Reston	VA
2	102	Sanderson	Lucy	Herndon	VA
3	103	Smith	Larry	Kensington	MD
7	107	Zeibermann	Daniel	Arlington	VA

An identical set of commands could be stored within a program, named "TEST.PRG", as shown in the following example:

```
NOTE**TEST.PRG
*This is an example of a command file.
USE BUYERS
INDEX ON LASTNAME TAG NAMES
LIST LASTNAME, FIRSTNAME, CITY, STATE, ZIPCODE
```

The lines within the program that begin with NOTE, or with an asterisk (*), are comment lines. Comment lines are ignored by FoxPro when the program is executed. Comment lines are helpful (and highly recommended) for documenting the operation of a program.

Once the commands are stored in the file, those commands can be executed in sequential order by entering the single command,

```
DO TEST
```

which produces the following result:

```
Record#  CUSTID  LASTNAME      FIRSTNAME    CITY           STATE
     10  110     Anderson      Harry        Santa Monica   CA
      9  109     Bannerton     Alicia       Falls Church   VA
      5  105     Hernandez     Maria        Towson         MD
      4  104     Jones         Nikki        Washington     DC
      6  106     Jones         Jarel        McLean         VA
      8  108     O'Neill       John         Merrifield     VA
      1  101     Roberts       Jamie        Reston         VA
      2  102     Sanderson     Lucy         Herndon        VA
      3  103     Smith         Larry        Kensington     MD
      7  107     Zeibermann    Daniel       Arlington      VA
```

Creating a Program

Programs can be created with the FoxPro Editor or a text editor of your choice. If you use a text editor, it must have the capability to create ASCII text files without any control characters. Program files are normally assigned an extension of .PRG. If you use a different extension, you must specify the extension as a part of the filename when running the program with the DO command.

To create a program with the FoxPro Editor, choose File, New from the menus, and in the dialog box that appears, click Program, then click New. You can also enter MODIFY COMMAND in the Command Window. The syntax for this command is:

```
MODIFY COMMAND <filename>
```

where "filename" is the name of the program file to be created. If no extension is specified, the .PRG extension is assigned. If no filename is supplied, the Editor opens a window called "Untitled", and you are asked for a filename when you close the window. For example, entering the command

```
MODIFY COMMAND TEST
```

creates a file, called "TEST.PRG". and causes the FoxPro Editor to appear within a window. Commands can then be typed, a line at a time, with the return key pressed upon completion of each line.

Typing errors can be corrected with the cursor keys, and the backspace and delete keys. Pressing the Insert key switches back and forth between the "Insert" and "Overwrite" modes of the FoxPro Editor. When in the Insert mode, all characters typed are inserted at the cursor position. If any existing characters occupy the cursor position, these characters are pushed to the right to make room for the new characters. In the overwrite mode of operation, new typed characters write over existing characters. Various combinations of control keys can also be used with the FoxPro Editor for scrolling the screen, moving the cursor, and for deleting various characters, words, and entire lines. A complete listing of these keys is provided in Table 19.1. Once editing with the FoxPro Editor is completed, files can be saved to disk by choosing File, Save from the menus, or with the Ctrl+End key combination. The Escape key can be used to abort an editing process without saving the text.

Table 19.1. The Editing Keys for FoxPro Editor.

Key	Result
Up Arrow	Cursor up one line
Down Arrow	Cursor down one line
Left Arrow	Cursor left one space
Right Arrow	Cursor right one space
Ins	Switches between Insert and overwrite modes
Del	Deletes character at cursor
Backspace	Deletes character to left of cursor
Home	Cursor to beginning to line
End	Cursor to end of line
PgUp	Scroll up by one screen
PgDn	Scroll down by one screen
Ctrl+End	Saves file to disk
Esc	Abort editing; don't save file

Operators

Each FoxPro data type (with the exception of memo and general fields) has specific operators than can be used with those data elements. Operators perform various operations on data to produce a value. Mathematic, character string or alphanumeric, logical, and relational operators are available in the FoxPro language.

Math operators (used to perform operations that yield numeric results) are:

```
+ and -  (unary) signs
^ and ** exponentiation
*        multiplication
/        division
+        addition
-        subtraction
()       grouping
```

Note that the order or precedence among the math operators is unary, then exponentiation, then multiplication or division, then addition or subtraction. In cases where operators maintain equal precedence (such as multiplication and division), the order of precedence is from left to right. Parentheses can be used within the expression, to force a different order. When parentheses are used, FoxPro calculates from the innermost pair of parentheses, and works outward.

Character string operators are:

```
+    Concatenation
-    Concatenation (strips any trailing spaces)
```

When used with character strings, the plus sign concatenates, or combines, strings of characters. As an example, "Mr." + "Smith" equates to the character string, "Mr.Smith".

Relational Operators are:

```
=        Equal to
<> or #  Not equal to
<        Less than
>        Greater than
<=       Less than or equal to
>=       Greater than or equal to
$        Substring contained within a string
```

Logical Operators are:

```
.NOT.   (Negation or complement)
.AND.   (Logical AND)
.OR.    (Logical OR)
()      grouping
```

The order of precedence for logical operators is NOT, then AND, then OR. If different types of operators are used within a single expression, the order of precedence is math and string operators, followed by relational operators, followed by logical operators.

Expressions

Expressions are combinations of fields, memory variables, constants, functions, and/or operators. The only rule governing what may be placed in expressions states that all elements of the expression must be of the same type. You cannot, for example, combine numeric elements and character elements within the same expression. Examples of valid expressions include:

```
(SALARY-(TAXES+2.78))
"Ms. " + LAST_NAME
"Robinson"
3.14159
```

The most commonly-used expressions in FoxPro programs are numeric expressions. These can consist of numeric memory variables, numeric fields, constants, or any combination of these, linked by any combination of math operators. Assuming that fields of a table named SALARY and HOURS are numeric fields, all of the following are numeric expressions:

```
48
SALARY + 500.50
SALARY * HOURS
((SALARY * HOURS)+2.75)
```

Character expressions are also found throughout FoxPro programs. Character expressions consist of character variables, the contents of character fields, or literal character strings enclosed in quotation marks, usually joined by a plus sign. Examples of character expressions are:

```
"Bob Smith"
FIRST_NAME + LAST_NAME
"Client name is: " + LAST_NAME
```

Memory Variables

FoxPro allocates an area of memory for the storage of memory variables. Memory variables are storage areas set aside to contain data, which can be characters, numbers, dates, or logical (true/false) expressions. Memory variables are designated by assigning a value to a name for the variable. Memory variable names are limited to a maximum of 10 characters, and the first character must be a letter.

In the FoxPro programming language, memory variables must be created or initialized, before they can be used within the program. This is in direct contrast to a programming language like BASIC, where memory variables can be created "on the fly." Memory variables can be initialized in one of two ways: with the STORE command, or as a part of an assignment statement. The syntax of the STORE command is:

```
STORE <value> TO <memory variable>
```

while the syntax of an assignment statement is:

```
<memory variable> = <value>
```

The value stored to a memory variable can be a literal value, the contents of a table field, or the contents of another memory variable. As an example, to store the word "Robert" to a memory variable called FNAME, either of the following commands could be used:

```
STORE "Robert" TO FNAME
FNAME = "Robert"
FoxPro allows four types of memory variables: character, numeric, logical, and date.
Character variables will contain strings of characters, which can be composed of a
```

combination of letters, numbers, and punctuation symbols. Numeric values contain
numbers, which are recognized as numbers and not as characters by FoxPro. You can
perform calculations on numeric variables. Numbers stored in numeric variables can be
whole numbers, or they can be fractional (decimal) numbers. Date variables contain dates
that follow the FoxPro date format. Examples of commands for initializing all four types
of memory variables are shown below.

```
STORE "PS/2" TO SYSTYPE
STORE 1344.85 TO SYSCOST
STORE {12/21/93} TO PURCHDATE
STORE .T. TO SRCONTRACT
```

The first example stores a character string, "PS/2", to the character variable named
SYSTYPE. The second example stores a numeric value, 1344.85, to a numeric variable
named SYSCOST. In the third example, a date value is indicated, by the presence of curly
braces around it. The last example stores a logical value, True, to the variable
SRCONTRACT.

Note that in each case, the type of memory variable (character, numeric, date, or logical)
is ascertained by FoxPro from the manner in which the data is supplied. For example,
single or double quotation marks identify data as a character string. The letters T,F,Y,
and N surrounded by two periods identify the data as a logical variable. Numbers are assumed to be numeric variables unless the numbers are enclosed in quotation marks. Dates
are stored to a memory variable by surrounding them with curly braces. Use the proper
syntax when declaring memory variables. You could get into trouble with a command
like

```
STORE "1344.85" TO SYSCOST
```

because the quotation marks tell FoxPro that this is a character variable. If you later tried
to perform math calculations directly on the variable, FoxPro responds with an error
message.

Displaying Memory Variables

To display the contents of memory variables at any time, use the DISPLAY MEMORY
and LIST MEMORY commands. The commands perform the same function with one
difference: LIST MEMORY displays the contents of all memory variables without paus-
ing, while DISPLAY MEMORY pauses every window full of data, requiring the press of
a key before the window of data is displayed. Both commands show the name of the
memory variable, its type, the contents, and whether the memory variable is public or
private (public vs. private memory variables are discussed in a later chapter). If you enter
DISPLAY MEMORY in the Command Window, you see a display whose first few lines
resemble those shown here:

```
INDEX     Pub    N   45        (      45.00000000)
PDATE     Pub    D   02/28/93
```

```
    2 variables defined,    0 bytes used
 1022 variables available
```

The ? command can also be used to display the contents of a single memory variable. The syntax of the command, when used in this manner, is:

```
? <memory variable name>
```

For example, the following commands produce the results shown:

```
? systype
PS/2

? syscost
1344.85

? purchdate
12/21/93
```

Functions

FoxPro also has a number of functions available for use by the programmer for performing various tasks. Functions can be thought of as special-purpose programs which perform tasks that would otherwise be difficult or impossible. In FoxPro, functions are used to convert data from one type to another, to perform specialized math operations, to test for various conditions, and to manipulate data in various ways. Functions always provide a value, and functions are used either as an expression or within an expression. The common format for a function is:

```
name of function(expression)
```

As an example, the Square Root (SQRT) function can be combined with an expression (in this case, a given number) to determine the square root of that number, as shown:

```
? SQRT(9)
3.00
```

Some functions are not used with an expression. These functions require only the name of the function to operate. An example is the Date() function, which returns the date maintained by the system clock:

```
? DATE()
04/18/93
```

Commonly used functions are described in the following groups of functions.

MIN() and MAX()

The MIN() and MAX() functions return the minimum and maximum values, respectively, of two numeric expressions. The syntax for the functions is:

```
MIN (<numeric expression 1>,<numeric expression 2>)
MAX (<numeric expression 1>,<numeric expression 2>)
```

The MIN() function returns the lower of the two expressions, while the MAX() function returns the higher of the two expressions. Often in a program, one expression is the contents of a numeric field, and the other expression is a memory variable that contains some pre-defined high or low value.

For instance, the following code determines the higher of two expressions: one is a ceiling of repair costs, and the other is an actual figure for repair costs contained within a table.

```
*Exceeds.PRG lists ceilings exceeded for building repairs.
INPUT "Enter maximum value for repairs: " TO MAXVAL
USE REPAIRS
LIST COST, MAX(MAXVAL, COST)

do exceeds
Enter maximum value for repairs: 150.00

Record#   COST MAX(MAXVAL, COST)
     1   56.00       150.00
     2  128.53       150.00
     3   69.90       150.00
     4  218.54       218.54
     5   78.77       150.00
     6  432.95       432.95
     7   45.67       150.00
```

ROUND()

The ROUND() function rounds off numbers, with a specific number of decimal places retained. The syntax for the ROUND function is:

```
ROUND(<numeric expression>,<number of decimal places>)
```

Example:

```
? ROUND(5.867,2)
5.870

? ROUND(5.867,0)
6.000
```

Note that if the numeric expression used to specify the number of decimal places is a negative value, the resultant value is a rounded whole number, as shown in the following examples:

```
? ROUND(5.867,-0)
6
? ROUND(5.867,-1)
10
```

```
LTRIM()
```

The `LTRIM()` function removes any leading blanks from a character string. The syntax of the function is:

```
LTRIM(<character expression>)
```

Example:

```
STORE 21 TO NUMBER
? STR(NUMBER)
      21
? LTRIM(STR(NUMBER))
21
```

```
LOWER()
```

The `LOWER()` function is used to convert uppercase letters to lowercase. The `LOWER()` function has no effect on lowercase letters, numbers, spaces, or punctuation marks. The syntax for the `LOWER()` function is:

```
LOWER(<character expression>)
```

Example:

```
STORE LOWER("SMITH") TO TEST
? TEST
smith
```

```
UPPER()
```

The `UPPER()` function performs the reverse of the `LOWER()` function—it converts lowercase letters to uppercase. The `UPPER()` function has no effect on uppercase letters, numbers, spaces, or punctuation marks. The syntax for the `UPPER()` function is:

```
UPPER(<character expression>)
```

Example:

```
STORE "rotunda" TO TEST
? UPPER(TEST)
ROTUNDA
```

The `LOWER()` and `UPPER()` functions are useful to force consistency and to overcome problems caused by the case-sensitive nature of FoxPro. For example, if a record contains the name "JOHNSON" in a lastname field, and the name is stored as shown (in all uppercase letters), a `LOCATE` statement using the following syntax would NOT find the record:

```
LOCATE FOR LASTNAME = "johnson"
```

But with a `LOWER()` function used as shown, the name is found regardless of whether it is stored in the table as lowercase letters, uppercase letters, or a combination of both:

```
LOCATE FOR LOWER(LASTNAME) = "johnson"
```

TRIM()

The TRIM() function strips trailing spaces from a character string. The syntax for the TRIM() function is:

```
TRIM(<character expression>)
```

The TRIM() function is useful for removing undesired gaps of "white space" between the contents of character fields that are combined as part of an expression, such as:

```
USE MAILER
GO 5
? FIRSTNAME + LASTNAME
Maria          Hernandez
? TRIM(FIRSTNAME) + " " + LASTNAME
Maria Hernandez
```

SPACE()

The SPACE() function creates a character string containing a specified number of blank spaces. The syntax for the SPACE() function is:

```
SPACE(<numeric expression>)
```

where <numeric expression> translates to a value between 1 and 254.

Example:

```
STORE SPACE(15) TO GAP
? "System" + GAP + "Main" + GAP + "Menu"
System          Main          Menu
```

DATE() and TIME()

The DATE() and TIME() functions provide the current date and time. The value provided by the DATE() function takes the form of a date variable, while the value provided by the TIME() function takes the form of a character variable. FoxPro does not provide any function for setting the system clock date or time.

Examples:

```
? date()
03/01/94
? time()
22:09:29
store date() to today
03/01/94
store time() to rightnow
22:09:42
display memory
TODAY     pub  D 03/01/94
RIGHTNOW  pub  C "22:09:42"
```

CTOD()

The CTOD() function is the character-to-date conversion function. CTOD() converts a character expression containing a string of characters formatted as a date into a date variable. The default for the format of the characters is MM/DD/YY, but this format can be changed with the SET DATE command. The syntax for the CTOD() function is:

```
CTOD(<character expression>)
```

The character string supplied by the expression can vary from "1/1/100" to "12/31/9999".

Example:

```
STORE CTOD("07/06/94") TO WEDDING
07/06/94
DISPLAY MEMORY
WEDDING    pub  D 07/06/94
```

DTOC()

The DTOC() function is the date-to-character conversion function. DTOC() converts a date expression into a string of characters. The format of the characters supplied by DTOC() follows the current settings for display of dates, which can be altered by means of the SET DATE command. The syntax for the DTOC() function is:

```
DTOC(<date expression>)
```

Example:

```
STORE DTOC(WEDDING) TO TEST
07/06/93
? TEST
07/06/93
```

DISPLAY MEMORY

```
WEDDING    pub  D 07/06/93
TEST     pub  C "07/06/93"
  2 variables defined,    19 bytes used
 254 variables available,  5981 bytes available
```

BOF()

The BOF() function is the beginning-of-file function. BOF() provides a logical value of true if the record pointer is at the beginning of the table, and a logical value of false if the record pointer is not at the beginning of the file. The syntax for the BOF() function is:

```
BOF()
```

Example:

```
USE MAILER
? BOF()
.T.
SKIP
? BOF()
.F.
```

```
EOF()
```

The EOF() function is the end-of-file function. EOF() provides a logical value of true if the record pointer is at the end of the table, and a logical value of false if the record pointer is not at the end of the table. The syntax for the EOF() function is:

```
EOF()
```

Example:

```
USE CLIENTS
? EOF()
.F.
GO BOTTOM
? EOF()
.T.
```

```
FOUND()
```

The FOUND() function is used to test for the successful find of a record with a LOCATE, CONTINUE, SEEK, or FIND command. If the command used to search for the record is successful, the FOUND() function provides a logical value of true. Programs can use a statement containing the FOUND() function to test for a successful find, as shown in this program:

```
USE IFILES
SET ORDER TO STOCKNO
INPUT "Stock number? " TO SNUMB
SEEK SNUMB
IF .NOT. FOUND()
    ? "No such record!"
    RETURN
ENDIF
```

```
IIF()
```

The IIF(), or Immediate IF function performs a conditional IF test of a logical expression, and returns one of two expressions if the condition is true. The syntax for the IIF() function is:

```
IIF(<logical expression>,<expression 1>,<expression 2>)
```

As an example of the IIF() function, the following line uses IIF() to evaluate whether a company employee is salaried or non-salaried. If the individual is non-salaried, an amount of zero is stored to the variable, BENEFITS; if the individual is salaried, an amount equal to 5.7 percent of the salary is stored to the variable, BENEFITS.

```
BENEFITS = IIF(SALARIED = .T., .057*SALARY, 0)
```

The IIF() function is faster than the IF...ENDIF construction it can replace, and can also be used within reports and labels.

Chapter Summary

This chapter examined FoxPro programming with a view toward providing the familiarity needed to begin working with the FoxPro programming language. In the next four chapters, you'll see how these techniques can be used to manage tasks in the specific areas of database management, such as data entry, reporting, and the building of complete applications.

Program Flow In A FoxPro Program

20

A well-known rule of programming states that any problem, no matter how large, can be easily solved if it is broken down into smaller, manageable pieces. FoxPro lends itself to this philosophy by providing commands that enable control within a program to be passed back and forth between smaller parts, or modules. Until now, examples of FoxPro programs have been fairly simple, with most programs following a simple flow from beginning to end. In real life, applications are never simple enough to warrant a program flow that runs uninterrupted from start to finish without changing direction. Most programming languages offer three types of control structures that let the user control the flow of a program. FoxPro is no exception. The different types of control structures are conditional structures, repetitive structures, and branching structures. Control structures are commonly used throughout a FoxPro program to provide users with flexibility. Using control structures, you can design a program to deal with any one of a number of conditions or to respond to varying user requests.

Branching Controls: DO, RETURN, and RETURN TO MASTER

In a branching control structure, one program calls, or executes, another program. A branching structure lets the program deviate from its normal (sequential) path. A program that performs no branching, as opposed to a program that does, could be graphically depicted with the following illustration:

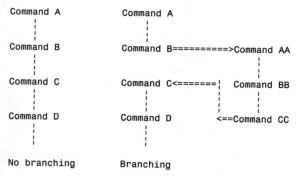

As outlined in the previous chapter, the DO command is used to run a FoxPro command file, or program. However, the DO command can also be used within a program to call (or, branch to) another program. Once that program has finished its tasks, control can be passed back to the original (calling) program with the RETURN command. In a sense, it's as if the commands contained within the other program file have become a part of the first program file. This type of program flow is illustrated here.

```
     MAIN.PRG              NOFIND.PRG


IF MZIPCODE <> ZIPCODE
    CONTINUE
    IF EOF()
    DO NOFIND            *NOFIND.PRG
    RETURN               *Prints a message if person isn't in database
    LOOP                 CLEAR
ENDIF                    @7,10 SAY "This person not in database!"
                         @8,10 SAY "Return to menu to enter"
                         @9,10 SAY "new names, or to try different"
                         @10,10 SAY "name."
                         WAIT
                         RETURN
```

In this example of program code, NOFIND.PRG can be considered to be a subprogram, or module, of the main program. When used within a program, the DO command transfers program control to the first line of the command file named by the DO command. Program control remains in that command file until a RETURN command is encountered (or until the end of the command file is encountered). When the RETURN command is encountered, program control returns to the line immediately following the DO command that originally called the module.

The DO command is the only available method for transferring program control to another program module within FoxPro. The FoxPro programming language encourages structured programming by default—there is no equivalent to the GOTO command present in BASIC and similar unstructured languages. You cannot transfer program control to another part of the same program with the DO command—you can only branch to another module, or subprogram.

Branches to a submodule can be conditional (only occurring when a specified condition is met), or unconditional (always occurring at a given point within the program). The previous example of a branch is conditional; the program, NOFIND.PRG, is run only if the test for End-Of-File in the main program returns a value of true.

FoxPro supports multiple nesting of subroutines, or submodules, within a program. Such nesting takes place when one program uses a DO statement to run another program, which uses a DO statement to run yet another program, and so on, as shown here:

```
    MainMenu.PRG

    DO PrinMenu =====>  PrinMenu.PRG

                        DO Label1.PRG =====>  Label1.PRG
```

In most cases, RETURN is sufficient to end the execution of the submodule. However, a useful option of the RETURN command is RETURN TO MASTER. This option causes program control to be passed to the highest-level module of a program. Complex applications often result in programs that are a number of levels deep. In such cases, a user request to return to the main menu (assuming the main menu is in the highest-level program) can be performed with a RETURN TO MASTER command. Effective use of the RETURN TO MASTER command makes it unnecessary for the user to wade through an annoying number of menus in a large application, just to get back to the first menu to choose an option to leave the application.

CONDITIONAL CONTROL WITHIN A PROGRAM

Conditional controls are used to alter the flow of a program depending on the outcome of an evaluated condition. The most common use of conditional commands in a FoxPro program is within the construction of the menus used in an application. FoxPro offers two commands for conditional controls: the IF..ELSE..ENDIF command, and the DO CASE command.

Using The If/EndIf Commands

The IF...ENDIF command provides a true/false evaluation of a given condition, enabling FoxPro to perform one operation if the condition is true, and a different operation if the condition is false. The syntax for the statement bears a resemblance to English, and in planning a program it helps to think of the statement as following the way in which the syntax is written:

```
IF <condition>
  <commands>
ENDIF
or, as an alternate method,
IF <condition>
  <commands>
ELSE
  <commands>
ENDIF
```

The IF and ENDIF commands are a matched set. Each IF command sequence must be closed with an ENDIF command. The ELSE command is optional, and can be used to denote an alternative path for program flow. If the ELSE command is omitted, then all statements contained within the IF and the ENDIF commands are carried out, if the condition specified is true. If the condition is not true, program control passes to the first statement following the ENDIF command. In the following example, an IF...ENDIF set of commands is used to evaluate whether a printing program is executed.

```
IF CHOICE = 1
  DO PRINTER
ENDIF
```

In this example, no alternate path is provided; either the condition is true, and the PRINTER program is run, or the condition is false, and program control passes to the command immediately following the ENDIF command. In cases where an alternate path is desired, the ELSE statement can be used to specify commands that are executed if the evaluated condition is false, as shown in the following example:

```
IF CHOICE = 1
   DO PRINTER1
ELSE
   DO PRINTER2
ENDIF
```

In this case, if the condition is false (memory variable CHOICE not equal to 1), the command file named PRINTER2 is run. Simple conditions can be replaced with very complex conditions, when necessary, to form the basis for the desired condition.

Using Immediate IF

The IIF(), or "Immediate IF" function lets you duplicate an IF...ENDIF conditional structure within a single command, enabling the use of IF conditionals both within a program and from the dot prompt. The syntax for the command is

```
IIF(<logical expression>,<expression 1>,<expression 2>
```

It helps to think of the function as actually working something like this:

```
IF(<logical expression is true, then>,<expression 1>, OTHERWISE
<expression 2>)
```

For example, consider the following IF...ENDIF construction:

```
IF AGE >= 21
    STORE "Legal drinking age" TO MSTRING
ELSE
    STORE "No alcohol to minors" TO MSTRING
ENDIF
```

Using the Immediate IF function, the entire construction could be accomplished within one line of a program:

```
MSTRING = IIF(AGE >= 21,"Legal drinking age","No alcohol to minors")
```

Use of the Immediate IF function provides two significant benefits. First, it speeds program execution time. Secondly, it can be used within an expression inside of a report or label form, providing the ability to produce reports or labels containing different data based on the logical expression provided by the IIF() function.

When using complex conditions as a part of a program, care should be taken to ensure that the conditional statements are designed to achieve the proper results. The following program code shows how things can get complicated with complex conditionals:

```
IF SALARY >= 22500
     IF EXEMPTION > 1
          DO TAXCALC1
     ELSE
          DO TAXCALC2
     ENDIF
ELSE
     IF EXEMPTION > 1
          DO TAXCALC3
     ELSE
          DO TAXCALC4
     ENDIF
ENDIF
```

The most common error when designing such conditionals is the omission of a closing statement, with possibly bizarre results.

Using DO CASE and ENDCASE

The DO CASE and ENDCASE commands are used when it is necessary to make decisions on any one of several conditions. The syntax for the DO CASE and ENDCASE commands are

```
DO CASE
  CASE <first condition>
    <commands>
  CASE <second condition>
    <commands>
  CASE <third condition>
    <commands>
  CASE <fourth condition>
    <commands>
  <OTHERWISE>
    <other commands>
ENDCASE
```

When FoxPro encounters a DO CASE command, it begins evaluating the specified condition following each CASE statement, beginning with the first one, until it finds a CASE statement whose condition can be evaluated as true. Once such a statement is found, the commands identified by that statement are carried out. Execution then continues with the next command that follows the ENDCASE command. If no CASE statement in the series evaluates as true, then program control proceeds to the next command following the ENDCASE command, unless you have included the optional OTHERWISE statement. If the OTHERWISE statement is included, commands identified by that statement are executed if no other CASE statements can be executed.

DO CASE commands are regularly used to design and implement menus, where one choice of a number of possible choices is normally appropriate, as shown in the following example:

```
STORE SPACE " " TO ANS
@ 17,33 SAY " select choice: "
@ 17,50 GET ANS
READ
DO CASE
  CASE selectnum = 0
    CLEAR ALL
    QUIT

  CASE selectnum = 1
    SET FORMAT TO MYFORM
    APPEND
    STORE ' ' TO wait_subst
    @ 23,0 SAY 'Press any key to continue...' GET wait_subst
    READ

  CASE selectnum = 2
    SET FORMAT TO MYFORM
    DO MyEdit
    STORE ' ' TO wait_subst
    @ 23,0 SAY 'Press any key to continue...' GET wait_subst
    READ

  CASE selectnum = 3
    DO Eraser
    STORE ' ' TO wait_subst
    @ 23,0 SAY 'Press any key to continue...' GET wait_subst
    READ

  CASE selectnum = 4
    DO Reporter
    STORE ' ' TO wait_subst
    @ 23,0 SAY 'Press any key to continue...' GET wait_subst
    READ
  ENDCASE
ENDDO
```

In the example, a number entered by the user is stored as a memory variable (selectnum). The CASE statements then compare the contents of the memory variable selectnum to each of the possible alternatives listed between the DO CASE and ENDCASE commands. When a match is found, the statements following that CASE statement are carried out, and the remaining CASE statements in the set are ignored.

Any choices made with a CASE command could also be carried out with multiple IF..ENDIF commands, so you may wonder when one approach is preferred over the other. Generally, if more than two pairs of IF..ENDIF commands are required, it is better to make use of CASE statements. Consider the following example, which shows a simplified menu program using DO CASE, and its equivalent using IF...ENDIF commands.

```
? "Enter selection of 1 to 4."        ? "Enter selection of 1 to 4."
INPUT TO CHOOSY                        INPUT TO CHOOSY
DO CASE                                IF CHOOSY = 1
     CASE CHOOSY = 1                        DO MAKEREC
          DO MAKEREC                   ENDIF
     CASE CHOOSY = 2                   IF CHOOSY = 2
          DO CHANGREC                       DO CHANGREC
     CASE CHOOSY = 3                   ENDIF
          DO REMOVE                    IF CHOOSY = 3
     CASE CHOOSY = 4                        DO REMOVE
          DO PRINTED                   ENDIF
     OTHERWISE                         IF CHOOSY = 4
          ? "Invalid entry!"               DO PRINTED
ENDCASE                                ELSE
                                            ? "Invalid entry!"
                                       ENDIF
```

Not only are CASE statements easier to read, but they are executed by the FoxPro interpreter slightly faster than an equivalent number of IF..ENDIF commands.

Repetitive Controls with DO WHILE and ENDDO

Many sequential processes performed by programs require some kind of repetitive, or looping process. Often, sequential processing of records in a database requires that some sort of operation be repeated once for each record in the database. The DO WHILE and ENDDO commands provide repetitive, or looping, capability within a FoxPro program. The syntax for the DO WHILE and ENDDO commands are

```
DO WHILE <condition>
    <commands>
ENDDO
```

All loops within a FoxPro program are performed by a DO WHILE...ENDDO structure. Most loops are conditional; the loop is terminated when a specified condition changes. Some loops are unconditional. These loops never terminate on their own, but the looping procedure is effectively ended by a branch within the loop that calls another submodule of the program.

The process specified by the commands contained between the DO WHILE and ENDDO commands are repeated until the condition specified as a part of the DO WHILE command is no longer true. Usually, the commands contained within the DO WHILE and ENDDO commands include a statement that causes a change in the specified condition, resulting in the termination of the repetitive loop. Without such a statement, the loop would repeat endlessly. In the following example,

```
DO WHILE .NOT. EOF()
   ? TRIM(FIRSTNAME) + " " + LASTNAME
   ? ADDRESS + CITY + STATE
   ? ZIP
   SKIP
ENDDO
```

the statements between the DO WHILE and ENDDO commands are repeated, until the SKIP command causes the record pointer to reach the end of the database (EOF). Once this occurs, the condition specified as a part of the DO WHILE statement (.NOT. EOF()) is no longer true, so the loop terminates, and program control passes to the statement immediately following the ENDDO statement.

The common use of an unconditional, or endless loop within a FoxPro program is when the popular DO WHILE TRUE construction is used, usually to cause a prompt or a menu to be displayed until an appropriate choice is made by the user. Since no condition is specified following the DO WHILE command, a DO WHILE TRUE loop is always true, and the commands contained in the loop are repeated until one of the commands causes an exit, usually by running another module in the program. This use of the DO WHILE command is illustrated:

```
DO WHILE .T.
   ? "Enter 1 for trial report, or 2 for summary report."
   INPUT TO CHOICE
   IF CHOICE = 1
      DO REPORT1
      RETURN
   ENDIF
   IF CHOICE = 2
      DO REPORT2
      RETURN
   ENDIF
   CLEAR
ENDDO
```

The user is asked to enter a choice for printed reports. If any response other than 1 or 2 is entered, the loop is repeated, and the user is again asked to supply a valid choice.

Programmers should keep in mind that the DO WHILE..ENDDO loop provided by FoxPro is a leading test loop, meaning that the condition to be tested is evaluated at the start of the loop. If the condition is not true, the loop is never executed. In some cases, it is desirable to execute a loop once, and then test for a condition to determine whether the loop should then terminate or be repeated. In such cases, it may be better to use an endless DO WHILE TRUE loop, and use an IF..ENDIF conditional statement just prior to the end of the loop, to determine whether program execution should continue within the loop.

Using LOOP, EXIT to Terminate Loops

A repetitive loop can also be terminated with the LOOP and EXIT commands. The LOOP command causes program flow to return to the DO WHILE command that started the loop, for another test of the condition. LOOP is used to skip any conditional tests that follow the LOOP command, possibly saving some program execution time by immediately returning program control to the start of the DO WHILE loop. The EXIT command, which is considerably more abrupt in its action, causes program flow to leave the DO WHILE loop, and continue at the first command following the ENDDO command. Both LOOP and EXIT should be used sparingly, as both commands interrupt the structured flow of a program, making the program logic more difficult to follow and debug. This is an example of how to terminate a repetitive loop:

```
        (LOOP)                                    (EXIT)


                   (loop causes
                    another test of                          (exit causes
                    condition.)                               branch to
DO WHILE AMOUNT > 50<***<***    DO WHILE AMOUNT > 50    first command
    <commands...>         *         <commands...>       after ENDDO.)
    IF ZIP <= 10000          *      IF ZIP <= 10000
        LOOP *******>*****>             EXIT******>***********>
    ENDIF                              ENDIF                  *
    <more commands...>                 <more commands...>     *
ENDDO                              ENDDO                      *
STORE 1 + COUNTER TO COUNTER      STORE 1 + COUNTER TO COUNTER<***
<more commands...>                <more commands...>
```

Single Choice Versus Multiple Choice Logic

Which types of conditional commands are appropriate often depends upon whether the programming task requires a single choice decision or a multiple choice decision. Single choice decisions present a simple task to the programmer. Normally, a simple IF..ENDIF set of commands is sufficient to perform the job, as shown here:

```
IF CURRSTOCK < 1
    STORE .T. TO OUTSTOCK
ENDIF
```

This type of decision is common in FoxPro programs. Multiple choice decisions, on the other hand, often require planning due to the variety of ways in which the choices can affect the flow of a program. When a multiple-choice decision is evaluated, a single course of action may be taken as a result; a number of choices of action may be taken as a result; or one course of action may be taken as a result of a number of decisions. When a program contains a number of possible choices—of which only one choice is to be executed—the CASE..ENDCASE commands are usually appropriate, as shown in this portion of the menu program:

```
DO CASE
   CASE UPPER(CHOICE) = 1
       DO ADDER
   CASE UPPER(CHOICE) = 2
       DO EDITREC
   CASE UPPER(CHOICE) = 3
       DO PRINTREC
ENDCASE
```

In the example, only one course of action will result from among the three possible choices. A different approach is needed in programming situations where a number of processes must be performed as a result of one condition being satisfied. In such cases, it is usually more effective to use a combination of IF..ENDIF commands to test for all required conditions. Consider the following example, if a value of 2 is entered in response to the user prompt:

```
? "Current inventory level?"
INPUT TO AMOUNT
IF AMOUNT < 10
   STORE AMOUNT TO REORDER
ENDIF
IF AMOUNT < 5
   STORE PARTNO TO XPRESSHIP
ENDIF
IF AMOUNT < 3
   DO NOTIFY
ENDIF
```

In the example, a value of 2 satisfies all three IF...ENDIF conditional tests. Each condition is tested independently of the other conditions.

Still another approach can be taken when a decision must be based on a combination of conditions. One way to handle this task is to nest various IF..ENDIF commands within each other. The following example uses this approach to test for matching last names, first names, and ZIP codes in a mailing list program:

```
IF MLAST = LASTNAME
   IF MFIRST = FIRSTNAME
      IF MZIP = ZIPCODE
         EDIT
      ENDIF
   ENDIF
ENDIF
```

In the example, each condition is evaluated in sequential order. For the second condition to be evaluated, the first must be true, and for the third condition to be evaluated, the second must be true. If any of the conditions test as false, the desired action (execution of the EDIT command) is not carried out. The same type of logic can be carried out with a single IF...ENDIF series of commands and logical functions, as demonstrated here:

```
IF MLAST = LASTNAME .AND. MFIRST = FIRSTNAME .AND. MZIP = ZIPCODE
   EDIT
ENDIF
```

Both examples result in the same analysis taking place within the program. Neither approach is necessarily correct for a given application. The first style is easier for the programmer to understand at a glance. When decisions grow complex (and they will), it becomes visually difficult to follow the logic in a command structured like the one in the second example. When complex logic is required within a program, it often helps to try executing various conditions from the dot prompt. This is an excellent way to discover what does and doesn't work before you write a complex condition as a part of a program.

Each of the basic control structures can be nested within other control structures, to any level required by the program, as depicted in the following illustration. When designing such programs, it often helps to draw lines between the matching statements to avoid leaving out any closing statements.

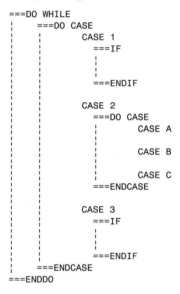

```
===DO WHILE
 |    ===DO CASE
 |     |      CASE 1
 |     |        ===IF
 |     |         |
 |     |         |
 |     |        ===ENDIF
 |     |
 |     |      CASE 2
 |     |        ===DO CASE
 |     |         |        CASE A
 |     |         |
 |     |         |      CASE B
 |     |         |
 |     |         |        CASE C
 |     |        ===ENDCASE
 |     |
 |     |      CASE 3
 |     |        ===IF
 |     |         |
 |     |         |
 |     |        ===ENDIF
 |    ===ENDCASE
===ENDDO
```

Terminating Program Execution

Programs can be halted with the CANCEL and QUIT commands. The CANCEL command causes a program to halt and program control returns to the Command Window. The QUIT command causes the program to halt and FoxPro terminates all operation and returns the user to the Windows environment. It is common to use CANCEL in a FoxPro program during the development and testing phase. Before the program is turned over to the users, any CANCEL command should be replaced with a QUIT command that is normally an option from the application's main menu. Users should not be presented with an unexplained FoxPro desktop and Command Window, which will confuse the inexperienced.

General Hints when Programming for Logic

Some things may not improve your program's performance, but may make it easier for you and other humans to decipher your programs. These hints include plenty of indentation in repetitive and decision-making structures. Indentations reveal the logic structure of your programs and make the logic simple to decipher. In addition, place plenty of comments immediately after the END statements; ENDIF, ENDDO, and ENDCASE. FoxPro ignores the rest of the line following any of these statements, so it is one of the few places within a program where you can add comments without slowing down execution. Finally, you gain added flexibility by using conditional (IF...ENDIF) structures inside of repetitive loops. If you use this technique, you can control repetitions of the loop based on a wide range of conditions. If you instead resort to the condition that is a part of the loop itself (DO WHILE <condition>), you are more limited as to the number and the variety of conditions which control the loop.

Chapter Summary

This chapter detailed the logic structures which are an integral part of controlling program flow in your FoxPro programs. In the next two chapters, you'll examine how you can put the programming constructs covered in this chapter and Chapter 19, "FoxPro Programming Basics," to work in the areas of data entry and editing, and in reporting.

Programming for Data Entry and Editing

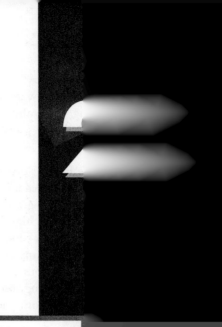

IN THIS CHAPTER

This chapter covers ways to add and edit data within a program. Verification and error trapping of invalid data, editing and deleting under the control of a program, user-defined windows, and effective use validation techniques within programs are all addressed in this chapter.

Because FoxPro offers all the power of XBase (and because XBase has been around for more than a decade), there are a number of ways to do data entry and editing under the control of a program. One thing this book aims to do is save you time and effort, so the approach that's highlighted in this chapter is to use programming code along with one of FoxPro's power tools—the Screen Designer. The Screen Designer, as outlined in Chapter 11, "Designing and Customizing Screens," lets you quickly design data entry/editing screens to fit your own liking. Once you've designed and saved the screen that you want to use for editing, use the following overall procedures (implemented through the program code of your choice) to add or edit data:

- Query the user for the desired data to edit. If an addition to the table is needed, you also can use the APPEND BLANK command within the program to add an empty record to the end of the table.

- For editing, use search techniques to find the desired record to edit. For appending, you also can move the record pointer to the blank record.

- Open a screen and enable the user to make changes through the screen.

- After the screen is cleared, perform any desired housekeeping on the table.

Adding New Records

Adding records within a program can be done with the APPEND BLANK command, which adds a blank record to the end of the table. For example, the program shown here is designed to add a new record to a parts inventory table. The program assumes the existence of a screen called PARTS, with that screen's source code generated and stored in a file called PARTS.SPR.

```
***Invent.prg***
*Adds items to inventory
*last update 03/15/94
SET TALK OFF
USE MAINFILE
SET ORDER TO PARTS
*query user for new part number.
CLEAR
STORE "    " TO MPARTNO
@2,30 TO 5,70
@3,40 SAY "Enter part number:"
@4,40 SAY "(press RETURN to exit)"
@3,59 GET MPARTNO
READ
```

```
IF MPARTNO = " "
   CLEAR
   RETURN
ENDIF
SEEK MPARTNO
IF FOUND()
    *Duplicate entry attempted.
    @3,40 CLEAR TO 4,69
    @3,40 SAY "Part number already exists!"
    @4,40 SAY "Press a key to return to menu."
    ? CHR(7)
    WAIT" "
    CLOSE DATABASES
    RETURN
ENDIF
*Valid new part number.
CLEAR
DO PARTS.SPR
RETURN
*end of subroutine
```

The program opens the database file, MAINFILE, and the associated index file. The user is prompted for a new part number, and the response is stored to a variable, MPARTNO. If the value of MPARTNO is zero (meaning the user most likely pressed return without entering a value), program flow returns to the calling program. If a value is entered, a SEEK command does a fast search on the indexed database for a matching part number. If a match is found, the user is told that the part number already exists, and program execution returns to the calling program. If the part number is a new part number, the main FoxPro window is cleared with the CLEAR command, and the DO PARTS.SPR statement calls the screen to display the data. After the user finishes making changes and exists from the screen, the RETURN statement returns program control to the calling program.

The advantage of this methodology is that the stored screen code does the work behind the editing. The alternative to this method (which involves a lot more work as far as writing program code goes) is to manually design your own data entry screen, with a series of @...SAY...GET commands for each field in the table. (For those who like tedium or just prefer to stick with the old ways, this technique of using @...SAY...GET commands to display data is detailed later in the chapter.)

Editing Records

Programs for editing and deleting records are often very similar to those used for adding records, with one significant difference. In place of an APPEND BLANK statement to add a new record, a search routine is used to find the desired record to edit or delete.

Finding the desired record is always easier if the file is indexed on a unique field (such as an employee ID number, part number, or social security number). In such cases, FIND or SEEK should be used to perform a fast search of the indexed field. If there is no unique field, FIND or SEEK can still be used, but since only the first occurrence will be found, your program may need to display a succession of records following the found record until the desired one is verified by the user. If the database is not indexed, you must resort to the LOCATE command, which operates at a snail's pace when compared to FIND and SEEK. This alone is a good reason for indexing the database. The following command file is used to find a record and edit that record. The file design is adapted from the program used to add data, described previously.

```
***EditInv.prg***
*Edits items in inventory
*last update 03/15/94
SET TALK OFF
USE MAINFILE INDEX PARTS
*query user for part number to edit.
CLEAR
STORE 0 TO MPARTNO
@2,30 TO 5,70
@3,40 SAY "Enter part number:"
@4,40 SAY "(press RETURN to exit)"
@3,59 GET MPARTNO
READ
IF MPARTNO = 0
   CLEAR
   RETURN
ENDIF
SEEK MPARTNO
IF EOF()
    *No such P/N found.
    @3,40 CLEAR TO 4,69
    @3,40 SAY "No such part number!"
    @4,40 SAY "Press a key to return to menu."
    ? CHR(7)
    WAIT""
    CLOSE DATABASES
    RETURN
ENDIF
*Valid part number.
STORE PARTDESC TO MPARTDESC
STORE WHOLCOST TO MWHOLCOST
STORE RETLCOST TO MRETLCOST
STORE QUANTITY TO MQUANTITY
CLEAR
@  6,  3  TO 18, 50
@  1,  0  TO 19, 54  DOUBLE
@  2, 15  SAY "INVENTORY MASTER FILE"
@  4, 15  SAY "Editing Screen"
@  7, 12  SAY "Part Number: "
@  7, 26  SAY MPARTNO
@  9, 12  SAY "Description:"
@  9, 25  GET  MPARTDESC
@ 11,  9  SAY "Wholesale Cost:"
@ 11, 25  GET  MWHOLCOST
@ 13, 12  SAY "Retail Cost:"
@ 13, 25  GET  MRETLCOST
@ 15,  7  SAY "Initial Quantity:"
@ 15, 25  GET  MQUANTITY
```

```
READ
REPLACE PARTDESC with MPARTDESC, QUANTITY with MQUANTITY
REPLACE WHOLCOST with MWHOLCOST, RETLCOST with MRETLCOST
CLOSE DATABASES
RETURN
*end of subroutine
```

A similar program can be used to delete records while under program control. In place of the @...SAY...GETs for editing, use @...SAY commands to display the data, and ask for confirmation of the deletion. Once confirmation is provided, you can use the DELETE command, as illustrated in the portion of the following program:

```
STORE .T. TO ANSWER
@ 20,5 SAY "Delete this record? " GET ANSWER PICTURE 'Y'
READ
IF ANSWER
     DELETE
ENDIF
```

Of course, these methods of finding records to edit or to delete work with a simple case: the table has a field that contains a unique entry for each record in the table. In this case, it is the part number for the inventory item. Tables that keep track of people often use social security numbers for this purpose; if those are not available, some sort of unique account number can be chosen. If at all possible, find something that is unique about each record, and use that item as an indexed key to perform searches. If you are building an application, and the users have not specified a unique field for the table specification, strongly suggest one. It will save you much coding (and users' time) if the program can perform searches on a unique, indexed field.

Nevertheless, there are times when an application doesn't have a unique field, or has one, but the user can't recall John Smith's social security number, so the search must be more generic. For example, the user may recall that the person's last name is Smith, so the user wants to search for Smith (despite the fact that there are 1,057 "Smiths" in the table). The LOCATE and CONTINUE commands will spring to mind only if you've never used them in a sizeable table. Use them once, and you are likely to abandon them for life because of their lack of speed. A workable alternative is to index the file on the field that will be searched, use FIND or SEEK to find the first record in a group of records, and then display the records and let the user pick the record to edit. The display of the records can be one by one, using @...SAY commands to display each possible match, until the desired record is found.

Using @...SAY...GET Commands to Display and Retrieve Data

If you're working with data entry, you'll often find a need for the @...SAY and @...GET commands of the FoxPro language. These commands can be used to place data at a given screen location, and to retrieve data (stored in fields or as memory variables) from the user. The @...SAY command can be used to place data at any screen location. The basic syntax for the command is @ (*row,col*) SAY *expression*. If the expression is a character expression, it must be enclosed in quotes. For instance, to display the contents of the field LASTNAME at the screen position of row 5, column 30, the command would be:

```
@ 5,30 SAY LASTNAME
```

The positions begin at 0,0 for the upper-left corner of the main FoxPro window. In the days of the DOS predecessors for FoxPro/Windows (like FoxPro for DOS and other XBase products), the numbers stood for a precisely defined location, based on rows down from the top of the screen, and characters across from the left edge. Under the DOS products, a screen location of 0,0 meant the upper-left corner, and a screen location of 23,79 was at the lower-right corner. Since Windows is not a character-based environment, the actual numbers become somewhat variable depending on your screen hardware, but they are still used to maintain compatibility with XBase programs. The old maximum of 23,79 for DOS-based screens places data at the right edge and about two-thirds down in a maximized FoxPro desktop window under FoxPro for Windows, on a machine running in standard (600×480) VGA mode.

The expression used as a part of the @...SAY command can contain any combination of valid field names, character strings, or numeric data. Functions can also be used with the @...SAY command to provide desired formatting. For example, the command:

```
@ 12,5 SAY "Employee " + NAME + " is " + STR(AGE) + " years old."
```

results in the text, "Employee Bill Smith is 34 years old" displayed beginning at row 12, column 5.

The GET option displays a blank fill-in field that is highlighted in reverse video. The GET option can be used alone, or in combination with SAY to display a prompt and allow user entry of data. After one or more @...GET or @...SAY commands are encountered, a READ command is used to cause FoxPro to read the values supplied by the user and store those values to the memory variables or fields specified after the GET. If variables are used with GET, those variables must be initialized prior to the use of GET or an error message occurs. For example, you can initialize memory variables and then use a series of @...SAY...GET commands, followed by a READ command to prompt for user data, as shown:

```
CLEAR
STORE SPACE(30) TO NAME
STORE 0 TO AGE
STORE 0.00 TO SALARY
@ 5,10 SAY "Name?"
@ 5,20 GET NAME
@ 7,10 SAY "Age?"
@ 7,20 GET AGE
```

```
@ 9,10 SAY "Salary?"
@ 9,20 GET SALARY
READ
```

When the commands are encountered, the prompts and blanks for data entry appear on the screen. (See Figure 21.1.)

FIGURE 21.1.

The Prompts and Fill-In Fields from @...Says and Gets.

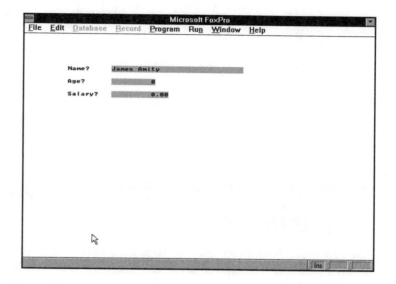

If fieldnames are used instead of variables, the data entered into the highlighted fill-in fields is stored directly in the database. In the past, such use of @...SAY...GET commands was common as a replacement for the less-attractive EDIT and APPEND commands. However, the use of the Screen Designer in FoxPro makes this technique somewhat cumbersome by comparison. In general, coding your own statements using @...SAY...GET commands makes sense if you have a small number of fields or a small amount of data to display or to prompt the user for. But if you have a screen full of fields, use the Screen Designer along with the data entry and editing techniques detailed previously in this chapter.

Using CLEAR

The CLEAR command can be used to clear all or a portion of the screen. The syntax for the CLEAR command is:

```
CLEAR
@(row,column) CLEAR
@(row,column) TO (row,column) CLEAR
```

The first usage of the CLEAR command, used without any screen coordinates, clears the entire active window (which is the FoxPro main window, unless you've defined and activated a window with the DEFINE WINDOW and ACTIVATE WINDOW commands). The second type of usage of CLEAR clears the screen to the right of and below the specified cursor location. The final type of usage clears a rectangular area extending from the first specified location to the second specified location. For instance, the command,

```
@ 5,10 CLEAR
```

clears all areas of the active window to the right of column 10, and below row 5. The command,

```
@ 15,40 TO 19,60 CLEAR
```

clears a rectangular area in the active window whose upper-left corner is located at row 15, column 40, and whose lower-right corner is located at row 19, column 60.

Working with Windows in FoxPro for Windows

You can place your prompts and your data entry fields (created by means of the @...SAY...GET commands) in separate windows that you define by means of the DEFINE WINDOW command. The basic syntax for the DEFINE WINDOW command is:

```
DEFINE WINDOW window-name FROM row1,col1 TO row2,col2 [TITLE character-expression]
[SYSTEM] [CLOSE/NOCLOSE] [GROW/NOGROW]
```

The *row1,col1* coordinates indicate the row and column location for the window's upper-left corner, while the *row2,col2* coordinates indicate the row and column location for the window's lower-right corner. The TITLE clause, followed by an optional character expression, puts that character expression in the window's title bar. Use the SYSTEM clause to define a window that resembles the standard FoxPro windows. The CLOSE/NO CLOSE option specifies whether the window contains a Close box in the upper-left corner which the user can use to close the window, and the GROW/NOGROW option controls whether the user can change the size of the window. (There are additional optional clauses that make the DEFINE WINDOW command compatible with its FoxPro for DOS counterpart, but these options are not discussed here.)

As an example of a window's definition, the command

```
DEFINE WINDOW MyWind FROM 10,5 TO 18,50 SYSTEM CLOSE GROW
```

defines a window with the upper-left corner at row 10, column 5, and the lower-right corner at row 18, column 50. The window resembles the standard FoxPro windows, and is sizable and closable with the mouse. After defining the window, activate it when you want to display data inside the window with the ACTIVATE WINDOW command. The syntax for this command is:

```
ACTIVATE WINDOW window-name / ALL
```

where *window-name* is the name of the window defined earlier with the DEFINE WIN-DOW command. Using the ALL option activates all windows previously defined.

Once you have activated the window, all screen operations take place relative to the window, which means that screen coordinates of 0,0 are referenced to the upper-left corner of the window you activated, not the entire FoxPro main window. If you've activated a series of windows with the ALL option of the ACTIVATE WINDOW command, the last window defined is the one that will be in current use. As you use the DEACTIVATE WINDOW command, any multiple windows are closed in successive order until the first window you defined is closed. You can use this effect to present a "layered," or "tiled" look to data entry or help screens.

For simple editing of a large character field, you could define a window with the DEFINE WINDOW command, activate that window with the ACTIVATE WINDOW command, and display the data for the desired fields at desired locations within the window, using coordinates 0,0 as the window's upper-left corner as a reference point. Consider the following simple program as an example:

```
USE LITIGATE
INPUT "Enter record number to edit: " TO ANS
GOTO ANS
CLEAR
@ 5,5 SAY "Please enter names of the people involved."
DEFINE WINDOW MYWIND FROM 6,5 TO 18,60 SYSTEM CLOSE
ACTIVATE WINDOW MYWIND
@ 1,1 SAY "Document Number:" GET DOCNUMB
@ 3,1 GET PERSONS
@ 7,1 SAY "Date of the document: " GET DOCDATE
READ
DEACTIVATE WINDOW MyWind
RETURN
*end of program*
```

After positioning the record pointer to the desired record with the GOTO statement, the DEFINE WINDOW statement is used to define a window that will be used for editing the desired fields. The ACTIVATE WINDOW statement is used to activate the window. The @...SAY...GETs then display the desired data inside the window. If a field is too long to fit on a single line within the window, it is automatically wrapped to the next line at the window borders. The results of the program are shown in Figure 21.2.

FIGURE 21.2.

The use of User-defined Windows.

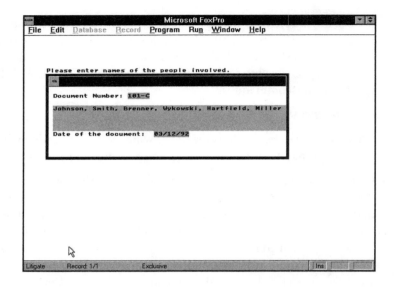

After the desired entries or edits are made and Ctrl+End is pressed (or the cursor moves past the last field), the DEACTIVATE WINDOW statement clears the window from the screen. When the window is deactivated, any screen text that was underneath the window prior to its being activated reappears.

Using WAIT, ACCEPT, and INPUT

The WAIT, ACCEPT, and INPUT commands are also used to obtain input from users. These commands are most appropriate when a single-character or one-line response is all that's needed by the program.

The WAIT command causes a pause in program execution, and waits for a single key to be pressed. Once a key is pressed, program execution continues. The key pressed can be stored to a character variable for later use by the program. The syntax of the WAIT command is:

```
WAIT <message> TO <variable>
```

The message is optional, and if used, must be enclosed in quotes. If no message is included, a default message of "Press any key to continue..." appears. The following example uses WAIT to indicate when a program can proceed.

```
? "Make sure the printer is turned on, then-"
WAIT
SET PRINT ON
LIST L_Name, F_Name_M_I, SCHOOL, CITY, STATE
EJECT
SET PRINT OFF
```

If no message is desired, the default message can be shut off by using a null character variable (" ").

Some programmers use WAIT as a way to obtain variables for a choice within menus. This is a matter of style. Contrary to its name, however, WAIT does not wait around for user confirmation; the program continues after the first key is pressed. If the user presses the wrong key, there is no opportunity to immediately recover. When prompting users for a response, ACCEPT, INPUT, or an @...SAY...GET command often provides a better option.

The ACCEPT command requests input from the user, and stores that input as a character string. The user entry is terminated by pressing return. An optional message can be included as a part of the ACCEPT command; if included, it must be enclosed in quotes. The syntax for the command is:

```
ACCEPT <message> TO <variable>
```

It is not necessary for the variable to be initialized before using ACCEPT. If no variable by the specified name exists, ACCEPT creates a new character variable by the name, and stores the entry supplied to that variable. The following example illustrates the use of ACCEPT.

```
ACCEPT "Enter name:" TO MNAME
Enter name: Douglas
ACCEPT "Enter amount:" TO MAMOUNT
Enter amount: 245

DISPLAY MEMORY

MNAME       Pub   C   "Douglas"
MAMOUNT     Pub   C   "245"
    2 variables defined,    24 bytes used
 1022 variables available
```

The INPUT command also requests input from the user and stores the data to a memory variable. However, INPUT is a more flexible command, in that it does not necessarily store the data as a character variable. INPUT accepts any type of value or expression—even fieldnames or the names of other variables can be entered. If an expression is entered, INPUT first evaluates the expression, then stores the result as the named variable. If a character string is to be supplied to INPUT, it must be enclosed in quotes. An optional message can be included as a part of the INPUT command; if included, it must be enclosed in quotes. The syntax for the command is:

```
INPUT <message> TO <variable>
```

Note the following examples of INPUT:

```
INPUT "Enter name, in quotes: " TO VAR1
Enter name, in quotes: "Johnson"

INPUT "Enter age: " TO VAR2
Enter age: 22

INPUT "Enter a valid expression: " TO VAR3
Enter a valid expression: CTOD("02/24/52")

DISPLAY MEMORY
VAR1         pub  C  "Johnson"
VAR2         pub  N         22  (        22.00000000)
VAR3         pub  D  02/24/52
    3 variables defined,       27 bytes used
  253 variables available,   5973 bytes available
```

Validating Data

Programs can check for valid data using a number of techniques. One effective technique is to use the PICTURE and RANGE options of the @...SAY...GET commands, to restrict the values accepted by the GETs. The syntax for the @...SAY...GET command, when used with the PICTURE or RANGE option, is:

```
@(<row>,<column>)[SAY<expression>][PICTURE<clause>][GET<variable>]

[PICTURE<clause>][RANGE<expression,expression>]
```

The clauses that follow PICTURE contain template symbols and/or template functions. Template symbols restrict the display or entry of a single character, and one symbol is used to represent each position in the blank. Template functions affect the entire display for the entry field instead of for single characters. Functions are preceded by an @ sign, and both the template functions and the template symbols are enclosed in quotes. If functions and templates are combined in one clause, they must be separated with a space. A complete list of functions and templates is provided in Table 21.1.

Table 21.1. Picture Functions and Templates.

Template	Result
!	Forces letters to uppercase
$	Leading zeroes are displayed as dollar signs
*	Leading zeroes are displayed as asterisks
.	Identifies a decimal position
,	Identifies a comma, if numbers exist to the left of the comma
#	Permits digits, blanks, and signs only

Template	Result
9	Permits digits for character data, digits and signs for numeric data
A	Permits letters only
L	Permits logical data (true/false)
N	Permits letters and digits only
X	Permits any characters
Y	Permits logical data as Y or N only

Function	Result
!	Forces letters to uppercase
(	Negative numbers will be surrounded by parentheses
^	Numbers displayed in scientific notation
A	Accepts alphabetic characters only
B	Numeric data will be left-justified
C	Letters CR (credit) displayed following positive numbers
D	American date format
E	European date format
I	Centers text
J	Right-justifies text
L	Shows leading zeroes
M	Permits list of choices for GET
S*n*	Limits display to *n* characters wide, and scrolls text within field
T	Trims leading and trailing blanks
X	Letters DB (debit) are displayed following negative numbers
Z	Zeroes displayed as blanks

As an example of the use of PICTURE to restrict data entry, the ! template can be used to convert all character data to uppercase, reducing the possibility of confusing searches due to some names stored in uppercase and others stored in lowercase:

```
@ 5,6 SAY "Enter name: " GET L_Name PICTURE '@!'
```

For numbers, specific places for digits, decimal points, and asterisks in place of leading zeroes can be displayed by means of the following example:

```
@ 10,12 GET AMOUNT PICTURE '*****.99'
```

With this template, leading zeroes in the amount appear as asterisks, and two decimal places are provided following the decimal point. Only digits are accepted during data entry. Any attempt to enter alpha characters causes a beep. If you are using logical fields, the Y template allows the entry of the letters Y or N only, and lowercase entries of these letters will be converted to uppercase. While PICTURE functions and templates can't perform all necessary validation for you, they can provide a needed hand in preventing data entry errors.

Using RANGE

The RANGE option of the @...SAY...GET command can also be used during the data validation process to limit entries to an acceptable range of data. RANGE works with numeric data, and with dates if appropriate conversion functions are used. The syntax for the RANGE option is:

```
@(row,column) GET variable/fieldname RANGE[lower limit],[upper limit]
```

For example, to restrict the entry of ZIP codes to the State of California:

```
@ 12,2 GET ZIPCODE RANGE 90000,99999
```

To restrict a single end of the range, include the comma and specify the value for the desired end. For instance,

```
@ 15,9 GET HOURLYPAY RANGE 2.70,
```

sets a minimum of 2.70 for the salary, with no maximum. The command,

```
@ 15,9 GET HOURLYPAY RANGE ,20.05
```

sets no minimum for the salary, and a maximum of 20.05. To use RANGE with dates, enclose the dates in curly braces. For example, the following command:

```
@15,5 GET HIREDATE RANGE {05/15/88}, {06/01/93}
```

restricts entries to valid dates that fall between 5/15/88 and 6/1/93. The command

```
@15,5 GET HIREDATE RANGE {05/15/88}, DATE()
```

restricts entries to valid dates that fall between 5/15/88 and the current date maintained in the system clock. Obviously, such a scheme means that the PC's clock must be correct. If it defaults to the 01/01/80 date because it was not properly set, users of such a program could find it impossible to enter what would otherwise be an acceptable date.

Chapter Summary

This chapter provided the techniques you'll commonly need to get data into your database, while under control of the FoxPro programs that you write. Chapter 22, "Programming for Reporting Needs," will help you put that existing data to use by showing how to generate reports while under program control.

Programming for Reporting Needs

22

Any database consultant knows that the job is half done, at best, when you get data into a database. Generating reports is the end result for most database users. (It is also a major weakness of many custom applications, if the popularity of add-on report writers is any indication.) FoxPro applications need not be constrained when it comes to flexibility in reporting, because the Report Writer can produce virtually any kind of report needed. If it is mailing labels you need, the Label Writer offers the same kind of flexibility in the design of mailing labels. Chapter 11, "Designing and Customizing Screens," and Chapter 14, "Producing Mailings," detailed how you can design reports and labels using the Report Writer and Label Writer in FoxPro. This chapter details how you can put reports and labels you create to work within FoxPro programs. Your reports or labels can be called from within your programs with the use of the REPORT FORM or LABEL FORM commands.

Another option for reporting (briefly detailed in this chapter), is to write your reports entirely in program code. This technique was commonly used by XBase programmers before built-in report writers (like FoxPro's) had the flexibility they offer today. The approach is worth noting now only because existing applications written in earlier XBase programs and brought into FoxPro may contain this sort of coding. It is up to you as a programmer to decide whether to maintain such coding or trash it in favor of stored reports done by FoxPro's Report Writer.

Using REPORT FORM and LABEL FORM

Reports can be run from within your programs with the REPORT FORM command, which offers a number of flexible options. Mailing labels can be produced with the similar LABEL FORM command. The syntax for the REPORT FORM command is

```
REPORT FORM filename / ? [ENVIRONMENT] [scope] [WHILE condition] [FOR condition] [PLAIN]
[HEADING character expression] [NOEJECT] [TO PRINT/TO FILE filename] [SUMMARY] [OFF]
```

As covered in Chapter 11, the command produces a report based on the report design saved as *filename* with FoxPro's Report Writer. You can include the FOR clause to specify a condition that must be met for records to be included in the report. Use the WHILE condition, along with an index, to specify that records to be included in the report while the specified condition is true. The ENVIRONMENT option tells FoxPro to use the same environmental settings that were in effect when the report was saved. An optional *scope* (All, Next *x*, or Rest) can be included. If the scope is omitted, FoxPro assumes all records.

The PLAIN option drops the system clock date and page numbers, while the Heading option, followed by a character expression, causes that heading to appear at the top of each page. (This is in addition to any heading that you may have specified within the report's design.) The NOEJECT option cancels the form feed that normally occurs when the TO PRINT option (which routes output to the printer) is used. The TO FILE option can be used to store the output to a text file. The text file is assigned a .TXT extension unless a different extension is specified. The SUMMARY option cancels the normal display or printing of detail lines within a report. If SUMMARY is used, only totals and subtotals appear.

For example, the command

```
REPORT FORM MYFILE
```

causes the specified report, with no conditions, to be displayed on the screen. The command

```
REPORT FORM MYFILE NEXT 30 FOR L_NAME = "Smith" PLAIN TO PRINT
```

causes only the next 30 records in the table to be included in the processing of the report. The FOR L_NAME = "Smith" would further refine the report contents to specified records, where "Smith" appears in the L_NAME field. The PLAIN option drops the page numbers and date normally printed in a report, and the TO PRINT option causes the report to be printed as well as displayed.

If you have designed the report with alias names to take advantage of multiple tables open in different work areas, you must set up the work areas and identify the relationships between files before using the REPORT FORM command. This step must be taken each time the report is run. Programming steps for a report designed to simultaneously use two tables, CUSTOMER and ORDERS, might resemble the following

```
SELECT 1
USE CUSTOMER
SET ORDER TO ACCTNUMB
SELECT 2
USE SALES
SET ORDER TO ACCTNUMB
SET RELATION TO ACCTNUMB INTO CUSTOMER
REPORT FORM SALES TO PRINT
```

If these commands are unfamiliar, you'll find details on using commands to establish relationships between multiple tables in Chapter 10, "Working with FoxPro's Relational Powers."

In the same manner, you can use the LABEL FORM command (detailed in Chapter 14) to generate mailing labels from within a program. The syntax, quite similar to the REPORT FORM command, is

```
LABEL FORM filename / ? [ENVIRONMENT] [scope] [WHILE condition] [FOR condition]
[NOCONSOLE] [PREVIEW] [SAMPLE] [TO PRINT/TO FILE filename]
```

The SAMPLE option lets you print a sample label (a label filled with X's), usually done to test the label alignment with dot-matrix printers before beginning a print run. The NOCONSOLE option suppresses the display of data in the active window. The

PREVIEW option causes the labels to be displayed in a preview window before printing. The other options work the same as they do with the REPORT FORM command described earlier.

As with reports, if you want the labels printed in a particular order, an index should be created or opened with the SET ORDER TO command prior to using the LABEL FORM command. As with the REPORT FORM command, the labels can be limited to a subset of records from within the table by using the WHILE or FOR clauses or by setting a filter with the SET FILTER command.

Setting Conditions for Reports Within a Program

Most reports require selective processing of some sort. A user rarely wants a report of every scrap of data contained in a table. The more common request is for reports of specific names, or ranges of ZIP codes, or last month's sales, or whatever. A variety of conditional commands can be combined with the REPORT FORM command to create conditional reports.

Probably the most common use of conditionals with a report is within the REPORT FORM command. For instance, if a car dealer wanted a report listing all customers who purchased subcompacts in 1993, you could use a command like this one:

```
REPORT FORM SALES FOR TYPE = UPPER(SUBCOMPACT) .AND. YEARSALE = 1993 TO PRINT
```

Depending on how the table is structured (and how large it is), you might or might not want to use this method. With a large table, FoxPro may spend inordinate amounts of time in what is, in effect, a slow sequential search as it qualifies each record. In a large table, it would be better to index the table and use the WHILE option, as shown with these commands:

```
INDEX ON TYPE + STR(YEARSALE) TAG MODELS93
REPORT FORM SALES WHILE TYPE = UPPER(SUBCOMPACT) .AND. YEARSALE = 1993 TO PRINT
```

Since the WHILE condition searches for the first record in the table meeting the specified condition and then processes records until the condition is no longer met, FoxPro will quickly jump to the first appropriate record and then "batch process" that group of records. Since the records are indexed, the chosen records fall into a contiguous group, making the WHILE option an effective one. You can include such commands as a result of menu options as desired to give users an ability to process records meeting selected conditions.

Using SET FILTER in Reporting Programs

The SET FILTER command can also be used to provide users with choices of conditions that apply to data printed with a report. The SET FILTER command applies a specified filter condition to the table in use, making it appear that the table contains fewer records than it actually has. The syntax for the command is

```
SET FILTER TO [condition]
```

For programmers' needs, you can provide a choice of conditions within the program code by specifying the desired condition within the command. For example, the command,

```
SET FILTER TO TYPE = UPPER(SUBCOMPACT)
```

would, in the case of our car dealer, restrict all output from the table to only those records containing the word "subcompact" in the TYPE field. Once a filter has been set with the SET FILTER command, the appropriate report can be printed with the REPORT FORM command.

The beauty of SET FILTER is that you can offer users various menu options that call up different filters, and then print the same report. With this technique, users can print reports based on selected conditions. You don't have to program your way around the conditions by opening and closing multiple index files to match a string of WHILE conditions. For instance, a user may want a report for a specific group of names or cities or states or a range of ZIP codes. You can use CASE choices within a menu to create a string of SET FILTER commands that activate specific filters for each menu selection. The following program shows such an approach:

```
**Reporter program.
**Sets filter, then prints report.
**Last update 03/22/94
CLEAR
@ 4,4 TO 10,42
@ 5,5 PROMPT " 1. All Members (no filter in effect.)"
@ 6,5 PROMPT " 2. By Last Name"
@ 7,5 PROMPT " 3. By School or Business Name"
@ 8,5 PROMPT " 4. By State"
@ 9,5 PROMPT " 5. Range of Zip Codes
@10,5 PROMPT " 6. Return to prior menu"
MENU TO SIFTIT
CLEAR
DO CASE
    CASE SIFTIT = 1
        SET FILTER TO
        *no filter used.
    CASE SIFTIT = 2
        STORE SPACE(15) TO ML_NAME
        @5,5 SAY "Last name: " GET ML_NAME
        READ
        STORE UPPER(ML_NAME) TO SIFTERS
        SET FILTER TO UPPER(L_NAME) = SIFTERS
    CASE SIFTIT = 3
        STORE SPACE(25) TO MSCHOOLBUS
        @5,5 SAY "School or Business Name: " GET MSCHOOLBUS
        READ
```

```
         STORE UPPER(MSCHOOLBUS) TO SIFTERS
         SET FILTER TO UPPER(SCHOOL_BUS) = SIFTERS
    CASE SIFTIT = 4
         STORE SPACE(2) TO MSTATE
         @5,5 SAY "State: " GET MSTATE
         READ
         STORE UPPER(MSTATE) TO SIFTERS
         SET FILTER TO UPPER(STATE) = SIFTERS
    CASE SIFTIT = 5
         STORE SPACE(10) TO MZIPSTART
         STORE SPACE(10) TO MZIPEND
         @5,5 SAY "Enter starting Zip Code: " GET MZIPSTART
         @7,5 SAY "Enter ending Zip Code: " GET MZIPEND
         @10,5 SAY "(enter same codes for a single zip code.)"
         READ
         SET FILTER TO ZIP > MZIPSTART .AND. ZIP < MZIPEND
    CASE SIFTIT = 6
            RETURN
ENDCASE
CLEAR
DEFINE WINDOW AskThem FROM 6,6 TO 12,60 SYSTEM
ACTIVATE WINDOW AskThem
? "Turn on your printer, and press any key when ready,"
? "or press C to cancel this report request."
WAIT "" TO PRINTANS
IF UPPER(PRINTANS) = "C"
    DEACTIVATE WINDOW AskThem
    RETURN
ENDIF
*Print the report.
GO TOP
REPORT FORM MEMBERS TO PRINT
*clear any filter.
SET FILTER TO
*back to the program that called this one.
DEACTIVATE WINDOW AskThem
RETURN
```

In the example, each set of commands following a CASE gets a user response, stores the response to a variable, and uses that variable to set an appropriate filter for the table. If your program runs multiple reports and mailing labels, you may decide to build a filter routine similar to this one as a submodule that is called by the other report and label-generating modules. If you use this approach, be sure to declare the variables used in the filter submodule as public variables, or the filters are lost when you pass program control back to the calling program. Also be sure to turn off any filters with a SET FILTER TO command (with no condition specified) after printing the reports. If you fail to do so, users will get thoroughly confused when they discover large numbers of records to be "missing" from the table.

One warning about how FoxPro handles a SET FILTER command: the current record may not always be checked right after implementing a SET FILTER command. Depending on how your programs are structured, this may result in a record being included in the report, even though it does not meet the filter condition. The simple solution to this problem is to issue a GO TOP to move the record pointer right after a SET FILTER command.

Writing Reports Under Program Control

If you are forced with maintaining reports written in an earlier XBase variant (or for masochistic reasons, you just prefer to hard code all your reports), you can produce reports entirely in program code. Line-oriented reports are probably the most common example. Table 22.1 shows a portion of program code used to print a line-oriented report based on a table of legal depositions:

Table 22.1. The table structure for LEGAL.DBF.

Field Name	Type
DOCUMENT	numeric/6
DOCDATE	date
DOCSOURCE	character/10
PERSONS	character/50
SUMMARY	character/254

Listing 22.1. Program code for line-oriented report.

```
**Report1.PRG
**Prints deposition summaries by person named.
CLEAR
ACCEPT "Name of person involved in deposition?" TO MPERSONS
STORE UPPER(MPERSONS) TO MPERSONS
USE LEGAL
STORE 1 TO PAGECOUNT
STORE 0 TO LINECOUNT
SET FILTER TO UPPER(PERSONS) = MPERSONS
SET PRINT ON
?
? "   ***Deposition Summaries for witness: " + MPERSONS
? "========================================================"
?
DO WHILE .NOT. EOF()
     ? "Document number: "
     ?? DOCUMENT
     ? "Date of document: "
     ?? DOCUDATE
     ? "Source of document: " + DOCSOURCE
```

continues

Listing 22.1. continued

```
    ? "Summary: " + SUMMARY
    ? "**************************************************"
    STORE 6 + LINECOUNT TO LINECOUNT
    IF LINECOUNT > 54
        STORE 0 TO LINECOUNT
        STORE 1 + PAGECOUNT TO PAGECOUNT
        EJECT
        ? "                                          —Page #"
        ?? PAGECOUNT
        ? "  ***Deposition Summaries for witness: " + MPERSONS
        ? "======================================================"
        ?
    ENDIF
ENDDO
? "***End of deposition report.***"
SET PRINT OFF
EJECT
RETURN
*end of print routine.
```

In this example the ? and ?? commands are used to print the data. Page breaks are handled with a counter (STORE 6 + LINECOUNT TO LINECOUNT), which increments by 6 for each record printed. Once the value of the variable, LINECOUNT, indicates that the total number of lines printed is greater than the desired number of 54 lines per page, an EJECT command causes a form feed to be sent to the printer, and the next page starts.

Printing Data

Two methods can be used for writing data to the printer. They are SET PRINT ON, combined with the ? and ?? commands, or SET DEVICE TO PRINT, combined with the @...SAY commands. The ? and ?? commands print a line at a time, not necessarily at a precise location. (The line simply prints at the next available horizontal printer position.) The ? command prints the contents of the expression following the ?, and sends a line feed to move the printer position to the next line. The ?? command prints the contents of the expression on the same line as the current printer location, and does not move the printer position. If @...SAY commands are used, the SET DEVICE TO PRINT command causes all results of the @...SAY commands to be routed to the printer instead of to the screen. Using @...SAY commands gives the programmer more direct control over where the data is printed—the row and column locations translate to the appropriate printhead row and column locations. When using this route, exercise care not to send the printer a row location that is lower in value than the previous row location. Such a command causes a form feed to be sent, which ejects the previous page. FoxPro cannot make your printer perform reverse indexing, even if the printer is actually capable of such feats (as are some dot matrix printers). For example, if you print the contents of a variable at printer location 9,15, and then try to print the next variable at location 8,50, the printer ejects the page and aligns the new page so the printhead is at position 8,50. A general outline you can follow to design a report that operates entirely under program control might be as follows:

1. Open any desired index files and set any desired filters.
2. Initialize variables for a line counter and page counter.
3. Use SET PRINT ON or SET DEVICE TO PRINT to route output to the printer.
4. Print any desired report headings.
5. Start a scan of the table with a DO WHILE loop.
6. Print the desired contents of a record.
7. After printing a record, check the value of the line and page counters. Perform a form feed and print new headings and page numbers when necessary.
8. SKIP to the next record and repeat the contents of the DO WHILE loop.
9. When the desired records have been printed, turn off printer output with SET PRINT OFF or SET DEVICE TO SCREEN. Clear any filters that were in effect.

When you build a report through programming, you must handle headings, page breaks, totals, and subtotals, and any spacing between lines and columns.

As an example of a more complex report than the one shown earlier, the following report makes use of the SET DEVICE TO PRINT command, combined with @...SAY commands, to place the data at the desired print locations.

```
*BenPrt.PRG is for benefits report to printer.*
GO TOP
CLEAR
@ 5, 5 SAY "Printing... please wait..."
STORE 10 TO LINES
STORE 1 TO PAGES
SET DEVICE TO PRINT
@ 1,  5 SAY "Page No." + LTRIM(STR(PAGES))
@ 2,  5 SAY DATE()
@ 3, 28 SAY "The Personnel Director"
@ 4, 28 SAY " Benefits Report"
@ 6,  5 SAY REPLICATE("=",70)
@ 7,  5 SAY "Name     Health Plan   Date of   Amount 1 Amount 2  Comments"
@ 8,  5 SAY "                       Plan"
DO WHILE .NOT. EOF()
   @ LINES, 5 SAY SUBSTR(LASTNAME,1,14)
   @ LINES, 20 SAY BPLAN1
   @ LINES, 31 SAY BDATE1
   @ LINES, 40 SAY BFAMOUNT1
   @ LINES, 50 SAY BSAMOUNT1
```

```
@ LINES, 60 SAY SUBSTR(BCOMMENT1,1,15)
STORE LINES + 1 TO LINES
@ LINES, 5 SAY TRIM(FIRSTNAME)
@ LINES, 20 SAY BPLAN2
@ LINES, 31 SAY BDATE2
@ LINES, 40 SAY BFAMOUNT2
@ LINES, 50 SAY BSAMOUNT2
@ LINES, 60 SAY SUBSTR(BCOMMENT2,1,15)
STORE LINES + 1 TO LINES
@ LINES, 20 SAY BPLAN3
@ LINES, 31 SAY BDATE3
@ LINES, 40 SAY BFAMOUNT3
@ LINES, 50 SAY BSAMOUNT3
@ LINES, 60 SAY SUBSTR(BCOMMENT3,1,15)
STORE LINES + 1 TO LINES
@ LINES, 20 SAY BPLAN4
@ LINES, 31 SAY BDATE4
@ LINES, 40 SAY BFAMOUNT4
@ LINES, 50 SAY BSAMOUNT4
@ LINES, 60 SAY SUBSTR(BCOMMENT4,1,15)
STORE LINES + 3 TO LINES
IF LINES > 50
   EJECT
   STORE PAGES + 1 TO PAGES
   STORE 10 TO LINES
   @ 1,  5 SAY "Page No." + LTRIM(STR(PAGES))
   @ 2,  5 SAY DATE()
   @ 3, 28 SAY "The Personnel Director"
   @ 4, 28 SAY " Benefits Report"
   @ 6,  5 SAY REPLICATE("=",70)
   @ 7,  5 SAY "Name  Health Plan Date of Amount 1 Amount 2  Comments"
   @ 8,  5 SAY "                    Plan"
ENDIF
SKIP
ENDIF
ENDDO
IF LINES > 10
   EJECT
ENDIF
SET DEVICE TO SCREEN
RETURN
```

This report also makes use of a report-coding technique known as relative cursor addressing. A memory variable named LINES is used to contain the row position for the printer. Data is then printed at the desired location on each row with a statement like

```
@ LINES,20 SAY BPLAN1
```

and when the data for an entire row has been printed, the variable is incremented for the next line with the statement

```
STORE LINES + 1 TO LINES
```

and a successive series of @...SAY statements prints the data for the next line. This continues throughout the DO...WHILE loop, until all of the data has been printed.

The Case of the Missing Last Line

When you generate reports using program code, you will occasionally find that the last line of a report doesn't print on the printer until the program begins another printing operation. When the second printing operation begins, the last line of the first printing operation prints along with the first lines of the second printing operation. (Most laser printers carry this problem a step further by not printing the final page of a report until another print operation begins.) This problem is caused by the buffers in some printers, which are not cleared unless a printer eject or a carriage return and linefeed code are received. To get around this problem, issue an EJECT command or send a carriage return and linefeed with a

```
? CHR(13) + CHR(10)
```

statement.

Using LIST and DISPLAY

At times, the simple ways may be best. If all you need is a columnar display that fills a single page or less with no special formatting, you can use a LIST command along with the TO PRINT option. As an example, the following commands

```
USE MEMBERS
LIST LASTNAME, FIRSTNAME, PHONE TO PRINT OFF
```

produce a listing like this:

Record#	LASTNAME	FIRSTNAME	PHONE
1	Roberts	Jamie	703-555-2321
2	Sanderson	Lucy	703-555-5681
3	Smith	Larry	301-555-2815
4	Jones	Nikki	202-555-1586
5	Hernandez	Maria	301-555-6725
6	Jones	Jarel	703-555-9091
7	Zeibermann	Daniel	703-555-2114
8	O'Neill	John	703-555-9256
9	Bannerton	Alicia	703-555-1200
10	Anderson	Harry	415-555-5555
11	Jenkins	Susan	703-555-9543
12	Johnson	Larry	703-555-6723
13	Jennings	Benjamin	516-555-4525

Record#	LASTNAME	FIRSTNAME	PHONE
14	Canion	Don	714-555-2578
15	Roberts	Clarissa	213-555-4506
16	Miller	Anna	214-555-1203
17	Smith	William	415-555-6821
18	Askew	Charles	415-555-2535
19	Baker	Jeanette	703-555-1218
20	Baker	Benjamin	415-555-6890
21	Harris	Daniel	415-555-2324
22	Jenkins	Renee	415-555-2003
23	Engel	Jordan	703-555-2301
24	Nguyen	Diem	415-555-2373
25	Flores	Alicia	510-555-7614
26	Sutton	Dario	809-555-1624
27	Wadsworth	J.Thorton	315-555-2987
28	Hayes	Rosario	716-555-2301
29	Miller	Ernest	415-555-7912
30	Jones	Edward	809-555-1234
31	Sutton	Derek	703-555-2525
32	Sutton	Tamar	703-555-2525

The TO PRINT clause causes all screen output that would normally be directed to the active window to be sent to the default Windows printer as well. (The OFF clause, also included in this example, turns off the display of records which normally appears with a LIST command.) You can use the DISPLAY command along with a scope to accomplish a similar result. For example, the command

```
DISPLAY NEXT 20 LASTNAME, FIRSTNAME, PHONE TO PRINT OFF
```

would display the next 20 records beginning with the location of the record pointer. Any arranging or selection of records can be done beforehand through indexing and the use of the SET FILTER command. You can also limit the records processed by adding a FOR or WHILE clause to the LIST or DISPLAY command. For example, a command like the following:

```
LIST LASTNAME, FIRSTNAME, PHONE TO PRINT OFF FOR STATE = "CA"
```

would produce a printed listing of records with the abbreviation "CA" in the State field. The LIST and DISPLAY commands work when all you need is the simple columnar format that results. When using these commands to print data, remember that some printers need an EJECT command following the LIST or DISPLAY command to force the last required sheet of paper from the printer. Also keep in mind that it is the responsibility of your program to warn users that printing is taking place. There will naturally be a delay between the time the command is executed and the time the printer starts (during this time, FoxPro is spooling the data to the Windows Print Manager). If the screen offers no helpful messages during that time, users may mistakenly assume the application has crashed.

Special Printer Effects

When you are printing data directly through program code, you can control many printer defaults with the use of certain system memory variables. The system memory variables appear when you enter the LIST MEMORY or DISPLAY MEMORY commands. The following listing shows an example of the system memory variables displayed with the LIST MEMORY command:

```
Print System Memory Variables

_ALIGNMENT   Pub   C   "LEFT"
_ASSIST      Pub   C   "D:\FPWIN\CATALOG.APP"
_BEAUTIFY    Pub   C   ""
_BOX         Pub   L   .T.
_CALCMEM     Pub   N   0.00          (        0.00000000)
_CALCVALUE   Pub   N   0.00          (        0.00000000)
_CUROBJ      Pub   N   -1            (       -1.00000000)
_DBLCLICK    Pub   N   0.50          (        0.50000000)
_DIARYDATE   Pub   D   03/27/94
_DOS         Pub   L   .F.
_FOXDOC      Pub   C   "D:\FPWIN\FOXDOC.APP"
_FOXGRAPH    Pub   C   ""
_GENGRAPH    Pub   C   "D:\FPWIN\GENGRAPH.APP"
_GENMENU     Pub   C   "D:\FPWIN\GENMENU.PRG"
_GENPD       Pub   C   "D:\FPWIN\GENPD.APP"
_GENSCRN     Pub   C   "D:\FPWIN\GENSCRN.FXP"
_GENXTAB     Pub   C   "D:\FPWIN\GENXTAB.PRG"
_INDENT      Pub   N   0             (        0.00000000)
_LMARGIN     Pub   N   0             (        0.00000000)
_MAC         Pub   L   .F.
_MLINE       Pub   N   0             (        0.00000000)
_PADVANCE    Pub   C   "FORMFEED"
_PAGENO      Pub   N   5             (        5.00000000)
_PBPAGE      Pub   N   1             (        1.00000000)
_PCOLNO      Pub   N   0.00          (        0.00000000)
_PCOPIES     Pub   N   1             (        1.00000000)
_PDRIVER     Pub   C   ""
_PDSETUP     Pub   C   ""
_PECODE      Pub   C   ""
_PEJECT      Pub   C   "NONE"
_PEPAGE      Pub   N   32767         (    32767.00000000)
_PLENGTH     Pub   N   66            (       66.00000000)
_PLINENO     Pub   N   6             (        6.00000000)
_PLOFFSET    Pub   N   0             (        0.00000000)
_PPITCH      Pub   C   "DEFAULT"
_PQUALITY    Pub   L   .F.
_PRETEXT     Pub   C   ""
```

```
_PSCODE      Pub   C   ""
_PSPACING    Pub   N   1            (         1.00000000)
_PWAIT       Pub   L   .F.
_RMARGIN     Pub   N   80           (        80.00000000)
_SHELL       Pub   C   ""
_SPELLCHK    Pub   C   "D:\FPWIN\SPELLCHK.APP"
_STARTUP     Pub   C   "D:\FPWIN\FOXSTART.APP"
_TABS        Pub   C   ""
_TALLY       Pub   N   120          (       120.00000000)
_TEXT        Pub   N   -1           (        -1.00000000)
_THROTTLE    Pub   N   0.00         (         0.00000000)
_TRANSPORT   Pub   C   "D:\FPWIN\TRANSPRT.PRG"
_UNIX        Pub   L   .F.
_WINDOWS     Pub   L   .T.
_WRAP        Pub   L   .F.
```

All system memory variables that begin with _p are used to control the print settings. The printer variables affect settings such as page length, page offset, number of copies printed in a report, and line spacing. The values that you can use are defined in the following list.

_PCOLNO: Repositions the printing position at the specified cursor location before any text is printed.

_PLINENO: Repositions the printing position at the specified line number before any text is printed.

_PAGENO: Defines the page number to begin numbering a report with, if something other than 1 is needed. Use an integer from 1 to 32,767.

_PLENGTH: Defines the length of the printed page. Default is 66; use 84 for U.S. legal (8.5 by 14 inch) paper.

_PCOPIES: Defines the number of copies printed of a report. Default is 1.

_PSPACING: Defines the overall line spacing for a report. Default is 1; possible options are 1, 2, and 3.

_PLOFFSET: Defines the offset from the left edge where printing begins. Use an integer value.

_PSCODE: Defines starting control or escape codes to be sent to a printer at the start of a report.

_PECODE: Defines ending control or escape codes to be sent to a printer at the end of a report.

_PBPAGE: Defines the first desired page in a report, if the entire report is not to be printed.

_PEPAGE: Defines the last desired page in a report, if the entire report is not to be printed.

_PADVANCE: Contains character string of "FORMFEED" or "LINEFEED" which determines whether page advances are done with formfeeds or linefeeds.

_PWAIT:	Contains logical "false" if printer should not pause between pages, or logical "true" if the printer should pause between pages.
_PEJECT:	Contains character string of "BEFORE" (if formfeed should occur before report), "AFTER" (if formfeed should occur after report), "BOTH" (if formfeed should occur before and after report), or "NONE" (if no formfeeds are needed).
_PQUALITY:	Contains logical "false" if normal print quality is desired, or logical "true" if emphasized print quality is desired.
_PPITCH:	Contains a character string which determines the print typestyle.
_PDRIVER:	Contains a character string with the name of a printer driver.
_PFORM:	Contains a character string with the name of a stored print form.

You can change these values from their default values by storing different values to the variables. For example, a statement like

```
_PSPACING = 3
```

would store a value of 3 to the print system memory variable _PSPACING. These memory variables are provided in FoxPro for Windows for backwards compatibility with FoxPro for DOS, FoxBase+, and dBASE IV, and can be useful if you are hard-coding reports. Remember that they will not have an effect if you use reports created with FoxPro's Report Writer, as the properties that you assign the report as a part of its design override any of these settings.

Chapter Summary

This chapter provided coding techniques that you can use for producing reports under program control from within your FoxPro applications. Probably the most time-saving hint in this entire area is to make full use of the FoxPro Report Writer and utilize stored reports created within the report writer in your programs. Doing so can save you an inordinate amount of time in coding. In Chapter 23, "Pulling It All Together," the techniques covered in this chapter and the three preceding chapters are combined with menu design techniques to form the basis for a complete application.

Pulling It All Together

23

This chapter examines the use of two of FoxPro's power tools, the Menu Builder and the Project Manager, in detail. The chapter also shows how you can use these tools, along with other FoxPro objects (queries, reports, screens, and labels) and a knowledge of FoxPro programming, to design and implement complete applications.

Using the Project Manager

One of FoxPro's power tools, the Project Manager, is aimed squarely at the needs of the FoxPro developer. Figure 23.1 shows the Project Manager containing various files that have been added to a project.

FIGURE 23.1.

The Project Manager in use.

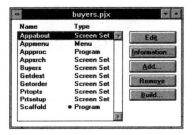

The Project Manager can be thought of as a central repository for all the discrete parts that make up a complete FoxPro application. The Project Manager is a logical first step in the design of an application. It not only keeps track of all the application's parts as you work with them, but also provides a launching point for performing the initial design and needed modifications to the separate parts of the application. For example, if an application uses two reports and a label, you can create and modify those report and label designs from within the Project Manager. (This sequence is not mandatory—objects which have already been created can also be added to a project.) The Project Manager tracks the overall relationship between the parts of the application. And the Project Manager is the only way you can pull together individual FoxPro programs into a single .APP file. (If you purchase FoxPro Professional which includes the FoxPro Distribution Kit, you can also use the Project Manager to build stand-alone executable (.EXE) files, which can be used on other machines without FoxPro.)

The Project Manager is similar in behavior to "Make" utilities that are provided with many programming languages for combining parts of an application into a single unit. But the Project Manager does more than just pull a number of program files into a single compiled procedure. It also serves as a central location from where you can manage the very design of a complete application. The overall steps to the use of the Project Manager are fairly straightforward. You create a new project, then add files to the project as needed. The files can be menus, screens, labels, reports, queries, or programs. In fact, you can add any type of file to a project. Once you've added all the desired files to the project, you use the Build button in the Project window to build the project.

Starting the Project Manager

To start the Project Manager, choose File, New, and in the New dialog box which appears, click Project, then click New. Or in the Command Window, enter CREATE PROJECT. With either method, an empty Project window appears and a new menu, titled "Project," gets added to the menu bar. (See Figure 23.2.)

FIGURE 23.2.

A New Project window.

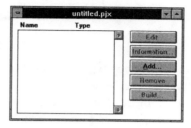

Project files appear in the list box at the left side of the window, and the window contains the options explained in Table 23.1.

Table 23.1. Project window options.

Option	Purpose
Edit push button	Opens the selected file for editing.
Information	Displays a File Information dialog box, containing information about the selected file.
Add	Displays the Add File dialog.
Remove	Deletes the selected file from the project.
Build	Displays the Build Option dialog.

Adding Files to a Project

To add a file to a project, click the Add button in the Project window. When you do so, the Add File dialog box appears. (See Figure 23.3.)

FIGURE 23.3.

The Add File dialog box.

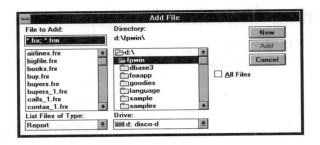

You can click in the List Files of Type list box and select the desired file type. The Project Manager lets you include any type of file, although there are good reasons for *not* including your tables and indexes, as explained shortly. You can navigate among the available drives and directories in the dialog box, and select the desired file. When you click Add, the selected file is added to the project. Note that you can also click New and supply a name for the new file. When you do so, a window launches into the appropriate design mode, and you can create the new file. For example, if you change the List Files of Type option to Report, then click New, a Save As dialog box first asks for a name for the new report, then a window into FoxPro's Report Writer opens where you can create the new report.

The Project Manager considers the first file that you add to a project to be the project's main file. Therefore, if you are building an application, and that application is structured around a main menu created with the Menu Builder, you should add that menu as the first file in the project. If you are accustomed to writing XBase code in classic XBase fashion (where a main .PRG file calls all associated procedures), you can add the main .PRG file as the first file in the project. When you click Build, the Project Manager automatically pulls all the other associated procedures that are referenced by the main file into the project.

> **NOTE**
>
> While you can add any type of file to a project, in the case of complete applications, you may *not* want to add the tables and indexes used by the application. When you build an application (.APP) file based on a project, all the files that can be executed by FoxPro (programs, menus, screens, labels, and reports) are combined into the .APP file. All other file types (including any tables and indexes in the project) are included in the application as *read-only* files, unless you highlight those files and choose Exclude from the Project menu before building the application. Therefore, if you include the tables or indexes that your application uses in

the project and don't choose Project, Exclude to mark those tables or indexes to be excluded from the .APP file, users of the application will not be able to modify the data—which is surely not what you had in mind. Since tables and indexes are the dynamic parts of an application that undergo constant change by nature, it makes sense in most cases to simply omit them from the project.

Building the Project or Application

When you are ready to build the project (or the application), click the Build button in the Project window. The Build Option dialog box appears. (See Figure 23.4.)

FIGURE 23.4.

The Build Option dialog box.

Select the desired type of file you want to build. Choose Rebuild Project to build a project (.PJX) file, which then contains a current record of all items in the project. Choose Build Application to build an application (.APP) file, which users can run by choosing Run, Application from the menus. Assuming the Distribution Kit provided with FoxPro Professional is installed, you also can choose Build Executable to build an .EXE file that can be used to run an application outside of FoxPro.

Turn on the Display Errors check box if you want errors that occur during the build process to appear in a window when the process is finished. Checking the Rebuild All check box tells FoxPro to refresh all files in the project, whether they have changed since the last project build or not.

If the project is untitled, FoxPro displays a Save As dialog box and asks for a name for the project. Enter a desired filename, and click Save to save the project.

Changing the Project Options

While a project is open you can change certain options, including developer information, where code gets saved, and other details, by choosing Project, Options from the menus. When you choose Project, Options, the Options dialog box appears. (See Figure 23.5.)

FIGURE 23.5.

The Options dialog box.

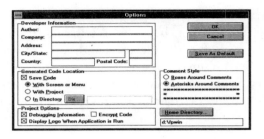

In the Developer Information portion of the dialog box, you can enter a name and address of the developer. (FoxPro uses this data in the headers of code that gets generated in screens and menus.) The Generated Code Location portion of the dialog box lets you specify whether code generated from screens and menus is saved with the screen or menu, or with the project, or in a specified directory. Under Project Options, turn on the Debugging Info option to add debugging information to your code; this is needed if you are to make effective use of the Trace and Debug windows. (See Chapter 24, "Debugging Techniques.") The Encrypt Code option, when turned on, encrypts your code so others cannot read it. The Display Logo When Application is Run option applies to the optional use of the Construction Kit in creating executable (.EXE) files. This option determines whether the FoxPro logo appears when an executable is started.

Use the Home Directory button to specify a home directory that contains the project and application files. The Save As Default button, when clicked, causes the information in the Options dialog box to be saved to the FOXUSER file. This information then is used as the default settings for all future projects that are created.

Viewing Information About a Project

You can display a listing of information about an entire project by choosing Project, Project Info from the menus. When you do so, a dialog box like that shown in Figure 23.6 appears.

In the dialog box, you see a listing of the number of types of files in the project and how many are current, as opposed to how many are out of data (meaning the files have been modified, but the project has not been rebuilt since the last modification.) To get information about a specific file in a project, select that file in the Project window, then click the Information button. A File Information dialog box appears. (See Figure 23.7.)

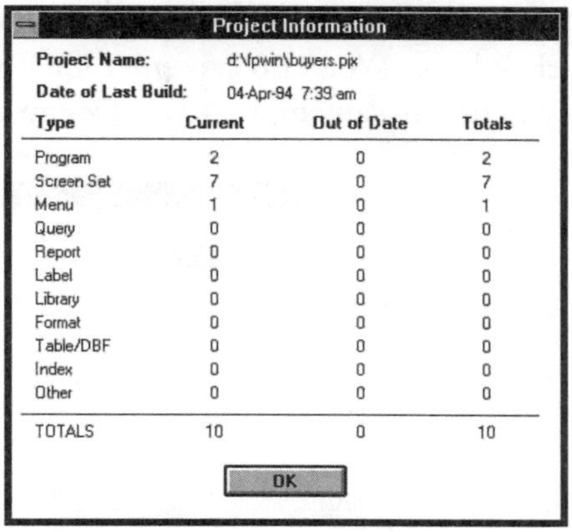

FIGURE 23.6.

The Project Info dialog box for entire project.

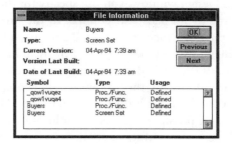

FIGURE 23.7.

The File Information dialog box.

In this dialog box, you are provided with the name and type of the file, the date and time of the current version, and the date of the last project build. Click the Previous and Next buttons in the dialog box to see information for the previous and next files in the project.

Using the Menu Builder

FoxPro's Menu Builder can be used to define a menu system, along the style of the default FoxPro menus. Like FoxPro's menus, the custom menus that you create with the Menu Builder place a horizontal menu bar across the top of the main window. The menu bar contains menu pads that are associated with menu popups.

To start the Menu Builder, choose File, New. In the New dialog box which appears click Menu, then click New. (You also can enter CREATE MENU in the Command Window.) When you do this, an empty Menu Design window appears. (See Figure 23.8.)

FIGURE 23.8.

An Empty Menu Design window.

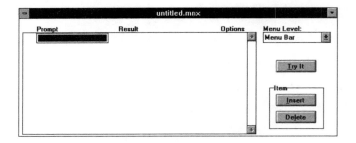

In the Menu Design window, you can specify (in the Prompt column) the prompts used for each of the menu pads and popups. In the Prompt column, you enter the desired prompts, or the text which appears on the menu pads or popups. Hot keys which serve as part of the menu text can be designated by including a backslash followed by a less-than symbol ahead of the desired character for the hot key. As an example, to assign "E" as a hot key for an Edit menu, the prompt would contain an entry like **\<Edit**. Another special character combination is the backslash followed by a hyphen (\-), which puts a separator line into the popup menu. Separator lines are used to group related menu items. For example, if you open FoxPro's File menu, you see separator lines above and below the Print and Print Setup menu options.

After choosing the desired prompt, you'll need to chose a desired result, or action that should take place when the menu option is chosen. Your choices in the Result list box (see Figure 23.9) are Submenu, Command, Pad Name, and Procedure. (If you are designing a submenu, the Pad Name option is replaced with a Bar # option.) Choose Submenu when you want the menu option to result in a submenu containing additional choices. Choose Command when you want the menu option to carry out a specific command, like BROWSE or DELETE. Choose Pad Name (or Bar #) to specify a choice from FoxPro's own system menus. Choose Procedure to create a procedure (or "code snippet" written in FoxPro program code). When you choose Procedure, a window opens where you can type the desired procedure. When the menu option is selected by the user, your procedure runs.

If you choose Command, a text box appears beside the Result column. (See Figure 23.9.) You can type the desired command directly into the text box.

Chapter 23

FIGURE 23.9.

A Menu Design window with entry in Result column and text box.

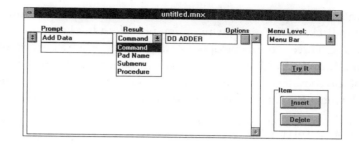

As an example of a custom menu created with the Menu Builder, consider Figure 23.10. In this figure, the top level menu in the menu design contains four menu pads labelled System, Database, Record, and Windows. Each menu option provides a hot key which happens to also be the first letter of the menu name. In this example, each menu, when chosen, leads to a submenu of additional choices, as indicated by the "Submenu" designations in the Result column beside each of the menu prompts.

FIGURE 23.10.

A completed menu design.

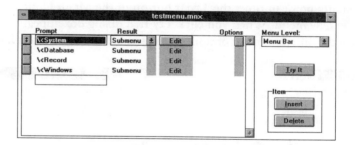

Clicking the Edit button to the right of any of the Submenu designations causes the submenu for that menu to appear in the Menu Design window. In Figure 23.11, the submenu for the Database menu is shown.

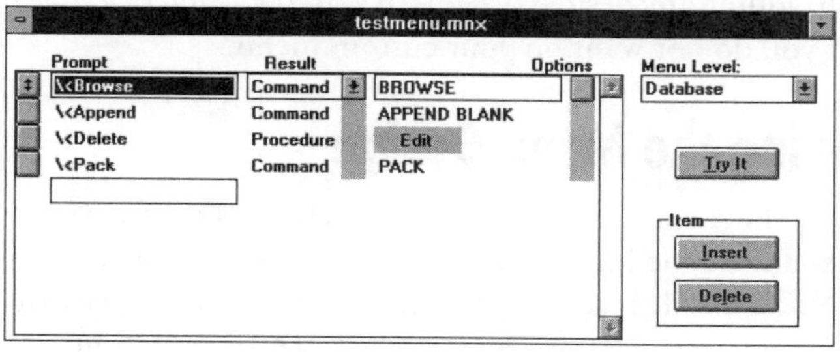

FIGURE 23.11.

A completed submenu design.

In this example, the submenu offers four menu options: Browse, Append Blank, Edit, and Pack. Again, each menu option provides a hot key that is the first letter of the menu name. Three of the menu options, when chosen, cause a FoxPro command to be executed—the Browse choice executes a BROWSE command, the Append choice executes an APPEND BLANK command, and the Pack choice executes a PACK command. The Delete option of the menu executes a short procedure containing the following program code:

```
WAIT WINDOW "Press C to cancel, any other key to delete." TO DOIT
IF UPPER(DOIT) <> "C"
     DELETE
ENDIF
```

and this procedure provides the user with a way to cancel the deletion of the record.

This particular example of a menu is designed to be used along with a screen, so the screen code within the screen opens the needed table and provides fields for the user to add and edit data. The custom menu provides the user with a way to generate reports, perform basic data management operations, and access the FoxPro desk accessories.

At any point in time, the Try It button in the Menu Design window can be used to try the new menu. When you click Try It, a dialog box appears. (See Figure 23.12.) As you try the different menu options, the designated results are displayed within the dialog box.

FIGURE 23.12.

The Try It dialog box.

Using the Quick Menu Option

When you initially create a new menu—before adding any options to it—you can choose Menu, Quick Menu from the menus, and FoxPro creates a menu structure that duplicates the design of the FoxPro system menus. You can then modify this structure as you wish, adding any desired options of your own, and deleting any of the FoxPro menu items that you do not want on your custom menu.

Saving the Menu Design

When the menu design is completed, choose File, Save from the menu, and if prompted, enter a filename for the menu design. The menu is saved to a file with the extension of .MNX. This file is actually a FoxPro table with a special extension, and the table contains the design specifications for the menu. (A corresponding memo field file for the table is also created, with an extension of .MNT.) With the Menu Builder still active, choose Program, Generate from the menus to generate the actual code that can be used by FoxPro to produce the menu. In the Generate dialog box which appears, accept the default name or enter a new name for the generated code, and click Generate. The code gets saved to a file with the same name as the menu design, but with an extension of .MPR. You can integrate the code of the menu into the design of your application, either by means of the Project Manager, or by manually merging the menu code with the code of your application in the FoxPro Editor.

Planning Your Application

With a knowledge of the Menu Builder and the Project Manager—and a familiarity with FoxPro's other power tools and FoxPro programming in general—you can design and implement your overall application. You can design the necessary tables and indexes, and use the Screen Builder or the Screen Wizards to create the screens you'll use for data entry and editing. You also can enter sample data and design and test reports that the application needs. Finally, use the Menu Builder to create a menu that provides the user with the ability to access the tables by means of the screens, and print the desired reports.

A significant part of the applications design approach which includes the use of the Menu Builder is the ability to store code snippets—portions of code which control various aspects of the system's behavior—as part of the menu's design. By choosing Procedure as the desired result for a given menu option during the menu design process and typing the desired code into the procedure window that appears, you integrate part of your application's code into the menu design. Certainly, not all of an application's code can necessarily be part of a main menu—there will always be a need for individual procedures, created with the Editor and stored in .PRG files, to accomplish needed tasks. However, the menu can serve as a focal point for the application, and certain menu options can call your individual program (.PRG) files where needed.

For example, consider the following structure of a main menu:

```
System              Records              Print
Calculator          Add/Edit Buyers      Print Buyers
Calendar/Diary      Add/Edit Donations   Print Donations
Puzzle
Quit
```

The menu structure shown here provides three menu options for a simple application: System, Records, and Print. Each of the individual menu pads provide the options shown below the pad name, within a pull-down menu. (For example, the System menu offers the choices of Calculator, Calendar/Diary, Puzzle, or Quit.) With the menu choices laid out on paper, you can use FoxPro's Menu Builder to create the menu code, and use it in your application as you see fit. The exercise that follows shows how the application described previously can be implemented.

An Example: Creating a Complete Application

You can use the following steps to see how the Project Manager and the Menu Builder, along with other FoxPro power tools such as the Screen and Report Wizards, can be used to quickly create a complete application. This application makes use of the Buyers.DBF and Donation.DBF tables that have been used as examples throughout this book. If you have not already created those tables (or copied them from the accompanying disk into your working directory), you need to do so before proceeding.

Before building the project and adding the main menu to the project, the application needs two reports and two screens. You can quickly create these needed items with the aid of the Screen Wizards and the Report Wizards. Perform the following steps to create the screen and the report that are used by the application for the Buyers table:

1. In the Command Window, enter USE BUYERS.
2. From the menus, choose Run, Wizard, Screen.
3. With Buyers selected in the dialog box for the Screen Wizard that appears, click the Finish button.
4. The last Screen Wizard dialog box appears. By default the "Save Screen for Later Use" option is checked. Click Finish.
5. In the Save As dialog box that now appears, enter BUY as a name for the screen file, then click Save to save the new screen.
6. From the menus, choose Run, Wizard, Report.
7. In the first Report Wizard dialog box that appears, click Report Wizard, then click Next.
8. With Buyers selected in the next dialog box for the Report Wizard that appears, click Next.
9. In the Style dialog box that next appears, click Next to accept the default style of report.
10. In the next dialog box, double-click Lastname, Firstname, City, State, and Phone. Then, click Finish.
11. The last Report Wizard dialog box appears. By default the "Save Report for Later Use" option is checked. Click Finish.
12. In the Save As dialog box that now appears, again enter BUY as a name for the report file. Click Save to save the new report.

Next, perform the following steps to create the screen and the report that are used by the application for the Donation table:

1. In the Command Window, enter USE DONATION.

2. From the menus, choose Run, Wizard, Screen.

3. With Donation selected in the dialog box for the Screen Wizard that appears, click the Finish button.

4. The last Screen Wizard dialog box appears. By default the "Save Screen for Later Use" option is checked. Click Finish.

5. In the Save As dialog box that now appears, enter DONATE as a name for the screen file. Click Save to save the new screen.

6. From the menus, choose Run, Wizard, Report.

7. In the first Report Wizard dialog box that appears, click Report Wizard, then click Next.

8. With Donation selected in the next dialog box for the Report Wizard that appears, click Next.

9. In the Style dialog box which next appears, click Next to accept the default style of report.

10. In the next dialog box that appears, click Finish.

11. The last Report Wizard dialog box appears, and by default the "Save Report for Later Use" option is checked. Click Finish.

12. In the Save As dialog box that now appears, again enter DONATE as a name for the report file, then click Save to save the new report.

With the screens and the reports to be used by this sample application created, proceed to create a project, create a menu, and add the other needed objects to the project. (Note that this sequence is not mandatory; the screens and reports could have been created from within the Project Manager, as well.) Perform the following steps:

1. In the Command Window, enter CREATE PROJECT to open a new Project window.

2. In the Project window, click the Add button.

3. In the Add Files dialog box, change the List Files of Type option to Menu. Click New in the dialog box.

4. The Save As dialog box now appears, asking for a name for the new menu. Enter MAINMENU and click Save. When you do so, the Menu Builder appears. (See Figure 23.8, shown previously.)

5. With the cursor currently in the first Prompt text box, type the following:

   \<System

   then tab over to the Create button and press Enter, or click the Create button to create the submenu for the application's System menu.

6. In the first Prompt box for the submenu, type **Ca\\<lculator**, then press Tab. Under Result, choose **Bar #**, then press Tab. In the text box beside Bar #, type **_mst_calcu**, then press Tab twice to get to the next line.

7. In the next Prompt box, type **Calendar/D\\<iary**, then press Tab. Under Result, choose **Bar #**, then press Tab. In the text box beside Bar #, type **_mst_diary**, then press Tab twice to get to the next line.

8. In the next Prompt box, type **\\<Puzzle**, then press Tab. Under Result, choose **Bar #**, then press Tab. In the text box beside Bar #, type **_mst_puzzle**, then press Tab twice to get to the next line.

9. In the next Prompt box, type **\\<Quit**, then press Tab. Under Result, choose **Procedure**, then press Tab. Click the Create button, to open a window where you can type a procedure. Type the following code into the window:

```
SET SYSMENU TO DEFAULT
CANCEL
```

Then press Ctrl+F4 to close the window. This completes the menu actions needed for the System submenu.

10. Click in the Menu Level list box at the right side of the Menu Builder, and choose Menu Bar to return to the top-level menu. Click in the Prompt text box beneath \\>System and type the following:

\\>Records

then press Tab twice and press Enter, or click the Create button, to create the submenu for the Records menu option.

11. In the first Prompt box for the submenu, type **Add/Edit \\<Buyers**, then press Tab. Under Result, choose **Command**, then press Tab. In the text box beside Command, type **DO BUY.SPR**, then press Tab twice to get to the next line.

12. In the next Prompt box for the submenu, type **Add/Edit \\<Donations** then press Tab. Under Result, choose **Command**, then press Tab. In the text box beside Command, type **DO DONATE.SPR**, then press Tab.

13. Click in the Menu Level list box at the right side of the Menu Builder, and choose Menu Bar to return to the top-level menu. Click in the Prompt text box beneath \\>Records, and type the following:

\\>Print

then press Tab twice and press Enter, or click the Create button, to create the submenu for the Print menu option.

14. In the first Prompt box for the submenu, type **Print \<Buyers**, then press Tab. Under Result, choose **Procedure**, then press Tab. Click the Create button to open a window where you can type a procedure. Type the following code into the window:

```
WAIT WINDOW "Press C to CANCEL, any other key to print." TO DOIT
IF UPPER(DOIT) <> "C"
     REPORT FORM BUY TO PRINT
ENDIF
```

Then press Ctrl+F4 to close the window.

15. In the next Prompt box for the submenu, type **Print \<Donations**, then press Tab. Under Result, choose **Procedure**, then press Tab. Click the Create button to open a window where you can type a procedure. Type the following code into the window:

```
WAIT WINDOW "Press C to CANCEL, any other key to print." TO DOIT
IF UPPER(DOIT) <> "C"
     REPORT FORM DONATE TO PRINT
ENDIF
```

Then press Ctrl+F4 to close the window.

You can click the Try It button in the Menu Builder to try out the new menu. As you click a menu's option, the chosen response appears in the Try It dialog box, similar to the example shown previously in Figure 23.12. When you are done trying the various menu options, click OK in the Try It dialog box.

16. Choose File, Save, to save the changes to the menu. When prompted for a name for the menu, enter **Mainmenu**.

17. From the menus, choose Program, Generate. In the dialog box that appears, click Generate to generate the screen code for the menu. Then, press Ctrl+F4 to close the menu builder. When you do so, the new menu's name, Mainmenu, appears in the Project window.

You can now proceed to add the screens and reports created earlier to the project, so that the project can keep track of any changes made in the future to those objects. Perform the following steps to do so:

1. In the Project window, click Add. In the Add File dialog box, change the List Files of Type option to Screen.

2. Click Buy.SCX, then click Add. An Edit Screen Set dialog box appears. No further editing is needed to the screen, so click OK to add the screen to the project.

3. In the Project window, click Add.

4. In the Add File dialog box, click Donate.SCX, then click Add. When you do so, the Edit Screen Set dialog box again appears; click OK to add the screen to the project.

5. In the Project window, click Add. In the Add File dialog box, change the List Files of Type option to Report.

6. Click Buy.FRX, then click Add to add the report to the project.

7. In the Project window, click Add.

8. In the Add File dialog box, click Donate.FRX, then click Add to add the report to the project.

9. Choose File, Save from the menus to save the project. A Save As dialog box appears, asking for a name for the project. Enter **mysystem** and click Save to save the project's specifications to the project (.PJX) file.

10. To build a complete application, click the Build button in the Project window. The Build Option dialog box appears. (See Figure 23.4, shown previously.)

11. Click Build Application, then click OK. FoxPro displays another Save As dialog box, asking for a name for the application (.APP) file. FoxPro assumes the same name as the project (mysystem). In this case, the default is fine, so click Build in the dialog box.

    FoxPro proceeds to build the application, during which time various progress indicators flash on the screen. When done with the process, FoxPro displays the message, "Build application completed" in the Status Bar.

12. Press Ctrl+F4 (or double-click the Menu Builder's Close button) to close the Menu Builder. You can run the completed application, by choosing Run, Application and selecting the application by name ("mysystem") in the dialog box, or by entering **DO mysystem.app** in the Command Window. The completed application's menu appears, and you can try the various menu options to perform the various tasks. Figure 23.13 shows the completed application (in the figure, the Command Window has been closed).

FIGURE 23.13.

The completed application.

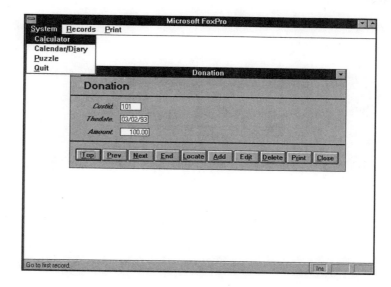

Chapter Summary

This chapter provided an examination of the workings of the Menu Builder and the Project Manager and a look at a design methodology you can use to develop complete applications. Remember that the flexibility FoxPro offers means you can choose any one of a number of approaches to applications design. A familiarity with the tools provided by FoxPro gives you the flexibility to choose an approach that suits you best.

Debugging
Techniques

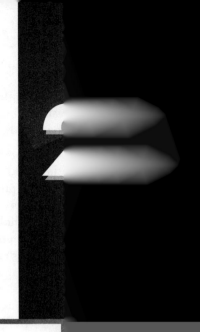

IN THIS CHAPTER

This chapter outlines various strategies for debugging programs, along with techniques for preventing bugs while in the design stage and techniques that enable a program to handle bugs without your assistance.

If you write programs of any complexity (and if you didn't, you wouldn't be reading this part of the book), you encounter bugs, which are mistakes in coding that cause errors in a program. All programmers face bugs in their code from time to time—nobody's perfect. FoxPro has a number of tools to aid in the eternal hunt for bugs in program code. These tools include the ON ERROR, RESUME, SET ECHO, SET STEP, and SUSPEND commands. Some other commands which were not intended solely for debugging but are nevertheless useful in this task are the SET ALTERNATE and SET TALK commands. And users of FoxPro can take advantage of a powerful debugger, which can be used to monitor program execution and trap errors, along with a Trace window, which shows you what is happening at any point in time within a program.

Using *SUSPEND* and *RESUME*

When an error serious enough to halt program execution occurs, FoxPro displays three choices within a dialog box: Cancel, Suspend, or Ignore. Of the three choices, Cancel and Suspend both halt the program, but with very different results. Cancel halts the program and clears all private variables from memory. Suspend, on the other hand, leaves the program files open, and leave all memory variables intact. SUSPEND is also designed to be used with the RESUME command, which restarts program execution at the point of interruption.

If faults in the program logic are causing your errors, you can use the Suspend option, and then use DISPLAY MEMORY or LIST MEMORY TO PRINT to examine the contents of the variables for possible clues to the problem. Once you have finished poking around memory from the Command Window, you can use the RESUME command to attempt to continue execution of the program. Entering RESUME causes a program to continue execution at the place in the file where the error interrupted the program.

An effective debugging technique is to use Suspend, then use STORE commands to change the contents of various memory variables, then try using RESUME and seeing what the results are with the new variables in use by the program.

Using the Trace Window

FoxPro provides a Trace window (see Figure 24.1), which you can use to see your program as it runs. Through this window, you can pass parameters to a program or an application and trace the program execution.

FIGURE 24.1.

The Trace Window.

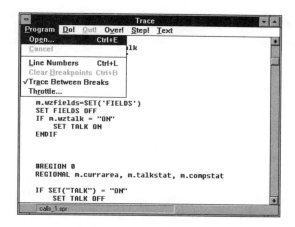

The Trace window has its own menu bar, which includes the menu options described in Table 24.1.

Table 24.1. Trace menu options.

Menu Option	Purpose
Program, Open	Displays Open dialog to open a program.
Program, Cancel	Stops execution of suspended program.
Program, Line Numbers	Turn this option on or off to display or hide program line numbers.
Program, Clear Breakpoints	Strips breakpoints from all programs displayed in the Trace window.
Program, Trace Between Breaks	Turn this option on or off to display and highlight each line of program code as it executes. If the Trace Between Breaks option is off, the last line executed remains highlighted until another line with a breakpoint is reached.
Program, Throttle	Displays Execution Throttle dialog, which you can use to specify the execution speed of programs.
Do/Resume	Displays Do dialog, which you can use to specify a program to run. Program execution is suspended at the first executable line. The Do... option changes to Resume after a program is chosen, to continue program execution.

continues

Table 24.1. continued

Menu Option	Purpose
Out!	Exits from a currently executing program, halting execution on the first line after the command that called the current program.
Over!	Continues program execution, without showing the lines executed within a subprocedure at the next statement of the same procedure.
Step!	Executes a program in single-step fashion, letting you step through each line of code in a program one line at a time.

To use the Trace window, perform these steps:

1. Choose Program, Trace to open the Trace window.
2. From the Program menu within the Trace window, choose Open, then select the desired program or application from the Open dialog box which appears.
3. Set a breakpoint on any executable line of the program, by clicking on the desired line.
4. In the Command window, enter DO *programname* or run the program by choosing Program, Do from the menus.

The program runs up to the breakpoint. You can then examine memory variables or other aspects of the program as desired. Click Resume in the Trace window's menu to continue execution of the program.

Using the Debug Window

FoxPro also provides a Debug window, which is useful for tracking various values during program execution. For example, you can monitor the value of certain fields or memory variables. To use the Debug window, choose Program, Debug from the menus. When you do so, the Debug window appears. (See Figure 24.2.)

To track any value in the Debug window, type the desired fieldnames, variables, or expressions that you want to monitor in the left side of the Debug window. Press Enter after typing each variable or expression. As the program runs, the values appear in the right side of the Debug window. You can set breakpoints based on a variable or expression by clicking in the breakpoint column (between the two partitions) next to the desired variable or expression. Breakpoints that you set in the Debug window halt execution of the program when the value of the expression changes.

FIGURE 24.2.

The Debug window.

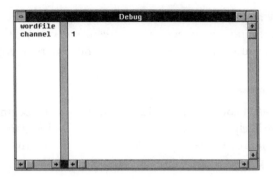

Using *SET TALK*

The SET TALK command may also be used to display the results of various processing operations within a program. For example, the results of STORE commands—that are often used to store values to variables or fields—will display those values in the active window unless SET TALK is off. Normally, programs turn off TALK with a SET TALK OFF command at the start of the program. When debugging, it may help to see the results of calculations and processing operations on various files, so you may want to include a SET TALK ON command in an appropriate location.

Using *SET ALTERNATE*

The SET ALTERNATE commands can be very useful for troubleshooting a large program, particularly if the errors seem to be occurring when the users are around and you aren't. Name a file with the SET ALTERNATE TO *filename* command, then open that file with the SET ALTERNATE ON command. Once the file is open, all data that is displayed on the screen (with the exception of full-screen commands like BROWSE and EDIT), also is stored in the file named in the SET ALTERNATE command. At some point, you must close the file with a CLOSE ALTERNATE command. The file is assigned a .TXT extension, unless another extension is specified. If your system is operating on a hard disk and you have plenty of space, you can open a file with SET ALTERNATE and leave that file open for a day of use. Then close the file, and examine its contents for possible indications of user techniques that are giving your program grief. These problems may include the selection of options that don't apply, or printing or disk operations which fail due to program errors.

Using *ON ERROR*

FoxPro has an ON ERROR command that can perform another command or transfer control to a submodule if a program error occurs. Before the ON ERROR command was available as part of the XBase language, program errors left users with any one of a number of unfriendly messages on the screen. You can use the ON ERROR command to provide a friendlier alternative if your program encounters an error. The syntax for the command is:

ON ERROR command

An ON ERROR command should be placed near the beginning of the program, before any errors are likely to occur. If an error occurs in the program, the command specified is carried out. In most cases, the command is a DO command that runs another program, such as in the example

ON ERROR DO WARNING

In this case, the command file, WARNING.PRG, is executed if an error occurs. That command file may contain something as simple as an error message informing the user that a problem has occurred, or it may contain procedures for handling the error. The ERROR() function can be used along with the ON ERROR command. The ERROR() function returns a numeric value that corresponds to the type of error that occurred. The MESSAGE() function can also be used to display the FoxPro error message that defines the type of error which has occurred.

The most comprehensive use of ON ERROR (along with the ERROR() function) is to run an error trapping routine, which is a section of programming code designed to deal with program errors. If you include such a section of code in your program, the program may be able to recover from errors without your assistance (a nice touch when the program bombs and you're on the beach in Honolulu). Even when the program cannot automatically recover from an error condition, the use of ON ERROR presents users with a less confusing set of error messages. The following program makes use of the ON ERROR command and the ERROR function to deal with program errors.

```
**Master.PRG
**Uses MASTER database; displays main menu.
**last update 04/15/94
ON ERROR DO PANIC WITH ERROR()
...commands...

**PANIC.PRG
**Error handling routine.
PARAMETERS Errorcode
*Interpret the code.
CLEAR
DO CASE

    CASE Errorcode = 1
        ? "I can't find that file on the disk. Please verify."
        WAIT
        RETRY

    CASE Errorcode = 41
```

```
            ? "The memo field file is not accessible to FoxPro."
            ? "Use the QUIT option and contact DP Tech Support immediately."
            WAIT
            RETURN TO MASTER

     CASE Errorcode = 56
            ? "The disk is full.  Return to the main menu, quit this"
            ? "system, erase some files from the disk, then try again."
            CLOSE DATABASES
            WAIT
            RETURN TO MASTER

     CASE Errorcode = 125
            ? "A NOT READY error code has been received from the printer."
            ? "please take corrective action and press a key to continue."
            WAIT
            RETRY

ENDCASE
*Errorcode unknown, so call for help!
? "An uncorrectable error has occurred.  The error code is: "
?? Errorcode
?
? "Contact DP Tech Support, and report this error code."
WAIT
SET ALTERNATE TO ERRNOTES
SET ALTERNATE ON
SET CONSOLE OFF
? "Error is: "
?? Errorcode
LIST MEMORY
LIST STATUS
SET CONSOLE ON
CLOSE ALTERNATE
QUIT
```

In the example, the ON ERROR statement at the start of the program causes the error-trapping submodule (PANIC.PRG) to be run if an error occurs. Parameter-passing is used to pass the value obtained by the ERROR() function to the submodule, PANIC.PRG. If an error occurs, the "PARAMETERS Errorcode" statement at the beginning of PANIC.PRG causes the value provided by the ERROR() function to be stored to a numeric variable, Errorcode. The CASE statements then act on that value, and appropriate user error messages are displayed. If the error code is a code that the program is not equipped to deal with, a message to that effect is displayed. An alternate file then opens to store status of the variables and files as an aid to the programmer. The QUIT command then closes all files and exits back to Windows.

Note that operating-system level errors (no disk in drive, lack of printer handshaking, error reading data file, and so forth) are not dealt with using this kind of error-trapping. You can guard against these types of problems by using FoxPro's system functions (such as SYS(13), which returns a logical true if the printer is online) to check the status of various aspects of FoxPro.

Avoiding the Bugs

Some general techniques help you avoid bugs while still in the program design stage. Bugs are caused by syntax errors or by errors in the program logic. Syntax errors are easy to spot, since these are a direct result of typos, missing spaces, or improper use of the XBase programming language. Logic errors can be far more difficult to detect, as they often don't interrupt the program—they may just case the program to accomplish something that's totally different than what you had in mind. The most common program bugs include the following:

Mismatched data types: you cannot interchange different data types (such as a numeric variable and a character field) within the same expression. If you do so, the common "Data type mismatch" error occurs.

Syntax errors in variable names, fieldnames, or in commands: FoxPro provides a "Syntax error" or "Unrecognized command verb" message if commands or options for commands are misspelled. If variable names or fieldnames are misspelled, you get a "Variable not found" message. Where you really get into trouble is if the fieldname or variable name is misspelled, but the misspelling matches a different fieldname or variable. Then you have a logic problem on your hands, as your program tries to work with the wrong data. The best safeguard against this flaw is to give fields and memory variables names that are distinctively different.

Improper construction of matching statements. Each IF command must be followed by an ENDIF command, each TEXT requires an ENDTEXT, each DO CASE requires an ENDCASE, and each DO WHILE command must have a matching ENDDO command. When such commands are nested to multiple levels, it is easy to leave out a closing command and cause problems that are hard to track down. It's also common to find program bugs that are caused by the incorrect nesting of control structures, as shown in this example:

```
DO WHILE .T.
    IF COUNTER < 5
    <commands...>
ENDDO
ENDIF
```

The ENDIF statement being placed after the ENDDO statement results in an overlapping control structure. Such a use of nested commands is improper, and causes bugs that are often particularly difficult to track down because they do not always occur upon execution of the code line causing the problem.

Missing punctuation (periods, commas, colons and semicolons, and character delimiters such as quotation marks). FoxPro almost always displays a "syntax error" message. On rare occasions, the error slips by FoxPro's error checking, producing possibly bizarre results.

Memory variables not initialized at point of program execution: An attempt to use a variable that has not been created with a STORE or assignment (=) statement causes a rather obvious "variable not found" error. A more subtle version of the same error crops up if you don't declare variables PUBLIC, transfer control to a higher level subroutine, and attempt to use that variable.

Debugging the Modular Program

Finally, consider one more plug for the merits of modular system design. Debugging is an area where modular design comes in quite handy. Small modules are far easier to debug than a large program. It can be argued that no single module should contain more than two letter-sized pages of FoxPro commands. If the program is any larger than that, it probably belongs in more than one module. If your programs are comprised of modules sufficiently small in size, you can effectively debug by running each module independently of the others. When the debugging process is complete, the modules can be compiled into a single application, with the aid of the Project Manager. If the error proves to be a baffling one, you can always rewrite the entire submodule, which is less intimidating because the module is small to begin with.

Chapter Summary

This chapter detailed debugging techniques with coverage of topics such as using the Trace and Debug windows, single-stepping through program code, and using error functions and error trapping within your programs. These techniques should prove helpful in finding the causes of errors in your FoxPro programs.

5

PART

Advanced Programming

The Event-Driven User Interface

25

In developing applications with FoxPro for Windows, you're faced with a new set of design choices that didn't exist in the early days of XBase. Since FoxPro is an XBase product, you can develop applications along the lines which XBase applications have been developed for years: With main menus and cascading menu choices that tightly control user access and let users accomplish one specific task at a time. You can also develop applications along the lines of Windows, which provides an *event-driven* approach to everything a user does. With the event-driven approach to applications design, the user isn't necessarily locked into a limited series of menu options or to doing a single task at a time. With an event-driven interface, the application must be prepared to respond to any one of a series of possible events which may occur. For example, Figure 25.1 shows an application written in the procedural style common to programs from the early days of XBase programming. User possibilities are limited to the menu options shown, and each user's choice often leads to additional menus, and eventually to the performing of a specific task (such as editing a record in a table, or printing a report).

FIGURE 25.1.

An application using procedural style of XBase programming.

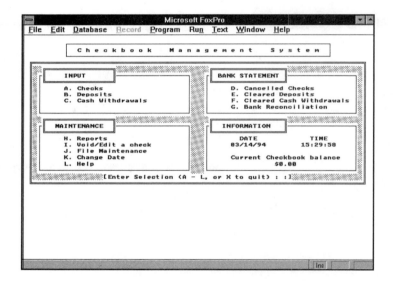

In contrast, consider the example shown in Figure 25.2. This example shows an application written along the style of event-driven programming. This application has an interface that presents the user with a number of possible options and waits to respond to any of the events triggered by the user's choices.

One important point to note is that the Windows "look" (meaning pull-down menus, dialog boxes, and mouse support) is not sufficient by itself to mark an application as being truly event-driven. With the power tools in FoxPro, it would be a relatively simple matter to design and implement an interface that made full use of pull-down menus, dialog boxes, and full mouse support. But if the application always restricted the user to doing one thing (and only one thing) at a time, the application would still be a classic "modal" application in the style of early dBASE, rather than being a "modeless" or event-driven application. To be event-driven, an application must be aware of any one of a number of actions that a user may take from a single point. A user might click in any one of a number of windows presented for browsing or editing, or the user might click a Print button within a Control Panel, or the user might choose an option from a menu bar at the top of the main FoxPro window. The application would need to respond appropriately to any of these events.

FIGURE 25.2.

An application using event-driven style of programming.

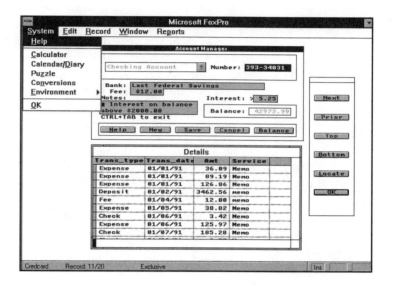

FoxPro's own interface is a classic example of an event-driven application. While working in FoxPro, you might have three Browse windows open, a report shown in a Page Preview window, and a screen's design visible in a Screen Builder window. Under these circumstances, you could move at will between any of the windows, accomplishing different tasks. This kind of multifunctionality is what one strives for when designing event-driven applications.

In FoxPro, a major part of event-driven applications design involves the effective use of FoxPro's power tools; in particular, the Screen Builder and the Menu Builder. With the Screen Builder (detailed in Chapter 11, "Designing and Customizing Screens"), you can design screens containing objects (such as push buttons and list boxes), and you can add code snippets to the screens which govern the behavior of the objects that you add. With the Menu Builder (detailed in Chapter 22, "Programming for Reporting Needs"), you can design a custom menu resembling those used by FoxPro, and your menu options can perform a wide variety of actions, such as opening screens, running reports, opening other menus, or executing FoxPro programs.

The Screen Builder as an Application Hub

The Screen Builder plays a vital role in designing event-driven applications without writing reams of program code. If you think of the Screen Builder as being a modern, Windows-era replacement for the data-entry screen design utilities from the early days of XBase, you are short-changing it. You can certainly build data-entry screens with the Screen Builder. But you can also define a significant amount of the logic behind the very design of an application. For example, you can place push buttons in a screen, and you can add code snippets to tell FoxPro what actions to take when the buttons are clicked. (Chapter 11 includes an exercise showing how this can be done.) If the push buttons that you add perform common data management tasks (such as adding, finding, or deleting records), you have in effect stored part of the application's design logic with the screen's design. Applications created with FoxPro's Applications Generator (detailed in Chapter 15, "Creating Applications with FoxPro") are a good example of event-driven programming. These applications use screens typical of what is possible with the Screen Builder as a central point of an application, and a customized menu provides users with the necessary choices for common data management tasks.

Veteran XBase programmers should recognize that, with FoxPro, *code snippets* (along with the use of the power tools to create screens and menus) are vital to creating event-driven applications. Code snippets are short routines, written in FoxPro program code, which are stored *with the screen or menu* at the time of its design. During the design process, when you add an object to a screen or a choice to a menu and tie that option or menu choice to a procedure, FoxPro opens a window into which you can type the program code that should be executed by the screen object or menu choice. When you close the window and later save the screen or menu, that code snippet gets saved as part of the screen or menu. If you ever want to modify the code that's associated with a code snippet, you do so through the Screen Builder or the Menu Builder.

In FoxPro, code snippets are needed to implement event-driven applications, because the events are directly linked to the code snippets; in effect, the code snippets tell FoxPro what action to take in response to the event. For those who are familiar with object-oriented programming, these code snippets closely resemble the methods which are associated with an object-oriented programming language.

Recognize, too, that using screens generated by the Screen Builder as the center of your application is one approach, and there are certainly others. A major disadvantage of the "screen as an applications hub" approach is that it emphasizes one table as the basis of your application, and most work done has a natural tendency to center around that table as a result. Perhaps your application is one that uses a number of tables, and no one table is used more extensively than the others. In such a case, it might make more sense to build the application around a menu bar which would let the user choose the desired table to work with. Appropriate screens could then be presented, depending on which table was chosen. Since the Screen Builder generates FoxPro program code, you can choose to take that code and use it as a basis for your application, while modifying it as heavily as you desire, to present the style of user interface that you think is appropriate. Finally, remember too that it's perfectly acceptable to bypass FoxPro's own methods of applications design entirely, and use a third-party code generator to build much or all of the application. Many FoxPro developers are comfortable with various third-party products, and these can provide solid applications while at the same time overcoming the limitations of FoxPro's own applications generator (which are substantial).

Using FoxPro's Event Handlers

As you are working with your program code, you'll want to work with FoxPro's *event handlers.* These are required tools of the programming language for those who want to implement an event-driven user interface. The event handlers are commands which begin with the word ON, and they include the commands, and their uses, shown in Table 25.1.

Table 25.1. FoxPro Event Handlers.

Command	Purpose
ON BAR	Activates a menu when a specific bar of a popup is selected.
ON ERROR	Executes a command when an error occurs. In most cases, the command runs an error-trapping routine, like the one shown in Chapter 24, "Debugging Techniques."
ON ESCAPE	Executes a command when the Esc key is pressed. The command is often a DO command that calls a routine designed to handle the user pressing the Esc key.
ON KEY	Traps for any key press during program execution, and branches to a subroutine when any key is pressed.
ON KEY LABEL	Traps for a specific key during program execution, and branches to a subroutine when the specific key is pressed.

continues

Table 25.1. continued

Command	Purpose
ON PAD	Links a specific pad in a bar menu to a specific popup, and displays that popup when the pad is selected.
ON SELECTION BAR	Executes a command upon selection of a specific bar in a bar menu.
ON SELECTION MENU	Executes a command upon selection of any bar in a bar menu.
ON SELECTION PAD	Executes a command upon selection of a specific pad within a menu.
ON SELECTION POPUP	Executes a command upon selection of a specific bar within a popup.

What sets the event handlers apart from other FoxPro commands is how they behave. With other FoxPro commands, as soon as the command is executed, a corresponding action is carried out. FoxPro's event handlers are different—they identify an action that will take place in the future, when a corresponding event occurs. In effect, an event handler tells FoxPro to watch for a specific occurrence of an event, and to take some action when that event occurs. For example, a specific bar of a menu popup could be used to launch the Windows clock, by calling the program (CLOCK.EXE) from within FoxPro with a RUN statement. Inside the program that constructs the main menu, you could have a statement like the following:

```
ON SELECTION BAR 2 of Windows RUN /N CLOCK.EXE
```

and when the specified event takes place (in this example, the choosing of the second bar in a menu popup), the corresponding action occurs.

You can see how the event-driven philosophy (and the use of FoxPro's event handlers) is put to work in the typical design of a FoxPro custom menu, if you look at any code generated by FoxPro's Menu Builder. (The use of the Menu Builder is covered in Chapter 23, "Pulling It All Together.") The following code was created by the Menu Builder. It produces the simple menu shown in Figure 25.3.

```
*       ***********************************************************
*       *
*       * 03/14/94            TESTMENU.MPR            09:53:48
*       *
*       ***********************************************************
*       * This program was automatically generated by GENMENU.
```

```
SET SYSMENU TO

SET SYSMENU AUTOMATIC

DEFINE PAD _qob0l7n4v OF _MSYSMENU PROMPT "\<System" COLOR SCHEME 3
DEFINE PAD _qob0l7n5y OF _MSYSMENU PROMPT "\<Database" COLOR SCHEME 3
DEFINE PAD _qob0l7n6a OF _MSYSMENU PROMPT "\<Record" COLOR SCHEME 3
DEFINE PAD _qob0l7n6o OF _MSYSMENU PROMPT "\<Windows" COLOR SCHEME 3
ON PAD _qob0l7n4v OF _MSYSMENU ACTIVATE POPUP system
ON PAD _qob0l7n5y OF _MSYSMENU ACTIVATE POPUP database
ON PAD _qob0l7n6a OF _MSYSMENU ACTIVATE POPUP record
ON PAD _qob0l7n6o OF _MSYSMENU ACTIVATE POPUP windows

DEFINE POPUP system MARGIN RELATIVE SHADOW COLOR SCHEME 4
DEFINE BAR _mst_calcu OF system PROMPT "Ca\<lculator"
DEFINE BAR _mst_diary OF system PROMPT "Calendar/D\<iary"
DEFINE BAR _mst_filer OF system PROMPT "\<Filer"
DEFINE BAR _mst_puzzle OF system PROMPT "Pu\<zzle"
DEFINE BAR 5 OF system PROMPT "\<Quit"
ON SELECTION BAR 5 OF system CANCEL

DEFINE POPUP database MARGIN RELATIVE SHADOW COLOR SCHEME 4
DEFINE BAR 1 OF database PROMPT "\<Browse"
DEFINE BAR 2 OF database PROMPT "\<Append"
DEFINE BAR 3 OF database PROMPT "\<Delete"
DEFINE BAR 4 OF database PROMPT "\<Pack"
ON SELECTION BAR 1 OF database BROWSE
ON SELECTION BAR 2 OF database APPEND BLANK
ON SELECTION BAR 3 OF database DELETE
ON SELECTION BAR 4 OF database PACK

DEFINE POPUP record MARGIN RELATIVE SHADOW COLOR SCHEME 4
DEFINE BAR 1 OF record PROMPT "\<Top"
DEFINE BAR 2 OF record PROMPT "\<Bottom"
DEFINE BAR 3 OF record PROMPT "\<Prior"
DEFINE BAR 4 OF record PROMPT "\<Next"
ON SELECTION BAR 1 OF record GO TOP
ON SELECTION BAR 2 OF record GO BOTTOM
ON SELECTION BAR 3 OF record SKIP -1
ON SELECTION BAR 4 OF record SKIP +1

DEFINE POPUP windows MARGIN RELATIVE SHADOW COLOR SCHEME 4
DEFINE BAR 1 OF windows PROMPT "\<Calendar"
DEFINE BAR 2 OF windows PROMPT "Cloc\<k"
ON SELECTION BAR 1 OF windows RUN /N CALENDAR.EXE
ON SELECTION BAR 2 OF windows RUN /N CLOCK.EXE
```

The menu uses ON SELECTION BAR statements to provide the menu with its event-driven nature. After this portion of code runs, the corresponding menu shown in the figure appears, and the program can go on to do other things (such as display specific records in a screen, or through a Browse window). When the user decides to choose a menu option, only then is the corresponding action which is tied to that option carried out.

FIGURE 25.3.

A custom menu.

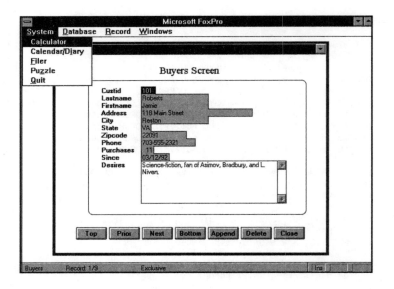

Another method of providing an event-driven nature to programs can be seen in the design of screens (generated by the Screen Builder) that contain control panels. For example, the end of Chapter 11 contains an exercise which shows how you can create screens containing a control panel for editing records and for navigating within a table. You can examine the program code generated by the Screen Builder in that exercise. If you carried out the exercise, the code is saved under the name Buyer1.SPR. The code looks like this:

```
*          ***********************************************************
*          *
*          * 03/13/94          BUYER1.SPR              08:32:03
*          *
*          ***********************************************************
*          *
*          * Author's Name
*          *
*          * Copyright (c) 1994 Company Name
*          * Address
*          * City,     Zip
*          *
*          * Description:
*          * This program was automatically generated by GENSCRN.
*          *
*          ***********************************************************


#REGION 0
REGIONAL m.currarea, m.talkstat, m.compstat

IF SET("TALK") = "ON"
     SET TALK OFF
     m.talkstat = "ON"
ELSE
     m.talkstat = "OFF"
```

```
        ENDIF
        m.compstat = SET("COMPATIBLE")
        SET COMPATIBLE FOXPLUS

        m.rborder = SET("READBORDER")
        SET READBORDER ON

        m.currarea = SELECT()


        *       ************************************************************
        *       *
        *       *          BUYER1/Windows Databases, Indexes, Relations
        *       *
        *       ************************************************************
        *

        IF USED("buyers")
             SELECT buyers
             SET ORDER TO 0
        ELSE
             SELECT 0
             USE (LOCFILE("buyers.dbf","DBF","Where is buyers?"));
                 AGAIN ALIAS buyers ;
                 ORDER 0
        ENDIF


        *       ************************************************************
        *       *
        *       *                Windows Window definitions
        *       *
        *       ************************************************************
        *

        IF NOT WEXIST("_qoa0iai0f")
             DEFINE WINDOW _qoa0iai0f ;
                 AT 0.000, 0.000 ;
                 SIZE 28.538,98.400 ;
                 FONT "MS Sans Serif", 8 ;
                 FLOAT ;
                 NOCLOSE ;
                 MINIMIZE ;
                 SYSTEM
        ENDIF


        *       ************************************************************
        *       *
        *       *                BUYER1/Windows Screen Layout
        *       *
        *       ************************************************************
        *

        #REGION 1
        IF WVISIBLE("_qoa0iai0f")
             ACTIVATE WINDOW _qoa0iai0f SAME
        ELSE
             ACTIVATE WINDOW _qoa0iai0f NOSHOW
```

```
ENDIF
@ 4.692,16.800 SAY "Custid"  ;
    FONT "MS Sans Serif", 8 ;
    STYLE "BT"
@ 4.692,31.600 GET buyers.custid ;
    SIZE 1.000,4.400 ;
    DEFAULT " " ;
    FONT "MS Sans Serif", 8 ;
    PICTURE "@K"
@ 5.769,16.800 SAY "Lastname"  ;
    FONT "MS Sans Serif", 8 ;
    STYLE "BT"
@ 5.769,31.600 GET buyers.lastname ;
    SIZE 1.000,23.600 ;
    DEFAULT " " ;
    FONT "MS Sans Serif", 8 ;
    PICTURE "@K"
@ 6.846,16.800 SAY "Firstname"  ;
    FONT "MS Sans Serif", 8 ;
    STYLE "BT"
@ 6.846,31.600 GET buyers.firstname ;
    SIZE 1.000,23.600 ;
    DEFAULT " " ;
    FONT "MS Sans Serif", 8 ;
    PICTURE "@K"
@ 7.923,16.800 SAY "Address"  ;
    FONT "MS Sans Serif", 8 ;
    STYLE "BT"
@ 7.923,31.600 GET buyers.address ;
    SIZE 1.000,39.600 ;
    DEFAULT " " ;
    FONT "MS Sans Serif", 8 ;
    PICTURE "@K"
@ 9.000,16.800 SAY "City"  ;
    FONT "MS Sans Serif", 8 ;
    STYLE "BT"
@ 9.000,31.600 GET buyers.city ;
    SIZE 1.000,23.600 ;
    DEFAULT " " ;
    FONT "MS Sans Serif", 8 ;
    PICTURE "@K"
@ 10.077,16.800 SAY "State"  ;
    FONT "MS Sans Serif", 8 ;
    STYLE "BT"
@ 10.077,31.600 GET buyers.state ;
    SIZE 1.000,2.800 ;
    DEFAULT " " ;
    FONT "MS Sans Serif", 8 ;
    PICTURE "@K"
@ 11.154,16.800 SAY "Zipcode"  ;
    FONT "MS Sans Serif", 8 ;
    STYLE "BT"
@ 11.154,31.600 GET buyers.zipcode ;
    SIZE 1.000,15.600 ;
    DEFAULT " " ;
    FONT "MS Sans Serif", 8 ;
    PICTURE "@K"
@ 12.231,16.800 SAY "Phone"  ;
    FONT "MS Sans Serif", 8 ;
```

```
        STYLE "BT"
@ 12.231,31.600 GET buyers.phone ;
        SIZE 1.000,18.800 ;
        DEFAULT " " ;
        FONT "MS Sans Serif", 8 ;
        PICTURE "@K"
@ 13.308,16.800 SAY "Purchases"  ;
        FONT "MS Sans Serif", 8 ;
        STYLE "BT"
@ 13.308,31.600 GET buyers.purchases ;
        SIZE 1.000,3.800 ;
        DEFAULT 0 ;
        FONT "MS Sans Serif", 8 ;
        PICTURE "@K"
@ 14.385,16.800 SAY "Since"  ;
        FONT "MS Sans Serif", 8 ;
        STYLE "BT"
@ 14.385,31.600 GET buyers.since ;
        SIZE 1.000,9.400 ;
        DEFAULT {  /  /  } ;
        FONT "MS Sans Serif", 8 ;
        PICTURE "@K"
@ 15.462,16.800 SAY "Desires"  ;
        FONT "MS Sans Serif", 8 ;
        STYLE "BT"
@ 15.462,31.600 EDIT Buyers.desires ;
        SIZE 6.000,52.600,0.000 ;
        PICTURE "@K" ;
        DEFAULT " " ;
        FONT "MS Sans Serif", 8 ;
        SCROLL
@ 3.692,12.000 TO 23.154,91.400 ;
        PEN 1, 8 ;
        STYLE "16" ;
        COLOR RGB(0,0,255,,,,)
@ 1.538,38.000 SAY "Buyers Screen"  ;
        FONT "Times New Roman", 14 ;
        STYLE "T"
@ 24.923,7.600 GET chooser ;
        PICTURE "@*HN Top;Prior;Next;Bottom;Append;Delete;Close" ;
        SIZE 1.769,9.333,0.667 ;
        DEFAULT 1 ;
        FONT "MS Sans Serif", 8 ;
        STYLE "B" ;
        VALID _qoa0iakgd()

IF NOT WVISIBLE("_qoa0iai0f")
        ACTIVATE WINDOW _qoa0iai0f
ENDIF

READ CYCLE

RELEASE WINDOW _qoa0iai0f

*       **********************************************************
*       *
*       *               Windows Closing Databases
*       *
*       **********************************************************
*
```

```
IF USED("buyers")
     SELECT buyers
     USE
ENDIF

SELECT (m.currarea)


#REGION 0

SET READBORDER &rborder

IF m.talkstat = "ON"
     SET TALK ON
ENDIF
IF m.compstat = "ON"
     SET COMPATIBLE ON
ENDIF


*      ************************************************************
*      *
*      * _QOA0IAKGD           chooser VALID
*      *
*      * Function Origin:
*      *
*      * From Platform:       Windows
*      * From Screen:         BUYER1,      Record Number:    27
*      * Variable:            chooser
*      * Called By:           VALID Clause
*      * Object Type:         Push Button
*      * Snippet Number:      1
*      *
*      ************************************************************
*
FUNCTION _qoa0iakgd      &&  chooser VALID
#REGION 1
DO CASE
CASE chooser = 1
     GO TOP
CASE chooser = 2
     IF EOF()
         GO TOP
     ELSE
         SKIP -1
     ENDIF
CASE chooser = 3
     IF EOF()
         GO BOTTOM
     ELSE
         SKIP 1
     ENDIF
CASE chooser = 4
     GO BOTTOM
CASE chooser = 5
     APPEND BLANK
CASE chooser = 6
     DELETE
CASE chooser = 7
```

```
      CLEAR READ
ENDCASE
SHOW GETS
RETURN
```

The event-driven ability of the screen to simultaneously respond to edits, or to clicks of buttons in the control panel, are due to the use of ACTIVATE WINDOW statements bracketed by IF...ENDIF statements, and followed by READ CYCLE statements. For example, near the end of the program, the following code appears:

```
IF NOT WVISIBLE("_qoa0iai0f")
    ACTIVATE WINDOW _qoa0iai0f
ENDIF

READ CYCLE
```

The IF NOT WVISIBLE statement activates the window containing the screen, and the READ CYCLE statement forces FoxPro to go back to the first GET statement after the last GET statement is acted upon. This forces FoxPro into an endless loop, waiting for an event (such as a menu selection or the click of a control panel button) to occur.

Chapter Summary

The overall point of this entire section is that event-driven applications come easy in FoxPro if you use FoxPro's power tools—the Screen Builder, the Menu Builder, the Report Writer, the RQBE Window, and the Project Manager—to create your application. (Since each of these power tools offers its own complex array of features and deals with a specific area, they are covered at various other locations throughout this book.) For veteran XBase programmers, event-driven programming is a different way of thinking, and may take some getting used to. Since the early days of XBase, programmers have always been accustomed to writing a main menu that leads to all available tasks, and programming an entire application from the top down. While applications development in FoxPro still requires good top-down planning (as does any development language), programmers must resist any urge to code every part of an application. Instead programmers should take full advantage of FoxPro's power tools to achieve an application that is event driven and easier for end users to use. In the long run, helping users get the job done with the least amount of hassle is what it all comes down to.

Multiuser Programming and Techniques

This chapter explains programming tools and techniques for writing programs in a network environment. The chapter assumes the installation of the multiuser version of FoxPro on a network.

Introduction to FoxPro on a Network

FoxPro is network ready out of the box; you can install it on a single-user PC, or on a network workstation. As of this writing, FoxPro is compatible with the Novell networks, and with any networks that are 100 percent NETBIOS compatible.

In addition to the commands and functions you use with FoxPro on a single PC, FoxPro also offers commands and functions for use on a network to lock and unlock records and files.

Programming Concerns for a Network

This chapter assumes that FoxPro is installed on the network, and that your prime concern is how to effectively program within a network environment. Database integrity is endangered when the program is not designed to deal with multiple users, and two or more users attempt a record modification or a global update to a database at the same time. At best, one user overwrites another's changes. At worst, the network operating system crashes, which brings the entire network down and possibly damages the table.

A second common problem with database software on a network is the potential problem of file deadlock, also known as a "deadly embrace." A file deadlock can result if two programs contend for the same files, and the error-tapping routine causes an unconditional retry of the file access. To guard against potential problems that can arise in a multiple-user environment, FoxPro offers the programmer manual file and record-locking facilities, automatic file and record locking, and a means of designating whether files are available for shared or for private use. FoxPro's ability to lock individual records prevents contention problems encountered by some database managers that do not support record-locking, and instead lock a buffer that often contains multiple records.

Also useful when operating on a network are the List and Display Status commands, which now indicate the status of file and record locks, and the List Users command, which shows all users logged onto FoxPro on the network.

File Attribute Modes

Tables can be opened in one of two attribute modes: exclusive or shared. When a table is opened in exclusive mode, no other network user can access that table with FoxPro until the file is closed, or the attribute is in some way changed from exclusive to shared. If the table is opened in shared mode, any number of network users can gain access to the table. Exclusive use of a file is granted on a first-come, first-served basis. The default attribute for a table is exclusive. FoxPro opens any table in exclusive mode unless told otherwise by your programs, or by entering Set Exclusive Off at the command window.

While Set Exclusive On prevents other FoxPro users from accessing the table, be aware that other XBase-compatible programs (like dBASE) will not respect what you do in FoxPro. Other programs can trample your data while you have an exclusive lock in effect in FoxPro, and nothing can be done in FoxPro to avoid this.

Most other types of files opened by FoxPro are also opened in exclusive mode by default. A simple way to remember whether a file is opened in exclusive mode is this: If the command results in a file being written to (such as the Copy To, Index, or any command that begins with the reserved words Create or Modify), it is opened exclusive by default. If the command results in the file being read from but not written to (such as with Report Form, Label Form, Set Format To, or Set Procedure To), it is opened on a shared basis by default. This rule applies to all types of files directly used by FoxPro.

The default manner in which index and the associated memo field files are opened is always the same as for the table associated with those files.

Lock Commands and Functions

As a programmer, it is up to you to determine what should and should not be locked by the program. Once you have made that decision, FoxPro offers locksmith's tools composed of three commands and three functions. The commands are Set Exclusive, Use Exclusive, and Unlock. The functions are Lock(), Flock(), and Rlock().

As mentioned previously, Set Exclusive On causes all files opened following the Set Exclusive On command at the start of the program to be opened in exclusive mode. If you prefer not to lock the files, use Set Exclusive Off. As an alternate to Set Exclusive On, you can use the Use Exclusive <filename> command to open a database. This variation of Use opens the named file in the exclusive mode.

The locking functions—Lock(), Flock(), and Rlock()—provide the ability to test for the presence of a file or record lock and to lock the file or record at the same time. In this respect, these functions differ from all other functions in FoxPro. Where other functions simply return a value, the Locking functions return a True or False value and perform an action. If the file or record is not previously locked, the locking function places a lock on the file or record. The Flock() function tests for file locking, while the Rlock() function and its Synonym, Lock(), test for record locking. The functions can be used in the interactive mode or from within a program. In the interactive mode, you can enter

```
? Flock()
```

or

```
? Rlock()
```

if the file or record was unlocked prior to the command, FoxPro responds with True (.T.), which indicates a successful lock. Enter a List or Display Status command to show the file or record to be locked, for example:

```
.? flock()
.T.
. display status
```

If either function returns a logical false, the record or file in question has been locked by another user.

Within a program, you can use the locking functions as part of a conditional statement that tests to a lock and performs the desired operation if the lock is successful. An example of such use is:

```
**CHANGEIT.PRG LOCKS, EDITS RECORD
**LAST UPDATE 03/31/94
CLEAR
INPUT "Enter stock number of record to be edited." TO MNUMB
USE INVFILES INDEX STOCKNO
SEEK MNUMB
IF EOF()
    ? "Sorry...no such stock number."
    WAIT
    RETURN
ENDIF
CLEAR
*Found the record, so test for a previous lock, and
*if not already locked, lock the record
IF RLOCK()
    STORE DISCRIPT TO MDESCRIPT
    STORE UNITCOST TO MUNITCOST
    STORE QUANTITY TO MQUANTITY
    @ 5,5 SAY "Item description:  "  GET MDESCRIPT
    @ 7,5 SAY "Unit cost:  "  GET MUNITCOST PICTURE "99999.99"
    @ 9,5 SAY "Quantity:  "  GET MQUANTITY PICTURE "999"
    READ
    REPLACE DESCRIPTION WITH MDESCRIPT
    REPLACE UNITCOST WITH MUNITCOST, QUANTITY WITH MQUANTITY
    CLOSE DATABASES
    RETURN
ELSE
    ? CHR(7)
    @ 5,5 SAY "Sorry...another network user is updating that record."
    @ 7,5 SAY "Try your request again later."
    WAIT
ENDIF
```

The program tests for the value returned by the RLOCK() function with the IF...ELSE...ENDIF statements. If RLOCK() returns the value of true, the temporary variables are created, and the @...SAY...GET commands followed by the REPLACE commands permit editing of the record. If the record is already locked, control passes to the ELSE statement, which advises the user that the record is not presently available for editing.

Using UNLOCK

The UNLOCK command is used to unlock a previously locked record or file.

The syntax for the command is:

```
UNLOCK [ALL]
```

If you don't specify the ALL option, UNLOCK removes the last lock implemented in the active work area. If you include the ALL option, UNLOCK removes all locks in all work areas. The following example shows the effects of the UNLOCK command:

```
.display status
. unlock all
. display status
```

As a general rule, your programs are most efficient on a network if you lock records when individual updates must be performed and lock files only when global updates (such as a REINDEX command) are performed. It's also important to note that any access granted by locking commands and functions in a program can be overridden by the network operating system software. For example, if you use a network command to designate a file as read-only, users are not able to update the file, regardless of whether the file is locked or not.

In addition to programming control of locking functions, certain FoxPro commands automatically place a lock on the file before these commands can take effect. The commands that perform a mandatory file lock are:

```
AVERAGE
CALCULATE
COPY TO
COPY TO ARRAY
COUNT
DISPLAY <scope>
INDEX
JOIN
LIST
LABEL
REPORT
SORT
SUM
TOTAL
```

This brings up the question of what happens to your program's execution if the record or file cannot be locked (because another user has already placed a lock on the file or record).

If this occurs, FoxPro reports that the record or file has been locked by another. This happens often on a network when many users share files, so error trapping to handle expected locking failures within your programs is a necessity.

Handling Failures to Lock with Error Trapping

Error-trapping routines, which you add to an application's design, must include commands to handle locking failures if you offer shared access to files within a program. The ERROR() function provides values that indicate the failure of a file-lock or record-lock attempt. In the error-handling routine, include an IF...ENDIF or CASE statement that detects an error value of 109 ("locked record error") and the error values of 108 ("locked file error").

Your program should also test for a possible error code of 148, which indicates to a network server busy conditions caused by the network operating system software. Such use of error trapping is shown in this example:

```
**ERRTRAP.PRG
**Error-trapping routine for INVENT.PRG on a Novell network
**Last update 03/30/94
DO CASE
CASE ERROR() = 108 .OR. ERROR() = 109 .OR ERROR = 158
   ? "The file or record is currently in use by another user."
   ACCEPT "Shall I continue trying to access it? (Y/N): " TO ANS
    IF UPPER (ANS) = "Y"
    CLEAR
    ? "...retrying access..."
    STORE 1 TO COUNT
    DO WHILE COUNT<100
            STORE 1 + COUNT TO COUNT
    ENDDO
    RETRY
   ENDIF
   *User wants no retry, so give up and back out
   CLOSE DATABASES
   RETURN TO MASTER
CASE ERROR() = 148
   ? "Getting a net server busy MESSAGE FOR THE FILE SERVER."
   ? " ... Please try again later."
   WAIT
   RETURN TO MASTER
CASE ERROR() =1
   ? "Cannot find the file.  Contact Network Administrator."
   CLEAR ALL
   WAIT
   QUIT
CASE ERROR() = 20 .OR. ERROR() = 26
   ? "The index seems to be missing a record.  Please wait,"
   ? "while I repair the index."
```

```
      SET TALK ON
      INDEX ON STOCKNO TAG STACKNO
      SET TALK OFF
      RETRY
OTHERWISE
      ? "A serious error has occurred.  Please record the following"
      ? "message, and contact the DP Department."
      ?
      ?MESSAGE()
      WAIT
      SET ALTERNATE TO ERRORS
      SET ALTERNATE ON
      DISPLAY MEMORY
      DISPLAY STATUS
      CLOSE ALTERNATE
      QUIT
ENDCASE
```

Precisely how you handle the error is a matter of programming style. Some programmers prefer to tell the user to try the operation again later and pass control back to a higher-level module in the program. Other programmers prefer to start a timing loop and retry the operation at the end of the loop. If your thoughts lean toward the second method, include the RETRY command, to use SET REPROCESS (covered in the following section). RETRY causes the program control to return to the program that called the error-trapping routine at the same line of the program that caused the error. This is different than the RETURN command, which passes control to the program that called the error-trapping routine, but which starts the execution at the line following the one that called the program.

Using RETRY, you can repeat the access attempt on the file or the record indefinitely— or until the user indicates that he or she is tired of waiting for the record or file to become available. The error-trapping program listed previously uses a timing loop along with an optional abort of the RETRY operation. The option is chosen when the user decides whether to make repeated tries for access of return to the calling program without accessing the file.

Performing Automated Retries

You can use the SET REPROCESS command to perform automated retries of a record lock or file lock attempt. The syntax for this command is:

```
SET REPROCESS TO <n>/AUTOMATIC
```

where <n> is a numeric value from one to 32,000. The default for SET REPROCESS is zero, meaning FoxPro immediately reports an error condition if the lock cannot be placed. By entering the SET REPROCESS TO <n> command, you tell FoxPro to retry any locking attempt by the specified number of times before the error condition is reported. Note that you can also enter a negative number as the value, in which case FoxPro retries the attempt on a infinite basis. If you use the AUTOMATIC clause, FoxPro retries the attempt on an infinite basis, and displays a system message "Attempting to lock... press Esc to cancel."

Other Network-Specific Commands

Other FoxPro commands can prove useful with a network. These are DISPLAY STATUS, LIST STATUS, and, SET PRINTER.

The DISPLAY STATUS and LIST STATUS commands perform the same functions as when you are not on a network (display of the default drives and paths, database names, work area numbers and alias names, and index filenames.) Displayed by these commands, the status of any active file locks or record locks is included. Status of the locks appears along with the information identifying the filenames, work areas, and alias names, as shown in the following example:

```
. display status
```

Both DISPLAY STATUS and LIST STATUS can make use to of the TO PRINT option in the network environment. The output is directed to the default printer (LPT1), unless you have changed the default printer status with a network operating system command.

The SET PRINTER command provides a means for redirecting printer output to another printer on the network. Print output can be sent to the local printer attached to the workstation, or to a server. To send printer output to a printer other than the one attached to that workstation, the syntax for the command is:

```
SET PRINTER TO \\ <computer name> \<printer name> = <destination>
```

where <computer name> is the workstation name assigned under the network software and <printer name> is the network assigned printer name. The <destination> designation is LPT1, LPT2, or LPT3, as appropriate with the particular setup.

To redirect printer output back to the local printer (the one attached to that workstation), the command is:

```
SET PRINTER TO LPT1/LPT2/LPT3
```

By default, the assigned printer is the shared printer on the network (often attached to the file server). Users of Novell can enter a shorter command for choosing the default printer, which is:

```
SET PRINTER TO \\SPOOLER
```

The SET REFRESH command sets the interval for the updating of the screen display when the user is in a full-screen mode such as EDIT or BROWSE. Each time the screen is updated, any changes made by other users appear. The syntax for the command is:

```
SET REFRESH TO <n>
```

where <N> is a numeric value from 1 to 3600. The value represents the time, measured in seconds, between the screen updates. If the command is not used, FoxPro defaults to an interval value of zero.

Moving Your Single-User Applications to a Network

FoxPro's automatic file and record locking do much toward making it easy to bring an application previously written for a single-user environment onto a network. The performance of the application under multiple users improves if you take full advantage of selective locking. However, you can perform a few minimal steps to quickly get an application "up and running" on a network. Once the application is network-ready, you can then concentrate on ways to improve the performance by implementing selective locking functions and error routines. The following steps can be considered as the least you should do when moving an application to a network.

At or near the start of the program, add a SET EXCLUSIVE OFF statement. Without this statement, FoxPro defaults to exclusive mode, and your network users will be very upset when only one user can access a table at a time.

Add a SET REPROCESS TO <n> statement, so that FoxPro does not immediately present a user with an error message every time an attempt is made to access a locked record. The number provided should not be so high that users get tired of waiting to gain access to the locked record or file.

If there are any locations in the program where you prefer not to have the automatic record locking of FoxPro in effect, add a SET LOCK OFF statement at that location in the program. Be sure to restore the automatic locking capability when necessary with SET LOCK ON.

Chapter Summary

This chapter has detailed network-related topics, with a view toward how FoxPro programs can be implemented on a network. Effective use of FoxPro's network tools, for file and record locking and for exclusive use of files when needed, is the key to making your FoxPro applications work well on a LAN.

Programming with DDE

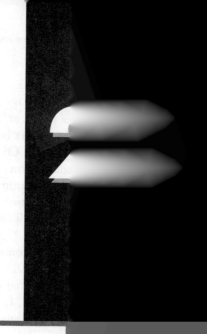

IN THIS CHAPTER

A major advantage of moving from FoxPro for DOS to FoxPro for Windows is the availability of DDE, and all that it entails. Windows can use Dynamic Data Exchange (DDE) to exchange data between different applications. The DDE protocols have been around for longer than OLE (Object Linking and Embedding), so with older applications you may find that you can use DDE where you cannot use OLE. DDE is by nature a tool that requires programming code to use in a truly comprehensive manner. Therefore, it is covered in this portion of the book, while the use of OLE (which does not necessarily require programming) is covered previously. (Note that in cases where you can accomplish a task using either OLE or DDE, you should use OLE, because it is more stable and easier to work with.) A common example of the use of DDE is when you need to obtain individual values from a Windows spreadsheet. You can link a group of spreadsheet cells to a report in FoxPro, so that each time the report is printed, FoxPro prints the current value from the spreadsheet. Using DDE, you can add capabilities to your FoxPro applications that let the applications exchange data with spreadsheets, word processors, graphics packages, and other Windows applications while under the control of a FoxPro program. DDE can be used to perform tasks like the following:

- Retrieve data stored in word processing documents or in spreadsheets
- Send data to a spreadsheet, so that calculations beyond the capabilities of FoxPro can be performed
- Configure FoxPro to respond as a DDE server to requests for data sent by Word Basic or Excel macros

The Basics of DDE

Data exchange using DDE consists of *conversations* between FoxPro and the other Windows application. The application which initiates the conversation is called the *client*, and the application which responds to the conversation is called the *server*. FoxPro for Windows can act as both a DDE client and DDE server. This means it can send DDE data to other Windows applications and receive DDE data from other Windows applications. When working with DDE, you'll need to use a specific naming convention that includes *service names*, *topic names*, and *item names*.

A *service name* is a name which the DDE Server responds to when it receives a DDE conversation from a client. The name of an application can often be used as a default service name. For example, the service name for FoxPro is "FoxPro." DDE Servers can (and often do) support more than one service name.

A *topic name* identifies a specific data set within the application, such as a spreadsheet or word processing document. With file-based applications, topic names are usually the names of files; other applications use topic names that vary depending on the application's design. For instance, a Word for Windows document could be referred to with a topic name like REPORT5.DOC, while a topic name for an Excel spreadsheet might be BUDGET94.XLS.

An *item name* specifies a unit of data contained within the topic. When the server requests the unit of data, the client can then pass along that specific data by means of a DDE conversation. In Word for Windows, an item name would be the name of a bookmark (such as "NT1" or "ITEM"). In Excel and most other Windows spreadsheets, a topic name would be a cell reference (such as "R2C5" in Excel, or "A:A4" in Lotus 1-2-3 for Windows). In other Windows database managers, an item name often is the name of a field in a table.

Under Windows, you can have two different types of DDE conversations: *asynchronous,* and *synchronous.* With *asynchronous* conversations, the DDE client sends the data to the server, then continues its own processes without waiting for a response from the server. With *synchronous* conversations, the DDE client sends the data to the server and waits for a response before continuing. (With synchronous conversations, FoxPro waits two seconds before returning an error message if the server does not respond.) Also, when you establish a link to a DDE server, the link is of the *notify* type, or of the *automatic* type. (You use the DDEAdvise() function to specify the type of link.) When a notify link is created, the server notifies the client if a specified item changes. If an automatic link is created, the server application notifies the client if a specified item changes, and the server automatically passes the new data to the client.

DDE Functions as the Key to DDE

FoxPro provides a group of DDE functions, which you use to initiate DDE conversations and exchange the data with the other application. The general idea behind using FoxPro as a DDE client is that you first open a channel to the other application with the DDEInitiate() function, then use the other DDE functions as desired to request data from the other application. If FoxPro is to play the role of a DDE Server, you use the DDESetService() function to create a service name, then you use the DDESetTopic() function to identify topics and settings for each service name. The names of the DDE functions, and their purposes, are shown in Table 27.1.

Table 27.1. The DDE Functions.

DDE Function	*Description*
DDEAbortTrans( )	Aborts an asynchronous DDE transaction.
DDEAdvise( )	Creates a notify link or an automatic link used in DDE.
DDEEnabled( )	Enables or disables DDE processing, or returns the status of DDE processing.

continues

Table 27.1. continued

DDE Function	Description
DDEExecute( )	Using DDE, sends a command to another application.
DDEInitiate( )	Establishes a DDE channel between FoxPro for Windows and another Windows-based application.
DDELastError( )	Returns an error number for the last DDE function.
DDEPoke( )	Sends data between client and server applications in a DDE conversation.
DDERequest( )	Requests data from a server application in a DDE conversation.
DDESetOption( )	Changes or returns DDE settings.
DDESetService( )	Creates, releases or modifies service names and settings in FoxPro.
DDESetTopic( )	In a DDE conversation, creates or releases a topic name from a service name.
DDETerminate( )	Closes a DDE channel established with DDEInitiate( ).

Note that these functions differ from other FoxPro functions in the following ways: the first four characters of these functions aren't unique, and the function names are longer than 10 characters and can't be abbreviated.

Steps Involved in a DDE Conversation

If you want to use FoxPro as a client, you can write FoxPro program code which establishes FoxPro for Windows as a DDE client. To do this, use the following steps:

1. Use the DDEInitiate() function to establish a link to the server application.
2. If the link is successful, use the DDERequest() function to request data from the server application. (You can use DDERequest() repeatedly to request additional data.)
3. Once the data is received, use the DDETerminate() function to terminate the link to the server application. (This isn't required, but it's a good idea, as leaving links active ties up system resources under Windows.)

If you want to use FoxPro as a server, you can use the following steps:

1. Use the DDESetService() function to create a service and specify the type of service.

2. Use the DDESetTopic() function to create a service topic and specify the FoxPro program to execute when the topic is specified by a request sent by a DDE client.

3. Create the FoxPro program specified in DDESetTopic() to accept the parameters passed to the program. Within the program, process the request and return any requested data to the client.

Before Starting the Conversation

Before you can begin a DDE conversation, the DDE server must be running under Windows. If the application isn't running and you use DDEInitiate() to try to open a channel to the application, FoxPro displays a dialog box asking if the application should be started. (See Figure 27.1.)

FIGURE 27.1.

The "Remote data not accessible" dialog box.

As an option, you can automate the launching of the other application by including the RUN command with the /N option, which launches another Windows application from FoxPro. For example, the statement

```
RUN /N C:\EXCEL\EXCEL.EXE
```

would launch Microsoft Excel from FoxPro. If you take this approach, you should include program code in your application that first checks to see if the other Windows application is already running. If you don't include this code, your application could launch needless extra copies of an already-running Windows application, which would use up precious system resources.

Initiating the Conversation

Once the application is running, you initiate the conversation with the DDEInitiate() function. The syntax of this function is as follows:

```
DDEInitiate(expC1, expC2)
```

where *expC1* is the service name of the server application. In most cases, this is the name of the executable program, minus its extension. If you are establishing a channel to Excel, *expC1* is Excel; with Word for Windows, *expC1* is Winword. (The default service name for FoxPro for Windows is FoxPro.)

expC2 identifies the topic name. Topic naming conventions vary from application to application; you can refer to the application's documentation for specifics on acceptable topic names for a given application. (Most DDE servers provide a default topic name of "system.")

The function returns a numeric value which identifies the DDE channel to the application. You need to use this channel number with the other DDE functions to communicate with the application. (The number of channels you can establish with other applications is limited only by your system's available resources.) If for some reason the link to the application is unsuccessful, the function returns a -1.

> **TIP**
>
> The main reasons for a "failure to communicate" (as far as DDE is concerned) are incorrect topic names and incorrect application names.

Communicating with the Other Application

With the conversation established, you can use the appropriate DDE functions to carry out the desired tasks. Three of the more commonly-used functions are DDEExecute(), DDERequest(), and DDEPoke().

Use the DDEExecute() function to send a command to the other application. (Note that some, but not all, applications let you execute their commands by way of DDE.) The syntax of the function is:

```
DDEExecute(expN, expC1 [, expC2])
```

where *expN* is the channel number, *expC1* is the command to send to the other application, and *expC2* is an optional character expression which, when used, allows asynchronous communications requests. (*expC2* can name a user-defined function, in which case the UDF is called when the server completes the command.) For example, assuming a DDE channel named "word" had been opened with the DDEInitiate() function, you might use a statement like

```
=DDEExecute(word, '[FilePrintSetup "Epson FX-80 on LPT1:"]')
```

to choose File, Print Setup in Word for Windows, and select a specific printer in the resulting dialog box.

Use the `DDERequest()` function to request data from the other application. The syntax for the function is:

```
DDERequest(expN, expC1[, expC2[, expC3]])
```

where *expN* is the channel number, *expC1* is the item name, *expC2* is an optional character expression which specifies a format for the data, and *expC3* is an optional character expression which, when used, allows asynchronous communications requests. (*expC3* can name a user-defined function, in which case the UDF is called when the server completes the command.)

The function returns the requested data as a character string. If the request fails, a null string ("") is returned by the function. For instance, the statement shown here requests the paragraph containing a bookmark called "MyMark" from a Word for Windows document, and stores the paragraph to a character string named ThePara.

```
ThePara = DDERequest(word,"\MyMark")
```

Use the `DDEPoke()` function to send data between the client and the server. `DDEPoke()` sends data as a character string to the item name specified by the channel number. If the data is successfully sent, `DDEPoke()` returns a logical true (.T.). If the data cannot be sent, the function returns a logical false (.F.). The syntax for the function is:

```
DDEPoke(expN, expC1, expC2[, expC3[, expC4]])
```

where *expN* is the channel number, *expC1* is the item name, *expC2* is the data to be sent, *expC3* is an optional character expression which specifies a format for the data, and *expC4* is an optional character expression which, when used, allows asynchronous communications requests. (*expC4* can name a user-defined function, in which case the UDF is called when the server completes the command.) For example, assuming a DDE channel named "ssheet" had been opened into an Excel spreadsheet with the `DDEInitiate()` function, you could use a statement like the following to store the formula =B3+B4+B7 in a cell of the spreadsheet:

```
=DDEPoke(ssheet, "R2C5", "=B3+B4+B7")
```

The `DDEPoke()` function is also routinely used when you design your code to have FoxPro act as a server, and respond to DDE requests from other applications.

Terminating the Conversation

When the DDE conversation is no longer needed, you can end it with the `DDETerminate()` function. The syntax for the function is:

```
DDETerminate(expN ¦ expC)
```

where *expN* is the channel number to close. In place of the channel number, you can specify *expC*, which is a service name. If you use the service name, all open channels to that service are closed by the function. When the channel is closed, the function returns a logical true (.T.). If for some reason the channel cannot be closed, the function returns a logical false (.F.).

Handling DDE Errors

The process of using DDE is rather complex and tends to be error-prone, so it is generally a wise idea to include code in your application that checks to make sure that each DDE call you made executed successfully. When a DDE function fails, the function returns a logical false; if the function executes successfully, it returns a logical true. You can structure your code to test for the failure of a DDE function, and then use the DDELastError() function to return the error code for the failure and respond accordingly. For example, the following code shows a portion of an error-handling routine that acts on the failure of a DDE function.

```
CHANNEL = DDEInitiate("EXCEL","SYSTEM")
IF .NOT. CHANNEL
     *Attempt to open channel to Excel failed.*
     The Error = DDELastError()
     *Handle the error.*
     DO CASE
        CASE TheError = 7
        WAIT WINDOW "Insufficient memory for this operation."
        RETURN
        CASE TheError = 16
        WAIT WINDOW "Can't establish connection. Call PC support."
          *...more code to handle possible errors here...*
     ENDCASE
ENDIF
*...more code follows...*
```

An Example of DDE Use

As an example of the use of DDE, the following program, when run from FoxPro, lets the user choose any existing Word for Windows document. This program then prints that document.

■ This program demonstrates the use of DDE to call WinWord.*

■ The program prints a Word document from FoxPro.*

■ First, get a filename of a Word document to print.*

```
    TheFile = GETFILE("DOC","Print what document?")
```

■ Turn off the want to start Word? message.*

```
A=DDESetOption("safety",.F.)
```

■ Launch Word for Windows.*

```
Channel = DDEInitiate("WINWORD","SYSTEM")
IF Channel = -1
```

■ failed to open channel, so Word must not be in the path...*

■ open a dialog box and ask user where is Word.*

```
WORDFILE = LOCFILE("winword.exe","exe","Where is Word?")
IF WORDFILE == ""
   WAIT WINDOW "Can't find Word for Windows!"
   CANCEL
   ENDIF
```

■ launch Word based on selection in dialog box.*

```
RUN /N &WORDFILE
Channel = DDEInitiate("WINWORD","System")
IF Channel = -1
   WAIT WINDOW "DDE Error trying to start WinWord."
   CANCEL
ENDIF
ENDIF
```

■ Word commands follow to open & print file, then exit Word.*

```
A=DDEExecute(Channel, '[FileOpen .name='+'"'+TheFile+'"]')
B=DDEExecute(Channel, '[FilePrint]')
C=DDEExecute(Channel, '[FileClose]')
D=DDEExecute(Channel, '[FileExit]')
E=DDESetOption("safety",.T.)
RETURN
```

When run, the GETFILE() function causes FoxPro's Open dialog box to be displayed, and the chosen document name is stored to the memory variable called TheFile. The DDESetOption() function is used to turn off the error message that appears if a DDEInitiate() function fails to find an application. The DDEInitiate() function is then used to initiate a DDE conversation with Word for Windows. Once the conversation has been initiated, the program uses a series of DDEExecute() functions to perform Word's File, Open; File, Print; File, Close; and File, Exit commands.

Chapter Summary

This chapter detailed how you can use DDE functions within your FoxPro programs to communicate with other Windows applications, by means of DDE. One point to keep in mind is that since the effective use of DDE requires a considerable amount of programming, you should resort to the use of DDE only when you cannot accomplish the same tasks with less complex methods.

Working with the FoxPro API

28

For those familiar with C programming, the Application Program Interface (API) significantly extends FoxPro's capabilities. You can write your own routines in C or in assembler, and use your compiler to assemble those routines into a library file. FoxPro is made aware of the library file with the SET LIBRARY command, and the routines in the library then become available to FoxPro as functions. Use of the API overcomes the limitations of LOAD and CALL statements and assembly-language (.BIN) routines, which have been commonly used in XBase. Assembly-language routines loaded into memory and executed with LOAD and CALL statements have always had disadvantages. Allocating memory was nearly impossible (and where possible, often a good way to crash the system); only a limited number of routines could be loaded into memory at one time; and parameter passing between the routines and XBase was odd, to say the least. All these limitations are overcome by the use of C routines and the API. In addition to this, C, with all of its challenges, is still inherently easier to code for than assembler. (For those diehard fans of assembly language, you can also choose to code your API routines in assembler.) Besides having the ability to replace LOAD and CALL statements, API routines let developers tap all of FoxPro's own features. You can use API routines to manage memory, perform file input/output operations, manipulate windows, and work with data in tables.

To develop routines in C, you need the FoxPro Library Construction Kit (available separately with version 2.5 of FoxPro, and provided as a part of FoxPro Professional with version 2.6). In the Library Construction Kit, you'll find libraries, make files, and object files needed to create your routines. Of course, you also need a C compiler if you are going to write routines in C. The Library Construction Kit supports Watcom C (version 8.5), Microsoft C/C++ version 7, or Microsoft Visual C++. While the Microsoft documentation makes no reference to other compilers, numerous FoxPro users in the past have used Borland's C++ as well.

This chapter won't discuss the actual programming of API routines in C—the subject of C programming is a tad beyond the scope of this book. This chapter shows how you can activate API routines from within FoxPro, how you can pass parameters between your API routines and FoxPro, and some guidelines you can follow when writing API routines.

Making FoxPro Aware of Your API Routines

After writing a library of routines (whether in C or in assembler), compile and link the routines to a .FLL file. (Technically, you can use any extension you want, but the SET LIBRARY command in FoxPro assumes the use of .FLL as an extension. If you use a different extension, you'll need to include the extension along with the filename in FoxPro.) Back in FoxPro, you use the SET LIBRARY TO *.fll filename* command to open the API routine library. Once the library is opened, you can use the API functions just as if they were FoxPro's own functions. If you use a DISPLAY STATUS or a LIST STATUS command, the added functions are shown in the command's results. The complete syntax of the command is:

```
SET LIBRARY TO [.FLL FILENAME[ADDITIVE]]
```

with *.fll filename* being the name of the library file to open. Using SET LIBRARY TO with no filename specified removes all API libraries from memory. The ADDITIVE clause is included when you want to load an API library and retain any existing libraries already in memory. (Note, too, that individual libraries can be released from memory with the RELEASE LIBRARY *library name* command.)

Since API routines are hardware-specific, you cannot use API routines written for other platforms (such as FoxPro for DOS) in FoxPro for Windows, nor can you use routines written for FoxPro for Windows with other platform versions of FoxPro.

The Structure of API Routines

Your API routines must include a "FoxInfo" data structure, which defines how your functions are named, the number of parameters you can pass to them, and what kinds of parameters are required. The structure of FoxInfo is defined as follows:

```
typedef struct{
    char FAR * funcName;    /*function name in caps*/
    FPFI       function;    /*address of function*/
    Short      parmCount;   /*number of parameters*/
    Char FAR * parmTypes;   /*data types for parameters*/
    }FoxInfo;
```

and parmTypes (the type of parameter) is a letter indicating any of the following parameter types:

C	character string
D	date
I	integer
L	logical
N	numeric
R	variable, or array passed by reference
?	permits any data type

For example, if your API library contained three functions named FILLBOX, BEGFILL, and ENDFILL, the FoxInfo structure might resemble the following:

```
FoxInfo DrawBox[]={
    {"FILLBOX", (FPFI) fillbox, 2, "C", "N"},
    {"BEGFILL", (FPFI) begfill, 1, "N"},
    {"ENDFILL", (FPFI) endfill, 1, "N"},
    };
```

and the functions could be referred to in FoxPro as `FILLBOX()`, `BEGFILL()`, and `ENDFILL()`. The first function accepts two parameters (one character and one numeric). The second and third functions each accept a numeric parameter.

In addition to creating a FoxInfo structure in your API routine, you must also create a "FoxTable" structure. The FoxTable structure defines the number of functions in the library, and provides FoxPro with the address of each function. The structure for FoxTable is shown here:

```
FoxTable _FoxTable = {
    (FoxTable FAR *)0,
    SIZEOF(DrawBox)/SIZEOF(FoxInfo),
    DrawBox};
```

Regardless of the compiler you use to write your API routines, you'll need to use the large memory model for any routines written to work with FoxPro for Windows. (See your compiler's documentation for details on developing code using the large memory model.)

Parameter Passing

FoxPro can pass parameters to API routines by value, or by reference, depending on the setting of SET UDFPARMS (VALUE or REFERENCE). When a parameter is passed by value, FoxPro retains the original value of the parameter, no matter what the function does with the passed value. When a parameter is passed by reference, the API routine can change the value of the variable. You can force a parameter to be passed by value or by reference. To force parameter passing by value, refer to the function with the form,

```
thefunct((memvar))
```

and you can force parameter passing by reference by preceding the name of the function with the @ symbol, as in

```
thefunct(@memvar)
```

Returning the Results

Included in the API Library (as part of the Library Construction Kit) are functions you can use to return data from your routines back to FoxPro. Table 28.1 describes the purpose of each of these functions. The functions pass data to FoxPro, but they do not terminate your external routines. Therefore, all the functions are of the VOID type, declared as returning nothing.

Table 28.1. The API Functions used to return data to FoxPro.

Function	Purpose
_RetChar(char FAR *the string*)	Returns a string terminated with a null.
_RetDateStr(char FAR *the string*)	Returns a date in the format of a character string. The date you supply as *the string* must have the format of "MM/DD/YY" or "MM/DD/YYYY."
__RetFloat(*the double value*, intwidth, intdecimals)	Returns a double-precision floating point value.
_RetInt(*the long ival*, intwidth)	Returns a long integer. Intwidth is the number of columns used to display the number.
_RetLogical(int *the logical value*)	Returns a logical value.
_RetVal(value FAR *the value*)	Returns a complete value structure. Can be used to pass any data type except memo; can also be used to pass a string with embedded nulls.

Chapter Summary

This chapter provided an introduction to the FoxPro Application Program Interface (API). (Additional details can be found in the documentation which accompanies the FoxPro Library Construction Kit, part of FoxPro Professional as of version 2.6.) You can use the API to dramatically extend the power of FoxPro 2.5 by creating external libraries in C, calling them from FoxPro, and calling your FoxPro routines from these libraries. You can use the FoxPro API to seamlessly integrate your custom routines into any FoxPro application.

Cross-Platform and Migration Tips and Techniques

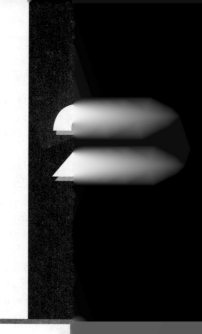

This chapter details the techniques you can use when working with FoxPro applications across platforms and when migrating applications from other database managers into FoxPro. One of FoxPro's significant strengths is that it is truly a cross-platform product. You can develop applications on any platform running FoxPro and use those applications on a different platform. FoxPro currently supports three different platforms: FoxPro for Windows, FoxPro for DOS, and FoxPro for the Macintosh. According to Microsoft, FoxPro for Unix is under development at the time of this writing. FoxPro is the first database development environment that has provided the ability to move applications seamlessly between DOS and Windows. With the Macintosh version available and the Unix version in the works, developers—for the first time—can code applications that can run, unchanged, on a variety of platforms. Figure 29.1 shows an application written in FoxPro for DOS and running under FoxPro for DOS. Figure 29.2 shows the same application, running unchanged under FoxPro for Windows.

FIGURE 29.1.

An application running under FoxPro for DOS.

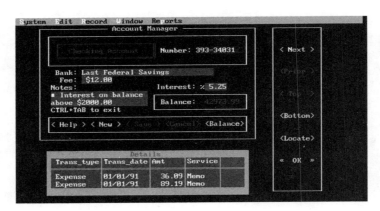

This capability brings up another question that an application developer must address: given that you can write code that runs unchanged across all FoxPro platforms, do you want to? The "GUI" versions of the product (FoxPro for Windows and FoxPro for the Macintosh) have capabilities that the character-based versions lack. For example, in FoxPro for Windows and FoxPro for the Macintosh, you can add graphic design elements to a screen. In your FoxPro for Windows program code, you can use DDE functions to exchange data with other Windows software. If you choose to develop your application using platform-specific features like these, you can't run it unchanged on one of the other platforms. So, FoxPro gives you a choice: you can develop applications which don't take advantage of platform-specific features and which run unchanged across all platforms, or you can develop applications to take advantage of a particular platform, and then make changes where needed to move the application to another platform.

FIGURE 29.2.

An application running under FoxPro for Windows.

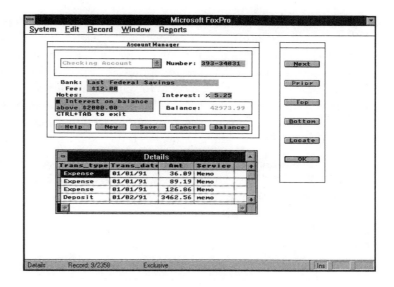

When designing cross-platform applications, much of the same code can be used transparently across platforms. You should try to separate this code from platform specific code. Code that involves database operations can usually be generic across platforms. Code which affects the appearance of the user interface, on the other hand, can vary across platforms.

Choosing a Development Platform

If you work in an organization where multiple platforms are supported, a question that arises is: which platform should be used to develop your application? Often, the answer is dictated by the realities of the real world, and the hardware that's available. If the person doing the development has a 286 running FoxPro for DOS, then that's what the application will be developed under. When you do have a choice, and the application is going to run on multiple platforms, there are advantages to doing the initial application development in FoxPro for DOS. Microsoft considers FoxPro for DOS to be the "lowest common denominator" among the different versions of FoxPro. All objects in FoxPro for DOS have corresponding objects in FoxPro for Windows, and in FoxPro for the Macintosh. As a result, an application written using FoxPro for DOS runs, unchanged, on the other platforms regardless of what design elements you use. Since the GUI versions (FoxPro for Windows and FoxPro for the Macintosh) offer design elements that are unique to those environments, you must be careful when using either FoxPro for Windows or FoxPro for the Macintosh as the development environment. You must avoid depending on any special features that aren't available in the character-based versions of FoxPro. The use of FoxPro's Screen Builder to design screens provides an advantage when developing the interface for an application, because by default the Screen Builder writes code that is compatible with all platforms. When a screen is run, each respective version of FoxPro runs the code within the screen that is compatible with that respective version. (A corresponding disadvantage is that screens are sometimes larger in disk size than needed, because they sometimes contain code that's specific to multiple platforms. When you generate code for a screen as detailed in Chapter 11, "Designing and Customizing Screens," if you click More in the Generate Screen dialog box and turn on the Windows Objects Only option, the code that the Screen Builder generates is then specific only to FoxPro for Windows.)

As you write code for multiple platforms, keep in mind the existence of the system memory variables _WINDOWS, _DOS, _MAC, and _UNIX. Each of these system memory variables returns a logical true (.T.) if FoxPro is running on that respective platform, and a logical false (.F.) otherwise. You can use these system memory variables to control IF...ENDIF or CASE statements within an application, to do one thing if FoxPro for Windows is running the application, and something else if another version of FoxPro is running the application. For example, if you wanted to display a company logo stored in a bit map file under FoxPro for Windows and in its place, display the name of the company under FoxPro for DOS, your program might contain a portion of program code like the following:

```
IF _WINDOWS
     @ 5,5 SAY "MYLOGO.BMP" BIT MAP
ELSE
     @ 5,5 SAY "AlphaBeta Systems"
ENDIF
```

FoxPro uses these same system memory variables when it generates screens containing design elements that are platform-specific, to bracket the code so that each version of FoxPro runs its respective code when the screen runs.

Bringing FoxPro for DOS Applications to Windows

Given the size of the installed base (and that the first version of FoxPro was FoxPro for DOS), the most common tasks under cross-platform development are going to involve DOS applications and Windows applications. As mentioned earlier, you can bring any FoxPro for DOS application directly into Windows with no changes, but you may or may not choose to do so. You have three basic strategies available when bringing FoxPro for DOS applications to the Windows platform. The strategies are:

■ You can run the DOS application completely unchanged under FoxPro for Windows.

■ You can use the Transporter to convert all screens, reports, and labels so that they take on a true graphical appearance under Windows.

■ You can make platform-specific changes to the design of the application, optimizing it to run under the Windows platform.

It's important to note that with the second and third options you won't change how the interface of the application appears under DOS, so you maintain compatibility back to the DOS platform. These options simply increase the amount of work necessary on your part. In return for the extra work, you get a Windows application that is more in tune with the benefits of the Windows environment.

Running FoxPro for DOS Applications

To run a FoxPro 2.5 for DOS application as is, you simply choose Program, Do from the menus to open the Do dialog box, and select the desired application, then click the Do button. You can also use the DO *filename.APP* command, where *filename* is the name of the application.

To run a FoxPro 2.0 for DOS application (stored as an .APP file), you must perform a few additional steps, because the object code used to build applications is different for version 2.0 than it is for version 2.5 and above. You can rebuild .APP files from FoxPro version 2.0 to run in either the DOS or Windows versions of FoxPro 2.6 with the following steps:

1. From the menus, choose File, Open.
2. In the Open dialog box, change the List Files of Type option to Project to display all the project files.
3. Select the desired project file, and click Open. A dialog box appears, asking if you want to convert the project file to FoxPro 2.6 format.
4. Click Yes. (You may also be asked for permission to relocate the home directory for the project.)
5. Click Build.
6. Select Build Application, then click OK.
7. Click Yes, to save the new project file. Choose Build to accept the existing filename, and choose Yes again to overwrite the existing file.

Note that when you convert a project from FoxPro 2.0 file format, you can no longer use that same project in FoxPro 2.0.

Running FoxPro for DOS Programs

Since FoxPro recompiles source code as is needed, no changes are necessary to run any program code written in FoxPro for DOS. To run a program, simply choose Program, Do from the menus, click the desired program file to select it, and click Do. You can also enter DO *filename* in the Command Window, where *filename* is the name of the program.

Running FoxPro for DOS Executables

If executable (.EXE) files have been created under earlier versions of FoxPro for DOS, you must convert those files back to application (.APP) files before they can run under FoxPro for Windows. To convert a FoxPro for DOS application that's stored as an .EXE file, perform the following steps:

1. Choose File, Open.
2. Click Project in the List Files of Type list box and select the desired project file, then click Open.
3. If a dialog box appears asking for permission to convert the file to 2.6 format, click Yes. (You may also be asked for permission to relocate the home directory for the project.)
4. Click Build.
5. Select Build Application, then click OK.
6. Click Yes, to save the changes to the existing new project file.
7. Click Build, to accept the same filename as the original application, and choose Yes again to overwrite the existing file.

Using the Transporter

FoxPro for Windows provides the Transporter, a built-in utility that helps add the "Windows look" to screens, reports, and labels created under FoxPro for DOS. The Transporter dialog box appears automatically whenever you open a FoxPro for DOS screen, report, or label in FoxPro for Windows. The Transporter can be a significant aid in creating cross platform screens, reports, and labels.

When you first open a FoxPro for DOS screen, report, or label, the Transporter dialog box appears. (See Figure 29.3.)

FIGURE 29.3.

*The Transporter
dialog box.*

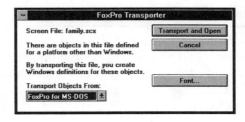

The Transporter dialog contains the options as explained in Table 29.1.

Table 29.1. The Transporter dialog box options.

Option	Meaning
Transports Objects From popup	Select the platform you want to convert the screen from.
Transport and Open push button	Transports the file and opens the appropriate editing window.
Cancel push button	Exits the dialog without making changes to your screen. You can still open the screen in FoxPro 2.0 but not in FoxPro for Windows.
Font... push button	Opens the Font dialog so you can choose the default font for your transported screen, report, or label.

The options shown in Table 29.2 are included in the dialog box when you partially transport items.

Table 29.2. Transporter options when objects are partially transported.

Option	Meaning
Objects New to Windows check box	Check this option to have all objects that are new to the Windows version of the file included in the partial transport.

continues

Table 29.2. continued

Option	Meaning
Objects More Recently Modified Than Windows Equivalent Objects check box	Check this option when you want to include existing objects that have been modified in another platform.
All Objects Replace Existing Definitions check box	Check this option to replace all the object definitions.

For example, Figure 29.4 shows a FoxPro for DOS application running under Windows, with no changes made.

FIGURE 29.4.

A FoxPro for DOS application running under Windows.

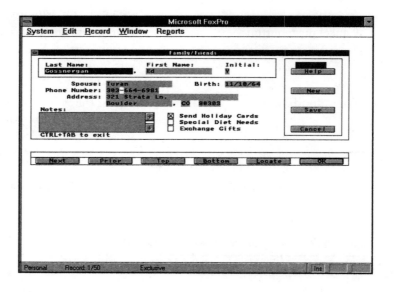

Figure 29.5 shows the same application, after the screen which serves as the application's main menu has been run through the Transporter. Notice that in the second figure, screen objects have been rearranged, fonts have been modified, and buttons have been changed in size to give the application more of a Windows appearance.

FIGURE 29.5.

A DOS application after use of the Transporter.

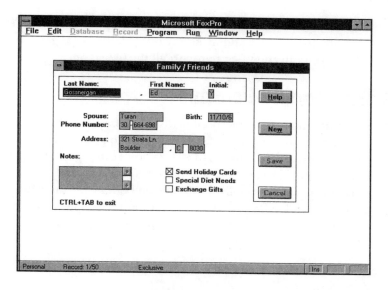

To transport a screen, report, or label, first select the desired screen, report, or label in the Project window. (Choose File, Open and select Project to open an existing project, or use File, New to create a new project, and add the screens, report, and labels to the project.) When you select the screen, label, or report and click Open, the Transport dialog box appears. (See Figure 29.3, shown previously.)

Next, click the Transport and Open button, to transport the screen, label, or report. After you have transported the object, it appears in design mode. You can then use the usual methods to save the object and return to the Project window, where you can transport additional objects.

Taking FoxPro for Windows Applications to FoxPro for DOS

Running your applications developed under FoxPro for Windows on the DOS platform is also a simple matter. You can take an application from the Windows to the DOS environment with these steps:

1. Under FoxPro for DOS, choose File, Open.
2. Click Project in the List Files of Type list box and select the desired project file, then click Open.
3. In the dialog box which appears, select a file and click Edit. The Transport dialog box appears.

4. For each file in the project, choose Transport and Open. You can transport the files individually and make any other desired changes to each file as you go along, or you can choose to transport all the files at once.

Transporting Elements

When transporting applications across platforms, you may need to adjust some screens, especially if you are going from a character to graphical environment. If you intend to port Windows applications to MS-DOS, leave extra space in screens because there are more pixels in a graphical environment than there are rows and columns in a character environment. Also, try to use objects available on both platforms. OLE and picture objects cannot be used in FoxPro for MS-DOS. According to Microsoft, the Transporter makes the following changes in the process of transporting from FoxPro for Windows to FoxPro for DOS:

With Screens Transported to DOS:

Transported picture buttons become regular controls with the bit map (.BMP) file name as the text prompt.

Transported rounded rectangles become regular rectangles.

Transported spinners become numeric GET fields.

Rectangles, lines, and text colors are transported; the DOS version of FoxPro accepts them as an individual color pair.

Fonts, font styles, and font sizes are not transported. Instead, FoxPro removes the attributes and places them on-screen as monospaced character mode text.

Multiple-line text objects are broken into separate objects, with each line becoming its own object.

Multiple-line text objects that have 1 1/2 line spacing transport to single line spacing.

Pictures fields are ignored.

Grouped objects are no longer grouped after being transported.

Coordinates in FoxPro for Windows are fractional. After transporting, these become whole numbers based on an internal algorithm used by FoxPro.

Pen sizes transport as shown in the following table (the two values indicate the pen size in FoxPro for Windows and the equivalent pen size after transporting to FoxPro for DOS):

Pen Size	Equivalent
1	Single
2	Double
4	Panel
6	Single

With Reports Transported to DOS:

Multi-column reports are transported as single column reports and the column headers and footers are merged into the page headers and footers.

Colors in reports do not transport.

Individual fields in FoxPro for Windows can have the blank lines suppressed option turned on or off. If one field in a FoxPro for Windows report has this option turned on, then the Transporter turns the option on for the entire report in FoxPro for MS-DOS.

Group header and group footer fields that are marked to stretch, are cut off at the group header or group footer band when transported to FoxPro for DOS.

Fonts, font styles, and font sizes are not transported. Instead, FoxPro removes their attributes and places them on the screen as monospaced character mode text.

Multiple-line text objects are broken into separate objects. Each line becomes its own object.

Multiple-line text objects that have 1 1/2 line spacing transport to single line spacing.

Pictures fields are ignored.

Grouped objects are no longer grouped after they are transported.

Coordinates in FoxPro for Windows are fractional. After transporting, these become whole numbers based on an internal algorithm used by FoxPro.

Pen sizes transport as shown in the following table (the two values indicate the pen size in FoxPro for Windows and the equivalent pen size after transporting to FoxPro for DOS):

Pen Size	Equivalent
1	Single
2	Double
4	Panel
6	Single

With Labels Transported to DOS:

Rectangles and lines do not transport.

Objects that are determined by the Transporter to be on the same line are merged into a single, comma-delimited expression. (This means horizontal information is not transported.)

Single-column labels are transported to FoxPro for MS-DOS as labels with a width of 80.

Fonts, font styles, and font sizes are not transported. Instead, FoxPro removes their attributes and places them on the screen as monospaced character mode text.

Multiple-line text objects are broken into separate objects. Each line becomes its own object.

Multiple-line text objects that have 1 1/2 line spacing transport to single line spacing.

Pictures fields are ignored.

Grouped objects are no longer grouped after they are transported.

Coordinates in FoxPro for Windows are fractional. After transporting, these become whole numbers based on a complex algorithm.

Pen sizes transport as shown in the following table (the two values indicate the pen size in FoxPro for Windows and the equivalent pen size after transporting to FoxPro for DOS):

Pen Size	Equivalent
1	Single
2	Double
4	Panel
6	Single

Updating Cross-Platform Applications

You can run FoxPro 2.5 applications transparently on different platforms. However, remember that some changes you make on one platform are not automatically reflected on other platforms. Changes made in one platform do not necessarily update all platforms. For example, if you add a new object to a screen in FoxPro for Windows and recompile the application, that new object does not appear when you run the .APP in FoxPro for MS-DOS. You must open the screen in FoxPro for MS-DOS and rebuild the application. The Transporter dialog appears, showing that new objects were added on another platform and asking if you'd like to make the same changes on the current platform.

Migrating Applications from Other XBase Environments

Version 2.6 of FoxPro was specifically designed to appeal to users of dBASE IV and dBASE III Plus. FoxPro's command set encompasses virtually all of dBASE IV's command set and all of the command set of dBASE III Plus, which makes it highly compatible with dBASE IV and fully compatible with dBASE III Plus and dBASE III. (The only dBASE commands not supported by FoxPro are those dBASE IV commands that deal mainly with transaction processing on a network; BEGIN TRANSACTION, END TRANSACTION, ROLLBACK, PROTECT, and COMMIT.) This high degree of dBASE compatibility makes FoxPro version 2.6 extremely compatible with dBASE, and very compatible with most other XBase products, including Clipper (summer 87 version) and Quicksilver. (Because Clipper and Quicksilver both added their own extensions to the dBASE III Plus command set on which they were based, there may be parts of your program code which will need modification before Clipper or Quicksilver program code runs in FoxPro.)

If your application is written in dBASE IV, dBASE III Plus, or dBASE III, you can run it with these simple steps:

1. In the Command Window, enter SET COMPATIBLE DB4.
2. Run the dBASE program as you would run any other program, by entering DO *filename* in the Command Window, or by choosing Program, Do from the menus.

For the most part, your dBASE programs run unchanged in FoxPro. As soon as you run the program (.PRG) file, FoxPro recompiles the program into a FoxPro compiled program file (.FXP), and runs it. Note that due to differences in the way SQL is implemented, FoxPro cannot run dBASE IV SQL programs (these have a .PRS extension).

If you are running XBase applications written with a product other than dBASE IV or dBASE III Plus/dBASE III, you can identify any possible program errors with the use of FoxPro's Project Manager, and the error log that the Project Manager automatically creates. (For more on the use of the Project Manager, refer to Chapter 23, "Pulling It All Together.") After placing all of the application's files together in a single subdirectory, you can perform these steps in FoxPro:

1. Choose File, New.
2. In the New dialog box, click Project, then click New.
3. In the Untitled dialog box which appears, click Add.
4. Using the Add File dialog box which appears, add the main program (.PRG) file from the XBase application. (The main program file is whatever file is used to start the application.)

5. Click Build.

6. In the Build Option dialog box which appears, select Build Application, then click Build. FoxPro automatically pulls all the associated program files into the project, along with the main program file.

When the process is complete, you can examine any error log created by FoxPro's Project Manager. If the Project Manager ran across any commands that it could not deal with, messages about those commands are stored in an error log. The error log is a text file with the same name as the project, and with an extension of .ERR. You can examine the error log to see the source of the incompatibilities, go into the source code and remedy the problem, then build and run the application.

Dealing with Runtime Errors

If a dBASE program produces a runtime error or other unexpected results, you can debug the program using FoxPro's debugging tools, the Trace and Debug windows. Using the Trace window, you can step through the program code a line at a time. Using the Debug window, you can enter field names, memory variables, or function names in the left panel of the window, and display the runtime values assigned to the variables or returned by the functions in the right panel of the window. For more on using the Trace and Debug windows (and on debugging programs in general), refer to Chapter 24, "Debugging Techniques."

Migrating Applications from Non-XBase Environments

If you are faced with the task of migrating an application from a non-XBase product to FoxPro (such as Paradox, Access, or database applications from mainframe or minicomputers), you face a major task. The mere phrase "converting an application" must be taken in a very liberal context. What you can do is to transfer the *overall design* of your non-XBase application to a FoxPro application. Here are the overall steps you can follow to perform such a task.

Start with the Tables

Begin with the existing data files and table structures in the original application. If you want to avoid the tedious process of re-keying all the data, you must bring the data into FoxPro's data format (which is, of course, dBASE-compatible). You can use the APPEND FROM and IMPORT commands as an aid in bringing data from foreign files into FoxPro.

(See Chapter 16, "Sharing Data with Other Programs," for hints on how you can do this.) If the database is one that makes use of relational capabilities, you need to use the techniques outlined in Chapter 12, "Designing and Customizing Reports," to add relational capabilities where needed in FoxPro.

Next, the Screens

Once the data exists in FoxPro, you can create screens to facilitate the adding and editing of data. (The Screen Wizards, accessible through the Catalog Manager or by choosing Run, Wizard from the menus, can be a significant aid in the creation of screens for adding and editing data.) Also keep in mind that if you are duplicating the functionality of an application that was originally written in a character-based environment (like DOS), you should not feel limited to the constraints of the old system when you design screens under the Windows environment.

Next, the Reports

With the needed screens created for each table, the next logical task is to create the reports and to duplicate the reports generated by the original application. If you plan to base those reports on queries created with relational query-by-example (RQBE), you also need to create the queries that those reports should be based upon. You'll also need to decide how you are going to handle putting data in order before the reports are generated. If the reports are based on queries, you can use the Order By specifications within the queries to establish a sort order. If you don't use queries as a data source for the reports, you need to establish and activate the necessary indexes to support the reports.

Add the Menus and Any Needed Procedures

You can use FoxPro's Menu Builder to design a main menu for the application. With this done, you are left with what is likely to be the most challenging step in the entire process. You must examine all the nuances of the code which underlies the other application, and where necessary, duplicate the functionality of that code in FoxPro. In some cases, you must look at doing things differently. For example, any database application must provide a way to delete records from a table. But FoxPro, being XBase-compatible, uses the two-step method of delete the record, then pack the table. If you are duplicating an application that was originally written in a DOS version of Borland's Paradox, for example, you would need to decide how to handle this difference in how the two products handle deleted records.

Finally, a Word on Aesthetics...

If you are duplicating the functionality of a character-based application, remember that there is such a thing as bringing too much of a character-based application into the Windows environment. Windows uses a graphical environment that makes some things you would do under DOS unnecessary. Many aspects of DOS-based applications come across as being in poor design taste when copied under Windows. An ideal transfer from a DOS-based application to FoxPro for Windows provides users with an equal or enhanced ability to produce desired results, while taking full advantage of the user interface. If you can use the enhancements present under Windows and in FoxPro for Windows to make the process easier for the users of the application, then you have gained something in porting the application over to FoxPro.

Chapter Summary

This chapter examined the techniques you'll need to move FoxPro applications across platforms, and to bring XBase and non-XBase applications into FoxPro. If you are faced with maintaining applications compatible with more than one platform, you can use FoxPro's capabilities described in this chapter to maintain applications in Windows, in DOS, in Macintosh, and in Unix, with little or no redevelopment work necessary.

Developing Online Help

30

Any serious developer of a FoxPro application must at some point deal with the issue of providing users with online help. Help screens that are context-sensitive, or attuned to the area of an application that a user is in, have come to be expected by PC users. Given that Windows programs typically offer an extensive series of help screens, users of an application running under FoxPro for Windows are likely to expect the same. As the developer, it's up to you to provide custom help in your applications.

Before moving on to the actual process of implementing your help screens, you should effectively plan the design of the help screens. In doing so, you must consider what the help screens are intended to do. The help screens that are built into major Windows applications (like FoxPro and Windows itself) can provide an excellent example of how professional online help should be designed. When you build custom database applications, there are unique aspects to each of your screens, and these must be explained to the user who requests help when those screens are in use. Virtually any custom database application will contain some common general areas: selecting the desired tables, adding new records, editing existing records, deleting unwanted records, selecting groups of records for a report, printing reports, and so on. These general areas can be identified, and help text written explaining each of the specific areas. Once the help text for all the important areas has been written, it can be tied to the specific topics using the techniques outlined in this chapter.

How FoxPro Provides Help

FoxPro for Windows offers unique possibilities when it comes to providing online help. The original implementation of FoxPro (FoxPro for DOS 1.0) stored its online help in the memo fields of a table called FOXHELP.DBF. To provide the context-sensitive aspect of help, FoxPro would search the help table for a record matching the requested topic, and display the contents of the record's memo field. Besides being efficient in terms of design, this method of providing help offered another major advantage: it left FoxPro's internal help system open to customization by developers. FoxPro's originators wisely added two unique commands to FoxPro's implementation of the XBase language: SET HELP TO, and SET TOPIC TO. The SET HELP TO command lets you change the help table for FoxPro-style help from the default (FOXHELP.DBF) to any table that you specify. The SET TOPIC TO command can be used throughout an application to determine which record in the help file is used to display a message when the Help key (F1) is pressed. Note that these commands work with FoxPro-style help, which is one of two ways FoxPro for Windows can supply online help. Because FoxPro for Windows is a Windows application, it makes use of Windows-style help screens by default. However, you can use the previously mentioned commands to make use of FoxPro-style help, which can be readily customized.

NOTE

During the installation process, FoxPro provides a custom installation setup, and one option during the custom setup portion of the installation lets you turn off the normal installation of FoxPro-style help. If you turned off this option during installation, you will not find FOXHELP.DBF or its associated memo files on your system.

With FoxPro for Windows, making use of FoxPro's internal help system is just one of two ways of providing online help to an application. The second way is to create true Windows-style help by creating a help executable with the Windows Help compiler. This second method is far more complex than the first, and requires the use of tools (like an editor and the Windows Help compiler) which are not provided with FoxPro. For that reason, this chapter shows how to implement online help using FoxPro-style help. The end of this chapter provides an overview of the steps involved in implementing online help using the Windows Help compiler.

Since FoxPro-style help is stored in a table (named FOXHELP.DBF) with a corresponding memo field file (FOXHELP.FPT), you can choose to use it and append it to the file, adding your own records. You can also create another table and tell FoxPro to use it as a source of the help data. (FoxPro doesn't make use of any index files with the help table.) The structure of FoxPro's default help file, FOXHELP.DBF, is shown in Table 30.1.

Table 30.1. The structure of FoxPro's Help file.

Fieldname	Type	Purpose
TOPIC	character	Contains the topic that appears in the scrolling help window
DETAILS	memo	The memo field which contains the help text
CLASS	character	A class of help topic that the particular help topic falls into

You can examine the contents of the help file by first turning off FoxPro's access to it with a SET HELP TO command with no table name specified, and entering USE FOXHELP followed by BROWSE. For example, if you now enter the following commands in the Command Window:

```
SET HELP OFF
USE FOXHELP
BROWSE
```

you see the contents of FoxPro's own help file. (See Figure 30.1.)

FIGURE 30.1

The contents of the Help file.

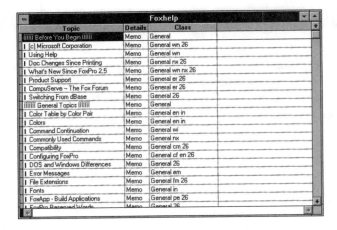

Since the Help file is a FoxPro table, you can modify it just as you would modify any other FoxPro table. You can add, edit, and delete data at will. (If you are going to make major changes to FOXHELP.DBF, it may be a wise idea to make a backup copy of the .DBF and the associated .FPT file. That way, if you ever want to restore the online help to its original configuration, you won't need to completely reinstall FoxPro to do so.)

By default, FoxPro assumes FOXHELP.DBF as the help file, and it opens this table upon start up in a special work area. If you want to examine or modify the help file, you must first enter a SET HELP OFF command before you open the file with a USE FOXHELP statement.

Specifying Your Own Online Help

To implement your own help that's completely separate from FoxPro's, first create a table (giving it any name other than FOXHELP.DBF). The table must contain at least two fields. The first field must be a character field. You can name the field whatever you like. The second field must be a memo field. Again, you can name this field whatever you like. The first field contains your help topics, while the second contains the text that appears in the Help window while the application is running.

To activate the custom help file in your application, you need two commands such as these near the start of the application:

```
SET HELP TO myhelp
ON KEY = 315 HELP
```

where *myhelp* is the name of your custom help file. The second statement tells FoxPro to launch the help system when the help key (F1) is pressed; this is needed because FoxPro normally disables the help system when a program runs.

With these statements in your application, pressing F1 causes the contents of your custom help file to be accessible in a FoxPro-style help window. However, if you want to add context-sensitive capability to your help system, you need to complete one more task. You need to add SET TOPIC TO topic name statements throughout your application, so that FoxPro knows which help topic to display at any point when F1 is pressed. For instance, you might create a record in your custom help table with an entry of "Add a Buyer" in the first field, and with corresponding text explaining the topic in the second field of the table. At an appropriate place in the application (such as just prior to opening a screen to add records to the Buyers table), you could include a statement such as this:

```
SET TOPIC TO "Add a Buyer"
```

and if the F1 key was pressed at any time after the SET TOPIC TO statement was executed, the Help window would show the help topic corresponding to the Add a Buyers entry. For example, Figure 30.2 shows a custom help window created using these techniques.

FIGURE 30.2.

A custom help window.

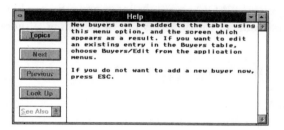

When you implement a custom help system in this manner, FoxPro searches the named help file using the equivalent of a LOCATE command for the specified help topic. If FoxPro can't find a topic in the help file that matches the one named by the last SET TOPIC TO statement, FoxPro displays the table of contents for the help file. The table of contents lists the contents of the first field for every record in the help file. It's important to remember this fact when designing the entries in your help table—it is better to use clear topic names that are understandable when viewed through the table of contents by a user.

Implementing Windows-Style Help

If you want to provide true Windows-style help, you'll need to take an entirely different route than the one described so far throughout this chapter (and one that requires considerably more effort). True Windows-style help is provided with the Windows Help

Engine, which is an integral part of Windows. To create help files that are compatible with the Windows Help Engine, you need a word processor that can save files in Rich Text Format (also known as RTF files), such as any version of Word for Windows. You also need the Microsoft Help Compiler (HC31.EXE), which converts rich text format files to a file format that's readable by the Windows Help Engine. The Microsoft Help Compiler is not provided with FoxPro, but you can purchase it directly from Microsoft, and it is provided as part of the Windows Software Development Kit (SDK), as well as with Microsoft's Visual Basic Professional. You can find complete details on creating the help files in the documentation that accompanies the Microsoft Help Compiler. If faced with a significant amount of development of help files under Windows, you may also want to seriously consider a commercial help authoring tool. While your RTF-compatible word processor and the Microsoft Help Compiler are technically all that is needed, this combination is not the easiest way to write help systems. The help files you create must follow a very specific format, and this means a great deal of word processing work on your part. Commercial help authoring systems can save you a significant amount of work by automating many of the text formatting tasks (like adding footnotes and assigning the needed Help context strings to the file). One popular help authoring system is RoboHelp, produced by Blue Sky Software of San Diego, CA. Also, if you use Word for Windows and Visual Basic, you can use a Word for Windows template that's provided with Visual Basic (called VBHELP.DOT). While not as powerful as a help authoring system, the template does take some of the drudgery out of designing Windows-style help.

Chapter Summary

This chapter provided a look at the techniques you can use to implement help in your FoxPro applications. The effort behind developing effective help can pay off handsomely, as support calls can be significantly reduced. Keep in mind too, that online help is no substitute for printed documentation. Providing your users with both is a necessity when developing professional applications.

6

PART

Reference

Command Reference

31

This chapter contains a reference for all FoxPro commands. Each command name that appears is followed by the syntax for the command and a description of how the command is used. Due to space limitations, the use for every syntax option is not detailed in this chapter. The syntaxes that are provided assume a familiarity with FoxPro command usage and programming. Where deemed appropriate, explanations of syntax options are provided for the more commonly used commands. For specific details on the options of each syntax, refer to the Command and Function reference provided by the FoxPro documentation.

Some options for certain commands are so common throughout FoxPro's command set that they are defined here, as follows:

[NOOPTIMIZE]: Where used, this option disables FoxPro's use of Rushmore, its internal technology for speeding searches and data retrievals.
[IN SCREEN]: Where used, this option forces the display of data to the main FoxPro window (or to the screen when under FoxPro for DOS).
[IN WINDOW *windowname*]: Where used, this option forces the display of data to a user-defined window identified by *windowname*.
[COLOR *standard/enhanced*] and [COLOR SCHEME *expN*]: These options let you define colors of objects (such as Browse and Edit windows) under FoxPro. The *standard/enhanced* expression refers to a color pair (such as R/B meaning red/blue), and a color scheme is a predefined set of 10 color pairs.
[TO PRINT] and [TO FILE]: Where used, the TO PRINT option causes output of a command to be directed to the default printer. Where TO FILE is used, the output of a command is stored in a disk file.

\ (or) \ \

Syntax

```
\ <<text line>>
\ \ <<text line>>
```

The \ and \\ commands are used to output a line of text to the current text merge output file (specified with the SET TEXTMERGE command), and to the active window. The \ command precedes the output with a carriage return and linefeed, while the \\ command does not.

? or ??

Syntax

```
?/?? [expression] [PICTURE clause] [FUNCTION functionlist] [AT expN]
```

The ? command sends the characters specified by the *expression* to the printer, without changing the current row or column cursor locations. Control codes can be specified as part of the expression by enclosing them in curly {} braces.

```
???
```

Syntax

```
??? [expC]
```

The ??? command sends the specified characters to the printer, without changing the position of the printhead.

```
@
```

Syntax

```
@ row,col [SAY expression] [PICTURE expression] [FUNCTION list] [GET variable] [PICTURE
expression] [FUNCTION list] [RANGE] [VALID condition] [ERROR expC] [COLOR standard/
enhanced] [COLOR SCHEME expN]
```

The @ command draws a single or double line or box between the specified coordinates. If the coordinates share the same horizontal and vertical planes, a horizontal or vertical line is drawn. Clear erases characters below and to the right of the coordinates.

```
@...BOX
```

Syntax

```
@ row1,col1,row2,col2 BOX expC
```

This command draws a box in the main FoxPro window or in a window defined by the user. Note that boxes can be easily drawn with FoxPro's Screen Builder.

```
@...CLEAR TO
```

Syntax

```
@ row,col CLEAR/CLEAR TO row,col
```

This variation of the @ command clears part of the main window or a window previously defined by the user.

@...EDIT

Syntax

@ *row, column* EDIT *memvar* ¦ field SIZE *expN1, expN2*[,*expN3*] [FUNCTION *expC1*] [FONT *expC2*[, *expN4*]] [STYLE *expC3*] [DEFAULT expr] [ENABLE ¦ DISABLE] [MESSAGE *expC4*] [VALID *expL1* ¦ *expN5* [ERROR *expC5*]] [WHEN *expL2*] [NOMODIFY] [SCROLL] [TAB] [COLOR SCHEME *expN6* ¦ COLOR *color-pair list*]

The @...EDIT command is used to create an editing region. Editing regions are typically used to edit the contents of memo fields. Note that edit regions can be easily created with FoxPro's Screen Builder.

@...FILL TO

Syntax

@ row1,col1 FILL TO row2,col2 [COLOR *standard/enhanced*] [COLOR SCHEME *expN*]

Under FoxPro for DOS, the ...FILL command changes the screen colors within the defined area. If the COLOR option is omitted, FoxPro clears the screen within the defined area.

@...GET TO Make Check Boxes

Syntax

@ row,col GET variable FUNCTION *expC1*/PICTURE *expC2* [DEFAULT expr] [FONT *expC3*] [STYLE *expC4*] [SIZE *expN1, expN2*] [ENABLE/DISABLE] [MESSAGE *expC5*] [OPEN WINDOW window name] [RANGE] [VALID *expL1*] [ERROR *expC6*] [WHEN *expL2*] [COLOR SCHEME *expN3*/COLOR *color-pair list*]

This variation of the @...GET command enables the creation of check boxes or picture check boxes. Note that check boxes can be easily created with FoxPro's Screen Builder.

@...GET TO Make Invisible Buttons

Syntax

@ row,col GET variable FUNCTION *expC1*/PICTURE *expC2* [DEFAULT expr] [FONT *expC3*] [STYLE *expC4*] [SIZE *expN1, expN2*] [ENABLE/DISABLE] [MESSAGE *expC5*] [VALID *expL1*] [ERROR *expC6*] [WHEN *expL2*] [COLOR SCHEME *expN3*/COLOR *color-pair list*]

This variation of the @...GET command is used to create invisible buttons, which are regions of the main window or a previously defined window that can be selected. Note that invisible buttons can be easily created with FoxPro's Screen Builder.

```
@...GET TO Make List Boxes
```

Syntax

```
@ row,col GET variable FROM array[RANGE expN1[, expN2]] /POPUP popupname [FUNCTION
expC1]/[PICTURE expC2] [FONT expC3[,expN3]] [STYLE expC4] [DEFAULT expr] [SIZE expN2,
expN3] [ENABLE/DISABLE] [MESSAGE expC5] [OPEN WINDOW window name] [RANGE] [VALID expL1]
[WHEN expL2] [ERROR expC6] [COLOR SCHEME expN5/COLOR color-pair list]
```

This variation of the @...GET command is used to create list boxes from which one can choose options by double-clicking on them. Note that list boxes can be easily created with FoxPro's Screen Builder.

```
@...GET TO Make Popups
```

Syntax

```
@ row,col GET variable [FUNCTION expC1]/[PICTURE expC2] [FONT expC3[,expN3]] [STYLE
expC4] [DEFAULT expr] FROM array [RANGE expN1[, expN2]] [SIZE expN3, expN4] [ENABLE/
DISABLE] [MESSAGE expC5]  [OPEN WINDOW window name] [VALID expL1] [WHEN expL2] [COLOR
SCHEME expN5/COLOR color-pair list]
```

This variation of the @...GET command is used to create popups. Note that popups can be easily created with FoxPro's Screen Builder.

```
@...GET TO Make Pushbuttons
```

Syntax

```
@ row,col GET variable [FUNCTION expC1]/[PICTURE expC2] [FONT expC3[,expN3]] [STYLE
expC4][DEFAULT expr] [SIZE expN1, expN2[, expN3]] [ENABLE/DISABLE] [MESSAGE expC5]
[VALID expL1] [WHEN expL2] [COLOR SCHEME expN4/COLOR color-pair list]
```

This variation of the @...GET command is used to create a set of picture push buttons. Note that push buttons can be easily created with FoxPro's Screen Builder.

@...GET TO Make Radio Buttons

Syntax

@ row,col GET variable [FUNCTION *expC1*]/[PICTURE *expC2*] [FONT *expC3*[,*expN3*]] [STYLE *expC4*] [DEFAULT expr] [SIZE *expN1*, *expN2*[, *expN3*]] [ENABLE/DISABLE] [MESSAGE *expC5*] [VALID *expL1*] [WHEN *expL2*] [COLOR SCHEME *expN4*/COLOR *color-pair list*]

This variation of the @...GET command is used to create picture radio buttons. Note that radio buttons can be easily created with FoxPro's Screen Builder.

@...GET TO Make Spinners

Syntax

@ *row, column* GET *memvar* ¦ field SPINNER *expN1*[, *expN2*[, *expN3*]] [FUNCTION *expC1*] [PICTURE *expC2*] [FONT *expC3*[, *expN4*]] [STYLE *expC4*] [DEFAULT *expN5*] [SIZE *expN6*, *expN7*] [ENABLE ¦ DISABLE] [MESSAGE *expC5*] [RANGE [*expN8*] [, *expN9*]] [VALID *expL1* ¦ *expN10* [ERROR *expC6*]] [WHEN *expL2* [COLOR SCHEME *expN11* ¦ COLOR *color-pair list*]

This variation of the @...GET command is used to create spinners. Note that spinners can be easily created with FoxPro's Screen Builder.

@...MENU

Syntax

@ row,col MENU *array*, *expN1*[, *expN2*] [TITLE *expC*] [SHADOW]

This command is used to create a menu popup. Note that menus can be easily created with FoxPro's Menu Builder.

@...PROMPT

Syntax

@ row,col PROMPT *expC* [MESSAGE *expC*]

This command, along with the MENU TO command, is used to create light-bar menus. (These commands for menu design are compatible with FoxBASE+ and Clipper. For compatibility with dBASE IV , use the DEFINE POPUP and DEFINE BAR commands instead.) Note that menus can be easily created with FoxPro's Menu Builder.

@...SAY

Syntax

@ *row, column* SAY expr [FUNCTION *expC1*] [PICTURE *expC2*] [SIZE *expN1, expN2*] [FONT *expC3*[, expN3*]] [STYLE *expC4*] [COLOR SCHEME *expN4* ¦ COLOR *color-pair list*]

This command displays the contents of the expression at the defined location in the active window (the main FoxPro window if no user-defined window is active).

@...SAY (with Bitmaps)

Syntax

@ *row, column* SAY file BIT MAP ¦ *general field* [STYLE *expC1*] [CENTER] [ISOMETRIC ¦ STRETCH] [SIZE *expN1, expN2*] [NOWAIT]

This variation of the @...SAY command is used to display the contents of a general field or a bit map stored as a .BMP file on the screen or in the active window.

@...TO

Syntax

@ row,col TO row,col [DOUBLE/PANEL/*border string*] [COLOR *standard* [,*enhanced*]] [PATTERN *expN1*] [PEN *expN2*[, expN3*]] [STYLE *expC*][COLOR SCHEME *expN4*]

This variation of the @ command creates a line or a rectangle, using the specified coordinates. Note that lines and boxes can be easily created with FoxPro's Screen Builder.

ACCEPT

Syntax

ACCEPT [*expC*] TO *memvar*

The ACCEPT command displays a prompt and stores a character string as a prompt. The value provided in response to ACCEPT will be stored as a character variable.

ACTIVATE MENU

Syntax

ACTIVATE MENU *menuname* [PAD *padname*] [NOWAIT]

The ACTIVATE MENU command activates a predefined menu and displays the menu on the screen. If PAD is specified, the highlight appears at the named pad; otherwise, the first pad in the menu is highlighted.

ACTIVATE POPUP

Syntax

ACTIVATE POPUP *popupname* [AT *row, column*] [BAR *expN*] [NOWAIT] [REST]

The ACTIVATE POPUP command activates a predefined popup menu and displays that popup menu on the screen.

ACTIVATE SCREEN

Syntax

ACTIVATE SCREEN

The ACTIVATE SCREEN command provides a full-screen display of the contents of a predefined window.

ACTIVATE WINDOW

Syntax

ACTIVATE WINDOW *windowname list*/ALL [BOTTOM/TOP/SAME] [NOSHOW] [IN WINDOW *windowname*/IN SCREEN]

The ACTIVATE WINDOW command activates a window (the window must have been previously defined in memory). After the ACTIVATE WINDOW command is executed, all screen output appears in the window. If the ALL clause is used, all windows currently defined in memory are displayed in the order in which they were defined.

APPEND

Syntax

APPEND [BLANK]

The APPEND command adds a record to the end of a table and opens an Edit window into the new record. If you include the BLANK option with APPEND, it adds a blank record to the end of the table, and FoxPro does not open an Edit window.

APPEND FROM

Syntax

APPEND FROM *filename* [FIELDS *fieldlist*] [FOR *condition*] [TYPE *filetype*] [DELIMITED [WITH *delimiter*/BLANK/TAB]]

The APPEND FROM command copies records from the table identified by *filename,* and adds them to the active table. Use the FOR/WHILE clause to specify a condition that must be met before any records are copied. When the file is a foreign file, an acceptable TYPE must be specified.

APPEND FROM ARRAY

Syntax

APPEND FROM ARRAY *array* FOR *condition* [FIELDS *fieldlist* ¦ FIELDS LIKE *skeleton* ¦ FIELDS EXCEPT *skeleton*]

The APPEND FROM ARRAY command appends records to a table from a named array. (APPEND FROM ARRAY is compatible with dBASE IV; if you want compatibility with FoxBASE+, use the GATHER FROM command instead.)

APPEND GENERAL

Syntax

APPEND GENERAL *general field* FROM file [LINK] [CLASS ole class]

The APPEND GENERAL command imports an OLE object from a file and inserts it into a general field. If LINK is included, an OLE link is created; otherwise, the object is embedded. Include the CLASS option to specify a class other than the default OLE class.

APPEND MEMO

Syntax

APPEND MEMO *memofield* FROM *filename* [OVERWRITE]

The APPEND MEMO command reads a text file into a memo field. The contents of the file are added to the end of any existing text in the memo field. If the OVERWRITE option is used, the contents of the file overwrite existing text in the memo field. The file should have an extension of .TXT, or the extension must be specified along with the filename.

ASSIST

Syntax

ASSIST

The ASSIST command causes the FoxPro Catalog Manager to appear.

AVERAGE

Syntax

AVERAGE *fieldlist* [*scope*] [FOR *condition*] [WHILE *condition*] [TO *memvarlist*/TO ARRAY *array*] [NOOPTIMIZE]

The AVERAGE command averages expressions involving numeric fields. If the TO option is used, the results are stored to the memory variables specified in the variable list. If the TO ARRAY option is used, the results are stored in the named array.

BLANK

Syntax

BLANK [FIELDS *fieldlist*] [*scope*] [FOR *expL1*] [WHILE *expL2*] [NOOPTIMIZE]

The BLANK command clears the contents of a record.

BROWSE

Syntax

BROWSE [FIELDS *fieldlist*] [FONT *expC1*[, *expN1*]] [STYLE *expC2*] [FOR *expL1*] [FORMAT]

```
[FREEZE field] [KEY expr1[, expr2]] [LAST ¦ NOINIT] [LEDIT] [REDIT] [LOCK expN2]
[LPARTITION] [NOAPPEND] [NOCLEAR] [NODELETE] [NOEDIT ¦ NOMODIFY] [NOLGRID] [NORGRID]
[NOLINK] [NOMENU] [NOOPTIMIZE] [NOREFRESH] [NORMAL] [NOWAIT] [PARTITION expN3]
[PREFERENCE expC3] [REST] [SAVE] [TIMEOUT expN4] [TITLE expC4] [VALID [:F] expL2 [ERROR
expC5]] [WHEN expL3] [WIDTH expN5] [[WINDOW window name1] [IN [WINDOW] window name2 ¦ IN
SCREEN]] [COLOR SCHEME expN6 ¦ COLOR color-pair list]
```

The BROWSE command provides the full-screen editing capability of a table. If no fields are specified, BROWSE displays all fields. The LOCK option locks a specified number of columns at the left side of the screen, while remaining columns are allowed to pan. FREEZE allows editing of only the named field. NOINIT forces BROWSE to use the settings in effect at the last use of BROWSE. NOFOLLOW can reposition the record pointer after a field's content is altered. NOMENU makes the Menu Bar inaccessible. WIDTH limits the characters displayed in the fields. With NOAPPEND, records can't be added to the current file using BROWSE. NODELETE prevents deletions while in Browse. NOCLEAR leaves the BROWSE display on the screen after the Browse mode is exited. NOEDIT prevents edits to records. FORMAT causes BROWSE to use any picture or function settings in effect due to an active format file. WINDOW causes the display to appear within a specified window.

The syntax for the FIELDS clause, where used with the BROWSE command, is shown here:

```
BROWSE FIELDS fieldname1 [/R] [/expN1] [/V = expr1 [:E = expC1] [:F]]
[:B = expr2, expr3] [:W = expL1] [, fieldname2] [/R]...
```

The optional switches perform the following tasks:

> **/R:** Specifies field as a read-only field; no changes will be allowed in that field.
> **/expN1:** Specifies the width of a field in the Browse window. Just the width of the column is changed while in the Browse display. This does not change the actual size of the field in the table.
> **/V:** This option lets you perform data validation within a Browse window. The contents of the field are compared to expr1, which can be a numeric or a logical expression.
> **/F:** This controls how validation is performed. If this option is included along with the /V option, the comparison is made whether the field contents are modified or not. If this option is omitted, comparisons caused by the /V option are made only when the contents of the field are changed.
> **/E:** Normally, if the validation expression (expr1) evaluates to true, a normal exit from the field is permitted. If the expression evaluates to false, an exit is not permitted, and an error message Invalid Input appears. Including the :E option causes the contents of the expression expr1 to be displayed instead of the Invalid Input error message, and the bell sounds (if SET BELL is ON).

/**B = Expr2,:** Use this option to specify a range, or a set of limits between which the data entered in the field must fall. Expr2 specifies the lower limit, and expr3 specifies the upper limit.

/**W = Expl1:** This option prohibits entry into a field, depending on the value of the logical expression *expL1*. The :W option causes the expression to be evaluated when the BROWSE command is executed. If the expression evaluates to a logical false, data entry into the named field is prohibited.

BUILD APP

Syntax

```
BUILD APP app file FROM project file
```

The BUILD APP command creates an application file with the .APP file extension. The BUILD APP command is used to convert data stored in a project file (extension .PJX) into an application (extension .APP).

BUILD EXE

Syntax

```
BUILD EXE .exe filename FROM project [STANDALONE] [EXTENDED]
```

The BUILD EXE command (available only to users of FoxPro Professional) is used to build an executable (.EXE) file.

BUILD PROJECT

Syntax

```
BUILD PROJECT project file FROM program/menu/report/label/screen/library
```

The BUILD PROJECT command builds a project file with the .PJX file extension. This is done by the opening and processing of several program, menu, report, label, screen, and library files that are specified.

CALCULATE

Syntax

```
CALCULATE [scope] options [FOR condition] [WHILE condition] [TO memvarlist/TO ARRAY
```

array] [NOOPTIMIZE]

The CALCULATE command uses standard financial and statistical functions to calculate amounts. The functions are defined as part of the options list. All records are processed until the condition is no longer true, or until the scope is completed.

CALL

Syntax

CALL *modulename* [WITH *expC/memvar*] [SAVE/NOSAVE]

The CALL command executes a binary file placed in memory by LOAD. The routine must first be loaded into memory with the LOAD command (see LOAD). The WITH option is used to pass a parameter to the binary routine. The SAVE option, when used, causes any changes to the video caused by the binary routine to be saved to memory, and the video is restored when the routine completes. If NOSAVE is used (or the option is omitted), FoxPro ignores any changes made to the video display by the routine.

CANCEL

Syntax

CANCEL

The CANCEL command cancels execution of a program, returning program control to the Command Window.

CHANGE

Syntax

CHANGE

[FIELDS *fieldlist*] [*scope*] [FOR *expL1*] [WHILE *expL2*] [FONT *expC1*[, *expN1*]] [STYLE *expC2*]
[FREEZE field name] [KEY expr1[, expr2]] [LAST] [LEDIT] [REDIT] [LPARTITION] [NOAPPEND]
[NOCLEAR] [NODELETE] [NOEDIT ¦ NOMODIFY] [NOLINK] [NOMENU] [NOOPTIMIZE] [NORMAL]
[NOWAIT] [PARTITION *expN2*] [PREFERENCE *expC3*] [REST] [SAVE] [TIMEOUT *expN3*] [TITLE
expC4] [VALID [:F] *expL3* [ERROR *expC5*]] [WHEN *expL4*] [WIDTH *expN4*] [[WINDOW *window
name1*] [IN [WINDOW] *window name2* ¦ IN SCREEN]] [COLOR SCHEME *expN5* ¦ COLOR *color-pair
list*]

The CHANGE command allows full-screen editing of a record in the table. The CHANGE command allows the selection of specific fields for editing. If a list of fields is provided, only those fields can be edited. If no list is provided, all fields are available for editing. Note that the CHANGE command is functionally equivalent to the EDIT command. For more specifics on the options, see EDIT.

CLEAR

Syntax

CLEAR

The CLEAR command erases the active window, or the main FoxPro window if no user-defined window has been specified.

CLEAR ALL

Syntax

CLEAR ALL

The CLEAR ALL command closes all open table, memo, index, and format files, and resets the current work area to the default of work area 1.

CLEAR FIELDS

Syntax

CLEAR FIELDS

The CLEAR FIELDS command cancels a fields list previously chosen with the SET FIELDS command.

CLEAR GETS

Syntax

CLEAR GETS

The CLEAR GETS command clears current variables provided by GET from a READ access.

CLEAR MACROS

Syntax

CLEAR MACROS

The CLEAR MACROS command clears all keyboard macros from memory.

CLEAR MEMORY

Syntax

CLEAR MEMORY

The CLEAR MEMORY command clears all current memory variables from memory. If any array elements are in memory, they are also cleared by CLEAR MEMORY. Note that the CLEAR MEMORY and RELEASE ALL commands have different effects from within FoxPro programs. CLEAR MEMORY clears all existing memory variables, while RELEASE ALL clears only private memory variables or those variables local to the subroutine where RELEASE ALL was used.

CLEAR MENUS

Syntax

CLEAR MENUS

The CLEAR MENUS command clears all menus from the screen and erases all menus from memory.

CLEAR POPUPS

Syntax

CLEAR POPUPS

The CLEAR POPUPS command clears all popup menus from the screen and erases all popup menus from memory.

CLEAR PROGRAM

Syntax

CLEAR PROGRAM

The CLEAR PROGRAM command clears the program buffer.

CLEAR PROMPT

Syntax

CLEAR PROMPT

The CLEAR PROMPT command clears from the active window all menu prompts created with the @...PROMPT command.

CLEAR READ

Syntax

CLEAR READ [ALL]

The CLEAR READ command exits the active READ. Program control is returned to the previous READ level, if the READ is nested.

CLEAR TYPEAHEAD

Syntax

CLEAR TYPEAHEAD

The CLEAR TYPEAHEAD command empties the typehead buffer. (See SET TYPEAHEAD.)

CLEAR WINDOWS

Syntax

CLEAR WINDOWS

The CLEAR WINDOWS command removes all user-defined windows from memory. The CLEAR WINDOWS command also clears all active windows from the screen and removes all windows from memory.

```
CLOSE
```

Syntax

```
CLOSE filetype/ALL
```

The CLOSE command closes all file types listed as *filetype*. Filetype can be ALTERNATE, DATABASES, FORMAT, INDEX, or PROCEDURE. If the ALL option is used, all open files are closed.

```
CLOSE MEMO
```

Syntax

```
CLOSE MEMO memofield1[, memofield2...]/ALL
```

The CLOSE MEMO command is used to close any open memo editing windows.

```
COMPILE
```

Syntax

```
COMPILE filename/skeleton [ENCRYPT] [NODEBUG]
```

The COMPILE command loads a FoxPro command (.PRG) file and creates a FoxPro object (.DBO) file. The ENCRYPT option encrypts the compiled file, making it unreadable by any utilities. The NODEBUG option strips the characters which would otherwise be used by FoxPro's Debugger when debugging programs.

```
CONTINUE
```

The CONTINUE command continues a search begun by LOCATE. It finds the next record that meets the specific condition outlined with the LOCATE command.

```
COPY
```

Syntax

```
COPY TO filename [scope] [FIELDS fieldlist] [FOR condition] [WHILE condition] [[WITH]
CDX ¦ PRODUCTION] [NOOPTIMIZE] [TYPE] [FOXPLUS/DIF/MOD/SDF/SYLK/WK1/WKS/WR1/WRK/XLS/
DELIMITED [WITH delimiter/WITH BLANK/WITH TAB]]
```

The COPY command is used to copy data from a table to another table, or to a foreign file.

COPY FILE

Syntax

COPY FILE *sourcefile* TO *destinationfile*

The COPY FILE command creates a copy of any type of file.

COPY INDEXES

Syntax

COPY INDEXES *indexfile list*/ALL [TO .CDX*filename*]

The COPY INDEXES command converts .IDX-style index files to index tags in a .CDX (compound index) file. If the TO clause is specified, the .IDX files are added as tags to the .CDX file named in the TO clause. If the TO clause is omitted, the .IDX files are added as tags to the production .CDX file.

COPY MEMO

Syntax

COPY MEMO *memofield*name TO *filename* [ADDITIVE]

The COPY MEMO command copies the contents of a memo field to a text file. Drive and path identifiers are optional in the filename. If the ADDITIVE clause is used, the text of the memo field is added to the end of an existing filename. If the ADDITIVE clause is omitted, any existing file with the same name is overwritten.

COPY STRUCTURE

Syntax

COPY STRUCTURE TO filename [FIELDS *fieldlist* ¦ FIELDS LIKE *skeleton* ¦ FIELDS EXCEPT *skeleton*] [[WITH] CDX ¦ [WITH] PRODUCTION]

The COPY STRUCTURE command is used to copy the structure of the current table to a new table.

```
COPY STRUCTURE EXTENDED
```

Syntax

```
COPY TO filename STRUCTURE EXTENDED [FIELDS fieldlist ¦ FIELDS LIKE skeleton ¦ FIELDS
EXCEPT skeleton]
```

The COPY STRUCTURE EXTENDED command creates a table that contains four fields and is a structural representation of the table in use when the COPY STRUCTURE EXTENDED command was entered. The file created with the COPY STRUCTURE EXTENDED command contains five fields: FIELD_NAME, FIELD_LEN, FIELD_DEC, AND FIELD_TYPE, and one record corresponding to each field in the original table.

```
COPY TAG
```

Syntax

```
COPY TAG tagname [OF .CDX filename] TO indexfile
```

The COPY TAG command converts the tag information in a .CDX (compound index) file to a FoxBase-style (.IDX) index file. If the To Clause is omitted, the .IDX file is given the same name as the active .CDX file.

```
COPY TO ARRAY
```

Syntax

```
COPY TO ARRAY array [FIELDS fieldlist] [scope] [FOR condition] [WHILE condition]
[NOOPTIMIZE]
```

The COPY TO ARRAY command copies data from the fields of the active table into an array. For each record in the table, the first field is stored in the first column for the array, the second field in the second column, and so on. If the table has more fields than the array has columns, the contents of extra fields are ignored. If the array has more columns than the table has fields, the extra columns in the array are unchanged. Memo fields are not added to the array.

COUNT

Syntax

COUNT [*scope*] [FOR *condition*] [WHILE *condition*] [TO *memvar*] [NOOPTIMIZE]

The COUNT command totals the number of records that meet a specific condition or totals all records if condition and scope options are not used. If the TO option is used, the resultant total is stored as the specified memory variable.

CREATE

Syntax

CREATE *filename* / [?]

The CREATE command is used to create a new table. When the command is entered, the Table Structure window appears, and you can define the table's structure (field names, types, lengths, and number of decimal places). If the question mark is substituted for a filename, the Save As dialog box initially appears, where you can enter a name.

CREATE COLOR SET

Syntax

CREATE COLOR SET color set name

The CREATE COLOR SET command is used to create a color set from the current color settings.

CREATE CURSOR

Syntax

CREATE CURSOR tablename (fname1 type [(precision[, scale]) [, fname2 ...]]) ¦ FROM ARRAY *arrayname*

The CREATE CURSOR command is a SQL command, which creates a temporary table called a "cursor."

CREATE FROM

Syntax

CREATE *file1* FROM *file2*

The CREATE FROM command is used to create a table having a structure based on the contents of a file created earlier with the COPY STRUCTURE EXTENDED command.

CREATE LABEL

Syntax

CREATE LABEL [*filename*] [IN WINDOW *windowname*/IN SCREEN] [NOWAIT] [SAVE]

The CREATE LABEL command creates a label form used for generating labels.

CREATE MENU

Syntax

CREATE MENU [*filename*/?] [WINDOW *windowname*1] [IN [WINDOW] *windowname*2/IN SCREEN]
[NOWAIT] [SAVE]

The CREATE MENU command enables the user to create popup menus with the menu builder.

CREATE PROJECT

Syntax

CREATE PROJECT [*filename*/?] [WINDOW *windowname*1] [IN [WINDOW] *windowname*2/IN SCREEN]
[NOWAIT] [SAVE]

The CREATE PROJECT command opens FoxPro's Project window, which can then be used to create a project file.

CREATE QUERY

Syntax

CREATE QUERY [*filename*/?]

The CREATE QUERY command opens the RQBE window which can be used to create a query that limits available records or that links multiple tables.

CREATE REPORT

Syntax

CREATE REPORT [*filename*] [IN WINDOW *windowname*/IN SCREEN] [NOWAIT] [SAVE]

The CREATE REPORT command creates a report form file for generating reports.

CREATE REPORT FROM

Syntax

CREATE REPORT *filename*1/? FROM *filename*2 [FORM/COLUMN] [FIELDS *fieldlist*] [FIELDS LIKE *skeleton* / FIELDS EXCEPT *skeleton*] [ALIAS] [NOOVERWRITE] [WIDTH *expN*]

The CREATE REPORT FROM command enables you to create a quick report directly from the Command Window or under program control.

CREATE SCREEN

Syntax

CREATE SCREEN [*filename*/?] [WINDOW *windowname*1] [IN [WINDOW *windowname*2/IN SCREEN] [NOWAIT] [SAVE]

The CREATE SCREEN command opens a window into FoxPro's Screen Builder, which can then be used to design a screen.

CREATE SCREEN FROM

Syntax

CREATE SCREEN file1 ¦ ? FROM file2 [ROW ¦ COLUMN] [FIELDS *fieldlist* ¦ FIELDS LIKE *skeleton* ¦ FIELDS EXCEPT *skeleton*] [ALIAS] [NOOVERWRITE] [SIZE *expN1*, *expN2*] [SCREEN]

This variation of the CREATE SCREEN command creates a quick screen directly from the Command Window, or under program control.

CREATE TABLE

Syntax

CREATE TABLE ¦ DBF dbf_name (fname1 type [(precision[, scale]) [, fname2 ...]]) ¦ FROM
ARRAY *array*

The CREATE TABLE command is a SQL command which creates a table.

CREATE VIEW [FROM ENVIRONMENT]

Syntax

CREATE VIEW [FROM ENVIRONMENT]

The CREATE VIEW command creates an environment file, containing the names of all open tables, indexes, and relational links. The command performs the same task with or without the FROM ENVIRONMENT clause; the CREATE VIEW command (without the clause) is provided for backwards compatibility with dBASE.

DEACTIVATE MENU

Syntax

DEACTIVATE MENU *menu name1*[, *menu name2* ...] ¦ ALL

The DEACTIVATE MENU command deactivates the active menu and clears the menu from the screen. The menu remains in memory until a RELEASE MENU command is issued, and it can be recalled with ACTIVATE MENU.

DEACTIVATE POPUP

Syntax

DEACTIVATE POPUP *popup name1*[, *popup name2* ...] ¦ ALL

The DEACTIVATE POPUP command deactivates the active popup menu and erases the menu from the screen. The popup menu remains in memory until a RELEASE POPUP command is issued, and it can be recalled to the screen with ACTIVATE POPUP.

DEACTIVATE WINDOW

Syntax

DEACTIVATE WINDOW *windowname1* [,*windowname2...*] / ALL

The DEACTIVATE WINDOW command deactivates the windows named within the window name clause, and clears them from the screen. The windows remain in memory until RELEASE WINDOW is used, and they can be restored to the screen with ACTI-VATE WINDOW. If the ALL option is not used, the last window activated is deactivated. If a window is underlying the last window activated, it becomes the active window. If the ALL option is included, all active windows are deactivated.

DECLARE

Syntax

DECLARE *array1* [*rows, columns*] [*array2*] [*rows, columns*]

The DECLARE command is used for the creation of arrays. The arguments are used to specify the name of the array and the array dimensions (the number of rows and columns).

DEFINE BAR

Syntax

DEFINE BAR linenumber/System option name OF *popupname* PROMPT *expC* [BEFORE *expN*/AFTER *expN*] [KEY *key label*] [MARK *expC*] [MESSAGE *expC*] [SKIP [FOR *expL*]] [COLOR *color-pair list*/COLOR SCHEME *expN*]

The DEFINE BAR command defines a bar option in a popup menu. Line number identifies the line number within the popup menu; line 1 appears on the first line of the popup, line 2 on the second line of the popup, and so on. The text specified with PROMPT appears as text in the bar of the menu. The popup name refers to a popup which must have been previously defined with the DEFINE POPUP command. The MESSAGE option specifies optional text which is displayed in the message line when the specified bar is highlighted. The SKIP option causes the bar to be displayed but not to be selected by the user. The COLOR and COLOR SCHEME options let you define colors for menus.

DEFINE BOX

Syntax

DEFINE BOX FROM *printcolumn1* TO *printcolumn2* HEIGHT *expr*[AT LINE *print line*] [SINGLE/
DOUBLE/*border definition string*]

The DEFINE BOX command defines a box which surrounds text in a report. Use the specified options in the command to mark the leftmost starting column, the rightmost ending column, the starting line for the top of the box, and the height of the box. The border definition string clause is used to specify a character which appears as the box border. The default, if the option is omitted, is a single line. Note that boxes around report elements can be easily created using FoxPro's Report Writer.

DEFINE MENU

Syntax

DEFINE MENU *menuname* [BAR [AT LINE *expN*]] [IN [WINDOW *windowname*/IN SCREEN] [KEY *key
label*] [MARK *expC*] [MESSAGE *expC*] [NOMARGIN] [COLOR *color-pair list*/COLOR SCHEME *expN*]

The DEFINE MENU command enables you to create a horizontal menu bar. Use the BAR clause to create bar-style menus. IN WINDOW denotes a specified window, and IN SCREEN denotes the full screen. Use KEY to assign a specified key to a menu option. MARK denotes the placement of a check mark (for compatibility with FoxPro/DOS only). MESSAGE denotes a message which appears in the Status Bar when the menu is active. The COLOR and COLOR SCHEME options let you define colors for menus. Note that menus can easily be created with FoxPro's Menu Builder.

DEFINE PAD

Syntax

DEFINE PAD *padname* OF *menuname* PROMPT *expC* [AT *row,col*] [BEFORE *padname*/AFTER *padname*]
[KEY *key label* [MARK *expC*] [MESSAGE *expC*] [SKIP [FOR *expL*]] [COLOR *color-pair list*/COLOR
SCHEME *expN*]]

The DEFINE PAD command defines a pad of a bar menu. The text specified with PROMPT is displayed within the menu pad. If the AT row, col clause is omitted, the first pad appears at the far left, and each successive pad appears one space to the right of the previous pad. MARK denotes the placement of a check mark (for compatibility with FoxPro/DOS only). MESSAGE denotes a message which appears in the Status Bar when the menu is active. The COLOR and COLOR SCHEME options let you define colors for menu pads. Note that menus can easily be created with FoxPro's Menu Builder.

```
DEFINE POPUP
```

Syntax

```
DEFINE POPUP popupname [FROM row1,col1 [TO row2,col2] [IN [WINDOW windowname/IN SCREEN]
[FOOTER expC] [KEY key label] [MARGIN] [MARK expC] [MESSAGE expC] [MOVER] [MULTISELECT]
[PROMPT FIELD field/PROMPT FILES [LIKE skeleton]/PROMPT STRUCTURE] [RELATIVE] [SCROLL]
[SHADOW] [TITLE expC] [COLOR color-pair list/COLOR SCHEME expN]
```

Use the DEFINE POPUP command to define a popup menu. Use the FROM and TO row and column coordinates to define the upper-left and lower-right corners of the popup menu. If the TO coordinate is omitted FoxPro sizes the menu as needed to contain the prompts. The PROMPT FIELD, PROMPT FILE, and PROMPT STRUCTURE clauses are optional. These are used to display selection lists of the contents of table fields, list of filenames, or lists of fieldnames from a table structure. The COLOR and COLOR SCHEME options let you define colors for menu popups. Note that menus can easily be created with FoxPro's Menu Builder.

```
DEFINE WINDOW
```

Syntax

```
DEFINE WINDOW windowname FROM row1,col1 TO row2,col2 AT row3, column3 SIZE row4, column4
[IN [WINDOW] window name2 ¦ IN SCREEN ¦ IN DESKTOP] [FONT expC1[, expN1]] [STYLE expC2]
[FOOTER expC3] [TITLE expC4] [HALFHEIGHT] [DOUBLE ¦ PANEL ¦ NONE ¦ SYSTEM ¦ border
string] [CLOSE ¦ NOCLOSE] [FLOAT ¦ NOFLOAT] [GROW ¦ NOGROW] [MDI ¦ NOMDI] [MINIMIZE]
[SHADOW] [ZOOM ¦ NOZOOM] [ICON FILE expC5] [FILL expC6 ¦ FILL FILE bmp file] [COLOR
SCHEME expN2 ¦ COLOR color-pair list]
```

The DEFINE WINDOW command defines screen coordinates and display attributes for a window. Use the FROM and TO coordinates to plot the upper-left and lower-right corners of the window. The default border is a single line box; use the DOUBLE, PANEL, NONE, or border definition character options to specify a different border for the window. (ASCII codes are used with the border definition option.) The COLOR and COLOR SCHEME options let you define colors for windows.

DELETE

Syntax

DELETE [*scope*] [FOR *condition*] [WHILE *condition*] [NOOPTIMIZE]

The DELETE command marks certain records for deletion. The scope, FOR, and WHILE *condition* options specify conditions that must apply before records are marked for deletion. (See also PACK.)

DELETE FILE

Syntax

DELETE FILE *filename.ext*/[?]

The DELETE FILE command deletes a file from the disk. If the filename includes an extension, the extension must be included. When the optional question mark is used in place of a filename, a list box of all files in the current directory appears, and the user can choose a file from the list box for deletion.

DELETE TAG

Syntax

DELETE TAG *tagname1* [OF *.CDXfile1*][, *tagname2* [OF *.CDXfile2*]].../ALL

The DELETE TAG command deletes the tag specified by *tagname* from the compound index file named by *.CDXfile*. If no .CDX filename is specified, FoxPro assumes that the tag to be removed is in the structural compound index file.

DIMENSION

Syntax

DIMENSION *array1* [*rows, columns*] [*array2*] [*rows, columns*]...[*arrayX*] [*rows, columns*]

Several arrays can be created by a single DIMENSION command. (The DIMENSION command provides backward compatibility with FoxBase+. For compatibility with dBASE IV, use the DECLARE command.)

DIR

Syntax

DIR [drive:] [ON drive] [[LIKE] [path] [skeleton]] [TO PRINTER [PROMPT] ¦ TO FILE filename]

The DIR command displays a directory of all tables. If filenames or DOS wildcards are provided, specific files or types of files are shown.

DISPLAY

Syntax

DISPLAY [scope] [fieldlist] [FOR condition] [WHILE condition] [OFF] [TO PRINT/TO FILE filename] [NOCONSOLE] [NOOPTIMIZE]

The DISPLAY command displays fields or records from the table that is active. The DIS-PLAY command pauses every 24 lines. The scope, fields, and FOR/WHILE option specify records and fields to be displayed; the OFF option stops the record number from being shown.

DISPLAY FILES

Syntax

DISPLAY FILES [ON drive/dir] [LIKE skeleton] [TO PRINT[PROMPT]/TO FILE filename]

The DISPLAY FILES command performs a directory display in the same manner as the DIR command. (See DIR.)

DISPLAY MEMORY

Syntax

DISPLAY MEMORY [LIKE skeleton] [TO PRINTER [PROMPT] ¦ TO FILE filename] [NOCONSOLE]

The DISPLAY MEMORY command causes FoxPro to display all active memory variables.

```
DISPLAY STATUS
```

Syntax

```
DISPLAY STATUS [TO PRINTER [PROMPT] ¦ TO FILE filename] [NOCONSOLE]
```

The DISPLAY STATUS command displays information about currently active files and system settings. The display pauses every 24 lines. The status includes function key settings, ON/OFF status of SET commands, and names of open table and indexes in work areas.

```
DISPLAY STRUCTURE
```

Syntax

```
DISPLAY STRUCTURE [IN alias] [TO PRINTER [PROMPT] ¦ TO FILE filename] [NOCONSOLE]
```

The DISPLAY STRUCTURE command displays the structure of the table in use. The display pauses every 24 lines. The display shows the names of fields, fields types, field lengths, and number of decimal places.

```
DO
```

Syntax

```
DO filename [WITH parameter-list] [IN filename]
```

The DO command begins execution of a FoxPro program (command file). Optional parameters can be passed to the command file using the WITH option. The IN *filename* option can be used to run a procedure that is stored inside another program file.

```
DO CASE
```

Syntax

```
DO CASE
   CASE condition
      commands...
   [CASE condition]
      [commands...]
   [OTHERWISE]
      [commands...]
ENDCASE
```

The DO CASE command chooses one path from among a number of possible paths within a program. All possible paths are identified by CASE statements, bracketed by DO CASE and ENDCASE statements. The first CASE statement evaluated as a logical true is performed by the program.

DO WHILE

Syntax

```
DO WHILE condition
  commands...
  [LOOP]
  [EXIT]
ENDDO
```

The DO WHILE command allows command statements to be repeated as a loop as long as a specified condition evaluates as true.

EDIT

Syntax

```
[FIELDS fieldlist] [scope] [FOR expL1] [WHILE expL2] [FONT expC1[, expN1]] [STYLE expC2]
[FREEZE field name] [KEY expr1[, expr2]] [LAST] [LEDIT] [REDIT] [LPARTITION] [NOAPPEND]
[NOCLEAR] [NODELETE] [NOEDIT ¦ NOMODIFY] [NOLINK] [NOMENU] [NOOPTIMIZE] [NORMAL]
[NOWAIT] [PARTITION expN2] [PREFERENCE expC3] [REST] [SAVE] [TIMEOUT expN3] [TITLE
expC4] [VALID [:F] expL3 [ERROR expC5]] [WHEN expL4] [WIDTH expN4] [[WINDOW window
name1] [IN [WINDOW] window name2 ¦ IN SCREEN]] [COLOR SCHEME expN5 ¦ COLOR color-pair
list]
```

The EDIT command permits full-screen editing of the table. PgUp and PgDn keys move the record pointer to prior and successive records for editing. If a record number is provided, editing begins at that record. NOINIT forces EDIT to use the settings in effect at the last use of EDIT. NOFOLLOW causes movement between records to follow natural order, rather than the index order, as edits to the indexed field are changed. NOAPPEND, NOEDIT, and NODELETE prevent additions, edits, and deletions, respectively. NOMENU prevents access to the Edit Menu pad. FREEZE followed by a field list restricts editing to the specified fields. LAST forces FoxPro to use the window settings for the last Browse window. In a split window, LEDIT puts the left half of a window in Edit mode, while REDIT puts the right half of a window in Edit mode. Also with split windows, LPARTITION can be included to force the cursor to appear in the first field of the left partition, and NOLINK causes the partitions to not be linked.

Under FoxPro for DOS, the NORMAL option causes the window to take on normal color attributes instead of those of a defined window. (In FoxPro for Windows, the option is ignored.) NOWAIT causes execution of a program to continue after the Edit window is displayed. SAVE leaves the Edit window visible after editing is completed. TIMEOUT specifies a number of seconds that the Edit window remains active waiting for changes until it closes. TITLE specifies a title which appears at the top of the window. The VALID clause can be used to test validity of data, using a user-defined function. ERROR defines an error message which appears if the validation fails. WHEN denotes a logical expression which, when used, determines whether or not editing is allowed. The WIDTH clause defines the width of the Edit window. The COLOR and COLOR SCHEME clauses are used to establish colors other than the default ones.

EJECT

Syntax

EJECT

The EJECT command causes the printer to perform a form feed, advancing the paper to the top of the next page. The EJECT command sends a formfeed code (ASCII 12) to the printer by means of the Windows Print Manager.

EJECT PAGE

Syntax

EJECT PAGE

The EJECT PAGE command sends a form feed to the printer. The difference between EJECT PAGE and the EJECT command is that the form feed sent with EJECT PAGE is also sent to all destinations available with the ? command.

ENDCASE

Syntax

ENDCASE

The ENDCASE command is the ending command used within the DO CASE construction. See DO CASE for specifics about the ENDCASE command.

ENDDO

Syntax

ENDDO

The ENDDO command is the ending command used within the DO WHILE...ENDDO loop. See DO WHILE for specifics on the ENDDO command.

ENDIF

Syntax

ENDIF

The ENDIF command is the ending command used within the IF...ENDIF construction. See IF for specifics on the ENDIF command.

ENDPRINTJOB

Syntax

ENDPRINTJOB

The ENDPRINTJOB command identifies the end of a print job, as specified with the PRINTJOB command. See PRINTJOB/ENDPRINTJOB for specifics on ENDPRINTJOB.

ENDSCAN

Syntax

ENDSCAN

The ENDSCAN command is the ending command used within the SCAN...ENDSCAN loop. See SCAN for specifics on the ENDSCAN command.

ENDTEXT

Syntax

ENDTEXT

The ENDTEXT command identifies the end of text that is displayed with the TEXT command. See TEXT for specifics on ENDTEXT.

ERASE

Syntax

```
ERASE filename.ext/[?]
```

The ERASE command is used to erase a file from disk. If the optional question mark is used instead of a *filename*, a dialog box appears, and the user can select the desired file to be erased.

EXIT

Syntax

```
EXIT
```

The EXIT command exits a DO WHILE, FOR, or SCAN loop and proceeds to the first command which follows the end of the loop (the command after the ENDDO, ENDFOR, or ENDSCAN command).

EXPORT

Syntax

```
EXPORT TO filename [FIELDS fieldlist] [scope] [FOR condition] [WHILE condition]
[NOOPTIMIZE] [TYPE] DIF/MOD/SYLK/WK1/WKS/WR1/WRK/XLS
```

The EXPORT command exports the contents of the active table to a foreign file. Use the TYPE option to specify the type of foreign file that should be created. The FIELDS clause can be used to specify a list of fields that should be included in the foreign file. If this clause is omitted, the contents of all fields are copied to the foreign file.

EXTERNAL

Syntax

```
EXTERNAL ARRAY/LABEL/LIBRARY/MENU/PROCEDURE/REPORT/ SCREEN filename/arrayname
```

The EXTERNAL command resolves references that are undefined in projects created in the FoxPro Project Manager.

FILER

Syntax

FILER [LIKE *skeleton*] [NOWAIT] [IN WINDOW *windowname*/IN SCREEN]

The FILER command opens the Filer desk accessory, which provides a simple way to create directories and move and delete files.

FIND

Syntax

FIND character-string

The FIND command moves the record pointer to the first record having an index key matching the specified character string. If no such match is located, the record pointer is placed at the end of the file, and EOF() is set to True.

FLUSH

Syntax

FLUSH

The FLUSH command flushes FoxPro's internal buffers, writing all changes to tables and indexes to disk.

FOR

Syntax

```
FOR memvar = expN1 TO expN2 [STEP expN3]
...commands...
   [EXIT]
   [LOOP]
ENDFOR
```

The FOR and accompanying ENDFOR statements are used to establish a repetitive loop. The loop repeats the number of times as defined by *expN1* to *expN2*. The optional STEP *expN3* can be used to define an incremental value other than 1.

FUNCTION

Syntax

```
FUNCTION procedurename
```

The FUNCTION command identifies a procedure as a user-defined function.

GATHER FROM

Syntax

```
GATHER FROM array [FIELDS fieldlist / FIELDS LIKE skeleton / FIELDS EXCEPT skeleton]
[MEMO]
```

The GATHER FROM command is used to save memory variables or array elements to the current table.

GETEXPR

Syntax

```
GETEXPR [expC1] TO memvar [TYPE expC2[; expC3]] [DEFAULT expC4]
```

The GETEXPR command opens the expression builder and allows the saving of preconstructed expressions to memory or array elements.

GO or GOTO

Syntax

```
GO or GOTO BOTTOM/TOP/expn [IN alias]
```

The GO and GOTO commands move the record pointer to a specified location. GOTOP and GO BOTTOM move the pointer to the start and end of a table, respectively. GO X or GOTO X moves the pointer to the record number specified by the numeric expression, X.

HELP

Syntax

```
HELP [commandname or functionname] [IN WINDOW window name/IN SCREEN] [NOWAIT]
```

The HELP command displays an explanation of the specified FoxPro command, function, or other information. Entering HELP followed by a valid command or function displays the help screen for that command or function. Entering HELP without a name displays a help menu.

HIDE MENU

Syntax

HIDE MENU [[*name1*][, *name2*...]]/[ALL] [SAVE]

The HIDE MENU command removes menu bars from the main window. You may also specify all menu bars currently displayed with the ALL option. Use the SAVE option to save an image of the menu bar to a screen or a window.

HIDE POPUP

Syntax

HIDE POPUP [[*name1*][, *name2*...]]/[ALL] [SAVE]

The HIDE POPUP command removes popups from the main window. You may also specify all popups currently displayed with the ALL option. Use the SAVE option to save an image of the popup to a screen or a window.

HIDE WINDOW

Syntax

HIDE WINDOW [[*name1*][, *name2*...]]/[ALL] [IN WINDOW *windowname*/IN SCREEN] [BOTTOM ¦ TOP ¦ SAME] [SAVE]

The HIDE WINDOW command removes windows from the main window. You may also specify all windows currently on the screen with the ALL option. Hiding the window does not close it—it remains active in the memory of FoxPro.

IF

Syntax

```
IF condition
   commands...
[ELSE]
```

```
    commands...
ENDIF
```

The IF command permits conditional processing of commands in a command file. If the condition identified by the IF statement is true, all commands between IF and ENDIF are carried out. Otherwise, execution passes to the statement following the ENDIF command (unless the optional ELSE statement is used, in which case execution passes to the statements following the ELSE statement).

IMPORT

Syntax

IMPORT FROM *filename* [TYPE] DIF/FW2/MOD/PDOX/RPD/SYLK/WK1/WK3/WKS/WR1/WRK/XLS

The IMPORT command imports data from a foreign file into a FoxPro table. The type of foreign file is specified by one of the acceptable TYPE options shown.

INDEX

Syntax

INDEX ON expr TO .IDX *filename*/TAG tagname [OF .CDXfile] [FOR *expL*] [COMPACT]
[ASCENDING/DESCENDING] [UNIQUE] [ADDITIVE]

The INDEX command creates an index file based on a specified key field or expression. The expression can be a field, a list of fields, or a combination of fields and values. If TAG is used, the index is part of a compound index (.CDX) file. If TO is used, the index is stored in a FoxBase+ style (.IDX) file. If multiple records contain the same key field value, UNIQUE includes only the first record.

INPUT

Syntax

INPUT [*expC*] [TO *memvar*]

The INPUT command waits for the user to enter data and stores the entry to a memory variable. If the response is enclosed in quotes, data is stored as a numeric variable. If a valid expression is entered, the expression is first acted upon, and the results are stored to the appropriate type of variable. If an optional prompt is provided, the prompt is displayed ahead of the cursor that waits for the user input.

INSERT

Syntax

INSERT [BLANK] [BEFORE]

The INSERT command adds a new record at a specific position in the table. The record is inserted immediately following the current record, unless the BEFORE option is used. BEFORE inserts the record ahead of the current record. In either case, all records following the inserted record are renumbered. The BLANK option inserts a blank record; otherwise, FoxPro permits full-screen editing of the new record.

INSERT - SQL

Syntax

INSERT INTO dbf name [(field *name1*[, field *name2*[, ...]])] VALUES (expr1[, expr2[, ...]])

This variation of the INSERT command inserts data into a row of a table.

JOIN

Syntax

JOIN WITH alias TO *filename* FOR *condition* [FIELDS *fieldlist* / FIELDS LIKE *skeleton* / FIELDS EXCEPT *skeleton*] [FOR *condition*] [NOOPTIMIZE]

The JOIN command builds a new table by duplicating chosen records and fields from two existing tables. The optional FOR condition specifies which records are included. An optional list of fields limits the fields that are duplicated. If no list is provided, all fields are duplicated.

KEYBOARD

Syntax

KEYBOARD *expC* [PLAIN] [CLEAR]

The KEYBOARD command stuffs the keyboard buffer with an arbitrary character string that remains in the buffer until FoxPro looks for input. This command is used often in demonstration programs, to simulate keyboard input.

LABEL FORM

Syntax

LABEL FORM label-*filename*/? [*scope*] [SAMPLE] [FOR *condition*] [WHILE *condition*] [TO
PRINT[PROMPT]] / [TO FILE *filename*] [ENVIRONMENT] [NOCONSOLE] [NOOPTIMIZE] [PDSETUP]
[PREVIEW]

The LABEL FORM command prints mailing labels using a label form file. The FOR and WHILE *condition* options limit labels printed to a range of records. The SAMPLE option prints a sample label (a series of X's) prior to the printing of the first label. If the TO PRINT option is specified, output is directed to the default print device. If the TO FILE option is specified, output is stored in a disk file. ENVIRONMENT restores the environment (assuming it was saved) that existed when the label was created. NOCONSOLE turns off output to the active window while the labels are printed. The PREVIEW option causes the labels to be displayed in a Page Preview window. The OFF option suppresses the display to the active window.

LIST

Syntax

LIST [OFF] [*scope*] [*fieldlist*] [FOR *condition*] [WHILE *condition*] [TO PRINT [PROMPT] / TO
FILE *filename*] [NOOPTIMIZE]

The LIST command supplies a list of the records in the current table. A scope (Records No., NEXT X ALL, or REST) can be used to limit the records that are listed. The FOR and WHILE *condition* options can be used to further limit the list to a range of records. If a list of fields is specified, only those fields are listed; otherwise, all fields are listed. The OFF option omits record numbers from the list. If the TO PRINT option is used, output is simultaneously directed to the default printer. The TO FILE option directs the output to an ASCII text file.

LIST FILES

Syntax

LIST FILES [ON drive/dir [LIKE *skeleton*] [TO PRINT [PROMPT] / TO FILE *filename*]

The LIST FILES command performs a directory display in the same manner as the DIR command (see DIR).

```
LIST MEMORY
```

Syntax

```
LIST MEMORY [LIKE skeleton] [TO PRINT [PROMPT] / TO FILE filename]
```

The LIST MEMORY command lists names, sizes, and types of memory variables for the table in the use. If the TO PRINT option is used, output is simultaneously directed to the default printer. The TO FILE option directs the output to an ASCII text file.

```
LIST STATUS
```

Syntax

```
LIST STATUS [TO PRINT [PROMPT] / TO FILE filename]
```

The LIST STATUS command lists information about currently active files and system settings. The status includes function key settings, ON/OFF status of SET commands, and names of open table and indexes in respective work areas. If the TO PRINT option is used, output is simultaneously directed to the default printer. The TO FILE option directs the output to an ASCII text file.

```
LIST STRUCTURE
```

Syntax

```
LIST STRUCTURE [TO PRINT [PROMPT] / TO FILE filename]
```

The LIST STRUCTURE command lists the structure of the currently active table. The structure shows names of fields, field types, field lengths, and number of decimal places. If the TO PRINT option is used, output is simultaneously directed to the default printer. The TO FILE option directs the output to an ASCII text file.

```
LOAD
```

Syntax

```
LOAD binary filename [SAVE/NOSAVE]
```

The LOAD command is used to load a binary (assembly-language) routine into memory. The routine must have an extension of .BIN, or the extension must be specified along with the filename. Once loaded, the routine can be executed with the CALL command (see CALL).

LOCATE

Syntax

`LOCATE [scope] [FOR condition] [WHILE condition] [NOOPTIMIZE]`

The LOCATE command locates a record that matches the condition specified. A scope (Record No., NEXT X, ALL, or REST) can be used to limit the records that are searched for the condition.

LOOP

Syntax

LOOP

The LOOP command causes a loop back to the beginning of a DO WHILE loop. It is normally used as part of a conditional statement (IF...ENDIF or DOCASE) to prevent execution of commands following the LOOP command.

MENU

Syntax

```
MENU BAR array1, expN1
MENU expN2, array2, expN3[, expN4]
READ MENU BAR TO var1, var2 [SAVE]
```

The MENU BAR, MENU, and READ MENU BAR TO commands can be used to create a horizontal menu bar. The MENU BAR command places the contents of the array (which contains character expressions that name the menu pads) into the menu bar. The MENU command is used to insert the menu popups into the menu bar, and the READ MENU TO command is used to activate the menus. These commands provide backward compatibility with XBase, but FoxPro's Menu Builder should be used to create menus.

MENU TO

Syntax

`MENU TO memvar`

The MENU TO command is used along with the @...PROMPT command to implement light-bar menus. See @...PROMPT for specifics on the use of the MENU TO command.

MODIFY COMMAND/MODIFY FILE

Syntax

MODIFY COMMAND/FILE *filename* [*skeleton*] [NOEDIT] [NOWAIT] [RANGE *expN1*[, *expN2*] [WINDOW *windowname*] [IN WINDOW *windowname*/IN SCREEN] [SAME] [SAVE]

The MODIFY COMMAND and MODIFY FILE commands launch the FoxPro editor, which can be used to create and edit programs or text files. MODIFY COMMAND assigns the file an extension of .PRG, unless a specific extension is specified. MODIFY FILE assigns no extension, unless one is specified. Use the NOEDIT clause to open the file as read-only. Use the WAIT option to open the file and continue program execution. The SAME option keeps the window from coming forward as the active window. The SAVE option leaves the window visible after editing is completed.

MODIFY GENERAL

Syntax

MODIFY GENERAL *general field*1[, *general field*2 ...] [NOMODIFY] [NOWAIT] [[WINDOW *window name1*] [IN [WINDOW] *window name2* ¦ IN SCREEN]]

The MODIFY GENERAL command opens an editing window into a general field of the current record.

MODIFY LABEL

Syntax

MODIFY LABEL *filename*/? [[WINDOW *windowname1*] [IN [WINDOW] *windowname2*/IN SCREEN]] [NOENVIRONMENT] [NOWAIT] [SAVE]

The MODIFY LABEL command modifies a label form file used to generate mailing labels.

MODIFY MEMO

Syntax

MODIFY MEMO *memofield*1[, *memofield*2...] [NOEDIT] [NOWAIT] [RANGE *expN1*[, *expN2*]] [WINDOW *windowname*] [SAME] [SAVE] [IN WINDOW *windowname*/IN SCREEN]

The MODIFY MEMO command allows the viewing or modification of the contents of the memo field. An editing window can be opened for each memo field if there is more than one memo field listed with the command.

MODIFY MENU

Syntax

```
MODIFY MENU [filename/?] [[WINDOW windowname1] [IN [WINDOW] windowname2/SCREEN]]
[NOWAIT] [SAVE]
```

The MODIFY MENU command is used to modify an existing menu. Entering MODIFY MENU causes FoxPro's Menu Builder to appear in the active window. MODIFY MENU is synonymous with the CREATE MENU command. See CREATE MENU for specifics on this command.

MODIFY PROJECT

Syntax

```
MODIFY PROJECT [filename/?] [[WINDOW windowname1] [IN [WINDOW] windowname2/SCREEN]]
[SAVE]
```

The MODIFY PROJECT command is used to modify an existing project. The command opens the project window. MODIFY PROJECT is synonymous with the CREATE PROJECT command. See CREATE PROJECT for specifics on this command.

MODIFY QUERY

Syntax

```
MODIFY QUERY [filename/?] [NOWAIT]
```

The MODIFY QUERY command is used to modify an existing query. The command causes the RQBE window to appear, containing a query saved previously.

MODIFY REPORT

Syntax

```
MODIFY REPORT filename/? [[WINDOW windowname1] [IN [WINDOW] windowname2/IN SCREEN]]
[NOENVIRONMENT] [NOWAIT] [SAVE]
```

The MODIFY REPORT command modifies a report form file for generating reports.

MODIFY SCREEN

Syntax

MODIFY SCREEN [*filename*/?] [[WINDOW *windowname1*] [IN [WINDOW] *windowname2*/IN SCREEN]] [NOENVIRONMENT] [NOWAIT] [SAVE]

The MODIFY SCREEN command is used to modify an existing screen, created earlier with the CREATE SCREEN command. See CREATE SCREEN for additional details.

MODIFY STRUCTURE

Syntax

MODIFY STRUCTURE

The MODIFY STRUCTURE command allows the modification of the current table structure. Entering the command causes the Table Structure window to appear, where desired modification of field names, sizes and types can be made.

MODIFY WINDOW

Syntax

MODIFY WINDOW window name ¦ SCREEN [FROM row1, column1 TO row2, column2 ¦ AT row3, column3 SIZE row4, column4] [FONT *expC1*[, *expN1*]] [STYLE *expC2*] [TITLE *expC3*] [HALFHEIGHT] [DOUBLE ¦ PANEL ¦ NONE ¦ SYSTEM] [CLOSE ¦ NOCLOSE] [FLOAT ¦ NOFLOAT] [GROW ¦ NOGROW] [MINIMIZE] [ZOOM ¦ NOZOOM] [ICON FILE *expC4*] [FILL FILE bmp *filename*] [COLOR SCHEME *expN2* ¦ COLOR *color-pair list*]

The MODIFY WINDOW command is used to change the attributes of a user-defined window or of the main FoxPro window.

MOVE POPUP

Syntax

MOVE POPUP *popupname* TO row,col / BY rows,cols

The MOVE POPUP command moves a popup menu to another location within the active window.

```
MOVE WINDOW
```

Syntax

```
MOVE WINDOW windowname TO row,col / BY rows,cols [CENTER]
```

The MOVE WINDOW command moves a predefined window to a new location.

```
NOTE or * or &&
```

Syntax

```
NOTE / * / &&
```

The NOTE or * or && command marks the beginning of a nonexecuting comment used to place comments in program files.

```
ON BAR
```

Syntax

```
ON BAR expN OF popup1 [ACTIVATE POPUP popup2/ACTIVATE MENU menuname]
```

The ON BAR command activates a popup when a specified option is chosen. ON SELECTION BAR or ON SELECTION POPUP can be used to execute a command when an option is chosen from a menu popup.

```
ON ERROR
```

Syntax

```
ON ERROR command
```

The ON ERROR command causes a specified command (usually a DO command to branch to another program) to be carried out when an error occurs within a program.

```
ON ESCAPE
```

Syntax

```
ON ESCAPE command
```

The ON ESCAPE command causes a specified command (usually a DO command to branch to another program) to be carried out when the user presses Esc during program execution.

```
ON KEY
```

Syntax

```
ON KEY command
```

The ON KEY command causes a specified command (usually a DO command to branch to another program) to be carried out when the user presses any key.

```
ON KEY =
```

Syntax

```
ON KEY = expN [command]
```

The ON KEY = command executes a specific command when the named key is pressed during a READ operation.

```
ON KEY LABEL
```

Syntax

```
ON KEY LABEL key label command
```

The ON KEY LABEL command executes a specified program when a key or key combination is pressed, or when the mouse is clicked.

```
ON PAD
```

Syntax

```
ON PAD padname OF menuname [ACTIVATE POPUP popupname/ACTIVATE MENU menuname]
```

The ON PAD command links a specified pad in a bar menu to a specific popup menu. When the pad is chosen from the bar menu, the associated popup menu appears.

```
ON PAGE
```

Syntax

```
ON PAGE [AT LINE expN command]
```

The ON PAGE command executes the command named after the ON PAGE command, each time the end of the page is reached. The page length is controlled by the system print variables when PRINTJOB is active (see PRINTJOB).

ON READERROR

Syntax

ON READERROR [command]

The ON READERROR command executes a named command, procedure, or program after detecting an error condition. ON READERROR is called as a result of improper responses to a VALID clause, improper entries when a RANGE clause is in effect, or improper date entries.

ON SELECTION BAR

Syntax

ON SELECTION BAR *expN* OF *popupname* [command]

The ON SELECTION BAR command specifies a command that is executed when a specific popup option is chosen.

ON SELECTION MENU

Syntax

ON SELECTION MENU *menuname*/ALL [command]

The ON SELECTION MENU command specifies a command that is executed when any pad on a menu bar is chosen.

ON SELECTION PAD

Syntax

ON SELECTION PAD *padname* OF *menuname* [command]

The ON SELECTION PAD command links a command, procedure, or program file to a pad in a bar menu. When the pad is chosen from the bar menu, the command, procedure, or program file named in the ONSELECTION statement is executed.

ON SELECTION POPUP

Syntax

ON SELECTION POPUP *popupname*/ALL [command]

The ON SELECTION POPUP command names a command, procedure, or program file which executes when a selection is chosen from a popup menu. If no command or procedure is named, the active popup is deactivated. If the ALL clause is used, the command, procedure, or program file applies to all popups.

ON SHUTDOWN

Syntax

ON SHUTDOWN [command]

The ON SHUTDOWN command is used to specify a command that executes when you shut down FoxPro for Windows. (Note that this command is supported only by FoxPro for Windows.)

PACK

Syntax

PACK [MEMO] [DBF]

The PACK command removes records marked for deletion. It renumbers remaining records in the table. The DBF clause can be included to force a pack of the table without packing the associated memo field file. The MEMO option can be included to force a pack of the associated memo field file, without packing the table. (Also see DELETE.)

PARAMETERS

Syntax

PARAMETERS *parameter-list*

The PARAMETERS command passes parameters from one program to another, when the second program is called with a WITH option of the DO command.

PLAY MACRO

Syntax

PLAY MACRO macroname [TIME *n seconds*]

The PLAY MACRO command plays a macro. Use the optional numeric argument to specify a number of seconds between keystrokes of the macro.

POP KEY

Syntax

POP KEY [ALL]

The POP KEY command restores ON KEY LABEL assignments that were placed on the stack with PUSH KEY.

POP MENU

Syntax

POP MENU *menuname* [TO MASTER]

The POP MENU command restores menu bar definitions that were placed on the stack with PUSH MENU. When used in combination with the PUSH MENU command, it enables you to save menu definitions, change the menu definitions, and restore them. POP MENU is provided for compatibility with the XBase language, but FoxPro's menu builder should be used to create menus.

POP POPUP

Syntax

POP POPUP *popupname*

The POP POPUP command restores popup definitions that were placed on the stack with the PUSH POPUP command. When used in combination with the PUSH POPUP command, it enables you to save popup definitions, change the popup definitions, and restore them. POP POPUP is provided for compatibility with the XBase language, but FoxPro's menu builder should be used to create menus.

```
PRINTJOB/ENDPRINTJOB
```

Syntax

```
PRINTJOB
...commands...
ENDPRINTJOB
```

The PRINTJOB command puts stored print settings in effect for the duration of a print job and activates the ON PAGE command (if ON PAGE was used earlier). The desired print settings are stored to the system printer memory variables before the PRINTJOB command is encountered. When PRINTJOB is executed, any starting codes stored to _PSCODES are sent to the printer, a form feed is sent if _PEJECT contains BEFORE or BOTH, _PCOLNO is initialized at zero, and _PLINENO and ON PAGE are activated. When printing is completed and ENDPRINTJOB is encountered, any ending print codes stored to _PECODES are sent to the printer. Also a form feed is repeated if the _PCOPIES variable contains more than 1 (that is, if more than one copy of the report is desired), and _PLINENO and ON PAGE are deactivated. Note that PRINTJOB and ENDPRINTJOB provide program compatibility with FoxPro for DOS. However, under Windows, printing is controlled by the Windows Print Manager.

```
PRIVATE
```

Syntax

```
PRIVATE ALL [LIKE/EXCEPT skeleton/memvarlist/ARRAY array definition list]
```

The PRIVATE command creates memory variables that are not public to higher-level parts of a program.

```
PROCEDURE
```

Syntax

```
PROCEDURE procedurename
```

The PROCEDURE command indicates the beginning of each procedure in a procedure file.

```
PUBLIC
```

Syntax

```
PUBLIC memvarlist/[ARRAY array definition list]
```

The PUBLIC command declares memory variables as public; those variables are then available to higher-level programs.

PUSH KEY

Syntax

PUSH KEY [CLEAR]

The PUSH KEY command puts all current ON KEY LABEL command settings on a stack in memory.

PUSH MENU

Syntax

PUSH MENU *menuname*

The PUSH MENU command places the definition of a menu bar in a stack of menu definitions in memory. When used in combination with the POP MENU command, PUSH MENU enables you to save, make changes to, and then restore the menu bar. PUSH MENU is provided for compatibility with the XBase language, but FoxPro's menu builder should be used to create menus.

PUSH POPUP

Syntax

PUSH POPUP *popupname*

The PUSH POPUP command places the definition of a popup in a stack of popup definitions in memory. When used in combination with the POP POPUP command, it enables you to save, make changes to, and then restore the popup definition. PUSH POPUP is provided for compatibility with the XBase language, but FoxPro's menu builder should be used to create menus.

QUIT

Syntax

QUIT

The QUIT command closes all open files, exits FoxPro, and returns you to the Windows environment.

READ

Syntax

```
READ [CYCLE] [ACTIVATE expL1] [DEACTIVATE expL2] [MODAL] [WITH window title list] [SHOW
expL3] [VALID expL4/expN1] [WHEN expL5] [OBJECT expN2] [TIMEOUT expN3] [SAVE] [NOMOUSE]
[LOCK/NOLOCK] [COLOR [color-pair list]/COLOR SCHEME expN4]
```

The READ command permits full-screen data entry as well as editing of a field or memory variable displayed using a @...GET statement. If the SAVE option is used, the GETs are not cleared following the READ command.

READ MENU

Syntax

```
READ MENU TO memvar [SAVE]
```

The READ MENU command activates a menu popup made by the @... MENU command.

RECALL

Syntax

```
RECALL [scope] [FOR condition] [WHILE condition] [NOOPTIMIZE]
```

The RECALL command unmarks records that have been marked for deletion. A scope (Record No., NEXT X, ALL, or REST) can be used to limit the records that are recalled. The FOR and WHILE *condition* options can be used to further limit recalled records to a range of records.

REINDEX

Syntax

```
REINDEX [COMPACT]
```

The REINDEX command rebuilds all open indexes. The COMPACT option causes the reindexed file to be stored in the compact format.

RELEASE

Syntax

```
RELEASE memvarlist/ALL [LIKE/EXCEPT wildcards]

RELEASE MODULE modulename/MENUS menuname list/POPUP popupname list/WINDOW windowname
list
```

The RELEASE command erases memory variables from memory . Memory variables can be identified with a list, or the ALL LIKE and ALL EXCEPT options can be used, with names or with wildcards, to specify variables to be released.

The RELEASE MODULE command removes a loaded module from memory. RELEASE MENUS removes the named menus. RELEASE WINDOW removes the named windows.

RENAME

Syntax

```
RENAME oldfile.ext TO newfile.ext
```

The RENAME command renames an existing file. If the old filename includes an extension, it must be provided. Path designations and drive designations can be provided, if the file is not located within the default drive and directory.

REPLACE

Syntax

```
REPLACE [scope] field WITH expression [ADDITIVE] [...field2 WITH expression2...]
[ADDITIVE] [FOR condition] [WHILE condition][NOOPTIMIZE]
```

The REPLACE command replaces the contents of specific fields within a range of records with new values based on the expression provided. A scope (Record No., NEXT X, ALL, or REST) can be used to limit the records that will have fields replaced. The FOR and WHILE *condition* options can be used to further limit replacements to a range of records. Use the ADDITIVE option to build a memo field using the contents of character strings.

```
REPLACE FROM ARRAY
```

Syntax

```
REPLACE FROM ARRAY array [FIELDS fieldlist] [scope] [FOR expL1] [WHILE expL2]
[NOOPTIMIZE]
```

The REPLACE FROM ARRAY command is used to replace data in fields with values stored in an array in memory.

```
REPORT FORM
```

Syntax

```
REPORT FORM filename/? [scope] [FOR condition] [WHILE condition] [PLAIN] [HEADING expC]
[SUMMARY] [NOEJECT] [TO PRINT [PROMPT] / TO FILE filename] [OFF] [ENVIRONMENT]
[NOCONSOLE] [NOOPTIMIZE] [PDSETUP] [PREVIEW]
```

The REPORT FORM command uses a report form file to generate a report. (The report must have been created previously with the CREATE REPORT or MODIFY REPORT command.) A scope (Record No., NEXT X, ALL, or REST) can be used to limit the records that appear in the report. The FOR and WHILE *condition* options can be used to further limit records printed to a range of records. The PLAIN option drops headings from the report. The HEADING option, followed by a character string, provides an additional header. The NOEJECT option cancels the form feed command that normally precedes a printed report. If the TO PRINT option is used, output is directed to the Windows Print Manager. If the TO FILE option is included, output is directed to a disk file. ENVIRONMENT restores the environment (assuming it was saved) that existed when the label was created. NOCONSOLE turns off output to the active window while the labels are printed. The PREVIEW option causes the labels to be displayed in a Page Preview window.

```
RESTORE
```

Syntax

```
RESTORE FROM filename/MEMO memofield [ADDITIVE]
```

The RESTORE command restores memory variables from a memory variable (.MEM) file. If the ADDITIVE option is used, current memory variables are not erased from memory when the new variables are read into memory.

RESTORE MACROS

Syntax

RESTORE MACROS FROM *macroname*/MEMO *memofieldname*

The RESTORE MACROS command restores macros saved in a macro file to active memory. Any macros existing in memory which are assigned the same keys are overwritten by the macros loaded with RESTORE MACROS.

RESTORE SCREEN

Syntax

RESTORE SCREEN [FROM *memvar*]

The RESTORE SCREEN command restores the main FoxPro window or a user-created window from the screen buffer. The SAVE SCREEN command can be used to save the active user-defined window or the main FoxPro window to the screen buffer, a memory variable, or an array element.

RESTORE WINDOW

Syntax

RESTORE WINDOW *windowname list*/ALL FROM [*filename*/MEMO *memofield*]

The RESTORE WINDOW command restores window definitions previously stored to a file with SAVE WINDOW (see SAVE WINDOW).

RESUME

Syntax

RESUME

The RESUME command resumes execution of a command file previously suspended, either when the user answers S to the Cancel, Suspend, or Ignore? prompt displayed at the time of a program error, or when a SUSPEND command has been placed within a program.

RETRY

Syntax

RETRY

The RETRY command passes control to a higher-level program, at the same line that called the program containing the RETRY statement. Normally it is used within an error-trapping routine to return program control to the point of the error.

RETURN

Syntax

RETURN [TO MASTER/*expression*/TO *procedurename*]

The RETURN command ends execution of a procedure or a command file. Program control returns to the next higher-level program. If there is no higher-level program, program control returns to the Command Window. The TO MASTER option can be specified to cause program control to return to the highest-level program (usually the Main Menu). Use *expression* to return a value from a user-defined function to a higher-level calling program.

RUN

Syntax

RUN [/N [K]] *filename*

or

! [/N [K]] *filename*

The RUN command runs an executable non-FoxPro program. The program can be any .COM, .EXE, or .BAT file, or any resident DOS command. Parameters can also be passed to the called program, if the called program normally accepts parameters. Upon completion of the program, batch file, or DOS command, control returns to FoxPro. The K option is used along with the /N option under FoxPro for DOS, but is ignored under FoxPro for Windows. Under FoxPro for Windows, the /N option specifies that the program to be run is a Windows program. Under FoxPro for DOS, the /N (or /NK) option is used to specify an amount of memory that should be freed.

SAVE

Syntax

SAVE TO *filename*/MEMO *memofield*name [ALL LIKE/EXCEPT *skeleton*]

The SAVE command stores memory variables in a file. Memory variables to be saved can be identified with a list, or the ALL, LIKE, and ALL EXCEPT options can be used, with names or with wildcards, to specify the variables to be saved. The SAVE TO MEMO memofieldname syntax is used to save the variables to a memo field of the current table.

SAVE MACROS

Syntax

SAVE MACROS TO *macroname*/MEMO *memofieldname*

The SAVE MACROS command is used to save keyboard macros to a keyboard macro file or to a memo field of the current table.

SAVE SCREEN

Syntax

SAVE SCREEN [TO *memvar*]

The SAVE SCREEN command saves screens or window images to a buffer, memory variable, or an array element. This image, stored with the SAVE SCREEN command, can be displayed again with the RESTORE SCREEN command.

SAVE WINDOW

Syntax

SAVE WINDOW *windownamelist*/ALL TO *windowname*/MEMO *memofield*

The SAVE WINDOW command saves the windows named in the window list to a disk file. If the ALL option is used, all windows in active memory are stored in the file. Use the RESTORE WINDOW command to restore the saved windows to memory.

SCAN

Syntax

```
SCAN [scope] [FOR condition] [WHILE condition] [NOOPTIMIZE]
[commands...]
   [LOOP]
   [commands...]
   [EXIT]
ENDSCAN
```

The SCAN and ENDSCAN commands form a repetitive loop, where all commands between the SCAN command and the ENDSCAN command are repeated for the condition named within the SCAN statement. The commands between SCAN and ENDSCAN will be processed for all records which meet the specified conditions.

SCATTER TO

Syntax

```
SCATTER TO [FIELDS fieldlist ¦ FIELDS LIKE skeleton ¦ FIELDS EXCEPT skeleton] [MEMO] TO
array ¦ TO array BLANK ¦ MEMVAR ¦ MEMVAR BLANK
```

The SCATTER TO command is used to copy data from a current record to a set of memory variables or to a memory array. This command also creates memory variables or arrays if they don't already exist.

SCROLL

Syntax

```
SCROLL row1,col1,row2,col2,expN
```

The SCROLL command scrolls a window vertically or horizontally.

SEEK

Syntax

```
SEEK expression
```

The SEEK command moves the record pointer to the first record having an index key matching the specified expression. If no such match is located, the record pointer is placed at the end of the file, and EOF() is set to True.

SELECT

Syntax

SELECT *n* or SELECT *alias*

The SELECT command selects from among 225 possible work areas for opening of tables and indexes. A number from 1 to 225 can be specified, or alias names can be used.

SELECT - SQL

Syntax

SELECT [ALL/DISTINCT] [alias.] selectitem [AS columnname] [, [alias.] selectitem [AS columnname]...] FROM table [local_alias] [, table [local_alias]...] [[INTO destination]/ [TO FILE *filename* [ADDITIVE]/TO PRINTER]] [NOCONSOLE] [PLAIN] [NOWAIT] [WHERE joincondition [AND joincondition...] [AND/OR filtercondition [AND/OR filtercondition...]]] [GROUP BY groupcolumn [, groupcolumn...]] [HAVING filtercondition] [UNION [ALL] SELECTcommand] [ORDER BY order_item [ASC/DESC] [, orderitem [ASC/DESC]...]]

This variation of the SELECT command is used to retrieve data from a table (made up of fields from one or more FoxPro tables). SELECT commands can be generated by means of a query designed within the RQBE Window, or they can be typed directly into the Command Window. The use of the SQL SELECT statement is beyond the scope of this chapter. For specifics on using SQL, refer to your FoxPro documentation or to a text file on the SQL Data Retrieval language.

SET

Syntax

SET

The SET command displays the View window, which can then be used to set various FoxPro parameters.

SET ALTERNATE

Syntax

SET ALTERNATE ON/OFF and SET ALTERNATE TO *filename* [ADDITIVE]

The SET ALTERNATE TO command is used to direct the screen or printer output to a text file. SET ALTERNATE ON turns on the storing of output to the text file, and SET ALTERNATE OFF turns it off.

SET ANSI

Syntax

SET ANSI ON/OFF

The SET ANSI command specifies how comparisons are made in the FoxPro SQL commands.

SET AUTOSAVE

Syntax

SET AUTOSAVE ON/OFF

The SET AUTOSAVE command, when on, tells FoxPro to save changes to disk after each I/O operation, reducing the chances of data loss due to power failures or hardware faults. The default for SET AUTOSAVE is OFF.

SET BELL

Syntax

SET BELL ON/OFF

The SET BELL command determines whether audible beeps sound during certain operations. SET BELL ON enables the beep, and SET BELL OFF disables the beep. The default for SET BELL is ON.

SET BELL TO

Syntax

SET BELL TO frequency/duration

The SET BELL TO command controls the frequency and duration of the bell. The frequency is the desired tone measured in Hertz while each unit of duration is approximately .0549 seconds.

SET BLINK

Syntax

SET BLINK ON/OFF

The SET BLINK command, in FoxPro for DOS, determines whether screen elements—such as borders or text—blink or not. The SET BLINK command is ignored by FoxPro for Windows.

SET BLOCKSIZE

Syntax

SET BLOCKSIZE TO *expN*

The SET BLOCKSIZE command changes the block size used for storing data within memo fields. The default value of 1 is the only size compatible with dBASE III and dBASE III Plus. The value multiplied by 512 represents the actual size of the blocks in bytes. Larger block sizes tend to speed performance when storing large amounts of text.

SET BORDER

Syntax

SET BORDER TO [SINGLE/DOUBLE/PANEL/NONE/*border-definition string1*] [,*border-definition string2*]

The SET BORDER command changes the default border from a single-line box to the type of border described. Use the SINGLE option to choose a single line, the DOUBLE option to choose a double line, the PANEL option to choose a panel composed of the ASCII-219 character, and NONE to omit the border. Under FoxPro for DOS, the border definition string option can be used; it should contain eight ASCII values separated by commas. Value one specifies the top of the border; value two the bottom; values three and four the left and right sides; and values five, six, seven, and eight the upper-left, upper-right, lower-left, and lower-right corners, respectively. Note that this command is provided for compatibility with FoxPro for DOS. In FoxPro for Windows, the DOUBLE option creates a PANEL border for popups and windows, and the *border string* option is ignored.

SET BRSTATUS

Syntax

SET BRSTATUS ON/OFF

The SETBRSTATUS command is used to enable or disable the display of the Status Bar in a Browse window.

SET CARRY

Syntax

SET CARRY ON/OFF

SET CARRY TO *fieldlist* [ADDITIVE]

The SET CARRY command specifies whether entries are duplicated from the previous record into a new record when the APPEND or INSERT command is used.

SET CENTURY

Syntax

SET CENTURY ON/OFF

The SET CENTURY command turns on (or off) the display of dates with four-digit years.

SET CLEAR

Syntax

SET CLEAR ON/OFF

The SET CLEAR command is used to determine whether the main window in FoxPro is cleared with the issuing of the SET FORMAT command.

SET CLOCK

Syntax

SET CLOCK ON/OFF/STATUS

The SET CLOCK command displays the system clock in a specified location, or determines whether it is shown at all. OFF disables the clock, ON causes it to appear in the upper-right corner of the main FoxPro window, and STATUS causes it to appear in the Status Bar.

```
SET CLOCK TO
```

Syntax

```
SET CLOCK TO row, col
```

The SET CLOCK TO command specifies a location for the clock.

```
SET COLLATE
```

Syntax

```
SET COLLATE TO expC
```

The SET COLLATE command specifies a language-specific collation order for indexing and sorting.

```
SET COLOR OF
```

Syntax

```
SET COLOR OF NORMAL / MESSAGES / TITLES / BOX / HIGHLIGHT / INFORMATION / FIELDS TO
[color-pair list]
```

The SET COLOR OF command sets the colors of the user-created windows and system windows.

```
SET COLOR OF SCHEME
```

Syntax

```
SET COLOR OF SCHEME expN TO [color-pair list]
```

The SET COLOR OF SCHEME command sets the colors of the color scheme or copies a color scheme to another scheme.

```
SET COLOR ON/OFF
```

Syntax

```
SET COLOR ON/OFF
```

The SET COLOR ON/OFF command sets the screen colors on or off.

```
SET COLOR SET TO
```

Syntax

```
SET COLOR SET TO [ColorSetname]
```

The SET COLOR SET TO command is used to load colors from a previously defined Color Setname.

```
SET COLOR TO
```

Syntax

```
SET COLOR TO color-pair list
```

The SET COLOR TO command sets the screen color intensity.

```
SET COMPATIBLE
```

Syntax

```
SET COMPATIBLE [ON/DB4]/[OFF/FOXPLUS]
```

The SET COMPATIBLE command is used for the controlling of compatibility with FoxBase+ and other Xbase languages. Entering SET COMPATIBLE OFF or SET COMPATIBLE FOXPLUS makes FoxPro fully compatible with the FoxBase Plus command and function set. Entering SET COMPATIBLE ON or SET COMPATIBLE DB4 makes FoxPro more compatible with the dBASE IV command and function set.

```
SET CONFIRM
```

Syntax

```
SET CONFIRM ON/OFF
```

The SET CONFIRM command controls the method of cursor advance between full-screen editing fields. When SET CONFIRM is ON, the Enter key must be pressed to move the cursor out of a field. When SET CONFIRM is OFF, the arrow keys can also be used to move the cursor out of a field.

SET CONSOLE

Syntax

SET CONSOLE ON/OFF

The SET CONSOLE command turns screen output off (or on). This command can be used within programs to hide operations normally viewed on the screen or to speed up program execution by temporarily disabling the screen.

SET CURRENCY

Syntax

SET CURRENCY TO [*expC*]

The SET CURRENCY command changes the symbol used for currency. Any character expression having up to nine characters can be used as the currency symbol.

SET CURRENCY LEFT/RIGHT

Syntax

SET CURRENCY LEFT/RIGHT

The SET CURRENCY LEFT/RIGHT command changes the placement of the currency symbol, causing the symbol to appear to the left or the right of the value.

SET CURSOR

Syntax

SET CURSOR ON/OFF

The SET CURSOR command determines whether the cursor appears during a pending @...GET.

```
SET DATE
```

Syntax

```
SET DATE AMERICAN/ANSI/BRITISH/ITALIAN/FRENCH/GERMAN/ JAPAN/USA/MDY/DMY/YMD
```

The SET DATE command controls the date format for display of dates. Acceptable types are American, ANSI, British, Italian, French, German, Japanese, USA, MDY, DMY, and, YMD. American format is mm/dd/yy, ANSI is yy.mm.dd, British and French formats are dd/mm/yy, Italian format is dd-mm-yy, and German format is dd.mm.yy. Japanese format is yy/mm/dd. If the SET DATE command is not used, FoxPro defaults to the American date display.

```
SET DEBUG
```

Syntax

```
SET DEBUG ON/OFF
```

The SET DEBUG command turns on or off access to the Trace and Debug windows.

```
SET DECIMALS
```

Syntax

```
SET DECIMALS TO expN
```

The SET DECIMALS command controls the number of decimals displayed in a numerical expression.

```
SET DEFAULT
```

Syntax

```
SET DEFAULT TO drive:directory
```

The SET DEFAULT command sets the default drive and/or directory.

```
SET DELETED
```

Syntax

```
SET DELETED ON/OFF
```

The SET DELETED command displays (or hides) records marked for deletion from processing by most FoxPro commands.

SET DELIMITER

Syntax

```
SET DELIMITER TO character-string / [DEFAULT]
SET DELIMITER ON/OFF
```

The SET DELIMITER command specifies characters to be used as the starting and ending delimiters for full-screen fields. If one character is specified, that character is used as the beginning and ending delimiter. If two characters are specified, the first is used as the beginning delimiter, and the second character becomes the ending delimiter.

SET DEVELOPMENT

Syntax

```
SET DEVELOPMENT ON/OFF
```

The SET DEVELOPMENT command, if on, causes FoxPro to compare the dates of creation for .PRG files and compiled (.FXP) files. For this reason when a program is run, outdated .FXP files are not used. Old .FXP files are automatically deleted as the programs are updated. Therefore, the SET DEVELOPMENT command is not necessary if the FoxPro Editor is used to create programs. If another editor is used to modify and create program files, SET DEVELOPMENT ON must be used at the command level before you begin to run and modify your programs.

SET DEVICE

Syntax

```
SET DEVICE TO PRINTER [PROMPT] / TO SCREEN / TO FILE filename
```

The SET DEVICE command is used to direct the output of @...SAY commands to a printer, the screen, or to a disk file.

SET DISPLAY TO

Syntax

```
SET DISPLAY TO MONO / COLOR / CGA / EGA25 / EGA43 / MONO43 / VGA25 / VGA43 / VGA50
```

Under FoxPro for DOS, the SET DISPLAY command selects the desired monitor and sets the number of lines displayed. Note that the graphics hardware used must support the type chosen before the command has any effect. In FoxPro for Windows, this command changes the font used by the main FoxPro window.

SET DOHISTORY

Syntax

SET DOHISTORY ON/OFF

The SET DOHISTORY command enables you to store the commands from a program in the Command Window. When SET DOHISTORY is ON, commands executed within a program are stored in the Command Window.

SET ECHO

Syntax

SET ECHO ON/OFF

The SET ECHO command determines whether commands within a program will be duplicated or "echoed" to the screen during program execution. The SET ECHO command is a debugging tool primarily used when hunting for errors within a program.

SET ESCAPE

Syntax

SET ESCAPE ON/OFF

The SET ESCAPE command controls whether the Esc key interrupts program execution. If SET ESCAPE is OFF, pressing the Esc key while a program runs has no effect. The default for SET ESCAPE is ON.

SET EXACT

Syntax

SET EXACT ON/OFF

The SET EXACT command sets the precision of comparisons between two character strings. If SET EXACT is ON, character strings must match precisely; if SET EXACT is

OFF, only the first X characters of the larger string must match the smaller string with a length of X characters.

SET FIELDS

Syntax

SET FIELDS ON/OFF

The SET FIELDS command is used to specify which fields in a table can be accessed.

SET FIELDS TO

Syntax

SET FIELDS TO [*fieldlist*/ALL]

The SET FIELDS TO command specifies a list of fields that will be available to other FoxPro commands once the list of fields has been specified. The list of fields is made active with the SET FIELDS ON command; the setting is canceled with the SET FIELDS OFF command. If the ALL option is used, all fields in the active table are made available.

SET FILTER

Syntax

SET FILTER TO [*condition*]

The SET FILTER command causes a table to appear as if it contains only records that meet a specific condition. All records not meeting the specified filter condition are excluded from most FoxPro operations.

SET FIXED

Syntax

SET FIXED ON/OFF

The SET FIXED command determines whether a specific number of decimal places are displayed with all numerical output. It is used with the SET DECIMALS command (see SET DECIMALS).

SET FORMAT

Syntax

SET FORMAT TO *filename*/?

The SET FORMAT command opens a format file for use with full-screen commands. The command is provided for backward compatibility with dBASE. However, in FoxPro, the purpose of format files can be replaced with the use of FoxPro screens created with the Screen Wizards and the Screen Builder.

SET FULLPATH

Syntax

SET FULLPATH ON/OFF

The SET FULLPATH command, when off, suppresses the inclusion of file extensions in functions that return filenames.

SET FUNCTION

Syntax

SET FUNCTION *expN/key label* TO *character-string*

The SET FUNCTION command stores strings in the function keys (to a maximum of 75 characters). For example, the semicolon can be used to indicate a carriage return. The F1 function key cannot be reprogrammed with the SET FUNCTION command.

SET HEADING

Syntax

SET HEADING ON/OFF

The SET HEADING command turns off (or on) the display of column headings that appear with LIST, DISPLAY, SUM, and AVERAGE commands.

```
SET HELP
```

Syntax

```
SET HELP ON/OFF
SET HELP TO filename
```

The SET HELP command turns on FoxPro's on-line help facility. If SET HELP is ON, pressing F1 causes the Help window to appear. If SET HELP is OFF, pressing F1 has no effect. The SET HELP TO *filename* variation of the command can be used to specify a different help filename.

```
SET HELPFILTER
```

Syntax

```
SET HELPFILTER [AUTOMATIC] TO expL
```

The SET HELPFILTER command limits the available topics shown in the Help window to a specified subset of topics. Only records in the Help file meeting the logical *condition* are included in the Help window. If the AUTOMATIC option is used, the effects of the SET HELPFILTER command are cancelled when the Help window is closed.

```
SET HOURS
```

Syntax

```
SET HOURS TO [12/24]
```

The SET HOURS command sets the format for the time display to 12 (English) or 24 (military) hours.

```
SET INDEX
```

Syntax

```
SET INDEX TO [indexfile list/?] [ORDER expN/.IDXfile/[TAG] tagname [OF .CDXfile]]
[ASCENDING/DESCENDING] [ADDITIVE]
```

The SET INDEX command opens the index tags or index files named in the list. Up to seven indexes can be opened at once by specifying more than one index name.

SET INTENSITY

Syntax

SET INTENSITY ON/OFF

In FoxPro for DOS, the SET INTENSITY command sets reverse video on (or off) while full-screen operations are used. The command is provided for compatibility with FoxPro for DOS, but it is ignored in FoxPro for Windows.

SET KEY

Syntax

SET KEY TO [*expr1* ¦ RANGE *expr2*, *expr3*] [IN *expC* ¦ *expN*]

The SET KEY command is used to limit available records, based on an index key.

SET KEYCOMP

Syntax

SET KEYCOMP TO DOS / WINDOWS

The SET KEYCOMP command specifies whether navigation keystrokes follow FoxPro for DOS conventions, or FoxPro for Windows conventions. (Note that this command is supported only in FoxPro for Windows.)

SET LIBRARY

Syntax

SET LIBRARY TO *filename* [ADDITIVE]

The SET LIBRARY command opens an external library file. This allows the use of Application Program Interface functions as if they were FoxPro functions. These functions can be displayed by the DISPLAY STATUS or LIST STATUS commands.

SET LOCK

Syntax

SET LOCK ON/OFF

The SET LOCK command enables or disables automatic record locking on a network.

SET LOGERRORS

Syntax

SET LOGERRORS ON/OFF

The SET LOGERRORS command enables you to save compilation error messages to a text file during the program compilation process.

SET MACKEY

Syntax

SET MACKEY TO *expC*

The SET MACKEY command specifies a key (other than the default of Shift+F10), which is used to display the Macros dialog box.

SET MARGIN

Syntax

SET MARGIN TO *expN*

The SET MARGIN command sets the left margin that the printer uses. The value is in spaces for any printer. The default, if no value is specified, is zero.

SET MARK

Syntax

SET MARK TO *expC*

The SET MARK command specifies a delimiter used to separate the month, day, and year of a date. The character expression must translate to a single character. If a literal character is supplied, it must be surrounded by quotes.

SET MARK OF

Syntax

SET MARK OF MENU *menuname* TO *expC1*/*expL1*

```
SET MARK OF PAD padname  OF menuname TO expC2/expL2
SET MARK OF POPUP popupname TO expC3/expL3
SET MARK OF BAR expN  OF popupname TO expC4/expL4
```

Under FoxPro for DOS, the SET MARK OF command is used to display or remove the mark character for a menu pad or popup option. The command is provided for compatibility with FoxPro for DOS, but is ignored under FoxPro for Windows.

```
SET MEMOWIDTH
```

Syntax

```
SET MEMOWIDTH TO expN
```

The SET MEMOWIDTH command sets the width of the contents of memo fields when they are displayed or printed.

```
SET MESSAGE
```

Syntax

```
SET MESSAGE OFF/ON
SET MESSAGE TO [expC/LEFT/CENTER/RIGHT]
```

The SET MESSAGE command specifies a message that appears in the Status Bar when SET MESSAGE is ON.

```
SET MOUSE
```

Syntax

```
SET MOUSE TO expN
```

Under FoxPro for DOS, the SET MOUSE command allows or prohibits the use of the mouse and controls the sensitivity of the mouse. The command is ignored by FoxPro for Windows, as mouse usage is defined by the Windows environment.

```
SET MULTILOCKS
```

Syntax

```
SET MULTILOCKS ON/OFF
```

The SET MULTILOCKS command determines whether you can set multiple locks when using the RLOCK() and LOCK() functions.

```
SET NEAR
```

Syntax

```
SET NEAR ON/SET NEAR OFF
```

The SET NEAR command places the record pointer at the nearest record following an unsuccessful SEEK or FIND operation. When SET NEAR is ON, the record pointer is placed at the next record following the expression that could not be found. When SET NEAR is OFF, the record pointer is placed at the end of the file if the expression is not found.

```
SETNOCPTRANS
```

Syntax

```
SET NOCPTRANS TO [field1 [, field2 ...]]
```

The SET NOCPTRANS command prevents the automatic translation of character and memo fields that contain binary data.

```
SET NOTIFY
```

Syntax

```
SET NOTIFY ON/OFF
```

The SET NOTIFY command determines whether certain system messages appear under FoxPro.

```
SET ODOMETER
```

Syntax

```
SET ODOMETER TO [expN]
```

The SET ODOMETER command specifies how often commands that display a record count update the screen display. The default value for SET ODOMETER is 1, and the maximum value is 32,767.

SET OPTIMIZE

Syntax

SET OPTIMIZE ON/OFF

The SET OPTIMIZE command turns on or off Rushmore optimization, FoxPro's own internal technology for rapid data retrieval.

SET ORDER

Syntax

SET ORDER TO [*expN*/.IDXfile/[TAG] *tagname* [OF *.CDXfile*] [IN *work area/alias*] [ASCENDING/DESCENDING]] [ADDITIVE]

The SET ORDER command selects the controlling index tag or index file. *expN* is a numerical value referring to the indexes in the order in which they were opened. This means that a value of four would refer to the fourth index opened. Note that the SET ORDER TO command can also be used with no index name specified or with a value of zero. In these cases, no index is used to arrange the records, and they then appear in the natural order of the table.

SET PALETTE

Syntax

SET PALETTE ON/OFF

The SET PALETTE command determines whether or not the Color Palette is used. Note that this command is supported only by FoxPro for Windows.

SET PATH

Syntax

SET PATH TO pathname

The SET PATH command specifies a DOS path to search if a file is not in the default directory.

```
SET PDSETUP
```

Syntax

```
SET PDSETUP TO [[expC[, expr1[, expr2 ...]]]] [WITH expr3[, expr4 ...]]]
```

The SET PDSETUP command is used to load a printer driver setup, or to clear the current printer driver setup. Printer driver setups are used in FoxPro for Windows when printing character-based reports originally created in FoxPro for DOS.

```
SET POINT
```

Syntax

```
SET POINT TO expC
```

The SET POINT command specifies the decimal character displayed in numerical expressions.

```
SET PRINT
```

Syntax

```
SET PRINT ON [PROMPT] / OFF
```

The SET PRINT command echoes screen output to the printer in addition to the screen. In FoxPro for Windows, the use of the PROMPT option causes a dialog box to appear before printing begins.

```
SET PRINTER TO
```

Syntax

```
SET PRINTER TO LPT1/COM1/COM2/other DOS device/filename [ADDITIVE]
```

Under FoxPro for DOS, the SET PRINTER TO command specifies the DOS device that is used as a default printer. Standard DOS names (LPT1, LPT2, COM1, COM2) can be used. Note that under FoxPro for Windows, all print output is sent to the Windows Print Manager.

SET PROCEDURE

Syntax

SET PROCEDURE TO procedure*filename*

The SET PROCEDURE command opens the specified procedure file.

SET READBORDER

Syntax

SET READBORDER ON/OFF

The SET READBORDER command determines whether single-line borders appear around edit regions placed with @...GET commands.

SET REFRESH

Syntax

SET REFRESH TO *expN1* [, *expN2*]

The SET REFRESH command determines whether or not FoxPro displays changes that are made to records by other users on a network.

SET RELATION

Syntax

SET RELATION TO [*expression*1 INTO *alias*] [ADDITIVE] [[, *expression*2 INTO *alias*]
[ADDITIVE]...]

The SET RELATION command links the table in use to another in a different work area.

SET RELATION OFF

Syntax

SET RELATION OFF INTO *alias*

The SET RELATION OFF command breaks an existing relation between two tables (see SET RELATION). The parent table must be the table which is open in the current work area, and alias indicates the related (child) table. Alias can be the alias name, or a work area number.

```
SET REPROCESS
```

Syntax

```
SET REPROCESS TO expN [SECONDS] ¦ TO AUTOMATIC
```

The SET REPROCESS command specifies how long FoxPro retries a locking attempt on a file or a record when the initial attempt is unsuccessful.

```
SET RESOURCE
```

Syntax

```
SET RESOURCE ON/OFF
```

The SET RESOURCE command turns the resource file on or off. When the resource file is off, the environment is not saved upon leaving FoxPro.

```
SET RESOURCE TO
```

Syntax

```
SET RESOURCE TO filename
```

The SET RESOURCE TO command lets you specify a resource file other than the default FOXUSER.DBF. This is useful when there is more than one user to a computer, as it allows the environment to be saved to a different file for each user.

```
SET SAFETY
```

Syntax

```
SET SAFETY ON/OFF
```

The SET SAFETY command determines whether a confirmation message is provided before existing files are overwritten by commands like SORT or COPY. The default for SET SAFETY is ON.

SET SCOREBOARD

Syntax

SET SCOREBOARD ON/OFF

Under FoxPro for DOS, the SET SCOREBOARD command determines where FoxPro displays the status of the Num Lock, Caps Lock, and Ins keys. The command is provided in FoxPro for Windows for backward compatibility, but it is ignored.

SET SEPARATOR

Syntax

SET SEPARATOR TO *expC*

The SET SEPARATOR command specifies the symbol used to separate hundreds in numerical amounts. The default is the comma, and the expression used can be any single character, surrounded by quotes.

SET SHADOWS

Syntax

SET SHADOWS ON/OFF

Under FoxPro for DOS, the SET SHADOWS command is used to add or remove shadows from user-created windows, popups created by DEFINE POPUP, and the normal system windows and popups. The command is provided for compatibility with FoxPro for DOS, but is ignored by FoxPro for Windows.

SET SKIP

Syntax

SET SKIP TO [*alias1*[, *alias2*...]]

The SET SKIP command lets you access all records within a linked file that match a particular index key value. Use SET SKIP along with the SET RELATION command.

SET SPACE

Syntax

SET SPACE ON/OFF

The SET SPACE command activates and deactivates the addition of a space between expressions printed with the ? and ?? commands. The default for SET SPACE is ON.

SET STATUS BAR

Syntax

SET STATUS BAR ON/OFF

The SET STATUS command turns on or off the display of a Windows-style Status Bar. Note that the command is supported only in FoxPro for Windows.

SET STATUS

Syntax

SET STATUS ON/OFF/TIMEOUT TO *expN*

The SET STATUS command turns on or off the display of a character-style Status Bar.

SET STEP

Syntax

SET STEP ON/OFF

The SET STEP command determines if execution of a command file halts after each command. Normally, SET STEP is used as a debugging aid.

SET STICKY

Syntax

SET STICKY ON/OFF

Under FoxPro for DOS, the SET STICKY command affects selections made by the mouse. It specifies how menus are displayed by the mouse in the FoxPro menu system. The command is provided for compatibility with FoxPro for DOS, but is ignored by FoxPro for Windows.

SET SYSMENU

Syntax

SET SYSMENU ON/OFF/AUTOMATIC/TO [*System menu popup list/pad list*]/TO [DEFAULT] [SAVE/ NOSAVE]

The SET SYSMENU command allows or prohibits the access of the FoxPro system menu bar during the execution of programs. Note that after using a custom menu, SET SYSMENU TO DEFAULT can be used to restore the default FoxPro menus.

SET TALK

Syntax

SET TALK ON/OFF [WINDOW *windowname* / NOWINDOW]

The SET TALK command turns off (or on) screen responses to most FoxPro operations and calculations within a program.

SET TEXTMERGE

Syntax

SET TEXTMERGE [ON/OFF] [TO [*filename*] [ADDITIVE]] [WINDOW *windowname*] [SHOW/NOSHOW]

The SET TEXTMERGE command allows or prohibits the evaluating of fields, functions, or expressions surrounded by the text merge delimiters.

SET TEXTMERGE DELIMITERS

Syntax

SET TEXTMERGE DELIMITERS [TO *expC1*[, *expC2*]]

The SET TEXTMERGE DELIMITERS command is used to change the default delimiters for textmerge operations.

SET TRBETWEEN

Syntax

SET TRBETWEEN ON/OFF

The SET TRBETWEEN command enables or disables tracing between breakpoints in FoxPro's Trace window during debugging operations.

SET TOPIC

Syntax

SET TOPIC TO [*expC/expL*]

The SET TOPIC command specifies the initial help topic which appears in the Help window when FoxPro help is activated.

SET TYPEAHEAD

Syntax

SET TYPEAHEAD TO *expN*

The SET TYPEAHEAD command changes the size of the typeahead buffer. Its default value is 20; valid entries are from zero to 33,000.

SET UDFPARMS

Syntax

SET UDFPARMS TO VALUE/REFERENCE

The SET UDFPARMS command controls whether parameters to a user-defined function are passed by value, or by reference.

SET UNIQUE

Syntax

SET UNIQUE ON/OFF

The SET UNIQUE command is used in combination with indexes to create indexes with no duplicate key expressions or fields.

SET VIEW

Syntax

SET VIEW ON/OFF

The SET VIEW command enables (or disables) the View window.

SET VIEW TO

Syntax

SET VIEW TO *filename*

The SET VIEW TO command activates the View file specified by *filename* and places all its settings into effect.

SET WINDOW OF MEMO

Syntax

SET WINDOW OF MEMO TO *windowname*

The SET WINDOW OF MEMO command identifies windows which can be used to edit a memo field.

SHOW GET

Syntax

SHOW GET variable[, *expN* [PROMPT *expC*]] [ENABLE/DISABLE] [LEVEL *expN*] [COLOR *color-pair list*/COLOR SCHEME *expN*]

The SHOW GET command is used to display the @... GET object used to represent a specified memory variable.

```
SHOW GETS
```

Syntax

```
SHOW GETS variable [ENABLE/DISABLE] [LEVEL expN] [OFF/ONLY] [LOCK] [WINDOW windowname]
[COLOR color-pair list/COLOR SCHEME expN]
```

The SHOW GETS command is used to redisplay all @... GET controls.

```
SHOW MENU
```

Syntax

```
SHOW MENU menuname/ALL [PAD padname] [SAVE]
```

The SHOW MENU command displays a menu without activating the menu, SHOW MENU can be used while designing the menu, to check its appearance.

```
SHOW OBJECT
```

Syntax

```
SHOW OBJECT expN [PROMPT expC] [ENABLE/DISABLE] [LEVEL expN] [COLOR color-pair list/
COLOR SCHEME expN]
```

The SHOW OBJECT command is used to redisplay an object having the specified object number.

```
SHOW POPUP
```

Syntax

```
SHOW POPUP popupname/ALL [SAVE]
```

The SHOW POPUP command is used to show a popup or group of menu popups without activating it.

```
SHOW WINDOW
```

Syntax

```
SHOW WINDOW windowname/ALL [SAVE] [TOP/BOTTOM/SAME] [IN WINDOW windowname/IN SCREEN]
```

The SHOW WINDOW command is used to show a user-defined or system window without activating it.

SIZE POPUP

Syntax

SIZE POPUP *popupname* TO *expN1*, *expN2*/BY *expN3*, *expN4*

The SIZE POPUP command enables you to size a popup menu.

SKIP

Syntax

SKIP *expN* [IN *alias*]

The SKIP command moves the record pointer. The command moves the record pointer forward by one record if *expN* is omitted. Values can be expressed as constants or as memory variables. Include the IN *alias* option to move the record pointer within a table that is open in a different work area.

SORT

Syntax

SORT TO *filename* ON *field1* [/A][/C][/D][, *field2* [/A][/C][/D]...] [ASCENDING / DESCENDING] [*scope*] [FOR *condition*] [WHILE *condition*] [FIELDS *fieldlist* / FIELDS LIKE *skeleton* / FIELDS EXCEPT *skeleton*] [NOOPTIMIZE]

The SORT command creates a sorted duplicate of a table. The new table contains records arranged in the order specified by the fields listed. A scope (Record No., NEXT X, ALL, or REST) can be used to limit the records that are included in the sorted table.

STORE

Syntax

STORE *expression* TO *memvarlist/array element list*

The STORE command stores a specified expression to the memory variable named. If the memory variable does not exist prior to the use of the STORE command, an appropriate memory variable is created. The ARRAY option stores the values to the named array.

SUM

Syntax

```
SUM [expression list] [scope] [TO memvarlist] [TO ARRAY array] [FOR condition] [WHILE
condition] [NOOPTIMIZE]
```

The SUM command provides a total of expressions involving numerical fields. If the TO option is specified, totals are stored to the memory variables identified with TO; otherwise, totals are displayed on the screen. The FOR and WHILE *condition* options can be used to limit totals to include numerical fields to a range of records. The ARRAY option stores the values to the named array.

SUSPEND

Syntax

```
SUSPEND
```

The SUSPEND command suspends program execution while keeping files open and memory variables intact. It is used primarily for debugging purposes; execution can be restarted with the RESUME command.

TEXT

Syntax

```
TEXT
...text to be displayed...
ENDTEXT
```

The TEXT command displays all text that appears between the TEXT and ENDTEXT commands in the active window.

TOTAL

Syntax

```
TOTAL TO filename ON key [scope] [FIELDS fieldlist / FIELDS LIKE skeleton / FIELDS
EXCEPT skeleton] [FOR condition] [WHILE condition] [NOOPTIMIZE]
```

The TOTAL command adds the numerical fields within the active table and creates a new table that contains a single record for each group of records in the original table. The single record shows the total for the records in the original table.

TYPE

Syntax

TYPE *filename.ext* [AUTO] [WRAP] [TO PRINT [PROMPT] / TO FILE *filename*] [NUMBER]

The TYPE command displays the contents of a disk file in the active window. If the TO PRINT option is used, the file is printed. The TO FILE option sends the output of the TYPE command to the named disk file. The NUMBER option causes line numbers to be included in the output.

UNLOCK

Syntax

UNLOCK [IN *expN* ¦ *expC* ¦ ALL]

The UNLOCK command releases one or more locks from records or from files.

UPDATE

Syntax

UPDATE [RANDOM] ON *keyfield* FROM *alias* REPLACE *field* WITH *expression*[, field2 WITH expression2...]

The UPDATE command uses data from a specified table to make changes to the active table. The changes are made by matching records in both tables on one key field.

USE

Syntax

USE [*filename*/?] [IN *work area*] [AGAIN] [INDEX *indexfile list*/? [ORDER [*expN*/.IDXfile/ [TAG] *tag name* [OF .CDXfile] [ASCENDING/DESCENDING]]]] [ALIAS alias] [EXCLUSIVE] [SHARED] [NOUPDATE]

The USE command opens a table and related indexes in the chosen work area. If ? is used instead of a filename, a picklist of available filenames appears. The INDEX and ORDER options are used to specify open indexes and active index tags. The IN option is used to open a table in a different work area. ALIAS can be used to specify an alias name for the table. Use the EXCLUSIVE option on a local area network, when the file is to be opened for exclusive (non-shared) use, and use the SHARED option to open the table for shared use. Use NOUPDATE to open the table as read-only.

WAIT

Syntax

WAIT [expC] [TO memvar] [WINDOW [NOWAIT]] [CLEAR] [TIMEOUT expN]

The WAIT command halts operation of a command file and displays an optional prompt until a key is pressed. If the TO option is used, the key pressed is stored to the memory variable named *memvar*.

ZAP

Syntax

ZAP

The ZAP command removes all records from the active table. Using a ZAP command is the same as entering a DELETE ALL command, followed by a PACK command.

ZOOM WINDOW

Syntax

ZOOM WINDOW windowname MIN/MAX/NORM [AT row1,col1/FROM row1,col1 [SIZE row2,col2/TO row2,col2]]

The ZOOM WINDOW command is used to change the size and the position of a system or user-defined window.

Function Reference

32

This chapter describes the FoxPro functions. Each function's name is followed by its proper syntax, and a description of that function. For a similar description of the FoxPro commands, see Chapter 31, "Command Reference."

Throughout this chapter, any parameters which are enclosed in brackets [ ] are optional. *expC* means a character *expression*, *expN* means a numeric expression, *expD* means a date expression, and *expL* means a logical expression. If the data type does not matter, the term *expression* or *expr* is used. Also note that where a function allows an *alias* argument, you can use the alias name (in quotes), or you can use the number of the work area.

ABS

Syntax

ABS(*expN*)

The ABS( ) function provides the absolute (positive) value of the specified numeric expression.

ACOPY

Syntax

ACOPY(*expC1, expC2*[, *expN1*[, *expN2*[, *expN3*]]])

The ACOPY( ) function copies elements from the source array <*expC1*> to elements of the destination array <*expC2*>. The elements in the destination array are replaced by those copied from the source array. *expN1* specifies an optional starting position in the source array, and *expN2* denotes the number of elements to copy, beginning with *expN1*. (If *expN1* is omitted, copying begins with the first element of the array.) *expN3* specifies an optional starting position in the destination array.

The arrays can be one- or two-dimensional. If the destination array doesn't exist, FoxPro creates it. When FoxPro creates the array, the size of the destination array will be the same as the size of the source array.

ACOS

Syntax

ACOS(*expN*)

The ACOS( ) function provides the angle size, as measured in radians, for a given cosine value. (To convert degrees to radians, use the RTOD( ) function.) The value supplied to the numeric expression must be between -1 and +1. Acceptable values for *expN* range from 0 to +1.

ADEL

Syntax

ADEL (*expC, expN*[, 2])

The ADEL( ) function deletes an element from a one-dimensional array, or deletes a row or a column from a two-dimensional array. (Deleting an element, row or column from an array does not change the size of the array.) Instead, the trailing elements, rows or columns are moved to the start of the array, and the last element, row or column in the array is set to a logical false (.F.). *expC* is the name of the array, and *expN* is the element to be deleted. Use the optional ,2 argument to delete a column from a two-dimensional array. If the element, row or column is successfully deleted, 1 is returned.

ADIR

Syntax

ADIR(*expC1*[, *expC2*[, *expC3*]])

The ADIR( ) function places information about all files in the current directory or all files that match a file skeleton into an array, and then returns the number of files. *expC1* denotes the name of the array. *expC2* is a DOS file skeleton, and the optional *expC3* identifies information that should be returned by the function: "D" for subdirectory data, "H" for hidden files, "S" for system files, or "V" for volume names.

AELEMENT

Syntax

AELEMENT(*expC, expN1*[, *expN2*])

The AELEMENT( ) function returns the number of an array element from the element's subscripts. *expC* denotes the name of the array. *expN1* denotes the row subscript, and *expN2* denotes the column subscript. Where the array is two-dimensional, include both *expN1* and *expN2*.

AFIELDS

Syntax

AFIELDS(*expC*)

The AFIELDS( ) function inserts information about the structure of the current table into an array, and returns the number of fields in the table. Use *expC* to name the array. The information inserted in the array includes the data from the four columns which normally appear when you perform a LIST STRUCTURE command.

AFONT

Syntax

AFONT(*array*[, *expC*[, *expN*]])

The AFONT( ) function inserts the names of all available Windows fonts into an array. *array* specifies the name of the array. The optional *expC* can be used to name a font where you want to create an array that contains the available font sizes for a specific font. The optional *expN* can be used to name a specific font size and determine whether a font size is available for a font. If the array is successfully created, AFONT( ) returns a logical true (.T.); otherwise, AFONT( ) returns a logical false (.F.).

AINS

Syntax

AINS(*expC*, *expN*[, 2])

The AINS( ) function inserts a new element into an array. *expC* denotes the name of the array. *expN* denotes an element number (in the case of one-dimensional arrays), or a row or column number (in the case of two-dimensional arrays). The optional ,2 argument denotes that *expN2* refers to a column; if omitted, reference to a row is assumed.

ALEN

Syntax

ALEN(*expC*[, *expN*])

The ALEN( ) function provides the number of elements, rows, or columns in an array. ExpC is the array name. ExpN indicates whether the function should return the number of elements, rows, or columns. Where *expN* is 0 (or is omitted), the number of elements is provided. If *expN* is 1, the number of rows is provided. If *expN* is 2, the number of columns is provided.

ALIAS

Syntax

ALIAS([*expN*])

The ALIAS( ) function provides the table alias for the work area specified by the numeric expression *expN* or the alias name *expC*. If <*expN*> or <*expC*> are omitted, ALIAS( ) returns the alias of the table which is open in the current work area. If no table is open in the current or specified work area, a null string is returned.

ALLTRIM

Syntax

ALLTRIM(*expC*)

The ALLTRIM( ) function provides the character expression *expC*, minus all leading and trailing blanks. The ALLTRIM( ) function is the equivalent of the use of LTRIM(RTRIM(*expC*)).

ANSITOOEM

Syntax

ANSITOOEM(*expC*)

The ANSITOOEM( ) function converts each character in the character expression to the corresponding character in the OEM character set. (Note that this function is not supported by other versions of FoxPro.) The ANSITOOEM( ) function can be used to move data from FoxPro for Windows to FoxPro for DOS.

ASC

Syntax

ASC(*expC*)

The ASC( ) function converts a character or the leftmost character in a character string as defined by *expC*, into its equivalent ASCII value.

ASCAN

Syntax

ASCAN(*expC, expression*[, *expN1*[, *expN2*]])

The ASCAN( ) function searches an array for an element containing the same data and data type as *<expr>*. If a match is found, the number of the element which contains the expression is returned. If a match is not found, the function returns a 0. *expC* denotes the array to be searched, and expression is the search term. *expN1* denotes an optional starting element for the search (when omitted, the search begins at the array's first element), and *expN2* denotes an optional number of elements to be searched (when omitted, the entire array is searched).

ASIN

Syntax

ASIN(*expN*)

The ASIN( ) function provides the angle, as measured in radians, for a given sine value. (To convert radians into degrees, use the RTOD( ) function.) The value supplied to the numeric expression must be between -1 and +1.

ASORT

Syntax

ASORT(*expC*[, *expN1*[, *expN2*[, *expN3*]]])

The ASORT( ) function sorts the elements in an array, in ascending or descending order. *expC* is the array's name. *expN1* denotes an optional starting element for the sort (when omitted, the sort begins at the array's first element), and *expN2* denotes a starting column for the sort. (If *expN2* is included, then *expN1* is assumed to refer to a row.) The optional *expN3* denotes the sort order, 0 for ascending and 1 for descending. When *expN3* is omitted, an ascending sort is assumed.

ASUBSCRIPT

Syntax

ASUBSCRIPT(*expC, expN1, expN2*)

The ASUBSCRIPT( ) function provides the row or column subscript of an element from the element's number. *expC* is the array name. *expN1* denotes the element number, and *expN2* is 1 if the row location should be returned by the function, or 2 if the column location should be returned by the function.

AT

Syntax

AT(*expC1*, *expC2*[, *expN*])

The AT( ) function provides a numeric value indicating the starting position of a substring denoted by *expC1* within the character string denoted by *expC2*. The optional *expN* tells FoxPro to search for the expNth occurrence of *expC1* in *expC2*.

ATAN

Syntax

ATAN(*expN*)

The ATAN( ) function provides the angle, as measured in radians, for a given tangent angle. (To convert radians to degrees, use the RTOD( ) function.) The value specified by the numeric expression is the tangent of the angle. It can range between pi/2 and -pi/2.

ATC

Syntax

ATC(*expC1*, *expC2*[, *expN*])

The ATC( ) function searches *expC2* for *expC1*, without regard for the case of these two expressions. If you want a case-sensitive search, use the AT( ) function. The optional *expN* tells FoxPro to search for the expNth occurrence of *expC1* in *expC2*.

ATCLINE

Syntax

ATCLINE(*expC1*, *expC2*)

The ATCLINE( ) function searches *expC2* for the occurrence of *expC1* without concern for the case (upper or lower) of the characters in either expression. If the search is successful, the function returns the number of the line containing the first character expression.

If the search is unsuccessful, the function returns a 0. If you want a case-sensitive search, use the ATLINE( ) function.

ATLINE

Syntax

ATLINE(*expC1, expC2*)

The ATLINE( ) function searches *expC2* for the occurrence of *expC1*. The case of the search term must match that of the data being searched for the search to be successful. If the search is successful, the function returns the number of the line containing the first character expression. If the search is unsuccessful, the function returns a 0. If you want a search that ignores the case of the characters, use the ATCLINE( ) function.

ATN2

Syntax

ATN2(*expN1, expN2*)

The ATN2( ) functions as the angle, as measured in radians, where the cosine and the sine of a given point are specified. Use <*expN1*> to specify the sine of the angle, and use <*expN2*> to specify the cosine of the angle. The value of <*expN1*>/<*expN2*> must range between pi and -pi. To convert the resulting value to degrees, use the RTOD( ) function.

BAR

Syntax

BAR( )

The BAR( ) function provides a number representing the most recently selected option from the active popup menu. If no popup menu is active, the BAR( ) function provides a 0.

BETWEEN

Syntax

BETWEEN(expr1, expr2, expr3)

The BETWEEN( ) function provides a logical true (.T.) when expr1 is greater than or equal to expr2 and less than or equal to expr3; otherwise, the function provides a logical false (.F.). The expressions supplied must be of the same type.

BOF

Syntax

BOF([alias])

The BOF( ) function provides a logical true (.T.) if the record pointer is at the beginning of the file (above the first record in the active table). The optional alias can be used to test for the beginning of the file in another work area.

CAPSLOCK

Syntax

CAPSLOCK([*expL*])

The CAPSLOCK( ) function turns the Caps Lock keyboard mode on or off, or it provides the current state of Caps Lock. CAPSLOCK(.T.) turns the Caps Lock mode on, and CAPSLOCK(.F.) turns the Caps Lock mode off. When *expL* is omitted, the keyboard state is not changed, and the status of CAPSLOCK( ) is provided.

CDOW

Syntax

CDOW(*expD*)

The CDOW( ) function provides the name for the day of the week, for a given date value.

CDX

Syntax

CDX(*expN*[, alias])

The CDX( ) function provides the filename of the multiple index file specified by the order number. (The CDX( ) function is identical in operation to the MDX( ) function.) The numeric expression specifies the position of the .CDX index file, as controlled by the

SET INDEX TO command. Use the optional alias to return the filename of a .CDX file open in a different work area.

CEILING

Syntax

CEILING(*expN*)

The CEILING( ) function returns the smallest integer greater than or equal to a numeric value.

CHR

Syntax

CHR(*expN*)

The CHR( ) function provides the character whose decimal ASCII code is equivalent to *expN*.

CHRSAW

Syntax

CHRSAW([*expN*])

The CHRSAW( ) function determines whether or not a character is present in the keyboard buffer. CHRSAW( ) returns a logical true (.T.) if a character is present in the keyboard buffer, and a logical false (.F.) if a character is not present in the buffer.

CHRTRAN

Syntax

CHRTRAN(*expC1*, *expC2*, *expC3*)

The CHRTRAN( ) function replaces each character in *expC1* that matches a character in *expC2* with the corresponding character in *expC3*.

CMONTH

Syntax

CMONTH(*expD*)

The CMONTH( ) function provides the name of the month which corresponds to a date value.

CNTBAR

Syntax

CNTBAR(*expC*)

The CNTBAR( ) function provides the number of bars in the popup menu named by *expC*.

CNTPAD

Syntax

CNTPAD(*expC*)

The CNTPAD( ) function provides the number of menu pads in the menu bar named by *expC*.

COL

Syntax

COL( )

The COL( ) function provides the current column location of the cursor.

COS

Syntax

COS(*expN*)

The COS( ) function provides a cosine value for an angle as measured in radians. The numeric expression supplied is the angle measured in radians. If the size is known in degrees, use the DTOR( ) function first to convert the size to radians, then use the COS( ) function. To convert the result back to degrees, use the RTOD( ) function.

CPCONVERT

Syntax

CPCONVERT(*expN1, expN2, expC*)

The CPCONVERT( ) function converts the character expression named in *expC* from one code page specified by *expN1* to another specified by *expN2*.

CPCURRENT

Syntax

CPCURRENT([1])

The CPCURRENT( ) function provides the code page setting in your configuration file (if one exists), or it provides the code page for the current operating system. If the optional 1 parameter is included, the function returns the code page for the current operating system, regardless of the code page setting in the configuration file.

CPDBF

Syntax

CPDBF([*expC | expN*])

The CPDBP( ) function returns the code page with which an open table has been marked. The function assumes the current work area. You can include the optional *expC* (as a work area number) or *expN* (as an alias name) if the table you specify is open in a different work area.

CTOD

Syntax

CTOD(*expC*)

The CTOD( ) function converts a character expression containing a string of characters formatted as a date into a date variable. The character string supplied by the expression can vary from "1/1/100" to "12/31/9999."

CURDIR

Syntax

CURDIR([expC])

The CURDIR( ) function provides the name of the current directory. The optional *expC* denotes a specific disk drive; where omitted, the current drive is assumed. If *expC* is provided and the specified drive does not exist, the function returns a null string.

DATE

Syntax

DATE( )

The DATE( ) function provides the current system date, as measured by the system clock.

DAY

Syntax

DAY(expD)

The DAY( ) function provides the numeric day of the month that corresponds to a date value.

DBF

Syntax

DBF([alias])

The DBF( ) function provides the name of the currently active database file in the currently selected work area.

DELETED

Syntax

DELETED([alias])

The DELETED( ) function provides a logical true (.T.) if the current record is marked for deletion. The function provides a logical false (.F.) if the record is not marked for deletion. The optional alias can be used to test for deleted records in a table that is open in another work area.

DESCENDING

Syntax

DESCENDING([cdx file,] *expN1*[, *expN2* ¦ *expC*])

The DESCENDING( ) function returns a logical value which indicates whether an index tag was created with the DESCENDING keyword or the DESCENDING keyword was included as part of a USE, SET INDEX or SET ORDER statement. *expN1*, which is required, is a number beginning at 1 which specifies which index file or index tag should be tested. (The value corresponds to the order in which the indexes were opened.) Use the optional *cdx file* name to specify a compound index file other than the structural compound index. By default, the function assumes the table that's open in the current work area. The optional *expN2* (as a work area number) or *expC* (as an alias) can be used to specify a table open in another work area.

DIFFERENCE

Syntax

DIFFERENCE(*expC1*, *expC2*)

The DIFFERENCE( ) function returns a numeric value representing the difference between two character strings. The numeric value returned is a number between 0 and 4, and is calculated by converting both strings to equivalent SOUNDEX codes and comparing the two SOUNDEX codes. Two expressions that have no letters in common return a value of 0, while two expressions which are a close match phonetically return a value of 4.

DISKSPACE

Syntax

DISKSPACE( )

The DISKSPACE( ) function provides the number of bytes available on the default drive.

DMY

Syntax

DMY(*expD*)

The DMY( ) function provides a date expression, using the European date format (DD Month YY) for the expression. The resultant format is DD-Month-YY if SET CENTURY is OFF, or DD-Month-YYYY if SET CENTURY is ON.

DOW

Syntax

DOW(*expD*)

The DOW( ) function provides a number representing the day of the week which corresponds to the date expression. The value provided ranges from 1 (Sunday) to 7 (Saturday).

DTOC

Syntax

DTOC(*expD*[, 1])

The DTOC( ) function converts the specified date expression into a string of characters. If you include the optional 1 parameter, the character string is returned in a YYYYMMDD format, which is useful as part of an expression used in indexing.

DTOR

Syntax

DTOR(*expN*)

The DTOR( ) function takes the angle specified by *expN*, and converts it from degrees to radians.

DTOS

Syntax

DTOS(*expD*)

The DTOS( ) function provides a character string in the format YYYYMMDD for the specified date expression, regardless of the SET DATE or SET CENTURY settings. The DTOS function is useful for maintaining proper chronological order when indexing on date fields.

EMPTY

Syntax

EMPTY(*expression*)

The EMPTY( ) function returns a logical true (.T.) when the value of expression is blank (in the case of character expressions), or 0 (in the case of numeric expressions), or false (in the case of logical expressions). The function also returns a logical true if expression refers to a memo field and the memo field is empty.

EOF

Syntax

EOF([alias])

The EOF( ) function provides a logical true (.T.) if the record pointer is at the end of a database, and a logical false (.F.) if the record pointer is not at the end of the database.

ERROR

Syntax

ERROR( )

The ERROR( ) function provides a value that corresponds to an error detected during the execution of a FoxPro program. (An ON ERROR routine must be in effect, or the ERROR( ) function will return a value of 0.)

EVALUATE

Syntax

EVALUATE(*expC*)

The EVALUATE( ) function evaluates the character expression named as *expC*, and provides the result of the expression.

EXP

Syntax

EXP(*expN*)

The EXP( ) function provides an exponential value of a numeric expression.

FCLOSE

Syntax

FCLOSE(*expN*)

The FCLOSE( ) function flushes and closes a file that was opened with a low-level file function. *expN* identifies the numeric handle of the file, which was returned by the FCREATE( ) or FOPEN( ) function when the file was created.

FCOUNT

Syntax

FCOUNT([alias])

The FCOUNT( ) function provides the number of fields in a database. The optional [alias] can be used to return the number of fields in a database that are open in another work area.

FCREATE

Syntax

FCREATE(*expC*[, *expN*])

The FCREATE( ) function creates and opens a low-level file. *expC* specifies the filename, and the optional *expN* assigns an attribute to the file according to the following table. If omitted, the file is opened with an attribute of read/write.

0   Read/write

1   Read only

2   Hidden

3   Read only and hidden

4   System

5   Read only and system

6   System and hidden

7   Read only, system, and hidden

FEOF

Syntax

FEOF(*expN*)

The FEOF( ) function provides a logical true (.T.) when the file pointer is positioned at the end of the file (EOF), and a logical false (.F.) when it is not. ExpN indicates the numeric handle of the file to test for the end-of-file condition.

FERROR

Syntax

FERROR( )

The FERROR( ) function is used to test whether a low-level file function was successful. FERROR( ) provides a 0 if the last low-level function was successful. If the last function was unsuccessful, a value other than 0 is provided.

FFLUSH

Syntax

FFLUSH(*expN*)

The FFLUSH( ) function flushes a file whose handle is *expN*. If the file was written to, FFLUSH( ) writes all data stored in the buffers to disk.

FGETS

Syntax

FGETS(*expN1*[, *expN2*])

The FGETS( ) function returns a series of bytes from a file or a communications port opened with a low-level file function until it reaches a carriage return. *expN1* denotes the file's handle as established with the FCREATE( ) or FOPEN( ) function. The optional *expN2* specifies the number of bytes the function should return, unless a carriage return is encountered first.

FIELD

Syntax

FIELD(*expN1*[, alias])

The FIELD( ) function provides the field name matching the numeric position of the field within the database structure.

FILE

Syntax

FILE(*expC*)

The FILE( ) function provides a logical true (.T.) when the character expression matches the name for an existing file in the default directory. If no file by the specified name can be found, the function provides a logical false (.F.).

FILTER

Syntax

FILTER([alias])

The FILTER( ) function provides the filter expression of the current work area. The optional alias can be used to return a filter from another work area. If no filter is in effect, a null string is provided.

FKLABEL

Syntax

FKLABEL(*expN*)

The FKLABEL( ) function provides the name of the function key which corresponds to *expN*.

FKMAX

Syntax

FKMAX( )

The FKMAX( ) function provides the number of programmable function keys present on the computer. On an IBM compatible computer with 10 function keys, the FKMAX( ) function returns a value of 28, because F1 is not considered to be a programmable key, and Shift+F10 is reserved for use by FoxPro macros. Also, F11 and F12 are not programmable.

FLOCK

Syntax

FLOCK(*expN ¦ expC*)

The FLOCK( ) function attempts to lock a table, and returns a logical true (.T.) if the locking operation was successful, and a logical false (.F.) otherwise. By default, the function assumes the table that's open in the current work area. The optional *expN* (as a work area number) or *expC* (as an alias) can be used to specify a table open in another work area.

FLOOR

Syntax

FLOOR(*expN*)

The FLOOR( ) function returns the largest integer less than or equal to the value specified by the expression.

FONTMETRIC

Syntax

FONTMETRIC(*expN1*[, *expC1*, *expN2*[, *expC2*]])

The FONTMETRIC( ) function returns the font attributes for the current installed Windows fonts. *expN1* is a numeric value, as indicated in the table which follows, that identifies the font attribute.

value	font attribute
1	Character height in pixels
2	Character ascent (units above baseline) in pixels
3	Character descent (units below baseline) in pixels
4	Leading (space between lines) in pixels
5	Extra leading in pixels
6	Average character width in pixels
7	Maximum character width in pixels
8	Font weight
9	Italic (0 =no, non-zero=yes)
10	Underlined (0 = no, non-zero = yes)
11	Strikeout (0 = no, non-zero = yes)
12	First character defined in font
13	Last character defined in font
14	Default character (substituted for characters not in font)
15	Word break character
16	Pitch and family
17	Character set
18	Overhang (extra added width)
19	Horizontal aspect for font device
20	Vertical aspect for font device

Use the optional *expN2* to denote the point size of a font specified by the optional *expC1*. Use the optional *expC2* to denote a font style code, to return an attribute for a specific font style. Where *expC2* is omitted, the attribute is returned for the normal font style.

FOPEN

Syntax

FOPEN(*expC*[, *expN*])

The FOPEN( ) function opens a file for use with the low-level file functions. *expC* denotes the filename, and the optional *expN* specifies a file attribute with a value of 0 for read only, 1 for write only, or 2 for read-write. If *expN* is omitted, the file is opened read-only. If the file cannot be found, FOPEN( ) returns a value of -1.

FOR

Syntax

```
FOR([expN1[, expN2 ¦ expC]])
```

The FOR( ) function returns the index filter expression of a single-entry .IDX index file or of an index tag which is open. All arguments are optional. *expN1*, where used, specifies a filter expression which should be used to return from the open index files or tags. By default, the function assumes the table that's open in the current work area. The optional *expN* (as a work area number) or *expC* (as an alias) can be used to specify a table open in another work area.

FOUND

Syntax

```
FOUND([alias])
```

The FOUND( ) function provides a logical true (.T.) if the last CONTINUE, FIND, LOCATE, or SEEK command was successful; otherwise, a logical false (.F.) is provided. The optional alias can be used to test for a successful search in another work area.

FPUTS

Syntax

```
FPUTS(expN1, expC[, expN2])
```

The FPUTS( ) function writes a character string, carriage return and line feed to a file which was opened with a low-level file function. *expN1* denotes the name of the file, and *expC* is the character string which gets written to the file. *expN2*, which is optional, specifies the number of bytes to write to the file.

FREAD

Syntax

FREAD(*expN1, expN2*)

The FREAD( ) function provides a specified number of bytes from a file which was opened with a low-level function. *expN1* identifies the numeric handle of the file, which was returned by the FCREATE( ) or FOPEN( ) function when the file was created. *expN2* denotes the number of bytes to read from the file, beginning with the current position of the file pointer.

FSEEK

Syntax

FSEEK(*expN1, expN2*[, *expN3*])

The FSEEK( ) function moves the file pointer within a file that was opened with a low-level function. *expN1* identifies the numeric handle of the file, which was returned by the FCREATE( ) or FOPEN( ) function when the file was created. *expN2* denotes the number of bytes to move the pointer. (If *expN2* is a positive value, the pointer is moved forward in the file, and if *expN2* is a negative value, the pointer is moved backwards in the file.) By default, the file pointer is moved relative to the start of the file. You can alternatively move the file pointer relative to the current file pointer position, or the end of the file by including the optional *expN3*. If *expN3* is zero (the default), movement is relative to the start of the file. If *expN3* is 1, movement is relative to the current file pointer position. If *expN3* is 2, movement is relative to the end of the file.

FSIZE

Syntax

FSIZE(*expC*[, alias])

The FSIZE( ) function provides the size of *expC*, representing the specified field, in bytes. The optional alias can be used to select a field from a file in another work area.

FULLPATH

Syntax

FULLPATH(*expC*[, 1])

The FULLPATH( ) function provides the complete DOS pathname for the file named as *expC*. By default, FoxPro uses the FoxPro path to search for the file. You can include the optional ,1 argument to tell FoxPro to search the DOS path.

FV

Syntax

FV(payment, rate, periods)

The FV( ) function provides the future value of an investment. <payment> is the payment amount and can be negative or positive. <rate> is a positive number representing the interest rate, compounded per period. <periods> is a number representing the number of payments. If the payments are compounded monthly and the interest rate is compounded annually, divide the interest rate by 12 to obtain the monthly interest rate before using the function.

FWRITE

Syntax

FWRITE(*expN1*, *expC*[, *expN2*])

The FWRITE( ) function writes a character string to a file that was opened with a low-level file function. *expN1* denotes the name of the file, and *expC* is the character string which gets written to the file. *expN2*, which is optional, specifies the number of bytes to write to the file. FWRITE( ) is different from FPUTS( ) in that the FWRITE( ) function does not add a carriage return and linefeed.

GETBAR

Syntax

GETBAR(*expC*, *expN*)

The GETBAR( ) function provides the number of a bar at a specific position in a popup menu. *expC* specifies the popup name, and *expN* specifies a position within the popup.

GETDIR

Syntax

GETDIR([expC1[, expC2]])

The GETDIR( ) function displays the Select Directory dialog box, and returns the name of the chosen directory as a character string. Use the optional *expC1* to denote the directory initially displayed in the dialog box. Use the optional *expC2* to denote the prompt for the directory list in the Select Directory dialog box.

GETENV

Syntax

GETENV(expC)

The GETENV( ) function provides a character string which contains the contents of the DOS environmental variable named as *expC*.

GETEXPR

Syntax

GETEXPR [expC1] TO memvar [TYPE expC2[; expC3]] [DEFAULT expC4]

The GETEXPR( ) function displays the Expression Builder, and stores the expression constructed in the Expression Builder to a memory variable, or to an array. *memvar* denotes the name of the variable or array element where the expression should be stored. Include the optional TYPE *expC2*[; *expC3*] to denote the expression type, where C is character, N is numeric, D is date, and L is logical, and use *expC3* to specify an error message which is displayed if the expression is not valid. Where *expC3* is included with *expC2*, *expC2* and *expC3* must be separated by a semicolon (;), and the entire combination of *expC2*, the semicolon, and *expC3* must be enclosed in quotes. Use the optional DEFAULT *expC4* clause to display an initial default expression in the Expression Builder.

GETFILE

Syntax

GETFILE([expC1][, expC2][,expC3][,expN])

The GETFILE( ) function displays the Open dialog box, and returns the name of the file you choose from that dialog box. All the arguments are optional. *expC1* denotes a file extension; if included, only files with that extension are displayed in the Open dialog box. *expC2* denotes a prompt which appears at the top of the dialog box. *expC3* replaces the text which appears in the Open button. *expN* is a value of 1 or 2 which denotes the buttons which appear in the dialog box. A value of 1 causes Open, New, and Cancel buttons to be included in the dialog box. A value of 2 causes Open, None, and Cancel buttons to be included in the dialog box.

GETFONT

Syntax

GETFONT( )

The GETFONT( ) function displays the Font dialog box, and returns the name, size, and style of the font you chose from the dialog box. Your choice is returned as a character string with the font name, size and style separated by commas.

GETPAD

Syntax

GETPAD(*expC, expN*)

The GETPAD( ) function provides the name of a menu pad that appears at a specific location in a bar menu. *expC* specifies the menu name, and *expN* identifies the position in the bar menu.

GOMONTH

Syntax

GOMONTH(*expD, expN*)

The GOMONTH( ) function provides a date value that is *expN* months from *expD*. If *expN* is a positive value, the function returns a date which is *expN* months after *expD*. If *expN* is a negative value, the function returns a date which is *expN* months before *expD*.

HEADER

Syntax

HEADER([alias])

The HEADER( ) function provides the number of bytes in the header of the current or specified table/.DBF file. The optional alias may be used to specify a table that is open in another work area.

HOME( )

Syntax

HOME( )

The HOME( ) function returns the name of the directory that FoxPro was started from.

IDXCOLLATE( )

Syntax

IDXCOLLATE([.cdx file,] *expN1* [, *expN2* ¦ *expC*])

The IDXCOLLATE( ) function returns the collation sequence for an index or index tag. This function lets you delete an index file and rebuild it correctly, using a series of SET COLLATE and INDEX commands.

The numeric expression *expN1* denotes for which index or index tag the collation sequence is returned. IDXCOLLATE( ) returns the collation sequence for indexes and index tags in the following order:

1. Collation sequences for single-entry .IDX index files are returned first. The order in which the single-entry index files are included in USE or SET INDEX determines how the collation sequences are returned.

2. The collation sequences for tags in the structural compound index are returned next. The collation sequences are returned for the tags in the order in which the tags were created in the structural compound index.

3. Collation sequences for tags in any open independent compound indexes are returned last. The collation sequences are returned for the tags in the order in which the tags were created in the independent compound indexes.

A null string is returned if *expN1* is greater than the total number of open single-entry .IDX files and structural compound and independent compound index tags.

If you omit the work area and alias, collation sequences are returned from index files which are open for the table in the current work area. To return collation sequences from index files open in another work area, include the work area number denoted as *expN2*, or the table alias specified as *expC*.

IIF

Syntax

IIF(*expL*, expr1, expr2)

The IIF( ) function (Immediate IF) provides a value of expr1 if the logical expression is true, or a value of expr2 if the logical expression is false.(Note that Expr1 and expr2 must be of the same data type.)

INKEY

Syntax

INKEY([*expN*])

The INKEY( ) function provides an integer value between 0 and 255, which corresponds to the ASCII code for the key that was pressed. (The function provides a zero if no key has been pressed.)

INLIST

Syntax

INLIST(expr1, expr2[, expr3...])

The INLIST( ) function determines if an expression can be found within a series of expressions of the same data type. If expr1 can be located in expr2, expr3, and so on, the function returns a logical true (.T.).

INSMODE

Syntax

INSMODE([*expL*])

The INSMODE( ) function changes the Insert/Overwrite mode of the keyboard, depending on the value of *expL*. INSMODE(.T.) turns on the Insert mode, and INSMODE(.F.)

turns off the Insert mode. Where *expL* is omitted, the function provides the current setting of the Insert mode. If the Insert mode is on, .T. is provided. If the Insert mode is off, .F. is provided.

INT

Syntax

INT(*expN*)

The INT( ) function provides the integer portion of *expN*. No rounding occurs with this function; any decimal values are simply dropped.

ISALPHA

Syntax

ISALPHA(*expC*)

The ISALPHA( ) function provides a logical true (.T.) when the first character of *expC* is "a" through "z," or "A" through "Z." A logical false (.F.) is provided if *expC* begins with any other character (such as a number or a punctuation symbol).

ISBLANK

Syntax

ISBLANK(*expr*)

The ISBLANK( ) function returns a logical true (.T.) if the expression *expr* is blank, or a logical false (.F.) if the expression is not blank.

ISCOLOR

Syntax

ISCOLOR( )

The ISCOLOR( ) function provides a logical true (.T.) if the system has color capability (whether or not a color monitor is being used) and provides a logical false (.F.) if the system has only monochrome capability. This function is provided for backwards compatibility with FoxPro for DOS. On systems running Windows, ISCOLOR( ) always returns a logical true.

ISDIGIT

Syntax

ISDIGIT(*expC*)

The ISDIGIT( ) function provides a logical true (.T.) if the first character of *expC* is a digit (0 to 9).

ISLOWER

Syntax

ISLOWER(*expC*)

The ISLOWER( ) function provides a logical true (.T.) when the first character in *expC* is a lowercase alphabetical character. The function returns a logical false (.F.) when the first character is any character other than a lowercase alphabetical character.

ISREADONLY

Syntax

ISREADONLY([*expC* ¦ *expN*])

The ISREADONLY( ) function returns a logical true if a table/.DBF is opened read-only; otherwise, a logical false (.F.) is returned. FoxPro assumes the table that is open in the current work area. You can include the optional *expC* to name an alias of a table open in another work area, or the optional *expN* to indicate a work area number.

ISUPPER

Syntax

ISUPPER(*expC*)

The ISUPPER( ) function provides a logical true (.T.) when the first character in *expC* is an uppercase alphabetical character. The function returns a logical false (.F.) when the first character is any character other than an uppercase alphabetical character.

KEY

Syntax

KEY(*expN*[, alias])

The KEY( ) function provides the key expression of the specified index file. If a multiple index file is named, the numeric expression supplied in the function refers to the desired index tag in the multiple index file. If no index file is named, the numeric expression refers to the desired index among all open index files in the work area. Use the optional alias to return the index expression for an index open in a different work area.

KEYMATCH( )

Syntax

KEYMATCH(index key [, *expN1* [, *expN2* ¦ *expC*]])

The KEYMATCH( ) function searches an index file or index tag for an index key, and returns a logical true (.T.) if the index key is found. *expN1* denotes which index file or index tag should be searched. If you omit the work area and alias, KEYMATCH( ) searches index files or tags open for the table that is in the current work area. To search index files or tags open in another work area, include the work area number *expN2* or the alias name represented by *expC*.

LASTKEY

Syntax

LASTKEY( )

The LASTKEY( ) function provides the decimal ASCII value for the last key pressed. The LASTKEY( ) function provides the same ASCII values as the INKEY( ) function. In programs, LASTKEY( ) can be useful for determining which key was used to terminate a wait state.

LEFT

Syntax

LEFT(*expC*, *expN*)

The LEFT( ) function provides a character string containing the number of characters specified by the numeric expression, beginning with the leftmost character in the string.

LEN

Syntax

LEN(*expC*)

The LEN( ) function provides a number indicating the length of a character string.

LIKE

Syntax

LIKE(*expC1, expC2*)

The LIKE( ) function compares the pattern with the character string indicated by the expression. The function returns a logical true (.T.) if the character string contained in the expression contains the characters indicated by the patterns. Wildcards * and ? can be used in the pattern. The LIKE function is commonly used with predicates in the SQL language.

LINENO

Syntax

LINENO( )

The LINENO( ) function provides the line number of the next statement in the program which is currently running.

LOCFILE

Syntax

LOCFILE(*expC1*[, *expC2*][, *expC3*])

The LOCFILE( ) function locates a disk file and provides the filename with its complete search path. The Open File dialog box appears if the file cannot be found in the current directory or within the FoxPro path. *expC1* specifies the filename. *expC2* specifies extensions to appear in the Open File dialog box, while *expC3* appears as a prompt.

LOCK

Syntax

```
LOCK([expN | expC1] | [expC2, expN | expC1])
```

The LOCK( ) function attempts to lock a table. (The LOCK( ) function is identical in operation to the RLOCK( ) function.) If the lock is successful, the function returns a logical true. If the lock cannot be placed for any reason, the function returns a logical false. By default, LOCK( ) attempts to lock the table in the current work area. Use *expN* (a work area number) or *expC1* (an alias) to specify a table open in another work area. The optional *expC2* is used to specify multiple records to be locked. For example, if you wanted to lock records one, two, and three, *expC2* would contain the character string "1,2,3". Note that if you plan to lock multiple records at one time, the setting of SET MULTILOCKS must be ON.

LOG

Syntax

```
LOG(expN)
```

The LOG( ) function provides the natural logarithm of the number specified in *expN*. (ExpN must be a value greater than zero.)

LOG10

Syntax

```
LOG10(expN)
```

The LOG10( ) function provides the common (or "base 10") logarithm of the number specified by *expN*. (ExpN must be a value greater than zero.)

LOOKUP

Syntax

```
LOOKUP(<field1>, <search expr>, <field2>[, expC])
```

The LOOKUP( ) function searches a table for the first record with a field that matches the expression specified. Field 1 denotes the field which should return the value, and field 2 denotes the field to search. Use the optional *expC* to name a compact index tag for LOOKUP( ) to search; including this speeds up the search.

LOWER

Syntax

LOWER(*expC*)

The LOWER( ) function converts uppercase letters to lowercase. The LOWER function has no effect on lowercase letters, numbers, spaces, or punctuation marks.

LTRIM

Syntax

LTRIM(*expC*)

The LTRIM( ) function trims leading blanks from the character expression named in *expC*.

LUPDATE

Syntax

LUPDATE([alias])

The LUPDATE( ) function provides a date value representing the last update of the active table. The optional alias can be used to return the last update for a table that is open in another work area.

MAX

Syntax

MAX(expr1, expr2[, expr3...])

The MAX( ) function provides the maximum value of two numeric expressions.

MCOL( )

Syntax

MCOL([*expC*])

The MCOL( ) function provides the screen or window column position of the mouse pointer. Use *expC* to denote a window name; if omitted, MCOL( ) assumes the current window.

MDOWN( )

Syntax

MDOWN( )

The MDOWN( ) function provides a logical value which represents the state of the left mouse button. When the left mouse button is pressed, MDOWN( ) provides a logical true (.T.); otherwise, MDOWN( ) provides a logical false (.F.).

MDX( )

Syntax

MDX(*expN*[, alias])

The MDX( ) function provides the filename of the multiple index file specified by the order number. The numeric expression specifies the position of the .MDX index file, as controlled by the SET INDEX TO command. Use the optional alias to return the filename of an .MDX file open in a different work area.

MDY

Syntax

MDY(*expD*)

The MDY( ) function converts a valid date expression to a format of Month, DD, YY if SET CENTURY is OFF, or to a format of Month, DD,YY if SET CENTURY is ON. The automatic inclusion of a comma after the day makes the MDY( ) function useful for the printing of dates in a spelled-out format, as is commonly used when writing checks.

MEMLINES

Syntax

MEMLINES(*expC*)

The MEMLINES( ) function provides the number of lines in *expC*, which represents a memo field of the current record. The number of lines in the memo field are affected by the current value of SET MEMOWIDTH.

MEMORY

Syntax

MEMORY( )

The MEMORY( ) function provides the amount of free conventional (base) memory, as a numeric value in kilobytes.

MENU

Syntax

MENU( )

The MENU( ) function provides the name of the currently active menu. If a menu is not active, MENU( ) provides a null string ("").

MESSAGE

Syntax

MESSAGE([1])

The MESSAGE( ) function provides a character string provided as an error message in situations where FoxPro detects an error in a program.

MIN

Syntax

MIN(expr1, expr2[, expr3...])

The MIN( ) function provides a minimum value from two or more numeric expressions.

MLINE

Syntax

MLINE(*expC, expN*)

The MLINE( ) function provides the specified line *expN* from *expC*, which represents a memo field in the current record. The value of SET MEMOWIDTH will affect the number of lines in a memo field.

MOD

Syntax

MOD(*expN1*, *expN2*)

The MOD( ) function provides the remainder of a division, where *expN1* is the dividend, and *expN2* is the divisor.

MONTH

Syntax

MONTH(*expD*)

The MONTH( ) function provides the numeric month (1 to 12) which corresponds to a date value. The numbers 1 through 12 correspond to January through December.

MRKBAR

Syntax

MRKBAR(*expC*, *expN*)

The MRKBAR( ) function determines whether a bar located on a popup (defined with the DEFINE POPUP command) or on a FoxPro menu system popup is marked with the SET MARK OF command. Use *expC* to specify the name of the popup that contains the bar. Use *expN* to specify the number of the bar with *expN*.

MRKPAD

Syntax

MRKPAD(*expC1*, *expC2*)

The MRKPAD( ) function determines whether a pad located on a user-defined menu bar or on the FoxPro system menu bar is marked with the SET MARK OF command. Use *expC1* to specify the name of the menu bar which contains the menu pad. Use *expC2* to specify the name of the menu pad.

MROW( )

Syntax

MROW(*expC*)

The MROW( ) function provides the screen or window row position of the mouse pointer. Use *expC* to denote a window name; if omitted, MROW( ) assumes the current window.

MWINDOW( )

Syntax

MWINDOW([<window name>])

The MWINDOW( ) function returns a character string or a logical value indicating the name of a window the mouse is positioned over, or whether the mouse is positioned over a window. If no window name is specified, the function returns the name of the window that the mouse pointer is over, or a null string if the mouse pointer is not over a window. If a window name is specified, the function returns a logical true (.T.) if the mouse pointer is positioned over the specified window, and a logical false (.F.) if it is not.

NDX( )

Syntax

NDX(*expN*[, alias])

The NDX( ) function provides the name of any open index file in the selected work area. The numeric expression is a value between 1 and 7. The value provided by the function indicates the position, in sequential order, of the index file. For example, the second index file named would be number 2, the fourth index file named would be number 4, and so on.

NUMLOCK

Syntax

NUMLOCK([*expL*])

The NUMLOCK( ) function returns the status of the Num Lock key, or it changes the mode of the Num Lock key. NUMLOCK(.T.) turns on Num Lock, and NUMLOCK(.F.)

turns off Num Lock. If the logical expression *expL* is omitted, NUMLOCK( ) returns the status of the Num Lock key.

OBJNUM

Syntax

OBJNUM(*expC*[, *expN*])

The OBJNUM( ) function provides the object number assigned to a GET object. *expC* denotes the variable used to create the GET object, and the optional *expN* can be used to denote an object at a READ level other than the current one.

OBJVAR

Syntax

OBJVAR([<*expN1*> [, <*expN2*>]])

The OBJVAR( ) function provides the name of the memory variable, array element or field associated with an object. Use the optional *expN1* to return the memory variable, array element or field for a specific object, where *expN1* corresponds to the order in which the objects are created. (If omitted, the currently active object is assumed.) Use the optional *expN* to denote an object at a READ level other than the current one.

OCCURS

Syntax

OCCURS(*expC1*, *expC2*)

The OCCURS( ) function provides an integer that represents the number of times *expC1* occurs in *expC2*. If *expC1* does not occur in *expC2*, the function provides a value of zero.

OEMTOANSI

Syntax

OEMTOANSI(<*expC*>)

The OEMTOANSI( ) function converts each character in the character expression to the corresponding character in the ANSI character set. (Note that this function is not supported by other versions of FoxPro.) The OEMTOANSI( ) function can be used to move data from FoxPro for DOS to FoxPro for Windows.

ON

Syntax

ON(<expC1>[, <expC2>])

The ON( ) function provides a character string representing the command assigned to ON ERROR, ON ESCAPE, ON KEY, ON KEY LABEL, ON PAGE or ON READERROR. *expC* is ERROR, ESCAPE, KEY, PAGE, or READERROR. Use the optional *expC2* to name the function key if the name of a key label is to be returned by the function.

ORDER

Syntax

ORDER([alias])

ORDER( ) provides the name of the active index file in the current work area. The optional alias can be used to return the name of the active index in another work area.

OS

Syntax

OS( )

The OS( ) function provides the name and version of the current operating system.

PAD

Syntax

PAD( )

The PAD( ) function provides the name of the pad which was last selected from the active menu bar. If no menu is active, the function provides a null string.

PADC, PADL, PADR

Syntax

PADC(*expression*, expN[, expC])
PADL(*expression*, expN[, expC])

```
PADR(expression, expN[, expC])
```

These functions are used to return a character string from a character expression, padded to a specified length. PADL( ) inserts padding on the left, PADR( ) inserts padding on the right and PADC( ) inserts padding on both sides. *expression* is the expression to be padded. *expN* denotes the total number of characters in the expression after it is padded, and the optional *expC* is the character used to pad the string. If omitted, the string is padded with spaces.

PARAMETERS

Syntax

```
PARAMETERS( )
```

The PARAMETERS( ) function provides a numeric value which indicates the number of parameters passed to the procedure most recently called.

PAYMENT

Syntax

```
PAYMENT(principal, rate, periods)
```

The PAYMENT( ) function provides a payment amount of a loan, given the principal, interest rate, and periods. <principal> can be expressed as a positive or negative number. <rate> is the interest rate, expressed as a positive value. <periods> represents the number of periods (that is, payments) of the loan. If the payments are compounded monthly and the interest rate is compounded yearly, divide the interest rate by 12 to obtain the monthly interest rate before using the function. Note that fractional amounts are rounded to whole numbers.

PCOL

Syntax

```
PCOL( )
```

The PCOL( ) function provides the current column position of the printer.

PI

Syntax

PI( )

The PI( ) function provides the numeric constant pi (approximately 3.14159).

POPUP

Syntax

POPUP( )

The POPUP( ) function provides the name of the active popup menu. If no popup menu is active, the POPUP( ) function returns a null string.

PRINTSTATUS

Syntax

PRINTSTATUS( )

The PRINTSTATUS( ) function provides a logical true (.T.) if the printer is ready and a logical false (.F.) if it is not.

PRMBAR

Syntax

PRMBAR(*expC, expN*)

The PRMBAR( ) function provides the prompt text for a specific option of a popup menu. ExpC specifies the popup name, and *expN* specifies the bar number of the popup menu.

PRMPAD

Syntax

PRMPAD(*expC1, expC2*)

The PRMPAD( ) function provides the prompt text for a specific pad of a bar menu. ExpC1 specifies the menu name, and *expC2* specifies the pad name in the bar menu.

PROGRAM

Syntax

PROGRAM([*expN*])

The PROGRAM( ) function provides the name of the program currently running or the program that was running when an error occurred. Include the optional *expN* when nesting programs (calling a program from a program). When used, the value of *expN* indicates how many levels back FoxPro should look for the program name.

PROMPT

Syntax

PROMPT( )

The PROMPT( ) function provides a prompt representing the last option chosen from the active menu pad or popup menu. If no popup menu is active, the function provides a null string.

PROPER

Syntax

PROPER(*expC*)

The PROPER( ) function converts a character string to one having its initial letter capitalized, and all other letters as lowercase. *expC* denotes the character string to be properly capitalized.

PROW

Syntax

PROW( )

The PROW( ) function provides the current row position of the printer. When an EJECT command is issued, PROW( ) is reset to zero.

PRTINFO

Syntax

PRTINFO(*expN*)

The PRTINFO( ) function returns the current printer settings under FoxPro for Windows. *expN* is a code where 1 is page orientation, 2 is paper size, 3 is paper length, and 4 is paper width. According to the code used, corresponding printer settings are returned.

PUTFILE

Syntax

PUTFILE([*expC1*][, *expC2*][, *expC3*])

The PUTFILE( ) function displays the Save As dialog box, and returns a character string representing the file name chosen or entered in the dialog box. All arguments are optional with this function. *expC1*, when used, denotes a prompt that appears above the text box within the Save As dialog box. *expC2*, when used, specifies a default filename which appears in the text box. *expC3*, when used, specifies a default file extension.

PV

Syntax

PV(*payment, rate, periods*)

The PV( ) function provides the present value of an investment, or the amount that must be invested at a given rate to earn a known future value. *payment* is the payment amount and can be negative or positive. *rate* is a positive number representing the interest rate, compounded per period. *periods* is a number representing the number of payments. If the payments are compounded monthly and the interest rate is compounded annually, divide the interest rate by 12 to obtain the monthly interest rate before using the function.

RAND

Syntax

RAND([*expN*])

The RAND( ) function returns a random number between 0 and 0.999999. The optional numeric expression can be included to provide a seed for generating the random number.

A negative number may also be used in the expression, in which case the system clock is used as the seed for the random number.

RAT

Syntax

RAT(*expC1*, *expC2*[, *expN*])

The RAT( ) function (Reverse AT( )) looks for *expC1* in *expC2*, starting from the rightmost character. The function provides the starting numeric position of the first occurrence of one character expression (or memo field) in another character expression (or memo field). *expC1* and *expC2* can be memo fields. If *expN* is included, the function searches for the expNth occurrence of *expC1* in *expC2*.

RATLINE

Syntax

RATLINE(*expC1*, *expC2*)

The RATLINE( ) function (Reverse ATLINE( )) looks in *expC2* for the last occurrence of *expC1*. The function provides a line number, indicating the line where *expC1* was found. (If *expC1* is not found, the function returns a value of zero.) *expC2* can be a memo field.

RDLEVEL

Syntax

RDLEVEL( )

The RDLEVEL( ) function provides a numeric value which represents the level of the current READ.

READKEY

Syntax

READKEY( )

The READKEY( ) function provides an integer value which indicates what key was pressed when exiting from the editing commands APPEND, BROWSE, CHANGE, CREATE,

EDIT, INSERT, MODIFY, and READ. READKEY( ) provides a value between 0 and 36 if no changes were made to the data. If changes were made to the data, a value between 256 and 292 is provided.

RECCOUNT

Syntax

```
RECCOUNT([alias])
```

The RECCOUNT( ) function provides the number of records in the database open in the current work area. (When no database is open, RECCOUNT( ) provides a zero.) The optional alias can be used to return the number of records in a database open in another work area.

RECNO

Syntax

```
RECNO([alias])
```

The RECNO( ) function provides the current record number. The optional alias can be used to return the current record number in a database open in another work area.

RECSIZE

Syntax

```
RECSIZE([alias])
```

The RECSIZE( ) function provides the size of a table's record in the current work area. The optional alias can be used to return the size of the record for a table that is open in another work area. If no table is open, RECSIZE( ) provides a zero.

RELATION

Syntax

```
RELATION(expN[, alias])
```

The RELATION( ) function provides a specified relational expression for a table open in a specific work area. *expN* denotes the relation by number. For example, if the number 2 is specified, the function returns the relational expression for the second relation created. The optional alias specifies a different work area than the current one.

REPLICATE

Syntax

REPLICATE(*expC, expN*)

The REPLICATE( ) function causes repetition of the specified character expression. Characters are repeated the number of times identified within the numeric expression.

RGBSCHEME

Syntax

RGBSCHEME(*expN1*[, *expN2*])

The RGBSCHEME( ) function returns an RGB color pair, or an RGB color pair list from the color scheme indicated by *expN1*. The optional *expN2* can be used to return a single RGB color pair from a color scheme. Where used, *expN2* denotes the position of the RGB color pair in the color scheme. For example, if *expN2* is 3, the third RGB color pair is returned.

RIGHT

Syntax

RIGHT(*expC* or *memvar, expN*)

The RIGHT( ) function provides a character string containing the number of characters specified by the numeric expression, beginning with the rightmost character in the string.

RLOCK

Syntax

RLOCK([*expN ¦ expC1*] ¦ [*expC2, expN ¦ expC1*])

The RLOCK( ) function attempts to lock a table. If the lock is successful, the function returns a logical true. If the lock cannot be placed for any reason, the function returns a logical false. By default, RLOCK( ) attempts to lock the table in the current work area. Use *expN* (a work area number) or *expC1* (an alias) to specify a table open in another work area. The optional *expC2* is used to specify multiple records to be locked. For example, if you wanted to lock records one, two, and three, *expC2* would contain the character string "1,2,3". Note that if you plan to lock multiple records at one, the setting of SET MULTILOCKS must be ON.

ROUND

Syntax

ROUND(*expN1*, *expN2*)

The ROUND( ) function rounds off numbers, retaining the number of decimal places specified.

ROW

Syntax

ROW( )

The ROW( ) function provides the current row location of the cursor.

RTOD

Syntax

RTOD(*expN*)

The RTOD( ) function converts radians to degrees. The expression *expN* represents the value in radians, and the value provided by the function is the equivalent value measured in degrees.

RTRIM

Syntax

RTRIM(*expC*)

The RTRIM( ) function strips the trailing spaces from the character string named as *expC*. (The RTRIM( ) function is equivalent to the TRIM( ) function.)

SCHEME

Syntax

SCHEME(*expN1*[, *expN2*])

The SCHEME( ) function provides a color pair or a color pair list from the color scheme indicated by *expN1*. The optional *expN2* can be used to return a single RGB color pair from a color scheme. Where used, *expN2* denotes the position of the RGB color pair in the color scheme. As an example, if *expN2* is 3, the third RGB color pair is returned.

SCOLS

Syntax

SCOLS( )

The SCOLS( ) function provides the number of columns available in the main window in FoxPro for Windows.

SECONDS

Syntax

SECONDS( )

The SECONDS( ) function provides the value stored in the system clock represented as the number of seconds past midnight, in seconds.thousandths format.

SEEK

Syntax

SEEK(*expression*[, alias])

The SEEK( ) function provides a logical true (.T.) when the search term represented by *expression* can be found in the active index. If the search term cannot be found, the function provides a logical false (.F.), and the record pointer is moved to the end of the file. The optional alias can be used to search an open index in another work area.

SELECT

Syntax

SELECT( )

The SELECT( ) function provides the number of the current work area if SET COMPATIBLE is OFF. If SET COMPATIBLE is ON, the function provides the number of the highest unused work area.

SET

Syntax

SET(*expC*[, 1])

The SET( ) function provides a character string indicating the status of the SET command named within the function.

SIGN

Syntax

SIGN(*expN*)

The SIGN( ) function provides a numeric value that represents the sign of the numeric expression. When *expN* is positive, SIGN( ) provides a value of 1. When *expN* is negative, SIGN( ) provides a value of -1. When *expN* is zero, SIGN( ) provides a zero.

SIN

Syntax

SIN(*expN*)

The SIN( ) function provides the sine of *expN*, where *expN* is an angle as measured in radians.

SKPBAR

Syntax

SKPBAR(*expC*,*expN*)

The SKPBAR( ) function returns a logical value which indicates whether a popup has been enabled or disabled with the SET SKIP OF command. Use *expC* to specify the name of the popup, and use *expN* to denote the desired bar within the popup. The function returns true (.T.) if the popup bar is disabled, and false (.F.) if the popup bar is enabled.

SKPPAD

Syntax

SKPPAD(*expC*,*expN*)

The SKPPAD function returns a logical value which indicates whether a menu pad has been enabled or disabled with the SET SKIP OF command. Use *expC* to specify the name of the menu bar, and use *expN* to denote the desired pad within the menu bar. The function returns true (.T.) if the menu pad is disabled, and false (.F.) if the menu pad is enabled.

SOUNDEX

Syntax

SOUNDEX(*expC*)

The SOUNDEX( ) function provides a phonetic ("SOUNDEX") code for a given character expression. The code returned by the function is derived from the SOUNDEX( ) algorithm, which is as follows:

1. The first letter of the character expression becomes the first character in the code.
2. All occurrences of the letters A, E, H, I, O, U, W, and Y are dropped.
3. The remaining letters are assigned a number according to the following:

b,p,v	1
c,g,j,k,q,s,x,z	2
d,t	3
l	4
m,n	5
r	6

4. When two or more adjacent letters have the same code, all but the first letter in the group are dropped.
5. A code in the format of "letter digit digit digit" is returned. If less than three digits are in the code, trailing zeroes are added. If more than three digits are in the code, excess digits are dropped.

6. If the first character is not a letter, "0000" is returned as the code. If leading blanks exist in the character string, these are skipped. The calculation of the code stops at the first character that is not a letter.

The four-character code returned by the SOUNDEX( ) function can be useful for finding similar-sounding names, or for building an index to perform lookups based on the sound of a word.

SPACE

Syntax

SPACE(*expN*)

The SPACE( ) function provides a character string containing the specified number of blank spaces.

SQRT

Syntax

SQRT(*expN*)

The SQRT( ) function provides the square root of the numeric expression *expN*. (The value of *expN* must be a positive number.)

SROWS

Syntax

SROWS( )

The SROWS( ) function provides the number of rows available in the main window in FoxPro for Windows.

STR

Syntax

STR(*expN*[, *expN2*[, *expN3*]])

The STR( ) function converts a numeric expression specified by *expN* into a character string. Use the optional *expN2* to denote the length of the character string returned by the function. The optional *expN3* is used to specify the number of decimal places in the character string.

STRTRAN

Syntax

STRTRAN(*expC1, expC2[, expC3][, expN1][, expN2]*)

The STRTRAN( ) function searches a character expression (or memo field) denoted by *expC1* for occurrences of a second character expression or memo field (*expC2*), and then replaces each occurrence with a third character expression or memo field (*expC3*). The optional *expN2* denotes that occurrence of *expC2* where the replacements should begin; if omitted, replacements begin at the start of the string. The optional *expN2* denotes the number of replacements to make. If omitted, all needed replacements are made.

STUFF

Syntax

STUFF(*expC1, expN1, expN2, expC2*)

The STUFF( ) function inserts or removes characters from any part of a character string. Use *expN1* to denote the position in *expC1* where the replacement starts, and use *expN2* to specify the number of characters to be replaced. Where *expN2* is zero, the replacement string *expC2* gets inserted into *expC1*. Use *expC2* to specify the replacement characters. If *expC2* is a null string, the number of characters specified by *expN2* are removed from *expC1*.

SUBSTR

Syntax

SUBSTR(*expC, expN1[, expN2]*)

The SUBSTR( ) function extracts a portion of a character string from a character string. If the number of characters is not provided, the character expression produced by SUBSTR( ) will begin with the starting position specified and end with the last character of the character expression.

SYS

Syntax

SYS(*expN*)

The SYS( ) functions return character strings that contain various system data. ExpN is a numeric value which corresponds to an appropriate system function. The more commonly used system functions are shown here. You can refer to the FoxPro documentation for a complete listing.

SYS(0)	Provides the machine number and name when on a network
SYS(1)	Provides the current system date
SYS(2)	Provides the number of seconds since midnight
SYS(3)	Provides a unique legal filename
SYS(5)	Provides the current default device
SYS(6)	Provides the current print device
SYS(7)	Provides the name of the current format file
SYS(9)	Provides your FoxPro serial number
SYS(12)	Provides the amount of free memory
SYS(13)	Provides the printer status
SYS(16)	Provides the name of the executing program
SYS(17)	Provides the name of the type of processor in use
SYS(23)	Provides the amount of EMS memory used by FoxPro
SYS(24)	Provides the EMS limit specified in CONFIG.FP
SYS(2003)	Provides the current directory name

SYSMETRIC

Syntax

SYSMETRIC(*expN*)

The SYSMETRIC( ) function returns the size of a Windows display element. Use *expN* to denote the display element, according to the following table. (Note also that SYSMETRIC( ) is not supported by other versions of FoxPro.)

Value of expN	Display Element
1	Windows screen width
2	Windows screen height
3	Width of sizable window frame
4	Height of sizable window frame
5	Width of scroll arrows on vertical scroll bar
6	Height of scroll arrows on vertical scroll bar
7	Width of scroll arrows on horizontal scroll bar
8	Height of scroll arrows on horizontal scroll bar
9	Height of window title
10	Width of non-sizable window frame
11	Height of non-sizable window frame

12	Width of DOUBLE or PANEL window frame
13	Height of DOUBLE or PANEL window frame
14	Thumb width on horizontal scroll bar in text editing windows
15	Thumb height on vertical scroll bar in text editing windows
16	Minimized window icon width
17	Minimized window icon height
18	Maximum cursor width
19	Maximum cursor height
20	Single line menu bar height
21	Maximized window width
22	Maximized window height
23	Kanji window height
24	Minimum sizable window width
25	Minimum sizable window height
26	Minimum window width
27	Minimum window height
28	Window controls width
29	Window controls height
30	1 if mouse hardware present; 0 otherwise
31	1 for Windows debugging version; 0 otherwise
32	1 if mouse buttons swapped; 0 otherwise

TAG

Syntax

TAG([expC,] expN[, alias])

The TAG( ) function returns a character string representing the name of an index (.NDX) file or index (.MDX) tag specified by the numeric expression. If a multiple index file name (.MDX) is not used, the function assumes that the numeric expression supplied refers to all open index files. Use the optional alias to refer to an index file open in a different work area.

TAN

Syntax

TAN(expN)

The TAN( ) function provides the tangent of *expN*, where *expN* is measured in radians.

TARGET

Syntax

TARGET(*expN*[, *expression*])

The TARGET( ) function returns the alias of a table which is the target for a relation as specified in the INTO clause of the SET RELATION command. *expN* denotes a number, from 1 to the number of relationships set out of the specified work area. By default, the function assumes a relation set out of the current work area. Use the optional *expression* to name a work area number or an alias for a table open in another work area.

TIME

Syntax

TIME([*expN*])

The TIME( ) function provides the current system time, in the format HH:MM:SS AM/PM (if SET HOURS is set to 12), or in the format of HH:MM:SS (if SET HOURS is set to 24).

TRANSFORM

Syntax

TRANSFORM(*expression*, *expC*)

The TRANSFORM( ) function formats alphanumerics with PICTURE options without requiring @...SAY commands.

TRIM

Syntax

TRIM(*expC*)

The TRIM( ) function trims trailing spaces from a character string. (The TRIM( ) function is equivalent in operation to the RTRIM( ) function.) If the character string is composed entirely of spaces, TRIM( ) provides a null string.

TXTWIDTH

Syntax

TXTWIDTH(*expC1*[, *expC2*, *expN*[, *expC3*]])

The TXTWIDTH( ) function returns the number of characters a character expression *expC1* occupies, based on the average character width of a specified font. Include <*expC2*> to return the length of a character expression with a specific font, where *expC2* is the name of the font. Include *expN* to return the length of a character expression with a specific font size, where *expN* is a number which corresponds to the font size in points. Include *expC3* to specify a special font style for the character expression. *expC3* is a font style code as outlined in the following table. The normal font style is used if *expC3* is omitted.

Character	*Font Style*
B	Bold
I	Italic
N	Normal
O	Outline
Q	Opaque
S	Shadow
-	Strikeout
T	Transparent
U	Underline

TYPE

Syntax

TYPE(*expC*)

The TYPE( ) function provides a character indicating the type of expression. C denotes character expression, N denotes numeric expression, L denotes logical expression, and U denotes undefined expression.

UPDATED

Syntax

UPDATED( )

The UPDATED( ) function returns a logical true (.T.) if any data was changed during the most recent READ operation.

UPPER

Syntax

UPPER(*expC*)

The UPPER( ) function converts all alphabetic characters in *expC* to uppercase letters.

USED

Syntax

USED([alias])

The USED( ) function provides a logical true (.T.) if a table is open in the current work area. The optional alias can be used to identify another work area by its alias, number, or letter. If no table is open in the specified work area, a logical false (.F.) is provided by the function.

VAL

Syntax

VAL(*expC*)

The VAL( ) function converts strings of numeric characters into numeric expressions. If the character string begins with a non-numeric character that is not a space, the VAL function will provide a value of zero.

VARREAD

Syntax

VARREAD( )

The VARREAD( ) function returns the name of the field or memory variable currently being edited. The function is useful when designing context-sensitive help systems, to display different help screens for different fields.

VERSION

Syntax

VERSION( )

The VERSION( ) function provides a character string indicating the version number of FoxPro.

WBORDER

Syntax

WBORDER(*expC*)

The WBORDER( ) function returns a logical true (.T.) if the specified window has a border, and a logical false (.F.) if the window has no border. By default, the active window is assumed. The optional *expC* can be used to denote another window by name.

WCHILD

Syntax

WCHILD([*expC*/*expN*])

The WCHILD( ) function provides a numeric value that indicates the number of child windows in a parent window, or it provides the names of the child windows in the order in which they are stacked in the parent window. The optional *expC* denotes the name of the parent window. The optional *expN* can be zero, or any positive value. If *expN* is zero, the function returns the name of the child window at the bottom of the stack of windows. If *expN* is any positive number, the function returns the name of the next child window in the stack.

WCOLS

Syntax

WCOLS([*expC*])

The WCOLS( ) function provides a numeric value that indicates the number of columns in a window. By default, the active window is assumed. The optional *expC* can be used to denote another window by name.

WEXIST

Syntax

WEXIST(*expC*)

The WEXIST( ) function provides a logical true (.T.) if the window named in *expC* has been previously defined.

WFONT

Syntax

WFONT( )

The WFONT( ) function provides the font name, font size, or font style of the current font for a window. (Note that the use of WFONT( ) is not compatible with FoxPro for DOS.) *expN* is a number from 1 to 3 which specifies the desired attribute, where 1 indicates the font name, 2 indicates the font size, and 3 indicates the font style according to the table below. By default, the active window is assumed. The optional *expC* can be used to denote another window by name.

Code	Font Styles
B	Bold
I	Italic
N	Normal
O	Outline
Q	Opaque
S	Shadow
-	Strikeout
T	Transparent
U	Underline

WLAST

Syntax

WLAST([expC])

The WLAST( ) function provides the name of the window that was active before the current window, or determines whether or not the named window was active prior to the current window. If the optional *expC* is omitted, WLAST( ) returns the name of the last active window. When *expC* (which denotes the name of a window) is included, WLAST( ) returns a logical true (.T.) if the window named was the last window to be activated.

WLCOL

Syntax

WLCOL([*expC*])

The WLCOL( ) function provides a numeric value that indicates the column location of the upper left corner of a window. By default, the active window is assumed. The optional *expC* can be used to denote another window by name. If the upper left corner of a window resides outside of the FoxPro main window, the function returns a negative value.

WLROW

Syntax

WLROW([*expC*])

The WLROW( ) function provides a numeric value that indicates the row location of the upper left corner of a window. By default, the active window is assumed. The optional *expC* can be used to denote another window by name. If the upper left corner of a window resides outside of the FoxPro main window, the function returns a negative value.

WMAXIMUM

Syntax

WMAXIMUM([*expC*])

The WMAXIMUM( ) function returns a logical true if a window is maximized. The function assumes the current window; the optional *expC* can be used to specify a window other than the current one.

WMINIMUM

Syntax

WMINIMUM([*expC*])

The WMINIMUM( ) function returns a logical true if a window is minimized. The function assumes the current window. The optional *expC* can be used to specify a window other than the current one.

WONTOP

Syntax

WONTOP([expC])

The WONTOP( ) function provides the name of the window that is frontmost on the screen. When the optional *expC* is used to name a window, WONTOP( ) provides a logical true (.T.) if the named window is frontmost.

WOUTPUT

Syntax

WOUTPUT([expC])

The WOUTPUT( ) function indicates whether output is currently being directed to a window. If the function returns a logical true (.T.), output is currently being directed to the window. The function assumes the current window. The optional *expC* can be used to specify a window other than the current one.

WPARENT

Syntax

WPARENT([expC])

The WPARENT( ) function provides the name of a parent window for a specific child window. By default, the active window is assumed to be the child window. The optional *expC* can be used to denote another child window by name. If the window has no parent window, the function returns a null string.

WREAD

Syntax

WREAD([expC])

The WREAD( ) function returns a logical true (.T.) if the specified window is participating in the current READ, or a logical false (.F.) if the specified window isn't involved in the current READ or if the window does not exist. The function assumes the current window. The optional *expC* can be used to specify a window other than the current one.

WROWS

Syntax

WROWS([*expC*])

The WROWS( ) function provides a numeric value that indicates the number of rows in a window. By default, the active window is assumed. The optional *expC* can be used to denote another window by name.

WTITLE

Syntax

WTITLE([*expC*])

The WTITLE( ) function returns the title of a specified window. By default, the active window is assumed. The optional *expC* can be used to denote another window by name.

WVISIBLE

Syntax

WVISIBLE(*expC*)

The WVISIBLE( ) function provides a logical true (.T.) if the window named by *expC* has been activated and is not hidden. The function provides a logical false (.F.) if the window has not been activated, has been deactivated, or is hidden.

YEAR

Syntax

YEAR(*expD*)

The YEAR( ) function provides the numeric year corresponding to the date value.

Third-Party Products

This appendix provides a representative listing of third-party add-ons that can be used with FoxPro.

Fox SQL

FoxSQL is a family of libraries that lets you use FoxPro to access SQL database servers, such as Microsoft SQL Server, Gupta SQL base, Sybase, and Oracle. FoxSQL enables you to access an unlimited number of tables simultaneously. It supports all SQL commands, and lets you retrieve, update, or delete rows, and create or delete tables.

Source:

Aladdin Publishing
126 S. Helberta Ave., #4
Redondo Beach, CA 90277
Phone (310) 798-6488

Fox Med

Fox Med, complete with source code in FoxPro, is a 10-module, fully-integrated medical practice management application. Dealers can sell Fox Med on a royalty-free basis.

The Fox Med system includes patient and insurance billing, electronic claims filing in the National Standard format, patient history, patient communications, patient scheduling, general ledger, custom reporting, and clinical applications, all integrated into a single application.

Source:

ACC Incorporated
12500 San Pedro, Suite 460
San Antonio, Texas 78216-2858
Phone: (210) 545-1010

Flash Development Toolkit

The Flash Development Toolkit is a collection of software tools and guidelines that makes large-scale application development easier by reducing maintenance hassles and development errors. It includes the Flash Design Standards, a Data Dictionary that is integrated into the FoxPro screen builder, a Version control Systems Link, and more.

The Data Dictionary enables you to define all of your field information such as PICTURE, VALID, RANGE, and so forth, in one central location. Data Dictionary information is automatically propagated to all screens that use those fields. It includes support for domains, which are developer-created field types (such as ZIP codes, Social Security numbers, and so on).

The version control link works with major version control software packages such as Intersolv's PVCS products, Borland's Sorcerer's Apprentice, Burton Systems' TLIB, and One Tree's SourceSafe. Developers can "check out" a screen, program, or any FoxPro module, knowing that no one else can modify it at the same time.

The Multiuser Project Builder works like the FoxPro Project Builder, but automatically enables multiple developers to use it at once. It is well-suited to larger development projects.

Source:

Flash Creative Management INC.
1060 Main St.
River Edge, NJ 07661
Phone (201) 489-2500

Portmanteau

Portmanteau, from The Information Management Group, automates key workgroup activities: contact tracking, project management, time and billing, and group scheduling. Modules are sold on an integrated or stand-alone basis. Written in FoxPro, Portmanteau interfaces seamlessly with other FoxPro-based applications, and is portable to all FoxPro environments.

Portmanteau is entirely event-driven and makes extensive use of IMG's Common Objects technology. It runs on all popular PC-based LAN operating systems. Source code and support agreements are available.

Source:

The Information Management Group
720 North Franklin, Suite 300
Chicago, IL 60610
Phone: (800) 922-2019

STAGE

STAGE provides a new way to develop applications in the '90s. STAGE has improved application templates, a better simulation environment, more object attributes, and more features than the application generator provided by FoxPro. It even has an Active Data Dictionary not available in FoxPro.

STAGE users worldwide have developed applications ranging from accounting to mission critical with productivity gains not offered by other tools for FoxPro.

Source:

IS Technology
Dept. 240, P.O. Box 64742
Los Angeles, CA 90064
Phone: (818) 304-0614

CommTools

CommTools lets you add communications capabilities to your FoxPro-based programs. CommTools takes advantage of FoxPro 2.x library capabilities, providing you with a powerful set of communications functions in a PLB file. You just use a SET LIBRARY TO call and then write CommTools' functions right into your code—you don't have to shell to DOS. The command features fit seamlessly with your user interface and have instant access to your database fields.

Your users can call CompuServe and download electronic mail; send faxes at the press of a key; upload information from branch offices to their main office; interface with credit card readers, bar-code scanners, scales, and other electronic equipment; and even set up a bulletin board system (BBS) so that outside callers can download information directly from you program.

Source:

Pinnacle Publishing, Inc.
P.O. Box 888
Kent, WA 98035-2888
Phone: (206) 251-1900

NetLib for FoxPro

NetLib for FoxPro lets you add powerful performance and security features to FoxPro version 2.x-based programs running on Novell NetWare, Banyan VINES, and NetBIOS networks. Because NetLib takes advantage of FoxPro 2.x library capabilities, you just use a SET LIBRARY TO call and then build the networking functions (contained in a PLB file) into you FoxPro-based code.

A total of 16 NetLib functions let you query and update the NetWare Bindery. You can check and modify user and group names, determine if a user has access to a print queue, create "pick lists" of available print queues, and more. Another 11 functions let you read and modify network and DOS environment settings-like the station number, user ID and access rights, server name, DOS environment strings (PATH, PROMPT), and more— all within FoxPro.

Source:

Pinnacle Publishing, Inc.
P.O. Box 888
Kent, WA 98035-2888
Phone: (206) 251-1900

RaSQL/B for FoxPro

RaSQL/B for FoxPro, Pinnacle Publishing's Btrieve Library, opens up FoxPro 2.x to the multiuser capabilities of Novell's Btrieve file format. You just add RaSQL/B's functions to your FoxPro code to read and write Btrieve files and enjoy the benefits of Btrieve's sophisticated data and index structures, automatic encryption, and decreased network traffic. You can also access information from existing Btrieve programs, including many of today's popular accounting packages.

RaSQL/B gives you automatic conversion between DBF and Btrieve data types. You can even open both file formats in the same program. RaSQL/B for FoxPro gives programmers access to the client/server performance of Novell's NetWare SQL database manager. You can read and write NetWare SQL data with commands inserted into your FoxPro code, combining SQL's network possibilities with development ease of FoxPro.

RaSQL/B gives you automatic conversions between DBF and SQL data types, so you can easily convert you FoxPro data to NetWare SQL for better multiuser database performance. You can also use ANSI-standard SQL commands, access the SQL data dictionary, and open multiple tables and views at once.

Source:

Pinnacle Publishing, Inc.
P.O. Box 888
Kent, WA 98035-2888
Phone: (206) 251-1900

Word Wrapper

Word Wrapper is a word processor that stores free-form text directly in .DBF fields. It provides a very reliable data storage format while giving your applications more word-processing power. Users can copy or move text from one memo to another an search and replace across one, some or all memos. Additionally, you can customize any aspect of its operation or user interface. Word Wrapper is written in FoxPro and comes with complete royalty-free source code.

Source:

Strategic Edge
2062 Union St., Suite 300
San Francisco, CA 94123
Phone: (415) 563-3755

SBT Professional Series

SBT's Professional Series is a high-performance LAN-based application that provides business users with significant power and important business information in real-time. Ideal for small- to medium-sized business and departments, the Professional Series takes advantage of FoxPro technology and brings increased speed and control to accounting software. It includes source code to modify the product to fit your specific business needs. Applications include: System Manager, General Ledger, Accounts Receivable, Accounts Payable, Inventory Control, Sales Orders, and Purchase Orders.

Source:

SBT Systems
One Harbor Dr., Suite 300
Sausalito, CA 94965
Phone (800) 944-1000

Query Maker

Query Maker is a relational Query-by-Example builder that can be included royalty free in your FoxPro applications. It can now be easy for end users to create and run their own queries.

The query's field names are shown with plain English descriptions and can be taken from multiple databases. You can include character, memo, date, numeric and logical fields in the query. The resulting query is also displayed in plain English and can be used to filter records in a mail-merge, filter records in a report (including R&R reports) or to fund and record in your application's databases.

Query Maker can generate and execute a SQL select statement. It can show the records matching the query in a browse window. You can also direct the output to a SQL cursor file to be used by the FoxPro report writer or to one of 12 different file formats. Query Maker comes with a front-end application called the Query List Manager. It can store an unlimited number of queries with user supplied titles.

Source:

Strategic Edge
2062 Union St., Suite 300
San Francisco, CA 94123
Phone: (415) 563-3755

Liaison

Liaison is a Contact Management System for developers and Integrators. It offers contact/account history, unlimited contacts per account, user-defined fields, personal planner, report, label writer, contact notebook/profiler, telemarketing scripts, and mail-merge/data export. It comes with complete source code.

Source:

Galaxy Systems & Resources, Inc.
10035 Greenleaf Ave.
Santa Fe Springs, CA 90670
Phone: (310) 946-1102

Fox Frame 2

Fox Frame 2 is a complete application generator that guides you through the creation of every component of your application, from screens to menus to reports.

Fox Frame 2 creates 100-percent modeless applications. You can even create BROWSE-only applications. Fox Frame 2 also has the ability to change generated code without losing the ability to regenerate source code.

Source:

UFO Computing, Inc.
28924 S. Western Ave., Suite 207
Rancho Palos Verdes, CA 90732
Phone: (310) 519-0545

SoftCode

SoftCode is an advanced, template-based program generator. SoftCode provides a simple way to create high-quality, heavily-customized applications. Menus and submenus are designed visually, and you tell the application what to do by attaching actions to the menu choices and hot keys. Templates included with the product provide standard database actions, such as adding and editing data, navigating between records, querying the database, and performing maintenance operations.

Source:

BottleWorks Development Corp.
333 Hempstead Ave.
Malverne, NY 11565

R & R Report Writer for Windows

R & R Report Writer for Windows is a powerful and flexible report writer which lets you create reports that can be called from within or outside of FoxPro. R & R can provide reports that range from simple queries to complex financial analysis and it offers spreadsheet calculations that can be used to analyze financial data or build financial models. The XBase version of R & R supports FoxPro for Windows, and also supports Clipper and dBASE.

Source:

Concentric Data Systems, Inc.
110 Turnpike Rd.
Westborough, MA 01581

Visual XBase

Visual XBase is an application development system which enables you to define FoxPro applications through an interactive screen painter type of process. Visual XBase includes an integrated data dictionary that you can use to enforce data integrity, and support for calculated fields, cascading deletions, parent-child relationships and screens, and more. Visual XBase generates source code that's optimized for use in FoxPro for Windows, or in FoxPro for DOS.

Source:

RyTech
2 Stamford Landing, Suite 100
Stamford, CT 06902

FoxFire

FoxFire is a query and report development system, written in FoxPro, that can be distributed with your own custom applications on a royalty-free basis. When customers express a need to create their own ad-hoc reports and queries from within your custom application, you can use FoxFire to allow the creation of user-customizable queries and reports. FoxFire uses the FoxPro "look and feel" to seamlessly integrate into your application, and it comes with complete source code.

Source:

Micromega Systems
832 Baker St.
San Francisco, CA 94115

HeadFix and QuickFix-2

HeadFix and QuickFix-2 are file recovery packages, designed to recover damaged database (table) files. HeadFix automatically repairs damaged headers in .DBF files, and QuickFix-2 repairs damaged .DBF files.

Source:

Hilco Software
11266 Barnett Valley Rd.
Sebastopol, CA 95472-9255

INDEX

Add to Your Sams Library Today with the Best Books for Programming, Operating Systems, and New Technologies

The easiest way to order is to pick up the phone and call
1-800-428-5331
between 9:00 a.m. and 5:00 p.m. EST.
For faster service, please have your credit card available.

ISBN	Quantity	Description of Item	Unit Cost	Total Cost
0-672-30565-8		FoxPro 2.6 for Windows Developer's Guide (Book/Disk)	$45.00	
0-672-30466-X		The Internet Unleashed (Book/Disk)	$44.95	
0-672-30485-6		Navigating the Internet, Deluxe Edition (Book/Disk)	$29.95	
0-672-30160-1		Multimedia Developer's Guide (Book/CD-ROM)	$49.95	
0-672-30312-4		Mastering Windows Programming with Borland C++ 4 (Book/Disk)	$39.95	
0-672-30471-6		Teach Yourself Advanced C in 21 Days (Book/Disk)	$34.95	
0-672-30445-7		OS/2 2.11 Unleashed (Book/CD-ROM)	$39.95	
0-672-30514-3		Master Visual Basic 3 (Book/CD-ROM)	$45.00	
❏ 3 ½" Disk		Shipping and Handling: See information below.		
❏ 5 ¼" Disk		TOTAL		

Shipping and handling: $4.00 for the first book, and $1.75 for each additional book. Floppy disk: add $1.75 for shipping and handling. If you need to have it NOW, we can ship product to you in 24 hours for an additional charge of approximately $18.00, and you will receive your item overnight or in two days. Overseas shipping and handling adds $2.00 per book and $8.00 for up to three disks. Prices subject to change. Call for availability and pricing information on latest editions.

201 W. 103rd Street, Indianapolis, Indiana 46290

1-800-428-5331 — Orders   1-800-835-3202 — FAX   1-800-858-7674 — Customer Service

Book ISBN 0-672-30538-0

What's on the Disk

What's on the Disk

The *FoxPro 2.6 for Windows Unleashed* disk contains:

- The database tables (BUYERS, CARSALES, DONATION, and MEMBERS) and accompanying files used as examples throughout the text.
- **Stage 2**, a demonstration of the Applications Generator, along with sample application code for a complete order-entry system created using Stage 2.
- **FoxSQZ**, a full-featured file archiving and data compression system for FoxPro.
- **The ULTIMATE FoxPro Routines Library**, a comprehensive set of routines that will enable all FoxPro programmers, whether beginners or advanced, to produce professional and "smart" business applications and other useful utilities.
- **Nubrowse and Nubrowse Assistant**, utilities which enable you to create and use fully functional incremental browse routines.
- **PTX Editor**, a FoxPro application that allows extended editing power over the FoxPro Power Tools.
- **Comp5**, a limited version of the data compression system that can compress and decompress files within FoxPro.

Installing the Disk

The software included with this book is stored in a compressed form. You cannot use the software without first installing it to your hard drive. The installation program runs from within Windows.

> **NOTE**
>
> To install the files on the disk, you'll need at least 4MB of free space on your hard drive.

1. From File Manager or Program Manager, choose **R**un from the **F**ile menu.
2. Type `<drive>INSTALL` and press Enter, where `<drive>` is the letter of the drive that contains the installation disk. For example, if the disk is in drive B:, type `B:INSTALL` and press Enter.

Follow the on-screen instructions in the installation program. The files will be installed in the \FPU directory, unless you chose a different directory during installation. Be sure to read the file that is displayed at the end of the installation process; it contains information on the files and programs that were installed.